MACHINE LEARNING

The Art and Science of Algorithms that Make Sense of Data

PETER FLACH

CAMBRIDGE
UNIVERSITY PRESS

University Printing House, Cambridge CB2 8BS, United Kingdom

Cambridge University Press is part of the University of Cambridge.

It furthers the University's mission by disseminating knowledge in the pursuit of education, learning and research at the highest international levels of excellence.

www.cambridge.org
Information on this title: www.cambridge.org/9781107096394

First published 2012
9th printing 2016

Printed in the United Kingdom by Clays, St Ives plc.

A catalogue record for this publication is available from the British Library

ISBN 978-1-107-09639-4 Hardback
ISBN 978-1-107-42222-3 Paperback

Additional resources for this publication at www.cs.bris.ac.uk/home/flach/mlbook

To Hessel Flach (1923–2006)

Brief Contents

Contents

Preface

This book started life in the Summer of 2008, when my employer, the University of Bristol, awarded me a one-year research fellowship. I decided to embark on writing a general introduction to machine learning, for two reasons. One was that there was scope for such a book, to complement the many more specialist texts that are available; the other was that through writing I would learn new things – after all, the best way to learn is to teach.

The challenge facing anyone attempting to write an introductory machine learning text is to do justice to the incredible richness of the machine learning field without losing sight of its unifying principles. Put too much emphasis on the diversity of the discipline and you risk ending up with a 'cookbook' without much coherence; stress your favourite paradigm too much and you may leave out too much of the other interesting stuff. Partly through a process of trial and error, I arrived at the approach embodied in the book, which is is to emphasise both unity and diversity: unity by separate treatment of *tasks* and *features*, both of which are common across any machine learning approach but are often taken for granted; and diversity through coverage of a wide range of logical, geometric and probabilistic models.

Clearly, one cannot hope to cover all of machine learning to any reasonable depth within the confines of 400 pages. In the Epilogue I list some important areas for further study which I decided not to include. In my view, machine learning is a marriage of statistics and knowledge representation, and the subject matter of the book was chosen to reinforce that view. Thus, ample space has been reserved for tree and rule learning, before moving on to the more statistically-oriented material. Throughout the book I have placed particular emphasis on intuitions, hopefully amplified by a generous use of examples and graphical illustrations, many of which derive from my work on the use of ROC analysis in machine learning.

How to read the book

The printed book is a linear medium and the material has therefore been organised in such a way that it can be read from cover to cover. However, this is not to say that one couldn't pick and mix, as I have tried to organise things in a modular fashion.

For example, someone who wants to read about his or her first learning algorithm as soon as possible could start with Section 2.1, which explains binary classification, and then fast-forward to Chapter 5 and read about learning decision trees without serious continuity problems. After reading Section 5.1 that same person could skip to the first two sections of Chapter 6 to learn about rule-based classifiers.

Alternatively, someone who is interested in linear models could proceed to Section 3.2 on regression tasks after Section 2.1, and then skip to Chapter 7 which starts with linear regression. There is a certain logic in the order of Chapters 4–9 on logical, geometric and probabilistic models, but they can mostly be read independently; similar for the material in Chapters 10–12 on features, model ensembles and machine learning experiments.

I should also mention that the Prologue and Chapter 1 are introductory and reasonably self-contained: the Prologue does contain some technical detail but should be understandable even at pre-University level, while Chapter 1 gives a condensed, high-level overview of most of the material covered in the book. Both chapters are freely available for download from the book's web site at `www.cs.bris.ac.uk/~flach/mlbook`; over time, other material will be added, such as lecture slides. As a book of this scope will inevitably contain small errors, the web site also has a form for letting me know of any errors you spotted and a list of errata.

Acknowledgements

Writing a single-authored book is always going to be a solitary business, but I have been fortunate to receive help and encouragement from many colleagues and friends. Tim Kovacs in Bristol, Luc De Raedt in Leuven and Carla Brodley in Boston organised reading groups which produced very useful feedback. I also received helpful comments from Hendrik Blockeel, Nathalie Japkowicz, Nicolas Lachiche, Martijn van Otterlo, Fabrizio Riguzzi and Mohak Shah. Many other people have provided input in one way or another: thank you.

José Hernández-Orallo went well beyond the call of duty by carefully reading my manuscript and providing an extensive critique with many excellent suggestions for improvement, which I have incorporated so far as time allowed. José: I will buy you a free lunch one day.

Many thanks to my Bristol colleagues and collaborators Tarek Abudawood, Rafal Bogacz, Tilo Burghardt, Nello Cristianini, Tijl De Bie, Bruno Golénia, Simon Price, Oliver Ray and Sebastian Spiegler for joint work and enlightening discussions. Many thanks also to my international collaborators Johannes Fürnkranz, Cèsar Ferri, Thomas Gärtner, José Hernández-Orallo, Nicolas Lachiche, John Lloyd, Edson Matsubara and Ronaldo Prati, as some of our joint work has found its way into the book, or otherwise inspired bits of it. At times when the project needed a push forward my disappearance to a quiet place was kindly facilitated by Kerry, Paul and David, Renée, and Trijntje.

David Tranah from Cambridge University Press was instrumental in getting the process off the ground, and suggested the pointillistic metaphor for 'making sense of data' that gave rise to the cover design (which, according to David, is 'just a canonical silhouette' not depicting anyone in particular – in case you were wondering...). Mairi Sutherland provided careful copy-editing.

I dedicate this book to my late father, who would certainly have opened a bottle of champagne on learning that 'the book' was finally finished. His version of the problem of induction was thought-provoking if somewhat morbid: the same hand that feeds the chicken every day eventually wrings its neck (with apologies to my vegetarian readers). I am grateful to both my parents for providing me with everything I needed to find my own way in life.

Finally, more gratitude than words can convey is due to my wife Lisa. I started writing this book soon after we got married – little did we both know that it would take me nearly four years to finish it. Hindsight is a wonderful thing: for example, it allows one to establish beyond reasonable doubt that trying to finish a book while organising an international conference and overseeing a major house refurbishment is really not a good idea. It is testament to Lisa's support, encouragement and quiet suffering that all three things are nevertheless now coming to full fruition. Dank je wel, meisje!

Peter Flach, Bristol

Prologue: A machine learning sampler

YOU MAY NOT be aware of it, but chances are that you are already a regular user of machine learning technology. Most current e-mail clients incorporate algorithms to identify and filter out spam e-mail, also known as junk e-mail or unsolicited bulk e-mail. Early spam filters relied on hand-coded pattern matching techniques such as regular expressions, but it soon became apparent that this is hard to maintain and offers insufficient flexibility – after all, one person's spam is another person's ham![1] Additional adaptivity and flexibility is achieved by employing machine learning techniques.

SpamAssassin is a widely used open-source spam filter. It calculates a score for an incoming e-mail, based on a number of built-in rules or 'tests' in SpamAssassin's terminology, and adds a 'junk' flag and a summary report to the e-mail's headers if the score is 5 or more. Here is an example report for an e-mail I received:

```
-0.1 RCVD_IN_MXRATE_WL        RBL: MXRate recommends allowing
                              [123.45.6.789 listed in sub.mxrate.net]
 0.6 HTML_IMAGE_RATIO_02      BODY: HTML has a low ratio of text to image area
 1.2 TVD_FW_GRAPHIC_NAME_MID BODY: TVD_FW_GRAPHIC_NAME_MID
 0.0 HTML_MESSAGE             BODY: HTML included in message
 0.6 HTML_FONx_FACE_BAD       BODY: HTML font face is not a word
 1.4 SARE_GIF_ATTACH          FULL: Email has a inline gif
 0.1 BOUNCE_MESSAGE           MTA bounce message
 0.1 ANY_BOUNCE_MESSAGE       Message is some kind of bounce message
 1.4 AWL                      AWL: From: address is in the auto white-list
```

[1] Spam, a contraction of 'spiced ham', is the name of a meat product that achieved notoriety by being ridiculed in a 1970 episode of *Monty Python's Flying Circus*.

From left to right you see the score attached to a particular test, the test identifier, and a short description including a reference to the relevant part of the e-mail. As you see, scores for individual tests can be negative (indicating evidence suggesting the e-mail is ham rather than spam) as well as positive. The overall score of 5.3 suggests the e-mail might be spam. As it happens, this particular e-mail was a notification from an intermediate server that another message – which had a whopping score of 14.6 – was rejected as spam. This 'bounce' message included the original message and therefore inherited some of its characteristics, such as a low text-to-image ratio, which pushed the score over the threshold of 5.

Here is another example, this time of an important e-mail I had been expecting for some time, only for it to be found languishing in my spam folder:

```
2.5 URI_NOVOWEL            URI: URI hostname has long non-vowel sequence
3.1 FROM_DOMAIN_NOVOWEL    From: domain has series of non-vowel letters
```

The e-mail in question concerned a paper that one of the members of my group and I had submitted to the European Conference on Machine Learning (ECML) and the European Conference on Principles and Practice of Knowledge Discovery in Databases (PKDD), which have been jointly organised since 2001. The 2008 instalment of these conferences used the internet domain `www.ecmlpkdd2008.org` – a perfectly respectable one, as machine learning researchers know, but also one with eleven 'non-vowels' in succession – enough to raise SpamAssassin's suspicion! The example demonstrates that the importance of a SpamAssassin test can be different for different users. Machine learning is an excellent way of creating software that adapts to the user.

How does SpamAssassin determine the scores or 'weights' for each of the dozens of tests it applies? This is where machine learning comes in. Suppose we have a large 'training set' of e-mails which have been hand-labelled spam or ham, and we know the results of all the tests for each of these e-mails. The goal is now to come up with a weight for every test, such that all spam e-mails receive a score above 5, and all ham e-mails get less than 5. As we will discuss later in the book, there are a number of machine learning techniques that solve exactly this problem. For the moment, a simple example will illustrate the main idea.

Example 1 (Linear classification). Suppose we have only two tests and four training e-mails, one of which is spam (see Table 1). Both tests succeed for the

E-mail	x_1	x_2	Spam?	$4x_1 + 4x_2$
1	1	1	1	8
2	0	0	0	0
3	1	0	0	4
4	0	1	0	4

Table 1. A small training set for SpamAssassin. The columns marked x_1 and x_2 indicate the results of two tests on four different e-mails. The fourth column indicates which of the e-mails are spam. The right-most column demonstrates that by thresholding the function $4x_1 + 4x_2$ at 5, we can separate spam from ham.

spam e-mail; for one ham e-mail neither test succeeds, for another the first test succeeds and the second doesn't, and for the third ham e-mail the first test fails and the second succeeds. It is easy to see that assigning both tests a weight of 4 correctly 'classifies' these four e-mails into spam and ham. In the mathematical notation introduced in Background 1 we could describe this classifier as $4x_1 + 4x_2 > 5$ or $(4,4) \cdot (x_1, x_2) > 5$. In fact, any weight between 2.5 and 5 will ensure that the threshold of 5 is only exceeded when both tests succeed. We could even consider assigning different weights to the tests – as long as each weight is less than 5 and their sum exceeds 5 – although it is hard to see how this could be justified by the training data.

But what does this have to do with learning, I hear you ask? It is just a mathematical problem, after all. That may be true, but it does not appear unreasonable to say that SpamAssassin learns to recognise spam e-mail from examples and counter-examples. Moreover, the more training data is made available, the better SpamAssassin will become at this task. The notion of performance improving with experience is central to most, if not all, forms of machine learning. We will use the following general definition: *Machine learning is the systematic study of algorithms and systems that improve their knowledge or performance with experience.* In the case of SpamAssassin, the 'experience' it learns from is some correctly labelled training data, and 'performance' refers to its ability to recognise spam e-mail. A schematic view of how machine learning feeds into the spam e-mail classification task is given in Figure 2. In other machine learning problems experience may take a different form, such as corrections of mistakes, rewards when a certain goal is reached, among many others. Also note that, just as is the case with human learning, machine learning is not always directed at improving performance on a certain task, but may more generally result in improved knowledge.

There are a number of useful ways in which we can express the SpamAssassin classifier in mathematical notation. If we denote the result of the i-th test for a given e-mail as x_i, where $x_i = 1$ if the test succeeds and 0 otherwise, and we denote the weight of the i-th test as w_i, then the total score of an e-mail can be expressed as $\sum_{i=1}^{n} w_i x_i$, making use of the fact that w_i contributes to the sum only if $x_i = 1$, i.e., if the test succeeds for the e-mail. Using t for the threshold above which an e-mail is classified as spam (5 in our example), the 'decision rule' can be written as $\sum_{i=1}^{n} w_i x_i > t$.

Notice that the left-hand side of this inequality is linear in the x_i variables, which essentially means that increasing one of the x_i by a certain amount, say δ, will change the sum by an amount $(w_i\delta)$ that is independent of the value of x_i. This wouldn't be true if x_i appeared squared in the sum, or with any exponent other than 1.

The notation can be simplified by means of linear algebra, writing $\mathbf{w}$ for the vector of weights $(w_1,\ldots,w_n)$ and $\mathbf{x}$ for the vector of test results $(x_1,\ldots,x_n)$. The above inequality can then be written using a dot product: $\mathbf{w}\cdot\mathbf{x} > t$. Changing the inequality to an equality $\mathbf{w}\cdot\mathbf{x} = t$, we obtain the 'decision boundary', separating spam from ham. The decision boundary is a plane (a 'straight' surface) in the space spanned by the x_i variables because of the linearity of the left-hand side. The vector $\mathbf{w}$ is perpendicular to this plane and points in the direction of spam. Figure 1 visualises this for two variables.

It is sometimes convenient to simplify notation further by introducing an extra constant 'variable' $x_0 = 1$, the weight of which is fixed to $w_0 = -t$. The extended data point is then $\mathbf{x}^\circ = (1, x_1,\ldots,x_n)$ and the extended weight vector is $\mathbf{w}^\circ = (-t, w_1,\ldots,w_n)$, leading to the decision rule $\mathbf{w}^\circ \cdot \mathbf{x}^\circ > 0$ and the decision boundary $\mathbf{w}^\circ \cdot \mathbf{x}^\circ = 0$. Thanks to these so-called homogeneous coordinates the decision boundary passes through the origin of the extended coordinate system, at the expense of needing an additional dimension (but note that this doesn't really affect the data, as all data points and the 'real' decision boundary live in the plane $x_0 = 1$).

Background 1. SpamAssassin in mathematical notation. In boxes such as these, I will briefly remind you of useful concepts and notation. If some of these are unfamiliar, you will need to spend some time reviewing them – using other books or online resources such as `www.wikipedia.org` or `mathworld.wolfram.com` – to fully appreciate the rest of the book.

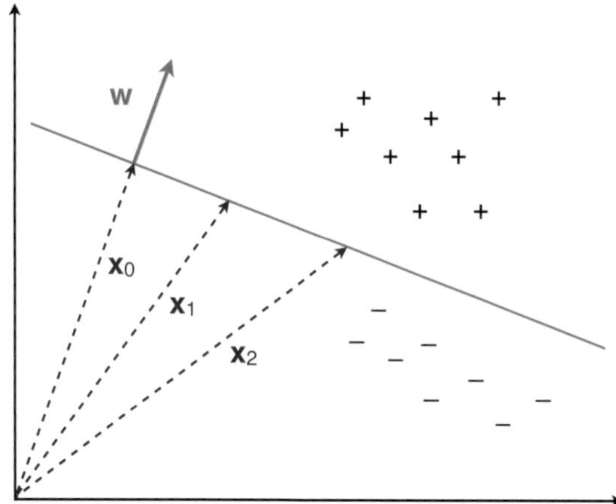

Figure 1. An example of linear classification in two dimensions. The straight line separates the positives from the negatives. It is defined by $\mathbf{w} \cdot \mathbf{x}_i = t$, where $\mathbf{w}$ is a vector perpendicular to the decision boundary and pointing in the direction of the positives, t is the decision threshold, and $\mathbf{x}_i$ points to a point on the decision boundary. In particular, $\mathbf{x}_0$ points in the same direction as $\mathbf{w}$, from which it follows that $\mathbf{w} \cdot \mathbf{x}_0 = ||\mathbf{w}||\ ||\mathbf{x}_0|| = t$ ($||\mathbf{x}||$ denotes the length of the vector $\mathbf{x}$). The decision boundary can therefore equivalently be described by $\mathbf{w} \cdot (\mathbf{x} - \mathbf{x}_0) = 0$, which is sometimes more convenient. In particular, this notation makes it clear that it is the orientation but not the length of $\mathbf{w}$ that determines the location of the decision boundary.

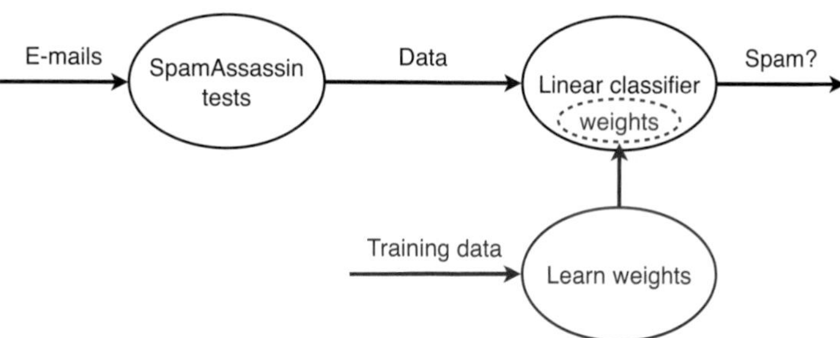

Figure 2. At the top we see how SpamAssassin approaches the spam e-mail classification task: the text of each e-mail is converted into a data point by means of SpamAssassin's built-in tests, and a linear classifier is applied to obtain a 'spam or ham' decision. At the bottom (in blue) we see the bit that is done by machine learning.

We have already seen that a machine learning problem may have several solutions, even a problem as simple as the one from Example 1. This raises the question of how we choose among these solutions. One way to think about this is to realise that we don't really care that much about performance on training data – we already know which of those e-mails are spam! What we care about is whether *future* e-mails are going to be classified correctly. While this appears to lead into a vicious circle – in order to know whether an e-mail is classified correctly I need to know its true class, but as soon as I know its true class I don't need the classifier anymore – it is important to keep in mind that good performance on training data is only a means to an end, not a goal in itself. In fact, trying too hard to achieve good performance on the training data can easily lead to a fascinating but potentially damaging phenomenon called *overfitting*.

Example 2 (Overfitting). Imagine you are preparing for your *Machine Learning 101* exam. Helpfully, Professor Flach has made previous exam papers and their worked answers available online. You begin by trying to answer the questions from previous papers and comparing your answers with the model answers provided. Unfortunately, you get carried away and spend all your time on memorising the model answers to all past questions. Now, if the upcoming exam completely consists of past questions, you are certain to do very well. But if the new exam asks different questions about the same material, you would be ill-prepared and get a much lower mark than with a more traditional preparation. In this case, one could say that you were *overfitting* the past exam papers and that the knowledge gained didn't *generalise* to future exam questions.

Generalisation is probably the most fundamental concept in machine learning. If the knowledge that SpamAssassin has gleaned from its training data carries over – generalises – to your e-mails, you are happy; if not, you start looking for a better spam filter. However, overfitting is not the only possible reason for poor performance on new data. It may just be that the training data used by the SpamAssassin programmers to set its weights is not representative for the kind of e-mails you get. Luckily, this problem does have a solution: use different training data that exhibits the same characteristics, if possible actual spam and ham e-mails that you have personally received. Machine learning is a great technology for adapting the behaviour of software to your own personal circumstances, and many spam e-mail filters allow the use of your own training data.

So, if there are several possible solutions, care must be taken to select one that doesn't overfit the data. We will discuss several ways of doing that in this book. What about the opposite situation, if there isn't a solution that perfectly classifies the training data? For instance, imagine that e-mail 2 in Example 1, the one for which both tests failed, was spam rather than ham – in that case, there isn't a single straight line separating spam from ham (you may want to convince yourself of this by plotting the four e-mails as points in a grid, with x_1 on one axis and x_2 on the other). There are several possible approaches to this situation. One is to ignore it: that e-mail may be atypical, or it may be mis-labelled (so-called *noise*). Another possibility is to switch to a more expressive type of classifier. For instance, we may introduce a second decision rule for spam: in addition to $4x_1 + 4x_2 > 5$ we could alternatively have $4x_1 + 4x_2 < 1$. Notice that this involves learning a different threshold, and possibly a different weight vector as well. This is only really an option if there is enough training data available to reliably learn those additional parameters.

Linear classification, SpamAssassin-style, may serve as a useful introduction, but this book would have been a lot shorter if that was the only type of machine learning. What about learning not just the weights for the tests, but also the tests themselves? How do we decide if the text-to-image ratio is a good test? Indeed, how do we come up with such a test in the first place? This is an area where machine learning has a lot to offer.

One thing that may have occurred to you is that the SpamAssassin tests considered so far don't appear to take much notice of the *contents* of the e-mail. Surely words and phrases like 'Viagra', 'free iPod' or 'confirm your account details' are good spam indicators, while others – for instance, a particular nickname that only your friends use – point in the direction of ham. For this reason, many spam e-mail filters employ text classification techniques. Broadly speaking, such techniques maintain a vocabulary of words and phrases that are potential spam or ham indicators. For each of those words and phrases, statistics are collected from a training set. For instance, suppose that the word 'Viagra' occurred in four spam e-mails and in one ham e-mail. If we then encounter a new e-mail that contains the word 'Viagra', we might reason that the odds that this e-mail is spam are 4:1, or the probability of it being spam is 0.80 and the probability of it being ham is 0.20 (see Background 2 for some basic notions of probability theory).

The situation is slightly more subtle than you might realise because we have to take into account the prevalence of spam. Suppose, for the sake of argument, that I receive on average one spam e-mail for every six ham e-mails (I wish!). This means that I would estimate the odds of the next e-mail coming in being spam as 1:6, i.e., non-negligible but not very high either. If I then learn that the e-mail contains the word 'Viagra', which occurs four times as often in spam as in ham, I somehow need to combine these two odds. As we shall see later, Bayes' rule tells us that we should simply multiply them: 1:6 times 4:1 is 4:6, corresponding to a spam probability of 0.4. In other words, despite the occurrence of the word 'Viagra', the safest bet is still that the e-mail is ham. That doesn't make sense, or does it?

Probabilities involve 'random variables' that describe outcomes of 'events'. These events are often hypothetical and therefore probabilities have to be estimated. For example, consider the statement '42% of the UK population approves of the current Prime Minister'. The only way to know this for certain is to ask everyone in the UK, which is of course unfeasible. Instead, a (hopefully representative) sample is queried, and a more correct statement would then be '42% of a sample drawn from the UK population approves of the current Prime Minister', or 'the proportion of the UK population approving of the current Prime Minister is estimated at 42%'. Notice that these statements are formulated in terms of proportions or 'relative frequencies'; a corresponding statement expressed in terms of probabilities would be 'the probability that a person uniformly drawn from the UK population approves of the current Prime Minister is estimated at 0.42'. The event here is 'this random person approves of the PM'.

The 'conditional probability' $P(A|B)$ is the probability of event A happening given that event B happened. For instance, the approval rate of the Prime Minister may differ for men and women. Writing $P(\text{PM})$ for the probability that a random person approves of the Prime Minister and $P(\text{PM}|\text{woman})$ for the probability that a random woman approves of the Prime Minister, we then have that $P(\text{PM}|\text{woman}) = P(\text{PM},\text{woman})/P(\text{woman})$, where $P(\text{PM},\text{woman})$ is the probability of the 'joint event' that a random person both approves of the PM and is a woman, and $P(\text{woman})$ is the probability that a random person is a woman (i.e., the proportion of women in the UK population).

Other useful equations include $P(A,B) = P(A|B)P(B) = P(B|A)P(A)$ and $P(A|B) = P(B|A)P(A)/P(B)$. The latter is known as 'Bayes' rule' and will play an important role in this book. Notice that many of these equations can be extended to more than two random variables, e.g. the 'chain rule of probability': $P(A,B,C,D) = P(A|B,C,D)P(B|C,D)P(C|D)P(D)$.

Two events A and B are independent if $P(A|B) = P(A)$, i.e., if knowing that B happened doesn't change the probability of A happening. An equivalent formulation is $P(A,B) = P(A)P(B)$. In general, multiplying probabilities involves the assumption that the corresponding events are independent.

The 'odds' of an event is the ratio of the probability that the event happens and the probability that it doesn't happen. That is, if the probability of a particular event happening is p, then the corresponding odds are $o = p/(1-p)$. Conversely, we have that $p = o/(o+1)$. So, for example, a probability of 0.8 corresponds to odds of 4:1, the opposite odds of 1:4 give probability 0.2, and if the event is as likely to occur as not then the probability is 0.5 and the odds are 1:1. While we will most often use the probability scale, odds are sometimes more convenient because they are expressed on a multiplicative scale.

Background 2. The basics of probability.

The way to make sense of this is to realise that you are combining two independent pieces of evidence, one concerning the prevalence of spam, and the other concerning the occurrence of the word 'Viagra'. These two pieces of evidence pull in opposite directions, which means that it is important to assess their relative strength. What the numbers tell you is that, in order to overrule the fact that spam is relatively rare, you need odds of at least 6:1. 'Viagra' on its own is estimated at 4:1, and therefore doesn't pull hard enough in the spam direction to warrant the conclusion that the e-mail is in fact spam. What it does do is make the conclusion 'this e-mail is ham' a lot less certain, as its probability drops from $6/7 = 0.86$ to $6/10 = 0.60$.

The nice thing about this 'Bayesian' classification scheme is that it can be repeated if you have further evidence. For instance, suppose that the odds in favour of spam associated with the phrase 'blue pill' is estimated at 3:1 (i.e., there are three times more spam e-mails containing the phrase than there are ham e-mails), and suppose our e-mail contains both 'Viagra' and 'blue pill', then the combined odds are 4:1 times 3:1 is 12:1, which is ample to outweigh the 1:6 odds associated with the low prevalence of spam (total odds are 2:1, or a spam probability of 0.67, up from 0.40 without the 'blue pill').

The advantage of not having to estimate and manipulate joint probabilities is that we can handle large numbers of variables. Indeed, the vocabulary of a typical Bayesian spam filter or text classifier may contain some 10 000 terms.[2] So, instead of manually crafting a small set of 'features' deemed relevant or predictive by an expert, we include a much larger set and let the classifier figure out which features are important, and in what combinations.

It should be noted that by multiplying the odds associated with 'Viagra' and 'blue pill', we are implicitly assuming that they are independent pieces of information. This is obviously not true: if we know that an e-mail contains the phrase 'blue pill', we are not really surprised to find out that it also contains the word 'Viagra'. In probabilistic terms:

- the probability $P(\text{Viagra}|\text{blue pill})$ will be close to 1;
- hence the joint probability $P(\text{Viagra}, \text{blue pill})$ will be close to $P(\text{blue pill})$;
- hence the odds of spam associated with the two phrases 'Viagra' and 'blue pill' will not differ much from the odds associated with 'blue pill' on its own.

Put differently, by multiplying the two odds we are counting what is essentially one piece of information twice. The product odds of 12:1 is almost certainly an overesti-

[2] In fact, phrases consisting of multiple words are usually decomposed into their constituent words, such that $P(\text{blue pill})$ is estimated as $P(\text{blue})P(\text{pill})$.

mate, and the real joint odds may be not more than, say, 5:1.

We appear to have painted ourselves into a corner here. In order to avoid overcounting we need to take joint occurrences of phrases into account; but this is only feasible computationally if we define the problem away by assuming them to be independent. What we want seems to be closer to a rule-based model such as the following:

1. if the e-mail contains the word 'Viagra' then estimate the odds of spam as 4:1;
2. otherwise, if it contains the phrase 'blue pill' then estimate the odds of spam as 3:1;
3. otherwise, estimate the odds of spam as 1:6.

The first rule covers all e-mails containing the word 'Viagra', regardless of whether they contain the phrase 'blue pill', so no overcounting occurs. The second rule *only* covers e-mails containing the phrase 'blue pill' but not the word 'Viagra', by virtue of the 'otherwise' clause. The third rule covers all remaining e-mails: those which neither contain neither 'Viagra' nor 'blue pill'.

The essence of such rule-based classifiers is that they don't treat all e-mails in the same way but work on a case-by-case basis. In each case they only invoke the most relevant features. Cases can be defined by several nested features:

1. Does the e-mail contain the word 'Viagra'?
   (a) If so: Does the e-mail contain the word 'blue pill'?
      i. If so: estimate the odds of spam as 5:1.
      ii. If not: estimate the odds of spam as 4:1.
   (b) If not: Does the e-mail contain the word 'lottery'?
      i. If so: estimate the odds of spam as 3:1.
      ii. If not: estimate the odds of spam as 1:6.

These four cases are characterised by logical conditions such as 'the e-mail contains the word "Viagra" but not the phrase "blue pill"'. Effective and efficient algorithms exist for identifying the most predictive feature combinations and organise them as rules or trees, as we shall see later.

We have now seen three practical examples of machine learning in spam e-mail recognition. Machine learners call such a task *binary classification*, as it involves assigning objects (e-mails) to one of two classes: spam or ham. This task is achieved by describing each e-mail in terms of a number of variables or features. In the SpamAssassin

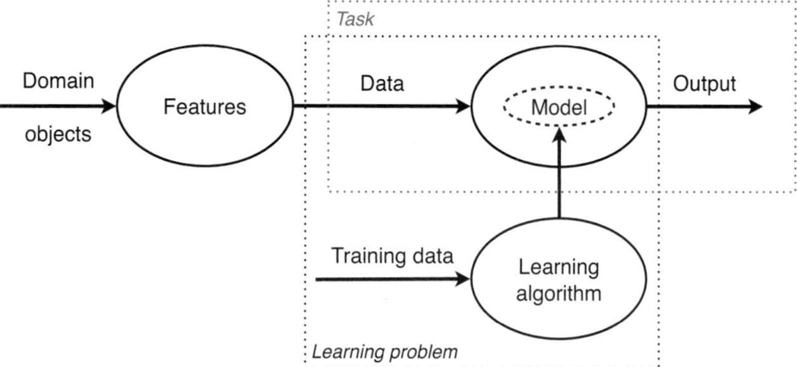

Figure 3. An overview of how machine learning is used to address a given task. A task (red box) requires an appropriate mapping – a model – from data described by features to outputs. Obtaining such a mapping from training data is what constitutes a learning problem (blue box).

example these features were handcrafted by an expert in spam filtering, while in the Bayesian text classification example we employed a large vocabulary of words. The question is then how to use the features to distinguish spam from ham. We have to somehow figure out a connection between the features and the class – machine learners call such a connection a *model* – by analysing a *training set* of e-mails already labelled with the correct class.

☞ In the SpamAssassin example we came up with a linear equation of the form $\sum_{i=1}^{n} w_i x_i > t$, where the x_i denote the 0–1 valued or 'Boolean' features indicating whether the i-th test succeeded for the e-mail, w_i are the feature weights learned from the training set, and t is the threshold above which e-mails are classified as spam.

☞ In the Bayesian example we used a decision rule that can be written as $\prod_{i=0}^{n} o_i > 1$, where $o_i = P(\mathsf{spam}|x_i)/P(\mathsf{ham}|x_i), 1 \leq i \leq n$, are the odds of spam associated with each word x_i in the vocabulary and $o_0 = P(\mathsf{spam})/P(\mathsf{ham})$ are the prior odds, all of which are estimated from the training set.

☞ In the rule-based example we built logical conditions that identify subsets of the data that are sufficiently similar to be labelled in a particular way.

Here we have, then, the main ingredients of machine learning: tasks, models and features. Figure 3 shows how these ingredients relate. If you compare this figure with Figure 2, you'll see how the model has taken centre stage, rather than merely being a set of parameters of a classifier otherwise defined by the features. We need this flexibility to incorporate the very wide range of models in use in machine learning. It is worth emphasising the distinction between tasks and learning problems: *tasks are addressed by models, whereas learning problems are solved by learning algorithms that produce models.* While the distinction is widely recognised, terminology may vary: for instance, you may find that other authors use the term 'learning task' for what we call a learning problem.

In summary, one could say that *machine learning is concerned with using the right features to build the right models that achieve the right tasks.* I call these 'ingredients' to emphasise that they come in many different forms, and need to be chosen and combined carefully to create a successful 'meal': what machine learners call an *application* (the construction of a model that solves a practical task, by means of machine learning methods, using data from the task domain). Nobody can be a good chef without a thorough understanding of the ingredients at his or her disposal, and the same holds for a machine learning expert. Our main ingredients of tasks, models and features will be investigated in full detail from Chapter 2 onwards; first we will enjoy a little 'taster menu' when I serve up a range of examples in the next chapter to give you some more appreciation of these ingredients.

CHAPTER 1

The ingredients of machine learning

Machine learning is all about using the right features to build the right models that achieve the right tasks – this is the slogan, visualised in Figure 3 on p.11, with which we ended the Prologue. In essence, *features* define a 'language' in which we describe the relevant objects in our domain, be they e-mails or complex organic molecules. We should not normally have to go back to the domain objects themselves once we have a suitable feature representation, which is why features play such an important role in machine learning. We will take a closer look at them in Section 1.3. A *task* is an abstract representation of a problem we want to solve regarding those domain objects: the most common form of these is classifying them into two or more classes, but we shall encounter other tasks throughout the book. Many of these tasks can be represented as a mapping from data points to outputs. This mapping or *model* is itself produced as the output of a machine learning algorithm applied to training data; there is a wide variety of models to choose from, as we shall see in Section 1.2.

We start this chapter by discussing tasks, the problems that can be solved with machine learning. No matter what variety of machine learning models you may encounter, you will find that they are designed to solve one of only a small number of tasks and use only a few different types of features. One could say that *models lend the machine learning field diversity, but tasks and features give it unity.*

1.1 Tasks: the problems that can be solved with machine learning

Spam e-mail recognition was described in the Prologue. It constitutes a binary classification task, which is easily the most common task in machine learning which figures heavily throughout the book. One obvious variation is to consider classification problems with more than two classes. For instance, we may want to distinguish different kinds of ham e-mails, e.g., work-related e-mails and private messages. We could approach this as a combination of two binary classification tasks: the first task is to distinguish between spam and ham, and the second task is, among ham e-mails, to distinguish between work-related and private ones. However, some potentially useful information may get lost this way, as some spam e-mails tend to look like private rather than work-related messages. For this reason, it is often beneficial to view *multi-class classification* as a machine learning task in its own right. This may not seem a big deal: after all, we still need to learn a model to connect the class to the features. However, in this more general setting some concepts will need a bit of rethinking: for instance, the notion of a decision boundary is less obvious when there are more than two classes.

Sometimes it is more natural to abandon the notion of discrete classes altogether and instead predict a real number. Perhaps it might be useful to have an assessment of an incoming e-mail's urgency on a sliding scale. This task is called *regression*, and essentially involves learning a real-valued function from training examples labelled with true function values. For example, I might construct such a training set by randomly selecting a number of e-mails from my inbox and labelling them with an urgency score on a scale of 0 (ignore) to 10 (immediate action required). This typically works by choosing a class of functions (e.g., functions in which the function value depends linearly on some numerical features) and constructing a function which minimises the difference between the predicted and true function values. Notice that this is subtly different from SpamAssassin learning a real-valued spam score, where the training data are labelled with classes rather than 'true' spam scores. This means that SpamAssassin has less information to go on, but it also allows us to interpret SpamAssassin's score as an assessment of how far it thinks an e-mail is removed from the decision boundary, and therefore as a measure of confidence in its own prediction. In a regression task the notion of a decision boundary has no meaning, and so we have to find other ways to express a models's confidence in its real-valued predictions.

Both classification and regression assume the availability of a training set of examples labelled with true classes or function values. Providing the true labels for a data set is often labour-intensive and expensive. Can we learn to distinguish spam from ham, or work e-mails from private messages, without a labelled training set? The answer is: yes, up to a point. The task of grouping data without prior information on the groups is called *clustering*. Learning from unlabelled data is called *unsupervised learning* and is quite distinct from *supervised learning*, which requires labelled training data. A typical clustering algorithm works by assessing the similarity between instances (the things we're trying to cluster, e.g., e-mails) and putting similar instances in the same cluster and 'dissimilar' instances in different clusters.

Example 1.1 (Measuring similarity). If our e-mails are described by word-occurrence features as in the text classification example, the similarity of e-mails would be measured in terms of the words they have in common. For instance, we could take the number of common words in two e-mails and divide it by the number of words occurring in either e-mail (this measure is called the *Jaccard coefficient*). Suppose that one e-mail contains 42 (different) words and another contains 112 words, and the two e-mails have 23 words in common, then their similarity would be $\frac{23}{42+112-23} = \frac{23}{130} = 0.18$. We can then cluster our e-mails into groups, such that the average similarity of an e-mail to the other e-mails in its group is much larger than the average similarity to e-mails from other groups. While it wouldn't be realistic to expect that this would result in two nicely separated clusters corresponding to spam and ham – there's no magic here – the clusters may reveal some interesting and useful structure in the data. It may be possible to identify a particular kind of spam in this way, if that subgroup uses a vocabulary, or language, not found in other messages.

There are many other patterns that can be learned from data in an unsupervised way. *Association rules* are a kind of pattern that are popular in marketing applications, and the result of such patterns can often be found on online shopping web sites. For instance, when I looked up the book *Kernel Methods for Pattern Analysis* by John Shawe-Taylor and Nello Cristianini on `www.amazon.co.uk`, I was told that 'Customers Who Bought This Item Also Bought' –

- *An Introduction to Support Vector Machines and Other Kernel-based Learning Methods* by Nello Cristianini and John Shawe-Taylor;
- *Pattern Recognition and Machine Learning* by Christopher Bishop;
- *The Elements of Statistical Learning: Data Mining, Inference and Prediction* by Trevor Hastie, Robert Tibshirani and Jerome Friedman;
- *Pattern Classification* by Richard Duda, Peter Hart and David Stork;

and 34 more suggestions. Such associations are found by data mining algorithms that zoom in on items that frequently occur together. These algorithms typically work by only considering items that occur a minimum number of times (because you wouldn't want your suggestions to be based on a single customer that happened to buy these 39 books together!). More interesting associations could be found by considering multiple items in your shopping basket. There exist many other types of associations that can be learned and exploited, such as correlations between real-valued variables.

Looking for structure

Like all other machine learning models, patterns are a manifestation of underlying structure in the data. Sometimes this structure takes the form of a single *hidden* or *latent variable*, much like unobservable but nevertheless explanatory quantities in physics, such as energy. Consider the following matrix:

$$\begin{pmatrix} 1 & 0 & 1 & 0 \\ 0 & 2 & 2 & 2 \\ 0 & 0 & 0 & 1 \\ 1 & 2 & 3 & 2 \\ 1 & 0 & 1 & 1 \\ 0 & 2 & 2 & 3 \end{pmatrix}$$

Imagine these represent ratings by six different people (in rows), on a scale of 0 to 3, of four different films – say *The Shawshank Redemption, The Usual Suspects, The Godfather, The Big Lebowski,* (in columns, from left to right). *The Godfather* seems to be the most popular of the four with an average rating of 1.5, and *The Shawshank Redemption* is the least appreciated with an average rating of 0.5. Can you see any structure in this matrix?

If you are inclined to say no, try to look for columns or rows that are combinations of other columns or rows. For instance, the third column turns out to be the sum of the first and second columns. Similarly, the fourth row is the sum of the first and second rows. What this means is that the fourth person combines the ratings of the first and second person. Similarly, *The Godfather*'s ratings are the sum of the ratings of the first two films. This is made more explicit by writing the matrix as the following product:

$$\begin{pmatrix} 1 & 0 & 1 & 0 \\ 0 & 2 & 2 & 2 \\ 0 & 0 & 0 & 1 \\ 1 & 2 & 3 & 2 \\ 1 & 0 & 1 & 1 \\ 0 & 2 & 2 & 3 \end{pmatrix} = \begin{pmatrix} 1 & 0 & 0 \\ 0 & 1 & 0 \\ 0 & 0 & 1 \\ 1 & 1 & 0 \\ 1 & 0 & 1 \\ 0 & 1 & 1 \end{pmatrix} \times \begin{pmatrix} 1 & 0 & 0 \\ 0 & 2 & 0 \\ 0 & 0 & 1 \end{pmatrix} \times \begin{pmatrix} 1 & 0 & 1 & 0 \\ 0 & 1 & 1 & 1 \\ 0 & 0 & 0 & 1 \end{pmatrix}$$

You might think I just made matters worse – instead of one matrix we now have three! However, notice that the first and third matrix on the right-hand side are now Boolean, and the middle one is diagonal (all off-diagonal entries are zero). Moreover, these matrices have a very natural interpretation in terms of film *genres*. The right-most matrix associates films (in columns) with genres (in rows): *The Shawshank Redemption* and *The Usual Suspects* belong to two different genres, say drama and crime, *The Godfather* belongs to both, and *The Big Lebowski* is a crime film and also introduces a new genre (say comedy). The tall, 6-by-3 matrix then expresses people's preferences in terms of genres: the first, fourth and fifth person like drama, the second, fourth and fifth person like crime films, and the third, fifth and sixth person like comedies. Finally, the middle matrix states that the crime genre is twice as important as the other two genres in terms of determining people's preferences.

Methods for discovering hidden variables such as film genres really come into their own when the number of values of the hidden variable (here: the number of genres) is much smaller than the number of rows and columns of the original matrix. For instance, at the time of writing `www.imdb.com` lists about 630 000 rated films with 4 million people voting, but only 27 film categories (including the ones above). While it would be naive to assume that film ratings can be completely broken down by genres – genre boundaries are often diffuse, and someone may only like comedies made by the Coen brothers – this kind of ☞*matrix decomposition* can often reveal useful hidden structure. It will be further examined in Chapter 10.

This is a good moment to summarise some terminology that we will be using. We have already seen the distinction between supervised learning from labelled data and unsupervised learning from unlabelled data. We can similarly draw a distinction between whether the model output involves the target variable or not: we call it a *predictive model* if it does, and a *descriptive model* if it does not. This leads to the four different machine learning settings summarised in Table 1.1.

- ☞ The most common setting is supervised learning of predictive models – in fact, this is what people commonly mean when they refer to supervised learning. Typical tasks are classification and regression.

- ☞ It is also possible to use labelled training data to build a descriptive model that is not primarily intended to predict the target variable, but instead identifies, say, subsets of the data that behave differently with respect to the target variable. This example of supervised learning of a descriptive model is called ☞*subgroup discovery*; we will take a closer look at it in Section 6.3.

- ☞ Descriptive models can naturally be learned in an unsupervised setting, and we have just seen a few examples of that (clustering, association rule discovery and matrix decomposition). This is often the implied setting when people talk about unsupervised learning.

- ☞ A typical example of unsupervised learning of a predictive model occurs when

	Predictive model	*Descriptive model*
Supervised learning	classification, regression	subgroup discovery
Unsupervised learning	predictive clustering	descriptive clustering, association rule discovery

Table 1.1. An overview of different machine learning settings. The rows refer to whether the training data is labelled with a target variable, while the columns indicate whether the models learned are used to predict a target variable or rather describe the given data.

we cluster data with the intention of using the clusters to assign class labels to new data. We will call this *predictive clustering* to distinguish it from the previous, *descriptive* form of clustering.

Although we will not cover it in this book, it is worth pointing out a fifth setting of *semi-supervised learning* of predictive models. In many problem domains data is cheap, but labelled data is expensive. For example, in web page classification you have the whole world-wide web at your disposal, but constructing a labelled training set is a painstaking process. One possible approach in semi-supervised learning is to use a small labelled training set to build an initial model, which is then refined using the unlabelled data. For example, we could use the initial model to make predictions on the unlabelled data, and use the most confident predictions as new training data, after which we retrain the model on this enlarged training set.

Evaluating performance on a task

An important thing to keep in mind with all these machine learning problems is that they don't have a 'correct' answer. This is different from many other problems in computer science that you might be familiar with. For instance, if you sort the entries in your address book alphabetically on last name, there is only one correct result (unless two people have the same last name, in which case you can use some other field as tie-breaker, such as first name or age). This is not to say that there is only one way of achieving that result – on the contrary, there is a wide range of sorting algorithms available: insertion sort, bubblesort, quicksort, to name but a few. If we were to compare the performance of these algorithms, it would be in terms of how fast they are, and how much data they could handle: e.g., we could test this experimentally on real data, or analyse it using computational complexity theory. However, what we wouldn't do is compare different algorithms with respect to the correctness of the result, because an algorithm that isn't guaranteed to produce a sorted list every time is useless as a sorting algorithm.

Things are different in machine learning (and not just in machine learning: see

Background 1.1). We can safely assume that the perfect spam e-mail filter doesn't exist – if it did, spammers would immediately 'reverse engineer' it to find out ways to trick the spam filter into thinking a spam e-mail is actually ham. In many cases the data is 'noisy' – examples may be mislabelled, or features may contain errors – in which case it would be detrimental to try too hard to find a model that correctly classifies the training data, because it would lead to overfitting, and hence wouldn't generalise to new data. In some cases the features used to describe the data only give an indication of what their class might be, but don't contain enough 'signal' to predict the class perfectly. For these and other reasons, machine learners take performance evaluation of learning algorithms very seriously, which is why it will play a prominent role in this book. We need to have some idea of how well an algorithm is expected to perform on new data, not in terms of runtime or memory usage – although this can be an issue too – but in terms of classification performance (if our task is a classification task).

Suppose we want to find out how well our newly trained spam filter does. One thing we can do is count the number of correctly classified e-mails, both spam and ham, and divide that by the total number of examples to get a proportion which is called the *accuracy* of the classifier. However, this doesn't indicate whether overfitting is occurring. A better idea would be to use only 90% (say) of the data for training, and the remaining 10% as a *test set*. If overfitting occurs, the test set performance will be considerably lower than the training set performance. However, even if we select the test instances randomly from the data, every once in a while we may get lucky, if most of the test instances are similar to training instances – or unlucky, if the test instances happen to be very non-typical or noisy. In practice this train–test split is therefore repeated in a process called ☞*cross-validation*, further discussed in Chapter 12. This works as follows: we randomly divide the data in ten parts of equal size, and use nine parts for training and one part for testing. We do this ten times, using each part once for testing. At the end, we compute the average test set performance (and usually also its standard deviation, which is useful to determine whether small differences in average performance of different learning algorithms are meaningful). Cross-validation can also be applied to other supervised learning problems, but unsupervised learning methods typically need to be evaluated differently.

In Chapters 2 and 3 we will take a much closer look at the various tasks that can be approached using machine learning methods. In each case we will define the task and look at different variants. We will pay particular attention to evaluating performance of models learned to solve those tasks, because this will give us considerable additional insight into the nature of the tasks.

Long before machine learning came into existence, philosophers knew that generalising from particular cases to general rules is not a well-posed problem with well-defined solutions. Such inference by generalisation is called *induction* and is to be contrasted with *deduction*, which is the kind of reasoning that applies to problems with well-defined correct solutions. There are many versions of this so-called *problem of induction*. One version is due to the eighteenth-century Scottish philosopher David Hume, who claimed that the only justification for induction is itself inductive: since it appears to work for certain inductive problems, it is expected to work for all inductive problems. This doesn't just say that induction cannot be deductively justified but that its justification is circular, which is much worse.

A related problem is stated by the *no free lunch theorem*, which states that no learning algorithm can outperform another when evaluated over all possible classification problems, and thus the performance of any learning algorithm, over the set of all possible learning problems, is no better than random guessing. Consider, for example, the 'guess the next number' questions popular in psychological tests: what comes after 1, 2, 4, 8, ...? If all number sequences are equally likely, then there is no hope that we can improve – on average – on random guessing (I personally always answer '42' to such questions). Of course, some sequences are very much more likely than others, at least in the world of psychological tests. Likewise, the distribution of learning problems in the real world is highly non-uniform. The way to escape the curse of the no free lunch theorem is to find out more about this distribution and exploit this knowledge in our choice of learning algorithm.

Background 1.1. Problems of induction and free lunches.

1.2 Models: the output of machine learning

Models form the central concept in machine learning as they are what is being learned from the data, in order to solve a given task. There is a considerable – not to say bewildering – range of machine learning models to choose from. One reason for this is the ubiquity of the tasks that machine learning aims to solve: classification, regression, clustering, association discovery, to name but a few. Examples of each of these tasks can be found in virtually every branch of science and engineering. Mathematicians, engineers, psychologists, computer scientists and many others have discovered – and sometimes rediscovered – ways to solve these tasks. They have all brought their specific background to bear, and consequently the principles underlying these models are also diverse. My personal view is that this diversity is a good thing as it helps to make machine learning the powerful and exciting discipline it is. It doesn't, however, make the task of writing a machine learning book any easier! Luckily, a few common themes can be observed, which allow me to discuss machine learning models in a somewhat more systematic way. I will discuss three groups of models: geometric models, probabilistic models, and logical models. These groupings are not meant to be mutually exclusive, and sometimes a particular kind of model has, for instance, both a geometric and a probabilistic interpretation. Nevertheless, it provides a good starting point for our purposes.

Geometric models

The *instance space* is the set of all possible or describable instances, whether they are present in our data set or not. Usually this set has some geometric structure. For instance, if all features are numerical, then we can use each feature as a coordinate in a Cartesian coordinate system. A *geometric model* is constructed directly in instance space, using geometric concepts such as lines, planes and distances. For instance, the linear classifier depicted in Figure 1 on p.5 is a geometric classifier. One main advantage of geometric classifiers is that they are easy to visualise, as long as we keep to two or three dimensions. It is important to keep in mind, though, that a Cartesian instance space has as many coordinates as there are features, which can be tens, hundreds, thousands, or even more. Such high-dimensional spaces are hard to imagine but are nevertheless very common in machine learning. Geometric concepts that potentially apply to high-dimensional spaces are usually prefixed with 'hyper-': for instance, a decision boundary in an unspecified number of dimensions is called a *hyperplane*.

If there exists a linear decision boundary separating the two classes, we say that the data is *linearly separable*. As we have seen, a linear decision boundary is defined by the equation $\mathbf{w} \cdot \mathbf{x} = t$, where $\mathbf{w}$ is a vector perpendicular to the decision boundary, $\mathbf{x}$ points to an arbitrary point on the decision boundary, and t is the decision threshold. A good way to think of the vector $\mathbf{w}$ is as pointing from the 'centre of mass' of the negative examples, $\mathbf{n}$, to the centre of mass of the positives $\mathbf{p}$. In other words, $\mathbf{w}$ is proportional (or equal) to $\mathbf{p} - \mathbf{n}$. One way to calculate these centres of mass is by averaging. For instance, if P is a set of n positive examples, then we can define $\mathbf{p} = \frac{1}{n} \sum_{x \in P} \mathbf{x}$, and similarly for $\mathbf{n}$. By setting the decision threshold appropriately, we can intersect the line from $\mathbf{n}$ to $\mathbf{p}$ half-way (Figure 1.1). We will call this the *basic linear classifier* in this book.[1] It has the advantage of simplicity, being defined in terms of addition, subtraction and rescaling of examples only (in other words, $\mathbf{w}$ is a *linear combination* of the examples). Indeed, under certain additional assumptions about the data it is the best thing we

[1] It is a simplified version of linear discriminants.

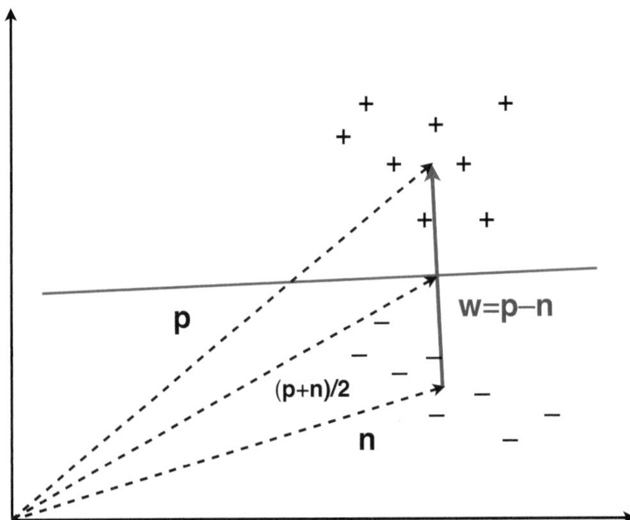

Figure 1.1. The basic linear classifier constructs a decision boundary by half-way intersecting the line between the positive and negative centres of mass. It is described by the equation $\mathbf{w}\cdot\mathbf{x} = t$, with $\mathbf{w} = \mathbf{p} - \mathbf{n}$; the decision threshold can be found by noting that $(\mathbf{p}+\mathbf{n})/2$ is on the decision boundary, and hence $t = (\mathbf{p}-\mathbf{n})\cdot(\mathbf{p}+\mathbf{n})/2 = (||\mathbf{p}||^2 - ||\mathbf{n}||^2)/2$, where $||\mathbf{x}||$ denotes the length of vector $\mathbf{x}$.

can hope to do, as we shall see later. However, if those assumptions do not hold, the basic linear classifier can perform poorly – for instance, note that it may not perfectly separate the positives from the negatives, even if the data is linearly separable.

Because data is usually noisy, linear separability doesn't occur very often in practice, unless the data is very sparse, as in text classification. Recall that we used a large vocabulary, say 10 000 words, each word corresponding to a Boolean feature indicating whether or not that word occurs in the document. This means that the instance space has 10 000 dimensions, but for any one document no more than a small percentage of the features will be non-zero. As a result there is much 'empty space' between instances, which increases the possibility of linear separability. However, because linearly separable data doesn't uniquely define a decision boundary, we are now faced with a problem: which of the infinitely many decision boundaries should we choose? One natural option is to prefer large margin classifiers, where the *margin* of a linear classifier is the distance between the decision boundary and the closest instance. ☞*Support vector machines*, discussed in Chapter 7, are a powerful kind of linear classifier that find a decision boundary whose margin is as large as possible (Figure 1.2).

Geometric concepts, in particular linear transformations, can be very helpful to understand the similarities and differences between machine learning methods (Background 1.2). For instance, we would expect most if not all learning algorithms

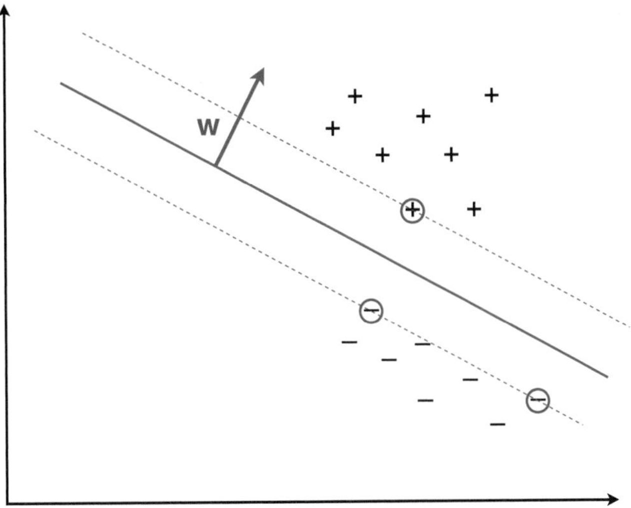

Figure 1.2. The decision boundary learned by a support vector machine from the linearly separable data from Figure 1. The decision boundary maximises the margin, which is indicated by the dotted lines. The circled data points are the support vectors.

to be translation-invariant, i.e., insensitive to where we put the origin of our coordinate system. Some algorithms may also be rotation-invariant, e.g., linear classifiers or support vector machines; but many others aren't, including Bayesian classifiers. Similarly, some algorithms may be sensitive to non-uniform scaling.

A very useful geometric concept in machine learning is the notion of *distance*. If the distance between two instances is small then the instances are similar in terms of their feature values, and so nearby instances would be expected to receive the same classification or belong to the same cluster. In a Cartesian coordinate system, distance can be measured by *Euclidean distance*, which is the square root of the sum of the squared distances along each coordinate:[2] $\sqrt{\sum_{i=1}^{d}(x_i - y_i)^2}$. A very simple distance-based classifier works as follows: to classify a new instance, we retrieve from memory the most similar training instance (i.e., the training instance with smallest Euclidean distance from the instance to be classified), and simply assign that training instance's class. This classifier is known as the *nearest-neighbour classifier*. Endless variations on this simple yet powerful theme exist: we can retrieve the k most similar training instances and take a vote (k-nearest neighbour); we can weight each neighbour's vote inversely to its distance; we can apply the same idea to regression tasks by averaging the training instances' function value; and so on. What they all have in common is that predictions are local in the sense that they are based on only a few training instances,

[2]This can be expressed in vector notation as $||\mathbf{x} - \mathbf{y}|| = \sqrt{(\mathbf{x}-\mathbf{y})\cdot(\mathbf{x}-\mathbf{y})} = \sqrt{\mathbf{x}\cdot\mathbf{x}-2\mathbf{x}\cdot\mathbf{y}+\mathbf{y}\cdot\mathbf{y}} = \sqrt{||\mathbf{x}||^2 - 2||\mathbf{x}||\,||\mathbf{y}||\cos\theta + ||\mathbf{y}||^2}$, where θ is the angle between $\mathbf{x}$ and $\mathbf{y}$.

Transformations in d-dimensional Cartesian coordinate systems can be conveniently represented by means of matrix notation. Let $\mathbf{x}$ be a d-vector representing a data point, then $\mathbf{x}+\mathbf{t}$ is the resulting point after *translating* over $\mathbf{t}$ (another d-vector). Translating a set of points over $\mathbf{t}$ can be equivalently understood as translating the origin over $-\mathbf{t}$. Using *homogeneous coordinates* – the addition of an extra dimension set to 1 – translations can be expressed by matrix multiplication: e.g., in two dimensions we have

$$\mathbf{x}^\circ = \begin{pmatrix} 1 \\ x_1 \\ x_2 \end{pmatrix} \qquad \mathbf{T} = \begin{pmatrix} 1 & 0 & 0 \\ t_1 & 1 & 0 \\ t_2 & 0 & 1 \end{pmatrix} \qquad \mathbf{T}\mathbf{x}^\circ = \begin{pmatrix} 1 \\ x_1 + t_1 \\ x_2 + t_2 \end{pmatrix}$$

A *rotation* is defined by any d-by-d matrix $\mathbf{D}$ whose transpose is its inverse (which means it is orthogonal) and whose determinant is 1. In two dimensions a rotation matrix can be written as $\mathbf{R} = \begin{pmatrix} \cos\theta & \sin\theta \\ -\sin\theta & \cos\theta \end{pmatrix}$, representing a clockwise rotation over angle θ about the origin. For instance, $\begin{pmatrix} 0 & 1 \\ -1 & 0 \end{pmatrix}$ is a 90 degrees clockwise rotation.

A *scaling* is defined by a diagonal matrix; in two dimensions $\mathbf{S} = \begin{pmatrix} s_1 & 0 \\ 0 & s_2 \end{pmatrix}$. A *uniform scaling* applies the same scaling factor s in all dimensions and can be written as $s\mathbf{I}$, where $\mathbf{I}$ is the identity matrix. Notice that a uniform scaling with scaling factor -1 is a rotation (over 180 degrees in the two-dimensional case).

A common scenario which utilises all these transformations is the following. Given an n-by-d matrix $\mathbf{X}$ representing n data points in d-dimensional space, we first calculate the centre of mass or mean vector $\boldsymbol{\mu}$ by averaging each column. We then zero-centre the data set by subtracting $-\boldsymbol{\mu}$ from each row, which corresponds to a translation. Next, we rotate the data such that as much variance (a measure of the data's 'spread' in a certain direction) as possible is aligned with our coordinate axes; this can be achieved by a matrix transformation known as ☞*principal component analysis*, about which you will learn more in Chapter 10. Finally, we scale the data to unit variance along each coordinate.

Background 1.2. Linear transformations.

rather than being derived from a global model built from the entire data set.

There is a nice relationship between Euclidean distance and the mean of a set of points: there is no other point which has smaller total squared Euclidean distance to the given points (see Theorem 8.1 on p.238 for a proof of this). Consequently, we can use the mean of a set of nearby points as a representative *exemplar* for those points. Suppose we want to cluster our data into K clusters, and we have an initial guess of how the data should be clustered. We then calculate the means of each initial cluster, and reassign each point to the nearest cluster mean. Unless our initial guess was a lucky one, this will have changed some of the clusters, so we repeat these two steps (calculating the cluster means and reassigning points to clusters) until no change occurs. This clustering algorithm, which is called ☞*K-means* and is further discussed in Chapter 8, is very widely used to solve a range of clustering tasks. It remains to be decided how we construct our initial guess. This is usually done randomly: either by randomly partitioning the data set into K 'clusters' or by randomly guessing K 'cluster centres'. The fact that these initial 'clusters' or 'cluster centres' will bear little resemblance to the actual data is not a problem, as this will quickly be rectified by running the algorithm for a number of iterations.

To summarise, geometric notions such as planes, translations and rotations, and distance are very useful in machine learning as they allow us to understand many key concepts in intuitive ways. Geometric models exploit these intuitions and are simple, powerful and allow many variations with little effort. For instance, instead of using Euclidean distance, which can be sensitive to outliers, other distances can be used such as *Manhattan distance*, which sums the distances along each coordinate: $\sum_{i=1}^{d} |x_i - y_i|$.

Probabilistic models

The second type of models are probabilistic in nature, like the Bayesian classifier we considered earlier. Many of these models are based around the following idea. Let X denote the variables we know about, e.g., our instance's feature values; and let Y denote the *target variables* we're interested in, e.g., the instance's class. The key question in machine learning is how to model the relationship between X and Y. The statistician's approach is to assume that there is some underlying random process that generates the values for these variables, according to a well-defined but unknown probability distribution. We want to use the data to find out more about this distribution. Before we look into that, let's consider how we could use that distribution once we have learned it.

Since X is known for a particular instance but Y may not be, we are particularly interested in the conditional probabilities $P(Y|X)$. For instance, Y could indicate whether the e-mail is spam, and X could indicate whether the e-mail contains the words 'Viagra' and 'lottery'. The probability of interest is then $P(Y|\mathsf{Viagra},\mathsf{lottery})$, with Viagra and lottery two Boolean variables which together constitute the feature vector X. For a particular e-mail we know the feature values and so we might write $P(Y|\mathsf{Viagra} =$

Viagra	lottery	$P(Y = \text{spam}\mid\text{Viagra}, \text{lottery})$	$P(Y = \text{ham}\mid\text{Viagra}, \text{lottery})$
0	0	0.31	**0.69**
0	1	**0.65**	0.35
1	0	**0.80**	0.20
1	1	0.40	**0.60**

Table 1.2. An example posterior distribution. 'Viagra' and 'lottery' are two Boolean features; Y is the class variable, with values 'spam' and 'ham'. In each row the most likely class is indicated in bold.

$1, \text{lottery} = 0)$ if the e-mail contains the word 'Viagra' but not the word 'lottery'. This is called a *posterior probability* because it is used *after* the features X are observed.

Table 1.2 shows an example of how these probabilities might be distributed. From this distribution you can conclude that, if an e-mail doesn't contain the word 'Viagra', then observing the word 'lottery' increases the probability of the e-mail being spam from 0.31 to 0.65; but if the e-mail does contain the word 'Viagra', then observing the word 'lottery' as well decreases the spam probability from 0.80 to 0.40. Even though this example table is small, it will grow unfeasibly large very quickly (with n Boolean variables 2^n cases have to be distinguished). We therefore don't normally have access to the full joint distribution and have to approximate it using additional assumptions, as we will see below.

Assuming that X and Y are the only variables we know and care about, the posterior distribution $P(Y|X)$ helps us to answer many questions of interest. For instance, to classify a new e-mail we determine whether the words 'Viagra' and 'lottery' occur in it, look up the corresponding probability $P(Y = \text{spam}\mid\text{Viagra}, \text{lottery})$, and predict spam if this probability exceeds 0.5 and ham otherwise. Such a recipe to predict a value of Y on the basis of the values of X and the posterior distribution $P(Y|X)$ is called a *decision rule*. We can do this even without knowing all the values of X, as the following example shows.

Example 1.2 (Missing values). Suppose we skimmed an e-mail and noticed that it contains the word 'lottery' but we haven't looked closely enough to determine whether it uses the word 'Viagra'. This means that we don't know whether to use the second or the fourth row in Table 1.2 to make a prediction. This is a problem, as we would predict spam if the e-mail contained the word 'Viagra' (second row) and ham if it didn't (fourth row).

The solution is to average these two rows, using the probability of 'Viagra' occurring in any e-mail (spam or not):

$$P(Y|\text{lottery}) = P(Y|\text{Viagra} = 0, \text{lottery})P(\text{Viagra} = 0) + P(Y|\text{Viagra} = 1, \text{lottery})P(\text{Viagra} = 1)$$

For instance, suppose for the sake of argument that one in ten e-mails contain the word 'Viagra', then $P(\text{Viagra} = 1) = 0.10$ and $P(\text{Viagra} = 0) = 0.90$. Using the above formula, we obtain $P(Y = \text{spam}|\text{lottery} = 1) = 0.65 \cdot 0.90 + 0.40 \cdot 0.10 = 0.625$ and $P(Y = \text{ham}|\text{lottery} = 1) = 0.35 \cdot 0.90 + 0.60 \cdot 0.10 = 0.375$. Because the occurrence of 'Viagra' in any e-mail is relatively rare, the resulting distribution deviates only a little from the second row in Table 1.2.

As a matter of fact, statisticians work very often with different conditional probabilities, given by the *likelihood function* $P(X|Y)$.[3] This seems counter-intuitive at first: why would we be interested in the probability of an event we know has occurred (X), conditioned on something we don't know anything about (Y)? I like to think of these as thought experiments: if somebody were to send me a spam e-mail, how likely would it be that it contains exactly the words of the e-mail I'm looking at? And how likely if it were a ham e-mail instead? 'Not very likely at all in either case', you might think, and you would be right: with so many words to choose from, the probability of any particular combination of words would be very small indeed. What really matters is not the magnitude of these likelihoods, but their ratio: how much more likely is it to observe this combination of words in a spam e-mail than it is in a non-spam e-mail. For instance, suppose that for a particular e-mail described by X we have $P(X|Y = \text{spam}) = 3.5 \cdot 10^{-5}$ and $P(X|Y = \text{ham}) = 7.4 \cdot 10^{-6}$, then observing X in a spam e-mail is nearly five times more likely than it is in a ham e-mail. This suggests the following decision rule: predict spam if the likelihood ratio is larger than 1 and ham otherwise.

So which one should we use: posterior probabilities or likelihoods? As it turns out, we can easily transform one into the other using *Bayes' rule*, a simple property of conditional probabilities which states that

$$P(Y|X) = \frac{P(X|Y)P(Y)}{P(X)}$$

Here, $P(Y)$ is the *prior probability*, which in the case of classification tells me how likely each of the classes is *a priori*, i.e., before I have observed the data X. $P(X)$ is the prob-

[3]It is called the likelihood function rather than the 'likelihood distribution' because, for fixed X, $P(X|Y)$ is a mapping from Y to probabilities, but these don't sum to 1 and therefore don't establish a probability distribution over Y.

ability of the data, which is independent of Y and in most cases can be ignored (or inferred in a normalisation step, as it is equal to $\sum_Y P(X|Y)P(Y)$). The first decision rule above suggested that we predict the class with maximum posterior probability, which using Bayes' rule can be written in terms of the likelihood function:

$$y_{\text{MAP}} = \arg\max_Y P(Y|X) = \arg\max_Y \frac{P(X|Y)P(Y)}{P(X)} = \arg\max_Y P(X|Y)P(Y)$$

This is usually called the *maximum a posteriori* (*MAP*) decision rule. Now, if we assume a uniform prior distribution (i.e., $P(Y)$ the same for every value of Y) this reduces to the *maximum likelihood* (*ML*) decision rule:

$$y_{\text{ML}} = \arg\max_Y P(X|Y)$$

A useful rule of thumb is: *use likelihoods if you want to ignore the prior distribution or assume it uniform, and posterior probabilities otherwise.*

If we have only two classes it is convenient to work with ratios of posterior probabilities or likelihood ratios. If we want to know how much the data favours one of two classes, we can calculate the *posterior odds*: e.g.,

$$\frac{P(Y = \text{spam}|X)}{P(Y = \text{ham}|X)} = \frac{P(X|Y = \text{spam})}{P(X|Y = \text{ham})} \frac{P(Y = \text{spam})}{P(Y = \text{ham})}$$

In words: the *posterior odds* are the product of the *likelihood ratio* and the *prior odds*. If the odds are larger than 1 we conclude that the class in the enumerator is the more likely of the two; if it is smaller than 1 we take the class in the denominator instead. In very many cases the prior odds is a simple constant factor that can be manually set, estimated from the data, or optimised to maximise performance on a test set.

Example 1.3 (Posterior odds). Using the data from Table 1.2, and assuming a uniform prior distribution, we arrive at the following posterior odds:

$$\frac{P(Y = \text{spam}|\text{Viagra} = 0, \text{lottery} = 0)}{P(Y = \text{ham}|\text{Viagra} = 0, \text{lottery} = 0)} = \frac{0.31}{0.69} = 0.45$$
$$\frac{P(Y = \text{spam}|\text{Viagra} = 1, \text{lottery} = 1)}{P(Y = \text{ham}|\text{Viagra} = 1, \text{lottery} = 1)} = \frac{0.40}{0.60} = 0.67$$
$$\frac{P(Y = \text{spam}|\text{Viagra} = 0, \text{lottery} = 1)}{P(Y = \text{ham}|\text{Viagra} = 0, \text{lottery} = 1)} = \frac{0.65}{0.35} = 1.9$$
$$\frac{P(Y = \text{spam}|\text{Viagra} = 1, \text{lottery} = 0)}{P(Y = \text{ham}|\text{Viagra} = 1, \text{lottery} = 0)} = \frac{0.80}{0.20} = 4.0$$

Using a MAP decision rule (which in this case is the same as the ML decision rule, since we assumed a uniform prior) we predict ham in the top two cases and spam

Y	$P(\text{Viagra} = 1\|Y)$	$P(\text{Viagra} = 0\|Y)$
spam	0.40	0.60
ham	0.12	0.88

Y	$P(\text{lottery} = 1\|Y)$	$P(\text{lottery} = 0\|Y)$
spam	0.21	0.79
ham	0.13	0.87

Table 1.3. Example marginal likelihoods.

in the bottom two. Given that the full posterior distribution is all there is to know about the domain in a statistical sense, these predictions are the best we can do: they are *Bayes-optimal*.

It is clear from the above analysis that the likelihood function plays an important role in statistical machine learning. It establishes what is called a *generative model*: a probabilistic model from which we can sample values of all variables involved. Imagine a box with two buttons labelled 'ham' and 'spam'. Pressing the 'ham' button generates a random e-mail according to $P(X|Y = \text{ham})$; pressing the 'spam' button generates a random e-mail according to $P(X|Y = \text{spam})$. The question now is what we put inside the box. Let's try a model that is so simplistic it's almost laughable. Assuming a vocabulary of 10 000 words, you have two bags with 10 000 coins each, one for each word in the vocabulary. In order to generate a random e-mail, you take the appropriate bag depending on which button was pressed, and toss each of the 10 000 coins in that bag to decide which words should go in the e-mail (say heads is in and tails is out).

In statistical terms, each coin – which isn't necessarily fair – represents a parameter of the model, so we have 20 000 parameters. If 'Viagra' is a word in the vocabulary, then the coin labelled 'Viagra' in the bag labelled 'spam' represents $P(\text{Viagra}|Y = \text{spam})$ and the coin labelled 'Viagra' in the bag labelled 'ham' represents $P(\text{Viagra}|Y = \text{ham})$. Together, these two coins represent the left table in Table 1.3. Notice that by using different coins for each word we have tacitly assumed that likelihoods of individual words are independent within the same class, which – if true – allows us to decompose the joint likelihood into a product of *marginal likelihoods*:

$$P(\text{Viagra}, \text{lottery}|Y) = P(\text{Viagra}|Y)P(\text{lottery}|Y)$$

Effectively, this independence assumption means that knowing whether one word occurs in the e-mail doesn't tell you anything about the likelihood of other words. The probabilities on the right are called marginal likelihoods because they are obtained by 'marginalising' some of the variables in the joint distribution: e.g., $P(\text{Viagra}|Y) = \sum_{\text{lottery}} P(\text{Viagra}, \text{lottery}|Y)$.

Example 1.4 (Using marginal likelihoods). Assuming these estimates come out as in Table 1.3, we can then calculate likelihood ratios (the previously calculated odds from the full posterior distribution are shown in brackets):

$$\frac{P(\mathsf{Viagra}=0|Y=\mathsf{spam})}{P(\mathsf{Viagra}=0|Y=\mathsf{ham})}\frac{P(\mathsf{lottery}=0|Y=\mathsf{spam})}{P(\mathsf{lottery}=0|Y=\mathsf{ham})}=\frac{0.60}{0.88}\frac{0.79}{0.87}=0.62 \qquad (0.45)$$
$$\frac{P(\mathsf{Viagra}=0|Y=\mathsf{spam})}{P(\mathsf{Viagra}=0|Y=\mathsf{ham})}\frac{P(\mathsf{lottery}=1|Y=\mathsf{spam})}{P(\mathsf{lottery}=1|Y=\mathsf{ham})}=\frac{0.60}{0.88}\frac{0.21}{0.13}=1.1 \qquad (1.9)$$
$$\frac{P(\mathsf{Viagra}=1|Y=\mathsf{spam})}{P(\mathsf{Viagra}=1|Y=\mathsf{ham})}\frac{P(\mathsf{lottery}=0|Y=\mathsf{spam})}{P(\mathsf{lottery}=0|Y=\mathsf{ham})}=\frac{0.40}{0.12}\frac{0.79}{0.87}=3.0 \qquad (4.0)$$
$$\frac{P(\mathsf{Viagra}=1|Y=\mathsf{spam})}{P(\mathsf{Viagra}=1|Y=\mathsf{ham})}\frac{P(\mathsf{lottery}=1|Y=\mathsf{spam})}{P(\mathsf{lottery}=1|Y=\mathsf{ham})}=\frac{0.40}{0.12}\frac{0.21}{0.13}=5.4 \qquad (0.67)$$

We see that, using a maximum likelihood decision rule, our very simple model arrives at the Bayes-optimal prediction in the first three cases, but not in the fourth ('Viagra' and 'lottery' both present), where the marginal likelihoods are actually very misleading. A possible explanation is that these terms are very unlikely to occur together in any e-mail, but slightly more likely in ham than spam – for instance, I might be making exactly this point in an e-mail!

One might call the independence assumption that allows us to decompose joint likelihoods into a product of marginal likelihoods 'naive' – which is exactly what machine learners do when they refer to this simplified Bayesian classifier as *naive Bayes*. This shouldn't be taken as a derogatory term – on the contrary, it illustrates a very important guideline in machine learning: *everything should be made as simple as possible, but not simpler*.[4] In our statistical context, this rule boils down to using the simplest generative model that solves our task. For instance, we may decide to stick to naive Bayes on the grounds that the cases in which the marginal probabilities are misleading are very unlikely to occur in reality and therefore will be difficult to learn from data.

We now have some idea what a probabilistic model looks like, but how do we learn such a model? In many cases this will be a matter of estimating the model parameters from data, which is usually achieved by straightforward counting. For example, in the coin toss model of spam recognition we had two coins for every word w_i in our vocab-

[4]This formulation is often attributed to Einstein, although the source is unclear. Other rules in the same spirit include 'Entities should not be multiplied unnecessarily' (called *Occam's razor*, after William of Ockham); 'We are to admit no more causes of natural things than such as are both true and sufficient to explain their appearances' (Isaac Newton); and 'Scientists must use the simplest means of arriving at their results and exclude everything not perceived by the senses' (Ernst Mach). Whether any of these rules are more than methodological rules of thumbs and point to some fundamental property of nature is heavily debated.

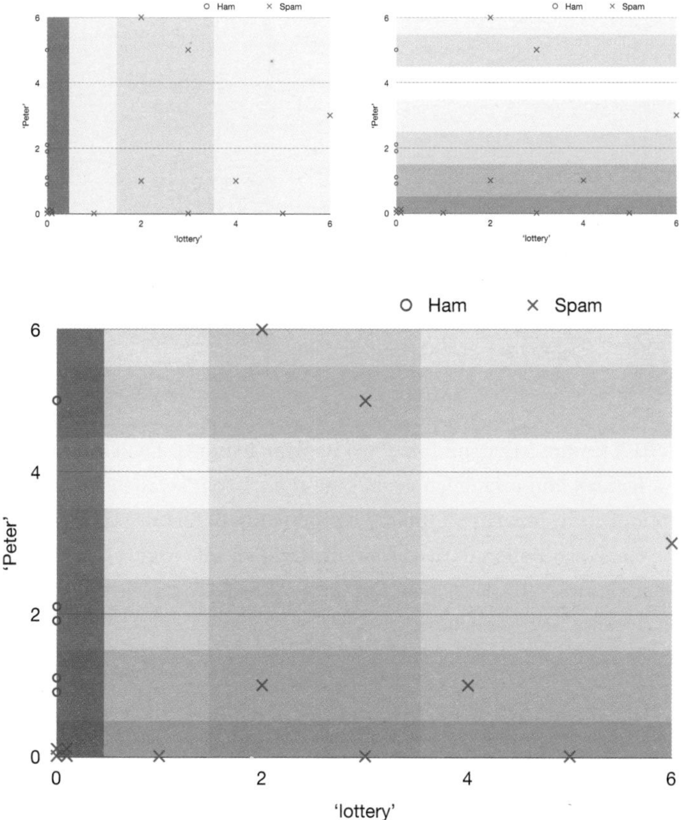

Figure 1.3. **(top)** Visualisation of two marginal likelihoods as estimated from a small data set. The colours indicate whether the likelihood points to spam or ham. **(bottom)** Combining the two marginal likelihoods gives a pattern not unlike that of a Scottish tartan. The colour of a particular cell is a result of the colours in the corresponding row and column.

ulary, one of which is to be tossed if we are generating a spam e-mail and the other for ham e-mails. Let's say that the spam coin comes up heads with probability $\theta_i^{\oplus}$ and the ham coin with probability $\theta_i^{\ominus}$, then these parameters characterise all the likelihoods:

$$P(w_i = 1|Y = \mathsf{spam}) = \theta_i^{\oplus} \qquad P(w_i = 0|Y = \mathsf{spam}) = 1 - \theta_i^{\oplus}$$
$$P(w_i = 1|Y = \mathsf{ham}) = \theta_i^{\ominus} \qquad P(w_i = 0|Y = \mathsf{ham}) = 1 - \theta_i^{\ominus}$$

In order to estimate the parameters $\theta_i^{\pm}$ we need a training set of e-mails labelled spam or ham. We take the spam e-mails and count how many of them w_i occurs in: dividing by the total number of spam e-mails gives us an estimate of $\theta_i^{\oplus}$. Repeating this for the ham e-mails results in an estimate of $\theta_i^{\ominus}$. And that's all there is to it![5]

[5]Sometimes we need to slightly adapt the raw counts for very frequent or very infrequent words, as we shall see in Section 2.3.

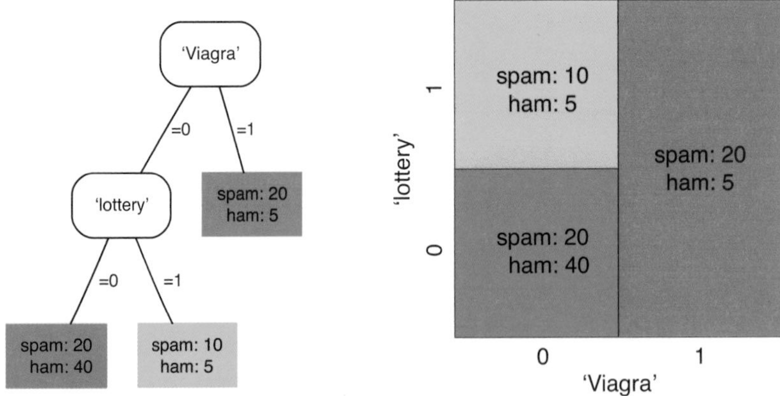

Figure 1.4. (left) A feature tree combining two Boolean features. Each internal node or split is labelled with a feature, and each edge emanating from a split is labelled with a feature value. Each leaf therefore corresponds to a unique combination of feature values. Also indicated in each leaf is the class distribution derived from the training set. **(right)** A feature tree partitions the instance space into rectangular regions, one for each leaf. We can clearly see that the majority of ham lives in the lower left-hand corner.

Figure 1.3 visualises this for a variant of the naive Bayes classifier discussed above. In this variant, we record the number of times a particular word occurs in an e-mail, rather than just whether it occurs or not. We thus need a parameter $p_{ij\pm}$ for each likelihood $P(w_i = j|Y = \pm)$, where $j = 0, 1, 2, \ldots$. For example, we see that there are two spam e-mails in which 'lottery' occurs twice, and one ham e-mail in which 'Peter' occurs five times. Combining the two sets of marginal likelihoods, we get the tartan-like pattern of Figure 1.3 (bottom), which is why I like to call naive Bayes the 'Scottish classifier'. This is a visual reminder of the fact that a multivariate naive Bayes model *decomposes* into a bunch of univariate ones. We will return to this issue of decomposition several times in the book.

Logical models

The third type of model we distinguish is more algorithmic in nature, drawing inspiration from computer science and engineering. I call this type 'logical' because models of this type can be easily translated into rules that are understandable by humans, such as ·**if** Viagra = 1 **then** Class = Y = spam·. Such rules are easily organised in a tree structure, such as the one in Figure 1.4, which I will call a *feature tree*. The idea of such a tree is that features are used to iteratively partition the instance space. The leaves of the tree therefore correspond to rectangular areas in the instance space (or hyper-rectangles, more generally) which we will call *instance space segments*, or segments for short. Depending on the task we are solving, we can then label the leaves with a class, a

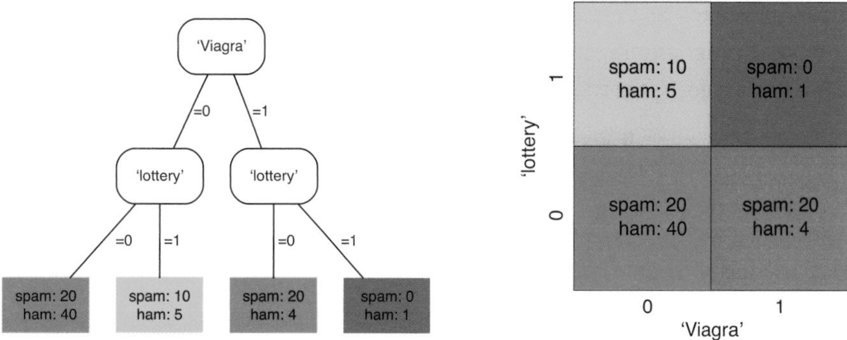

Figure 1.5. **(left)** A complete feature tree built from two Boolean features. **(right)** The corresponding instance space partition is the finest partition that can be achieved with those two features.

probability, a real value, and so on. Feature trees whose leaves are labelled with classes are commonly called *decision trees*.

Example 1.5 (Labelling a feature tree). The leaves of the tree in Figure 1.4 could be labelled, from left to right, as ham – spam – spam, employing a simple decision rule called *majority class*. Alternatively, we could label them with the proportion of spam e-mail occurring in each leaf: from left to right, 1/3, 2/3, and 4/5. Or, if our task was a regression task, we could label the leaves with predicted real values or even linear functions of some other, real-valued features.

Feature trees are very versatile and will play a major role in this book. Even models that do not appear tree-based at first sight can be understood as being built on a feature tree. Consider, for instance, the naive Bayes classifier discussed previously. Since it employs marginal likelihoods such as the ones in Table 1.3 on p.29, it partitions the instance space in as many regions as there are combinations of feature values. This means that it can be thought of as employing a *complete* feature tree, which contains all features, one at each level of the tree (Figure 1.5). Incidentally, notice that the rightmost leaf is the one where naive Bayes made a wrong prediction. Since this leaf covers only a single example, there is a danger that this tree is overfitting the data and that the previous tree is a better model. Decision tree learners often employ *pruning* techniques which delete splits such as these.

A *feature list* is a binary feature tree which always branches in the same direction, either left or right. The tree in Figure 1.4 is a left-branching feature list. Such feature lists can be written as nested if–then–else statements that will be familiar to anyone with a bit of programming experience. For instance, if we were to label the leaves in Figure 1.4 by majority class we obtain the following *decision list*:

·**if** Viagra = 1 **then** Class = Y = spam·
·**else if** lottery = 1 **then** Class = Y = spam·
·**else** Class = Y = ham·

Logical models often have different, equivalent formulations. For instance, two alternative formulations for this model are

·**if** Viagra = 1 ∨ lottery = 1 **then** Class = Y = spam·
·**else** Class = Y = ham·

·**if** Viagra = 0 ∧ lottery = 0 **then** Class = Y = ham·
·**else** Class = Y = spam·

The first of these alternative formulations combines the two rules in the original decision list by means of *disjunction* ('or'), denoted by ∨ . This selects a single non-rectangular area in instance space. The second model formulates a *conjunctive* condition ('and', denoted by ∧) for the opposite class (ham) and declares everything else as spam.

We can also represent the same model as un-nested rules:

·**if** Viagra = 1 **then** Class = Y = spam·
·**if** Viagra = 0 ∧ lottery = 1 **then** Class = Y = spam·
·**if** Viagra = 0 ∧ lottery = 0 **then** Class = Y = ham·

Here, every path from root to a leaf is translated into a rule. As a result, although rules from the same sub-tree share conditions (such as Viagra = 0), every pair of rules will have at least some mutually exclusive conditions (such as lottery = 1 in the second rule and lottery = 0 in the third). However, this is not always the case: rules can have a certain overlap.

Example 1.6 (Overlapping rules). Consider the following rules:

·**if** lottery = 1 **then** Class = Y = spam·
·**if** Peter = 1 **then** Class = Y = ham·

As can be seen in Figure 1.6, these rules overlap for lottery = 1 ∧ Peter = 1, for which they make contradictory predictions. Furthermore, they fail to make any predictions for lottery = 0 ∧ Peter = 0.

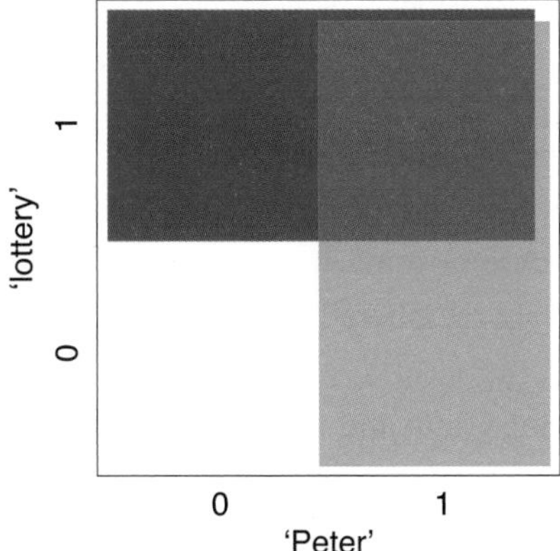

Figure 1.6. The effect of overlapping rules in instance space. The two rules make contradictory predictions in the top right-hand corner, and no prediction at all in the bottom left-hand corner.

A logician would say that rules such as these are both *inconsistent* and *incomplete*. To address incompleteness, we could add a *default rule* to predict, e.g., the majority class for instances not covered by any rule. There are a number of options to deal with overlapping rules, which will be further considered in Chapter 6.

Tree-learning algorithms typically work in a top–down fashion. The first task is to find a good feature to split on at the top of the tree. The aim here is to find splits that result in improved purity of the nodes on the next level, where the purity of a node refers to the degree in which the training examples belonging to that node are of the same class. Once the algorithm has found such a feature, the training set is partitioned into subsets, one for each node resulting from the split. For each of these subsets, we again find a good feature to split on, and so on. An algorithm that works by repeatedly splitting a problem into small sub-problems is what computer scientists call a divide-and-conquer algorithm. We stop splitting a node when all training examples belonging to that node are of the same class. Most rule learning algorithms also work in a top–down fashion. We learn a single rule by repeatedly adding conditions to the rule until the rule only covers examples of a single class. We then remove the covered examples of that class, and repeat the process. This is sometimes called a separate-and-conquer approach.

An interesting aspect of logical models, which sets them aside from most geometric and probabilistic models, is that they can, to some extent, provide *explanations* for their predictions. For example, a prediction assigned by a decision tree could be explained by reading off the conditions that led to the prediction from root to leaf. The model itself can also easily be inspected by humans, which is why they are sometimes called *declarative*. Declarative models do not need to be restricted to the simple rules that we have considered so far. The logical rule learning system Progol found the following set of conditions to predict whether a molecular compound is carcinogenic (causes cancer):

1. it tests positive in the Salmonella assay; or
2. it tests positive for sex-linked recessive lethal mutation in Drosophila; or
3. it tests negative for chromosome aberration; or
4. it has a carbon in a six-membered aromatic ring with a partial charge of -0.13; or
5. it has a primary amine group and no secondary or tertiary amines; or
6. it has an aromatic (or resonant) hydrogen with partial charge ≥ 0.168; or
7. it has a hydroxy oxygen with a partial charge ≥ -0.616 and an aromatic (or resonant) hydrogen; or
8. it has a bromine; or
9. it has a tetrahedral carbon with a partial charge ≤ -0.144 and tests positive on Progol's mutagenicity rules.[6]

The first three conditions concerned certain tests that were carried out for all molecules and whose results were recorded in the data as Boolean features. In contrast, the remaining six rules all refer to the structure of the molecule and were constructed entirely by Progol. For instance, rule 4 predicts that a molecule is carcinogenic if it contains a carbon atom with certain properties. This condition is different from the first three in that it is not a pre-recorded feature in the data, but a new feature that is constructed by Progol during the learning process because it helps to explain the data.

Grouping and grading

We have looked at three general types of models: geometric models, probabilistic models and logical models. As I indicated, although there are some underlying principles pertaining to each of these groups of models, the main reason for dividing things up along this dimension is one of convenience. Before I move on to the third main ingredient of machine learning, features, I want to briefly introduce another important but somewhat more abstract dimension that is in some sense orthogonal to the geometric–probabilistic–logical dimension. This is the distinction between *grouping models* and *grading models*. The key difference between these models is the way they handle the instance space.

Grouping models do this by breaking up the instance space into groups or *segments*, the number of which is determined at training time. One could say that grouping models have a fixed and finite 'resolution' and cannot distinguish between individual instances beyond this resolution. What grouping models do at this finest resolution

[6]Mutagenic molecules cause mutations in DNA and are often carcinogenic. This last rule refers to a set of rules that was learned earlier by Progol to predict mutagenicity.

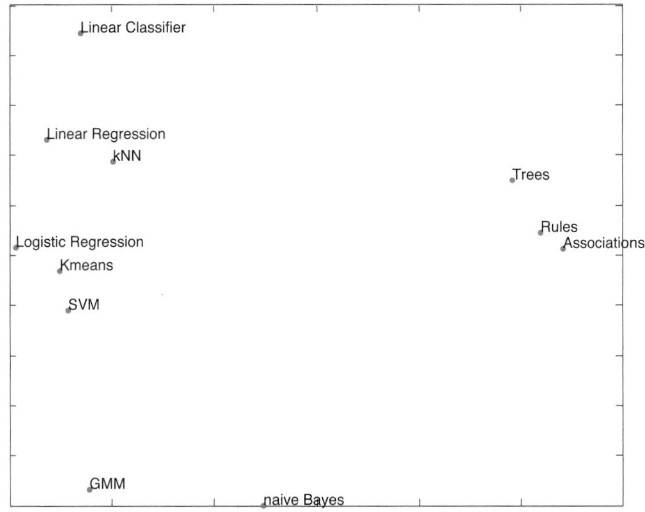

Figure 1.7. A 'map' of some of the models that will be considered in this book. Models that share characteristics are plotted closer together: logical models to the right, geometric models on the top left and probabilistic models on the bottom left. The horizontal dimension roughly ranges from grading models on the left to grouping models on the right.

is often something very simple, such as assigning the majority class to all instances that fall into the segment. The main emphasis of training a grouping model is then on determining the right segments so that we can get away with this very simple labelling at the local segment level. Grading models, on the other hand, do not employ such a notion of segment. Rather than applying very simple, local models, they form one global model over the instance space. Consequently, grading models are (usually) able to distinguish between arbitrary instances, no matter how similar they are. Their resolution is, in theory, infinite, particularly when working in a Cartesian instance space.

A good example of grouping models are the tree-based models we have just considered. They work by repeatedly splitting the instance space into smaller subsets. Because trees are usually of limited depth and don't contain all the available features, the subsets at the leaves of the tree partition the instance space with some finite resolution. Instances filtered into the same leaf of the tree are treated the same, regardless of any features not in the tree that might be able to distinguish them. Support vector machines and other geometric classifiers are examples of grading models. Because they work in a Cartesian instance space, they are able to represent and exploit the minutest differences between instances. As a consequence, it is always possible to come up with a new test instance that receives a score that has not been given to any previous test instance.

The distinction between grouping and grading models is relative rather than

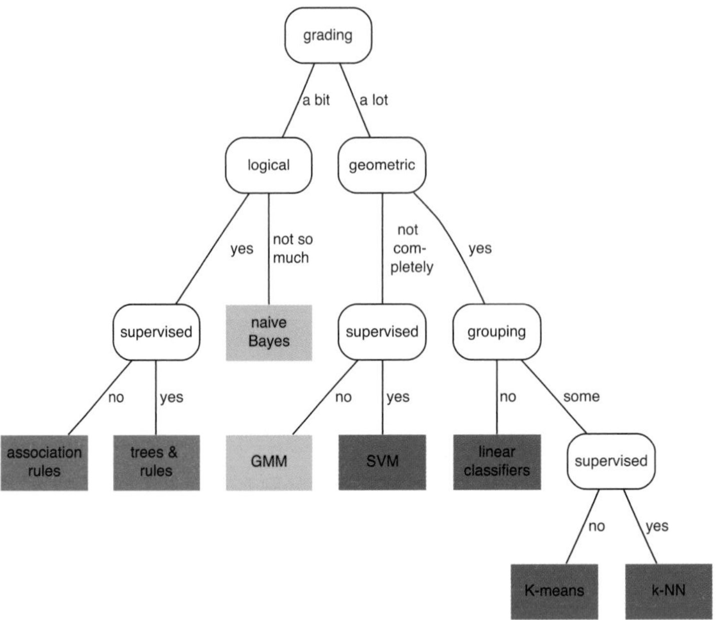

Figure 1.8. A taxonomy describing machine learning methods in terms of the extent to which they are grading or grouping models, logical, geometric or a combination, and supervised or unsupervised. The colours indicate the type of model, from left to right: logical (red), probabilistic (orange) and geometric (purple).

absolute, and some models combine both features. For instance, even though linear classifiers are a prime example of a grading model, it is easy to think of instances that a linear model can't distinguish, namely instances on a line or plane parallel to the decision boundary. The point is not so much that there aren't any segments, but that there are infinitely many. On the other end of the spectrum, regression trees combine grouping and grading features, as we shall see a little later. The overall picture is thus somewhat like what is depicted in Figure 1.7. A taxonomy of eight different models discussed in the book is given in Figure 1.8.[7] These models will be discussed in detail in Chapters 4–9.

1.3 Features: the workhorses of machine learning

Now that we have seen some more examples of machine learning tasks and models, we turn to the third and final main ingredient. Features determine much of the success of a machine learning application, because a model is only as good as its features. A fea-

[7] The figures have been generated from data explained in Example 1.7 below.

Model	geom	stats	logic	group	grad	disc	real	sup	unsup	multi
Trees	1	0	3	3	0	3	2	3	2	3
Rules	0	0	3	3	1	3	2	3	0	2
naive Bayes	1	3	1	3	1	3	1	3	0	3
kNN	3	1	0	2	2	1	3	3	0	3
Linear Classifier	3	0	0	0	3	1	3	3	0	0
Linear Regression	3	1	0	0	3	0	3	3	0	1
Logistic Regression	3	2	0	0	3	1	3	3	0	0
SVM	2	2	0	0	3	2	3	3	0	0
Kmeans	3	2	0	1	2	1	3	0	3	1
GMM	1	3	0	0	3	1	3	0	3	1
Associations	0	0	3	3	0	3	1	0	3	1

Table 1.4. The MLM data set describing properties of machine learning models. Both Figure 1.7 and Figure 1.8 were generated from this data.

ture can be thought of as a kind of measurement that can be easily performed on any instance. Mathematically, they are functions that map from the instance space to some set of feature values called the *domain* of the feature. Since measurements are often numerical, the most common feature domain is the set of real numbers. Other typical feature domains include the set of integers, for instance when the feature counts something, such as the number of occurrences of a particular word; the Booleans, if our feature is a statement that can be true or false for a particular instance, such as 'this e-mail is addressed to Peter Flach'; and arbitrary finite sets, such as a set of colours, or a set of shapes.

Example 1.7 (The MLM data set). Suppose we have a number of learning models that we want to describe in terms of a number of properties:

- the extent to which the models are geometric, probabilistic or logical;
- whether they are grouping or grading models;
- the extent to which they can handle discrete and/or real-valued features;
- whether they are used in supervised or unsupervised learning; and
- the extent to which they can handle multi-class problems.

The first two properties could be expressed by discrete features with three and two values, respectively; or if the distinctions are more gradual, each aspect could be rated on some numerical scale. A simple approach would be to measure each property on an integer scale from 0 to 3, as in Table 1.4. This table establishes a data set in which each row represents an instance and each column a feature. For example, according to this (highly simplified) data some models are purely grouping models (Trees, Associations) or purely grading models (the Linear models, Logistic Regression and GMM), whereas others are more mixed. We can also see that Trees and Rules have very similar values for most of the features, whereas GMM and Associations have mostly different values.

This small data set will be used in several examples throughout the book. In fact, the taxonomy in Figure 1.8 was adapted by hand from a decision tree learned from this small data set, using the models as classes. And the plot in Figure 1.7 was constructed using a dimensionality reduction technique which preserves pairwise distances as much as possible.

Two uses of features

It is worth noting that features and models are intimately connected, not just because models are defined in terms of features, but because a single feature can be turned into what is sometimes called a *univariate model*. We can therefore distinguish two uses of features that echo the distinction between grouping and grading models. A very common use of features, particularly in logical models, is to zoom in on a particular area of the instance space. Let f be a feature counting the number of occurrences of the word 'Viagra' in an e-mail, and let x stand for an arbitrary e-mail, then the condition $f(x) = 0$ selects e-mails that don't contain the word 'Viagra', $f(x) \neq 0$ or $f(x) > 0$ selects e-mails that do, $f(x) \geq 2$ selects e-mails that contain the word at least twice, and so on. Such conditions are called *binary splits*, because they divide the instance space into two groups: those that satisfy the condition, and those that don't. Non-binary splits are also possible: for instance, if g is a feature that has the value 'tweet' for e-mails with up to 20 words, 'short' for e-mails with 21 to 50 words, 'medium' for e-mails with 51 to 200 words, and 'long' for e-mails with more than 200 words, then the expression $g(x)$ represents a four-way split of the instance space. As we have already seen, such splits can be combined in a feature tree, from which a model can be built.

A second use of features arises particularly in supervised learning. Recall that a linear classifier employs a decision rule of the form $\sum_{i=1}^{n} w_i x_i > t$, where x_i is a numerical feature.[8] The linearity of this decision rule means that each feature makes an independent contribution to the score of an instance. This contribution depends on the weight w_i: if this is large and positive, a positive x_i increases the score; if $w_i \ll 0$, a positive x_i decreases the score; if $w_i \approx 0$, x_i's influence is negligible. Thus, the feature

---

[8]Notice we employ two different notations for features: sometimes we write $f(x)$ if it is more convenient to view a feature as a function applied to instance x, and sometimes we write x_i if it is more convenient to view an instance as a vector of feature values.

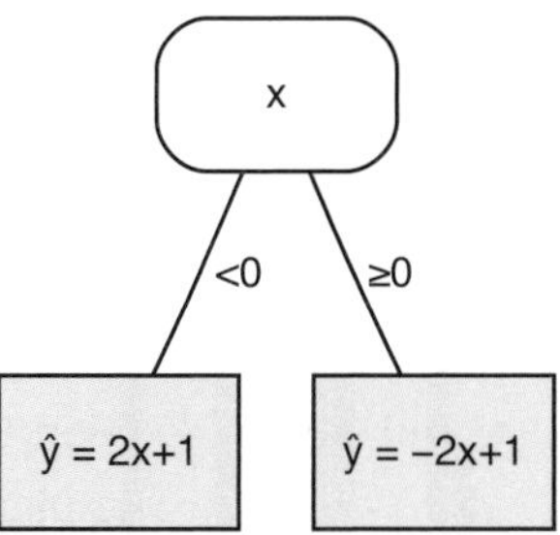

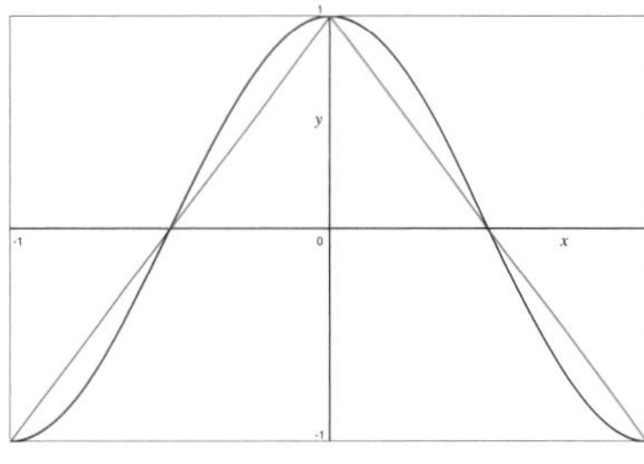

Figure 1.9. (left) A regression tree combining a one-split feature tree with linear regression models in the leaves. Notice how x is used as both a splitting feature and a regression variable. **(right)** The function $y = \cos\pi x$ on the interval $-1 \leq x \leq 1$, and the piecewise linear approximation achieved by the regression tree.

makes a precise and measurable contribution to the final prediction. Also note that that individual features are not 'thresholded', but their full 'resolution' is used in computing an instance's score. These two uses of features – 'features as splits' and 'features as predictors' – are sometimes combined in a single model.

Example 1.8 (Two uses of features). Suppose we want to approximate $y = \cos\pi x$ on the interval $-1 \leq x \leq 1$. A linear approximation is not much use here, since the best fit would be $y = 0$. However, if we split the x-axis in two intervals $-1 \leq x < 0$ and $0 \leq x \leq 1$, we could find reasonable linear approximations on each interval. We can achieve this by using x both as a splitting feature and as a regression variable (Figure 1.9).

Feature construction and transformation

There is a lot of scope in machine learning for playing around with features. In the spam filter example, and text classification more generally, the messages or documents don't come with built-in features; rather, they need to be constructed by the developer of the machine learning application. This *feature construction* process is absolutely crucial for the success of a machine learning application. Indexing an e-mail by the words that occur in it (called a *bag of words* representation as it disregards the order of the words in the e-mail) is a carefully engineered representation that manages to amplify the 'signal' and attenuate the 'noise' in spam e-mail filtering and related classification tasks. However, it is easy to conceive of problems where this would be exactly

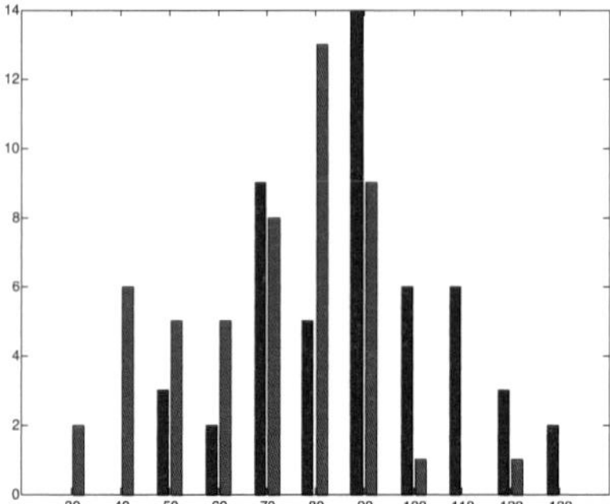

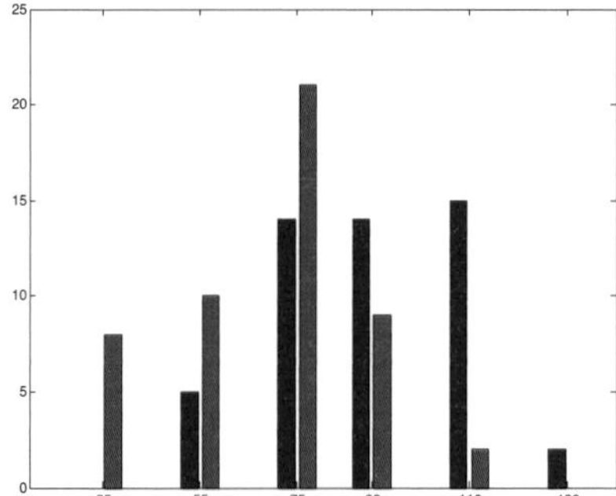

Figure 1.10. (left) Artificial data depicting a histogram of body weight measurements of people with (blue) and without (red) diabetes, with eleven fixed intervals of 10 kilograms width each. **(right)** By joining the first and second, third and fourth, fifth and sixth, and the eighth, ninth and tenth intervals, we obtain a discretisation such that the proportion of diabetes cases increases from left to right. This discretisation makes the feature more useful in predicting diabetes.

the wrong thing to do: for instance if we aim to train a classifier to distinguish between grammatical and ungrammatical sentences, word order is clearly signal rather than noise, and a different representation is called for.

It is often natural to build a model in terms of the given features. However, we are free to change the features as we see fit, or even to introduce new features. For instance, real-valued features often contain unnecessary detail that can be removed by *discretisation*. Imagine you want to analyse the body weight of a relatively small group of, say, 100 people, by drawing a histogram. If you measure everybody's weight in kilograms with one position after the decimal point (i.e., your precision is 100 grams), then your histogram will be sparse and spiky. It is hard to draw any general conclusions from such a histogram. It would be much more useful to discretise the body weight measurements into intervals of 10 kilograms. If we are in a classification context, say we're trying to relate body weight to diabetes, we could then associate each bar of the histogram with the proportion of people having diabetes among the people whose weight falls in that interval. In fact, as we shall see in Chapter 10, we can even choose the intervals such that this proportion is monotonically increasing (Figure 1.10).

The previous example gives another illustration of how, for a particular task such as classification, we can improve the signal-to-noise ratio of a feature. In more extreme cases of feature construction we transform the entire instance space. Consider Figure 1.11: the data on the left is clearly not linearly separable, but by mapping the instance space into a new 'feature space' consisting of the squares of the original features we see that the data becomes almost linearly separable. In fact, by adding in a third feature we can perform a remarkable trick: we can build this feature space classifier without actually constructing the feature space.

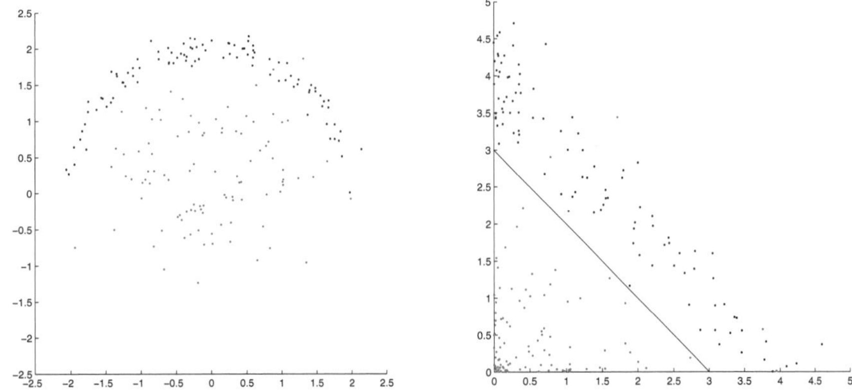

Figure 1.11. (left) A linear classifier would perform poorly on this data. **(right)** By transforming the original (x, y) data into $(x', y') = (x^2, y^2)$, the data becomes more 'linear', and a linear decision boundary $x' + y' = 3$ separates the data fairly well. In the original space this corresponds to a circle with radius $\sqrt{3}$ around the origin.

Example 1.9 (The kernel trick). Let $\mathbf{x}_1 = (x_1, y_1)$ and $\mathbf{x}_2 = (x_2, y_2)$ be two data points, and consider the mapping $(x, y) \mapsto (x^2, y^2, \sqrt{2}xy)$ to a three-dimensional feature space. The points in feature space corresponding to $\mathbf{x}_1$ and $\mathbf{x}_2$ are $\mathbf{x}'_1 = (x_1^2, y_1^2, \sqrt{2}x_1y_1)$ and $\mathbf{x}'_2 = (x_2^2, y_2^2, \sqrt{2}x_2y_2)$. The dot product of these two feature vectors is

$$\mathbf{x}'_1 \cdot \mathbf{x}'_2 = x_1^2x_2^2 + y_1^2y_2^2 + 2x_1y_1x_2y_2 = (x_1x_2 + y_1y_2)^2 = (\mathbf{x}_1 \cdot \mathbf{x}_2)^2$$

That is, by squaring the dot product in the original space we obtain the dot product in the new space *without actually constructing the feature vectors*! A function that calculates the dot product in feature space directly from the vectors in the original space is called a *kernel* – here the kernel is $\kappa(\mathbf{x}_1, \mathbf{x}_2) = (\mathbf{x}_1 \cdot \mathbf{x}_2)^2$.

We can apply this *kernel trick* to the basic linear classifier if we modify the way the decision boundary is calculated. Recall that the basic linear classifier learns a decision boundary $\mathbf{w} \cdot \mathbf{x} = t$ with $\mathbf{w} = \mathbf{p} - \mathbf{n}$ being the difference between the mean of the positive examples and the mean of the negative examples. As an example, suppose we have $\mathbf{n} = (0, 0)$ and $\mathbf{p} = (0, 1)$, and let's assume for the sake of argument that the positive mean has been obtained from two training examples $\mathbf{p}_1 = (-1, 1)$ and $\mathbf{p}_2 = (1, 1)$. This means that $\mathbf{p} = \frac{1}{2}(\mathbf{p}_1 + \mathbf{p}_2)$ and we can rewrite the decision boundary as $\frac{1}{2}\mathbf{p}_1 \cdot \mathbf{x} + \frac{1}{2}\mathbf{p}_2 \cdot \mathbf{x} - \mathbf{n} \cdot \mathbf{x} = t$. Applying the kernel trick we obtain the following decision boundary: $\frac{1}{2}\kappa(\mathbf{p}_1, \mathbf{x}) + \frac{1}{2}\kappa(\mathbf{p}_2, \mathbf{x}) - \kappa(\mathbf{n}, \mathbf{x}) = t$. Using the kernel defined earlier we have $\kappa(\mathbf{p}_1,\mathbf{x}) = (-x+y)^2$, $\kappa(\mathbf{p}_2,\mathbf{x}) = (x+y)^2$ and $\kappa(\mathbf{n},\mathbf{x}) = 0$, from which we derive the decision boundary $\frac{1}{2}(-x+y)^2 + \frac{1}{2}(x+y)^2 = x^2 + y^2 = t$, i.e., a circle around the origin with radius $\sqrt{t}$. Figure 1.11 illustrates this further for a larger data set.

The key point in this 'kernelisation' of the basic linear classifier is that we don't summarise the training data by the positive and negative means – rather, we keep the training data (here: $\mathbf{p}_1$, $\mathbf{p}_2$ and $\mathbf{n}$), so that when classifying a new instance we can evaluate the kernel on it paired with each training example. In return for this more elaborate calculation we get the ability to construct much more flexible decision boundaries.

Interaction between features

One fascinating and multi-faceted aspect of features is that they may interact in various ways. Sometimes such interaction can be exploited, sometimes it can be ignored, and sometimes it poses a challenge. We have already seen an example of feature interaction when we talked about Bayesian spam filtering. Clearly, if we notice the term 'Viagra' in an e-mail, we are not really surprised to find that the e-mail also contains the phrase 'blue pill'. Ignoring this interaction, as the naive Bayes classifier does, means that we are overestimating the amount of information conveyed by observing both phrases in the same e-mail. Whether we can get away with this depends on our task: in spam e-mail classification it turns out not to be a big problem, apart from the fact that we may need to adapt the decision threshold to account for this effect.

We can observe other examples of feature interaction in Table 1.4 on p.39. Consider the features 'grad' and 'real', which assess the extent to which models are of the grading kind, and the extent to which they can handle real-valued features. You may observe that the values of these two features differ by at most 1 for all but one model. Statisticians say that these features are positively correlated (see Background 1.3). Another pair of positively correlated features is 'logic' and 'disc', indicating logical models and the ability to handle discrete features. We can also see some negatively correlated features, where the value of one goes up when the other goes down: this holds naturally for 'split' and 'grad', indicating whether models are primarily grouping or grading models; and also for 'logic' and 'grad'. Finally, pairs of uncorrelated features are 'unsup' and 'multi', standing for unsupervised models and the ability to handle more than two classes; and 'disc' and 'sup', the latter of which indicates supervised models.

In classification, features may be differently correlated depending on the class. For instance, it is conceivable that for somebody whose last name is Hilton and who works for the Paris city council, e-mails with just the word 'Paris' or just the word 'Hilton'

Random variables describe possible outcomes of a random process. They can be either discrete (e.g., the possible outcomes of rolling a die are $\{1,2,3,4,5,6\}$) or continuous (e.g., the possible outcomes of measuring somebody's weight in kilograms). Random variables do not need to range over integer or real numbers, but it does make the mathematics quite a bit simpler so that is what we assume here.

If X is a discrete random variable with probability distribution $P(X)$ then the *expected value* of X is $\mathbb{E}[X] = \sum_x xP(x)$. For instance, the expected value of tossing a fair die is $1 \cdot \frac{1}{6} + 2 \cdot \frac{1}{6} + \ldots + 6 \cdot \frac{1}{6} = 3.5$. Notice that this is not actually a possible outcome. For a continuous random variable we need to replace the sum with an integral, and the probability distribution with a probability density function: $\mathbb{E}[X] = \int_{-\infty}^{+\infty} xp(x)\,dx$. The idea of this rather abstract concept is that if we take a sample $x_1, \ldots, x_n$ of outcomes of the random process, the expected value is what we expect the *sample mean* $\overline{x} = \frac{1}{n}\sum_{i=1}^{n} x_i$ to be – this is the celebrated *law of large numbers* first proved by Jacob Bernoulli in 1713. For this reason the expected value is often called the *population mean*, but it is important to realise that the latter is a theoretical value, while the sample mean is an empirical *estimate* of that theoretical value.

The expectation operator can be applied to functions of random variables. For instance, the (population) *variance* of a discrete random variable is defined as $\mathbb{E}\left[(X - \mathbb{E}[X])^2\right] = \sum_x (x - \mathbb{E}[X])^2 P(x)$ – this measures the spread of the distribution around the expected value. Notice that

$$\mathbb{E}\left[(X - \mathbb{E}[X])^2\right] = \sum_x (x - \mathbb{E}[X])^2 P(x) = \mathbb{E}\left[X^2\right] - \mathbb{E}[X]^2$$

We can similarly define the *sample variance* as $\sigma^2 = \frac{1}{n}\sum_{i=1}^{n}(x_i - \overline{x})^2$, which decomposes as $\frac{1}{n}\sum_{i=1}^{n} x_i^2 - \overline{x}^2$. You will sometimes see the sample variance defined as $\frac{1}{n-1}\sum_{i=1}^{n}(x_i - \overline{x})^2$: dividing by $n-1$ rather than n results in a slightly larger estimate, which compensates for the fact that we are calculating the spread around the sample mean rather than the population mean.

The (population) *covariance* between two discrete random variables X and Y is defined as $\mathbb{E}[(X - \mathbb{E}[X])(Y - \mathbb{E}[Y])] = \mathbb{E}[X \cdot Y] - \mathbb{E}[X] \cdot \mathbb{E}[Y]$ The variance of X is a special case of this, with $Y = X$. Unlike the variance, the covariance can be positive as well as negative. Positive covariance means that both variables tend to increase or decrease together; negative covariance means that if one variable increases, the other tends to decrease. If we have a sample of pairs of values of X and Y, *sample covariance* is defined as $\frac{1}{n}\sum_{i=1}^{n}(x_i - \overline{x})(y_i - \overline{y}) = \frac{1}{n}\sum_{i=1}^{n} x_i y_i - \overline{x}\,\overline{y}$. By dividing the covariance between X and Y by $\sqrt{\sigma_X^2 \sigma_Y^2}$ we obtain the *correlation coefficient*, which is a number between -1 and $+1$.

Background 1.3. Expectations and estimators.

are indicative of ham, whereas e-mails with both terms are indicative of spam. Put differently, within the spam class these features are positively correlated, while within the ham class they are negatively correlated. In such a case, ignoring these interactions will be detrimental for classification performance. In other cases, feature correlations may obscure the true model – we shall see examples of this later in the book. On the other hand, feature correlation sometimes helps us to zoom in on the relevant part of the instance space.

There are other ways in which features can be related. Consider the following three features that can be true or false of a molecular compound:

1. it has a carbon in a six-membered aromatic ring;
2. it has a carbon with a partial charge of −0.13;
3. it has a carbon in a six-membered aromatic ring with a partial charge of −0.13.

We say that the third feature is more *specific* (or less *general*) than the other two, because if the third feature is true, then so are the first and the second. However, the converse does not hold: if both first and second feature are true, the third feature may still be false (because the carbon in the six-membered ring may not be the same as the one with a partial charge of −0.13). We can exploit these relationships when searching for features to add to our logical model. For instance, if we find that the third feature is true of a particular negative example that we're trying to exclude, then there is no point in considering the more general first and second features, because they will not help us in excluding the negative either. Similarly, if we find that the first feature is false of a particular positive we're trying to include, there is no point in considering the more specific third feature instead. In other words, these relationships help us to structure our search for predictive features.

1.4 Summary and outlook

My goal in this chapter has been to take you on a tour to admire the machine learning landscape, and to raise your interest sufficiently to want to read the rest of the book. Here is a summary of the things we have been looking at.

☞ Machine learning is about using the right features to build the right models that achieve the right tasks. These tasks include: binary and multi-class classification, regression, clustering and descriptive modelling. Models for the first few of these tasks are learned in a supervised fashion requiring labelled training data. For instance, if you want to train a spam filter using machine learning, you need a training set of e-mails labelled spam and ham. If you want to know how good the model is you also need labelled test data that is distinct from the training data, as evaluating your model on the data it was trained on will paint too rosy a picture: a test set is needed to expose any overfitting that occurs.

- ☞ Unsupervised learning, on the other hand, works with unlabelled data and so there is no test data as such. For instance, to evaluate a particular partition of data into clusters, one can calculate the average distance from the cluster centre. Other forms of unsupervised learning include learning associations (things that tend to occur together) and identifying hidden variables such as film genres. Overfitting is also a concern in unsupervised learning: for instance, assigning each data point its own cluster will reduce the average distance to the cluster centre to zero, yet is clearly not very useful.

- ☞ On the output side we can distinguish between predictive models whose outputs involve the target variable and descriptive models which identify interesting structure in the data. Often, predictive models are learned in a supervised setting while descriptive models are obtained by unsupervised learning methods, but there are also examples of supervised learning of descriptive models (e.g., subgroup discovery which aims at identifying regions with an unusual class distribution) and unsupervised learning of predictive models (e.g., predictive clustering where the identified clusters are interpreted as classes).

- ☞ We have loosely divided machine learning models into geometric models, probabilistic models and logical models. Geometric models are constructed in Cartesian instance spaces, using geometric concepts such as planes and distances. The prototypical geometric model is the basic linear classifier, which constructs a decision plane orthogonal to the line connecting the positive and negative centres of mass. Probabilistic models view learning as a process of reducing uncertainty using data. For instance, a Bayesian classifier models the posterior distribution $P(Y|X)$ (or its counterpart, the likelihood function $P(X|Y)$) which tells me the class distribution Y after observing the feature values X. Logical models are the most 'declarative' of the three, employing if–then rules built from logical conditions to single out homogeneous areas in instance space.

- ☞ We have also introduced a distinction between grouping and grading models. Grouping models divide the instance space into segments which are determined at training time, and hence have a finite resolution. On each segment, grouping models usually fit a very simple kind of model, such as 'always predict this class'. Grading models fit a more global model, graded by the location of an instance in instance space (typically, but not always, a Cartesian space). Logical models are typical examples of grouping models, while geometric models tend to be grading in nature, although this distinction isn't clear-cut. While this sounds very abstract at the moment, the distinction will become much clearer when we discuss coverage curves in the next chapter.

☞ Last but not least, we have discussed the role of features in machine learning. No model can exist without features, and sometimes a single feature is enough to build a model. Data doesn't always come with ready-made features, and often we have to transform or even construct features. Because of this, machine learning is often an iterative process: we only know we have captured the right features after we have constructed the model, and if the model doesn't perform satisfactorily we need to analyse its performance to understand in what way the features need to be improved.

What you'll find in the rest of the book

In the next nine chapters, we will follow the structure laid out above, and look in detail at

☞ machine learning tasks in Chapters 2 and 3;

☞ logical models: concept learning in Chapter 4, tree models in Chapter 5 and rule models in Chapter 6;

☞ geometric models: linear models in Chapter 7 and distance-based models in Chapter 8;

☞ probabilistic models in Chapter 9; and

☞ features in Chapter 10.

Chapter 11 is devoted to techniques for training 'ensembles' of models that have certain advantages over single models. In Chapter 12 we will consider a number of methods for what machine learners call 'experiments', which involve training and evaluating models on real data. Finally, in the Epilogue we will wrap up the book and take a look ahead.

❦

CHAPTER 2

Binary classification and related tasks

IN THIS CHAPTER and the next we take a bird's-eye view of the wide range of different tasks that can be solved with machine learning techniques. 'Task' here refers to whatever it is that machine learning is intended to improve performance of (recall the definition of machine learning on p.3), for example, e-mail spam recognition. Since this is a classification task, we need to learn an appropriate classifier from training data. Many different types of classifiers exist: linear classifiers, Bayesian classifiers, distance-based classifiers, to name a few. We will refer to these different types as models; they are the subject of Chapters 4–9. Classification is just one of a range of possible tasks for which we can learn a model: other tasks that will pass the review in this chapter are class probability estimation and ranking. In the next chapter we will discuss regression, clustering and descriptive modelling. For each of these tasks we will discuss what it is, what variants exist, how performance at the task could be assessed, and how it relates to other tasks. We will start with some general notation that is used in this chapter and throughout the book (see Background 2.1 for the relevant mathematical concepts).

The objects of interest in machine learning are usually referred to as *instances*. The set of all possible instances is called the *instance space*, denoted $\mathscr{X}$ in this book. To illustrate, $\mathscr{X}$ could be the set of all possible e-mails that can be written using the Latin alphabet.[1] We furthermore distinguish between the *label space* $\mathscr{L}$ and the *output space* $\mathscr{Y}$. The label space is used in supervised learning to label the examples. In order to achieve the task under consideration we need a *model*: a mapping from the instance space to the output space. For instance, in classification the output space is a set of classes, while in regression it is the set of real numbers. In order to learn such a model we require a *training set* Tr of *labelled instances* $(x, l(x))$, also called *examples*, where $l : \mathscr{X} \to \mathscr{L}$ is a labelling function.

Based on this terminology and notation, and concentrating on supervised learning of predictive models for the duration of the chapter, Table 2.1 distinguishes a number of specific scenarios. The most commonly encountered machine learning scenario is where the label space coincides with the output space. That is, $\mathscr{Y} = \mathscr{L}$ and we are trying to learn an approximation $\hat{l} : \mathscr{X} \to \mathscr{L}$ to the true labelling function l, which is only known through the labels it assigned to the training data. This scenario covers both classification and regression. In cases where the label space and the output space differ, this usually serves the purpose of learning a model that outputs more than just a label – for instance, a score for each possible label. In this case we have $\mathscr{Y} = \mathbb{R}^k$, with $k = |\mathscr{L}|$ the number of labels.

Matters may be complicated by *noise*, which can take the form of *label noise* – instead of $l = l(x)$ we observe some corrupted label l' – or *instance noise* – instead of x we observe an instance x' that is corrupted in some way. One consequence of noisy data is that it is generally not advisable to try to match the training data exactly, as this may lead to overfitting the noise. Some of the labelled data is usually set aside for evaluating or testing a classifier, in which case it is called a *test set* and denoted by Te. We use superscripts to restrict training or test set to a particular class: e.g., $Te^{\oplus} = \{(x, l(x)) | x \in Te, l(x) = \oplus\}$ is the set of positive test examples, and $Te^{\ominus}$ is the set of negative test examples.

The simplest kind of input space arises when instances are described by a fixed number of *features*, also called attributes, predictor variables, explanatory variables or independent variables. Indicating the set of values or *domain* of a feature by $\mathscr{F}_i$, we then have that $\mathscr{X} = \mathscr{F}_1 \times \mathscr{F}_2 \times \ldots \times \mathscr{F}_d$, and thus every instance is a d-vector of feature values. In some domains the features to use readily suggest themselves, whereas in other domains they need to be constructed. For example, in the spam filter example in the Prologue we constructed a large number of features, one for each word in a vocabulary, counting the number of occurrences of that word in the e-mail. Even when features are given explicitly we often want to transform them to maximise their usefulness for the task at hand. We will discuss this in considerable detail in Chapter 10.

[1] It is perhaps worth emphasising that an instance space like this is an unimaginably vast set (e.g., the set of all possible text messages of 160 characters using only lower-case letters, spaces and full stops is 28^{160}, a number too large for most pocket calculators), and that only a minuscule fraction of this set carries enough meaning to be possibly encountered in the real world.

We briefly review some important concepts from discrete mathematics. A *set* is a collection of objects, usually of the same kind (e.g., the set of all natural numbers $\mathbb{N}$ or the set of real numbers $\mathbb{R}$). We write $x \in A$ if x is an element of set A, and $A \subseteq B$ if all elements of A are also elements of B (this includes the possibility that A and B are the same set, which is equivalent to $A \subseteq B$ and $B \subseteq A$). The *intersection* and *union* of two sets are defined as $A \cap B = \{x | x \in A \text{ and } x \in B\}$ and $A \cup B = \{x | x \in A \text{ or } x \in B\}$. The *difference* of two sets is defined as $A \setminus B = \{x | x \in A \text{ and } x \notin B\}$. It is customary to fix a *universe of discourse* U such that all sets under consideration are subsets of U. The *complement* of a set A is defined as $\overline{A} = U \setminus A$. Two sets are *disjoint* if their intersection is empty: $A \cap B = \emptyset$. The *cardinality* of a set A is its number of elements and is denoted $|A|$. The *powerset* of a set A is the set of all its subsets $2^A = \{B | B \subseteq A\}$; its cardinality is $|2^A| = 2^{|A|}$. The *characteristic function* of a set A is the function $f : U \rightarrow \{\mathsf{true}, \mathsf{false}\}$ such that $f(x) = \mathsf{true}$ if $x \in A$ and $f(x) = \mathsf{false}$ if $x \in U \setminus A$.

If A and B are sets, the *Cartesian product* $A \times B$ is the set of all pairs $\{(x, y) | x \in A \text{ and } y \in B\}$; this generalises to products of more than two sets. A (binary) *relation* is a set of pairs $R \subseteq A \times B$ for some sets A and B; if $A = B$ we say the relation is over A. Instead of $(x, y) \in R$ we also write xRy. A relation over A is (*i*) *reflexive* if xRx for all $x \in A$; (*ii*) *symmetric* if xRy implies yRx for all $x, y \in A$; (*iii*) *antisymmetric* if xRy and yRx implies $x = y$ for all $x, y \in A$; (*iv*) *transitive* if xRy and yRz implies xRz for all $x, y, z \in A$. (*v*) *total* if xRy or yRx for all $x, y \in A$.

A *partial order* is a binary relation that is reflexive, antisymmetric and transitive. For instance, the *subset* relation $\subseteq$ is a partial order. A *total order* is a binary relation that is total (hence reflexive), antisymmetric and transitive. The $\leq$ relation on real numbers is a total order. If xRy or yRx we say that x and y are *comparable*; otherwise they are *incomparable*. An *equivalence relation* is a binary relation $\equiv$ that is reflexive, symmetric and transitive. The *equivalence class* of x is $[x] = \{y | x \equiv y\}$. For example, the binary relation 'contains the same number of elements as' over any set is an equivalence relation. Any two equivalence classes are disjoint, and the union of all equivalence classes is the whole set – in other words, the set of all equivalence classes forms a *partition* of the set. If $A_1, \ldots, A_n$ is a partition of a set A, i.e. $A_1 \cup \ldots \cup A_n = A$ and $A_i \cap A_j = \emptyset$ for all $i \neq j$, we write $A = A_1 \uplus \ldots \uplus A_n$.

To illustrate this, let T be a feature tree, and define a relation $\sim_T \subseteq \mathscr{X} \times \mathscr{X}$ such that $x \sim_T x'$ if and only if x and x' are assigned to the same leaf of feature tree T, then $\sim_T$ is an equivalence relation, and its equivalence classes are precisely the instance space segments associated with T.

Background 2.1. Useful concepts from discrete mathematics.

The sections in this chapter are devoted to the first three scenarios in Table 2.1:

Task	*Label space*	*Output space*	*Learning problem*
Classification	$\mathscr{L} = \mathscr{C}$	$\mathscr{Y} = \mathscr{C}$	learn an approximation $\hat{c} : \mathscr{X} \to \mathscr{C}$ to the true labelling function c
Scoring and ranking	$\mathscr{L} = \mathscr{C}$	$\mathscr{Y} = \mathbb{R}^{\lvert\mathscr{C}\rvert}$	learn a model that outputs a score vector over classes
Probability estimation	$\mathscr{L} = \mathscr{C}$	$\mathscr{Y} = [0,1]^{\lvert\mathscr{C}\rvert}$	learn a model that outputs a probability vector over classes
Regression	$\mathscr{L} = \mathbb{R}$	$\mathscr{Y} = \mathbb{R}$	learn an approximation $\hat{f} : \mathscr{X} \to \mathbb{R}$ to the true labelling function f

Table 2.1. Predictive machine learning scenarios.

classification in Section 2.1, scoring and ranking in Section 2.2 and class probability estimation in Section 2.3. To keep things manageable we mostly restrict attention to two-class tasks in this chapter and deal with more than two classes in Chapter 3. Regression, unsupervised and descriptive learning will also be considered there.

Throughout this chapter I will illustrate key concepts by means of examples using simple models of the kind discussed in the Prologue. These models will either be simple tree-based models, representative of grouping models, or linear models, representative of grading models. Sometimes we will even construct models from single features, a setting that could be described as *univariate machine learning*. We will start dealing with the question of how to *learn* such models from Chapter 4 onwards.

2.1 Classification

Classification is the most common task in machine learning. A *classifier* is a mapping $\hat{c} : \mathscr{X} \to \mathscr{C}$, where $\mathscr{C} = \{C_1, C_2, \ldots, C_k\}$ is a finite and usually small set of *class labels*. We will sometimes also use C_i to indicate the set of examples of that class. We use the 'hat' to indicate that $\hat{c}(x)$ is an estimate of the true but unknown function $c(x)$. Examples for a classifier take the form $(x, c(x))$, where $x \in \mathscr{X}$ is an instance and $c(x)$ is the true class of the instance. Learning a classifier involves constructing the function $\hat{c}$ such that it matches c as closely as possible (and not just on the training set, but ideally on the entire instance space $\mathscr{X}$).

In the simplest case we have only two classes which are usually referred to as *positive* and *negative*, $\oplus$and $\ominus$, or $+1$ and -1. Two-class classification is often called *binary classification* (or *concept learning*, if the positive class can be meaningfully called

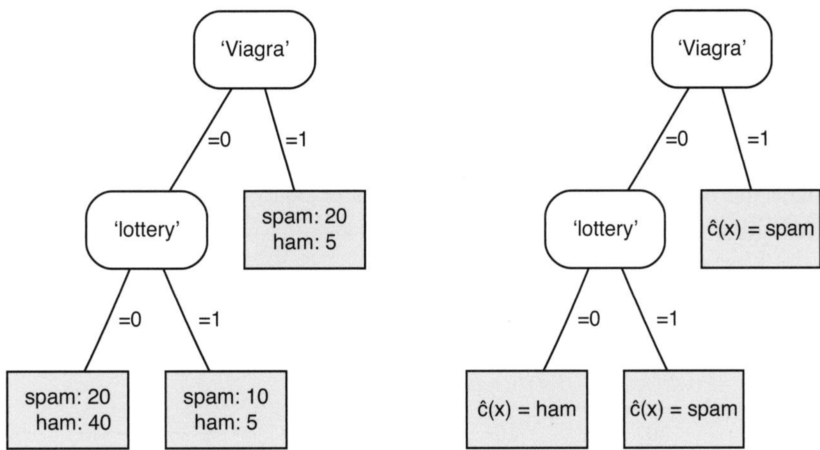

Figure 2.1. (left) A feature tree with training set class distribution in the leaves. **(right)** A decision tree obtained using the majority class decision rule.

a concept). Spam e-mail filtering is a good example of binary classification, in which spam is conventionally taken as the positive class, and ham as the negative class (clearly, positive here doesn't mean 'good'!). Other examples of binary classification include medical diagnosis (the positive class here is having a particular disease) and credit card fraud detection.

The feature tree in Figure 2.1 (left) can be turned into a classifier by labelling each leaf with a class. The simplest way to do this is by assigning the *majority class* in each leaf, resulting in the decision tree in Figure 2.1 (right). The classifier works as follows: if an e-mail contains the word 'Viagra' it is classified as spam (right-most leaf); otherwise, the occurrence of the word 'lottery' decides whether it gets labelled spam or ham.[2] From the numbers in Figure 2.1 we can get an idea how well this classifier does. The left-most leaf correctly predicts 40 ham e-mails but also mislabels 20 spam e-mails that contain neither 'Viagra' nor 'lottery'. The middle leaf correctly classifies 10 spam e-mails but also erroneously labels 5 ham e-mails as spam. The 'Viagra' test correctly picks out 20 spam e-mails but also 5 ham e-mails. Taken together, this means that 30 out of 50 spam e-mails are classified correctly, and 40 out of 50 ham e-mails.

Assessing classification performance

The performance of such classifiers can be summarised by means of a table known as a *contingency table* or *confusion matrix* (Table 2.2 (left)). In this table, each row refers to

[2] If you are keen to know how such a decision tree can be learned from data, you may want to take a sneak preview at Algorithm 5.1 on p.132.

actual classes as recorded in the test set, and each column to classes as predicted by the classifier. So, for instance, the first row states that the test set contains 50 positives, 30 of which were correctly predicted and 20 incorrectly. The last column and the last row give the *marginals* (i.e., column and row sums). Marginals are important because they allow us to assess statistical significance. For instance, the contingency table in Table 2.2 (right) has the same marginals, but the classifier clearly makes a random choice as to which predictions are positive and which are negative – as a result the distribution of actual positives and negatives in either predicted class is the same as the overall distribution (uniform in this case).

	Predicted ⊕	*Predicted* ⊖	
Actual ⊕	**30**	20	50
Actual ⊖	10	**40**	50
	40	60	100

	⊕	⊖	
⊕	**20**	30	50
⊖	20	**30**	50
	40	60	100

Table 2.2. (left) A two-class contingency table or confusion matrix depicting the performance of the decision tree in Figure 2.1. Numbers on the descending diagonal indicate correct predictions, while the ascending diagonal concerns prediction errors. **(right)** A contingency table with the same marginals but independent rows and columns.

From a contingency table we can calculate a range of performance indicators. The simplest of these is *accuracy*, which is the proportion of correctly classified test instances. In the notation introduced at the beginning of this chapter, accuracy over a test set *Te* is defined as

$$acc = \frac{1}{|Te|} \sum_{x \in Te} I[\hat{c}(x) = c(x)] \tag{2.1}$$

Here, the function $I[\cdot]$ denotes the *indicator function*, which is 1 if its argument evaluates to true, and 0 otherwise. In this case it is a convenient way to count the number of test instances that are classified correctly by the classifier (i.e., the estimated class label $\hat{c}(x)$ is equal to the true class label $c(x)$). For example, in Table 2.2 (left) the accuracy of the classifier is 0.70 or 70%, and in Table 2.2 (right) it is 0.50. Alternatively, we can calculate the *error rate* as the proportion of incorrectly classified instances, here 0.30 and 0.50, respectively. Clearly, accuracy and error rate sum to 1.

Test set accuracy can be seen as an *estimate* of the probability that an arbitrary instance $x \in \mathscr{X}$ is classified correctly: more precisely, it estimates the probability

$$P_{\mathscr{X}}(\hat{c}(x) = c(x))$$

(Notice that I write $P_{\mathscr{X}}$ to emphasise that this is a probability distribution over the instance space $\mathscr{X}$; I will often omit subscripts if this is clear from the context.) We typically only have access to the true classes of a small fraction of the instance space and so an estimate is all we can hope to get. It is therefore important that the test set is as representative as possible. This is usually formalised by the assumption that the occurrence of instances in the world – i.e., how likely or typical a particular e-mail is – is governed by an unknown probability distribution on $\mathscr{X}$, and that the test set *Te* is generated according to this distribution.

It is often convenient – not to say necessary – to distinguish performance on the classes. To this end, we need some further terminology. Correctly classified positives and negatives are referred to as *true positives* and *true negatives*, respectively. Incorrectly classified positives are, perhaps somewhat confusingly, called *false negatives*; similarly, misclassified negatives are called *false positives*. A good way to think of this is to remember that positive/negative refers to the classifier's prediction, and true/false refers to whether the prediction is correct or not. So, a false positive is something that was incorrectly predicted as positive, and therefore an actual negative (e.g., a ham e-mail misclassified as spam, or a healthy patient misclassified as having the disease in question). In the previous example (Table 2.2 (left)) we have 30 true positives, 20 false negatives, 40 true negatives and 10 false positives.

The *true positive rate* is the proportion of positives correctly classified, and can be defined mathematically as

$$tpr = \frac{\sum_{x \in Te} I[\hat{c}(x) = c(x) = \oplus]}{\sum_{x \in Te} I[c(x) = \oplus]} \tag{2.2}$$

True positive rate is an estimate of the probability that an arbitrary positive is classified correctly, that is, an estimate of $P_{\mathscr{X}}(\hat{c}(x) = \oplus | c(x) = \oplus)$. Analogously, the *true negative rate* is the proportion of negatives correctly classified (see Table 2.3 on p.57 for the mathematical definition), and estimates $P_{\mathscr{X}}(\hat{c}(x) = \ominus | c(x) = \ominus)$. These rates, which are sometimes called *sensitivity* and *specificity*, can be seen as per-class accuracies. In the contingency table, the true positive and negative rates can be calculated by dividing the number on the descending (good) diagonal by the row total. We can also talk about per-class error rates, which is the *false negative rate* for the positives (i.e., the number of misclassified positives or false negatives as a proportion of the total number of positives) and the *false positive rate* for the negatives (sometimes called the *false alarm rate*). These rates can be found by dividing the number on the ascending (bad) diagonal by the row total.

In Table 2.2 (left) we have a true positive rate of 60%, a true negative rate of 80%, a false negative rate of 40% and a false positive rate of 20%. In Table 2.2 (right) we have a true positive rate of 40%, a true negative rate of 60%, a false negative rate of 60% and a false positive rate of 40%. Notice that the accuracy in both cases is the average of the true positive rate and the true negative rate (and the error rate is the average of the false positive rate and the false negative rate). However, this is true only if the test set contains equal numbers of positives and negatives – in the general case we need to use a *weighted* average, where the weights are the proportions of positives and negatives in the test set.

Example 2.1 (Accuracy as a weighted average). Suppose a classifier's predictions on a test set are as in the following table:

	Predicted ⊕	*Predicted* ⊖	
Actual ⊕	**60**	15	75
Actual ⊖	10	**15**	25
	70	30	100

From this table, we see that the true positive rate is $tpr = 60/75 = 0.80$ and the true negative rate is $tnr = 15/25 = 0.60$. The overall accuracy is $acc = (60+15)/100 = 0.75$, which is no longer the average of true positive and negative rates. However, taking into account the proportion of positives $pos = 0.75$ and the proportion of negatives $neg = 1 - pos = 0.25$, we see that

$$acc = pos \cdot tpr + neg \cdot tnr \tag{2.3}$$

This equation holds in general: if the numbers of positives and negatives are equal, we obtain the unweighted average from the earlier example ($acc = (tpr + tnr)/2$).

Equation 2.3 has a neat intuition: good performance on either class contributes to good classification accuracy, but the more prevalent class contributes more strongly. In order to achieve good accuracy, a classifier should concentrate on the *majority class*, particularly if the class distribution is highly unbalanced. However, it is often the case that the majority class is also the least interesting class. To illustrate, suppose you issue a query to an internet search engine,[3] and suppose that for that particular query there is only one relevant page in every 1 000 web pages. Now consider a 'reluctant' search engine that doesn't return *any* answers – i.e., it classifies every web page as irrelevant to your query. Consequently, it will achieve 0% true positive rate and 100% true negative rate. Because $pos = 1/1000 = 0.1\%$ and $neg = 99.9\%$, the reluctant search engine's accuracy is very high (99.9%). Put differently, if we select a random web page uniformly

[3]An internet search engine can be seen as a binary classifier into the classes relevant and irrelevant, or interesting and not interesting, if we fix the query – not very realistic in practice, but a useful analogy for our purposes.

Measure	*Definition*	*Equal to*	*Estimates*
number of positives	$Pos = \sum_{x \in Te} I[c(x) = \oplus]$		
number of negatives	$Neg = \sum_{x \in Te} I[c(x) = \ominus]$	$\|Te\| - Pos$	
number of true positives	$TP = \sum_{x \in Te} I[\hat{c}(x) = c(x) = \oplus]$		
number of true negatives	$TN = \sum_{x \in Te} I[\hat{c}(x) = c(x) = \ominus]$		
number of false positives	$FP = \sum_{x \in Te} I[\hat{c}(x) = \oplus, c(x) = \ominus]$	$Neg - TN$	
number of false negatives	$FN = \sum_{x \in Te} I[\hat{c}(x) = \ominus, c(x) = \oplus]$	$Pos - TP$	
proportion of positives	$pos = \frac{1}{\|Te\|} \sum_{x \in Te} I[c(x) = \oplus]$	$Pos/\|Te\|$	$P(c(x) = \oplus)$
proportion of negatives	$neg = \frac{1}{\|Te\|} \sum_{x \in Te} I[c(x) = \ominus]$	$1 - pos$	$P(c(x) = \ominus)$
class ratio	$clr = pos/neg$	Pos/Neg	
(*) accuracy	$acc = \frac{1}{\|Te\|} \sum_{x \in Te} I[\hat{c}(x) = c(x)]$		$P(\hat{c}(x) = c(x))$
(*) error rate	$err = \frac{1}{\|Te\|} \sum_{x \in Te} I[\hat{c}(x) \neq c(x)]$	$1 - acc$	$P(\hat{c}(x) \neq c(x))$
true positive rate, sensitivity, recall	$tpr = \frac{\sum_{x \in Te} I[\hat{c}(x)=c(x)=\oplus]}{\sum_{x \in Te} I[c(x)=\oplus]}$	TP/Pos	$P(\hat{c}(x) = \oplus \| c(x) = \oplus)$
true negative rate, specificity, negative recall	$tnr = \frac{\sum_{x \in Te} I[\hat{c}(x)=c(x)=\ominus]}{\sum_{x \in Te} I[c(x)=\ominus]}$	TN/Neg	$P(\hat{c}(x) = \ominus \| c(x) = \ominus)$
false positive rate, false alarm rate	$fpr = \frac{\sum_{x \in Te} I[\hat{c}(x)=\oplus, c(x)=\ominus]}{\sum_{x \in Te} I[c(x)=\ominus]}$	$FP/Neg = 1 - tnr$	$P(\hat{c}(x) = \oplus \| c(x) = \ominus)$
false negative rate	$fnr = \frac{\sum_{x \in Te} I[\hat{c}(x)=\ominus, c(x)=\oplus]}{\sum_{x \in Te} I[c(x)=\oplus]}$	$FN/Pos = 1 - tpr$	$P(\hat{c}(x) = \ominus \| c(x) = \oplus)$
precision, confidence	$prec = \frac{\sum_{x \in Te} I[\hat{c}(x)=c(x)=\oplus]}{\sum_{x \in Te} I[\hat{c}(x)=\oplus]}$	$TP/(TP + FP)$	$P(c(x) = \oplus \| \hat{c}(x) = \oplus)$

Table 2.3. A summary of different quantities and evaluation measures for classifiers on a test set *Te*. Symbols starting with a capital letter denote absolute frequencies (counts), while lower-case symbols denote relative frequencies or ratios. All except those indicated with (*) are defined only for binary classification. The right-most column specifies the instance space probabilities that these relative frequencies are estimating.

over all web pages, the probability of selecting a positive is only 0.001, and these are the only pages on which the reluctant engine makes an error. However, we are not normally selecting pages from the web uniformly, and hence accuracy is not a meaningful quantity in this context. To be of any use at all, a search engine should achieve a much better true positive rate, which usually comes at the expense of a worse true negative rate (and hence a drop in accuracy).

We conclude from this example that, if the minority class is the class of interest and very small, accuracy and performance on the majority class are not the right quantities to optimise. For this reason, an alternative to true negative rate called *precision* is usually considered in such cases. Precision is a counterpart to true positive rate in the following sense: while true positive rate is the proportion of predicted positives among the actual positives, precision is the proportion of actual positives among the predicted positives. In Example 2.1 the classifier's precision on the test set is $60/70 = 85.7\%$. In

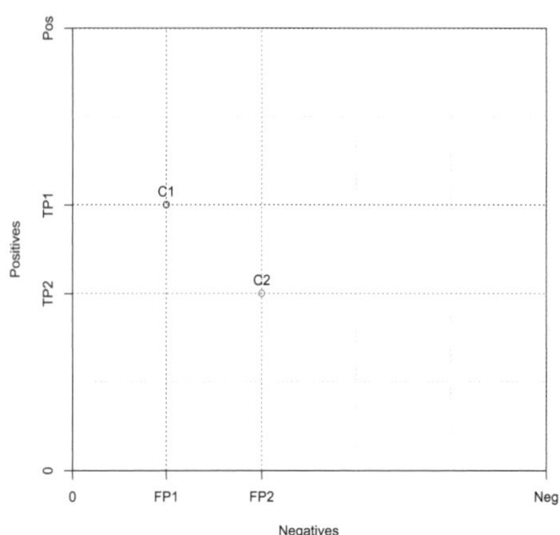

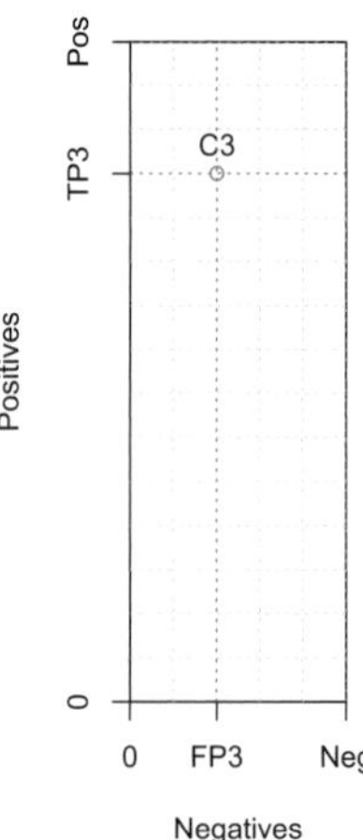

Figure 2.2. **(left)** A coverage plot depicting the two contingency tables in Table 2.2. The plot is square because the class distribution is uniform. **(right)** Coverage plot for Example 2.1, with a class ratio $clr = 3$.

the reluctant search engine example we have not only 0 true positive rate (which in this context is usually called *recall*) but also 0 precision, which clearly demonstrates the problem with a search engine that doesn't return any answers. Table 2.3 summarises the evaluation measures introduced in this section.

Visualising classification performance

I will now introduce an important tool for visualising the performance of classifiers and other models called a *coverage plot*. If you look at two-class contingency tables such as the ones depicted in Table 2.2, you realise that, even though the table contains nine numbers, only four of those can be chosen freely. For instance, once you've determined the true/false positives/negatives, the marginals are fixed. Or if you know the true positives, true negatives, total number of positives and size of the test set, you can reconstruct all other numbers. Statisticians say that the table has four *degrees of freedom*.[4]

Often we are particularly interested in the following four numbers that completely determine the contingency table: the number of positives *Pos*, the number of negatives *Neg*, the number of true positives *TP* and the number of false positives *FP*. A coverage plot visualises these four numbers by means of a rectangular coordinate system and a point. Imagine a rectangle with height *Pos* and width *Neg*. Imagine furthermore that all positives live on the y-axis of this rectangle, and all negatives on the x-axis. We don't

[4]More generally, a k-class contingency table has $(k+1)^2$ entries and k^2 degrees of freedom.

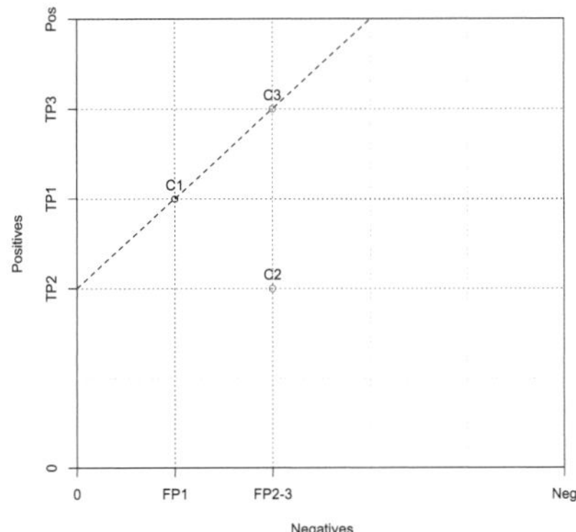

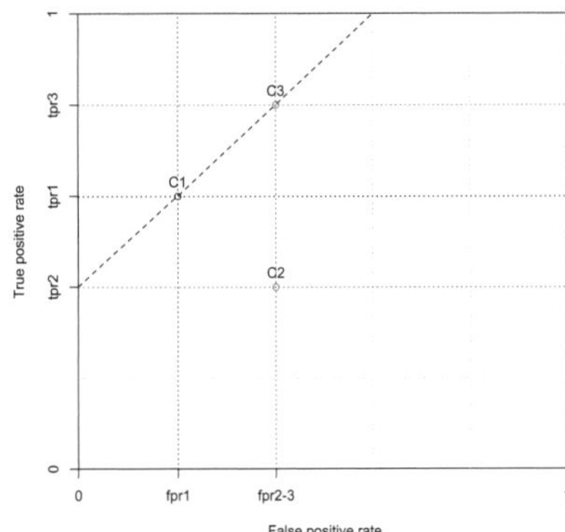

Figure 2.3. (left) C1 and C3 both dominate C2, but neither dominates the other. The diagonal line indicates that C1 and C3 achieve equal accuracy. **(right)** The same plot with normalised axes. We can interpret this plot as a merger of the two coverage plots in Figure 2.2, employing normalisation to deal with the different class distributions. The diagonal line now indicates that C1 and C3 have the same average recall.

really care how positives and negatives are ordered on their respective axes, as long as *positive predictions come before negative predictions.* This gives us enough information to depict the whole contingency table as a single point within the rectangle (Figure 2.2).

Consider the two classifiers marked C1 and C2 in Figure 2.2 (left). One reason why coverage plots are so useful is that we can immediately see that C1 is better than C2. How do we know that? Well, C1 has both more true positives and fewer false positives than C2, and so is better in both respects. Put differently, C1 achieves better performance than C2 on *both* classes. If one classifier outperforms another classifier on all classes, the first one is said to *dominate* the second.[5] However, things are not always that straightforward. Consider a third classifier C3, better than C1 on the positives but worse on the negatives (Figure 2.3 (left)). Although both C1 and C3 dominate C2, neither of them dominates the other. Which one we prefer depends on whether we put more emphasis on the positives or on the negatives.

We can make this a little bit more precise. Notice that the line segment connecting C1 and C3 has a slope of 1. Imagine travelling up that line: whenever we gain a true positive, we also lose a true negative (or gain a false positive, which is the same thing). This doesn't affect the sum of true positives and true negatives, and hence the accuracy is the same wherever we are on the line. It follows that C1 and C3 have the same accuracy. *In a coverage plot, classifiers with the same accuracy are connected by line segments with slope 1.* If true positives and true negatives are equally important, the

[5]This terminology comes from the field of *multi-criterion optimisation*. A dominated solution is one that is not on the *Pareto front*.

choice between C1 and C3 is arbitrary; if true positives are more important we should choose C3, if true negatives are more important we prefer C1.

Now consider Figure 2.3 (right). What I have done here is renormalise the axes by dividing the x-axis by *Neg* and the y-axis by *Pos*, resulting in a plot in the unit square with true positive rate on the y-axis and false positive rate on the x-axis. In this case the original coverage plot was already square (*Pos* = *Neg*), so the relative position of the classifiers isn't affected by the normalisation. However, since the normalised plot will be square regardless of the shape of the original plot, normalisation is a way to combine differently shaped coverage plots, and thus to combine results on test sets with different class distributions. Suppose you would normalise Figure 2.2 (right): since C3's true and false positive rates are 80% and 40%, respectively (see Example 2.1 on p.56), its position in a normalised plot is exactly the same as the one labelled C3 in Figure 2.3 (right)! In other words, classifiers occupying different points in different coverage spaces (e.g., C3 in Figure 2.2 (right) and C3 in Figure 2.3 (left)) can end up in the same point in a normalised plot.

What is the meaning of the diagonal line connecting C1 and C3 in Figure 2.3 (right)? It can't have the same meaning as in the coverage plot, because in a normalised plot we know the true and false positive rates but not the class distribution, and so we cannot calculate accuracy (refer back to Equation 2.3 on p.56 if you want to remind yourself why). The line is defined by the equation $tpr = fpr + y_0$, where y_0 is the y-intercept (the value of *tpr* where the line intersects the y-axis) . Now consider the average of the true positive rate and the true negative rate, which we will call *average recall*, denoted *avg-rec*.[6] On a line with slope 1 we have $avg\text{-}rec = (tpr + tnr)/2 = (tpr + 1 - fpr)/2 = (1 + y_0)/2$, which is a constant. *In a normalised coverage plot, line segments with slope 1 connect classifiers with the same average recall.* If recall on the positives and the negatives are equally important, the choice between C1 and C3 is arbitrary; if positive recall is more important we should choose C3, if negative recall is more important we prefer C1.

In the literature, normalised coverage plots are referred to as *ROC plots*, and we will follow that convention from now on.[7] ROC plots are much more common than coverage plots, but both have their specific uses. Broadly speaking, you should use a coverage plot if you explicitly want to take the class distribution into account, for instance when you are working with a single data set. An ROC plot is useful if you want to combine results from different data sets with different class distributions. Clearly, there are many connections between the two. Since an ROC plot is always square, lines of constant average recall (so-called average recall *isometrics*) do not only have

---

[6]Remember that recall is just a different name for true positive rate; negative recall is then the same as the true negative rate, and average recall is the average of positive recall (or true positive rate) and negative recall (or true negative rate). It is sometimes called *macro-averaged accuracy*.

[7]ROC stands for *receiver operating characteristic*, a term originating from *signal detection theory*.

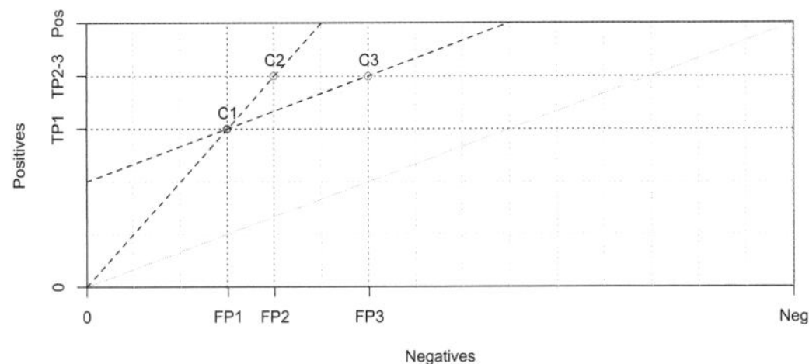

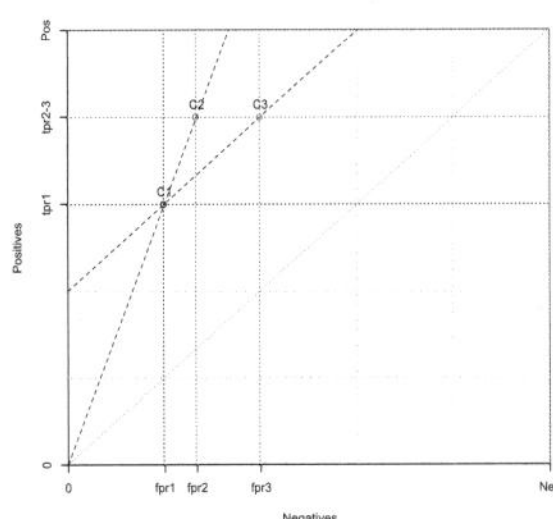

Figure 2.4. **(left)** In a coverage plot, accuracy isometrics have a slope of 1, and average recall isometrics are parallel to the ascending diagonal. **(right)** In the corresponding ROC plot, average recall isometrics have a slope of 1; the accuracy isometric here has a slope of 3, corresponding to the ratio of negatives to positives in the data set.

a slope of 1 but are parallel to the ascending diagonal. The latter property carries over to coverage plots. To illustrate, in the coverage plot in Figure 2.4, C1 and C2 have the same accuracy (they are connected by a line segment with slope 1), and C1 and C3 have the same average recall (they are connected by a line segment parallel to the diagonal). You can also argue that C2 has both higher accuracy and higher average recall than C3 (why?). In the corresponding ROC plot, the average recall isometric has a slope of 1, and the accuracy isometric's slope is $Neg/Pos = 1/clr$.

2.2 Scoring and ranking

Many classifiers compute scores on which their class predictions are based. For instance, in the Prologue we saw how SpamAssassin calculates a weighted sum from the rules that 'fire' for a particular e-mail. Such scores contain additional information that can be beneficial in a number of ways, which is why we perceive scoring as a task in its own right. Formally, a *scoring classifier* is a mapping $\hat{\mathbf{s}} : \mathscr{X} \rightarrow \mathbb{R}^k$, i.e., a mapping from the instance space to a k-vector of real numbers. The boldface notation indicates that a scoring classifier outputs a vector $\hat{\mathbf{s}}(x) = (\hat{s}_1(x), \ldots, \hat{s}_k(x))$ rather than a single number; $\hat{s}_i(x)$ is the score assigned to class C_i for instance x. This score indicates how likely it is that class label C_i applies. If we only have two classes, it usually suffices to consider the score for only one of the classes; in that case, we use $\hat{s}(x)$ to denote the score of the positive class for instance x.

Figure 2.5 demonstrates how a feature tree can be turned into a scoring tree. In order to obtain a score for each leaf, we first calculate the ratio of spam to ham, which is 1/2 for the left leaf, 2 for the middle leaf and 4 for the right leaf. Because it is often more convenient to work with an additive scale, we obtain scores by taking the logarithm of the class ratio (the base of the logarithm is not really important; here we have

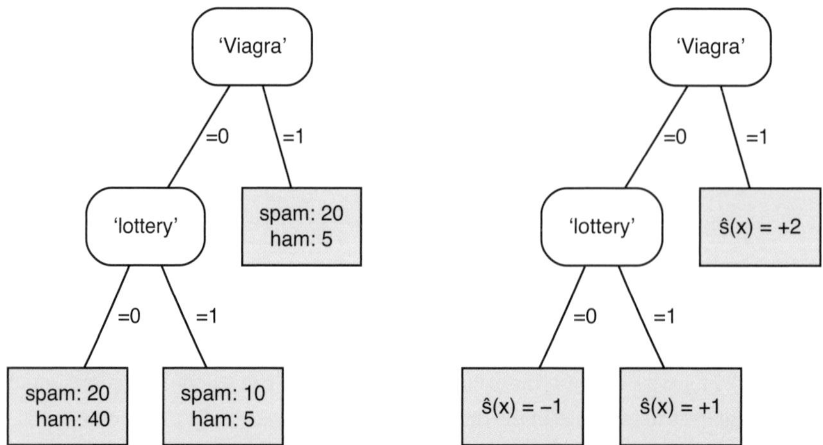

Figure 2.5. (left) A feature tree with training set class distribution in the leaves. **(right)** A scoring tree using the logarithm of the class ratio as scores; spam is taken as the positive class.

taken base-2 logarithms to get nice round numbers). Notice that the majority class decision tree corresponds to thresholding $\hat{s}(x)$ at 0: i.e., predict spam if $\hat{s}(x) > 0$ and ham otherwise.

If we take the true class $c(x)$ as $+1$ for positive examples and -1 for negative examples, then the quantity $z(x) = c(x)\hat{s}(x)$ is positive for correct predictions and negative for incorrect predictions: this quantity is called the *margin* assigned by the scoring classifier to the example.[8] We would like to reward large positive margins, and penalise large negative values. This is achieved by means of a so-called *loss function* $L : \mathbb{R} \mapsto [0, \infty)$ which maps each example's margin $z(x)$ to an associated loss $L(z(x))$. We will assume that $L(0) = 1$, which is the loss incurred by having an example on the decision boundary. We furthermore have $L(z) \geq 1$ for $z < 0$, and usually also $0 \leq L(z) < 1$ for $z > 0$ (Figure 2.6). The average loss over a test set Te is $\frac{1}{|Te|}\sum_{x \in Te} L(z(x))$.

The simplest loss function is *0–1 loss*, which is defined as $L_{01}(z) = 1$ if $z \leq 0$ and $L(z) = 0$ if $z > 0$. The average 0–1 loss is simply the proportion of misclassified test examples:

$$\frac{1}{|Te|}\sum_{x \in Te} L_{01}(z(x)) = \frac{1}{|Te|}\sum_{x \in Te} I[c(x)\hat{s}(x) \leq 0] = \frac{1}{|Te|}\sum_{x \in Te} I[c(x) \neq \hat{c}(x)] = err$$

where $\hat{c}(x) = +1$ if $\hat{s}(x) > 0$, $\hat{c}(x) = 0$ if $\hat{s}(x) = 0$, and $\hat{c}(x) = -1$ if $\hat{s}(x) < 0$. (It is sometimes more convenient to define the loss of examples on the decision boundary as $1/2$). In other words, 0–1 loss ignores the magnitude of the margins of the examples, only

[8] Remember that in Chapter 1 we talked about the margin of a classifier as the distance between the decision boundary and the nearest example. Here we use margin in a slightly more general sense: each example has a margin, not just the nearest one. This will be further explained in Section 7.3.

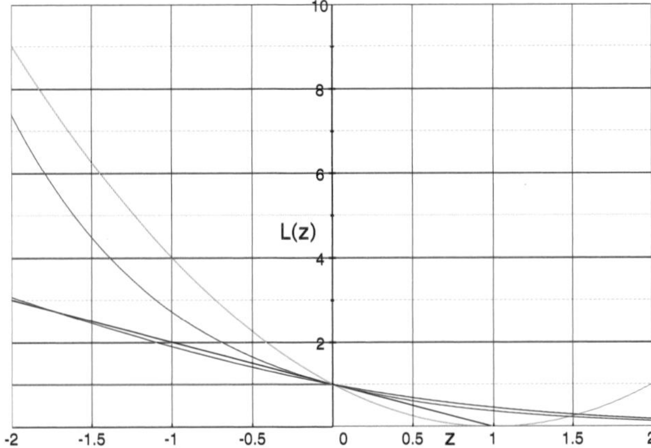

Figure 2.6. Loss functions: from bottom-left (*i*) 0–1 loss $L_{01}(z) = 1$ if $z \leq 0$, and $L_{01}(z) = 0$ if $z > 0$; (*ii*) hinge loss $L_h(z) = (1 - z)$ if $z \leq 1$, and $L_h(z) = 0$ if $z > 1$; (*iii*) logistic loss $L_{log}(z) = \log_2(1 + \exp(-z))$; (*iv*) exponential loss $L_{exp}(z) = \exp(-z)$; (*v*) squared loss $L_{sq}(z) = (1 - z)^2$ (this can be set to 0 for $z > 1$, just like hinge loss).

taking their sign into account. As a result, 0–1 loss doesn't distinguish between scoring classifiers, as long as their predictions agree. This means that it isn't actually that useful as a search heuristic or objective function when learning scoring classifiers. Figure 2.6 pictures several loss functions that are used in practice. Except for 0–1 loss, they are all *convex*: linear interpolation between any two points on the curve will never result in a point below the curve. Optimising a convex function is computationally more tractable.

One loss function that will be of interest later is the *hinge loss*, which is defined as $L_h(z) = (1 - z)$ if $z \leq 1$, and $L_h(z) = 0$ if $z > 1$. The name of this loss function comes from the fact that the loss 'hinges' on whether an example's margin is greater than 1 or not: if so (i.e., the example is on the correct side of the decision boundary with a distance of at least 1) the example incurs zero loss; if not, the loss increases with decreasing margin. In effect, the loss function expresses that it is important to avoid examples having a margin (much) less than 1, but no additional value is placed on achieving large positive margins. This loss function is used when training a ☞*support vector machine* (Section 7.3). We will also encounter *exponential loss* later when we discuss ☞*boosting* in Section 11.2.

Assessing and visualising ranking performance

It should be kept in mind that scores are assigned by a classifier, and are not a property inherent to instances. Scores are not estimated from 'true scores' – rather, a scoring classifier has to be learned from examples in the form of instances x labelled with classes $c(x)$, just as a classifier. (The task where we learn a function $\hat{f}$ from examples labelled with true function values $(x, f(x))$ is called ☞*regression* and is covered in Section 3.2.) Often it is more convenient to keep the order imposed by scores on a set of instances, but ignore their magnitudes – this has the advantage, for instance, of being much less sensitive to outliers. It also means that we do not have to make any assumptions about the scale on which scores are expressed: in particular, a ranker does not assume a particular score threshold for separating positives from negatives. A *ranking* is defined as a total order on a set of instances, possibly with ties.[9]

Example 2.2 (Ranking example). The scoring tree in Figure 2.5 produces the following ranking: [20+,5−][10+,5−][20+,40−]. Here, 20+ denotes a sequence of 20 positive examples, and instances in square brackets [...] are tied. By selecting a split point in the ranking we can turn the ranking into a classification. In this case there are four possibilities: (A) setting the split point before the first segment, and thus assigning all segments to the negative class; (B) assigning the first segment to the positive class, and the other two to the negative class; (C) assigning the first two segments to the positive class; and (D) assigning all segments to the positive class. In terms of actual scores, this corresponds to (A) choosing any score larger than 2 as the threshold; (B) choosing a threshold between 1 and 2; (C) setting the threshold between −1 and 1; and (D) setting it lower than −1.

Suppose x and x' are two instances such that x receives a lower score: $\hat{s}(x) < \hat{s}(x')$. Since higher scores express a stronger belief that the instance in question is positive, this would be fine except in one case: if x is an actual positive and x' is an actual negative. We will call this a *ranking error*. The total number of ranking errors can then be expressed as $\sum_{x \in Te^{\oplus}, x' \in Te^{\ominus}} I[\hat{s}(x) < \hat{s}(x')]$. Furthermore, for every positive and negative that receive the same score – a *tie* – we count half a ranking error. The maximum number of ranking errors is equal to $|Te^{\oplus}| \cdot |Te^{\ominus}| = Pos \cdot Neg$, and so the *ranking error rate* is defined as

$$rank\text{-}err = \frac{\sum_{x \in Te^{\oplus}, x' \in Te^{\ominus}} I[\hat{s}(x) < \hat{s}(x')] + \frac{1}{2} I[\hat{s}(x) = \hat{s}(x')]}{Pos \cdot Neg} \tag{2.4}$$

and analogously the *ranking accuracy*

$$rank\text{-}acc = \frac{\sum_{x \in Te^{\oplus}, x' \in Te^{\ominus}} I[\hat{s}(x) > \hat{s}(x')] + \frac{1}{2} I[\hat{s}(x) = \hat{s}(x')]}{Pos \cdot Neg} = 1 - rank\text{-}err \tag{2.5}$$

---

[9] A total order with ties should not be confused with a partial order (see Background 2.1 on p.51). In a total order with ties (which is really a total order on equivalence classes), any two elements are comparable, either in one direction or in both. In a partial order some elements are incomparable.

Ranking accuracy can be seen as an estimate of the probability that an arbitrary positive–negative pair is ranked correctly.

Example 2.3 (Ranking accuracy). We continue the previous example considering the scoring tree in Figure 2.5, with the left leaf covering 20 spam and 40 ham, the middle leaf 10 spam and 5 ham, and the right leaf 20 spam and 5 ham. The 5 negatives in the right leaf are scored higher than the 10 positives in the middle leaf and the 20 positives in the left leaf, resulting in $50 + 100 = 150$ ranking errors. The 5 negatives in the middle leaf are scored higher than the 20 positives in the left leaf, giving a further 100 ranking errors. In addition, the left leaf makes 800 half ranking errors (because 20 positives and 40 negatives get the same score), the middle leaf 50 and the right leaf 100. In total we have 725 ranking errors out of a possible $50 \cdot 50 = 2500$, corresponding to a ranking error rate of 29% or a ranking accuracy of 71%.

The coverage plots and ROC plots introduced in the previous section for visualising classifier performance provide an excellent tool for visualising ranking performance too. If *Pos* positives and *Neg* negatives are plotted on the vertical and horizontal axes, respectively, then each positive–negative pair occupies a unique 'cell' in this plot. If we order the positives and negatives on decreasing score, i.e., examples with higher scores are closer to the origin, then we can clearly distinguish the correctly ranked pairs at the bottom right, the ranking errors at the top left, and the ties in between (Figure 2.7). The number of cells in each area gives us the number of correctly ranked pairs, ranking errors and ties, respectively. The diagonal lines cut the ties area in half, so the area below those lines corresponds to the ranking accuracy multiplied by $Pos \cdot Neg$, and the area above corresponds to the ranking error rate times that same factor.

Concentrating on those diagonal lines gives us the piecewise linear curve shown in Figure 2.7 (right). This curve, which we will call a *coverage curve*, can be understood as follows. Each of the points marked A, B, C and D specifies the classification performance, in terms of true and false positives, achieved by the corresponding ranking split points or score thresholds from Example 2.2. To illustrate, C would be obtained by a score threshold of 0, leading to $TP2 = 20 + 10 = 30$ true positives and $FP2 = 5 + 5 = 10$ false positives. Similarly, B would be obtained by a higher threshold of 1.5, leading to $TP1 = 20$ true positives and $FP1 = 5$ false positives. Point A would result if we set the threshold unattainably high, and D if we set the threshold trivially low.

Why are these points connected by straight lines? How can we interpolate between, say, points C and D? Suppose we set the threshold exactly at -1, which is the score

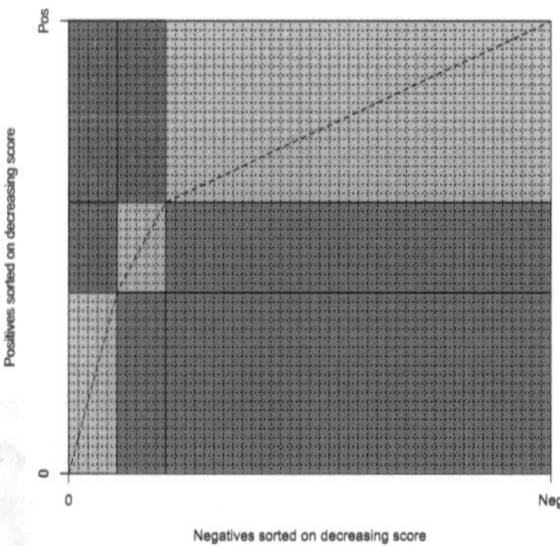

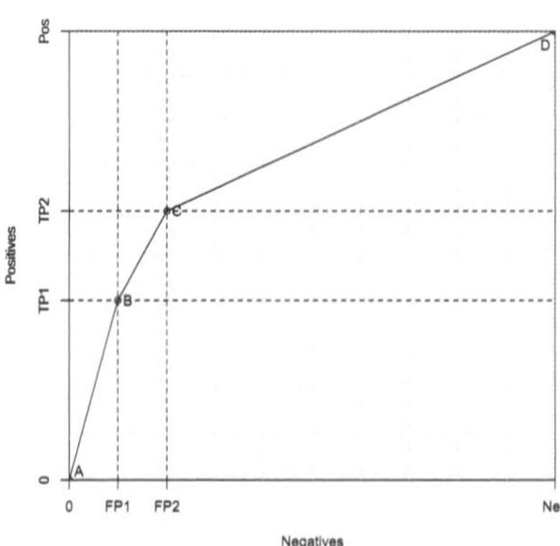

Figure 2.7. **(left)** Each cell in the grid denotes a unique pair of one positive and one negative example: the green cells indicate pairs that are correctly ranked by the classifier, the red cells represent ranking errors, and the orange cells are half-errors due to ties. **(right)** The coverage curve of a tree-based scoring classifier has one line segment for each leaf of the tree, and one (FP, TP) pair for each possible threshold on the score.

assigned by the left leaf of the tree. The question is now what class we predict for the 20 positives and 40 negatives that filter down to that leaf. It would seem reasonable to decide this by tossing a fair coin, leading to half of the positives receiving a positive prediction (on average) and half of them a negative one, and similar for the negatives. The total number of true positives is then $30 + 20/2 = 40$, and the number of false positives is $10 + 40/2 = 30$. In other words, we land exactly in the middle of the CD line segment. We can apply the same procedure to achieve performance half-way BC, by setting the threshold at 1 and tossing the same fair coin to obtain uniformly distributed predictions for the 10 positives and 5 negatives in the middle leaf, leading to $20 + 10/2 = 25$ true positives and $5 + 5/2 = 7.5$ false positives (of course, we cannot achieve a non-integer number of false positives in any trial, but this number represents the expected number of false positives over many trials). And what's more, by biasing the coin towards positive or negative predictions we can achieve expected performance anywhere on the line.

More generally, a coverage curve is a piecewise linear curve that rises monotonically from $(0,0)$ to (Neg, Pos) – i.e., TP and FP can never decrease if we decrease the decision threshold. Each segment of the curve corresponds to an equivalence class of the instance space partition induced by the model in question (e.g., the leaves of a feature tree). Notice that the number of segments is never more than the number of test instances. Furthermore, the slope of each segment is equal to the ratio of positive to negative test instances in that equivalence class. For instance, in our example the first segment has a slope of 4, the second segment slope 2, and the third segment slope 1/2

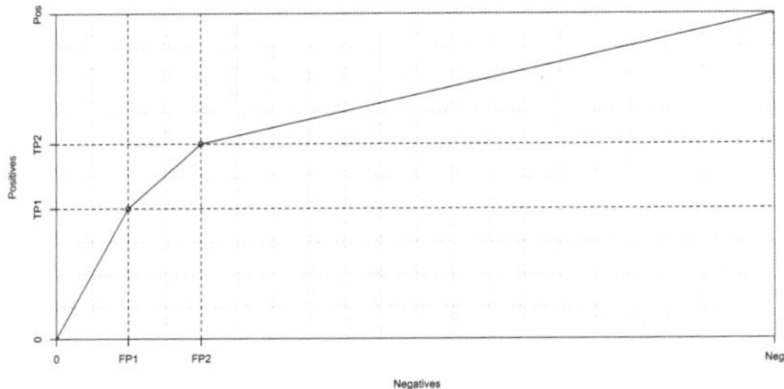

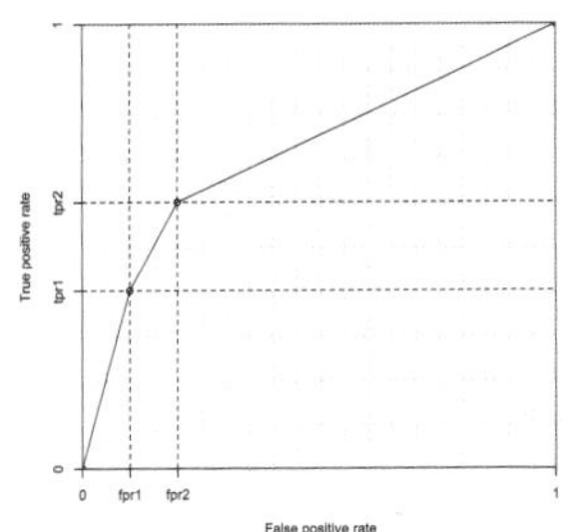

Figure 2.8. **(left)** A coverage curve obtained from a test set with class ratio $clr = 1/2$. **(right)** The corresponding ROC curve is the same as the one corresponding to the coverage curve in Figure 2.7 (right).

— exactly the scores assigned in each leaf of the tree! This is not true in general, since the coverage curve depends solely on the ranking induced by the scores, not on the scores themselves. However, it is not a coincidence either, as we shall see in the next section on class probability estimation.

An *ROC curve* is obtained from a coverage curve by normalising the axes to $[0, 1]$. This doesn't make much of a difference in our running example, but in general coverage curves can be rectangular whereas ROC curves always occupy the unit square. One effect this has is that slopes are multiplied by $Neg/Pos = 1/clr$. Furthermore, while in a coverage plot the area under the coverage curve gives the absolute number of correctly ranked pairs, in an ROC plot *the area under the ROC curve is the ranking accuracy* as defined in Equation 2.5 on p.64. For that reason people usually write *AUC* for 'Area Under (ROC) Curve', a convention I will follow.

Example 2.4 (Class imbalance). Suppose we feed the scoring tree in Figure 2.5 on p.62 an extended test set, with an additional batch of 50 negatives. The added negatives happen to be identical to the original ones, so the net effect is that the number of negatives in each leaf doubles. As a result the coverage curve changes (because the class ratio changes), but the ROC curve stays the same (Figure 2.8). Note that the AUC stays the same as well: while the classifier makes twice as many ranking errors, there are also twice as many positive–negative pairs, so the ranking error rate doesn't change.

Let us now consider an example of a coverage curve for a grading classifier. Figure 2.9 (left) shows a linear classifier (the decision boundary is denoted B) applied to a

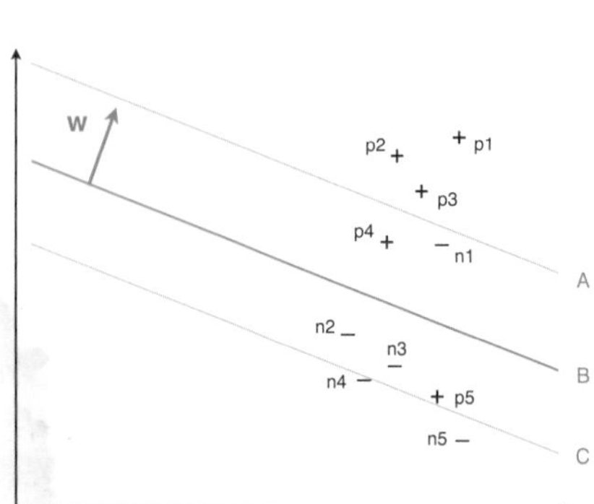

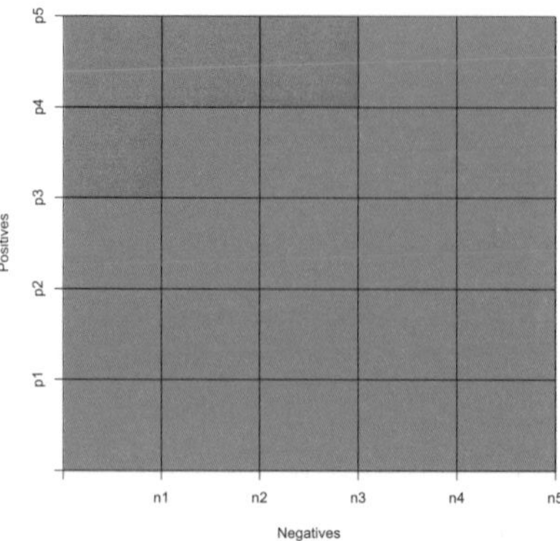

Figure 2.9. (left) A linear classifier induces a ranking by taking the signed distance to the decision boundary as the score. This ranking only depends on the orientation of the decision boundary: the three lines result in exactly the same ranking. **(right)** The grid of correctly ranked positive–negative pairs (in green) and ranking errors (in red).

small data set of five positive and five negative examples, achieving an accuracy of 0.80. We can derive a score from this linear classifier by taking the distance of an example from the decision boundary; if the example is on the negative side we take the negative distance. This means that the examples are ranked in the following order: p1 – p2 – p3 – n1 – p4 – n2 – n3 – p5 – n4 – n5. This ranking incurs four ranking errors: n1 before p4, and n1, n2 and n3 before p5. Figure 2.9 (right) visualises these four ranking errors in the top-left corner. The AUC of this ranking is 21/25 = 0.84.

From this grid we obtain the coverage curve in Figure 2.10. Because of its stepwise character, this curve looks quite different from the coverage curves for scoring trees that we saw earlier in this section. The main reason is the absence of ties, which means that all segments in the curve are horizontal or vertical, and that there are as many segments as examples. We can generate this stepwise curve from the ranking as follows: starting in the lower left-hand corner, we go up one step if the next example in the ranking is positive, and right one step if the next example is negative. The result is a curve that goes three steps up (for p1–3), one step to the right (for n1), one step up (p4), two steps to the right (n2–3), one step up (p5), and finally two steps to the right (n4–5).

We can actually use the same procedure for grouping models if we handle ties as follows: in case of a tie between p positive examples and n negative examples, we go p steps up and *at the same time* n steps to the right. Looking back at Figure 2.7 on p.66, you will see that this is exactly what happens in the diagonal segments spanning the orange rectangles which arise as a result of the ties in the leaves of the decision tree. Thus, the principles underlying coverage and ROC curves are the same for both grouping and grading models, but the curves themselves look quite different in each case. *Grouping model ROC curves have as many line segments as there are instance space segments in the model; grading models have one line segment for each example in the data set.* This is a concrete manifestation of something I mentioned in the Prologue: grading models have a much higher 'resolution' than grouping models; this is also called the model's *refinement*.

Notice the three points in Figure 2.10 labelled A, B and C. These points indicate the performance achieved by the decision boundaries with the same label in Figure 2.9. As an illustration, the middle boundary B misclassifies one out of five positives ($tpr = 0.80$) and one out of five negatives ($fpr = 0.80$). Boundary A doesn't misclassify any negatives, and boundary C correctly classifies all positives. In fact, while they should all have the same orientation, their exact location is not important, as long as boundary A is between p3 and n1, boundary B is between p4 and n2, and boundary C is between p5 and n4. There are good reasons why I chose exactly these three boundaries, as we shall see shortly. For the moment, observe what happens if we use all three boundaries to turn the linear model into a grouping model with four segments: the area above A, the region between A and B, the bit between B and C, and the rest below C. The result is that we no longer distinguish between n1 and p4, nor between n2–3 and p5. The ties just introduced change the coverage curve to the dotted segments in Figure 2.10. Notice that this results in a larger AUC of 0.90. Thus, *by decreasing a model's refinement we sometimes achieve better ranking performance*. Training a model is not just about amplifying significant distinctions, but also about diminishing the effect of misleading distinctions.

Turning rankers into classifiers

I mentioned previously that the main difference between rankers and scoring classifiers is that a ranker only assumes that a higher score means stronger evidence for the positive class, but otherwise makes no assumptions about the scale on which scores are expressed, or what would be a good score threshold to separate positives from negatives. We will now consider the question how to obtain such a threshold from a coverage curve or ROC curve.

The key concept is that of the accuracy isometric. Recall that in a coverage plot points of equal accuracy are connected by lines with slope 1. All we need to do, therefore, is to draw a line with slope 1 through the top-left point (which is sometimes called *ROC heaven*) and slide it down until we touch the coverage curve in one or more points. Each of those points achieves the highest accuracy possible with that model. In Figure 2.10 this method would identify points A and B as the points with highest accuracy (0.80). They achieve this in different ways: e.g., model A is more conservative on the positives.

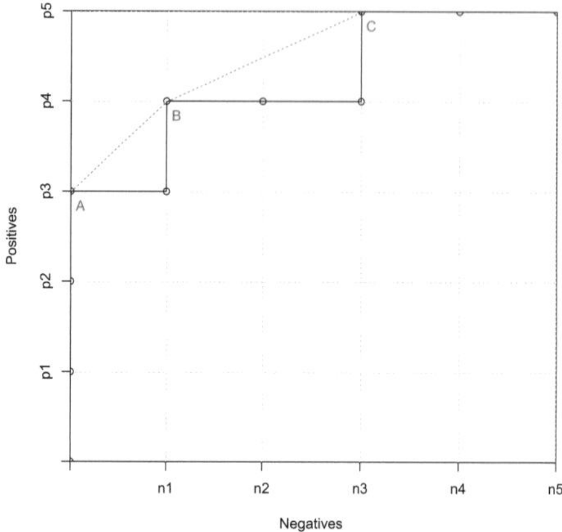

Figure 2.10. The coverage curve of the linear classifier in Figure 2.9. The points labelled A, B and C indicate the classification performance of the corresponding decision boundaries. The dotted lines indicate the improvement that can be obtained by turning the grading classifier into a grouping classifier with four segments.

A similar procedure can be followed with ROC plots, as long as you keep in mind that all slopes have to be multiplied by the reciprocal of the class ratio, $1/clr = Neg/Pos$.

Example 2.5 (Tuning your spam filter). You have carefully trained your Bayesian spam filter, and all that remains is setting the decision threshold. You select a set of six spam and four ham e-mails and collect the scores assigned by the spam filter. Sorted on decreasing score these are 0.89 (spam), 0.80 (spam), 0.74 (ham), 0.71 (spam), 0.63 (spam), 0.49 (ham), 0.42 (spam), 0.32 (spam), 0.24 (ham), and 0.13 (ham). If the class ratio of 3 spam against 2 ham is representative, you can select the optimal point on the ROC curve using an isometric with slope 2/3. As can be seen in Figure 2.11, this leads to putting the decision boundary between the sixth spam e-mail and the third ham e-mail, and we can take the average of their scores as the decision threshold (0.28).

An alternative way of finding the optimal point is to iterate over all possible split points – from before the top ranked e-mail to after the bottom one – and calculate the number of correctly classified examples at each split: 4 – 5 – 6 – 5 – 6 – 7 – 6 – 7 – 8 – 7 – 6. The maximum is achieved at the same split point, yielding an accuracy of 0.80. A useful trick to find out which accuracy an isometric in an ROC plot represents is to intersect the isometric with the descending diagonal.

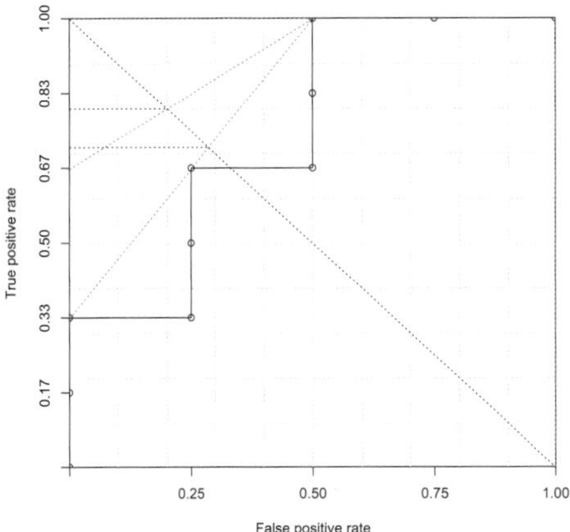

Figure 2.11. Selecting the optimal point on an ROC curve. The top dotted line is the accuracy isometric, with a slope of 2/3. The lower isometric doubles the value (or prevalence) of negatives, and allows a choice of thresholds. By intersecting the isometrics with the descending diagonal we can read off the achieved accuracy on the y-axis.

Since accuracy is a weighted average of the true positive and true negative rates, and since these are the same in a point on the descending diagonal, we can read off the corresponding accuracy value on the y-axis.

If the class distribution in the data is *not* representative, we can simply adjust the slope of the isometric. For example, if ham is in fact twice as prevalent, we use an isometric with slope 4/3. In the previous example this leads to three optimal points on the ROC curve.[10] Even if the class ratio in the data is representative, we may have other reasons to assign different weights to the classes. To illustrate, in the spam e-mail situation our spam filter may discard the false positives (ham e-mails misclassified as spam) so we may want to drive the false positive rate down by assigning a higher weight to the negatives (ham). This is often expressed as a *cost ratio* $c = c_{\text{FN}}/c_{\text{FP}}$ of the cost of false negatives in proportion to the cost of false positives, which in this case would be set to a value smaller than 1. The relevant isometrics then have a slope of $1/c$ in a coverage plot, and $1/(c \cdot clr)$ in an ROC plot. The combination of cost ratio and class ratio gives a precise context in which the classifier is deployed and is referred to as the

[10] It seems reasonable to choose the middle of these three points, leading to a threshold of 0.56. An alternative is to treat all e-mails receiving a score in the interval [0.28, 0.77] as lying on the decision boundary, and to randomly assign a class to those e-mails.

operating condition.

If the class or cost ratio is highly skewed, this procedure may result in a classifier that assigns the same class to all examples. For instance, if negatives are 1 000 times more prevalent than positives, accuracy isometrics are nearly vertical, leading to an unattainably high decision threshold and a classifier that classifies everything as negative. Conversely, if the profit of one true positive is 1 000 times the cost of a false positive, we would classify everything as positive – in fact, this is the very principle underlying spam e-mail! However, often such one-size-fits-all behaviour is unacceptable, indicating that accuracy is not the right thing to optimise here. In such cases we should use average recall isometrics instead. These run parallel to the ascending diagonal in both coverage and ROC plots, and help to achieve similar performance on both classes.

The procedure just described learns a decision threshold from labelled data by means of the ROC curve and the appropriate accuracy isometric. This procedure is often preferable over fixing a decision threshold in advance, particularly if scores are expressed on an arbitrary scale – for instance, this would provide a way to finetune the SpamAssassin decision threshold to our particular situation and preferences. Even if the scores are probabilities, as in the next section, these may not be sufficiently well estimated to warrant a fixed threshold of 0.5.

2.3 Class probability estimation

A *class probability estimator* – or probability estimator in short – is a scoring classifier that outputs probability vectors over classes, i.e., a mapping $\hat{\mathbf{p}} : \mathscr{X} \to [0,1]^k$. We write $\hat{\mathbf{p}}(x) = \big(\hat{p}_1(x), \ldots, \hat{p}_k(x)\big)$, where $\hat{p}_i(x)$ is the probability assigned to class C_i for instance x, and $\sum_{i=1}^{k} \hat{p}_i(x) = 1$. If we have only two classes, the probability associated with one class is 1 minus the probability of the other class; in that case, we use $\hat{p}(x)$ to denote the estimated probability of the positive class for instance x. As with scoring classifiers, we usually do not have direct access to the true probabilities $p_i(x)$.

One way to understand the probabilities $\hat{p}_i(x)$ is as estimates of the probability $P_{\mathscr{C}}(c(x') = C_i | x' \sim x)$, where $x' \sim x$ stands for 'x' is similar to x'. In other words, how frequent are instances of this class among instances similar to x? The intuition is that the more (or less) frequent they are, the more (or less) confident we should be in our belief that x belongs to that class as well. What we mean with similarity in this context will depend on the models we are considering – we will illustrate it here by means of a few two-class examples. First, assume a situation in which any two instances are similar to each other. We then have $P_{\mathscr{C}}(c(x') = \oplus | x' \sim x) = P_{\mathscr{C}}(c(x') = \oplus)$ which is simply estimated by the proportion *pos* of positives in our data set (I am going to drop the subscript $\mathscr{C}$ from now on). In other words, in this scenario we predict $\hat{p}(x) = pos$ regardless

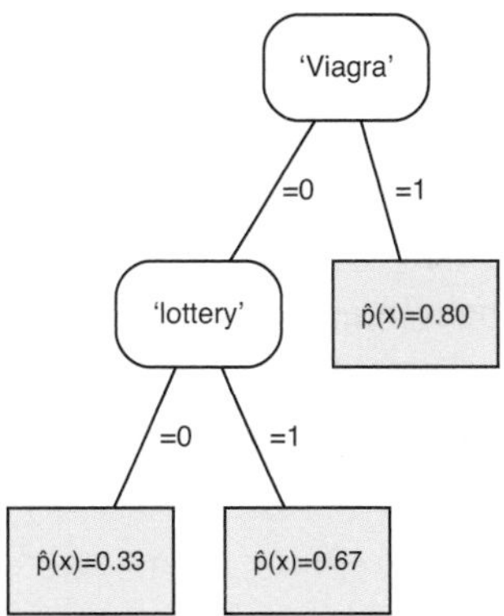

Figure 2.12. A probability estimation tree derived from the feature tree in Figure 1.4.

of whether we know anything about x's true class. At the other extreme, consider a situation in which no two instances are similar unless they are the same, i.e., $x' \sim x$ if $x' = x$, and $x' \not\sim x$ otherwise. In this case we have $P(c(x') = \oplus | x' \sim x) = P(c(x) = \oplus)$, which – because x is fixed – is 1 if $c(x) = \oplus$ and 0 otherwise. Put differently, we predict $\hat{p}(x) = 1$ for all known positives and $\hat{p}(x) = 0$ for all known negatives, but we can't generalise this to unseen instances.

A feature tree allows us to strike a balance between these extreme and simplistic scenarios, using the similarity relation $\sim_T$ associated with feature tree T: $x' \sim_T x$ if, and only if, x and x' are assigned to the same leaf of the tree. In each leaf we then predict the proportion of positives assigned to that leaf. For example, in the right-most leaf in Figure 1.4 on p.32 the proportion of positives is $40/50 = 0.80$, and thus we predict $\hat{p}(x) = 0.80$ for all instances x assigned to that leaf; similarly for the other two leaves (Figure 2.12). If we threshold $\hat{p}(x)$ at 0.5 (i.e., predict spam if the spam probability is 0.5 or more and predict ham otherwise), we get the same classifier as obtained by predicting the majority class in each leaf of the feature tree.

Assessing class probability estimates

As with classifiers, we can now ask the question of how good these class probability estimators are. A slight complication here is that, as already remarked, we do not have access to the true probabilities. One trick that is often applied is to define a binary vector $(I[c(x) = C_1], \ldots, I[c(x) = C_k])$, which has the i-th bit set to 1 if x's true class is C_i and all other bits set to 0, and use these as the 'true' probabilities. We can then define the *squared error* (*SE*) of the predicted probability vector $\hat{\mathbf{p}}(x) = \left(\hat{p}_1(x), \ldots, \hat{p}_k(x)\right)$ as

$$\mathrm{SE}(x) = \frac{1}{2} \sum_{i=1}^{k} (\hat{p}_i(x) - I[c(x) = C_i])^2 \tag{2.6}$$

and the *mean squared error* (*MSE*) as the average squared error over all instances in the test set:

$$\text{MSE}(Te) = \frac{1}{|Te|} \sum_{x \in Te} \text{SE}(x) \tag{2.7}$$

This definition of error in probability estimates is often used in *forecasting theory* where it is called the *Brier score*. The factor 1/2 in Equation 2.6 ensures that the squared error per example is normalised between 0 and 1: the worst possible situation is that the wrong class is predicted with probability 1, which means two 'bits' are wrong. For two classes this reduces to a single term $(\hat{p}(x) - I[c(x) = \oplus])^2$ only referring to the positive class. Notice that, if a class probability estimator is 'categorical' – i.e., it assigns probability 1 to one class and probability 0 to the rest – it is effectively a classifier, and MSE reduces to accuracy as defined in Section 2.1.

Example 2.6 (Squared error). Suppose one model predicts (0.70, 0.10, 0.20) for a particular example x in a three-class task, while another appears much more certain by predicting (0.99, 0, 0.01). If the first class is the actual class, the second prediction is clearly better than the first: the SE of the first prediction is $((0.70-1)^2 + (0.10-0)^2 + (0.20-0)^2)/2 = 0.07$, while for the second prediction it is $((0.99-1)^2 + (0-0)^2 + (0.01-0)^2)/2 = 0.0001$. The first model gets punished more because, although mostly right, it isn't quite sure of it.

However, if the third class is the actual class, the situation is reversed: now the SE of the first prediction is $((0.70-0)^2 + (0.10-0)^2 + (0.20-1)^2)/2 = 0.57$, and of the second $((0.99-0)^2 + (0-0)^2 + (0.01-1)^2)/2 = 0.98$. The second model gets punished more for not just being wrong, but being presumptuous.

Returning to the probability estimation tree in Figure 2.12, we calculate the squared error per leaf as follows (left to right):

$$\text{SE}_1 = 20(0.33-1)^2 + 40(0.33-0)^2 = 13.33$$
$$\text{SE}_2 = 10(0.67-1)^2 + 5(0.67-0)^2 = 3.33$$
$$\text{SE}_3 = 20(0.80-1)^2 + 5(0.80-0)^2 = 4.00$$

which leads to a mean squared error of $\text{MSE} = \frac{1}{100}(\text{SE}_1 + \text{SE}_2 + \text{SE}_3) = 0.21$. An interesting question is whether we can change the predicted probabilities in each leaf to obtain a lower mean squared error. It turns out that this is not possible: predicting probabilities obtained from the class distributions in each leaf is optimal in the sense of lowest MSE.

For instance, changing the predicted probabilities in the left-most leaf to 0.40 for spam and 0.60 for ham, or 0.20 for spam and 0.80 for ham, results in a higher squared error:

$$\mathrm{SE}'_1 = 20(0.40-1)^2 + 40(0.40-0)^2 = 13.6$$
$$\mathrm{SE}''_1 = 20(0.20-1)^2 + 40(0.20-0)^2 = 14.4$$

The reason for this becomes obvious if we rewrite the expression for two-class squared error of a leaf as follows, using the notation $n^{\oplus}$ and $n^{\ominus}$ for the numbers of positive and negative examples in the leaf:

$$\begin{aligned} n^{\oplus}(\hat{p}-1)^2 + n^{\ominus}\hat{p}^2 = (n^{\oplus}+n^{\ominus})\hat{p}^2 - 2n^{\oplus}\hat{p} + n^{\oplus} &= (n^{\oplus}+n^{\ominus})\left[\hat{p}^2 - 2\dot{p}\hat{p} + \dot{p}\right] \\ &= (n^{\oplus}+n^{\ominus})\left[(\hat{p}-\dot{p})^2 + \dot{p}(1-\dot{p})\right] \end{aligned}$$

where $\dot{p} = n^{\oplus}/(n^{\oplus}+n^{\ominus})$ is the relative frequency of the positive class among the examples covered by the leaf, also called the *empirical probability*. As the term $\dot{p}(1-\dot{p})$ does not depend on the predicted probability $\hat{p}$, we see immediately that we achieve lowest squared error in the leaf if we assign $\hat{p} = \dot{p}$.

Empirical probabilities are important as they allow us to obtain or finetune probability estimates from classifiers or rankers. If we have a set S of labelled examples, and the number of examples in S of class C_i is denoted n_i, then the empirical probability vector associated with S is $\dot{\mathbf{p}}(S) = (n_1/|S|, \ldots, n_k/|S|)$. In practice, it is almost always a good idea to *smooth* these relative frequencies to avoid issues with extreme values (0 or 1). The most common way to do this is to set

$$\dot{p}_i(S) = \frac{n_i + 1}{|S| + k} \tag{2.8}$$

This is called the *Laplace correction*, after the French mathematician Pierre-Simon Laplace, who introduced it for the case $k = 2$ (also known as Laplace's rule of succession). In effect, we are adding uniformly distributed *pseudo-counts* to each of the k alternatives, reflecting our prior belief that the empirical probabilities will turn out uniform.[11] We can also apply non-uniform smoothing by setting

$$\dot{p}_i(S) = \frac{n_i + m \cdot \pi_i}{|S| + m} \tag{2.9}$$

This smoothing technique, known as the *m-estimate*, allows the choice of the number of pseudo-counts m as well as the prior probabilities π_i. The Laplace correction is a special case of the m-estimate with $m = k$ and $\pi_i = 1/k$.

If all elements of S receive the same predicted probability vector $\hat{\mathbf{p}}(S)$ – which happens if S is a segment of a grouping model – then a similar derivation to the one above

[11]This can be modelled mathematically by a prior probability distribution known as a *Dirichlet prior*.

allows us to write the total incurred squared error over S in terms of estimated and empirical probabilities as

$$\begin{aligned}\mathrm{SE}(S) = \sum_{x\in S} \mathrm{SE}(x) &= \sum_{x\in S} \frac{1}{2}\sum_{i=1}^{k}(\hat{p}_i(x) - I[c(x) = C_i])^2 \\ &= \frac{1}{2}|S|\sum_{i=1}^{k}(\hat{p}_i(S) - \dot{p}_i(S))^2 + \frac{1}{2}|S|\sum_{i=1}^{k}(\dot{p}_i(S)(1-\dot{p}_i(S))\end{aligned}$$

The first term of the final expression is called the *calibration loss*, and measures squared error with respect to the empirical probabilities. It can be reduced to 0 in grouping models where we are free to choose the predicted probabilities for each segment, as in probability estimation trees. Models with low calibration loss are said to be well-calibrated. The second term is called the *refinement loss*; this depends only on the empirical probabilities, and is smaller if they are less uniform.

This analysis suggests that the best way of obtaining probability estimates is from empirical probabilities, obtained from the training set or from another set of labelled examples specifically set aside for the purpose. However, there are two issues we need to consider here. The first is that with some models we must make sure that the predicted probabilities obey the ranking imposed by the model. The second is that with grading models we don't have immediate access to empirical probabilities, since each example tends to get assigned an equivalence class of its own. We will now discuss this in a bit more detail.

Turning rankers into class probability estimators

Consider again Example 2.5 on p.70, and imagine the scores are not probabilities but on some unknown scale, so that the spam filter is a ranker rather than a class probability estimator. Since each test example receives a different score, the 'empirical probabilities' are either 0 (for negative examples) or 1 (for positive examples), leading to a sequence of $\dot{p}$-values of 1–1–0–1–1–0–1–1–0–0 in order of decreasing scores. The obvious problem is that these $\dot{p}$-values do not obey the order imposed by the scores, and so cannot be used directly to obtain probability estimates. Smoothing the empirical probabilities using Laplace correction doesn't really address this problem, since all it does is replace 0 with 1/3 and 1 with 2/3. We need a different idea.

Looking at Figure 2.11, we see that $\dot{p} = 1$ corresponds to a vertical segment of the ROC curve, and $\dot{p} = 0$ to a horizontal segment. The problem we have is caused by having a vertical segment following a horizontal one, or, more generally, a segment with steeper slope following a flatter segment. We will call a sequence of segments with increasing slope a *concavity*, as it forms a 'dent' in the ROC curve. A curve without concavities is a *convex* ROC curve. Our curve has two concavities: one formed by the third, fourth and fifth example, and the other by the sixth, seventh and eighth example.

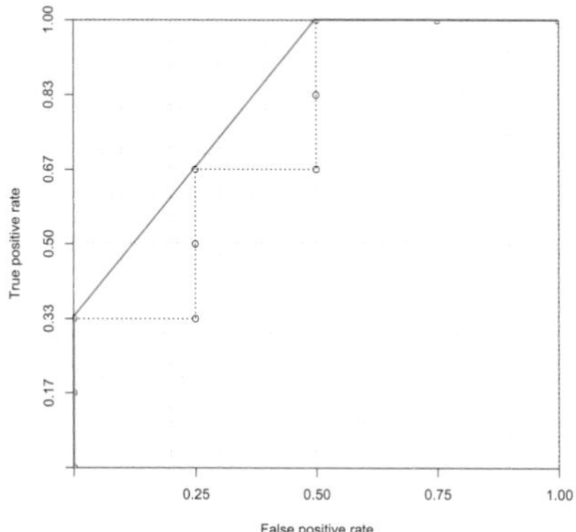

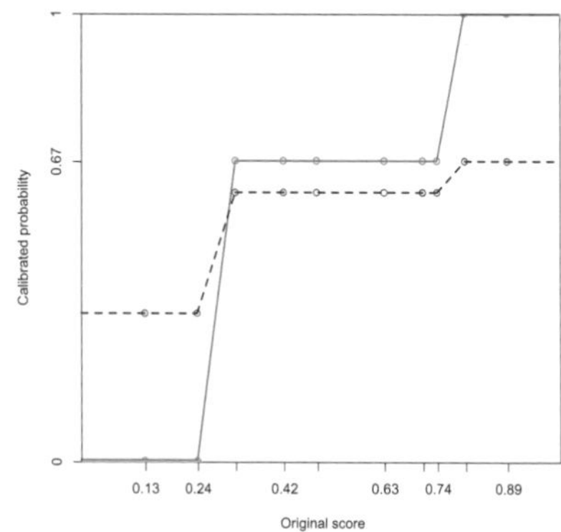

Figure 2.13. (left) The solid red line is the convex hull of the dotted ROC curve. **(right)** The corresponding calibration map in red: the plateaus correspond to several examples being mapped to the same segment of the convex hull, and linear interpolation between example scores occurs when we transition from one convex hull segment to the next. A Laplace-corrected calibration map is indicated by the dashed line in blue: Laplace smoothing compresses the range of calibrated probabilities but can sometimes affect the ranking.

Suppose now that the third to the fifth example all receive the same score, say 0.7; and the sixth to the eight example are also tied, say at 0.4. In that case the ROC curve would have six segments, with empirical probabilities 1 – 1 – 2/3 – 2/3 – 0 – 0. As we see, the $\dot{p}$-values are now decreasing with the scores; in other words, the concavities have disappeared and the ROC curve has become convex.

More generally speaking, *concavities in ROC curves can be remedied by combining segments through tied scores*. This is achieved by identifying what are sometimes called *adjacent violators*. For instance, in the sequence 1 – 1 – 0 – 1 – 1 – 0 – 1 – 1 – 0 – 0, the third and fourth example are adjacent violators, because they violate the rule that scores should be decreasing from left to right in the sequence (or, mathematically more accurate, they should be non-increasing). This is remedied by assigning them both their average score, leading to the sequence 1 – 1 – [1/2 – 1/2] – 1 – 0 – 1 – 1 – 0 – 0. The newly introduced segment now forms an adjacent violator pair with the fourth example, so we give them all their mean score, leading to the sequence 1 – 1 – [2/3 – 2/3 – 2/3] – 0 – 1 – 1 – 0 – 0.[12] The second 0 – 1 – 1 concavity is treated identically, and the final sequence is 1 – 1 – [2/3 – 2/3 – 2/3] – [2/3 – 2/3 – 2/3] – 0 – 0.

The result is illustrated in Figure 2.13. On the left, we see how the two concavities are replaced with two diagonal line segments with the same slope. These diagonal segments coincide with the accuracy isometric that gives the three 'outermost' points

[12]These two steps can be combined into one: once a pair of adjacent violators is found, we can scan to the left and right to include examples with the same score as the left and right example in the pair, respectively.

involved in the concavities the same accuracy (Figure 2.11 on p.71). Jointly, the red segments constitute the *convex hull* of the ROC curve, which is the unique convex curve through the outermost points of the original ROC curve. The convex hull has a higher AUC than the original curve, because it replaces (some of) the ranking errors of the original curve with half-errors due to ties. In our example the original ranking incurs 6 out of 24 ranking errors (AUC = 0.75), while the convex hull turns all of these into half-errors (AUC = 0.83).

Once we have determined the convex hull, we can use the empirical probabilities in each segment of the convex hull as calibrated probabilities. Figure 2.13 (right) shows the resulting *calibration map*, which is a piecewise linear, non-decreasing curve mapping original scores on the x-axis to calibrated probabilities on the y-axis. Also shown is an alternative calibration map giving probability estimates after Laplace correction: for the given sequence these are 2/3 – 2/3 – [3/5 – 3/5 – 3/5] – [3/5 – 3/5 – 3/5] – 1/3 – 1/3, giving rise to a much compressed range of probability estimates.

Let's now look at this process from the point of view of mean squared error, calibration and refinement. The original scores had a mean squared error of $\frac{1}{10}[(0.89-1)^2+(0.80-1)^2+(0.74-0)^2+(0.71-1)^2+(0.63-1)^2+(0.49-0)^2+(0.42-1)^2+(0.32-1)^2+(0.24-0)^2+(0.13-0)^2]=0.19$. Notice that this is entirely incurred by the calibration loss, as all empirical probabilities are either 0 or 1 and thus the refinement loss is zero. The calibrated scores have a mean squared error of $\frac{1}{10}[(1-1)^2+(1-1)^2+(0.67-0)^2+(0.67-1)^2+(0.67-1)^2+(0.67-0)^2+(0.67-1)^2+(0.67-1)^2+(0-0)^2+(0-0)^2]=0.13$. Now the entire mean squared error is incurred by refinement loss as the estimated probabilities are equal to the empirical ones in each segment by construction. We have traded an increase in refinement loss for a decrease in calibration loss; since the latter is larger than the former, the overall error decreases. The increase in refinement loss comes from the construction of the convex hull, which introduces diagonal segments. The technical term for this process of obtaining calibrated scores through the convex hull of the ROC curve is *isotonic calibration*, as the mathematical problem underlying it is called isotonic regression. Some caution is in order when applying isotonic calibration, as it is easy to overfit the data in this process. In the calibration map in Figure 2.13 (right), both the horizontal transition points and the vertical levels are directly obtained from the given data, and may not generalise well to unseen data. This is why it is advisable to apply the Laplace correction to the empirical probabilities, even though it will increase the calibration loss on the given data.

2.4 Binary classification and related tasks: Summary and further reading

In this chapter we have looked at binary classification, a ubiquitous task that forms the starting point of a lot of work in machine learning. Although we haven't talked much about learning in this chapter, my philosophy is that you will reach a better understanding of machine learning models and algorithms if you first study the tasks that these models are meant to address.

- ☞ In Section 2.1 we defined the binary classification task and introduced an important tool to assess performance at such a task, namely the two-by-two contingency table. A wide range of performance indicators are derived from the counts in a contingency table. I introduced the coverage plot, which visualises a contingency table as a rectangle with size *Pos* up and size *Neg* across, and within that rectangle a point with y-coordinate *TP* and x-coordinate *FP*. We can visualise several models evaluated on the same data set by several points, and use the fact that accuracy is constant along line segments with slope 1 to visually rank these classifiers on accuracy. Alternatively, we can normalise the rectangle to be a unit square with true and false positive rate on the axes. In this so-called ROC space, line segments with slope 1 (i.e., those parallel to the ascending diagonal) connect points with the same average recall (sometimes also called macro-accuracy). The use of these kinds of plot in machine learning was pioneered by Provost and Fawcett (2001). Unnormalised coverage plots were introduced by Fürnkranz and Flach (2003).

- ☞ Section 2.2 considered the more general task of calculating a score for each example (or a vector of scores in the general case of more than two classes). While the scale on which scores are expressed is unspecified, it is customary to put the decision threshold at $\hat{s}(x) = 0$ and let the sign of the score stand for the prediction (positive or negative). Multiplying the score with the true class gives us the margin, which is positive for a correct prediction and negative for an incorrect one. A loss function determines how much negative margins are penalised and positive margins rewarded. The advantage of working with convex and continuously differentiable 'surrogate' loss functions (rather than with 0–1 loss, which is the loss function we ultimately want to optimise) is that this often leads to more tractable optimisation problems.

- ☞ Alternatively, we can ignore the scale on which scores are measured altogether and only work with their order. Such a ranker is visualised in coverage or ROC space by a piecewise continuous curve. For grouping models the line segments in these curves correspond to instance space segments (e.g., the leaves of a tree model) whereas for grading models there is a segment for each unique score assigned by the model. The area under the ROC curve gives the ranking accuracy (an estimate of the probability that a random positive is ranked before a random negative) and is known in statistics as the Wilcoxon-Mann-Whitney statistic These curves can be used to find a suitable operating point by translating the operating condition (class and cost distribution) into an isometric in ROC or coverage space. The origins of ROC curves are in signal detection theory (Egan, 1975); accessible introductions can be found in (Fawcett, 2006; Flach, 2010*b*).

☞ In Section 2.3 we looked at scoring models whose scores can be interpreted as estimates of the probability that the instance belongs to a particular class. Such models were pioneered in forecasting theory by Brier (1950) and Murphy and Winkler (1984), among others. We can assess the quality of class probability estimates by comparing them to the 'ideal' probabilities (1 for a positive, 0 for a negative) and taking mean squared error. Since there is no reason why the true probabilities should be categorical this is quite a crude assessment, and decomposing it into calibration loss and refinement loss provides useful additional information. We have also seen a very useful trick for smoothing relative frequency estimates of probabilities by adding pseudo-counts, either uniformly distributed (Laplace correction) or according to a chosen prior (m-estimate). Finally, we have seen how we can use the ROC convex hull to obtain calibrated class probability estimates. The approach has its roots in isotonic regression (Best and Chakravarti, 1990) and was introduced to the machine learning community by Zadrozny and Elkan (2002). Fawcett and Niculescu-Mizil (2007) and Flach and Matsubara (2007) show that the approach is equivalent to calibration by means of the ROC convex hull. (Note that in this chapter we have seen two different uses of the term 'convex': one in relation to loss functions, where convexity means that linear interpolation between any two points on the curve depicting the loss function will never result in a point below the curve; and the other in relation to the ROC convex hull, where it refers to the linearly interpolated boundary of a convex set which envelopes all points in the set.)

CHAPTER 3

Beyond binary classification

THE PREVIOUS CHAPTER introduced binary classification and associated tasks such as ranking and class probability estimation. In this chapter we will go beyond these basic tasks in a number of ways. Section 3.1 discusses how to handle more than two classes. In Section 3.2 we consider the case of a real-valued target variable. Section 3.3 is devoted to various forms of learning that are either unsupervised or aimed at learning descriptive models.

3.1 Handling more than two classes

Certain concepts are fundamentally binary. For instance, the notion of a coverage curve does not easily generalise to more than two classes. We will now consider general issues related to having more than two classes in classification, scoring and class probability estimation. The discussion will address two issues: how to evaluate multi-class performance, and how to build multi-class models out of binary models. The latter is necessary for some models, such as linear classifiers, that are primarily designed to separate two classes. Other models, including decision trees, handle any number of classes quite naturally.

Multi-class classification

Classification tasks with more than two classes are very common. For instance, once a patient has been diagnosed as suffering from a rheumatic disease, the doctor will want to classify him or her further into one of several variants. If we have k classes, performance of a classifier can be assessed using a k-by-k contingency table. Assessing performance is easy if we are interested in the classifier's accuracy, which is still the sum of the descending diagonal of the contingency table, divided by the number of test instances. However, as before, this can obscure differences in performance on different classes, and other quantities may be more meaningful.

Example 3.1 (Performance of multi-class classifiers). Consider the following three-class confusion matrix (plus marginals):

	Predicted			
	15	2	3	20
Actual	7	**15**	8	30
	2	3	**45**	50
	24	20	56	100

The accuracy of this classifier is $(15+15+45)/100 = 0.75$. We can calculate per-class precision and recall: for the first class this is $15/24 = 0.63$ and $15/20 = 0.75$ respectively, for the second class $15/20 = 0.75$ and $15/30 = 0.50$, and for the third class $45/56 = 0.80$ and $45/50 = 0.90$. We could average these numbers to obtain single precision and recall numbers for the whole classifier, or we could take a weighted average taking the proportion of each class into account. For instance, the weighted average precision is $0.20 \cdot 0.63 + 0.30 \cdot 0.75 + 0.50 \cdot 0.80 = 0.75$. Notice that we still have that accuracy is weighted average per-class recall, as in the two-class case (see Example 2.1 on p.56).

Another possibility is to perform a more detailed analysis by looking at precision and recall numbers for each pair of classes: for instance, when distinguishing the first class from the third precision is $15/17 = 0.88$ and recall is $15/18 = 0.83$, while distinguishing the third class from the first these numbers are $45/48 = 0.94$ and $45/47 = 0.96$ (can you explain why these numbers are much higher in the latter direction?).

Imagine now that we want to construct a multi-class classifier, but we only have the ability to train two-class models – say linear classifiers. There are various ways to combine several of them into a single k-class classifier. The *one-versus-rest* scheme is to train k binary classifiers, the first of which separates class C_1 from $C_2,\dots,C_n$, the second of which separates C_2 from all other classes, and so on. When training the i-th classifier we treat all instances of class C_i as positive examples, and the remaining instances as negative examples. Sometimes the classes are learned in a fixed order, in which case we learn $k-1$ models, the i-th one separating C_i from $C_{i+1},\dots,C_n$ with $1 \le i < n$. An alternative to one-versus-rest is *one-versus-one*. In this scheme, we train $k(k-1)/2$ binary classifiers, one for each pair of different classes. If a binary classifier treats the classes asymmetrically, as happens with certain models, it makes more sense to train two classifiers for each pair, leading to a total of $k(k-1)$ classifiers.

A convenient way to describe all these and other schemes to decompose a k-class task into l binary classification tasks is by means of a so-called *output code* matrix. This is a k-by-l matrix whose entries are $+1$, 0 or -1. The following are output codes describing the two ways to transform a three-class task by means of one-versus-one:

$$\begin{pmatrix} +1 & +1 & 0 \\ -1 & 0 & +1 \\ 0 & -1 & -1 \end{pmatrix} \qquad \begin{pmatrix} +1 & -1 & +1 & -1 & 0 & 0 \\ -1 & +1 & 0 & 0 & +1 & -1 \\ 0 & 0 & -1 & +1 & -1 & +1 \end{pmatrix}$$

Each column of these matrices describes a binary classification task, using the class corresponding to the row with the $+1$ entry as positive class and the class with the -1 entry as the negative class. So, in the symmetric scheme on the left, we train three classifiers: one to distinguish between C_1 (positive) and C_2 (negative), one to distinguish between C_1 (positive) and C_3 (negative), and the remaining one to distinguish between C_2 (positive) and C_3 (negative). The asymmetric scheme on the right learns three more classifiers with the roles of positives and negatives swapped. The code matrices for the unordered and ordered version of the one-versus-rest scheme are as follows:

$$\begin{pmatrix} +1 & -1 & -1 \\ -1 & +1 & -1 \\ -1 & -1 & +1 \end{pmatrix} \qquad \begin{pmatrix} +1 & 0 \\ -1 & +1 \\ -1 & -1 \end{pmatrix}$$

On the left, we learn one classifier to distinguish C_1 (positive) from C_2 and C_3 (negative), another one to distinguish C_2 (positive) from C_1 and C_3 (negative), and the third one to distinguish C_3 (positive) from C_1 and C_2 (negative). On the right, we have ordered the classes in the order $C_1 - C_2 - C_3$, and thus only two classifiers are needed.

In order to decide the class for a new test instance, we collect predictions from all binary classifiers which can again be $+1$ for positive, -1 for negative and 0 for no prediction or *reject* (the latter is possible, for instance, with a rule-based classifier). Together, these predictions form a 'word' that can be looked up in the code matrix, a process also known as *decoding*. Suppose the word is -1 $+1$ -1 and the scheme is unordered one-versus-rest, then we know the decision should be class C_2. The question is: what should we with words that do not appear in the code matrix? For instance, suppose the word is $0\ +1\ 0$, and the scheme is symmetric one-versus-one (the first of the above four code matrices). In this case we could argue that the nearest code word is the first row in the matrix, and so we should predict C_1. To make this a little bit more precise, we define the distance between a word w and a code word c as $d(w,c) = \sum_i (1 - w_i c_i)/2$, where i ranges over the 'bits' of the words (the columns in the code matrix). That is, bits where the two words agree do not contribute to the distance; each bit where one word has $+1$ and the other -1 contributes 1; and if one of the bits is 0 the contribution is $1/2$, regardless of the other bit.[1] The predicted class for word w is then $\arg\min_j d(w, c_j)$, where c_j is the j-th row of the code matrix. So, if $w = 0\ +1\ 0$ then $d(w, c_1) = 1$ and $d(w, c_2) = d(w, c_3) = 1.5$, which means that we predict C_1.

However, the nearest code word is not always unique. For instance, suppose we use a four-class one-versus-rest scheme, and two of the binary classifiers predict positive and the other two negative, then this word is equidistant to two code words, and so we can't resolve which of the two classes corresponding to the two nearest code words to predict. We can improve the situation by adding more columns to our code matrix:

$$\begin{pmatrix} +1 & -1 & -1 & -1 \\ -1 & +1 & -1 & -1 \\ -1 & -1 & +1 & -1 \\ -1 & -1 & -1 & +1 \end{pmatrix} \qquad \begin{pmatrix} +1 & -1 & -1 & -1 & +1 & +1 & +1 \\ -1 & +1 & -1 & -1 & +1 & -1 & -1 \\ -1 & -1 & +1 & -1 & -1 & +1 & -1 \\ -1 & -1 & -1 & +1 & -1 & -1 & +1 \end{pmatrix}$$

On the left we see a standard four-class one-versus-rest code matrix, which has been extended with three extra columns (i.e., binary learning problems) on the right. As a result, the distance between any two code words has now increased from 2 to 4, increasing the likelihood that we can decode words that are not contained in the code matrix. The resulting scheme can be seen as a mix between one-versus-rest and one-versus-one classification. However, notice that the additional binary learning problems may be hard. For instance, if our four classes are spam e-mails, work e-mails, household e-mails (e.g., utility bills or credit card statements) and private e-mails, then each one-versus-rest binary classification task may be much easier than, say, distinguishing between spam and work e-mails on the one hand and household and private e-mails on the other.

The one-versus-rest and one-versus-one schemes are the most commonly used ways to turn binary classifiers into multi-class classifiers. In order to force a decision in the one-versus-rest scenario we can settle on a class ordering prior to or after learning. In the one-versus-one scheme we can use voting to arrive at a decision, which is actu-

[1] This is a slight generalisation of the *Hamming distance* for binary strings, which counts the number of positions in which the two strings differ.

ally equivalent to distance-based decoding as demonstrated by the following example.

Example 3.2 (One-versus-one voting). A one-versus-one code matrix for $k = 4$ classes is as follows:

$$\begin{pmatrix} +1 & +1 & +1 & 0 & 0 & 0 \\ -1 & 0 & 0 & +1 & +1 & 0 \\ 0 & -1 & 0 & -1 & 0 & +1 \\ 0 & 0 & -1 & 0 & -1 & -1 \end{pmatrix}$$

Suppose our six pairwise classifiers predict $w = +1\ -1\ +1\ -1\ +1\ +1$. We can interpret this as votes for $C_1 - C_3 - C_1 - C_3 - C_2 - C_3$; i.e., three votes for C_3, two votes for C_1 and one vote for C_2. More generally, the i-th classifier's vote for the j-th class can be expressed as $(1 + w_i c_{ji})/2$, where c_{ji} is the entry in the j-th row and i-th column of the code matrix. However, this overcounts the 0 entries in the code matrix; since every class participates in $k-1$ pairwise binary tasks, and there are $l = k(k-1)/2$ tasks, the number of zeros in every row is $k(k-1)/2 - (k-1) = (k-1)(k-2)/2 = l(k-2)/k$ (3 in our case). For each zero we need to subtract half a vote, so the number of votes for C_j is

$$\begin{aligned} v_j &= \left(\sum_{i=1}^{l} \frac{1 + w_i c_{ji}}{2}\right) - l\frac{k-2}{2k} = \left(\sum_{i=1}^{l} \frac{w_i c_{ji} - 1}{2}\right) + l - l\frac{k-2}{2k} \\ &= -d_j + l\frac{2k-k+2}{2k} = \frac{(k-1)(k+2)}{4} - d_j \end{aligned}$$

where $d_j = \sum_i (1 - w_i c_{ji})/2$ is the bit-wise distance we used earlier. In other words, the distance and number of votes for each class sum to a constant depending only on the number of classes; with three classes this is 4.5. This can be checked by noting that the distance between w and the first code word is 2.5 (two votes for C_1); with the second code word, 3.5 (one vote for C_2); with the third code word, 1.5 (three votes for C_3); and 4.5 with the fourth code word (no votes).

If our binary classifiers output scores, we can take these into account as follows. As before we assume that the sign of the scores s_i indicates the class. We can then use the appropriate entry in the code matrix c_{ji} to calculate a margin $z_i = s_i c_{ji}$, which we feed into a loss function L (margins and loss functions were discussed in Section 2.2). We thus define the distance between a vector of scores s and the j-th code word c_j as $d(s, c_j) = \sum_i L(s_i c_{ji})$, and we assign the class which minimises this distance. This way of arriving at a multi-class decision from binary scores is called *loss-based decoding*.

Example 3.3 (Loss-based decoding). Continuing the previous example, suppose the scores of the six pairwise classifiers are $(+5,-0.5,+4,-0.5,+4,+0.5)$. This leads to the following margins, in matrix form:

$$\begin{pmatrix} +5 & -0.5 & +4 & 0 & 0 & 0 \\ -5 & 0 & 0 & -0.5 & +4 & 0 \\ 0 & +0.5 & 0 & +0.5 & 0 & +0.5 \\ 0 & 0 & -4 & 0 & -4 & -0.5 \end{pmatrix}$$

Using 0–1 loss we ignore the magnitude of the margins and thus predict C_3 as in the voting-based scheme of Example 3.2. Using exponential loss $L(z) = \exp(-z)$, we obtain the distances $(4.67, 153.08, 4.82, 113.85)$. Loss-based decoding would therefore (just) favour C_1, by virtue of its strong wins against C_2 and C_4; in contrast, all three wins of C_3 are with small margin.

It should be noted that loss-based decoding assumes that each binary classifier scores on the same scale.

Multi-class scores and probabilities

If we want to calculate multi-class scores and probabilities from binary classifiers, we have a number of different options.

- ☞ We can use the distances obtained by loss-based decoding and turn them into scores by means of some appropriate transformation, just as we turned bit-wise distances into votes in Example 3.2. This method is applicable if the binary classifiers output calibrated scores on a single scale.

- ☞ Alternatively, we can use the output of each binary classifier as features (real-valued if we use the scores, binary if we only use the predicted class) and train a model that can produce multi-class scores, such as naive Bayes or tree models. This method is generally applicable but requires additional training.

- ☞ A simple alternative that is also generally applicable and often produces satisfactory results is to derive scores from *coverage counts*: the number of examples of each class that are classified as positive by the binary classifer. Example 3.4 illustrates this.

Example 3.4 (Coverage counts as scores). Suppose we have three classes and three binary classifiers which either predict positive or negative (there is no reject option). The first classifier classifies 8 examples of the first class as positive, no examples of the second class, and 2 examples of the third class. For the second classifier these counts are 2, 17 and 1, and for the third they are 4, 2 and 8. Suppose a test instance is predicted as positive by the first and third classifiers. We can add the coverage counts of these two classifiers to obtain a score vector of $(12,2,10)$. Likewise, if all three classifiers 'fire' for a particular test instance (i.e., predict positive), the score vector is $(14,19,11)$.

We can describe this scheme conveniently using matrix notation:

$$\begin{pmatrix} 1 & 0 & 1 \\ 1 & 1 & 1 \end{pmatrix} \begin{pmatrix} 8 & 0 & 2 \\ 2 & 17 & 1 \\ 4 & 2 & 8 \end{pmatrix} = \begin{pmatrix} 12 & 2 & 10 \\ 14 & 19 & 11 \end{pmatrix} \tag{3.1}$$

The middle matrix contains the class counts (one row for each classifier). The left 2-by-3 matrix contains, for each example, a row indicating which classifiers fire for that example. The right-hand side then gives the combined counts for each example.

With l binary classifiers, this scheme divides the instance space into up to 2^l regions. Each of these regions is assigned its own score vector, so in order to obtain diverse scores l should be reasonably large.

Once we have multi-class scores, we can ask the familiar question of how good these are. As we have seen in Section 2.1, an important performance index of a binary scoring classifier is the area under the ROC curve or AUC, which is the proportion of correctly ranked positive–negative pairs. Unfortunately ranking does not have a direct multi-class analogue, and so the most obvious thing to do is to calculate the average AUC over binary classification tasks, either in a one-versus-rest or one-versus-one fashion. For instance, the one-versus-rest average AUC estimates the probability that, taking a uniformly drawn class as positive, a uniformly drawn example from that class gets a higher score than a uniformly drawn example over all other classes. Notice that the 'negative' is more likely to come from the more prevalent classes; for that reason the positive class is sometimes also drawn from a non-uniform distribution in which each class is weighted with its prevalence in the test set.

Example 3.5 (Multi-class AUC). Assume we have a multi-class scoring classifier that produces a k-vector of scores $\hat{\mathbf{s}}(x) = (\hat{s}_1(x), \ldots, \hat{s}_k(x))$ for each test instance x. By restricting attention to $\hat{s}_i(x)$ we obtain a scoring classifier for class C_i against the other classes, and we can calculate the one-versus-rest AUC for C_i in the normal way.

By way of example, suppose we have three classes, and the one-versus-rest AUCs come out as 1 for the first class, 0.8 for the second class and 0.6 for the third class. Thus, for instance, all instances of class 1 receive a higher first entry in their score vectors than any of the instances of the other two classes. The average of these three AUCs is 0.8, which reflects the fact that, if we uniformly choose an index i, and we select an instance x uniformly among class C_i and another instance x' uniformly among all instances not from C_i, then the expectation that $\hat{s}_i(x) > \hat{s}_i(x')$ is 0.8.

Suppose now C_1 has 10 instances, C_2 has 20 and C_3 70. The weighted average of the one-versus-rest AUCs is then 0.68: that is, if we uniformly choose x *without reference to the class*, and then choose x' uniformly from among all instances not of the same class as x', the expectation that $\hat{s}_i(x) > \hat{s}_i(x')$ is 0.68. This is lower than before, because it is now more likely that a random x comes from class C_3, whose scores do a worse ranking job.

We can obtain similar averages from one-versus-one AUCs. For instance, we can define AUC_{ij} as the AUC obtained using scores $\hat{s}_i$ to rank instances from classes C_i and C_j. Notice that $\hat{s}_j$ may rank these instances differently, and so $\text{AUC}_{ji} \neq \text{AUC}_{ij}$. Taking an unweighted average over all $i \neq j$ estimates the probability that, for uniformly chosen classes i and $j \neq i$, and uniformly chosen $x \in C_i$ and $x' \in C_j$, we have $\hat{s}_i(x) > \hat{s}_i(x')$. The weighted version of this estimates the probability that the instances are correctly ranked if we don't pre-select the class.

The simplest way to turn multi-class scores into classifications is by assigning the class that achieves the maximum score – that is, if $\hat{\mathbf{s}}(x) = (\hat{s}_1(x), \ldots, \hat{s}_k(x))$ is the score vector assigned to instance x and $m = \arg\max_i \hat{s}_i(x)$, then the class assigned to x is $\hat{c}(x) = C_m$. However, just as in the two-class case such a fixed decision rule can be sub-optimal, and instead we may want to learn it from data. What this means is that we want to learn a weight vector $\mathbf{w} = (w_1, \ldots, w_k)$ to adjust the scores and assign $\hat{c}(x) = C_{m'}$ with $m' = \arg\max_i w_i \hat{s}_i(x)$ instead.[2] Since the weight vector can be multiplied with a constant without affecting m', we can fix one of the degrees of freedom by setting

[2]Notice that with two classes such a weighted decision rule assigns class C_1 if $w_1 \hat{s}_1(x) > w_2 \hat{s}_2(x)$, or equivalently, $\hat{s}_1(x)/\hat{s}_2(x) > w_2/w_1$. This can be interpreted as a threshold on suitably transformed scores,

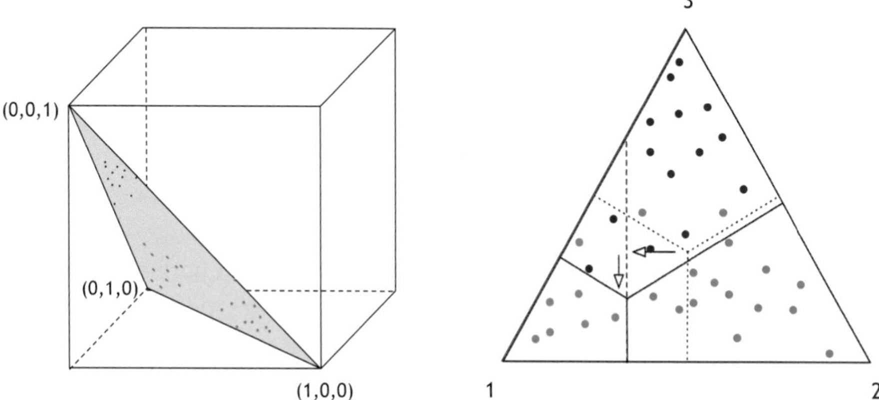

Figure 3.1. **(left)** Triples of probabilistic scores represented as points in an equilateral triangle connecting three corners of the unit cube. **(right)** The arrows show how the weights are adjusted from the initial equal weights (dotted lines), first by optimising the separation of C_2 against C_1 (dashed line), then by optimising the separation of C_3 against the other two classes (solid lines). The end result is that the weight of C_1 is considerably decreased, to the benefit of the other two classes.

$w_1 = 1$. Unfortunately, finding a globally optimal weight vector is computationally intractable. A heuristic approach that works well in practice is to first learn w_2 to optimally separate C_2 from C_1 as in the two-class case; then learn w_3 to separate C_3 from $C_1 \cup C_2$, and so on.

Example 3.6 (Reweighting multi-class scores). We illustrate the procedure for a three-class probabilistic classifier. The probability vectors $\hat{\mathbf{p}}(x) = \big(\hat{p}_1(x), \hat{p}_2(x), \hat{p}_3(x)\big)$ can be thought of as points inside the unit cube. Since the probabilities add up to 1, the points lie in an equilateral triangle connecting three corners of the cube (Figure 3.1 (left)). Each corner of this triangle represents one of the classes; the probability assigned to a particular class in a given point is proportional to the distance to the opposite side.

Any decision rule of the form $\arg\max_i w_i \hat{s}_i(x)$ cuts the triangle in three areas using lines perpendicular to the sides. For the unweighted decision rule these lines intersect in the triangle's centre of mass (Figure 3.1 (right)). Optimising the separation between C_2 against C_1 means moving this point along a line parallel to the base of the triangle, moving away from the class that receives greater weight. Once the optimal point on this line is found, we optimise the separation

---

so the weighted decision rule indeed generalises the two-class decision threshold.

of C_3 against the first two classes by moving in a direction perpendicular to the previous line.

Finally, we briefly look at the issue of obtaining calibrated multi-class probabilities. This is not a solved problem and several approaches have been suggested in the literature. One of the simplest and most robust of these calculates normalised coverage counts. Specifically, we take the summed or averaged coverage counts of all classifiers that fire, and normalise these to obtain probability vectors whose components sum to one. Equivalently, we can obtain probability vectors for each classifier separately, and take a weighted average of these with weights determined by the relative coverage of each classifier.

Example 3.7 (Multi-class probabilities from coverage counts). In Example 3.4 on p.87 we can divide the class counts by the total number of positive predictions. This results in the following class distributions: (0.80,0,0.20) for the first classifier, (0.10,0.85,0.05) for the second classifier, and (0.29,0.14,0.57) for the third. The probability distribution associated with the combination of the first and third classifiers is

$$\frac{10}{24}(0.80,0,0.20) + \frac{14}{24}(0.29,0.14,0.57) = (0.50,0.08,0.42)$$

which is the same distribution as obtained by normalising the combined counts (12,2,10). Similarly, the distribution associated with all three classifiers is

$$\frac{10}{44}(0.80,0,0.20) + \frac{20}{44}(0.10,0.85,0.05) + \frac{14}{44}(0.29,0.14,0.57) = (0.32,0.43,0.25)$$

Matrix notation describes this very succinctly as

$$\begin{pmatrix} 10/24 & 0 & 14/24 \\ 10/44 & 20/44 & 14/44 \end{pmatrix} \begin{pmatrix} 0.80 & 0.00 & 0.20 \\ 0.10 & 0.85 & 0.05 \\ 0.29 & 0.14 & 0.57 \end{pmatrix} = \begin{pmatrix} 0.50 & 0.08 & 0.42 \\ 0.32 & 0.43 & 0.25 \end{pmatrix}$$

The middle matrix is a row-normalised version of the middle matrix in Equation 3.1. *Row normalisation* works by dividing each entry by the sum of the entries in the row in which it occurs. As a result the entries in each row sum to one, which means that each row can be interpreted as a probability distribution. The left matrix combines two pieces of information: (*i*) which classifiers fire for each example (for instance, the second classifier doesn't fire for the first example); and (*ii*) the coverage of each classifier. The right-hand side then gives the class distribution for each example. Notice that the product of row-normalised matrices again gives a row-normalised matrix.

In this section we have seen that many interesting issues arise, once we have more than two classes. The general way of addressing a k-class learning problem with binary classifiers is to (*i*) break the problem up into l binary learning problems; (*ii*) train l binary classifiers on two-class versions of the original data; and (*iii*) combine the predictions from these l classifiers into a single k-class prediction. The most common ways to do the first and third step is one-versus-one or one-versus-rest, but the use of code matrices gives the opportunity of implementing other schemes. We have also looked at ways of obtaining multi-class scores and probabilities from the binary classifiers, and discussed a heuristic method to calibrate the multi-class decision rule by reweighting.

This concludes our discussion of classification, arguably the most common task in machine learning. In the remainder of this chapter we will look at one more supervised predictive task in the next section, before we turn our attention to unsupervised and descriptive learning in Section 3.3.

3.2 Regression

In all the tasks considered so far – classification, scoring, ranking and probability estimation – the label space was a discrete set of classes. In this section we will consider the case of a real-valued target variable. A *function estimator*, also called a *regressor*, is a mapping $\hat{f}: \mathscr{X} \to \mathbb{R}$. The regression learning problem is to learn a function estimator from examples $(x_i, f(x_i))$. For instance, we might want to learn an estimator for the Dow Jones index or the FTSE 100 based on selected economic indicators.

While this may seem a natural and innocuous generalisation of discrete classification, it is not without its consequences. For one thing, we switched from a relatively low-resolution target variable to one with infinite resolution. Trying to match this precision in the function estimator will almost certainly lead to overfitting – besides, it is highly likely that some part of the target values in the examples is due to fluctuations that the model is unable to capture. It is therefore entirely reasonable to assume that the examples are noisy, and that the estimator is only intended to capture the general trend or shape of the function.

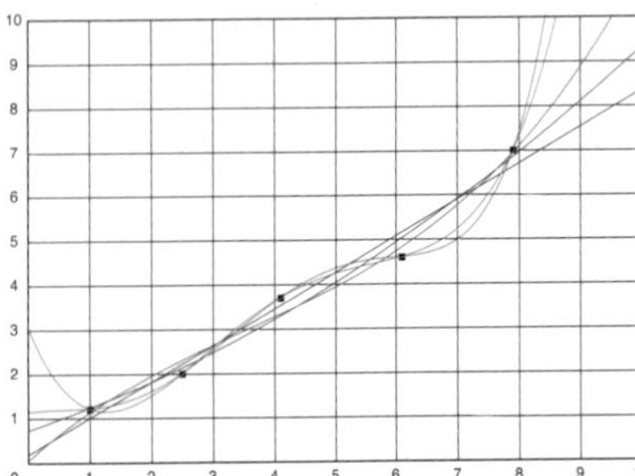

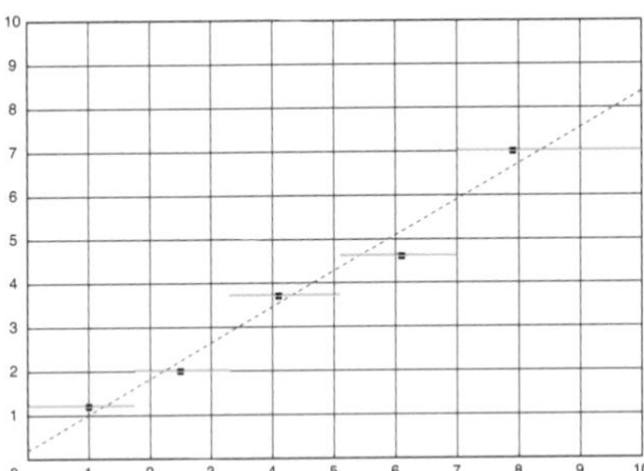

Figure 3.2. **(left)** Polynomials of different degree fitted to a set of five points. From bottom to top in the top right-hand corner: degree 1 (straight line), degree 2 (parabola), degree 3, degree 4 (which is the lowest degree able to fit the points exactly), degree 5. **(right)** A piecewise constant function learned by a grouping model; the dotted reference line is the linear function from the left figure.

Example 3.8 (Line fitting example). Consider the following set of five points:

x	y
1.0	1.2
2.5	2.0
4.1	3.7
6.1	4.6
7.9	7.0

We want to estimate y by means of a polynomial in x. Figure 3.2 (left) shows the result for degrees of 1 to 5 using ☞*linear regression*, which will be explained in Chapter 7. The top two degrees fit the given points exactly (in general, any set of n points can be fitted by a polynomial of degree no more than $n-1$), but they differ considerably at the extreme ends: e.g., the polynomial of degree 4 leads to a decreasing trend from $x = 0$ to $x = 1$, which is not really justified by the data.

To avoid overfitting the kind of data exemplified in Example 3.8 it is advisable to choose the degree of the polynomial as low as possible – often a simple linear relationship is assumed.

Regression is a task where the distinction between grouping and grading models comes to the fore. The philosophy of grouping models is to cleverly divide the instance space into segments and learn a local model in each segment that is as simple as possible. For instance, in decision trees the local model is a majority class classifier. In the same spirit, to obtain a regression tree we could predict a constant value in each leaf. In the univariate problem of Example 3.8 this would result in the piecewise constant curve of Figure 3.2 (right). Notice that such a grouping model is able to fit the given points exactly, just as a polynomial of sufficiently high degree, and the same caveat regarding overfitting applies.

We can understand the phenomenon of overfitting a bit better by looking at the number of parameters that each model has. An n-degree polynomial has $n+1$ parameters: e.g., a straight line $y = a \cdot x + b$ has two parameters, and the polynomial of degree 4 that fits the five points exactly has five parameters. A piecewise constant model with n segments has $2n-1$ parameters: n y-values and $n-1$ x-values where the 'jumps' occur. So the models that are able to fit the points exactly are the models with more parameters. A rule of thumb is that, *to avoid overfitting, the number of parameters estimated from the data must be considerably less than the number of data points.*

We have seen that classification models can be evaluated by applying a loss function to the margins, penalising negative margins (misclassifications) and rewarding positive margins (correct classifications). Regression models are evaluated by applying a loss function to the *residuals* $f(x) - \hat{f}(x)$. Unlike classification loss functions a regression loss function will typically be symmetric around 0 (although it is conceivable that positive and negative residuals have different weights). The most common choice here is to take the squared residual as the loss function. This has the advantage of mathematical convenience, and can also be justified by the assumption that the observed function values are the true values contaminated by additive, normally distributed noise. However, it is well-known that squared loss is sensitive to outliers: you can see an example of this in Figure 7.2 on p.199.

If we underestimate the number of parameters of the model, we will not be able to decrease the loss to zero, regardless of how much training data we have. On the other hand, with a larger number of parameters the model will be more dependent on the training sample, and small variations in the training sample can result in a considerably different model. This is sometimes called the *bias–variance dilemma*: a low-complexity model suffers less from variability due to random variations in the training data, but may introduce a systematic bias that even large amounts of training data can't resolve; on the other hand, a high-complexity model eliminates such bias but can suffer non-systematic errors due to variance.

We can make this a bit more precise by noting that expected squared loss on a training example x can be decomposed as follows:[3]

$$\mathbb{E}\left[\left(f(x) - \hat{f}(x)\right)^2\right] = \left(f(x) - \mathbb{E}\left[\hat{f}(x)\right]\right)^2 + \mathbb{E}\left[\left(\hat{f}(x) - \mathbb{E}\left[\hat{f}(x)\right]\right)^2\right] \tag{3.2}$$

[3]The derivation expands the squared difference term, making use of the linearity of $\mathbb{E}[\cdot]$ and that $\mathbb{E}\left[f(x)\right] = f(x)$, after which terms can be rearranged to yield Equation 3.2.

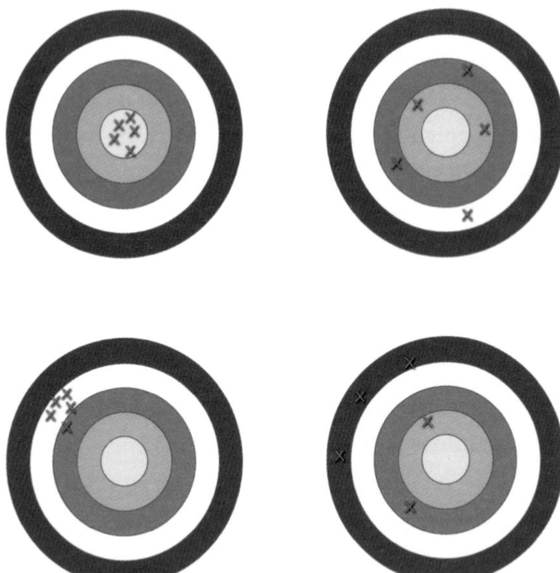

Figure 3.3. A dartboard metaphor illustrating the concepts of bias and variance. Each dartboard corresponds to a different learning algorithm, and each dart signifies a different training sample. The top row learning algorithms exhibit low bias, staying close to the bull's eye (the true function value for a particular x) on average, while the ones on the bottom row have high bias. The left column shows low variance and the right column high variance.

It is important to note that the expectation is taken over different training sets and hence different function estimators, but the learning algorithm and the example are fixed. The first term on the right-hand side in Equation 3.2 is zero if these function estimators get it right on average; otherwise the learning algorithm exhibits a systematic *bias* of some kind. The second term quantifies the *variance* in the function estimates $\hat{f}(x)$ as a result of variations in the training set. Figure 3.3 illustrates this graphically using a dartboard metaphor. The best situation is clearly achieved in the top left-hand corner of the figure, but in practice this is rarely achievable and we need to settle either for a low bias and a high variance (e.g., approximating the target function by a high-degree polynomial) or for a high bias and a low variance (e.g., using a linear approximation). We will return to the bias–variance dilemma at several places in the book: although the decomposition is not unique for most loss functions other than squared loss, it serves as a useful conceptual tool for understanding over- and underfitting.

3.3 Unsupervised and descriptive learning

So far, we have concerned ourselves exclusively with supervised learning of predictive models. That is, we learn a mapping from instance space $\mathscr{X}$ to output space $\mathscr{Y}$ using labelled examples $(x, l(x)) \in \mathscr{X} \times \mathscr{L}$ (or a noisy version thereof). This kind of learning is called 'supervised' because of the presence of the target variable $l(x)$ in the training data, which has to be supplied by a 'supervisor' or 'teacher' with some knowledge about the true labelling function l. Furthermore, the models are called 'predictive' because the outputs produced by the models are either direct estimates of the target variable or provide us with further information about its most likely value. Thus, we have only paid attention to the top-left entry in Table 3.1. In the remainder of this chapter we will briefly introduce the other three learning settings by means of selected examples:

- ☞ unsupervised learning of a predictive model in the form of predictive clustering;
- ☞ unsupervised learning of a descriptive model, exemplified by descriptive clustering and association rule discovery;
- ☞ supervised learning of a descriptive model, with subgroup discovery as practical realisation.

	Predictive model	*Descriptive model*
Supervised learning	classification, regression	**subgroup discovery**
Unsupervised learning	**predictive clustering**	**descriptive clustering, association rule discovery**

Table 3.1. The learning settings indicated in **bold** are introduced in the remainder of this chapter.

It is worthwhile reflecting for a moment on the nature of descriptive learning. The task here is to come up with a description of the data – to produce a descriptive model. It follows that the task output, being a model, is of the same kind as the learning output. Furthermore, it makes no sense to employ a separate training set to produce the descriptive model, as we want the model to describe our actual data rather than some hold-out set. In other words, *in descriptive learning the task and learning problem coincide* (Figure 3.4). This makes some things harder: for example, it is unlikely that a 'ground truth' or 'gold standard' is available to test the descriptive models against, and hence evaluating descriptive learning algorithms is much less straightforward than evaluating predictive ones. On the other hand, one could say that descriptive learning leads to the *discovery* of genuinely new knowledge, and it is often situated at the intersection of machine learning and data mining.

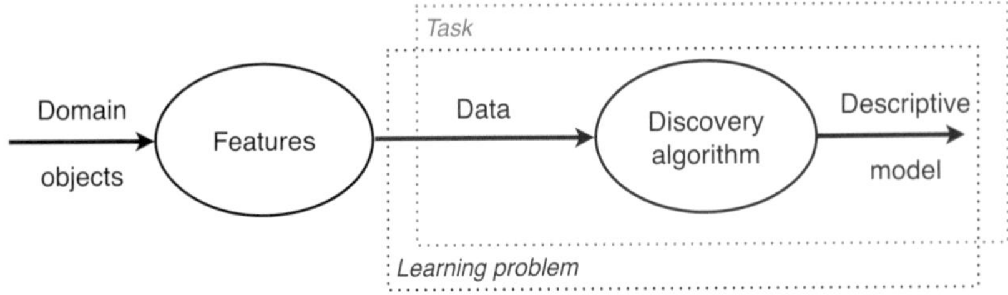

Figure 3.4. In descriptive learning the task and learning problem coincide: we do not have a separate training set, and the task is to produce a descriptive model of the data.

Predictive and descriptive clustering

The distinction between predictive and descriptive models can be clearly observed in clustering tasks. One way to understand clustering is as learning a new labelling function from unlabelled data. So we could define a 'clusterer' in the same way as a classifier, namely as a mapping $\hat{q}: \mathscr{X} \rightarrow \mathscr{C}$, where $\mathscr{C} = \{C_1, C_2, \ldots, C_k\}$ is a set of new labels. This corresponds to a *predictive* view of clustering, as the domain of the mapping is the entire instance space, and hence it generalises to unseen instances. A *descriptive* clustering model learned from given data $D \subseteq \mathscr{X}$ would be a mapping $\hat{q}: D \rightarrow \mathscr{C}$ whose domain is D rather than $\mathscr{X}$. In either case the labels have no intrinsic meaning, other than to express whether two instances belong to the same cluster. So an alternative way to define a clusterer is as an equivalence relation $\hat{q} \subseteq \mathscr{X} \times \mathscr{X}$ or $\hat{q} \subseteq D \times D$ (see Background 2.1 on p.51 for the definition of an equivalence relation), or, equivalently, as a partition of $\mathscr{X}$ or D.

The distinction between predictive and descriptive clustering is subtle and not always articulated clearly in the literature. Several well-known clustering algorithms including ☞*K-means* (discussed in more detail in Chapter 8) learn a predictive clustering. Thus, they learn a clustering model from training data that can subsequently be used to assign new data to clusters. This is in keeping with our distinction between the task (clustering arbitrary data) and the learning problem (learning a clustering model from training data). However, this distinction isn't really applicable to descriptive clustering methods: here, the clustering model learned from D can only be used to cluster D. In effect, the task becomes learning a suitable clustering model for the given data.

Without any further information, any clustering is as good as any other. What distinguishes a good clustering is that the data is partitioned into *coherent* groups or clusters. 'Coherence' here means that, on average, two instances from the same cluster have more in common – are more similar – than two instances from different clusters. This assumes some way of assessing the similarity or, as is usually more convenient, the dissimilarity or distance of an arbitrary pair of instances. If our features are numerical, i.e., $\mathscr{X} = \mathbb{R}^d$, the most obvious distance measure is Euclidean distance, but other choices are possible, some of which generalise to non-numerical features. Most distance-based clustering methods depend on the possibility of defining a 'centre of mass' or *exemplar* for an arbitrary set of instances, such that the exemplar minimises some distance-related quantity over all instances in the set, called its *scatter*. A good clustering is then one where the scatter summed over each cluster – the *within-cluster scatter* – is much smaller than the scatter of the entire data set.

This analysis suggests a definition of the clustering problem as finding a partition $D = D_1 \uplus \ldots \uplus D_K$ that minimises the within-cluster scatter. However, there are a few issues with this definition:

☞ the problem as stated has a trivial solution: set $K = |D|$ so that each 'cluster' contains a single instance from D and thus has zero scatter;

☞ if we fix the number of clusters K in advance, the problem cannot be solved efficiently for large data sets (it is NP-hard).

The first problem is the clustering equivalent of overfitting the training data. It could be dealt with by penalising large K. Most approaches, however, assume that an educated guess of K can be made. This leaves the second problem, which is that finding a globally optimal solution is intractable for larger problems. This is a well-known situation in computer science and can be dealt with in two ways:

☞ by applying a heuristic approach, which finds a 'good enough' solution rather than the best possible one;

☞ by relaxing the problem into a 'soft' clustering problem, by allowing instances a degree of membership in more than one cluster.

Most clustering algorithms follow the heuristic route, including the K-means algorithm. The soft clustering approach can be addressed in various ways, including ☞*Expectation-Maximisation* (Section 9.4) and ☞*matrix decomposition* (Section 10.3). Figure 3.5 illustrates the heuristic and soft clustering approaches. Notice that a soft clustering generalises the notion of a partition, in the same way that a probability estimator generalises a classifier.

The representation of clustering models depends on whether they are predictive, descriptive or soft. A descriptive clustering of n data points into c clusters could be represented by a *partition matrix*: an n-by-c binary matrix with exactly one 1 in each row (and at least one 1 in each column, otherwise there would be empty clusters). A soft clustering corresponds to a row-normalised n-by-c matrix. A predictive clustering partitions the whole instance space and is therefore not suitable for a matrix representation. Typically, predictive clustering methods represent a cluster by their *centroid* or *exemplar*: in that case, the cluster boundaries are a set of straight lines called a *Voronoi*

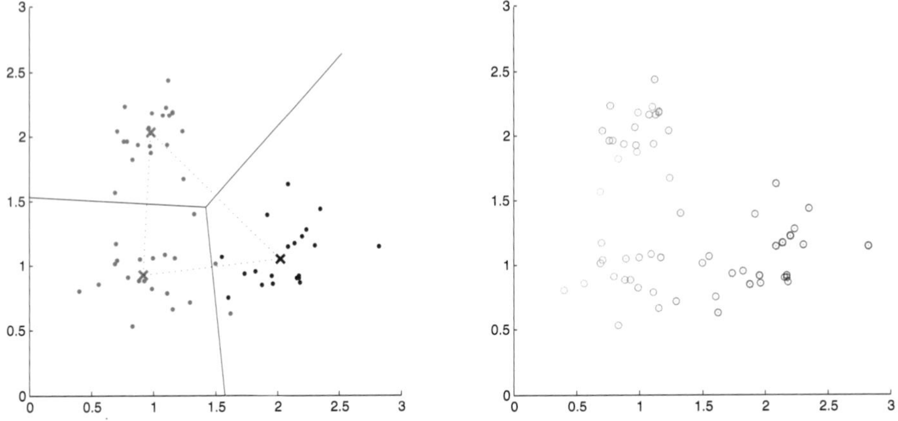

Figure 3.5. **(left)** An example of a predictive clustering. The coloured dots were sampled from three bivariate Gaussians centred at $(1,1)$, $(1,2)$ and $(2,1)$. The crosses and solid lines are the cluster exemplars and cluster boundaries found by 3-means. **(right)** A soft clustering of the same data found by matrix decomposition.

diagram (Figure 3.5 (left)). More generally, each cluster could be represented by a probability density, with the boundaries occurring where densities of neighbouring clusters are equal; this would allow non-linear cluster boundaries.

Example 3.9 (Representing clusterings). The cluster exemplars in Figure 3.5 (left) can be given as a c-by-2 matrix:

$$\begin{pmatrix} 0.92 & 0.93 \\ 0.98 & 2.02 \\ 2.03 & 1.04 \end{pmatrix}$$

The following n-by-c matrices represent a descriptive clustering (left) and a soft clustering (right) of given data points:

$$\begin{pmatrix} 1 & 0 & 0 \\ 0 & 1 & 0 \\ 1 & 0 & 0 \\ 0 & 0 & 1 \\ \cdots & \cdots & \cdots \end{pmatrix} \qquad \begin{pmatrix} 0.40 & 0.30 & 0.30 \\ 0.40 & 0.51 & 0.09 \\ 0.44 & 0.29 & 0.27 \\ 0.35 & 0.08 & 0.57 \\ \cdots & \cdots & \cdots \end{pmatrix}$$

An interesting question is how clustering models should be evaluated. In the absence of labelled data we cannot use a test set in the same way as we would in classification or regression. We can use within-cluster scatter as a measure of the quality of a clustering. For a predictive clustering it is possible to evaluate within-cluster scatter on hold-out data that wasn't used to build the clusters in the first place. An alternative way of evaluating a clustering arises if we have some knowledge about instances that should, or should not, be clustered together.

Example 3.10 (Evaluating clusterings). Suppose we have five test instances that we think should be clustered as $\{e1, e2\}, \{e3, e4, e5\}$. So out of the $5 \cdot 4 = 20$ possible pairs, 4 are considered 'must-link' pairs and the other 16 as 'must-not-link' pairs. The clustering to be evaluated clusters these as $\{e1, e2, e3\}, \{e4, e5\}$ – so two of the must-link pairs are indeed clustered together ($e1$–$e2$, $e4$–$e5$), the other two are not ($e3$–$e4$, $e3$–$e5$), and so on.

We can tabulate this as follows:

	Are together	*Are not together*	
Should be together	**2**	2	4
Should not be together	2	**14**	16
	4	16	20

We can now treat this as a two-by-two contingency table, and evaluate it accordingly. For instance, we can take the proportion of pairs on the 'good' diagonal, which is $16/20 = 0.8$. In classification we would call this accuracy, but in the clustering context this is known as the *Rand index*.

Note that there are usually many more must-not-link pairs than must-link pairs, and it is a good idea to compensate for this. One way to do that is to calculate the harmonic mean of precision and recall (the latter the same as true positive rate, see Table 2.3 on p.57), which in the information retrieval literature is known as the *F-measure*.[4] Precision is calculated on the left column of the contingency table and recall on the top row; as a result the bottom right-hand cell (the must-not-link pairs that are correctly not clustered together) are ignored, which is precisely what we want. In the example both precision and recall are $2/4 = 0.5$, and so is the F-measure. This shows that the relatively good Rand index is mostly accounted for by the must-not-link pairs that end up in different clusters.

[4]The harmonic mean of precision and recall is $\frac{2}{1/prec + 1/rec} = \frac{2\,prec \cdot rec}{prec + rec}$. The harmonic mean is appropriate for averaging ratios; see Background 10.1 on p.300.

Other descriptive models

To wrap up our catalogue of machine learning tasks we will briefly look at two other descriptive models, one learned in a supervised fashion from labelled data and the other entirely unsupervised.

Subgroup models don't try to approximate the labelling function, but rather aim at identifying subsets of the data exhibiting a class distribution that is significantly different from the overall population. Formally, a *subgroup* is a mapping $\hat{g} : D \rightarrow \{\text{true}, \text{false}\}$ and is learned from a set of labelled examples $(x_i, l(x_i))$, where $l : \mathscr{X} \rightarrow \mathscr{C}$ is the true labelling function. Note that $\hat{g}$ is the characteristic function of the set $G = \{x \in D | \hat{g}(x) = \text{true}\}$, which is called the *extension* of the subgroup. Note also that we used the given data D rather than the whole instance space $\mathscr{X}$ for the domain of a subgroup, since it is a descriptive model.

Example 3.11 (Subgroup discovery). Imagine you want to market the new version of a successful product. You have a database of people who have been sent information about the previous version, containing all kinds of demographic, economic and social information about those people, as well as whether or not they purchased the product. If you were to build a classifier or ranker to find the most likely customers for your product, it is unlikely to outperform the majority class classifier (typically, relatively few people will have bought the product). However, what you are really interested in is finding reasonably sized subsets of people with a proportion of customers that is significantly higher than in the overall population. You can then target those people in your marketing campaign, ignoring the rest of your database.

A subgroup is essentially a binary classifier, and so one way to develop a subgroup discovery system is to adapt an existing classifier training algorithm. This may not involve much more than adapting the search heuristic to reflect the specific objective of a subgroup (to identify subsets of the data with a significantly different class distribution). However, this would only give us a single subgroup. Rule learners are particularly appropriate for subgroup discovery since every rule can be interpreted as a separate subgroup.

How do we distinguish interesting subgroups from uninteresting ones? This can be determined by constructing a contingency table similar to the ones we use in binary classification. For three classes such a table looks as follows:

	In subgroup	*Not in subgroup*	
Labelled C_1	g_1	$C_1 - g_1$	C_1
Labelled C_2	g_2	$C_2 - g_2$	C_2
Labelled C_3	g_3	$C_3 - g_3$	C_3
	$\lvert G\rvert$	$\lvert D\rvert - \lvert G\rvert$	$\lvert D\rvert$

where $g_i = |\{x \in D | \hat{g}(x) = \mathsf{true} \wedge l(x) = C_i\}|$ and C_i is shorthand for $|\{x \in D | l(x) = C_i\}|$. From here there are a number of possibilities. One idea is to measure the extent to which the class distribution in the left column is different from the class distribution in the row marginals (the right-most column). As we shall see later (Example 6.6 on p.180), this boils down to using an adaptation of average recall as evaluation measure. Another idea is to treat the subgroup as a decision tree split and borrow splitting criteria from ☞*decision tree* learning (Section 5.1). It is also possible to use the χ^2 statistic to evaluate the extent to which each g_i differs from what would be expected on the basis of the marginals C_i and $|G|$. What these evaluation measures have in common is that they prefer different class distributions in the subgroup and its complement from the overall distribution in D, and also larger subgroups over smaller ones. Most of these measures are actually symmetric in that they assign the same evaluation to a subgroup and its complement, from which it follows that they also prefer larger complements over smaller ones – in other words, they prefer subgroups that are about half the size of the data (other things being equal).

I will now give an example of unsupervised learning of descriptive models. Associations are things that usually occur together. For example, in market basket analysis we are interested in items frequently bought together. An example of an association rule is ·**if** beer **then** crisps·, stating that customers who buy beer tend to also buy crisps. Association rule discovery starts with identifying feature values that often occur together. There is some superficial similarity with subgroups here, but these so-called frequent item sets are identified in a purely unsupervised manner, without need for labelled training data. Item sets then give rise to rules describing co-occurrences between feature values. These association rules are if-then rules similar to classification rules, except that the then-part isn't restricted to a particular class variable and can contain any feature (or even several features). Rather than adapting a given learning algorithm we need a new algorithm that first finds frequent item sets and then turns them into association rules. The process needs to take into account a mix of statistics in order to avoid generating trivial rules.

Example 3.12 (Association rule discovery). In a motorway service station most clients will buy petrol. This means that there will be many frequent item sets involving petrol, such as {newspaper, petrol}. This might suggest the construction of an association rule ·**if** newspaper **then** petrol· – however, this is predictable given that {petrol} is already a frequent item set (and clearly at least as frequent as {newspaper, petrol}). Of more interest would be the converse rule ·**if** petrol **then** newspaper· which expresses that a considerable proportion of the people buying petrol also buy a newspaper.

We clearly see a relationship with subgroup discovery in that association rules also identify subsets that have a different distribution when compared with the full data set, namely with respect to the then-part of the rule. The difference is that the then-part is not a fixed target variable but it is found as part of the discovery process. Both subgroup discovery and association rule discovery will be discussed in the context of rule learning in Section 6.3.

3.4 Beyond binary classification: Summary and further reading

While binary classification is an important task in machine learning, there are many other relevant tasks and in this chapter we looked at a number of them.

- In Section 3.1 we considered classification tasks with more than two classes. We shall see in the coming chapters that some models handle this situation very naturally, but if our models are essentially two-class (such as linear models) we have to approach it via a combination of binary classification tasks. One key idea is the use of a code matrix to combine the results of several binary classifiers, as proposed by Dietterich and Bakiri (1995) under the name 'error-correcting output codes' and developed by Allwein *et al.* (2000). We also looked at ways to obtain scores for more than two classes and to evaluate those scores using multi-class adaptations of the area under the ROC curve. One of these multi-class extensions of AUC was proposed and analysed by Hand and Till (2001). The heuristic procedure for reweighting multi-class scores in Example 3.6 on p.89 was proposed by Lachiche and Flach (2003); Bourke *et al.* (2008) demonstrated that it achieves good performance in comparison with a number of alternative approaches.

- Section 3.2 was devoted to regression: predicting a real-valued target value. This is a classical data analysis problem that was already studied by Carl Friedrich Gauss in the late eighteenth century. It is natural to use a quadratic loss function on the residuals, although this carries with it a certain sensitivity to outliers. Grading models are most common here, although it is also possible to learn a grouping model that divides the instance space into segments that admit a simple local model. Since it is often possible to fit a set of points exactly (e.g., with a high-degree polynomial), care must be taken to avoid overfitting. Finding the right balance between over- and underfitting is sometimes called the bias–variance dilemma; an extensive discussion (including the dartboard metaphor) can be found in Rajnarayan and Wolpert (2010).

☞ In Section 3.3 we considered unsupervised and descriptive learning tasks. We saw that in descriptive learning the task and learning problem coincide. A clustering model can be either predictive or descriptive: in the former case it is meant to construct classes in a wholly unsupervised manner, after which the learned model can be applied to unseen data in the usual way. Descriptive clustering, on the other hand, only applies to the data at hand. It should be noted that the distinction between predictive and descriptive clustering is not universally recognised in the literature; sometimes the term 'predictive clustering' is used in the slightly different sense of clustering simultaneously on the target variable and the features (Blockeel *et al.*, 1998).

☞ Like descriptive clustering, association rule discovery is another descriptive task which is wholly unsupervised. It was introduced by Agrawal, Imielinski and Swami (1993) and has given rise to a very large body of work in the data mining literature. Subgroup discovery is a form of supervised learning of descriptive models aimed at finding subsets of the data with a significantly different distribution of the target variable. It was first studied by Klösgen (1996) and extended to the more general notion of exceptional model mining in order to deal with, e.g., real-valued target variables by Leman *et al.* (2008). More generally, unsupervised learning of descriptive models is a large subject that was pioneered by Tukey (1977).

CHAPTER 4

Concept learning

HAVING DISCUSSED A VARIETY of tasks in the preceding two chapters, we are now in an excellent position to start discussing machine learning models and algorithms for learning them. This chapter and the next two are devoted to logical models, the hallmark of which is that they use logical expressions to divide the instance space into segments and hence construct grouping models. The goal is to find a segmentation such that the data in each segment is more homogeneous, with respect to the task to be solved. For instance, in classification we aim to find a segmentation such that the instances in each segment are predominantly of one class, while in regression a good segmentation is such that the target variable is a simple function of a small number of predictor variables. There are essentially two kinds of logical models: tree models and rule models. Rule models consist of a collection of implications or if–then rules, where the if-part defines a segment, and the then-part defines the behaviour of the model in this segment. Tree models are a restricted kind of rule model where the if-parts of the rules are organised in a tree structure.

In this chapter we consider methods for learning logical expressions or *concepts* from examples, which lies at the basis of both tree models and rule models. In concept learning we only learn a description for the positive class, and label everything that doesn't satisfy that description as negative. We will pay particular attention to the generality ordering that plays an important role in logical models. In the next two chapters

The simplest logical expressions are equalities of the form Feature = Value and, for numerical features, inequalities of the form Feature < Value; these are called *literals*. Complex Boolean expressions can be built using logical connectives: *conjunction* $\wedge$, *disjunction* $\vee$, *negation* $\neg$ and *implication* $\rightarrow$. The following equivalences hold (the left two are called the *De Morgan laws*):

$$\neg(A \wedge B) \equiv \neg A \vee \neg B \qquad \neg\neg A \equiv A$$

$$\neg(A \vee B) \equiv \neg A \wedge \neg B \qquad A \rightarrow B \equiv \neg A \vee B$$

If Boolean expression A is true of instance x, we say that A *covers* x. The set of instances covered by expression A is called its *extension* and denoted $\mathscr{X}_A = \{x \in \mathscr{X} | A \text{ covers } x\}$, where $\mathscr{X}$ denotes the instance space which acts as the universe of discourse (see Background 2.1 on p.51). There is a direct correspondence between logical connectives and operations on sets: e.g., $\mathscr{X}_{A \wedge B} = \mathscr{X}_A \cap \mathscr{X}_B$, $\mathscr{X}_{A \vee B} = \mathscr{X}_A \cup \mathscr{X}_B$ and $\mathscr{X}_{\neg A} = \mathscr{X} \setminus \mathscr{X}_A$. If $\mathscr{X}_A \supseteq \mathscr{X}_{A'}$, we say that A is *at least as general as* A', and if in addition $\mathscr{X}_A \not\subseteq \mathscr{X}_{A'}$ we say that A is *more general than* A'. This *generality ordering* is a partial order on logical expressions as defined in Background 2.1. (More precisely: it is a partial order on the equivalence classes of the relation of logical equivalence $\equiv$.)

A *clause* is an implication $P \rightarrow Q$ such that P is a conjunction of literals and Q is a disjunction of literals. Using the equivalences above we can rewrite such an implication as

$$(A \wedge B) \rightarrow (C \vee D) \equiv \neg(A \wedge B) \vee (C \vee D) \equiv \neg A \vee \neg B \vee C \vee D$$

and hence a clause can equivalently be seen as a disjunction of literals or their negations. Any logical expression can be rewritten as a conjunction of clauses; this is referred to as *conjunctive normal form* (*CNF*). Alternatively, any logical expression can be written as a disjunction of conjunctions of literals or their negation; this is called *disjunctive normal form* (*DNF*). A *rule* is a clause $A \rightarrow B$ where B is a single literal; this is also often referred to as a *Horn clause*, after the American logician Alfred Horn.

Background 4.1. Some logical concepts and notation.

we consider tree and rule models, which go considerably beyond concept learning as they can handle multiple classes, probability estimation, regression, as well as clustering tasks.

4.1 The hypothesis space

The simplest concept learning setting is where we restrict the logical expressions describing concepts to conjunctions of literals (see Background 4.1 for a review of important definitions and notation from logic). The following example illustrates this.[1]

Example 4.1 (Learning conjunctive concepts). Suppose you come across a number of sea animals that you suspect belong to the same species. You observe their length in metres, whether they have gills, whether they have a prominent beak, and whether they have few or many teeth. Using these features, the first animal can described by the following conjunction:

$$\mathsf{Length} = 3 \land \mathsf{Gills} = \mathsf{no} \land \mathsf{Beak} = \mathsf{yes} \land \mathsf{Teeth} = \mathsf{many}$$

The next one has the same characteristics but is a metre longer, so you drop the length condition and generalise the conjunction to

$$\mathsf{Gills} = \mathsf{no} \land \mathsf{Beak} = \mathsf{yes} \land \mathsf{Teeth} = \mathsf{many}$$

The third animal is again 3 metres long, has a beak, no gills and few teeth, so your description becomes

$$\mathsf{Gills} = \mathsf{no} \land \mathsf{Beak} = \mathsf{yes}$$

All remaining animals satisfy this conjunction, and you finally decide they are some kind of dolphin.

Despite the simplicity of this example, the space of possible concepts – usually called the *hypothesis space* – is already fairly large. Let's assume we have three different lengths: 3, 4 and 5 metres, while the other three features have two values each. We then have $3 \cdot 2 \cdot 2 \cdot 2 = 24$ possible instances. How many conjunctive concepts are there using these same features? We can answer this question if we treat the absence of a feature as an additional 'value'. This gives a total of $4 \cdot 3 \cdot 3 \cdot 3 = 108$ different concepts. While this seems quite a lot, you should realise that the number of possible extensions – sets of instances – is much larger: 2^{24}, which is more than 16 million! That is, if you pick a random set of instances, the odds that you can't find a conjunctive concept that exactly describes those instances are well over 100 000 to 1. This is actually a good thing, as it forces the learner to generalise beyond the training data and cover instances that it hasn't seen before. Figure 4.1 depicts this hypothesis space, making use of the general-

[1] Inspired by www.cwtstrandings.org.

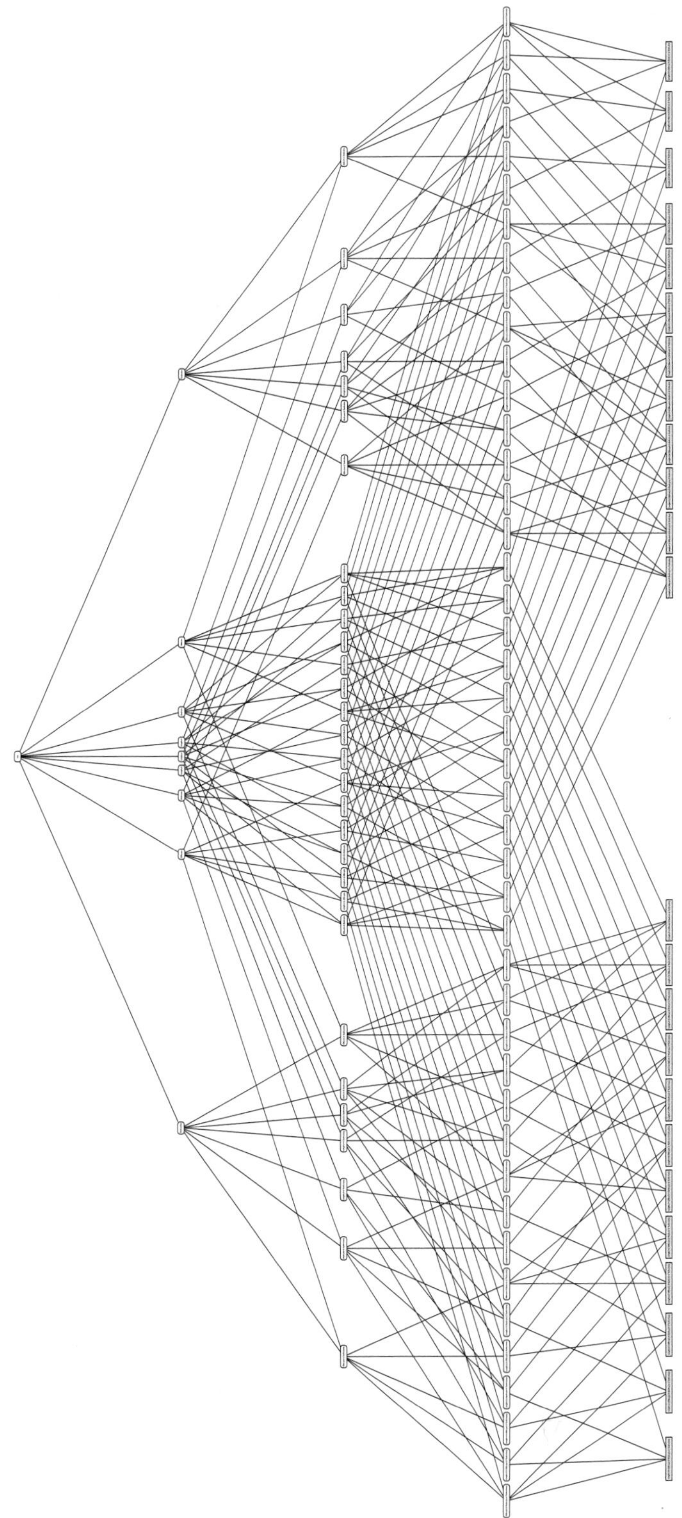

Figure 4.1. The hypothesis space corresponding to Example 4.1. The bottom row corresponds to the 24 possible instances, which are complete conjunctions with four literals each. The next row up are all 44 concepts with three literals each; then 30 concepts with two literals each; 9 concepts consisting of a single literal; and the top concept is the empty conjunction which is always true and hence covers all possible instances. A connecting line is drawn between concepts on consecutive layers if the higher one is more general than the lower one (i.e., the higher concept's extension is a superset of the lower's).

ity ordering (i.e., the subset relationship between concept extensions; see Background 4.1).

Least general generalisation

If we rule out all concepts that don't cover at least one of the instances in Example 4.1, the hypothesis space is reduced to 32 conjunctive concepts (Figure 4.2). Insisting that any hypothesis cover all three instances reduces this further to only four concepts, the least general one of which is the one found in the example – it is called their *least general generalisation* (*LGG*). Algorithm 4.1 formalises the procedure, which is simply to repeatedly apply a pairwise LGG operation (Algorithm 4.2) to an instance and the current hypothesis, as they both have the same logical form. The structure of the hypothesis space ensures that the result is independent of the order in which the instances are processed.

Intuitively, the LGG of two instances is the nearest concept in the hypothesis space where paths upward from both instances intersect. The fact that this point is unique is a special property of many logical hypothesis spaces, and can be put to good use in learning. More precisely, such a hypothesis space forms a *lattice*: a partial order in which each two elements have a *least upper bound* (*lub*) and a *greatest lower bound* (*glb*). So, the LGG of a set of instances is exactly the least upper bound of the instances in that lattice. Furthermore, it is the greatest lower bound of the set of all generalisations of the instances: all possible generalisations are at least as general as the LGG. In this very precise sense, *the LGG is the most conservative generalisation that we can learn from the data.*

If we want to be a bit more adventurous, we could choose one of the more general hypotheses, such as Gills = no or Beak = yes. However, we probably don't want to choose the most general hypothesis, which is simply that every animal is a dolphin,

Algorithm 4.1: LGG-Set(D) – find least general generalisation of a set of instances.

Input : data D.
Output : logical expression H.

```
x ←first instance from D;
H ←x;
while instances left do
    x ←next instance from D;
    H ←LGG(H, x) ;          // e.g., LGG-Conj (Alg. 4.2) or LGG-Conj-ID (Alg. 4.3)
end
return H
```

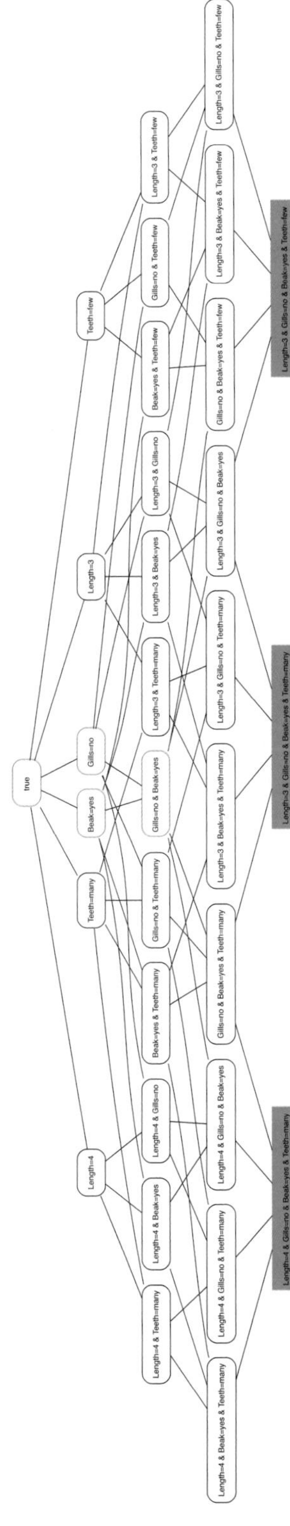

Figure 4.2. Part of the hypothesis space in Figure 4.1 containing only concepts that are more general than at least one of the three given instances on the bottom row. Only four conjunctions, indicated in green at the top, are more general than all three instances; the least general of these is Gills = no ∧ Beak = yes. It can be observed that the two left-most and right-most instances would be sufficient to learn that concept.

as this would clearly be an over-generalisation. Negative examples are very useful to prevent over-generalistion.

Example 4.2 (Negative examples). In Example 4.1 we observed the following dolphins:

p1: Length = 3 ∧ Gills = no ∧ Beak = yes ∧ Teeth = many
p2: Length = 4 ∧ Gills = no ∧ Beak = yes ∧ Teeth = many
p3: Length = 3 ∧ Gills = no ∧ Beak = yes ∧ Teeth = few

Suppose you next observe an animal that clearly doesn't belong to the species – a negative example. It is described by the following conjunction:

n1: Length = 5 ∧ Gills = yes ∧ Beak = yes ∧ Teeth = many

This negative example rules out some of the generalisations that were hitherto still possible: in particular, it rules out the concept Beak = yes, as well as the empty concept which postulates that everything is a dolphin.

The process is illustrated in Figure 4.3. We now have two hypotheses left, one which is least general and the other most general.

Internal disjunction

You might be tempted to conclude from this and the previous example that we always have a unique most general hypothesis, but that is not the case in general. To demonstrate that, we are going to make our logical language slightly richer, by allowing a restricted form of disjunction called *internal disjunction*. The idea is very simple: if you observe one dolphin that is 3 metres long and another one of 4 metres, you may want to add the condition 'length is 3 or 4 metres' to your concept. We will write this as Length = [3, 4], which logically means Length = 3 ∨ Length = 4. This of course only makes sense for features that have more than two values: for instance, the internal disjunction Teeth = [many, few] is always true and can be dropped.

Algorithm 4.2: LGG-Conj(x, y) – find least general conjunctive generalisation of two conjunctions.

Input : conjunctions x, y.
Output : conjunction z.

```
z ←conjunction of all literals common to x and y;
return z
```

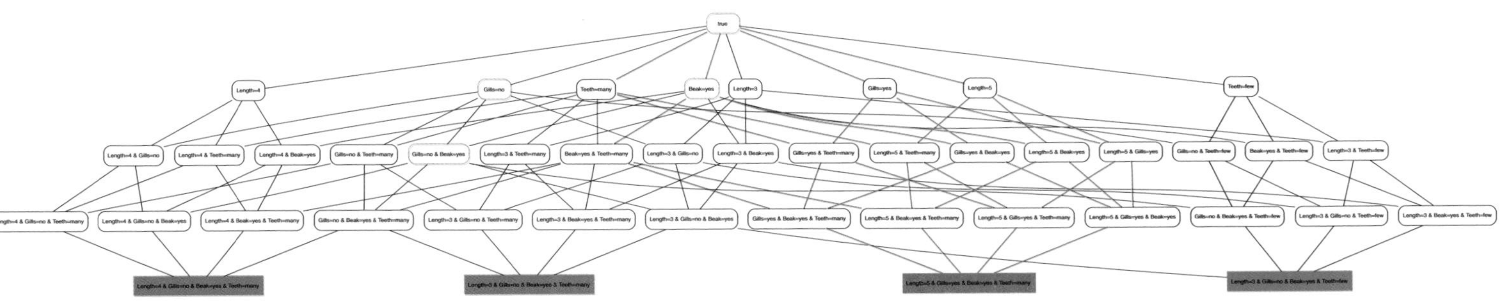

Figure 4.3. A negative example can rule out some of the generalisations of the LGG of the positive examples. Every concept which is connected by a red path to a negative example covers that negative and is therefore ruled out as a hypothesis. Only two conjunctions cover all positives and no negatives: Gills = no ∧ Beak = yes and Gills = no.

Example 4.3 (Internal disjunction). Using the same three positive examples as in Example 4.1, the second and third hypothesis are now

$$\text{Length} = [3,4] \land \text{Gills} = \text{no} \land \text{Beak} = \text{yes} \land \text{Teeth} = \text{many}$$

and

$$\text{Length} = [3,4] \land \text{Gills} = \text{no} \land \text{Beak} = \text{yes}$$

We can drop any of the three conditions in the latter LGG without covering the negative example from Example 4.2. Generalising further to single conditions, we see that Length = [3,4] and Gills = no are still OK but Beak = yes is not, as it covers the negative example.

Algorithm 4.3 details how we can calculate the LGG of two conjunctions employing internal disjunction. The function Combine-ID(v_x, v_y) returns $[v_x, v_y]$ if v_x and v_y are constants, and their union if v_x or v_y are already sets of values: e.g., Combine-ID([3,4],[4,5])= [3,4,5].

4.2 Paths through the hypothesis space

As we can clearly see in Figure 4.4, in this example we have not one but two most general hypotheses. What we can also notice is that *every concept between the least general one and one of the most general ones is also a possible hypothesis*, i.e., covers all the positives and none of the negatives. Mathematically speaking we say that the set of

Algorithm 4.3: LGG-Conj-ID(x, y) – find least general conjunctive generalisation of two conjunctions, employing internal disjunction.

```
Input  : conjunctions x, y.
Output : conjunction z.
z ←true;
for each feature f do
    if f = v_x is a conjunct in x and f = v_y is a conjunct in y then
        add f = Combine-ID(v_x, v_y) to z ;          // Combine-ID: see text
    end
end
return z
```

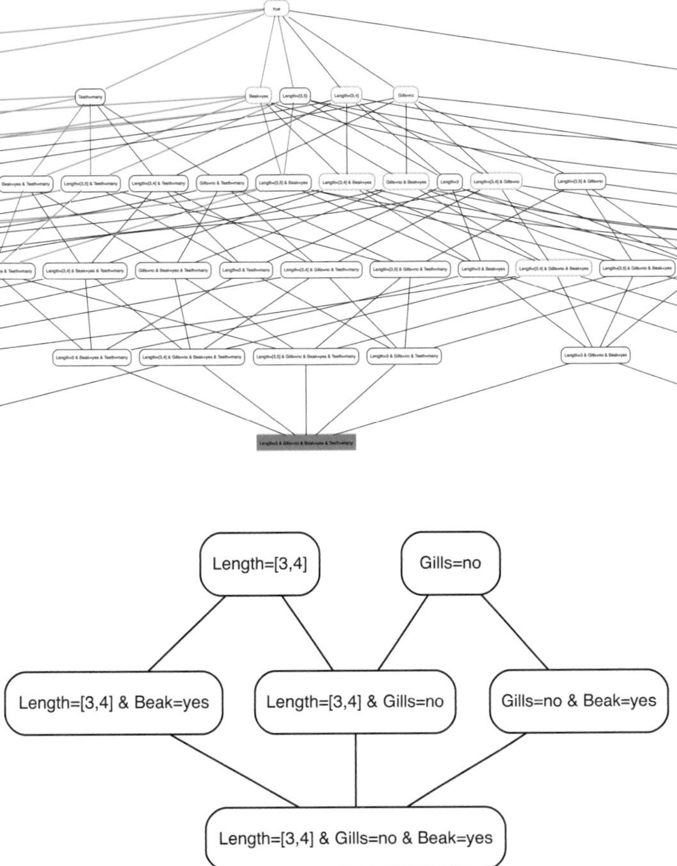

Figure 4.4. (top) A snapshot of the expanded hypothesis space that arises when internal disjunction is used for the 'Length' feature. We now need one more generalisation step to travel upwards from a completely specified example to the empty conjunction. **(bottom)** The version space consists of one least general hypothesis, two most general hypotheses, and three in between.

hypotheses that agree with the data is a *convex set*, which basically means that we can interpolate between any two members of the set, and if we find a concept that is less general than one and more general than the other then that concept is also a member of the set. This in turn means that we can describe the set of all possible hypotheses by its least and most general members. This is summed up in the following definition.

Definition 4.1 (Version space). *A concept is* complete *if it covers all positive examples. A concept is* consistent *if it covers none of the negative examples. The* version space *is the set of all complete and consistent concepts. This set is convex and is fully defined by its least and most general elements.*

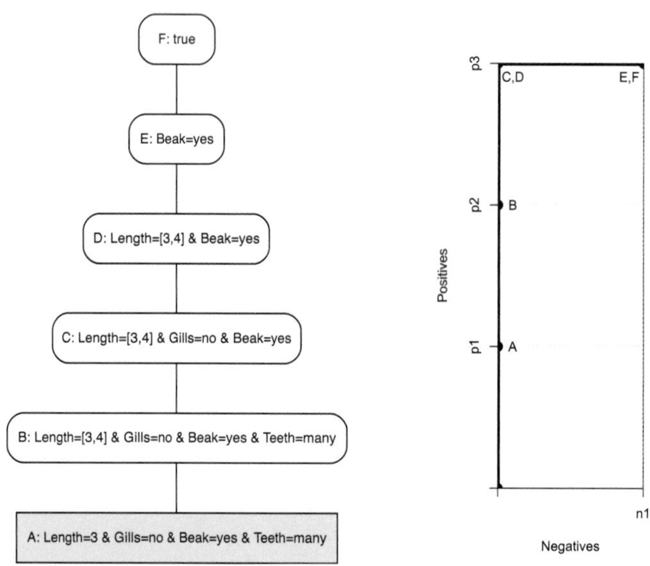

Figure 4.5. (left) A path in the hypothesis space of Figure 4.3 from one of the positive examples (p1, see Example 4.2 on p.110) all the way up to the empty concept. Concept A covers a single example; B covers one additional example; C and D are in the version space, and so cover all three positives; E and F also cover the negative. **(right)** The corresponding coverage curve, with ranking p1 – p2 – p3 – n1.

We can draw a useful connection between logical hypothesis spaces and the coverage plots introduced in Chapter 2. Suppose you were to follow a path in the hypothesis space from a positive example, through a selection of its generalisations, all the way up to the empty concept. The latter, by construction, covers all positives and all negatives, and hence occupies the top-right point (Neg, Pos) in the coverage plot. The starting point, being a single positive example, occupies the point $(0, 1)$ in the coverage plot. In fact, it is customary to extend the hypothesis space with a bottom element which doesn't cover any examples and hence is less general than any other concept. Taking that point as the starting point of the path means that we start in the bottom-left point $(0, 0)$ in the coverage plot.

Moving upwards in the hypothesis space by generalisation means that the numbers of covered positives and negatives can stay the same or increase, but never decrease. In other words, *an upward path through the hypothesis space corresponds to a coverage curve* and hence to a ranking. Figure 4.5 illustrates this for the running example. The chosen path is but one among many possible paths; however, notice that if a path, like this one, includes elements of the version space, the corresponding coverage curve passes through 'ROC heaven' $(0, Pos)$ and AUC = 1. In other words, such paths are optimal. Concept learning can be seen as the search for an optimal path through the hypothesis space.

What happens, you may ask, if the LGG of the positive examples covers one or more negatives? In that case, any generalisation of the LGG will be inconsistent as well. Conversely, any consistent hypothesis will be incomplete. It follows that the version space is empty in this case; we will say that the data is not *conjunctively separable*. The following example illustrates this.

Example 4.4 (Data that is not conjunctively separable). Suppose we have the following five positive examples (the first three are the same as in Example 4.1):

p1: Length = 3 ∧ Gills = no ∧ Beak = yes ∧ Teeth = many
p2: Length = 4 ∧ Gills = no ∧ Beak = yes ∧ Teeth = many
p3: Length = 3 ∧ Gills = no ∧ Beak = yes ∧ Teeth = few
p4: Length = 5 ∧ Gills = no ∧ Beak = yes ∧ Teeth = many
p5: Length = 5 ∧ Gills = no ∧ Beak = yes ∧ Teeth = few

and the following negatives (the first one is the same as in Example 4.2):

n1: Length = 5 ∧ Gills = yes ∧ Beak = yes ∧ Teeth = many
n2: Length = 4 ∧ Gills = yes ∧ Beak = yes ∧ Teeth = many
n3: Length = 5 ∧ Gills = yes ∧ Beak = no ∧ Teeth = many
n4: Length = 4 ∧ Gills = yes ∧ Beak = no ∧ Teeth = many
n5: Length = 4 ∧ Gills = no ∧ Beak = yes ∧ Teeth = few

The least general complete hypothesis is Gills = no ∧ Beak = yes as before, but this covers n5 and hence is inconsistent. There are seven most general consistent hypotheses, none of which are complete:

Length = 3	(covers p1 and p3)
Length = [3,5] ∧ Gills = no	(covers all positives except p2)
Length = [3,5] ∧ Teeth = few	(covers p3 and p5)
Gills = no ∧ Teeth = many	(covers p1, p2 and p4)
Gills = no ∧ Beak = no	
Gills = yes ∧ Teeth = few	
Beak = no ∧ Teeth = few	

The last three of these do not cover any positive examples.

Most general consistent hypotheses

As this example suggests, finding most general consistent hypotheses is considerably more involved than finding least general complete ones. Essentially, the process is one of enumeration. Algorithm 4.4 gives an algorithm which returns all most general consistent specialisations of a given concept, where a minimal specialisation of a concept is one that can be reached in one downward step in the hypothesis lattice (e.g., by adding a conjunct, or removing a value from an internal disjunction). Calling the algorithm with $C =$ true returns the most general consistent hypotheses.

Figure 4.6 shows a path through the hypothesis space of Example 4.4, and the corresponding coverage curve. We see that the path goes through three consistent hypotheses, which are consequently plotted on the y-axis of the coverage plot. The other three hypotheses are complete, and therefore end up on the top of the graph; one of these is, in fact, the LGG of the positives (D). The ranking corresponding to this coverage curve is p3 – p5 – [p1,p4] – [p2,n5] – [n1–4]. This ranking commits half a ranking error out of 25, and so AUC = 0.98. We can choose one concept from the ranking by applying the techniques discussed in Section 2.2. For instance, suppose that classification accuracy is the criterion we want to optimise. In coverage space, accuracy isometrics have slope 1, and so we see immediately that concepts C and D (or E) both achieve the best accuracy in Figure 4.6. If performance on the positives is more important we prefer the complete but inconsistent concept D; if performance on the negatives is valued more we choose the incomplete but consistent concept C.

Closed concepts

It is worthwhile to reflect on the fact that concepts D and E occupy the same point in coverage space. What this means is that generalising D into E by dropping Beak = yes does not change the coverage in terms of positive and negative examples. One could

Algorithm 4.4: MGConsistent(C, N) – find most general consistent specialisations of a concept.

Input : concept C; negative examples N.
Output : set of concepts S.

if C doesn't cover any element from N **then return** $\{C\}$;
$S \leftarrow \emptyset$;
for each minimal specialisation C' of C **do**
  $S \leftarrow S \cup$ MGConsistent(C', N);
end
return S

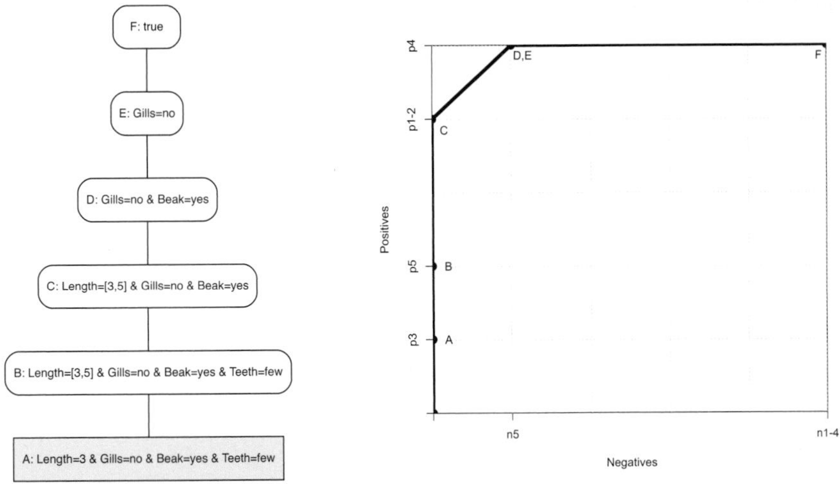

Figure 4.6. (left) A path in the hypothesis space of Example 4.4. Concept A covers a single positive (p3); B covers one additional positive (p5); C covers all positives except p4; D is the LGG of all five positive examples, but also covers a negative (n5), as does E. **(right)** The corresponding coverage curve.

say that the data suggests that, in the context of concept E, the condition Beak = yes is implicitly understood. A concept that includes all implicitly understood conditions is called a *closed concept*. Essentially, a closed concept is the LGG of all examples that it covers. For instance, D and E both cover all positives and n5; the LGG of those six examples is Gills = no ∧ Beak = yes, which is D. Mathematically speaking we say that the closure of E is D, which is also its own closure – hence the term 'closed concept'. This doesn't mean that D and E are logically equivalent: on the contrary, since $\mathscr{X}_{\mathrm{D}} \subset \mathscr{X}_{\mathrm{E}}$ – the extension of D is a proper subset of the extension of E – there exist instances in $\mathscr{X}$ that are covered by E but not by D. However, none of these 'witnesses' are present in the data, and thus, as far as the data is concerned, D and E are indistinguishable. As can be seen in Figure 4.7, limiting attention to closed concepts can considerably reduce the hypothesis space.

In this section we have looked at the problem of learning a single logical expression that covers most or all positive examples and few or no negative examples. We have seen that such concepts live in a hypothesis space ordered by generality, and learning a concept can be understood as finding a good path through that hypothesis space. Such a path has a natural interpretation as a ranker, which allows a connection with coverage curves and ROC curves. On the other hand, insisting on a single conjunction of feature-value literals is a strong limitation; in the next section we look at ways to relax it.

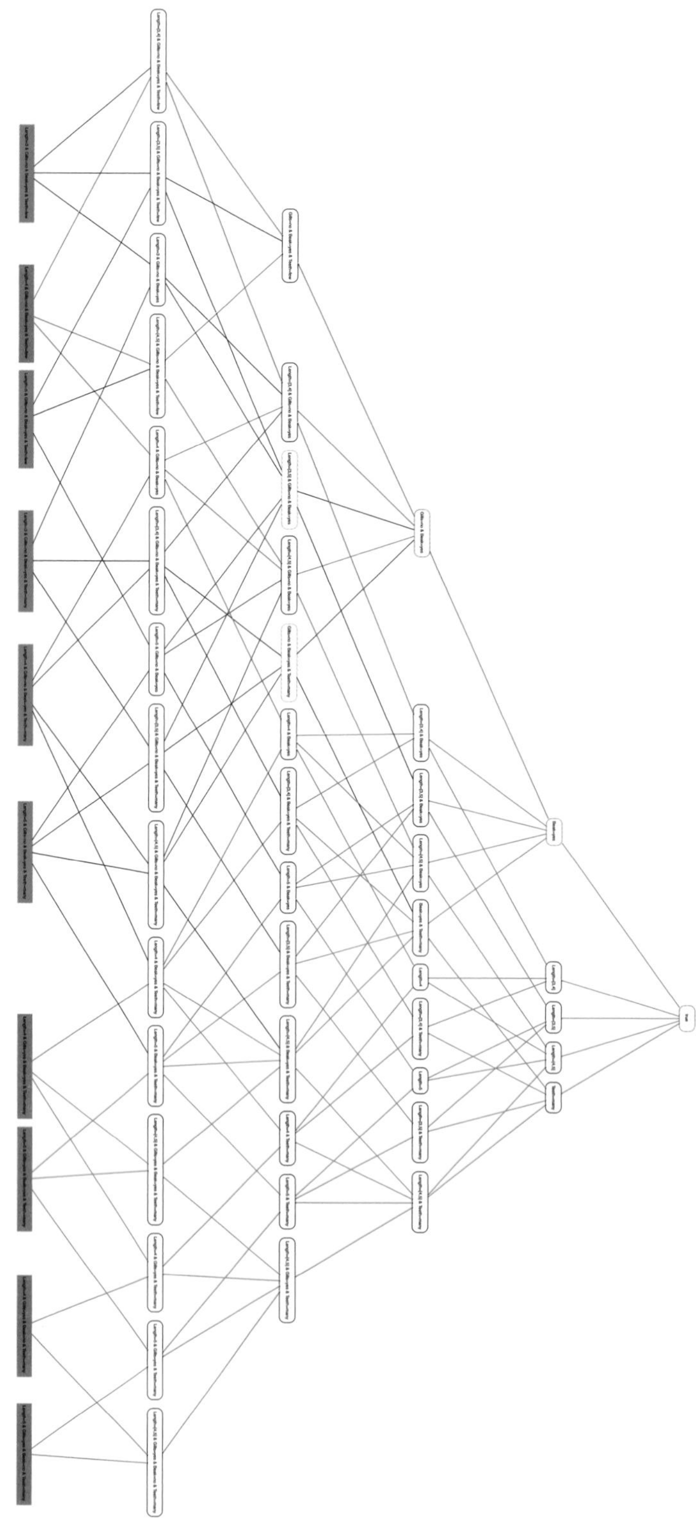

Figure 4.7. The hypothesis space is reduced considerably if we restrict attention to closed concepts. There are three, rather than four, complete concepts (in green), and two, rather than seven, most general consistent closed concepts (in orange). Notice that the latter are both specialisations of the LGG of the positives, and hence it is possible to select a path that includes both the LGG and a most general consistent hypothesis.

4.3 Beyond conjunctive concepts

Recall from Background 4.1 that a conjunctive normal form expression (CNF) is a conjunction of disjunctions of literals, or equivalently, a conjunction of clauses. The conjunctions of literals we have looked at until now are trivially in CNF where each disjunction consists of a single literal. CNF expressions are much more expressive, particularly since literals can occur in several clauses. We will look at an algorithm for learning Horn theories, where each clause $A \rightarrow B$ is a Horn clause, i.e., A is a conjunction of literals and B is a single literal. For ease of notation we will restrict attention to Boolean features, and write F for F = true and ¬F for F = false. In the example below we adapt the dolphins example to Boolean variables ManyTeeth (standing for Teeth = many), Gills, Short (standing for Length = 3) and Beak.

When we looked at learning conjunctive concepts, the main intuition was that uncovered positive examples led us to generalise by dropping literals from the conjunction, while covered negative examples require specialisation by adding literals. This intuition still holds if we are learning Horn theories, but now we need to think 'clauses' rather than 'literals'. Thus, if a Horn theory doesn't cover a positive we need to drop all clauses that violate the positive, where a clause $A \rightarrow B$ violates a positive if all literals in the conjunction A are true in the example, and B is false.

Things get more interesting if we consider covered negatives, since then we need to find one or more clauses to add to the theory in order to exclude the negative. For example, suppose that our current hypothesis covers the negative

$$\mathsf{ManyTeeth} \land \mathsf{Gills} \land \mathsf{Short} \land \neg\mathsf{Beak}$$

To exclude it, we can add the following Horn clause to our theory:

$$\mathsf{ManyTeeth} \land \mathsf{Gills} \land \mathsf{Short} \rightarrow \mathsf{Beak}$$

While there are other clauses that can exclude the negative (e.g., ManyTeeth → Beak) this is the most specific one, and hence least at risk of also excluding covered positives. However, the most specific clause excluding a negative is only unique if the negative has exactly one literal set to false. For example, if our covered negative is

$$\mathsf{ManyTeeth} \land \mathsf{Gills} \land \neg\mathsf{Short} \land \neg\mathsf{Beak}$$

then we have a choice between the following two Horn clauses:

$$\mathsf{ManyTeeth} \land \mathsf{Gills} \rightarrow \mathsf{Short}$$
$$\mathsf{ManyTeeth} \land \mathsf{Gills} \rightarrow \mathsf{Beak}$$

Notice that, the fewer literals are set to true in the negative example, the more general the clauses excluding the negative are.

The approach of Algorithm 4.5 is to add *all* of these clauses to the hypothesis. However, the algorithm applies two clever tricks. The first is that it maintains a list S of negative examples, from which it periodically rebuilds the hypothesis. The second is that, rather than simply adding new negative examples to the list, it tries to find negatives with fewer literals set to true, since this will result in more general clauses. This is possible if we assume we have access to a *membership oracle* Mb which can tell us whether a particular example is a member of the concept we're learning or not. So in line 7 of the algorithm we form the *intersection* of a new negative x and an existing one $s \in S$ – i.e., an example with only those literals set to true which are true in both x and s – and pass the result z to the membership oracle to check whether it belongs to the target concept. The algorithm also assumes access to an *equivalence oracle* Eq which either tells us that our current hypothesis h is logically equivalent to the target formula f, or else produces a *counter-example* that can be either a false positive (it is covered by h but not by f) or a false negative (it is covered by f but not by h).

Algorithm 4.5: Horn(Mb, Eq) – learn a conjunction of Horn clauses from membership and equivalence oracles.

```
   Input  : equivalence oracle Eq; membership oracle Mb.
   Output : Horn theory h equivalent to target formula f.
1  h ←true;                           // conjunction of Horn clauses, initially empty
2  S ←∅ ;                             // a list of negative examples, initially empty
3  while Eq(h) returns counter-example x do
4      if x violates at least one clause of h then              // x is a false negative
5          specialise h by removing every clause that x violates
6      else                                                     // x is a false positive
7          find the first negative example s ∈ S such that (i) z = s ∩ x has fewer true
           literals than s, and (ii) Mb(z) labels it as a negative;
8          if such an example exists then replace s in S with z, else append x to the
           end of S;
9          h ←true;
10         for all s ∈ S do                                     // rebuild h from S
11             p ←the conjunction of literals true in s;
12             Q ←the set of literals false in s;
13             for all q ∈ Q do h ←h ∧ (p → q);
14         end
15     end
16 end
17 return h
```

Example 4.5 (Learning a Horn theory). Suppose the target theory f is

$$(\text{ManyTeeth} \land \text{Short} \rightarrow \text{Beak}) \land (\text{ManyTeeth} \land \text{Gills} \rightarrow \text{Short})$$

This theory has 12 positive examples: eight in which ManyTeeth is false; another two in which ManyTeeth is true but both Gills and Short are false; and two more in which ManyTeeth, Short and Beak are true. The negative examples, then, are

n1: ManyTeeth ∧ Gills ∧ Short ∧ ¬Beak
n2: ManyTeeth ∧ Gills ∧ ¬Short ∧ Beak
n3: ManyTeeth ∧ Gills ∧ ¬Short ∧ ¬Beak
n4: ManyTeeth ∧ ¬Gills ∧ Short ∧ ¬Beak

S is initialised to the empty list and h to the empty conjunction. We call the equivalence oracle which returns a counter-example which has to be a false positive (since every example satisfies our initial hypothesis), say n1 which violates the first clause in f. There are no negative examples in S yet, so we add n1 to S (step 8 of Algorithm 4.5). We then generate a new hypothesis from S (steps 9–13): p is ManyTeeth ∧ Gills ∧ Short and Q is {Beak}, so h becomes (ManyTeeth ∧ Gills ∧ Short → Beak). Notice that this clause is implied by our target theory: if ManyTeeth and Gills are true then so is Short by the second clause of f; but then so is Beak by f's first clause. But we need more clauses to exclude all the negatives.

Now, suppose the next counter-example is the false positive n2. We form the intersection with n1 which was already in S to see if we can get a negative example with fewer literals set to true (step 7). The result is equal to n3 so the membership oracle will confirm this as a negative, and we replace n1 in S with n3. We then rebuild h from S which gives (p is ManyTeeth ∧ Gills and Q is {Short, Beak})

$$(\text{ManyTeeth} \land \text{Gills} \rightarrow \text{Short}) \land (\text{ManyTeeth} \land \text{Gills} \rightarrow \text{Beak})$$

Finally, assume that n4 is the next false positive returned by the equivalence oracle. The intersection with n3 on S is actually a positive example, so instead of intersecting with n3 we append n4 to S and rebuild h. This gives the previous two clauses from n3 plus the following two from n4:

$$(\text{ManyTeeth} \land \text{Short} \rightarrow \text{Gills}) \land (\text{ManyTeeth} \land \text{Short} \rightarrow \text{Beak})$$

The first of this second pair will subsequently be removed by a false negative from the equivalence oracle, leading to the final theory

$$(\mathsf{ManyTeeth} \land \mathsf{Gills} \rightarrow \mathsf{Short}) \land$$
$$(\mathsf{ManyTeeth} \land \mathsf{Gills} \rightarrow \mathsf{Beak}) \land$$
$$(\mathsf{ManyTeeth} \land \mathsf{Short} \rightarrow \mathsf{Beak})$$

which is logically equivalent (though not identical) to f.

The Horn algorithm combines a number of interesting new ideas. First, it is an *active learning* algorithm: rather than learning from a provided data set, it constructs its own training examples and asks the membership oracle to label them. Secondly, the core of the algorithm is the list of cleverly chosen negative examples, from which the hypothesis is periodically rebuilt. The intersection step is crucial here: if the algorithm just remembered negatives, the hypothesis would consist of many specific clauses. It can be shown that, in order to learn a theory consisting of m clauses and n Boolean variables, the algorithm requires $O(mn)$ equivalence queries and $O(m^2n)$ membership queries. In addition, the runtime of the algorithm is quadratic in both m and n. While this is probably prohibitive in practice, the Horn algorithm can be shown to always successfully learn a Horn theory that is equivalent to the target theory. Furthermore, if we don't have access to an equivalence oracle the algorithm is still guaranteed to 'almost always' learn a Horn theory that is 'mostly correct'. This will be made more precise in Section 4.4.

Using first-order logic

Another way to move beyond conjunctive concepts defined by simple features is to use a richer logical language. The languages we have been using so far are *propositional*: each literal is a proposition such as Gills = yes – standing for 'the dolphin has gills' – from which larger expressions are built using logical connectives. *First-order predicate logic*, or first-order logic for short, generalises this by building more complex literals from *predicates* and *terms*. For example, a first-order literal could be BodyPart(Dolphin42, PairOf(Gill)). Here, Dolphin42 and PairOf(Gill) are terms referring to objects: Dolphin42 is a constant, and PairOf(Gill) is a compound term consisting of the function symbol PairOf and the term Gills. BodyPart is a binary predicate forming a proposition (something that can be true or false) out of two terms. This richer language brings with it a number of advantages:

- ☞ we can use terms such as Dolphin42 to refer to individual objects we're interested in;

☞ the structure of objects can be explicitly described; and

☞ we can introduce variables to refer to unspecified objects and quantify over them.

To illustrate the latter point, the first-order literal BodyPart(x, PairOf(Gill)) can be used to refer to the set of all objects having a pair of gills; and the following expression applies universal quantification to state that everything with a pair of gills is a fish:

$$\forall x : \mathsf{BodyPart}(x, \mathsf{PairOf}(\mathsf{Gill})) \rightarrow \mathsf{Fish}(x)$$

Since we modified the structure of literals, we need to revisit notions such as generalisation and LGG. Remember that for propositional literals with internal disjunction we used the function Combine-ID for merging two internal disjunctions: thus, for example, LGG-Conj-ID(Length = [3,4], Length = [4,5]) returns Length = [3,4,5]. In order to generalise first-order literals we use variables. Consider, for example, the two first-order literals BodyPart(Dolphin42, PairOf(Gill)) and BodyPart(Human123, PairOf(Leg)): these generalise to BodyPart(x, PairOf(y)),signifying the set of objects that have a pair of some unspecified body part. There is a well-defined algorithm for computing LGGs of first-order literals called *anti-unification*, as it is the mathematical dual of the deductive operation of *unification*.

Example 4.6 (Unification and anti-unification). Consider the following terms:

BodyPart(x, PairOf(Gill))	describing the objects that have a pair of gills;
BodyPart(Dolphin42, PairOf(y))	describing the body parts that Dolphin42 has a pair of.

The following two terms are their unification and anti-unification, respectively:

BodyPart(Dolphin42, PairOf(Gill))	describing Dolphin42 as having a pair of gills;
BodyPart(x, PairOf(y))	describing the objects that have a pair of unspecified body parts.

So we see that in first-order logic literals already have quite a rich structure, owing to the use of variables. We will revisit this in Section 6.4 when we discuss how to learn classification rules in first-order logic.

4.4 Learnability

In this chapter we have seen several hypothesis languages for concept learning, including conjunctions of literals (possibly with internal disjunction), conjunctions of Horn clauses, and clauses in first-order logic. It is intuitively clear that these languages differ in expressivity: for example, a conjunction of literals is also a conjunction of Horn clauses with empty if-part, so Horn theories are strictly more expressive than conjunctive concepts. The downside of a more expressive concept language is that it may be harder to learn. The field of computational learning theory studies exactly this question of *learnability*.

To kick things off we need a *learning model*: a clear statement of what we mean if we say that a concept language is learnable. One of the most common learning models is the model of *probably approximately correct* (*PAC*) learning. PAC-learnability means that there exists a learning algorithm that gets it mostly right, most of the time. The model makes an allowance for mistakes on non-typical examples: hence the 'mostly right' or 'approximately correct'. The model also makes an allowance for sometimes getting it completely wrong, for example when the training data contains lots of non-typical examples: hence the 'most of the time' or 'probably'. We assume that typicality of examples is determined by some unspecified probability distribution D, and we evaluate the error rate err_D of a hypothesis with respect to this distribution D. More formally, for arbitrary allowable error rate $\epsilon < 1/2$ and failure rate $\delta < 1/2$ we require a PAC-learning algorithm to output with probability at least $1-\delta$ a hypothesis h such that $err_D < \epsilon$.

Let's assume for the moment that our data is noise-free, and that the target hypothesis is chosen from our hypothesis language. Furthermore, we assume our learner always outputs a hypothesis that is complete and consistent with the training sample. There is a possibility that this zero training error is misleading, and that the hypothesis is actually a 'bad' one, having a true error over the instance space that is larger than ϵ. We just want to make sure that this happens with probability less than δ. I will now show that this can be guaranteed by choosing the training sample large enough. Suppose our hypothesis space H contains a single bad hypothesis, then the probability it is complete and consistent on m independently sampled training examples is at most $(1-\epsilon)^m$. Since $1-\epsilon \le e^{-\epsilon}$ for any $0 \le \epsilon \le 1$, we have that this probability is at most $e^{-m\epsilon}$. We want this to be at most δ, which can be achieved by setting $m \ge \frac{1}{\epsilon}\ln\frac{1}{\delta}$. Now, H may contain several bad hypotheses, say $k \le |H|$; then the probability that at least one of them is complete and consistent on m independently sampled training examples is at most $k(1-\epsilon)^m \le |H|(1-\epsilon)^m \le |H|e^{-m\epsilon}$, which is at most δ if

$$m \ge \frac{1}{\epsilon}\left(\ln|H| + \ln\frac{1}{\delta}\right) \tag{4.1}$$

This is called the *sample complexity* of a complete and consistent learner. The good news is that it is linear in $1/\epsilon$ and logarithmic in $1/\delta$. Notice that this suggests that it is exponentially cheaper to reduce the failure rate than it is to reduce the error. Any learning algorithm that takes time polynomial in $1/\epsilon$ and $1/\delta$ to process a single training example will therefore also take polynomial training time, another requirement for PAC-learnability. However, finding a complete and consistent hypothesis is not tractable in many hypothesis languages.

Notice that the term $\ln|H|$ arose because in the worst case almost all hypotheses in H are bad. However, in practice this means that the bound in Equation 4.1 is overly pessimistic. Still, it allows us to see that concept languages whose size is exponential in some parameter n are PAC-learnable. For example, the number of conjunctions over n Boolean variables is 3^n, since each variable can occur unnegated, negated or not at all. Consequently, the sample complexity is $(1/\epsilon)(n\ln 3 + \ln(1/\delta))$. For example, if we set $\delta = 0.05$ and $\epsilon = 0.1$ then the sample complexity is approximately $10(n \cdot 1.1 + 3) = 11n + 30$. For our dolphin example with $n = 4$ this is clearly pessimistic, since there are only $2^4 = 16$ distinct examples! For larger n this is more realistic. Notice also that the PAC model is distribution-free: the learner is not given any information about the instance distribution D. This is another source for pessimism in the bound on the sample complexity.

We may not always be able to output a complete and consistent hypothesis: for instance, this may be computationally intractable, the target hypothesis may not be representable in our hypothesis language, or the examples may be noisy. A reasonable strategy would be to choose the hypothesis with lowest training error. A 'bad' hypothesis is then one whose true error exceeds the training error by at least ϵ. Using some results from probability theory, we find that this probability is at most $e^{-2m\epsilon^2}$. As a result, the $1/\epsilon$ factor in Equation 4.1 is replaced by $1/2\epsilon^2$: for $\epsilon = 0.1$ we thus need 5 times as many training examples compared to the previous case.

It has already been mentioned that the $|H|$ term is a weak point in the above analysis. What we need is a measure that doesn't just count the size of the hypothesis space, but rather gives its expressivity or capacity in terms of classification. Such a measure does in fact exist and is called the *VC-dimension* after its inventors Vladimir Vapnik and Alexey Chervonenkis. We will illustrate the main idea by means of an example.

Example 4.7 (Shattering a set of instances). Consider the following instances:

$m =$ ManyTeeth ∧ ¬Gills ∧ ¬Short ∧ ¬Beak

$g =$ ¬ManyTeeth ∧ Gills ∧ ¬Short ∧ ¬Beak

$s =$ ¬ManyTeeth ∧ ¬Gills ∧ Short ∧ ¬Beak

$b =$ ¬ManyTeeth ∧ ¬Gills ∧ ¬Short ∧ Beak

There are 16 different subsets of the set $\{m, g, s, b\}$. Can each of them be represented by its own conjunctive concept? The answer is yes: for every instance we want to exclude, we add the corresponding negated literal to the conjunction. Thus, $\{m, s\}$ is represented by ¬Gills ∧ ¬Beak, $\{g, s, b\}$ is represented by ¬ManyTeeth, $\{s\}$ is represented by ¬ManyTeeth ∧ ¬Gills ∧ ¬Beak, and so on. We say that this set of four instances is *shattered* by the hypothesis language of conjunctive concepts.

The VC-dimension is the size of the largest set of instances that can be shattered by a particular hypothesis language or model class. The previous example shows that the VC-dimension of conjunctive concepts over d Boolean literals is at least d. It is in fact equal to d, although this is harder to prove (since it involves showing that no set of $d+1$ instances can be shattered). This measures the capacity of the model class for representing concepts or binary classifiers. As another example, the VC-dimension of a linear classifier in d dimensions is $d+1$: a threshold on the real line can shatter two points but not three (since the middle point cannot be separated from the other two by a single threshold); a straight line in a two-dimensional space can shatter three points but not four; and so on.

The VC-dimension can be used to bound the difference between sample error and true error of a hypothesis (which is the step where $|H|$ appeared in our previous arguments). Consequently, it can also be used to derive a bound on the sample complexity of a complete and consistent learner in terms of the VC-dimension D rather than $|H|$:

$$m \geq \frac{1}{\epsilon} \max\left(8D\log_2 \frac{13}{\epsilon}, 4\log_2 \frac{2}{\delta}\right) \tag{4.2}$$

We see that the bound is linear in D, where previously it was logarithmic in $|H|$. This is natural, since to shatter D points we need at least 2^D hypotheses, and so $\log_2 |H| \geq D$. Furthermore, it is still logarithmic in $1/\delta$, but linear times logarithmic in $1/\epsilon$. Plugging in our previous values of $\delta = 0.05$ and $\epsilon = 0.1$, we obtain a sample complexity of $\max(562 \cdot D, 213)$.

We conclude that the VC-dimension allows us to derive the sample complexity of infinite concept classes, as long as they have finite VC-dimension. It is furthermore worth mentioning a classical result from computational learning theory which says that a concept class is PAC-learnable if and only if its VC-dimension is finite.

4.5 Concept learning: Summary and further reading

In this chapter we looked at methods for inductive concept learning: the process of constructing a logical expression defining a set of objects from examples. This problem was a focus of early work in artificial intelligence (Winston, 1970; Vere, 1975; Banerji, 1980), following the seminal work by psychologists Bruner, Goodnow and Austin (1956) and Hunt, Marin and Stone (1966).

☞ In Section 4.1 we considered the structure of the hypothesis space: the set of possible concepts. Every hypothesis has an extension (the set of instances it covers), and thus relationships between extensions such as subset relationships carry over to the hypothesis space. This gives the hypothesis space a lattice structure: a partial order with least upper bounds and greatest lower bounds. In particular, the LGG is the least upper bound of a set of instances, and is the most conservative generalisation that we can learn from the data. The concept was defined in the context of first-order logic by Plotkin (1971), who showed that it was the mathematical dual of the deductive operation of unification. We can extend the hypothesis language with internal disjunction among values of a feature, which creates a larger hypothesis space that still has a lattice structure. Internal disjunction is a common staple of attribute-value languages for learning following the work of Michalski (1973). For further pointers regarding hypothesis language and hypothesis space the reader is referred to (Blockeel, 2010*a*,*b*).

☞ Section 4.2 defined complete and consistent hypotheses as concepts that cover all positive examples and no negative examples. The set of complete and consistent concepts is called the version space, a notion introduced by Mitchell (1977). The version space can be summarised by its least general and most general members, since any concept between one least general hypothesis and another most general one is also complete and consistent. Alternatively, we can describe the version space by all paths from a least general to a most general hypothesis. Such upward paths give rise to a coverage curve which describes the extension of each concept on the path in terms of covered positives and negatives. Concept learning can then be seen as finding an upward path that goes through ROC heaven. Syntactically different concepts can have the same extension in a particular data set: a closed concept is the most specific one of these (technically, the LGG of the instances in its extension). The notion is studied in formal concept analysis (Ganter and Wille, 1999) and was introduced in a data mining context by Pasquier, Bastide, Taouil and Lakhal (1999); Garriga, Kralj and Lavrač (2008) investigate its usefulness for labelled data.

☞ In Section 4.3 we discussed the Horn algorithm for learning concepts described by conjunctions of Horn rules, first published in Angluin *et al.* (1992). The algorithm makes use of a membership oracle, which can be seen as an early form of active learning (Cohn, 2010; Dasgupta, 2010). Horn theories are superficially similar to classification rule models which will be studied in Chapter 6. However, there is an important difference, since those classification rules have the target variable in the then-part of the rule, while the Horn clauses we are looking at here can have any literal in the then-part. In fact, in this chapter the target variable is not part of the logical language at all. This setting is sometimes called *learning from interpretations*, since examples are truth-value assignments to our theory. The classification rule setting is called *learning from entailment*, since in order to find out whether a particular rule covers an example we need to apply logical inference. De Raedt (1997) explains and explores the differences between these two settings. Further introductions to first-order logic and its use in learning are given by Flach (2010*a*) and De Raedt (2010).

☞ Section 4.4 briefly reviewed some basic concepts and results in learnability theory. My account partly followed Mitchell (1997, Chapter 7); another excellent introduction is given by Zeugmann (2010). PAC-learnability, which allows an error rate of ϵ and a failure rate of δ, was introduced in a seminal paper by Valiant (1984). Haussler (1988) derived the sample complexity for complete and consistent learners (Equation 4.1), which is linear in $1/\epsilon$ and logarithmic in $1/\delta$ and the size of the hypothesis space. The VC-dimension as a measure of the capacity of a hypothesis language was introduced by Vapnik and Chervonenkis (1971) in order to quantify the difference between training error and true error. This allows a statement of the sample complexity in terms of the VC-dimension (Equation 4.2) which is due to Blumer, Ehrenfeucht, Haussler and Warmuth (1989). This same paper proved that a model class is PAC-learnable if and only if its VC-dimension is finite.

CHAPTER 5

Tree models

TREE MODELS ARE among the most popular models in machine learning. For example, the pose recognition algorithm in the Kinect motion sensing device for the Xbox game console has decision tree classifiers at its heart (in fact, an ensemble of decision trees called a random forest about which you will learn more in Chapter 11). Trees are expressive and easy to understand, and of particular appeal to computer scientists due to their recursive 'divide-and-conquer' nature.

In fact, the paths through the logical hypothesis space discussed in the previous chapter already constitute a very simple kind of tree. For instance, the feature tree in Figure 5.1 (left) is equivalent to the path in Figure 4.6 (left) on p.117. This equivalence is best seen by tracing the path and the tree from the bottom upward.

1. The left-most leaf of the feature tree represents the concept at the bottom of the path, covering a single positive example.
2. The next concept up in the path generalises the literal Length = 3 into Length = [3, 5] by means of internal disjunction; the added coverage (one positive example) is represented by the second leaf from the left in the feature tree.
3. By dropping the condition Teeth = few we add another two covered positives.
4. Dropping the 'Length' condition altogether (or extending the internal disjunction with the one remaining value '4') adds the last positive, and also a negative.
5. Dropping Beak = yes covers no additional examples (remember the discussion

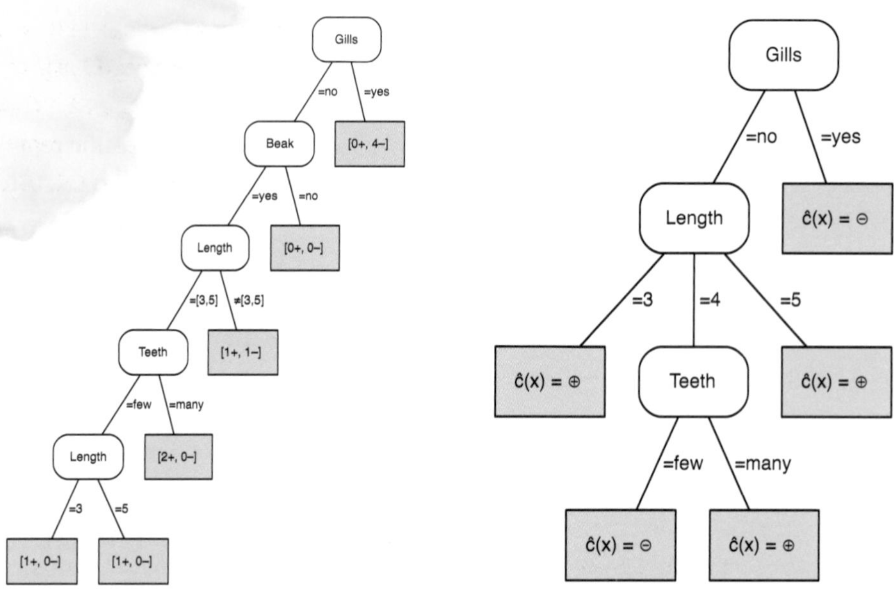

Figure 5.1. (left) The path from Figure 4.6 on p.117, redrawn in the form of a tree. The coverage numbers in the leaves are obtained from the data in Example 4.4. **(right)** A decision tree learned on the same data. This tree separates the positives and negatives perfectly.

about closed concepts in the previous chapter).

6. Finally, dropping Gills = no covers the four remaining negatives.

We see that a path through the hypothesis space can be turned into an equivalent feature tree. To obtain a tree that is equivalent to the i-th concept from the bottom in the path, we can either truncate the tree by combining the left-most i leaves into a single leaf representing the concept; or we can label the left-most i leaves positive and the remaining leaves negative, turning the feature tree into a decision tree.

Decision trees do not employ internal disjunction for features with more than two values, but instead allow branching on each separate value. They also allow leaf labellings that do not follow the left-to-right order of the leaves. Such a tree is shown in Figure 5.1 (right). This tree can be turned into a logical expression in many different ways, including:

$$(\mathsf{Gills} = \mathsf{no} \land \mathsf{Length} = 3) \lor (\mathsf{Gills} = \mathsf{no} \land \mathsf{Length} = 4 \land \mathsf{Teeth} = \mathsf{many})$$
$$\lor (\mathsf{Gills} = \mathsf{no} \land \mathsf{Length} = 5)$$
$$\mathsf{Gills} = \mathsf{no} \land [\mathsf{Length} = 3 \lor (\mathsf{Length} = 4 \land \mathsf{Teeth} = \mathsf{many}) \lor \mathsf{Length} = 5]$$
$$\neg[(\mathsf{Gills} = \mathsf{no} \land \mathsf{Length} = 4 \land \mathsf{Teeth} = \mathsf{few}) \lor \mathsf{Gills} = \mathsf{yes}]$$
$$(\mathsf{Gills} = \mathsf{yes} \lor \mathsf{Length} = [3,5] \lor \mathsf{Teeth} = \mathsf{many}) \land \mathsf{Gills} = \mathsf{no}$$

The first expression is in disjunctive normal form (DNF, see Background 4.1 on p.105) and is obtained by forming a disjunction of all paths from the root of the tree to leaves labelled positive, where each path gives a conjunction of literals. The second expression is a simplification of the first using the distributive equivalence $(A \wedge B) \vee (A \wedge C) \equiv A \wedge (B \vee C)$. The third expression is obtained by first forming a DNF expression representing the negative class, and then negating it. The fourth expression turns this into CNF by using the De Morgan laws $\neg(A \wedge B) \equiv \neg A \vee \neg B$ and $\neg(A \vee B) \equiv \neg A \wedge \neg B$.

There are many other logical expressions that are equivalent to the concept defined by the decision tree. Perhaps it would be possible to obtain an equivalent conjunctive concept? Interestingly, the answer to this question is no: some decision trees represent a conjunctive concept, but many trees don't and this is one of them.[1] *Decision trees are strictly more expressive than conjunctive concepts.* In fact, since decision trees correspond to DNF expressions, and since every logical expression can be equivalently written in DNF, it follows that decision trees are maximally expressive: the only data that they cannot separate is data that is inconsistently labelled, i.e., the same instance appears twice with different labels. This explains why data that isn't conjunctively separable, as in our example, can be separated by a decision tree.

There is a potential problem with using such an expressive hypothesis language. Let Δ be the disjunction of all positive examples, then Δ is in disjunctive normal form. Δ clearly covers all positives – in fact, Δ's extension is exactly the set of positive examples. In other words, in the hypothesis space of DNF expressions (or of decision trees), Δ is the LGG of the positive examples, but it doesn't cover any other instances. So Δ does not generalise beyond the positive examples, but merely memorises them – talk about overfitting! Turning this argument around, we see that *one way to avoid overfitting and encourage learning is to deliberately choose a restrictive hypothesis language*, such as conjunctive concepts: in such a language, even the LGG operation typically generalises beyond the positive examples. And if our language is expressive enough to represent any set of positive examples, we must make sure that the learning algorithm employs other mechanisms to force generalisation beyond the examples and avoid overfitting – this is called the *inductive bias* of the learning algorithm. As we will see, most learning algorithms that operate in expressive hypothesis spaces have an inductive bias towards less complex hypotheses, either implicitly through the way the hypothesis space is searched, or explicitly by incorporating a complexity penalty in the objective function.

Tree models are not limited to classification but can be employed to solve almost any machine learning task, including ranking and probability estimation, regression and clustering. The tree structure that is common to all those models can be defined

[1] If we allowed the creation of new conjunctive features, we could actually represent this tree as the conjunctive concept Gills = no ∧ F = false, where $F \equiv$ Length = 4 ∧ Teeth = few is a new conjunctive feature. The creation of new features during learning is called *constructive induction*, and as shown here can extend the representational power of a logical language.

as follows.

Definition 5.1 (Feature tree). *A* feature tree *is a tree such that each internal node (the nodes that are not leaves) is labelled with a feature, and each edge emanating from an internal node is labelled with a literal. The set of literals at a node is called a* split. *Each leaf of the tree represents a logical expression, which is the conjunction of literals encountered on the path from the root of the tree to the leaf. The extension of that conjunction (the set of instances covered by it) is called the* instance space segment *associated with the leaf.*

Essentially, a feature tree is a compact way of representing a number of conjunctive concepts in the hypothesis space. The learning problem is then to decide which of the possible concepts will be best to solve the given task. While rule learners (discussed in the next chapter) essentially learn these concepts one at a time, tree learners perform a top–down search for all these concepts at once.

Algorithm 5.1 gives the generic learning procedure common to most tree learners. It assumes that the following three functions are defined:

Homogeneous(D) returns true if the instances in D are homogeneous enough to be labelled with a single label, and false otherwise;

Label(D) returns the most appropriate label for a set of instances D;

BestSplit(D,F) returns the best set of literals to be put at the root of the tree.

These functions depend on the task at hand: for instance, for classification tasks a set of instances is homogeneous if they are (mostly) of a single class, and the most appropriate label would be the majority class. For clustering tasks a set of instances is homogenous if they are close together, and the most appropriate label would be some exemplar such as the mean (more on exemplars in Chapter 8).

Algorithm 5.1: GrowTree(D,F) – grow a feature tree from training data.

Input : data D; set of features F.
Output : feature tree T with labelled leaves.

if Homogeneous(D) **then return** Label(D) ; // Homogeneous, Label: see text
S ←BestSplit(D,F) ; // e.g., BestSplit-Class (Algorithm 5.2)
split D into subsets D_i according to the literals in S;
for each i **do**
  if $D_i \neq \emptyset$ **then** T_i ←GrowTree(D_i,F) **else** T_i is a leaf labelled with Label(D);
end
return a tree whose root is labelled with S and whose children are T_i

Algorithm 5.1 is a *divide-and-conquer* algorithm: it divides the data into subsets, builds a tree for each of those and then combines those subtrees into a single tree. Divide-and-conquer algorithms are a tried-and-tested technique in computer science. They are usually implemented recursively, because each subproblem (to build a tree for a subset of the data) is of the same form as the original problem. This works as long as there is a way to stop the recursion, which is what the first line of the algorithm does. However, it should be noted that such algorithms are *greedy*: whenever there is a choice (such as choosing the best split), the best alternative is selected on the basis of the information then available, and this choice is never reconsidered. This may lead to sub-optimal choices. An alternative would be to use a *backtracking search* algorithm, which can return an optimal solution, at the expense of increased computation time and memory requirements, but we will not explore that further in this book.

In the remainder of this chapter we will instantiate the generic Algorithm 5.1 to classification, ranking and probability estimation, clustering and regression tasks.

5.1 Decision trees

As already indicated, for a classification task we can simply define a set of instances D to be homogenous if they are all from the same class, and the function Label(D) will then obviously return that class. Notice that in line 5 of Algorithm 5.1 we may be calling Label(D) with a non-homogeneous set of instances in case one of the D_i is empty, so the general definition of Label(D) is that it returns the majority class of the instances in D.[2] This leaves us to decide how to define the function BestSplit(D, F).

Let's assume for the moment that we are dealing with Boolean features, so D is split into D_1 and D_2. Let's also assume we have two classes, and denote by $D^{\oplus}$ and $D^{\ominus}$ the positives and negatives in D (and likewise for $D_1^{\oplus}$ etc.). The question is how to assess the utility of a feature in terms of splitting the examples into positives and negatives. Clearly, the best situation is where $D_1^{\oplus} = D^{\oplus}$ and $D_1^{\ominus} = \emptyset$, or where $D_1^{\oplus} = \emptyset$ and $D_1^{\ominus} = D^{\ominus}$. In that case, the two children of the split are said to be *pure*. So we need to measure the impurity of a set of $n^{\oplus}$ positives and $n^{\ominus}$ negatives. One important principle that we will adhere to is that the impurity should only depend on the relative magnitude of $n^{\oplus}$ and $n^{\ominus}$, and should not change if we multiply both with the same amount. This in turn means that impurity can be defined in terms of the proportion $\dot{p} = n^{\oplus}/(n^{\oplus} + n^{\ominus})$, which we remember from Section 2.2 as the ☞*empirical probability* of the positive class. Furthermore, impurity should not change if we swap the positive and negative class, which means that it should stay the same if we replace $\dot{p}$ with $1 - \dot{p}$. We also want a function that is 0 whenever $\dot{p} = 0$ or $\dot{p} = 1$ and that reaches its maximum

[2] If there is more than one largest class we will make an arbitrary choice between them, usually uniformly random.

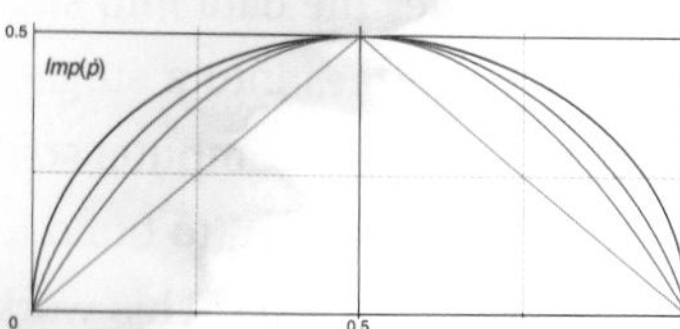

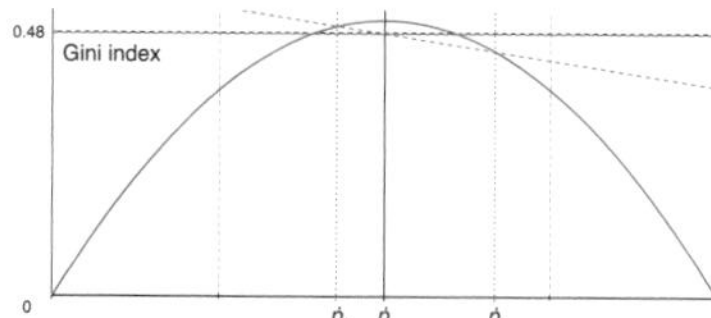

Figure 5.2. **(left)** Impurity functions plotted against the empirical probability of the positive class. From the bottom: the relative size of the minority class, $\min(\dot{p}, 1-\dot{p})$; the Gini index, $2\dot{p}(1-\dot{p})$; entropy, $-\dot{p}\log_2\dot{p}-(1-\dot{p})\log_2(1-\dot{p})$ (divided by 2 so that it reaches its maximum in the same point as the others); and the (rescaled) square root of the Gini index, $\sqrt{\dot{p}(1-\dot{p})}$ – notice that this last function describes a semi-circle. **(right)** Geometric construction to determine the impurity of a split (Teeth = [many, few] from Example 5.1): $\dot{p}$ is the empirical probability of the parent, and $\dot{p}_1$ and $\dot{p}_2$ are the empirical probabilities of the children.

for $\dot{p} = 1/2$. The following functions all fit the bill.

Minority class $\min(\dot{p}, 1-\dot{p})$ – this is sometimes referred to as the error rate, as it measures the proportion of misclassified examples if the leaf was labelled with the majority class; the purer the set of examples, the fewer errors this will make. This impurity measure can equivalently be written as $1/2 - |\dot{p} - 1/2|$.

Gini index $2\dot{p}(1-\dot{p})$ – this is the expected error if we label examples in the leaf randomly: positive with probability $\dot{p}$ and negative with probability $1-\dot{p}$. The probability of a false positive is then $\dot{p}(1-\dot{p})$ and the probability of a false negative $(1-\dot{p})\dot{p}$. [3]

entropy $-\dot{p}\log_2\dot{p}-(1-\dot{p})\log_2(1-\dot{p})$ – this is the expected information, in bits, conveyed by somebody telling you the class of a randomly drawn example; the purer the set of examples, the more predictable this message becomes and the smaller the expected information.

A plot of these three impurity measures can be seen in Figure 5.2 (left), some of them rescaled so that they all reach their maximum at (0.5, 0.5). I have added a fourth one: the square root of the Gini index, which I will indicate as $\sqrt{\text{Gini}}$, and which has an advantage over the others, as we will see later. Indicating the impurity of a single leaf D_j as $\text{Imp}(D_j)$, the impurity of a set of mutually exclusive leaves $\{D_1, \ldots, D_l\}$ is then

[3] When I looked up 'Gini index' on Wikipedia I was referred to a page describing the *Gini coefficient*, which – in a machine learning context – is a linear rescaling of the AUC to the interval $[-1, 1]$. This is quite a different concept, and the only thing that the Gini index and the Gini coefficient have in common is that they were both proposed by the Italian statistician Corrado Gini, so it is good to be aware of potential confusion.

defined as a weighted average

$$\mathrm{Imp}(\{D_1,\ldots,D_l\}) = \sum_{j=1}^{l} \frac{|D_j|}{|D|}\mathrm{Imp}(D_j) \tag{5.1}$$

where $D = D_1 \cup \ldots \cup D_l$. For a binary split there is a nice geometric construction to find $\mathrm{Imp}(\{D_1, D_2\})$ given the empirical probabilities of the parent and the children, which is illustrated in Figure 5.2 (right):

1. We first find the impurity values $\mathrm{Imp}(D_1)$ and $\mathrm{Imp}(D_2)$ of the two children on the impurity curve (here the Gini index).
2. We then connect these two values by a straight line, as any weighted average of the two must be on that line.
3. Since the empirical probability of the parent is also a weighted average of the empirical probabilities of the children, with the same weights (i.e., $\dot{p} = \frac{|D_1|}{|D|}\dot{p}_1 + \frac{|D_2|}{|D|}\dot{p}_2$ – the derivation is given in Equation 5.2 on p.139), $\dot{p}$ gives us the correct interpolation point.

This construction will work with any of the impurity measures plotted in Figure 5.2 (left). Note that, if the class distribution in the parent is very skewed, the empirical probability of both children may end up to the left or to the right of the $\dot{p} = 0.5$ vertical. This isn't a problem – except for the minority class impurity measure, as the geometric construction makes it clear that all such splits will be evaluated as having the same weighted average impurity. For this reason its use as an impurity measure is often discouraged.

Example 5.1 (Calculating impurity). Consider again the data in Example 4.4 on p.115. We want to find the best feature to put at the root of the decision tree. The four features available result in the following splits:

Length = [3,4,5]	[2+,0−][1+,3−][2+,2−]
Gills = [yes,no]	[0+,4−][5+,1−]
Beak = [yes,no]	[5+,3−][0+,2−]
Teeth = [many,few]	[3+,4−][2+,1−]

Let's calculate the impurity of the first split. We have three segments: the first one is pure and so has entropy 0; the second one has entropy $-(1/4)\log_2(1/4) - (3/4)\log_2(3/4) = 0.5 + 0.31 = 0.81$; the third one has entropy 1. The total entropy is then the weighted average of these, which is $2/10 \cdot 0 + 4/10 \cdot 0.81 + 4/10 \cdot 1 = 0.72$.

Similar calculations for the other three features give the following entropies:

Gills $4/10 \cdot 0 + 6/10 \cdot \big(-(5/6)\log_2(5/6) - (1/6)\log_2(1/6)\big) = 0.39;$

Beak $8/10 \cdot \big(-(5/8)\log_2(5/8) - (3/8)\log_2(3/8)\big) + 2/10 \cdot 0 = 0.76;$

Teeth $7/10 \cdot \big(-(3/7)\log_2(3/7) - (4/7)\log_2(4/7)\big)$
$+3/10 \cdot \big(-(2/3)\log_2(2/3) - (1/3)\log_2(1/3)\big) = 0.97.$

We thus clearly see that 'Gills' is an excellent feature to split on; 'Teeth' is poor; and the other two are somewhere in between.

The calculations for the Gini index are as follows (notice that these are on a scale from 0 to 0.5):

Length $2/10 \cdot 2 \cdot (2/2 \cdot 0/2) + 4/10 \cdot 2 \cdot (1/4 \cdot 3/4) + 4/10 \cdot 2 \cdot (2/4 \cdot 2/4) = 0.35;$

Gills $4/10 \cdot 0 + 6/10 \cdot 2 \cdot (5/6 \cdot 1/6) = 0.17;$

Beak $8/10 \cdot 2 \cdot (5/8 \cdot 3/8) + 2/10 \cdot 0 = 0.38;$

Teeth $7/10 \cdot 2 \cdot (3/7 \cdot 4/7) + 3/10 \cdot 2 \cdot (2/3 \cdot 1/3) = 0.48.$

As expected, the two impurity measures are in close agreement. See Figure 5.2 (right) for a geometric illustration of the last calculation concerning 'Teeth'.

Adapting these impurity measures to $k > 2$ classes is done by summing the per-class impurities in a one-versus-rest manner. In particular, k-class entropy is defined as $\sum_{i=1}^{k} -\dot{p}_i \log_2 \dot{p}_i$, and the k-class Gini index as $\sum_{i=1}^{k} \dot{p}_i(1-\dot{p}_i)$. In assessing the quality of a feature for splitting a parent node D into leaves $D_1, \ldots, D_l$, it is customary to look at the purity gain $\text{Imp}(D) - \text{Imp}(\{D_1, \ldots, D_l\})$. If purity is measured by entropy, this is called the *information gain* splitting criterion, as it measures the increase in information about the class gained by including the feature. However, note that Algorithm 5.1 only compares splits with the same parent, and so we can ignore the impurity of the parent and search for the feature which results in the lowest weighted average impurity of its children (Algorithm 5.2).

We now have a fully instantiated decision tree learning algorithm, so let's see what tree it learns on our dolphin data. We have already seen that the best feature to split on at the root of the tree is 'Gills': the condition Gills = yes leads to a pure leaf [0+, 4−] labelled negative, and a predominantly positive child [5+, 1−]. For the next split we have the choice between 'Length' and 'Teeth', as splitting on 'Beak' does not decrease the impurity. 'Length' results in a [2+, 0−][1+, 1−][2+, 0−] split and 'Teeth' in a [3+, 0−][2+, 1−] split; both entropy and Gini index consider the former purer than the latter. We then use 'Teeth' to split the one remaining impure node. The resulting tree is the one shown previously in Figure 5.1 on p.130, and reproduced in Figure 5.3 (left). We have learned

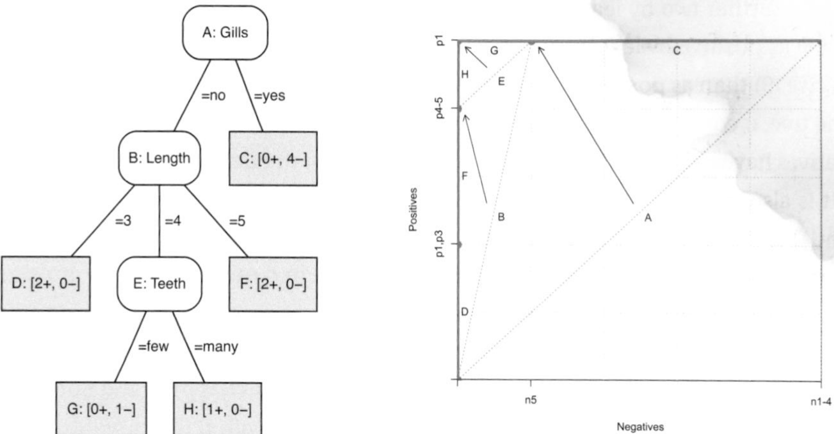

Figure 5.3. **(left)** Decision tree learned from the data in Example 4.4 on p.115. **(right)** Each internal and leaf node of the tree corresponds to a line segment in coverage space: vertical segments for pure positive nodes, horizontal segments for pure negative nodes, and diagonal segments for impure nodes.

our first decision tree!

The tree represents a partition of the instance space, and therefore also assigns a class to the 14 instances that were not part of the training set – which is why we can say that the tree generalises the training data. Leaf C leaves three feature values unspecified, with a total of $3 \cdot 2 \cdot 2 = 12$ possible combinations of values; four of these were supplied as training examples, so leaf C covers eight unlabelled instances and classifies them as negative. Similarly, two unlabelled instances are classified as positive by leaf

Algorithm 5.2: BestSplit-Class(D, F) – find the best split for a decision tree.

Input : data D; set of features F.
Output : feature f to split on.

$I_{\min} \leftarrow 1$;
for each $f \in F$ **do**
  split D into subsets $D_1, \ldots, D_l$ according to the values v_j of f;
  if $\text{Imp}(\{D_1, \ldots, D_l\}) < I_{\min}$ **then**
    $I_{\min} \leftarrow \text{Imp}(\{D_1, \ldots, D_l\})$;
    $f_{\text{best}} \leftarrow f$;
  end
end
return f_{best}

D, and a further two by leaf F; one is classified as negative by leaf G, and the remaining one as positive by leaf H. The fact that more unlabelled instances are classified as negative (9) than as positive (5) is thus mostly due to leaf C: because it is a leaf high up in the tree, it covers many instances. One could argue that the fact that four out of five negatives have gills is the strongest regularity found in the data.

It is also worth tracing the construction of this tree in coverage space (Figure 5.3 (right)). Every node of the tree, internal or leaf, covers a certain number of positives and negatives and hence can be plotted as a line segment in coverage space. For instance, the root of the tree covers all positives and all negatives, and hence is represented by the ascending diagonal A. Once we add our first split, segment A is replaced by segment B (an impure node and hence diagonal) and segment C, which is pure and not split any further. Segment B is further split into D (pure and positive), E (impure) and F (pure and positive). Finally, E is split into two pure nodes.

This idea of a decision tree coverage curve 'pulling itself up' from the ascending diagonal in a divide-and-conquer fashion is appealing – but unfortunately it is not true in general. The ordering of coverage curve segments is purely based on the class distributions in the leaves and does not bear any direct relationship to the tree structure. To understand this better, we will now look at how tree models can be turned into rankers and probability estimators.

5.2 Ranking and probability estimation trees

Grouping classifiers such as decision trees divide the instance space into segments, and so can be turned into rankers by learning an ordering on those segments. Unlike some other grouping models, decision trees have access to the local class distributions in the segments or leaves, which can directly be used to construct a leaf ordering that is optimal for the training data. So, for instance, in Figure 5.3 this ordering is [D – F] – H – G – C, resulting in a perfect ranking (AUC = 1). The ordering can simply be obtained from the empirical probabilities $\dot{p}$, breaking ties as much as possible by giving precedence to leaves covering a larger number of positives.[4] Why is this ordering optimal? Well, the slope of a coverage curve segment with empirical probability $\dot{p}$ is $\dot{p}/(1-\dot{p})$; since $\dot{p} \mapsto \frac{\dot{p}}{1-\dot{p}}$ is a monotonic transformation (if $\dot{p} > \dot{p}'$ then $\frac{\dot{p}}{1-\dot{p}} > \frac{\dot{p}'}{1-\dot{p}'}$) sorting the segments on non-increasing empirical probabilities ensures that they are also sorted on non-increasing slope, and so the curve is convex. This is an important point, so I'll say it again: *the ranking obtained from the empirical probabilities in the leaves of a decision tree yields a convex ROC curve on the training data.* As we shall see later in

[4]Tie breaking – although it does not alter the shape of the coverage curve and isn't essential in that sense – can also be achieved by subtracting $\epsilon \ll 1$ from the number of positives covered. The Laplace correction also breaks ties in favour of larger leaves but isn't a monotonic transformation and so might change the shape of the coverage curve.

the book, some other grouping models including ☞*rule lists* (Section 6.1) share this property, but no grading model does.

As already noted, the segment ordering cannot be deduced from the tree structure. The reason is essentially that, even if we know the empirical probability associated with the parent of a split, this doesn't constrain the empirical probabilities of its children. For instance, let $[n^{\oplus}, n^{\ominus}]$ be the class distribution in the parent with $n = n^{\oplus} + n^{\ominus}$, and let $[n_1^{\oplus}, n_1^{\ominus}]$ and $[n_2^{\oplus}, n_2^{\ominus}]$ be the class distributions in the children, with $n_1 = n_1^{\oplus} + n_1^{\ominus}$ and $n_2 = n_2^{\oplus} + n_2^{\ominus}$. We then have

$$\dot{p} = \frac{n^{\oplus}}{n} = \frac{n_1}{n}\frac{n_1^{\oplus}}{n_1} + \frac{n_2}{n}\frac{n_2^{\oplus}}{n_2} = \frac{n_1}{n}\dot{p}_1 + \frac{n_2}{n}\dot{p}_2 \tag{5.2}$$

In other words, the empirical probability of the parent is a weighted average of the empirical probabilities of its children; but this only tells us that $\dot{p}_1 \leq \dot{p} \leq \dot{p}_2$ or $\dot{p}_2 \leq \dot{p} \leq \dot{p}_1$. Even if the place of the parent segment in the coverage curve is known, its children may come much earlier or later in the ordering.

Example 5.2 (Growing a tree). Consider the tree in Figure 5.4 (top). Each node is labelled with the numbers of positive and negative examples covered by it: so, for instance, the root of the tree is labelled with the overall class distribution (50 positives and 100 negatives), resulting in the trivial ranking [50+,100−]. The corresponding one-segment coverage curve is the ascending diagonal (Figure 5.4 (bottom)). Adding split (1) refines this ranking into [30+,35−][20+,65−], resulting in a two-segment curve. Adding splits (2) and (3) again breaks up the segment corresponding to the parent into two segments corresponding to the children. However, the ranking produced by the full tree – [15+,3−][29+,10−][5+,62−][1+,25−] – is different from the left-to-right ordering of its leaves, hence we need to reorder the segments of the coverage curve, leading to the top-most, solid curve.

So, adding a split to a decision tree can be interpreted in terms of coverage curves as the following two-step process:

- ☞ split the corresponding curve segment into two or more segments;
- ☞ reorder the segments on decreasing slope.

The whole process of growing a decision tree can be understood as an iteration of these two steps; or alternatively as a sequence of splitting steps followed by one overall reordering step. It is this last step that guarantees that the coverage curve is convex (on the training data).

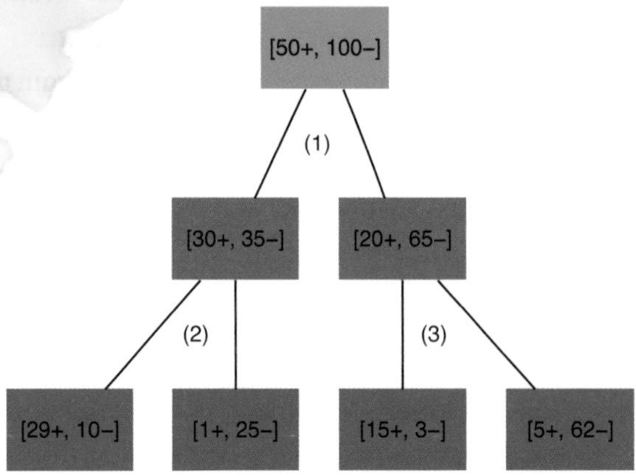

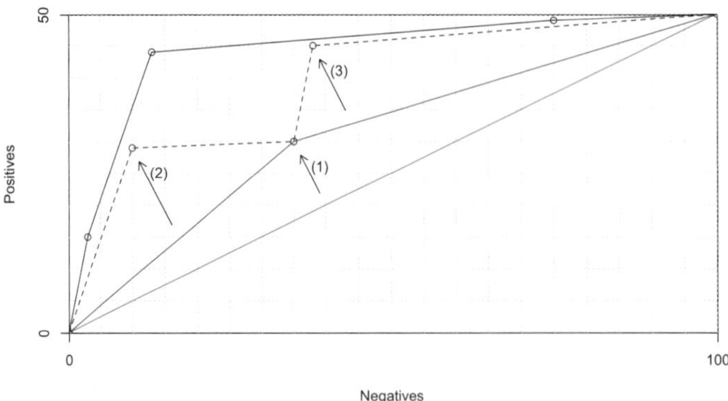

Figure 5.4. (top) Abstract representation of a tree with numbers of positive and negative examples covered in each node. Binary splits are added to the tree in the order indicated. **(bottom)** Adding a split to the tree will add new segments to the coverage curve as indicated by the arrows. After a split is added the segments may need reordering, and so only the solid lines represent actual coverage curves.

It is instructive to take this analysis a step further by considering all possible rankings that can be constructed with the given tree. One way to do that is to consider the tree as a feature tree, without any class labels, and ask ourselves in how many ways we can label the tree, and what performance that would yield, given that we know the numbers of positives and negatives covered in each leaf. In general, if a feature tree has l leaves and we have c classes, then the number of possible labellings of leaves with classes is c^l; in the example of Figure 5.4 this is $2^4 = 16$. Figure 5.5 depicts these 16 labellings in coverage space. As you might expect, there is a lot of symmetry in this

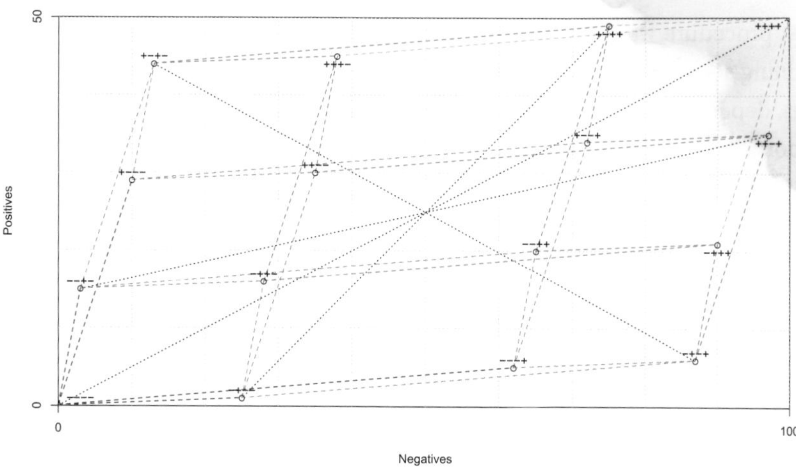

Figure 5.5. Graphical depiction of all possible labellings and all possible rankings that can be obtained with the four-leaf decision tree in Figure 5.4. There are $2^4 = 16$ possible leaf labellings; e.g., '$+-+-$' denotes labelling the first and third leaf from the left as $+$ and the second and fourth leaf as $-$. Also indicated are some pairwise symmetries (dotted lines): e.g., $+-+-$ and $-+-+$ are each other's inverse and end up at opposite ends of the plot. There are $4! = 24$ possible blue-violet-red-orange paths through these points which start in $----$ and switch each leaf to $+$ in some order; these represent all possible four-segment coverage curves or rankings.

plot. For instance, labellings occur in pairs (say $+-+-$ and $-+-+$) that occur in opposite locations in the plot (see if you can figure out what is meant by 'opposite' here). We obtain a ranking by starting in $----$ in the lower left-hand corner, and switching each leaf to $+$ in some order. For instance, the optimal coverage curve follows the order $----$, $--+-$, $+-+-$, $+-++$, $++++$. For a tree with l leaves there are $l!$ permutations of its leaves and thus $l!$ possible coverage curves (24 in our example).

If I were to choose a single image that would convey the essence of tree models, it would be Figure 5.5. What it visualises is that the class distributions in the leaves of an unlabelled feature tree can be used to turn one and the same tree into a decision tree, a ranking tree, or a probability estimation tree:

- to turn a feature tree into a ranker, we order its leaves on non-increasing empirical probabilities, which is provably optimal on the training set;
- to turn the tree into a probability estimator, we predict the empirical probabilities in each leaf, applying Laplace or m-estimate smoothing to make these estimates more robust for small leaves;
- to turn the tree into a classifier, we choose the operating conditions and find the

operating point that is optimal under those operating conditions.

The last procedure was explained in Section 2.2. We will illustrate it here, assuming the training set class ratio *clr* = 50/100 is representative. We have a choice of five labellings, depending on the expected cost ratio $c = c_{\text{FN}}/c_{\text{FP}}$ of misclassifying a positive in proportion to the cost of misclassifying a negative:

$+-+-$ would be the labelling of choice if $c = 1$, or more generally if $10/29 < c < 62/5$;

$+-++$ would be chosen if $62/5 < c < 25/1$;

$++++$ would be chosen if $25/1 < c$; i.e., we would always predict positive if false negatives are more than 25 times as costly as false positives, because then even predicting positive in the second leaf would reduce cost;

$--+-$ would be chosen if $3/15 < c < 10/29$;

$----$ would be chosen if $c < 3/15$; i.e., we would always predict negative if false positives are more than 5 times as costly as false negatives, because then even predicting negative in the third leaf would reduce cost.

The first of these options corresponds to the majority class labelling, which is what most textbook treatments of decision trees recommend, and also what I suggested when I discussed the function Label(D) in the context of Algorithm 5.1. In many circumstances this will indeed be the most practical thing to do. However, it is important to be aware of the underlying assumptions of such a labelling: these assumptions are that the training set class distribution is representative and the costs are uniform; or, more generally, that the product of the expected cost and class ratios is equal to the class ratio as observed in the training set. (This actually suggests a useful device for manipulating the training set to reflect an expected class ratio: to mimic an expected class ratio of c, we can oversample the positive training examples with a factor c if $c > 1$, or oversample the negatives with a factor $1/c$ if $c < 1$. We will return to this suggestion below.)

So let's assume that the class distribution is representative and that false negatives (e.g., not diagnosing a disease in a patient) are about 20 times more costly than false positives. As we have just seen, the optimal labelling under these operating conditions is $+-++$, which means that we only use the second leaf to filter out negatives. In other words, the right two leaves can be merged into one – their parent. Rather aptly, the operation of merging all leaves in a subtree is called *pruning* the subtree. The process is illustrated in Figure 5.6. The advantage of pruning is that we can simplify the tree without affecting the chosen operating point, which is sometimes useful if we want to communicate the tree model to somebody else. The disadvantage is that we lose ranking performance, as illustrated in Figure 5.6 (bottom). Pruning is therefore not recommended unless (*i*) you only intend to use the tree for classification, not for

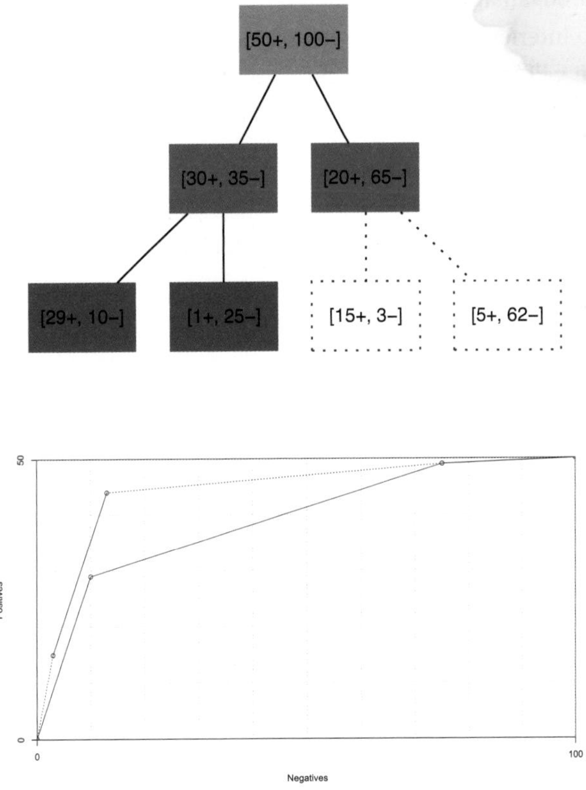

Figure 5.6. **(top)** To achieve the labelling $+-++$ we don't need the right-most split, which can therefore be pruned away. **(bottom)** Pruning doesn't affect the chosen operating point, but it does decrease the ranking performance of the tree.

ranking or probability estimation; and (*ii*) you can define the expected operating conditions with sufficient precision. One popular algorithm for pruning decision trees is called *reduced-error pruning*, and is given in Algorithm 5.3. The algorithm employs a separate *pruning set* of labelled data not seen during training, as pruning will never improve accuracy over the training data. However, if tree simplicity is not really an issue, I recommend keeping the entire tree intact and choosing the operating point through the leaf labelling only; this can similarly be done using a hold-out data set.

Sensitivity to skewed class distributions

I just mentioned in passing that one way to make sure the training set reflects the right operating conditions is to duplicate positives or negatives so that the training set class ratio is equal to the product of expected cost and class ratios in deployment of the model. Effectively, this changes the aspect ratio of the rectangle representing the coverage space. The advantage of this method is that it is directly applicable to any model, without need to interfere with search heuristics or evaluation measures. The disadvantage is that it will increase training time – and besides, it may not actually make a difference for the model being learned. I will illustrate this with an example.

Example 5.3 (Cost-sensitivity of splitting criteria). Suppose you have 10 positives and 10 negatives, and you need to choose between the two splits [8+,2−][2+,8−] and [10+,6−][0+,4−]. You duly calculate the weighted average entropy of both splits and conclude that the first split is the better one. Just to be sure, you also calculate the average Gini index, and again the first split wins. You then remember somebody telling you that the square root of the Gini index was a better impurity measure, so you decide to check that one out as well. Lo and behold, it favours the second split...! What to do?

You then remember that mistakes on the positives are about ten times as costly as mistakes on the negatives. You're not quite sure how to work out the maths, and so you decide to simply have ten copies of every positive: the splits are now [80+,2−][20+,8−] and [100+,6−][0+,4−]. You recalculate the three splitting criteria and now all three favour the second split. Even though you're slightly bemused by all this, you settle for the second split since all three splitting criteria are now unanimous in their recommendation.

So what is going on here? Let's first look at the situation with the inflated numbers of positives. Intuitively it is clear that here the second split is preferable, since one of the children is pure and the other one is fairly good as well, though perhaps not as

---

Algorithm 5.3: PruneTree(T, D) – reduced-error pruning of a decision tree.

Input : decision tree T; labelled data D.
Output : pruned tree T'.

for every internal node N of T, starting from the bottom **do**
  $T_N \leftarrow$ subtree of T rooted at N;
  $D_N \leftarrow \{x \in D | x \text{ is covered by } N\}$;
  if accuracy of T_N over D_N is worse than majority class in D_N **then**
    replace T_N in T by a leaf labelled with the majority class in D_N;
  end
end
return pruned version of T

---

good as [80+,2−]. But this situation changes if we have only one-tenth of the number of positives, at least according to entropy and Gini index. Using notation introduced earlier, this can be understood as follows. The Gini index of the parent is $2\frac{n^{\oplus}}{n}\frac{n^{\ominus}}{n}$, and the weighted Gini index of one of the children is $\frac{n_1}{n}2\frac{n_1^{\oplus}}{n_1}\frac{n_1^{\ominus}}{n_1}$. So the weighted impurity of the child *in proportion* to the parent's impurity is $\frac{n_1^{\oplus}n_1^{\ominus}/n_1}{n^{\oplus}n^{\ominus}/n}$; let's call this *relative impurity*. The same calculations for $\sqrt{\text{Gini}}$ give

- impurity of the parent: $\sqrt{\frac{n^{\oplus}}{n}\frac{n^{\ominus}}{n}}$;
- weighted impurity of the child: $\frac{n_1}{n}\sqrt{\frac{n_1^{\oplus}}{n_1}\frac{n_1^{\ominus}}{n_1}}$;
- relative impurity: $\sqrt{\frac{n_1^{\oplus}n_1^{\ominus}}{n^{\oplus}n^{\ominus}}}$.

The important thing to note is that this last ratio doesn't change if we multiply all numbers involving positives with a factor c. That is, $\sqrt{\text{Gini}}$ is designed to minimise relative impurity, and thus is insensitive to changes in class distribution. In contrast, relative impurity for the Gini index includes the ratio n_1/n, which changes if we inflate the number of positives. Something similar happens with entropy. As a result, these two splitting criteria emphasise children covering more examples.

A picture will help to explain this further. Just as accuracy and average recall have isometrics in coverage and ROC space, so do splitting criteria. Owing to their non-linear nature, these isometrics are curved rather than straight. They also occur on either side of the diagonal, as we can swap the left and right child without changing the quality of the split. One might imagine the impurity landscape as a mountain looked down on from above – the summit is a ridge along the ascending diagonal, representing the splits where the children have the same impurity as the parent. This mountain slopes down on either side and reaches ground level in ROC heaven as well as its opposite number ('ROC hell'), as this is where impurity is zero. The isometrics are the contour lines of this mountain – walks around it at constant elevation.

Consider Figure 5.7 (top). The two splits among which you needed to choose in Example 5.3 (before inflating the positives) are indicated as points in this plot. I have drawn six isometrics in the top-left of the plot: two splits times three splitting criteria. A particular splitting criterion prefers the split whose isometric is the *highest* (closest to ROC heaven) of the two: you can see that only one of the three ($\sqrt{\text{Gini}}$) prefers the split on the top-right. Figure 5.7 (bottom) demonstrates how this changes when inflating the positives with a factor 10 (a coverage plot would run off the page here, so I have plotted this in ROC space with the grid indicating how the class distribution has changed). Now all three splitting criteria prefer the top-right split, because the entropy

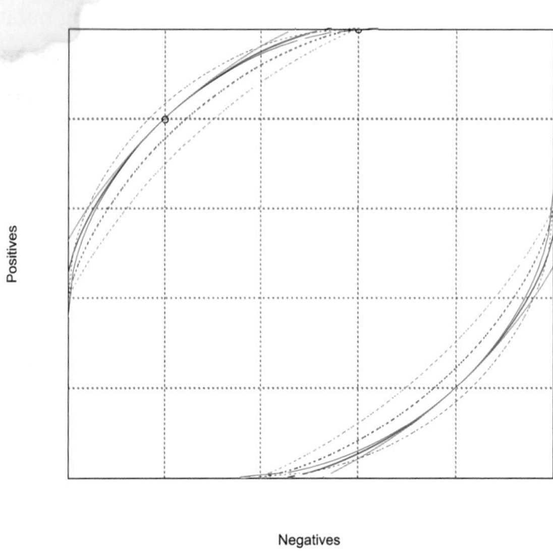

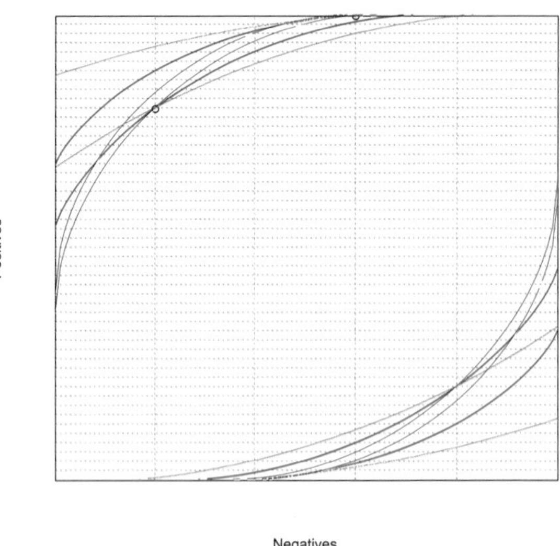

Figure 5.7. **(top)** ROC isometrics for entropy in blue, Gini index in violet and $\sqrt{\text{Gini}}$ in red through the splits [8+,2−][2+,8−] (solid lines) and [10+,6−][0+,4−] (dotted lines). Only $\sqrt{\text{Gini}}$ prefers the second split. **(bottom)** The same isometrics after inflating the positives with a factor 10. All splitting criteria now favour the second split; the $\sqrt{\text{Gini}}$ isometrics are the only ones that haven't moved.

and Gini index 'mountains' have rotated clockwise (Gini index more so than entropy), while the $\sqrt{\text{Gini}}$ mountain hasn't moved at all.

The upshot of all this is that if you learn a decision tree or probability estimation tree using entropy or Gini index as impurity measure – which is what virtually all available tree learning packages do – then your model will change if you change the class distribution by oversampling, while if you use $\sqrt{\text{Gini}}$ you will learn the same tree each time. More generally, *entropy and Gini index are sensitive to fluctuations in the class distribution, $\sqrt{\text{Gini}}$ isn't*. So which one should you choose? My recommendation echoes the ones I gave for majority class labelling and pruning: use a distribution-insensitive impurity measure such as $\sqrt{\text{Gini}}$ unless the training set operating conditions are representative.[5]

Let's wrap up the discussion on tree models so far. How would *you* train a decision tree on a given data set, you might ask me? Here's a list of the steps I would take:

1. First and foremost, I would concentrate on getting good ranking behaviour, because from a good ranker I can get good classification and probability estimation, but not necessarily the other way round.
2. I would therefore try to use an impurity measure that is distribution-insensitive, such as $\sqrt{\text{Gini}}$; if that isn't available and I can't hack the code, I would resort to oversampling the minority class to achieve a balanced class distribution.
3. I would disable pruning and smooth the probability estimates by means of the Laplace correction (or the m-estimate).
4. Once I know the deployment operation conditions, I would use these to select the best operating point on the ROC curve (i.e., a threshold on the predicted probabilities, or a labelling of the tree).
5. (optional) Finally, I would prune away any subtree whose leaves all have the same label.

Even though in our discussion we have mostly concentrated on binary classification tasks, it should be noted that decision trees can effortlessly deal with more than two classes – as, indeed, can any grouping model. As already mentioned, multi-class impurity measures simply sum up impurities for each class in a one-versus-rest manner. The only step in this list that isn't entirely obvious when there are more than two classes is step 4: in this case I would learn a weight for each class as briefly explained in Section 3.1, or possibly combine it with step 5 and resort to reduced-error pruning (Algorithm 5.3) which might be already implemented in the package you're using.

---

[5] It should be noted that it is fairly easy to make measures such as entropy and Gini index distribution-insensitive as well: essentially, this would involve compensating for an observed class ratio $clr \neq 1$ by dividing all counts of positives, or positive empirical probabilities, by clr.

5.3 Tree learning as variance reduction

We will now consider how to adapt decision trees to regression and clustering tasks. This will turn out to be surprisingly straightforward, and is based on the following idea. Earlier, we defined the two-class Gini index $2\dot{p}(1-\dot{p})$ of a leaf as the expected error resulting from labelling instances in the leaf randomly: positive with probability $\dot{p}$ and negative with probability $1-\dot{p}$. You can picture this as tossing a coin, prepared such that it comes up heads with probability $\dot{p}$, to classify examples. Representing this as a random variable with value 1 for heads and 0 for tails, the expected value of this random variable is $\dot{p}$ and its variance $\dot{p}(1-\dot{p})$ (look up 'Bernoulli trial' online if you want to read up on this). This leads to an alternative interpretation of the Gini index as a variance term: the purer the leaf, the more biased the coin will be, and the smaller the variance. For k classes we simply add up the variances of all one-versus-rest random variables.[6]

More specifically, consider a binary split into n_1 and $n_2 = n - n_1$ examples with empirical probabilities $\dot{p}_1$ and $\dot{p}_2$, then the weighted average impurity of these children in terms of the Gini index is

$$\frac{n_1}{n}2\dot{p}_1(1-\dot{p}_1) + \frac{n_2}{n}2\dot{p}_2(1-\dot{p}_2) = 2\left(\frac{n_1}{n}\sigma_1^2 + \frac{n_2}{n}\sigma_2^2\right)$$

where σ_j^2 is the variance of a Bernoulli distribution with success probability $\dot{p}_j$. So, finding a split with minimum weighted average Gini index is equivalent to minimising weighted average variance (the factor 2 is common to all splits and so can be omitted), and learning a decision tree boils down to partitioning the instance space such that each segment has small variance.

Regression trees

In regression problems the target variable is continuous rather than binary, and in that case we can define the variance of a set Y of target values as the average squared distance from the mean:

$$\mathrm{Var}(Y) = \frac{1}{|Y|}\sum_{y \in Y}(y - \overline{y})^2$$

where $\overline{y} = \frac{1}{|Y|}\sum_{y\in Y} y$ is the mean of the target values in Y; see Background 5.1 for some useful properties of variance. If a split partitions the set of target values Y into mutually exclusive sets $\{Y_1, \ldots, Y_l\}$, the weighted average variance is then

$$\mathrm{Var}(\{Y_1,\ldots,Y_l\}) = \sum_{j=1}^{l}\frac{|Y_j|}{|Y|}\mathrm{Var}(Y_j) = \sum_{j=1}^{l}\frac{|Y_j|}{|Y|}\left(\frac{1}{|Y_j|}\sum_{y\in Y_j} y^2 - \overline{y}_j^2\right) = \frac{1}{|Y|}\sum_{y\in Y} y^2 - \sum_{j=1}^{l}\frac{|Y_j|}{|Y|}\overline{y}_j^2 \tag{5.4}$$

[6] This implicitly assumes that the one-versus-rest variables are uncorrelated, which is not strictly true.

The *variance* of a set of numbers $X \subseteq \mathbb{R}$ is defined as the average squared difference from the mean:

$$\mathrm{Var}(X) = \frac{1}{|X|} \sum_{x \in X} (x - \overline{x})^2$$

where $\overline{x} = \frac{1}{|X|} \sum_{x \in X} x$ is the mean of X. Expanding $(x - \overline{x})^2 = x^2 - 2\overline{x}x + \overline{x}^2$ this can be written as

$$\mathrm{Var}(X) = \frac{1}{|X|} \left(\sum_{x \in X} x^2 - 2\overline{x} \sum_{x \in X} x + \sum_{x \in X} \overline{x}^2 \right) = \frac{1}{|X|} \left(\sum_{x \in X} x^2 - 2\overline{x}|X|\overline{x} + |X|\overline{x}^2 \right) = \frac{1}{|X|} \sum_{x \in X} x^2 - \overline{x}^2 \tag{5.3}$$

So the variance is the difference between the mean of the squares and the square of the mean.

It is sometimes useful to consider the average squared difference from another value $x' \in \mathbb{R}$, which can similarly be expanded:

$$\frac{1}{|X|} \sum_{x \in X} (x - x')^2 = \frac{1}{|X|} \left(\sum_{x \in X} x^2 - 2x'|X|\overline{x} + |X|x'^2 \right) = \mathrm{Var}(X) + (x' - \overline{x})^2$$

The last step follows because from Equation 5.3 we have $\frac{1}{|X|} \sum_{x \in X} x^2 = \mathrm{Var}(X) + \overline{x}^2$.

Another useful property is that the average squared difference between any two elements of X is twice the variance:

$$\frac{1}{|X|^2} \sum_{x' \in X} \sum_{x \in X} (x - x')^2 = \frac{1}{|X|} \sum_{x' \in X} (\mathrm{Var}(X) + (x' - \overline{x})^2) = \mathrm{Var}(X) + \frac{1}{|X|} \sum_{x' \in X} (x' - \overline{x})^2 = 2\mathrm{Var}(X)$$

If $X \subseteq \mathbb{R}^d$ is a set of d-vectors of numbers, we can define the variance $\mathrm{Var}_i(X)$ for each of the d coordinates. We can then interpret the sum of variances $\sum_{i=1}^{d} \mathrm{Var}_i(X)$ as the average squared Euclidean distance of the vectors in X to their vector mean $\overline{\mathbf{x}} = \frac{1}{|X|} \sum_{\mathbf{x} \in X} \mathbf{x}$.

(You will sometimes see sample variance defined as $\frac{1}{|X|-1} \sum_{x \in X} (x - \overline{x})^2$, which is a somewhat larger value. This version arises if we are estimating the variance of a population from which X is a random sample: normalising by $|X|$ would underestimate the population variance because of differences between the sample mean and the population mean. Here, we are only concerned with assessing the spread of the given values X and not with some unknown population, and so we can ignore this issue.)

Background 5.1. Variations on variance.

So, in order to obtain a regression tree learning algorithm, we replace the impurity measure Imp in Algorithm 5.2 with the function Var. Notice that $\frac{1}{|Y|} \sum_{y \in Y} y^2$ is constant for a given set Y, and so minimising variance over all possible splits of a given parent is the same as maximising the weighted average of squared means in the chil-

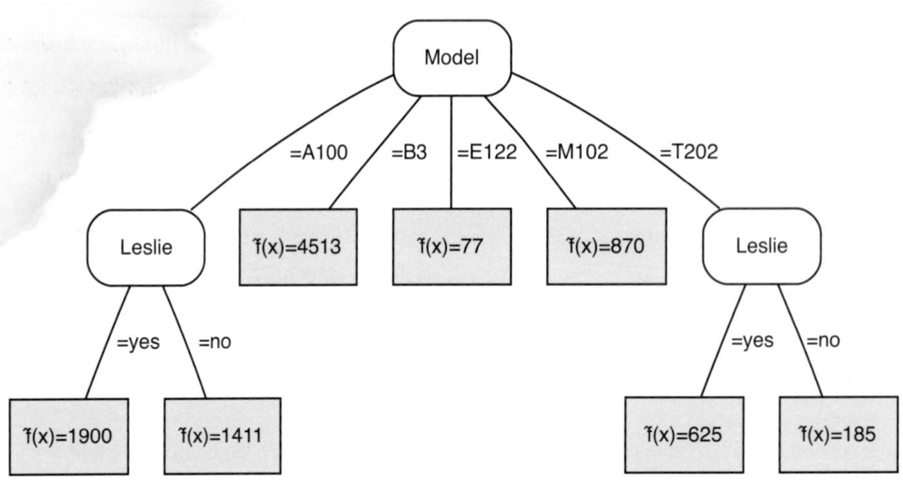

Figure 5.8. A regression tree learned from the data in Example 5.4.

dren. The function Label(Y) is similarly adapted to return the mean value in Y, and the function Homogeneous(Y) returns true if the variance of the target values in Y is zero (or smaller than a low threshold).

Example 5.4 (Learning a regression tree). Imagine you are a collector of vintage Hammond tonewheel organs. You have been monitoring an online auction site, from which you collected some data about interesting transactions:

#	Model	Condition	Leslie	Price
1.	B3	excellent	no	4513
2.	T202	fair	yes	625
3.	A100	good	no	1051
4.	T202	good	no	270
5.	M102	good	yes	870
6.	A100	excellent	no	1770
7.	T202	fair	no	99
8.	A100	good	yes	1900
9.	E112	fair	no	77

From this data, you want to construct a regression tree that will help you determine a reasonable price for your next purchase.

There are three features, hence three possible splits:

Model = [A100, B3, E112, M102, T202] [1051, 1770, 1900][4513][77][870][99, 270, 625]

Condition = [excellent, good, fair] [1770, 4513][270, 870, 1051, 1900][77, 99, 625]

Leslie = [yes, no] [625, 870, 1900][77, 99, 270, 1051, 1770, 4513]

The means of the first split are 1574, 4513, 77, 870 and 331, and the weighted average of squared means is $3.21 \cdot 10^6$. The means of the second split are 3142, 1023 and 267, with weighted average of squared means $2.68 \cdot 10^6$; for the third split the means are 1132 and 1297, with weighted average of squared means $1.55 \cdot 10^6$. We therefore branch on Model at the top level. This gives us three single-instance leaves, as well as three A100s and three T202s.

For the A100s we obtain the following splits:

Condition = [excellent, good, fair] [1770][1051, 1900][]

Leslie = [yes, no] [1900][1051, 1770]

Without going through the calculations we can see that the second split results in less variance (to handle the empty child, it is customary to set its variance equal to that of the parent). For the T202s the splits are as follows:

Condition = [excellent, good, fair] [][270][99, 625]

Leslie = [yes, no] [625][99, 270]

Again we see that splitting on Leslie gives tighter clusters of values. The learned regression tree is depicted in Figure 5.8.

Regression trees are susceptible to overfitting. For instance, if we have exactly one example for each Hammond model then branching on Model will reduce the average variance in the children to zero. The data in Example 5.4 is really too sparse to learn a good regression tree. Furthermore, it is a good idea to set aside a pruning set and to apply reduced-error pruning, pruning away a subtree if the average variance on the pruning set is lower without the subtree than with it (see Algorithm 5.3 on p.144). It should also be noted that predicting a constant value in a leaf is a very simple strategy, and methods exist to learn so-called *model trees*, which are trees with linear regression models in their leaves (☞*linear regression* is explained in Chapter 7). In that case, the splitting criterion would be based on correlation of the target variable with the regressor variables, rather than simply on variance.

Clustering trees

The simple kind of regression tree considered here also suggests a way to learn clustering trees. This is perhaps surprising, since regression is a supervised learning problem while clustering is unsupervised. The key insight is that regression trees find instance space segments whose target values are tightly clustered around the mean value in the segment – indeed, the variance of a set of target values is simply the (univariate) average squared Euclidean distance to the mean. An immediate generalisation is to use a vector of target values, as this doesn't change the mathematics in an essential way. More generally yet, we can introduce an abstract function $\text{Dis} : \mathscr{X} \times \mathscr{X} \to \mathbb{R}$ that measures the distance or *dissimilarity* of any two instances $x, x' \in \mathscr{X}$, such that the higher $\text{Dis}(x, x')$ is, the less similar x and x' are. The *cluster dissimilarity* of a set of instances D is then calculated as

$$\text{Dis}(D) = \frac{1}{|D|^2} \sum_{x \in D} \sum_{x' \in D} \text{Dis}(x, x') \tag{5.5}$$

The weighted average cluster dissimilarity over all children of a split then gives the *split dissimilarity*, which can be used to inform BestSplit(D, F) in the ☞*GrowTree algorithm* (Algorithm 5.1 on p.132).

Example 5.5 (Learning a clustering tree using a dissimilarity matrix).
Assessing the nine transactions on the online auction site from Example 5.4, using some additional features such as reserve price and number of bids (these features do not matter at the moment but are shown in Example 5.6), you come up with the following dissimilarity matrix:

$$\begin{array}{rrrrrrrrr}
0 & 11 & 6 & 13 & 10 & 3 & 13 & 3 & 12 \\
11 & \mathbf{0} & 1 & \mathbf{1} & 1 & 3 & \mathbf{0} & 4 & 0 \\
6 & 1 & \mathbf{0} & 2 & 1 & \mathbf{1} & 2 & \mathbf{2} & 1 \\
13 & \mathbf{1} & 2 & \mathbf{0} & 0 & 4 & \mathbf{0} & 4 & 0 \\
10 & 1 & 1 & 0 & 0 & 3 & 0 & 2 & 0 \\
3 & 3 & \mathbf{1} & 4 & 3 & \mathbf{0} & 4 & \mathbf{1} & 3 \\
13 & \mathbf{0} & 2 & \mathbf{0} & 0 & 4 & \mathbf{0} & 4 & 0 \\
3 & 4 & \mathbf{2} & 4 & 2 & \mathbf{1} & 4 & \mathbf{0} & 4 \\
12 & 0 & 1 & 0 & 0 & 3 & 0 & 4 & 0
\end{array}$$

This shows, for instance, that the first transaction is very different from the other eight. The average pairwise dissimilarity over all nine transactions is 2.94.

Using the same features from Example 5.4, the three possible splits are (now with transaction number rather than price):

Model = [A100, B3, E112, M102, T202] [3,6,8] [1] [9] [5] [2,4,7]

Condition = [excellent, good, fair] [1,6] [3,4,5,8] [2,7,9]

Leslie = [yes, no] [2,5,8] [1,3,4,6,7,9]

The cluster dissimilarity among transactions 3, 6 and 8 is $\frac{1}{3^2}(\mathbf{0+1+2+1+0+1+2+1+0}) = 0.89$; and among transactions 2, 4 and 7 it is $\frac{1}{3^2}(\mathbf{0+1+0+1+0+0+0+0+0}) = 0.22$. The other three children of the first split contain only a single element and so have zero cluster dissimilarity. The weighted average cluster dissimilarity of the split is then $3/9 \cdot 0.89 + 1/9 \cdot 0 + 1/9 \cdot 0 + 1/9 \cdot 0 + 3/9 \cdot 0.22 = 0.37$. For the second split, similar calculations result in a split dissimilarity of $2/9 \cdot 1.5 + 4/9 \cdot 1.19 + 3/9 \cdot 0 = 0.86$, and the third split yields $3/9 \cdot 1.56 + 6/9 \cdot 3.56 = 2.89$. The Model feature thus captures most of the given dissimilarities, while the Leslie feature is virtually unrelated.

Most of the caveats of regression trees also apply to clustering trees: smaller clusters tend to have lower dissimilarity, and so it is easy to overfit. Setting aside a pruning set to remove the lower splits if they don't improve the cluster coherence on the pruning set is recommended. Single examples can dominate: in the above example, removing the first transaction reduces the overall pairwise dissimilarity from 2.94 to 1.5, and so it will be hard to beat a split that puts that transaction in a cluster of its own.

An interesting question is: how should the leaves of a clustering tree be labelled? Intuitively, it makes sense to label a cluster with its most representative instance. We can define an instance as most representative if its total dissimilarity to all other instances is lowest – this is defined as the medoid in Chapter 8. For instance, in the A100 cluster transaction 6 is most representative because its dissimilarity to 3 and 8 is 1, whereas the dissimilarity between 3 and 8 is 2. Likewise, in the T202 cluster transaction 7 is most representative. However, there is no reason why this should always be uniquely defined.

A commonly encountered scenario, which both simplifies the calculations involved in determining the best split and provides a unique cluster label, is when the dissimilarities are Euclidean distances derived from numerical features. As shown in Background 5.1, if $\mathrm{Dis}(x, x')$ is squared Euclidean distance, then $\mathrm{Dis}(D)$ is twice the average squared Euclidean distance to the mean. This simplifies calculations because both the mean and average squared distance to the mean can be calculated in $O(|D|)$ steps (a single sweep through the data), rather than the $O(|D|^2)$ required if all we have is a dissimilarity matrix. In fact, the average squared Euclidean distance is simply the sum of the variances of the individual features.

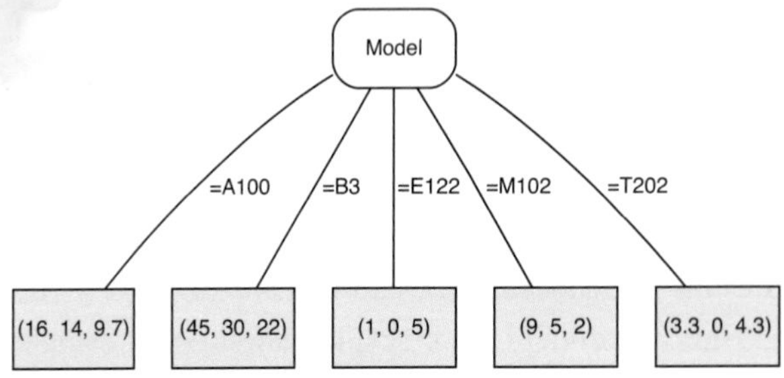

Figure 5.9. A clustering tree learned from the data in Example 5.6 using Euclidean distance on the numerical features.

Example 5.6 (Learning a clustering tree with Euclidean distance). We extend our Hammond organ data with two new numerical features, one indicating the reserve price and the other the number of bids made in the auction. Sales price and reserve price are expressed in hundreds of pounds in order to give the three numerical features roughly equal weight in the distance calculations.

Model	Condition	Leslie	Price	Reserve	Bids
B3	excellent	no	45	30	22
T202	fair	yes	6	0	9
A100	good	no	11	8	13
T202	good	no	3	0	1
M102	good	yes	9	5	2
A100	excellent	no	18	15	15
T202	fair	no	1	0	3
A100	good	yes	19	19	1
E112	fair	no	1	0	5

The means of the three numerical features are $(13.3, 8.6, 7.9)$ and their variances are $(158, 101.8, 48.8)$. The average squared Euclidean distance to the mean is then the sum of these variances, which is 308.6 (if preferred we can double this number to obtain the cluster dissimilarity as defined in Equation 5.5). For the A100 cluster these vectors are $(16, 14, 9.7)$ and $(12.7, 20.7, 38.2)$, with average squared distance to the mean 71.6; for the T202 cluster they are $(3.3, 0, 4.3)$ and $(4.2, 0, 11.6)$, with average squared distance 15.8. Using this split we can construct a clustering tree whose leaves are labelled with the mean vectors (Figure 5.9).

In this example we used categorical features for splitting and numerical features for distance calculations. Indeed, in all tree examples considered so far we have only used categorical features for splitting.[7] In practice, numerical features are frequently used for splitting: all we need to do is find a suitable threshold t so that feature F can be turned into a binary split with conditions $F \geq t$ and $F < t$. Finding the optimal split point is closely related to ☞*discretisation* of numerical features, a topic we will look at in detail in Chapter 10. For the moment, the following observations give some idea how we can learn a threshold on a numerical feature:

- ☞ Although in theory there are infinitely many possible thresholds, in practice we only need to consider values separating two examples that end up next to each other if we sort the training examples on increasing (or decreasing) value of the feature.
- ☞ We only consider consecutive examples of different class if our task is classification, whose target values are sufficiently different if our task is regression, or whose dissimilarity is sufficiently large if our task is clustering.
- ☞ Each potential threshold can be evaluated as if it were a distinct binary feature.

5.4 Tree models: Summary and further reading

Tree-based data structures are ubiquitous in computer science, and the situation is no different in machine learning. Tree models are concise, easy to interpret and learn, and can be applied to a wide range of tasks, including classification, ranking, probability estimation, regression and clustering. The tree-based classifier for human pose recognition in the Microsoft Kinect motion sensing device is described in Shotton *et al.* (2011).

- ☞ I introduced the feature tree as the common core for all these tree-based models, and the recursive GrowTree algorithm as a generic divide-and-conquer algorithm that can be adapted to each of these tasks by suitable choices for the functions that test whether a data set is sufficiently homogeneous, find a suitable label if it is, and find the best feature to split on if it isn't.

- ☞ Using a feature tree to predict class labels turns them into decision trees, the subject of Section 5.1. There are two classical accounts of decision trees in machine learning, which are very similar algorithmically but differ in details such as heuristics and pruning strategies. Quinlan's approach was to use entropy as impurity measure, and progressed from the ID3 algorithm (Quinlan, 1986), which

[7] Categorical features are features with a relatively small set of discrete values. Technically, they distinguish themselves from numerical features by not having a scale or an ordering. This is further explored in Chapter 10.

itself was inspired by Hunt, Marin and Stone (1966), to the sophisticated C4.5 system (Quinlan, 1993). The CART approach stands for 'classification and regression trees' and was developed by Breiman, Friedman, Olshen and Stone (1984); it uses the Gini index as impurity measure. The $\sqrt{\text{Gini}}$ impurity measure was introduced by Dietterich, Kearns and Mansour (1996), and is hence sometimes referred to as *DKM*. The geometric construction to find $\text{Imp}(\{D_1, D_2\})$ in Figure 5.2 (right) was also inspired by that paper.

☞ Employing the empirical distributions in the leaves of a feature tree in order to build rankers and probability estimators as described in Section 5.2 is a much more recent development (Ferri *et al.*, 2002; Provost and Domingos, 2003). Experimental results demonstrating that better probability estimates are obtained by disabling tree pruning and smoothing the empirical probabilities by means of the Laplace correction are presented in the latter paper and corroborated by Ferri *et al.* (2003). The extent to which decision tree splitting criteria are insensitive to unbalanced classes or misclassification costs was studied and explained by Drummond and Holte (2000) and Flach (2003). Of the three splitting criteria mentioned above, only $\sqrt{\text{Gini}}$ is insensitive to such class and cost imbalance.

☞ Tree models are grouping models that aim to minimise diversity in their leaves, where the appropriate notion of diversity depends on the task. Very often diversity can be interpreted as some kind of variance, an idea that already appeared in (Breiman *et al.*, 1984) and was revisited by Langley (1994), Kramer (1996) and Blockeel, De Raedt and Ramon (1998), among others. In Section 5.3 we saw how this idea can be used to learn regression and clustering trees (glossing over many important details, such as when we should stop splitting nodes).

It should be kept in mind that the increased expressivity of tree models compared with, say, conjunctive concepts means that we should safeguard ourselves against overfitting. Furthermore, the greedy divide-and-conquer algorithm has the disadvantage that small changes in the training data may lead to a different choice of the feature at the root of the tree, which will influence the choice of feature at subsequent splits. We will see in Chapter 11 how methods such as bagging can be applied to help reduce this kind of model variance.

CHAPTER 6

Rule models

RULE MODELS ARE the second major type of logical machine learning models. Generally speaking, they offer more flexibility than tree models: for instance, while decision tree branches are mutually exclusive, the potential overlap of rules may give additional information. This flexibility comes at a price, however: while it is very tempting to view a rule as a single, independent piece of information, this is often not adequate because of the way the rules are learned. Particularly in supervised learning, a rule model is more than just a set of rules: the specification of how the rules are to be combined to form predictions is a crucial part of the model.

There are essentially two approaches to supervised rule learning. One is inspired by decision tree learning: find a combination of literals – the *body* of the rule, which is what we previously called a concept – that covers a sufficiently homogeneous set of examples, and find a label to put in the *head* of the rule. The second approach goes in the opposite direction: first select a class you want to learn, and then find rule bodies that cover (large subsets of) the examples of that class. The first approach naturally leads to a model consisting of an ordered sequence of rules – a *rule list* – as will be discussed in Section 6.1. The second approach treats collections of rules as unordered *rule sets* and is the topic of Section 6.2. We shall see how these models differ in the way they handle rule overlap. The third section of the chapter covers discovery of subgroups and association rules.

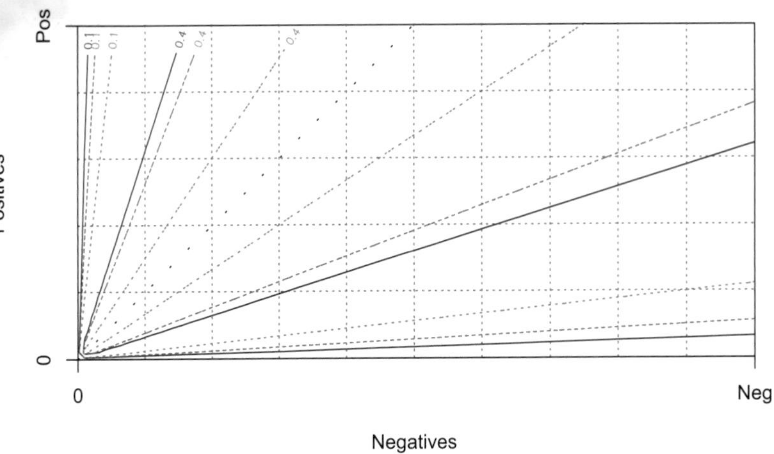

Figure 6.1. ROC isometrics for entropy (rescaled to have a maximum value of 1/2), Gini index and minority class. The grey dotted symmetry line is defined by $\dot{p} = 1/2$: each isometric has two parts, one above the symmetry line (where impurity decreases with increasing empirical probability $\dot{p}$) and its mirror image below the symmetry line (where impurity is proportional to $\dot{p}$). If these impurity measures are used as search heuristic, as they are in rule learning, only the shape of the isometrics matters but not the associated impurity values, and hence all three impurity measures are equivalent.

6.1 Learning ordered rule lists

The key idea of this kind of rule learning algorithm is to keep growing a conjunctive rule body by adding the literal that most improves its homogeneity. That is, we construct a downward path through the hypothesis space, of the kind discussed in Section 4.2, and we stop as soon as some homogeneity criterion is satisfied. It is natural to measure homogeneity in terms of purity, as we did with decision trees. You might think that adding a literal to a rule body is much the same as adding a binary split to a decision tree, as the added literal splits the instances covered by the original rule body in two groups: those instances for which the new literal is true, and those for which the new literal is false. However, one key difference is that in decision tree learning we are interested in the purity of *both* children, which is why we use the weighted average impurity as our search heuristic when constructing the tree. In rule learning, on the other hand, we are only interested in the purity of one of the children: the one in which the added literal is true. It follows that we can directly use any of the impurity measures we considered in the previous chapter (see Figure 5.2 on p.134 if you want to remind yourself which they are), without the need for averaging.

In fact, it doesn't even matter which of those impurity measures we use to guide the search, since they will all give the same result. To see this, notice that the impurity of a concept decreases with the empirical probability $\dot{p}$ (the relative frequency of covered positives) if $\dot{p} > 1/2$ and increases with $\dot{p}$ if $\dot{p} < 1/2$; see Figure 6.1. Whether this increase or decrease is linear or not matters if we are averaging the impurities of several concepts, as in decision tree learning, but not if we are evaluating single concepts. In other words, the difference between these impurity measures vanishes in rule learning, and we might as well take the proportion of the minority class $\min(\dot{p}, 1-\dot{p})$ (or, if you prefer, $1/2 - |\dot{p} - 1/2|$), which is arguably the simplest, as our impurity measure of choice in this section. Just keep in mind that if other authors use entropy or Gini index to compare the impurity of literals or rule bodies this will give the same results (not in terms of impurity values but in terms of which one is best).

We introduce the main algorithm for learning rule lists by means of an example.

Example 6.1 (Learning a rule list). Consider again our small dolphins data set with positive examples

p1: Length = 3 ∧ Gills = no ∧ Beak = yes ∧ Teeth = many
p2: Length = 4 ∧ Gills = no ∧ Beak = yes ∧ Teeth = many
p3: Length = 3 ∧ Gills = no ∧ Beak = yes ∧ Teeth = few
p4: Length = 5 ∧ Gills = no ∧ Beak = yes ∧ Teeth = many
p5: Length = 5 ∧ Gills = no ∧ Beak = yes ∧ Teeth = few

and negatives

n1: Length = 5 ∧ Gills = yes ∧ Beak = yes ∧ Teeth = many
n2: Length = 4 ∧ Gills = yes ∧ Beak = yes ∧ Teeth = many
n3: Length = 5 ∧ Gills = yes ∧ Beak = no ∧ Teeth = many
n4: Length = 4 ∧ Gills = yes ∧ Beak = no ∧ Teeth = many
n5: Length = 4 ∧ Gills = no ∧ Beak = yes ∧ Teeth = few

The nine possible literals are shown with their coverage counts in Figure 6.2 (top). Three of these are pure; in the impurity isometrics plot in Figure 6.2 (bottom) they end up on the x-axis and y-axis. One of the literals covers two positives and two negatives, and therefore has the same impurity as the overall data set; this literal ends up on the ascending diagonal in the coverage plot.

Although impurity in itself does not distinguish between pure literals (we will return to this point later), one could argue that Gills = yes is the best of the three as it covers more examples, so let's formulate our first rule as:

·**if** Gills = yes **then** Class = ⊖·

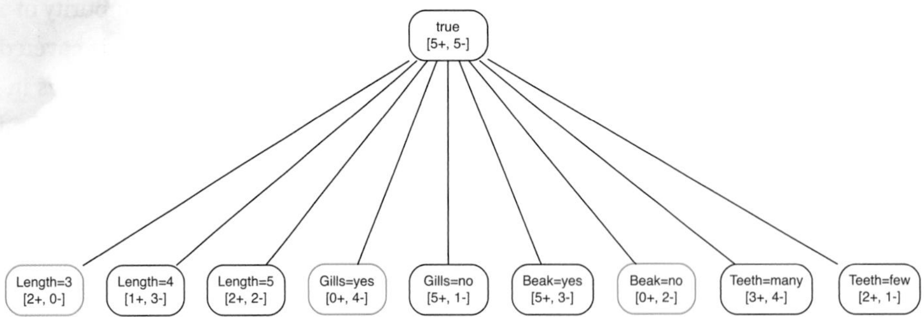

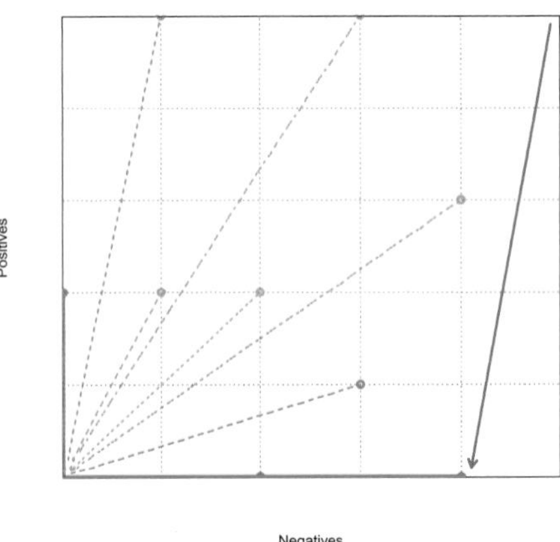

Figure 6.2. **(top)** All literals with their coverage counts on the data in Example 6.1. The ones in green (red) are pure for the positive (negative) class. **(bottom)** The nine literals plotted as points in coverage space, with their impurity values indicated by impurity isometrics (away from the ascending diagonal is better). Impurity values are colour-coded: towards green if $\dot{p} > 1/2$, towards red if $\dot{p} < 1/2$, and orange if $\dot{p} = 1/2$ (on a 45 degree isometric). The violet arrow indicates the selected literal, which excludes all five positives and one negative.

The corresponding coverage point is indicated by the arrow in Figure 6.2 (bottom). You can think of this arrow as the right-most bit of the coverage curve that results if we keep on following a downward path through the hypothesis space by adding literals. In this case we are not interested in following the path further because the concept we found is already pure (we shall see examples later where we have to add several literals before we hit one of the axes). One new thing that we haven't seen before is that this coverage curve lies below the diagonal – this is a consequence of the fact that we haven't fixed the class in advance, and therefore we are just as happy diving deep beneath the ascending

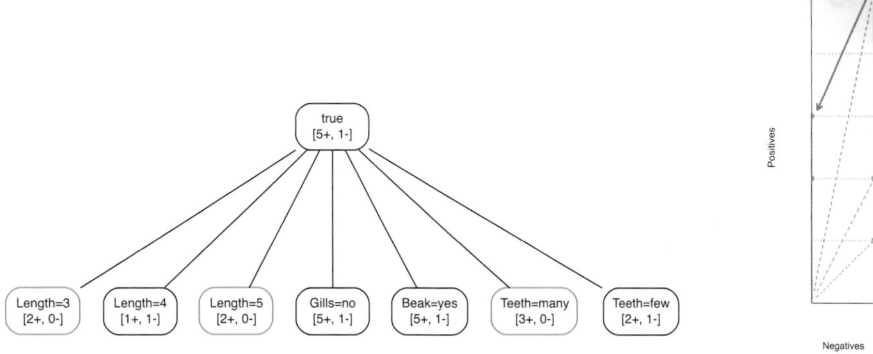

Figure 6.3. (left) Revised coverage counts after removing the four negative examples covered by the first rule found (literals not covering any examples are omitted). **(right)** We are now operating in the right-most 'slice' of Figure 6.2 on p.160.

diagonal as we would be flying high above it. Another way of thinking about this is that if we swap the labels this affects the heads but not the bodies of the learned rules.

Most rule learning algorithms now proceed as follows: they remove the examples covered by the rule just learned from consideration, and proceed with the remaining examples. This strategy is called *separate-and-conquer*, in analogy with the divide-and-conquer strategy of decision trees (the difference is that in separate-and-conquer we end up with one remaining subproblem rather than several as in divide-and-conquer). So we are left with five positive examples and one negative, and we again search for literals with minimum impurity. As is shown in Figure 6.3, we can understand this as working in a smaller coverage space. After going through the numbers, we find the next rule learned is

$$\cdot\textbf{if } \mathsf{Teeth} = \mathsf{many} \textbf{ then } \mathsf{Class} = \oplus\cdot$$

As I mentioned earlier, we should be cautious when interpreting this rule on its own, as against the original data set it actually covers more negatives than positives! In other words, the rule implicitly assumes that the previous rule doesn't 'fire'; in the final rule model we will precede it with 'else'.

We are now left with two positives and one negative (Figure 6.4). This time it makes sense to choose the rule that covers the single remaining negative, which is

$$\cdot\textbf{if } \mathsf{Length} = 4 \textbf{ then } \mathsf{Class} = \ominus\cdot$$

Since the remaining examples are all positive, we can invoke a *default rule* to cover those examples for which all other rules fail. Put together, the learned rule model is

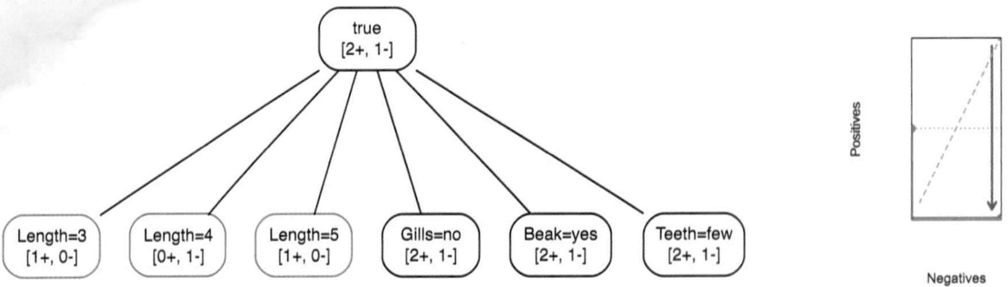

Figure 6.4. **(left)** The third rule covers the one remaining negative example, so that the remaining positives can be swept up by a default rule. **(right)** This will collapse the coverage space.

then as follows:

·**if** Gills = yes **then** Class = $\ominus$·
·**else if** Teeth = many **then** Class = $\oplus$·
·**else if** Length = 4 **then** Class = $\ominus$·
·**else** Class = $\oplus$·

Organising rules in a list is one way of dealing with overlaps among rules. For example, we know from the data that there are several examples with both Gills = yes and Teeth = many, but the rule list above tells us that the first rule takes precedence in such cases. Alternatively, we could rewrite the rule list such that the rules are mutually exclusive. This is useful because it means that we can use each rule without reference to the other rules, and also ignore their ordering. The only slight complication is that we need negated literals (or internal disjunction) for those features that have more than two values, such as 'Length':

·**if** Gills = yes **then** Class = $\ominus$·
·**if** Gills = no $\wedge$ Teeth = many **then** Class = $\oplus$·
·**if** Gills = no $\wedge$ Teeth = few $\wedge$ Length = 4 **then** Class = $\ominus$·
·**if** Gills = no $\wedge$ Teeth = few $\wedge$ Length $\neq$ 4 **then** Class = $\oplus$·

In this example we rely on the fact that this particular set of rules has a single literal in each rule – in the general case we would need non-conjunctive rule bodies. For example, consider the following rule list:

·**if** $P \wedge Q$ **then** Class = $\oplus$·
·**else if** R **then** Class = $\ominus$·

If we wanted to make these mutually exclusive the second rule would become

·**if** $\neg(P \wedge Q) \wedge R$ **then** Class = $\ominus$·

or equivalently,

·**if** $(\neg P \vee \neg Q) \wedge R$ **then** Class = $\ominus$·

Clearly, making rules mutually exclusive leads to less compact rules, which explains why rule lists are a powerful and popular format.

Algorithm 6.1 specifies the separate-and-conquer rule learning strategy in more detail. While there are still training examples left, the algorithm learns another rule and removes all examples covered by the rule from the data set. This algorithm, which is the basis for the majority of rule learning systems, is also called the *covering algorithm*. The algorithm for learning a single rule is given in Algorithm 6.2. Similar to decision trees, it uses the functions Homogeneous(D) and Label(D) to decide whether further specialisation is needed and what class to put in the head of the rule, respectively. It also employs a function BestLiteral(D, L) that selects the best literal to add to the rule from the candidates in L given data D; in our example above, this literal would be selected on purity.

Many variations on these algorithms exist in the literature. The conditions in the while-loops are often relaxed to other *stopping criteria* in order to deal with noisy data. For example, in Algorithm 6.1 we may want to stop when no class has more than a certain number of examples left, and include a default rule for the remaining examples. Likewise, in Algorithm 6.2 we may want to stop if D drops below a certain size.

Rule lists have much in common with decision trees. We can therefore analyse the construction of a rule list in the same way as we did in Figure 5.3 on p.137. This is shown for the running example in Figure 6.5. For example, adding the first rule is depicted in coverage space by splitting the ascending diagonal A into a horizontal segment B representing the new rule and another diagonal segment C representing the new coverage space. Adding the second rule causes segment C to split into vertical segment D (the second rule) and diagonal segment E (the third coverage space). Finally, E is split into a horizontal and a vertical segment (the third rule and the default rule, respectively). The remaining segments B, D, F and G are now all horizontal or vertical, signalling that the rules we learned are pure.

Algorithm 6.1: LearnRuleList(D) – learn an ordered list of rules.

Input : labelled training data D.
Output : rule list R.

$R \leftarrow \emptyset$;
while $D \neq \emptyset$ **do**
  $r \leftarrow$LearnRule(D) ; // LearnRule: see Algorithm 6.2
  append r to the end of R;
  $D \leftarrow D \setminus \{x \in D | x \text{ is covered by } r\}$;
end
return R

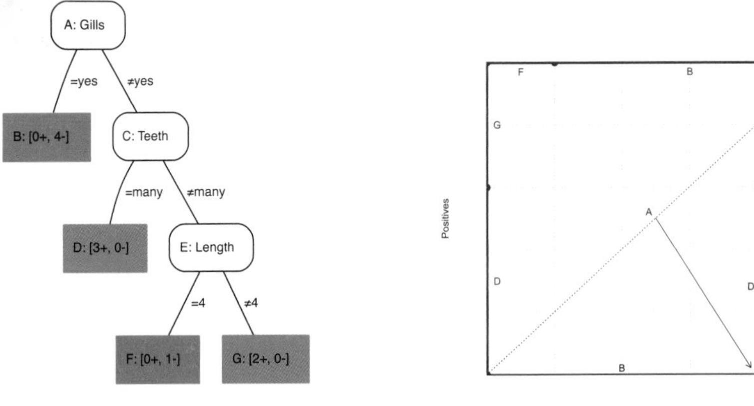

Figure 6.5. **(left)** A right-branching feature tree corresponding to a list of single-literal rules. **(right)** The construction of this feature tree depicted in coverage space. The leaves of the tree are either purely positive (in green) or purely negative (in red). Reordering these leaves on their empirical probability results in the blue coverage curve. As the rule list separates the classes this is a perfect coverage curve.

Rule lists for ranking and probability estimation

Turning a rule list into a ranker or probability estimator is as easy as it was for decision trees. Due to the covering algorithm we have access to the local class distributions

Algorithm 6.2: LearnRule(D) – learn a single rule.

Input : labelled training data D.
Output : rule r.

```
b ←true;
L ←set of available literals;
while not Homogeneous(D) do
    l ←BestLiteral(D, L) ;                    // e.g., highest purity; see text
    b ←b ∧ l;
    D ← {x ∈ D|x is covered by b};
    L ← L \ {l′ ∈ L|l′ uses same feature as l};
end
C ←Label(D) ;                                 // e.g., majority class
r ← ·if b then Class = C·;
return r
```

associated with each rule. We can therefore base our scores on the empirical probabilities. In the case of two classes we can rank the instances on decreasing empirical probability of the positive class, giving rise to a coverage curve with one segment for each rule. It is important to note that the ranking order of the rules is different from their order in the rule list, just as the ranking order of the leaves of a tree is different from their left-to-right order.

Example 6.2 (Rule lists as rankers). Consider the following two concepts:

(A)	Length = 4	p2	n2, n4–5
(B)	Beak = yes	p1–5	n1–2, n5

Indicated on the right is each concept's coverage over the whole training set. Using these concepts as rule bodies, we can construct the rule list AB:

·**if** Length = 4 **then** Class = ⊖·	[1+, 3−]
·**else if** Beak = yes **then** Class = ⊕·	[4+, 1−]
·**else** Class = ⊖·	[0+, 1−]

The coverage curve of this rule list is given in Figure 6.6. The first segment of the curve corresponds to all instances which are covered by B but not by A, which is why we use the set-theoretical notation B \ A. Notice that while this segment corresponds to the second rule in the rule list, it comes first in the coverage curve because it has the highest proportion of positives. The second coverage segment corresponds to rule A, and the third coverage segment denoted '-' corresponds to the default rule. This segment comes last, not because it represents the last rule, but because it happens to cover no positives.

We can also construct a rule list in the opposite order, BA:

·**if** Beak = yes **then** Class = ⊕·	[5+, 3−]
·**else if** Length = 4 **then** Class = ⊖·	[0+, 1−]
·**else** Class = ⊖·	[0+, 1−]

The coverage curve of this rule list is also depicted in Figure 6.6. This time, the first segment corresponds to the first segment in the rule list (B), and the second and third segment are tied between rule A (after the instances covered by B are taken away: A \ B) and the default rule.

Which of these rule lists is a better ranker? We can see that AB makes fewer ranking errors than BA (4.5 vs. 7.5), and thus has better AUC (0.82 vs. 0.70). We also see that,

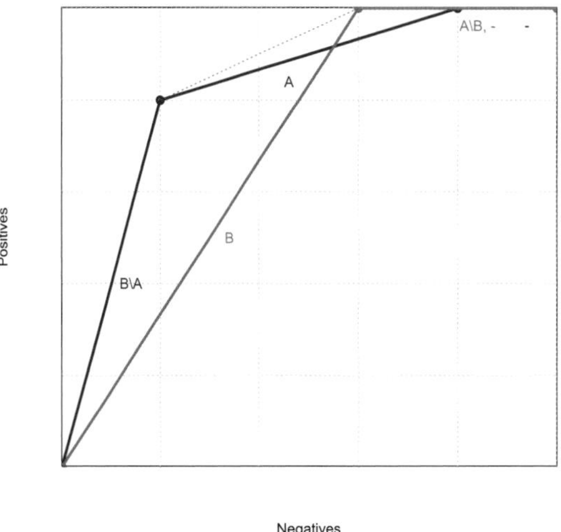

Figure 6.6. Coverage curves of two rule lists consisting of the rules from Example 6.2, in different order (AB in blue and BA in violet). B \ A corresponds to the coverage of rule B once the coverage of rule A is taken away, and '-' denotes the default rule. Neither curve dominates the other, and thus each has operating conditions under which it is superior. The dotted segment in red connecting the two curves corresponds to the overlap of the two rules A ∧ B, which is not accessible by either rule list.

if accuracy is our performance criterion, AB would be optimal, achieving 0.80 accuracy (*tpr* = 0.80 and *tnr* = 0.80) where BA only manages 0.70 (*tpr* = 1 and *tnr* = 0.40). However, if performance on the positives is 3 times as important as performance on the negatives, then BA's optimal operating point outperforms AB's. Hence, each rule list contains information not present in the other, and so neither is uniformly better.

The main reason for this is that the segment A ∧ B – the overlap of the two rules – is not accessible by either rule list. In Figure 6.6 this is indicated by the dotted segment connecting the segment B from rule list BA and the segment B \ A from rule list AB. It follows that this segment contains exactly those examples that are in B but not in B \ A, hence in A ∧ B. In order to access the rule overlap, we need to either combine the two rule lists or go beyond the power of rule lists. This will be investigated further at the end of the next section.

There are thus several connections between rule lists and decision trees. Furthermore, *rule lists are similar to decision trees in that the empirical probabilities associated with each rule yield convex ROC and coverage curves on the training data.* We have access to those empirical probabilities because of the coverage algorithm, which removes all training instances covered by one rule before learning the next (Algorithm 6.1). As a result, rule lists produce probabilities that are well-calibrated on the training set. Some rule learning algorithms in the literature reorder the rule list after all rules have been constructed. In this case, convexity cannot be guaranteed unless we re-evaluate the coverage of each rule in the reordered rule list.

6.2 Learning unordered rule sets

We next consider the alternative approach to rule learning, where rules are learned for one class at a time. This means we can further simplify our search heuristic: rather than minimising $\min(\dot{p}, 1-\dot{p})$, we can maximise $\dot{p}$, the empirical probability of the class we are learning. This search heuristic is conventionally referred to by its 'evaluation measure name' *precision* (see Table 2.3 on p.57).

Example 6.3 (Learning a rule set for one class). We continue the dolphin example. Figure 6.7 shows that the first rule learned for the positive class is

·**if** Length = 3 **then** Class = ⊕·

The two examples covered by this rule are removed, and a new rule is learned. We now encounter a new situation, as none of the candidates is pure (Figure 6.8). We thus start a second-level search, from which the following pure rule emerges:

·**if** Gills = no ∧ Length = 5 **then** Class = ⊕·

To cover the remaining positive, we again need a rule with two conditions (Figure 6.9):

·**if** Gills = no ∧ Teeth = many **then** Class = ⊕·

Notice that, even though these rules are overlapping, their overlap only covers positive examples (since each of them is pure) and so there is no need to organise them in an if-then-else list.

We now have a rule set for the positive class. With two classes this might be considered sufficient, as we can classify everything that isn't covered by the positive rules as negative. However, this might introduce a bias towards the negative class as all difficult cases we're unsure about get automatically classified as negative. So let's learn some rules for the negative class. By the same procedure as in Example 6.3 we find the following rules (you may want to check this): ·**if** Gills = yes **then** Class = ⊖· first, followed by ·**if** Length = 4 ∧ Teeth = few **then** Class = ⊖·. The final rule set with rules for

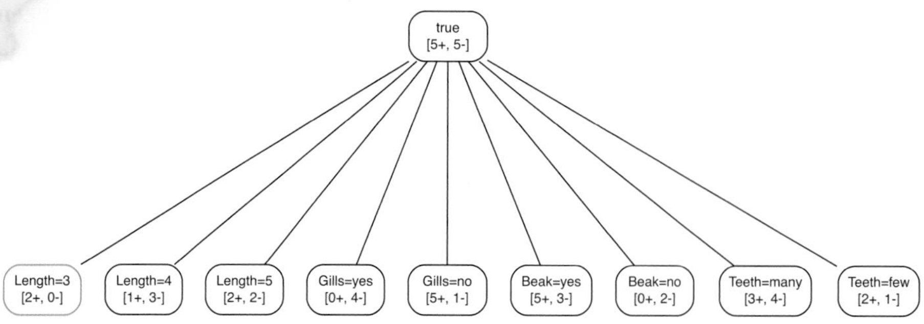

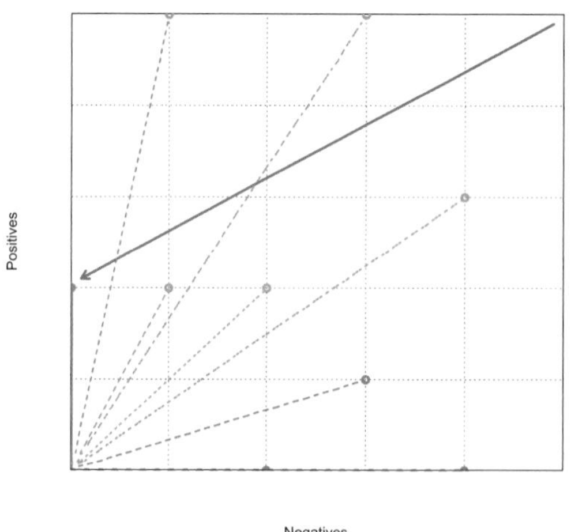

Figure 6.7. (top) The first rule is learned for the positive class. **(bottom)** Precision isometrics look identical to impurity isometrics (Figure 6.2); however, the difference is that precision is lowest on the x-axis and highest on the y-axis, while purity is lowest on the ascending diagonal and highest on both the x-axis and the y-axis.

both classes is therefore

(R1) ·**if** Length = 3 **then** Class = ⊕·
(R2) ·**if** Gills = no ∧ Length = 5 **then** Class = ⊕·
(R3) ·**if** Gills = no ∧ Teeth = many **then** Class = ⊕·
(R4) ·**if** Gills = yes **then** Class = ⊖·
(R5) ·**if** Length = 4 ∧ Teeth = few **then** Class = ⊖·

The algorithm for learning a rule set is given in Algorithm 6.3. The main differences

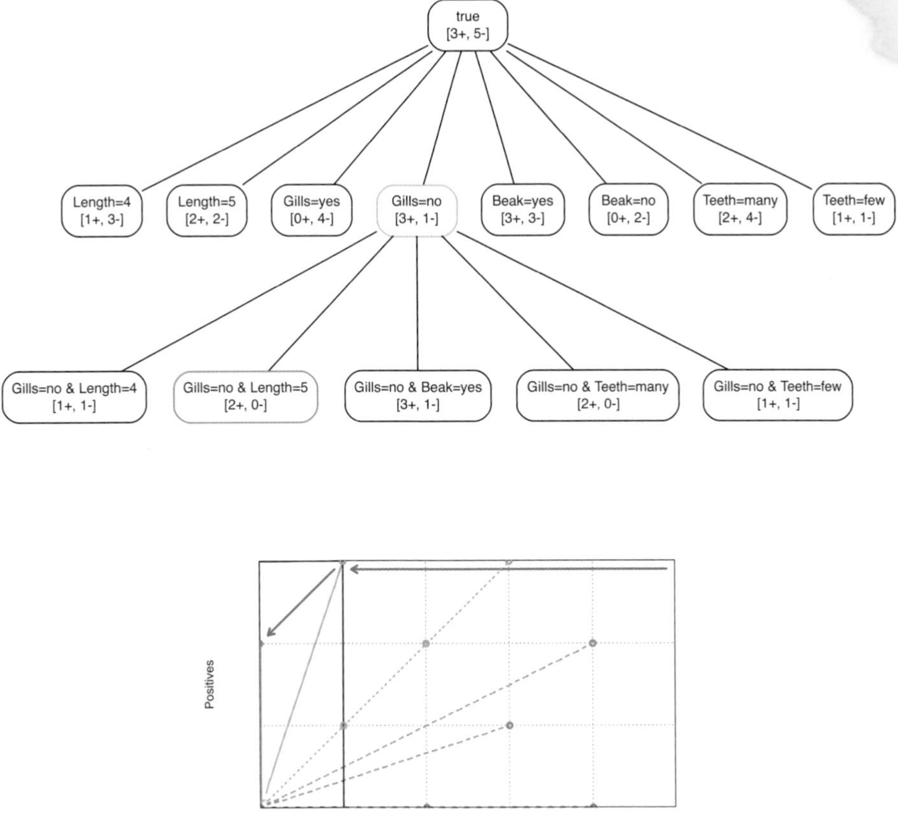

Figure 6.8. (top) The second rule needs two literals: we use maximum precision to select both. **(bottom)** The coverage space is smaller because the two positives covered by the first rule are removed. The blue box on the left indicates an even smaller coverage space in which the search for the second literal is carried out, after the condition Gills = no filters out four negatives. Inside the blue box precision isometrics overlap with those in the outer box (this is not necessarily the case with search heuristics other than precision).

with ☞*LearnRuleList* (Algorithm 6.1 on p.163) is that we now iterate over each class in turn, and furthermore that only covered examples for the class that we are currently learning are removed after a rule is found. The reason for this second change is that rule sets are not executed in any particular order, and so covered negatives are not filtered out by other rules. Algorithm 6.4 gives the algorithm for learning a single rule for a particular class, which is very similar to ☞*LearnRule* (Algorithm 6.2 on p.164) except (*i*) the best literal is now chosen with regard to the class to be learned, C_i; and(*ii*) the head of the rule is always labelled with C_i. An interesting variation that is sometimes

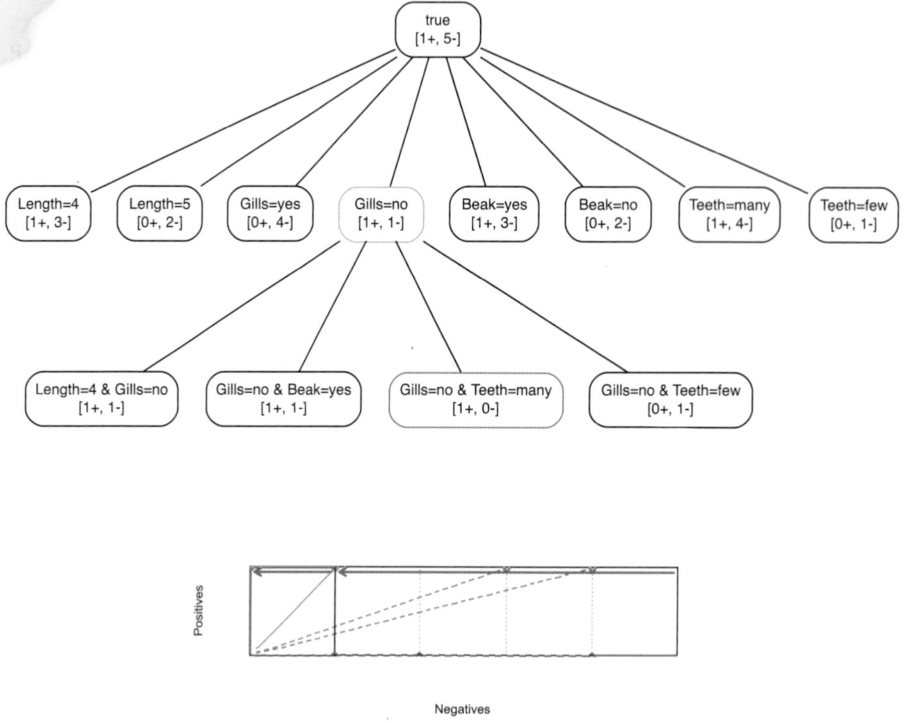

Figure 6.9. **(top)** The third and final rule again needs two literals. **(bottom)** The first literal excludes four negatives, the second excludes the one remaining negative.

encountered in the literature is to initialise the set of available literals L to those occurring in a given *seed example* belonging to the class to be learned: the advantage is that this cuts back the search space, but a possible disadvantage is that the choice of seed example may be sub-optimal.

One issue with using precision as search heuristic is that it tends to focus a bit too much on finding pure rules, thereby occasionally missing near-pure rules that can be specialised into a more general pure rule. Consider Figure 6.10 (top): precision favours the rule ·**if** Length = 3 **then** Class = ⊕·, even though the near-pure literal Gills = no leads to the pure rule ·**if** Gills = no ∧ Teeth = many **then** Class = ⊕·. A convenient way to deal with this 'myopia' of precision is the Laplace correction, which ensures that [5+,1−] is 'corrected' to [6+,2−] and thus considered to be of the same quality as [2+,0−] aka [3+,1−] (Figure 6.10 (bottom)). Another way to reduce myopia further and break such ties is to employ a *beam search*: rather than greedily going for the best candidate, we maintain a fixed number of alternate candidates. In the example, a small beam size would already allow us to find the more general rule:

- ☞ the first beam would include the candidate bodies Length = 3 and Gills = no;
- ☞ we then add all possible specialisations of non-pure elements of the beam;
- ☞ of the remaining set – i.e., elements of the original beam plus all added specialisations – we keep only the best few, preferring the ones that were already on the beam in case of ties, as they are shorter;
- ☞ we stop when all beam elements are pure, and we select the best one.

Now that we have seen how to learn a rule set, we turn to the question of how to employ a rule set model as a classifier. Suppose we encounter a new instance, say Length = 3 $\wedge$ Gills = yes $\wedge$ Beak = yes $\wedge$ Teeth = many. With the rule list on p.162 the

---

Algorithm 6.3: LearnRuleSet(D) – learn an unordered set of rules.

Input : labelled training data D.
Output : rule set R.

$R \leftarrow \emptyset$;
for every class C_i **do**
    $D_i \leftarrow D$;
    while D_i contains examples of class C_i **do**
        $r \leftarrow$ LearnRuleForClass(D_i, C_i) ; // LearnRuleForClass: see Algorithm 6.4
        $R \leftarrow R \cup \{r\}$;
        $D_i \leftarrow D_i \setminus \{x \in C_i | x$ is covered by $r\}$; // remove only positives
    end
end
return R

Algorithm 6.4: LearnRuleForClass(D, C_i) – learn a single rule for a given class.

Input : labelled training data D; class C_i.
Output : rule r.

$b \leftarrow$ true;
$L \leftarrow$ set of available literals ; // can be initialised by seed example
while not Homogeneous(D) **do**
    $l \leftarrow$ BestLiteral(D, L, C_i) ; // e.g. maximising precision on class C_i
    $b \leftarrow b \wedge l$;
    $D \leftarrow \{x \in D | x$ is covered by $b\}$;
    $L \leftarrow L \setminus \{l' \in L | l'$ uses same feature as $l\}$;
end
$r \leftarrow$ ·**if** b **then** Class = C_i·;
return r

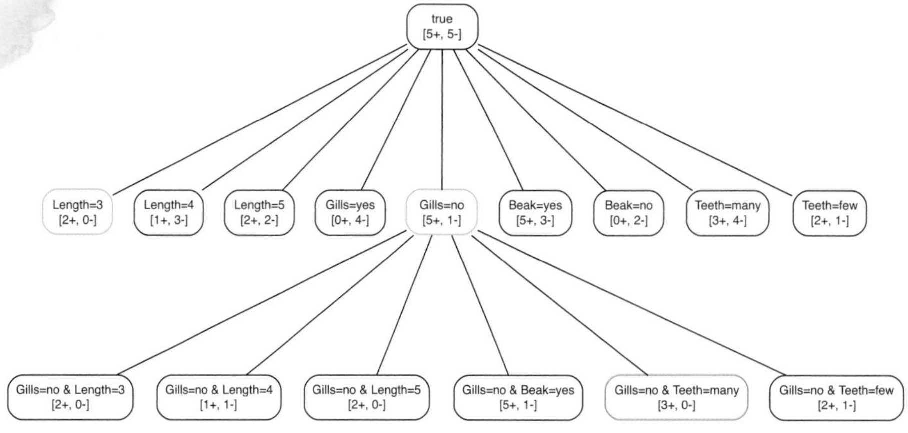

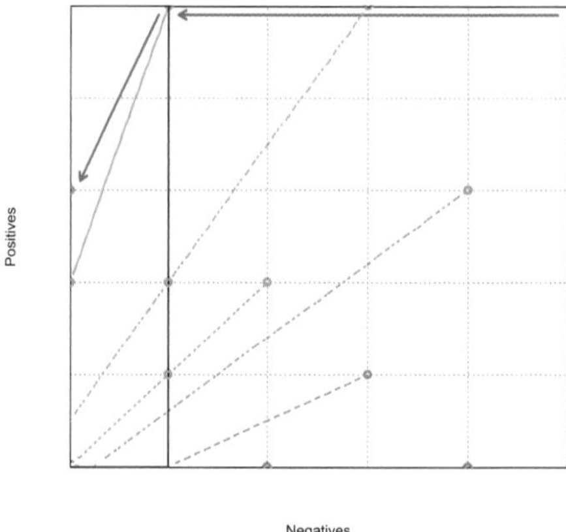

Figure 6.10. **(top)** Using Laplace-corrected precision allows learning a better rule in the first iteration. **(bottom)** Laplace correction adds one positive and one negative pseudo-count, which means that the isometrics now rotate around $(-1,-1)$ in coverage space, resulting in a preference for more general rules.

first rule would fire and hence the instance is classified as negative. With the rule set on p.168 we have that both R1 and R4 fire and make contradictory predictions. How can we resolve this? In order to answer that question, it is easier to consider a more general question first: how do we use a rule set for ranking and probability estimation?

Rule sets for ranking and probability estimation

In the general case, for a rule set consisting of r rules there are up to 2^r different ways in which rules can overlap, and hence 2^r instance space segments. Even though many of these segments will be empty because rules are mutually exclusive, in general we will have more instance space segments than rules. As a consequence, we have to estimate the coverage of some of these segments.

Example 6.4 (Rule sets as rankers). Consider the following rule set (the first two rules were also used in Example 6.2):

(A) ·**if** Length = 4 **then** Class = ⊖· [1+,3−]
(B) ·**if** Beak = yes **then** Class = ⊕· [5+,3−]
(C) ·**if** Length = 5 **then** Class = ⊖· [2+,2−]

The figures on the right indicate coverage of each rule over the whole training set. For instances covered by single rules we can use these coverage counts to calculate probability estimates: e.g., an instance covered only by rule A would receive probability $\hat{p}(\mathsf{A}) = 1/4 = 0.25$, and similarly $\hat{p}(\mathsf{B}) = 5/8 = 0.63$ and $\hat{p}(\mathsf{C}) = 2/4 = 0.50$.

Clearly A and C are mutually exclusive, so the only overlaps we need to take into account are AB and BC. A simple trick that is often applied is to average the coverage of the rules involved: for example, the coverage of AB is estimated as [3+,3−] yielding $\hat{p}(\mathsf{AB}) = 3/6 = 0.50$. Similarly, $\hat{p}(\mathsf{BC}) = 3.5/6 = 0.58$. The corresponding ranking is thus B – BC – [AB, C] – A, resulting in the orange training set coverage curve in Figure 6.11.

Let us now compare this rule set with the following rule list ABC:

·**if** Length = 4 **then** Class = ⊖· [1+,3−]
·**else if** Beak = yes **then** Class = ⊕· [4+,1−]
·**else if** Length = 5 **then** Class = ⊖· [0+,1−]

The coverage curve of this rule list is indicated in Figure 6.11 as the blue line. We see that the rule set outperforms the rule list, by virtue of being able to distinguish between examples covered by B only and those covered by both B and C.

While in this example the rule set outperformed the rule list, this cannot be guaranteed in general. Due to the fact that the coverage counts of some segments have to be estimated, a rule set coverage curve is not guaranteed to be convex even on the

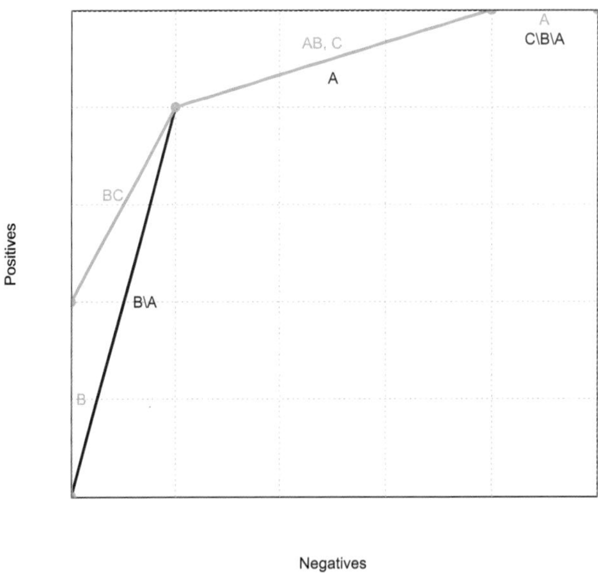

Figure 6.11. Coverage curves of the rule set in Example 6.4 (in orange) and the rule list ABC (in blue). The rule set partitions the instance space in smaller segments, which in this case lead to better ranking performance.

training set. For example, suppose that rule C also covers p1, then this won't affect the performance of the rule list (since p1 is already covered by B), but it would break the tie between AB and C in favour of the latter and thus introduce a concavity.

If we want to turn such a ranker into a classifier, we have to find the best operating point on the coverage curve. Assuming accuracy as our performance criterion, the point ($fpr = 0.2, tpr = 0.8$) is optimal, which can be achieved by classifying instances with $\hat{p} > 0.5$ as positive and the rest as negative. If such calibration of the decision threshold is problematic (for example, in the case of more than two classes), we can simply assign the class with the highest average coverage, making a random choice in case of a tie.

A closer look at rule overlap

We have seen that rule lists always give convex training set coverage curves, but that there is no globally optimal ordering of a given set of rules. The main reason is that rule lists don't give us access to the overlap of two rules $\mathsf{A} \wedge \mathsf{B}$: we either have access to $\mathsf{A} = (\mathsf{A} \wedge \mathsf{B}) \vee (\mathsf{A} \wedge \neg\mathsf{B})$ if the rule order is AB, or $\mathsf{B} = (\mathsf{A} \wedge \mathsf{B}) \vee (\neg\mathsf{A} \wedge \mathsf{B})$ if it is BA. More generally, a rule list of r rules results in only r instance space segments (or $r+1$

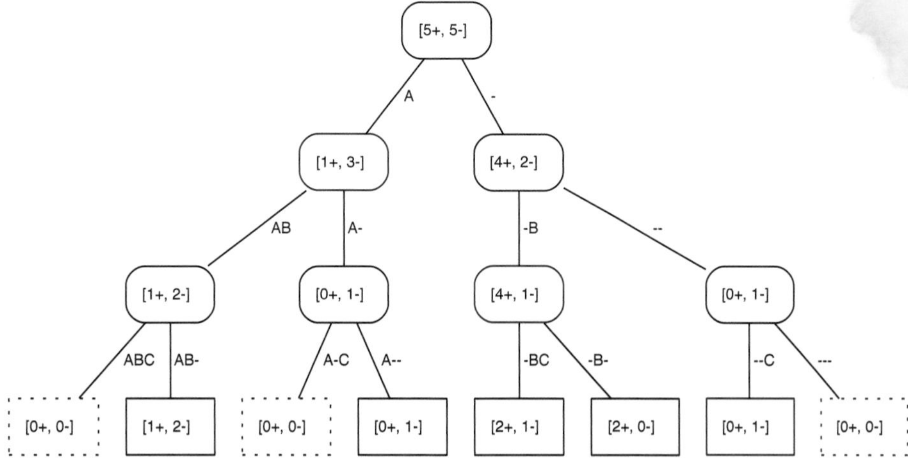

Figure 6.12. A rule tree constructed from the rules in Example 6.5. Nodes are labelled with their coverage (dotted leaves have empty coverage), and branch labels indicate particular areas in the instance space (e.g., A-C denotes $A \wedge \neg B \wedge C$). The blue nodes are the instance space segments corresponding to the rule list ABC: the rule tree has better performance because it is able to split them further.

in case we add a default rule). This means that we cannot take advantage of most of the 2^r ways in which rules can overlap. Rule sets, on the other hand, can potentially give access to such overlaps, but the need for the coverage counts of overlapping segments to be estimated means that we have to sacrifice convexity. In order to understand this further, we introduce in this section the concept of a *rule tree*: a complete feature tree using the rules as features.

Example 6.5 (Rule tree). From the rules in Example 6.4 we can construct the rule tree in Figure 6.12. The use of a tree rather than a list allows further splitting of the segments of the rule list. For example, the node labelled A is further split into AB ($A \wedge B$) and A- ($A \wedge \neg B$). As the latter is pure, we obtain a better coverage curve (the red line in Figure 6.13).

As we see in this example, the rule tree coverage curve dominates the rule list coverage curve. This is true in general: there is no other information regarding rule overlap than that contained in a rule tree, and any given rule list will usually convey only part of that information. Conversely, we may wonder whether any operating point on the rule tree curve is reachable by a particular rule list. The answer to this is negative, as a

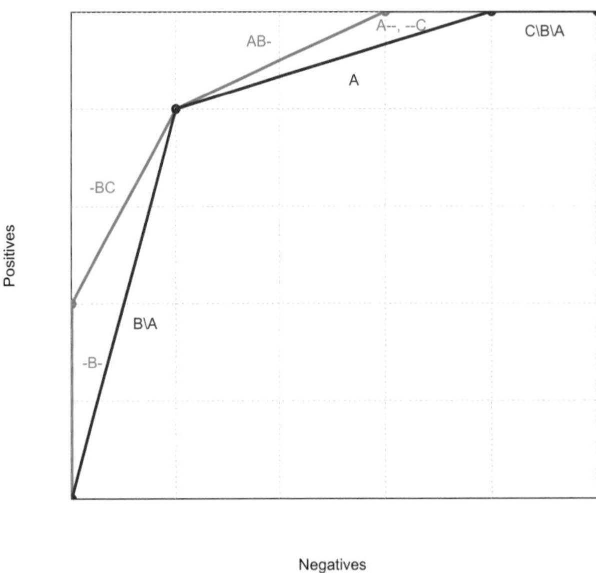

Figure 6.13. The blue line is the coverage curve of the rule list ABC in Example 6.4. This curve is dominated by the red coverage curve, corresponding to the rule tree in Figure 6.12. The rule tree also improves upon the rule set (orange curve in Figure 6.11), as it has access to exact coverage counts in all segments and thus recognises that AB- goes before - -C.

simple counter-example shows (Figure 6.14).

In summary, of the three rule models considered, only rule trees can unlock the full potential of rule overlap as they have the capacity to represent all 2^r overlap areas of r rules and give access to exact coverage counts for each area. Rule lists also convey exact coverage counts but for fewer segments; rule sets distinguish the same segments as rule trees but have to estimate coverage counts for the overlap areas. On the other hand, rule trees are expensive as their size is exponential in the number of rules. Another disadvantage is that the coverage counts have to be obtained in a separate step, after the rules have been learned. I have included rule trees here mainly for conceptual reasons: to gain a better understanding of the more common rule list and rule set models.

6.3 Descriptive rule learning

As we have seen, the rule format lends itself naturally to predictive models, built from rules with the target variable in the head. It is not hard to come up with ways to extend

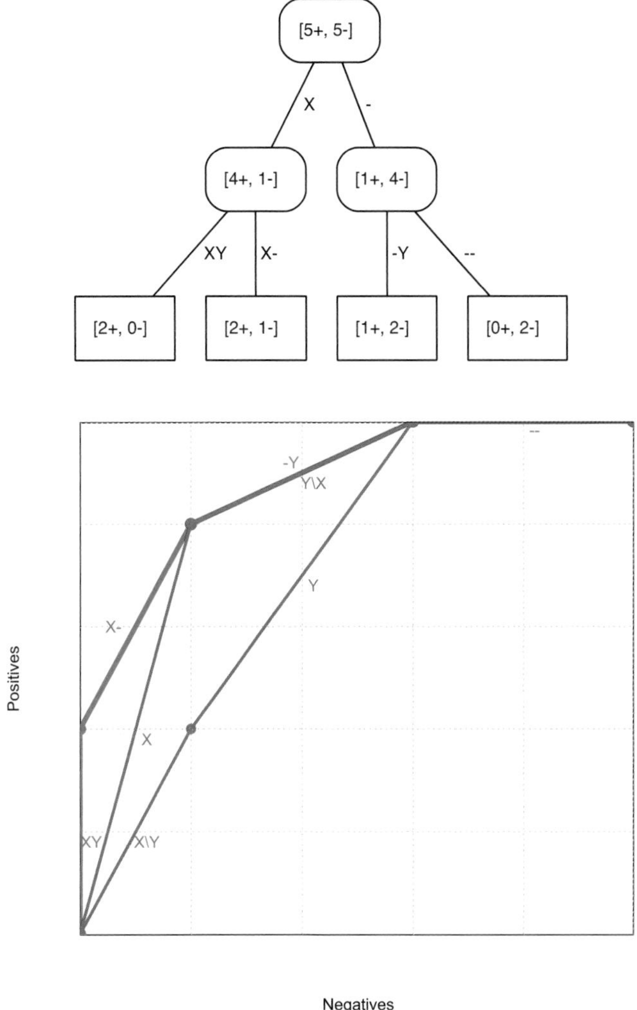

Figure 6.14. **(top)** A rule tree built on two rules X and Y. **(bottom)** The rule tree coverage curve strictly dominates the convex hull of the two rule list curves. This means that there is an operating point [2+,0−] that cannot be achieved by either rule list.

rule models to regression and clustering tasks, in a similar way to what we did for tree models at the end of Chapter 5, but I will not elaborate on that here. Instead I will show how the rule format can equally easily be used to build descriptive models. As explained in Section 1.1, descriptive models can be learned in either a supervised or an unsupervised way. As an example of the supervised setting we will discuss how to adapt the given rule learning algorithms to subgroup discovery. For unsupervised learning of descriptive rule models we will take a look at frequent item sets and association rule discovery.

Rule learning for subgroup discovery

When learning classification models it is natural to look for rules that identify pure subsets of the training examples: i.e., sets of examples that are all of the same class and that all satisfy the same conjunctive concept. However, as we have seen in Section 3.3, sometimes we are less interested in predicting a class and more interested in finding interesting patterns. We defined subgroups as mappings $\hat{g}: \mathscr{X} \rightarrow \{\text{true}, \text{false}\}$ – or alternatively, subsets of the instance space – that are learned from a set of labelled examples $(x_i, l(x_i))$, where $l: \mathscr{X} \rightarrow \mathscr{C}$ is the true labelling function. A good subgroup is one whose class distribution is significantly different from the overall population. This is by definition true for pure subgroups, but these are not the only interesting ones. For instance, one could argue that the complement of a subgroup is as interesting as the subgroup itself: in our dolphin example, the concept Gills = yes, which covers four negatives and no positives, could be considered as interesting as its complement Gills = no, which covers one negative and all positives. This means that we need to move away from impurity-based evaluation measures.

Like concepts, subgroups can be plotted as points in coverage space, with the positives in the subgroup on the y-axis and the negatives on the x-axis. Any subgroup plotted on the ascending diagonal has the same proportion of positives as the overall population; these are the least interesting subgroups as they have the same statistics as random samples. Subgroups above (below) the diagonal have a larger (smaller) proportion of positives than the population. So one way to measure the quality of subgroups is to take one of the heuristics used for rule learning and measure the absolute deviation from the default value on the diagonal. For example, the precision of any subgroup on the diagonal is equal to the proportion of positives, so this leads to $|prec - pos|$ as one possible quality measure. For reasons already discussed it is often better to use Laplace-corrected precision $prec^{\mathrm{L}}$, leading to the alternative measure $|prec^{\mathrm{L}} - pos|$. As can be seen in Figure 6.15 (left), the introduction of pseudo-counts means that [5+,1−] is evaluated as [6+,2−] and is thus as interesting as the pure concept [2+,0−] which is evaluated as [3+,1−].

However, this doesn't quite put complementary subgroups on an equal footing, as [5+,1−] is still considered to be of lower quality than [0+,4−]. In order to achieve this complementarity we need an evaluation measure whose isometrics all run parallel to the ascending diagonal. As it turns out, we have already seen such an evaluation measure in Section 2.1, where we called it *average recall* (see, e.g., Figure 2.4 on p.61). Notice that subgroups on the diagonal always have average recall 0.5, regardless of the class distribution. So, a good subgroup evaluation measure is $|avg\text{-}rec - 0.5|$. Average recall can be written as $(1 + tpr - fpr)/2$, and thus $|avg\text{-}rec - 0.5| = |tpr - fpr|/2$. It is sometimes desirable not to take the absolute value, so that the sign of the difference tells us whether we are above or below the diagonal. A related subgroup evaluation measure is

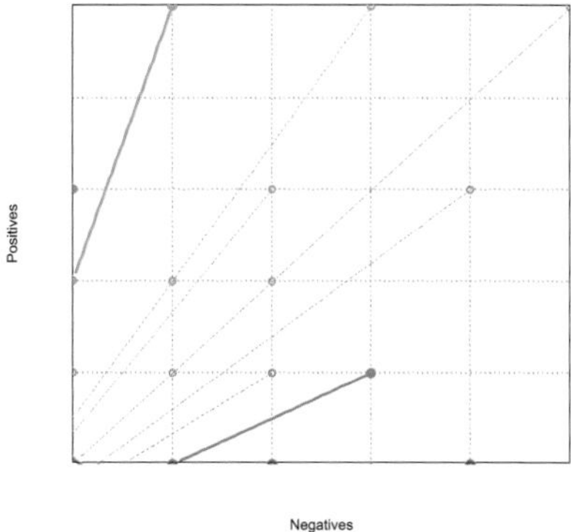

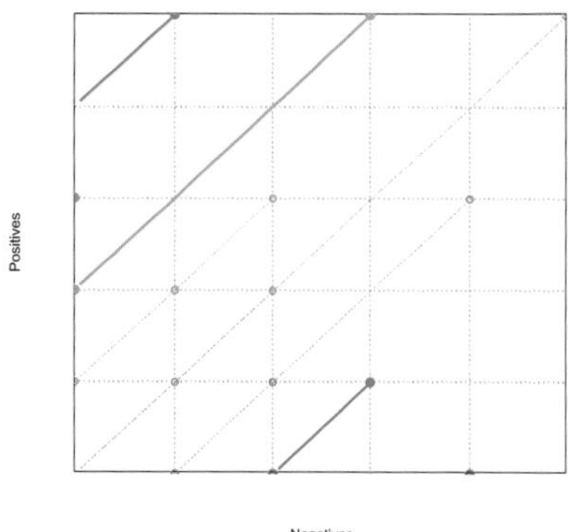

Figure 6.15. **(left)** Subgroups and their isometrics according to Laplace-corrected precision. The solid, outermost isometrics indicate the best subgroups. **(right)** The ranking changes if we order the subgroups on average recall. For example, [5+,1−] is now better than [3+,0−] and as good as [0+,4−].

Subgroup	*Coverage*	$prec^{L}$	*Rank*	*avg-rec*	*Rank*
Gills = yes	[0+,4−]	0.17	1	0.10	1–2
Gills = no ∧ Teeth = many	[3+,0−]	0.80	2	0.80	3
Gills = no	[5+,1−]	0.75	3–9	0.90	1–2
Beak = no	[0+,2−]	0.25	3–9	0.30	4–11
Gills = yes ∧ Beak = yes	[0+,2−]	0.25	3–9	0.30	4–11
Length = 3	[2+,0−]	0.75	3–9	0.70	4–11
Length = 4 ∧ Gills = yes	[0+,2−]	0.25	3–9	0.30	4–11
Length = 5 ∧ Gills = no	[2+,0−]	0.75	3–9	0.70	4–11
Length = 5 ∧ Gills = yes	[0+,2−]	0.25	3–9	0.30	4–11
Length = 4	[1+,3−]	0.33	10	0.30	4–11
Beak = yes	[5+,3−]	0.60	11	0.70	4–11

Table 6.1. Detailed evaluation of the top subgroups. Using Laplace-corrected precision we can evaluate the quality of a subgroup as $|prec^{L} - pos|$. Alternatively, we can use average recall to define the quality of a subgroup as $|avg\text{-}rec - 0.5|$. These two quality measures result in slightly different rankings.

weighted relative accuracy, which can be written as $pos \cdot neg(tpr - fpr)$.

As can be seen by comparing the two isometrics plots in Figure 6.15, using average recall rather than Laplace-corrected precision has an effect on the ranking of some of the subgroups. Detailed calculations are given in Table 6.1.

Subgroup	*Coverage*	*avg-rec*	*Wgtd coverage*	*W-avg-rec*	*Rank*
Gills = yes	[0+,4−]	0.10	[0+,3−]	0.07	1–2
Gills = no	[5+,1−]	0.90	[4.5+,0.5−]	0.93	1–2
Gills = no ∧ Teeth = many	[3+,0−]	0.80	[2.5+,0−]	0.78	3
Length = 5 ∧ Gills = yes	[0+,2−]	0.30	[0+,2−]	0.21	4
Length = 3	[2+,0−]	0.70	[2+,0−]	0.72	5–6
Length = 5 ∧ Gills = no	[2+,0−]	0.70	[2+,0−]	0.72	5–6
Beak = no	[0+,2−]	0.30	[0+,1.5−]	0.29	7–9
Gills = yes ∧ Beak = yes	[0+,2−]	0.30	[0+,1.5−]	0.29	7–9
Beak = yes	[5+,3−]	0.70	[4.5+,2−]	0.71	7–9
Length = 4	[1+,3−]	0.30	[0.5+,1.5−]	0.34	10
Length = 4 ∧ Gills = yes	[0+,2−]	0.30	[0+,1−]	0.36	11

Table 6.2. The 'Wgtd coverage' column shows how the weighted coverage of the subgroups is affected if the weights of the examples covered by Length = 4 are reduced to 1/2. 'W-*avg-rec*' shows how how the *avg-rec* numbers as calculated in Table 6.1 are affected by the weighting, leading to further differentiation between subgroups that were previously considered equivalent.

Example 6.6 (Comparing Laplace-corrected precision and average recall). Table 6.1 ranks ten subgroups in the dolphin example in terms of Laplace-corrected precision and average recall. One difference is that Gills = no ∧ Teeth = many with coverage [3+,0−] is better than Gills = no with coverage [5+,1−] in terms of Laplace-corrected precision, but worse in terms of average recall, as the latter ranks it equally with its complement Gills = yes.

The second difference between classification rule learning and subgroup discovery is that in the latter case we are naturally interested in overlapping rules, whereas the standard covering algorithm doesn't encourage this as examples already covered are removed from the training set. One way of dealing with this is by assigning weights to examples that are decreased every time an example is covered by a newly learned rule. A scheme that works well in practice is to initialise the example weights to 1 and halve them every time a new rule covers the example. Search heuristics are then evaluated in terms of the cumulative weight of covered examples, rather than just their number.

Example 6.7 (The effect of weighted covering). Suppose the first subgroup

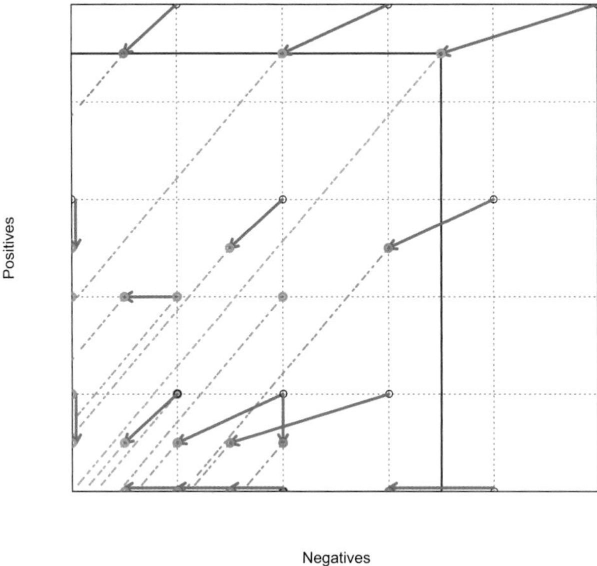

Figure 6.16. Visualisation of the effect of weighted covering. If the first subgroup found is Length = 4, then this halves the weight of one positive and three negatives, shrinking the coverage space to the blue box. The arrows indicate how this affects the weighted coverage of other subgroups, depending on which of the reduced-weight examples they cover.

found is Length = 4, reducing the weight of the one positive and three negatives covered by it to 1/2. Detailed calculations of how this affects the weighted coverage of subgroups are given in Table 6.2. We can see how the coverage space shrinks to the blue box in Figure 6.16. It also affects the weighted coverage of the subgroups overlapping with Length = 4, as indicated by the arrows. Some subgroups end up closer to the diagonal and hence lose importance: for instance, Length = 4 itself, which moves from [3+,1−] to [1.5+,0.5−]. Others move away from the diagonal and hence gain importance: for example Length = 5 ∧ Gills = yes at [0+,2−].

The *weighted covering* algorithm is given in Algorithm 6.5. Notice that this algorithm can be applied to discover subgroups over $k > 2$ classes, as long as the evaluation measure used to learn single rules can handle more than two classes. This is clearly the case for average recall used in our examples. Other possibilities include measures derived from the Chi-squared test and mutual information-based measures.

Association rule mining

I will now introduce a new kind of rule that can be learned in a wholly unsupervised manner and is prominent in data mining applications. Suppose we observed eight customers who each bought one or more of apples, beer, crisps and nappies:

Transaction	*Items*
1	nappies
2	beer, crisps
3	apples, nappies
4	beer, crisps, nappies
5	apples
6	apples, beer, crisps, nappies
7	apples, crisps
8	crisps

Each *transaction* in this table involves a set of *items*; conversely, for each item we can list the transactions in which it was involved: transactions 1, 3, 4 and 6 for nappies, transactions 3, 5, 6 and 7 for apples, and so on. We can also do this for sets of items: e.g., beer and crisps were bought together in transactions 2, 4 and 6; we say that item set {beer, crisps} *covers* transaction set $\{2,4,6\}$. There are 16 of such item sets (including the empty set, which covers all transactions); using the subset relation between transaction sets as partial order, they form a lattice (Figure 6.17).

Let us call the number of transactions covered by an item set I its *support*, denoted $\text{Supp}(I)$ (sometimes called frequency). We are interested in *frequent item sets*, which exceed a given support threshold f_0. Support is *monotonic*: when moving down a path in the item set lattice it can never increase. This means that the set of frequent item

Algorithm 6.5: WeightedCovering(D) – learn overlapping rules by weighting examples.

Input : labelled training data D with instance weights initialised to 1.
Output : rule list R.

```
R ← ∅;
while some examples in D have weight 1 do
    r ← LearnRule(D) ;                          // LearnRule: see Algorithm 6.2
    append r to the end of R;
    decrease the weights of examples covered by r;
end
return R
```

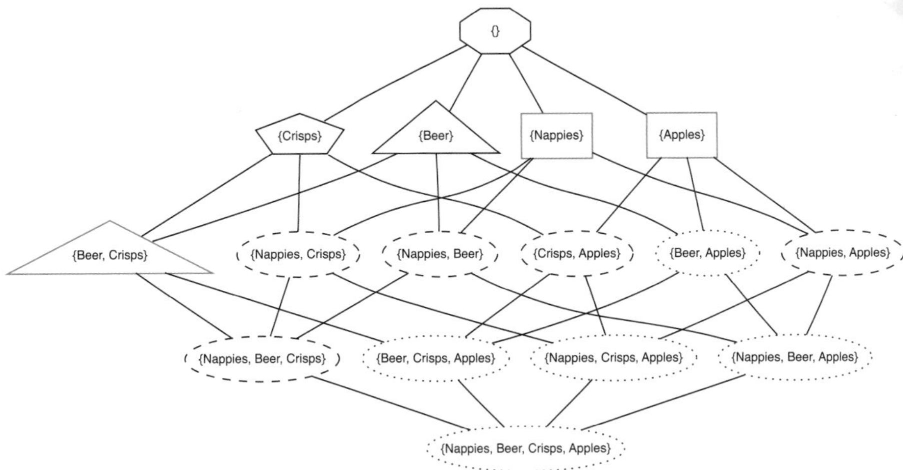

Figure 6.17. An item set lattice. Item sets in dotted ovals cover a single transaction; in dashed ovals, two transactions; in triangles, three transactions; and in polygons with n sides, n transactions. The maximal item sets with support 3 or more are indicated in green.

sets is *convex* and is fully determined by its lower boundary of largest item sets: in the example these maximal[1] frequent item sets are, for $f_0 = 3$: {apples}, {beer, crisps} and {nappies}. So, at least three transactions involved apples; at least three involved nappies; at least three involved both beer and crisps; and any other combination of items was bought less often.

Because of the monotonicity property of item set support, frequent item sets can be found by a simple enumerative breadth-first or level-wise search algorithm (Algorithm 6.6). The algorithm maintains a priority queue, initially holding only the empty item set which covers all transactions. Taking the next candidate item set I off the priority queue, it generates all its possible extensions (supersets containing one more item, the downward neighbours in the item set lattice), and adds them to the priority queue if they exceed the support threshold (at the back, to achieve the desired breadth-first behaviour). If at least one of I's extensions is frequent, I is not maximal and can be discarded; otherwise I is added to the set of maximal frequent item sets found.

We can speed up calculations by restricting attention to *closed item sets*. These are completely analogous to the ☞*closed concepts* discussed at the end of Section 4.2: a closed item set contains all items that are involved in every transaction it covers. For example, {beer, crisps} covers transactions 2, 4 and 6; the only items involved in each of those transactions are beer and crisps, and so the item set is closed. However, {beer} is not closed, as it covers the same transactions, hence its closure is {beer, crisps}. If two item sets that are connected in the lattice have the same coverage, the smaller item set

[1] 'Maximal' here means that no superset is frequent.

cannot be closed. The lattice of closed item sets is shown in Figure 6.18. Notice that maximal frequent item sets are necessarily closed (as extending them will decrease their coverage below the support threshold, otherwise they aren't maximal), and are thus unaffected by this restriction; but it does allow a more efficient search.

So what is the point of these frequent item sets? The answer is that we will use them to build *association rules*, which are rules of the form ·**if** B **then** H· where both body B and head H are item sets that frequently appear in transactions together. Pick any edge in Figure 6.17, say the edge between {beer} and {nappies, beer}. We know that the support of the former is 3 and of the latter, 2: that is, three transactions involve beer and two of those involve nappies as well. We say that the *confidence* of the association rule ·**if** beer **then** nappies· is 2/3. Likewise, the edge between {nappies} and {nappies, beer} demonstrates that the confidence of the rule ·**if** nappies **then** beer· is 2/4. There are also rules with confidence 1, such as ·**if** beer **then** crisps·; and rules with empty bodies, such as ·**if** true **then** crisps·, which has confidence 5/8 (i.e., five out of eight transactions involve crisps).

But we only want to construct association rules that involve frequent items. The rule ·**if** beer ∧ apples **then** crisps· has confidence 1, but there is only one transaction involving all three and so this rule is not strongly supported by the data. So we first use Algorithm 6.6 to mine for frequent item sets; we then select bodies B and heads H from

Algorithm 6.6: FrequentItems(D, f_0) – find all maximal item sets exceeding a given support threshold.

Input : data $D \subseteq \mathscr{X}$; support threshold f_0.
Output : set of maximal frequent item sets M.

```
M ← ∅;
initialise priority queue Q to contain the empty item set;
while Q is not empty do
    I ← next item set deleted from front of Q;
    max ← true ;                          // flag to indicate whether I is maximal
    for each possible extension I' of I do
        if Supp(I') ≥ f0 then
            max ← false ;                 // frequent extension found, so I is not maximal
            add I' to back of Q;
        end
    end
    if max = true then M ← M ∪ {I};
end
return M
```

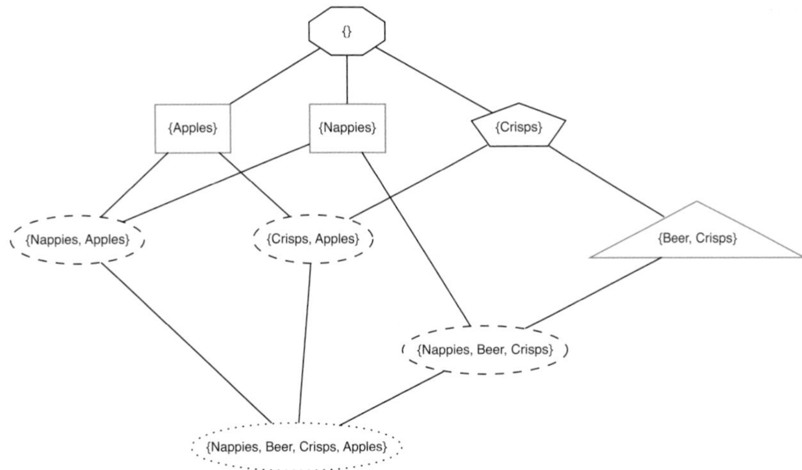

Figure 6.18. Closed item set lattice corresponding to the item sets in Figure 6.17. This lattice has the property that no two adjacent item sets have the same coverage.

the frequent sets m, discarding rules whose confidence is below a given confidence threshold. Algorithm 6.7 gives the basic algorithm. Notice that we are free to discard some of the items in the maximal frequent sets (i.e., $H \cup B$ may be smaller than m), because any subset of a frequent item set is frequent as well.

A run of the algorithm with support threshold 3 and confidence threshold 0.6 gives the following association rules:

·**if** beer **then** crisps· support 3, confidence 3/3

·**if** crisps **then** beer· support 3, confidence 3/5

Algorithm 6.7: AssociationRules(D, f_0, c_0) – find all association rules exceeding given support and confidence thresholds.

Input : data $D \subseteq \mathscr{X}$; support threshold f_0; confidence threshold c_0.
Output : set of association rules R.

$R \leftarrow \emptyset$;
$M \leftarrow$ FrequentItems(D, f_0) ; // FrequentItems: see Algorithm 6.6
for each $m \in M$ **do**
  for each $H \subseteq m$ and $B \subseteq m$ such that $H \cap B = \emptyset$ **do**
    if $\text{Supp}(B \cup H)/\text{Supp}(B) \geq c_0$ **then** $R \leftarrow R \cup \{$·**if** B **then** H·$\}$
  end
end
return R

·**if** true **then** crisps· support 5, confidence 5/8

Association rule mining often includes a *post-processing* stage in which superfluous rules are filtered out, e.g., special cases which don't have higher confidence than the general case. One quantity that is often used in post-processing is *lift*, defined as

$$\text{Lift}(\cdot\textbf{if } B \textbf{ then } H\cdot) = \frac{n \cdot \text{Supp}(B \cup H)}{\text{Supp}(B) \cdot \text{Supp}(H)}$$

where n is the number of transactions. For example, for the the first two association rules above we would have lifts of $\frac{8\cdot 3}{3\cdot 5} = 1.6$, as $\text{Lift}(\cdot\textbf{if } B \textbf{ then } H\cdot) = \text{Lift}(\cdot\textbf{if } H \textbf{ then } B\cdot)$. For the third rule we have $\text{Lift}(\cdot\textbf{if true then crisps}\cdot) = \frac{8\cdot 5}{8\cdot 5} = 1$. This holds for any rule with $B = \emptyset$, as

$$\text{Lift}(\cdot\textbf{if } \emptyset \textbf{ then } H\cdot) = \frac{n \cdot \text{Supp}(\emptyset \cup H)}{\text{Supp}(\emptyset) \cdot \text{Supp}(H)} = \frac{n \cdot \text{Supp}(H)}{n \cdot \text{Supp}(H)} = 1$$

More generally, a lift of 1 means that $\text{Supp}(B \cup H)$ is entirely determined by the *marginal* frequencies $\text{Supp}(B)$ and $\text{Supp}(H)$ and is not the result of any meaningful interaction between B and H. Only association rules with lift larger than 1 are of interest.

Quantities like confidence and lift can also be understood from a probabilistic context. Let $\text{Supp}(I)/n$ be an estimate of the probability $p(I)$ that a transaction involves all items in I, then confidence estimates the conditional probability $p(H|B)$. In a classification context, where H denotes the actual class and B the predicted class, this would be called precision (see Table 2.3 on p.57), and in this chapter we have already used it as a search heuristic in rule learning. Lift then measures whether the events 'a random transaction involves all items in B' and 'a random transaction involves all items in H' are statistically independent.

It is worth noting that the heads of association rules can contain multiple items. For instance, suppose we are interested in the rule ·**if** nappies **then** beer·, which has support 2 and confidence 2/4. However, {nappies, beer} is not a closed item set: its closure is {nappies, beer, crisps}. So ·**if** nappies **then** beer· is actually a special case of ·**if** nappies **then** beer ∧ crisps·, which has the same support and confidence but involves only closed item sets.

We can also apply frequent item set analysis to our dolphin data set, if we treat each literal Feature = Value as an item, keeping in mind that different values of the same feature are mutually exclusive. Item sets then correspond to concepts, transactions to instances, and the extension of a concept is exactly the set of transactions covered by an item set. The item set lattice is therefore the same as what we previously called the hypothesis space, with the proviso that we are not considering negative examples in this scenario (Figure 6.19). The reduction to closed concepts/item sets is shown in Figure 6.20. We can see that, for instance, the rule

·**if** Gills = no ∧ Beak = yes **then** Teeth = many·

has support 3 and confidence 3/5 (but you may want to check whether it has any lift!).

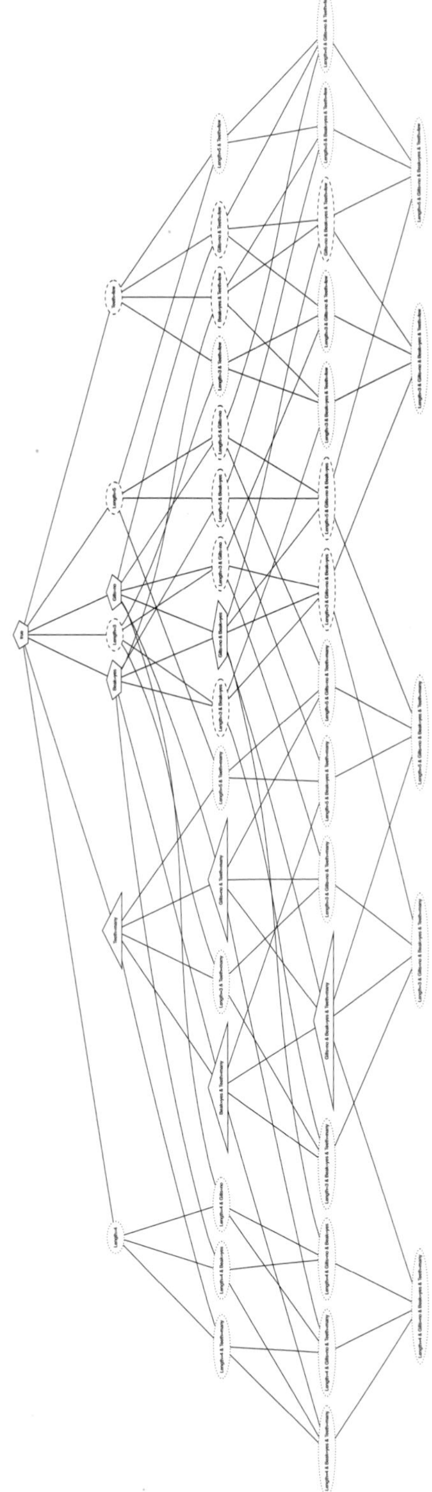

Figure 6.19. The item set lattice corresponding to the positive examples of the dolphin example in Example 4.4 on p.115. Each 'item' is a literal Feature = Value; each feature can occur at most once in an item set. The resulting structure is exactly the same as what was called the hypothesis space in Chapter 4.

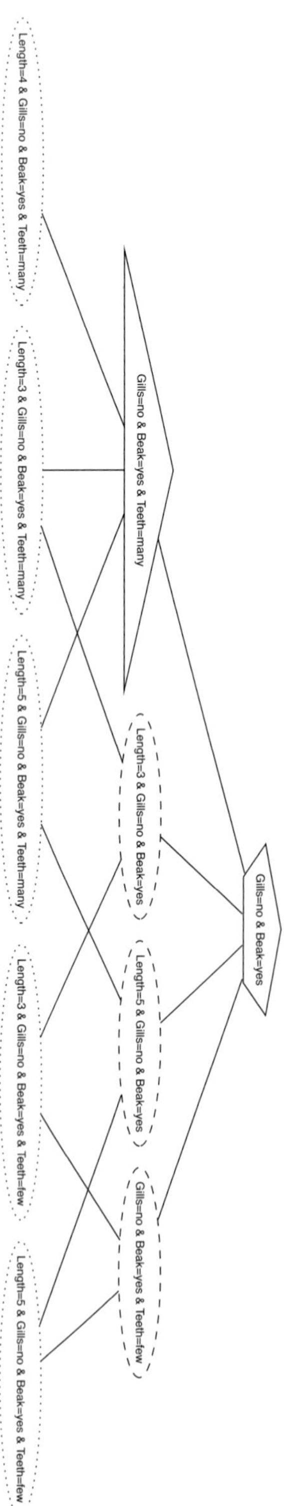

Figure 6.20. Closed item set lattice corresponding to the item sets in Figure 6.19.

6.4 First-order rule learning

In Section 4.3 we briefly touched upon using first-order logic as a concept language. The main difference is that literals are no longer simple feature-value pairs but can have a much richer structure. All rule learning approaches covered in this chapter have been upgraded in the literature to learn rules expressed in first-order logic. In this section we will take a brief look at how this might work.

Many approaches to learning in first-order logic are based on the logic programming language Prolog, and learning first-order rules is often called *inductive logic programming* (*ILP*). Logically speaking, Prolog rules are *Horn clauses* with a single literal in the head – we encountered Horn clauses before in Section 4.3. Prolog notation is slightly different from first-order logic notation. So, instead of

$$\forall x: \mathrm{BodyPart}(x, \mathrm{PairOf}(\mathrm{Gill})) \rightarrow \mathrm{Fish}(x)$$

we write

```
fish(X):-bodyPart(X,pairOf(gills)).
```

The main differences are:

- rules are written back-to-front in 'head-if-body' fashion;
- variables start with a capital letter; constants, predicates and function symbols (called *functors* in Prolog) start with lower-case;
- variables are implicitly universally quantified.

With regard to the third point, it is worth pointing out the difference between variables occurring in both head and body, and variables occurring in the body only. Consider the following Prolog clause:

```
someAnimal(X):-bodyPart(X,pairOf(Y)).
```

There are two equivalent ways of writing this rule in first-order logic:

$$\forall x: \forall y: \mathrm{BodyPart}(x, \mathrm{PairOf}(y)) \rightarrow \mathrm{SomeAnimal}(x)$$

$$\forall x: \left(\exists y: \mathrm{BodyPart}(x, \mathrm{PairOf}(y))\right) \rightarrow \mathrm{SomeAnimal}(x)$$

The first logical statement reads 'for all x and y, if x has a pair of ys as body parts then x is some kind of animal' whereas the second states 'for all x, if there exists a y such that x has a pair of ys as body parts then x is some kind of animal'. Crucially, in the second form the scope of the existential quantifier is the if-part of the rule, whereas universal quantifiers always range over the whole clause. Variables occurring in the body but not in the head of Prolog clauses are called *local variables*; they are the source of much additional complexity in learning first-order rules over propositional rules.

If we want to learn an ordered list of Prolog clauses, we can reuse ☞*LearnRuleList* (Algorithm 6.1 on p.163) in its entirety and most of ☞*LearnRule* (Algorithm 6.2 on p.164). What needs adjusting is the choice of literal to be added to the clause. Possible literals can be enumerated by listing the predicates, functors and constants that can be used to build a new literal. For example, if we have a binary predicate `bodyPart`, a unary functor `pairOf` and constants `gill` and `tail`, then we can build a variety of literals such as

```
bodyPart(X,Y)
bodyPart(X,gill)
bodyPart(X,tail)
bodyPart(X,pairOf(Y))
bodyPart(X,pairOf(gill))
bodyPart(X,pairOf(tail))
bodyPart(X,pairOf(pairOf(Y)))
bodyPart(X,pairOf(pairOf(gill)))
bodyPart(X,pairOf(pairOf(tail)))
```

and so on. Notice that the presence of functors means that our hypothesis language becomes infinite! Also, I have only listed literals that somehow 'made sense': there are many less sensible possibilities, such as `bodyPart(pairOf(gill),tail)` or `bodyPart(X,X)`, to name but a few. Although Prolog is an untyped language, many of these unwanted literals can be excluded by adding type information (in logic programming and ILP often done through 'mode declarations' which also specify particular input–output patterns of a predicate's arguments).

It is clear from these examples that there can be relationships between literals, and therefore between the clauses that contain them. For example, consider the following three clauses:

```
fish(X):-bodyPart(X,Y).
fish(X):-bodyPart(X,pairOf(Z)).
fish(X):-bodyPart(X,pairOf(gill)).
```

The first clause defines everything with some body part to be a fish. The second clause specialises this to everything with a pair of unspecified body parts. The third specialises this to everything with a pair of gills. A reasonable search strategy would be to try hypotheses in this order, and only move on to a specialised version if the more general clause is ruled out by negative examples. This is what in fact happens in top–down ILP systems. A simple trick is to represent substitution of terms for variables explicitly by adding equality literals, so the above sequence of clauses becomes

```
fish(X):-bodyPart(X,Y).
fish(X):-bodyPart(X,Y),Y=pairOf(Z).
fish(X):-bodyPart(X,Y),Y=pairOf(Z),Z=gill.
```

As an alternative for enumerating the literals to be considered for inclusion in a clause body we can derive them from the data in a bottom–up fashion. Suppose we have the following information about a dolphin:

```
bodyPart(dolphin42,tail).
bodyPart(dolphin42,pairOf(gills)).
bodyPart(dolphin42,pairOf(eyes)).
```

and this about a tunafish:

```
bodyPart(tuna123,pairOf(gills)).
```

By forming the LGG of each of the literals in the first example with the literal from the second example we obtain each of the generalised literals considered earlier.

This short discussion of rule learning in first-order logic has left out many important details and may therefore give an overly simplified view of the problem. While the problem of learning Prolog clauses can be stated quite succinctly, naive approaches are computationally intractable and 'the devil is in the detail'. The basic approaches sketched here can be extended to include background knowledge, which then affects the generality ordering of the hypothesis space. For example, if our background knowledge includes the clause

```
bodyPart(X,scales):-bodyPart(X,pairOf(gill)).
```

then the first of the following two hypotheses is more general than the second:

```
fish(X):-bodyPart(X,scales).
fish(X):-bodyPart(X,pairOf(gill)).
```

However, this cannot be determined purely by syntactic means and requires logical inference.

Another intriguing possibility offered by first-order logic is the possibility of learning recursive clauses. For instance, part of our hypothesis could be the following clause:

```
fish(X):-relatedSpecies(X,Y),fish(Y).
```

This blurs the distinction between background predicates that can be used in the body of hypotheses and target predicates that are to be learned, and introduces computational challenges such as non-termination. However, this doesn't mean that it cannot be done. Related techniques can be used to learn multiple, interrelated predicates at once, and to invent new background predicates that are completely unobserved.

6.5 Rule models: Summary and further reading

In a decision tree, a branch from root to a leaf can be interpreted as a conjunctive classification rule. Rule models generalise this by being more flexible about the way in which several rules are combined into a model. The typical rule learning algorithm is the covering algorithm, which iteratively learns one rule and then removes the examples covered by that rule. This approach was pioneered by Michalski (1975) with his AQ system, which became highly developed over three decades (Wojtusiak *et al.*, 2006). General overviews are provided by Fürnkranz (1999, 2010) and Fürnkranz, Gamberger and Lavrač (2012). Coverage plots were first used by Fürnkranz and Flach (2005) to achieve a better understanding of rule learning algorithms and demonstrate the close relationship (and in many cases, equivalence) of commonly used search heuristics.

☞ Rules can overlap and thus we need a strategy to resolve potential conflicts between rules. One such strategy is to combine the rules in an ordered rule list, which was the subject of Section 6.1. Rivest (1987) compares this approach with decision trees, calling the rule-based model a decision list (I prefer the term 'rule list' as it doesn't carry a suggestion that the elements of the list are single literals). Well-known rule list learners include CN2 (Clark and Niblett, 1989) and Ripper (Cohen, 1995), the latter being particularly effective at avoiding overfitting through incremental reduced-error pruning (Fürnkranz and Widmer, 1994). Also notable is the Opus system (Webb, 1995), which distinguishes itself by performing a complete search through the space of all possible rules.

☞ In Section 6.2 we looked at unordered rule sets as an alternative to ordered rule lists. The covering algorithm is adapted to learn rules for a single class at a time, and to remove only covered examples of the class currently under consideration. CN2 can be run in unordered mode to learn rule sets (Clark and Boswell, 1991). Conceptually, both rule lists and rule sets are special cases of rule trees, which distinguish all possible Boolean combinations of a given set of rules. This allows us to see that rule lists lead to fewer instance space segments than rule sets (over the set of rules); on the other hand, rule list coverage curves can be made convex on the training set, whereas rule sets need to estimate the class distribution in the regions where rules overlap.

☞ Rule models can be used for descriptive tasks, and in Section 6.3 we considered rule learning for subgroup discovery. The weighted covering algorithm was introduced as an adaption of CN2 by Lavrač, Kavšek, Flach and Todorovski (2004); Abudawood and Flach (2009) generalise this to more than two classes. Algorithm 6.7 learns association rules and is adapted from the well-known Apriori algorithm due to Agrawal, Mannila, Srikant, Toivonen and Verkamo (1996). There is a very wide choice of alternative algorithms, surveyed by Han *et al.* (2007). Association rules can also be used to build effective classifiers (Liu *et al.*, 1998; Li *et al.*, 2001).

☞ The topic of first-order rule learning briefly considered in Section 6.4 has been studied for the last 40 years and has a very rich history. De Raedt (2008) provides an excellent recent introduction, and an overview of recent advances and open problems is provided by Muggleton *et al.* (2012). Flach (1994) gives an introduction to Prolog and also provides high-level implementations of some of the key techniques in inductive logic programming. The FOIL system by Quinlan (1990) implements a top–down learning algorithm similar to the one discussed here. The bottom–up technique was pioneered in the Golem system (Muggleton and Feng, 1990) and further refined in Progol (Muggleton, 1995) and in Aleph (Srinivasan, 2007), two of the most widely used ILP systems. First-order rules can also be learned in an unsupervised fashion, for example by Tertius which learns first-order clauses (not necessarily Horn) (Flach and Lachiche, 2001) and Warmr which learns first-order association rules (King *et al.*, 2001). Higher-order logic provides more powerful data types that can be highly beneficial in learning (Lloyd, 2003). A more recent development is the combination of probabilistic modelling with first-order logic, leading to the area of statistical relational learning (De Raedt and Kersting, 2010).

CHAPTER 7

Linear models

AFTER DEALING WITH logical models in the preceding chapters we now move on to a quite different kind of model. The models in this chapter and the next are defined in terms of the geometry of instance space. Geometric models most often assume that instances are described by d real-valued features, and thus $\mathscr{X} = \mathbb{R}^d$. For example, we could describe objects by their position on a map in terms of longitude and latitude ($d = 2$), or in the real world by longitude, latitude and altitude ($d = 3$). While most real-valued features are not intrinsically geometric – think of a person's age or an object's temperature – we can still imagine them being plotted in a d-dimensional Cartesian coordinate system. We can then use geometric concepts such as lines and planes to impose structure on this space, for instance in order to build a classification model. Alternatively, we can use the geometric notion of distance to represent similarity, on the basis that if two points are close together they have similar feature values and thus can be expected to behave similarly with respect to the property of interest. Such distance-based models are the subject of the next chapter. In this chapter we will look at models that can be understood in terms of lines and planes, commonly called *linear models*.

Linearity plays a fundamental role in mathematics and related disciplines, and the mathematics of linear models is well-understood (see Background 7.1 for the most important concepts). In machine learning, linear models are of particular interest because of their simplicity (remember our rule of thumb 'everything should be made as

---

If x_1 and x_2 are two scalars or vectors of the same dimension and α and β are arbitrary scalars, then $\alpha x_1 + \beta x_2$ is called a *linear combination* of x_1 and x_2. If f is a *linear function* of x, then

$$f(\alpha x_1 + \beta x_2) = \alpha f(x_1) + \beta f(x_2)$$

In words, the function value of a linear combination of some inputs is a linear combination of their function values. As a special case, if $\beta = 1 - \alpha$ we are taking a weighted average of x_1 and x_2, and the linearity of f then means that the function value of the weighted average is the weighted average of the function values.

Linear functions take particular forms, depending on the domain and codomain of f. If x and $f(x)$ are scalars, it follows that f is of the form $f(x) = a + bx$ for some constants a and b; a is called the *intercept* and b the *slope*. If $\mathbf{x} = (x_1, \ldots, x_d)$ is a vector and $f(\mathbf{x})$ is a scalar, then f is of the form

$$f(\mathbf{x}) = a + b_1 x_1 + \ldots + b_d x_d = a + \mathbf{b} \cdot \mathbf{x} \tag{7.1}$$

with $\mathbf{b} = (b_1, \ldots, b_d)$. The equation $f(\mathbf{x}) = 0$ defines a plane in $\mathbb{R}^d$ perpendicular to the *normal vector* $\mathbf{b}$.

The most general case is where $f(\mathbf{x})$ is a d'-dimensional vector, in which case f is of the form $f(\mathbf{x}) = \mathbf{M}\mathbf{x} + \mathbf{t}$, where $\mathbf{M}$ is a d'-by-d matrix representing a *linear transformation* such as a rotation or a scaling, and $\mathbf{t}$ is a d'-vector representing a translation. In this case f is called an *affine transformation* (the difference between linear and affine transformations is that the former maps the origin to itself; notice that a linear function of the form of Equation 7.1 is a linear transformation only if the intercept is 0).

In all these forms we can avoid representing the intercept a or the translation $\mathbf{t}$ separately by using homogeneous coordinates. For instance, by writing $\mathbf{b}^\circ = (a, b_1, \ldots, b_d)$ and $\mathbf{x}^\circ = (1, x_1, \ldots, x_d)$ in Equation 7.1 we have $f(\mathbf{x}) = \mathbf{b}^\circ \cdot \mathbf{x}^\circ$ (see also Background 1.2 on p.24).

Examples of non-linear functions are the polynomials in x of degree $p > 1$: $g(x) = a_0 + a_1 x + a_2 x^2 + \ldots + a_p x^p = \sum_{i=0}^{p} a_i x^i$. Other non-linear functions can be approximated by a polynomial through their Taylor expansion. The *linear approximation* of a function g at x_0 is $g(x_0) + g'(x_0)(x - x_0)$, where $g'(x)$ is the derivative of x. A *piecewise linear* approximation is obtained by combining several linear approximations at different points x_0.

Background 7.1. Linear models.

simple as possible, but not simpler' that we introduced on p.30). Here are a couple of manifestations of this simplicity.

☞ Linear models are *parametric*, meaning that they have a fixed form with a small number of numeric parameters that need to be learned from data. This is different from tree or rule models, where the structure of the model (e.g., which features to use in the tree, and where) is not fixed in advance.

☞ Linear models are stable, which is to say that small variations in the training data have only limited impact on the learned model. Tree models tend to vary more with the training data, as the choice of a different split at the root of the tree typically means that the rest of the tree is different as well.

☞ Linear models are less likely to overfit the training data than some other models, largely because they have relatively few parameters. The flipside of this is that they sometimes lead to *underfitting*: e.g., imagine you are learning where the border runs between two countries from labelled samples, then a linear model is unlikely to give a good approximation.

The last two points can be summarised by saying that linear models have low variance but high bias. Such models are often preferable when you have limited data and want to avoid overfitting. High variance–low bias models such as decision trees are preferable if data is abundant but underfitting is a concern. It is usually a good idea to start with simple, high-bias models such as linear models and only move on to more elaborate models if the simpler ones appear to be underfitting.

Linear models exist for all predictive tasks, including classification, probability estimation and regression. Linear regression, in particular, is a well-studied problem that can be solved by the least-squares method, which is the topic of the next section. We will look at a number of other linear models in this chapter, including least-squares classification (also in Section 7.1), the perceptron in Section 7.2, and the support vector machine in Section 7.3. We will also find out how these models can be turned into probability estimators in Section 7.4. Finally, Section 7.5 briefly discusses how each of these methods could learn non-linear models by means of so-called kernel functions.

7.1 The least-squares method

We start by introducing a method that can be used to learn linear models for classification and regression. Recall that the regression problem is to learn a function estimator $\hat{f}: \mathscr{X} \to \mathbb{R}$ from examples $(x_i, f(x_i))$, where in this chapter we assume $\mathscr{X} = \mathbb{R}^d$. The differences between the actual and estimated function values on the training examples are called *residuals* $\epsilon_i = f(x_i) - \hat{f}(x_i)$. The *least-squares method*, introduced by Carl Friedrich Gauss in the late eighteenth century, consists in finding $\hat{f}$ such that $\sum_{i=1}^{n} \epsilon_i^2$ is minimised. The following example illustrates the method in the simple case of a single feature, which is called *univariate regression*.

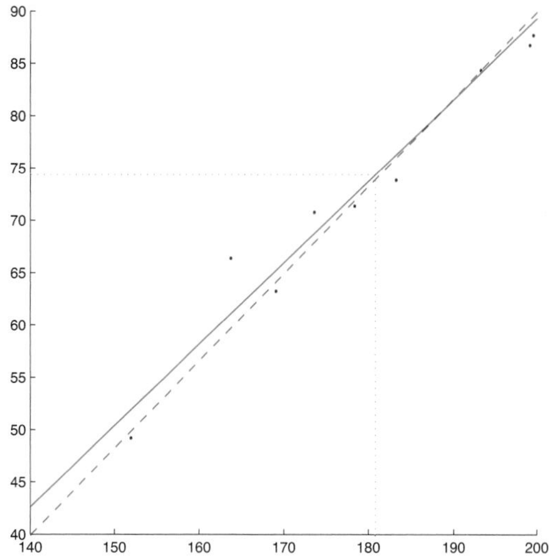

Figure 7.1. The red solid line indicates the result of applying linear regression to 10 measurements of body weight (on the y-axis, in kilograms) against body height (on the x-axis, in centimetres). The orange dotted lines indicate the average height $\overline{h} = 181$ and the average weight $\overline{w} = 74.5$; the regression coefficient $\hat{b} = 0.78$. The measurements were simulated by adding normally distributed noise with mean 0 and variance 5 to the true model indicated by the blue dashed line ($b = 0.83$).

Example 7.1 (Univariate linear regression). Suppose we want to investigate the relationship between people's height and weight. We collect n height and weight measurements $(h_i, w_i), 1 \leq i \leq n$. Univariate linear regression assumes a linear equation $w = a + bh$, with parameters a and b chosen such that the sum of squared residuals $\sum_{i=1}^{n}(w_i - (a + bh_i))^2$ is minimised. In order to find the parameters we take partial derivatives of this expression, set the partial derivatives to 0 and solve for a and b:

$$\frac{\partial}{\partial a}\sum_{i=1}^{n}(w_i - (a + bh_i))^2 = -2\sum_{i=1}^{n}(w_i - (a + bh_i)) = 0 \qquad \Rightarrow \hat{a} = \overline{w} - \hat{b}\overline{h}$$

$$\frac{\partial}{\partial b}\sum_{i=1}^{n}(w_i - (a + bh_i))^2 = -2\sum_{i=1}^{n}(w_i - (a + bh_i))h_i = 0$$

$$\Rightarrow \hat{b} = \frac{\sum_{i=1}^{n}(h_i - \overline{h})(w_i - \overline{w})}{\sum_{i=1}^{n}(h_i - \overline{h})^2}$$

So the solution found by linear regression is $w = \hat{a} + \hat{b}h = \overline{w} + \hat{b}(h - \overline{h})$; see Figure 7.1 for an example.

It is worthwhile to note that the expression for the *regression coefficient* or slope $\hat{b}$ derived in this example has n times the covariance between h and w in the enumerator and n times the variance of h in the denominator. This is true in general: for a feature x and a target variable y, the regression coefficient is

$$\hat{b} = n\frac{\sigma_{xy}}{n\sigma_{xx}} = \frac{\sigma_{xy}}{\sigma_{xx}}$$

(Here I use σ_{xx} as an alternative notation for σ_x^2, the variance of variable x.) This can be understood by noting that the covariance is measured in units of x times units of y (e.g., metres times kilograms in Example 7.1) and the variance in units of x squared (e.g., metres squared), so their quotient is measured in units of y per unit of x (e.g., kilograms per metre).

We can notice a few more useful things. The intercept $\hat{a}$ is such that the regression line goes through $(\overline{x},\overline{y})$. Adding a constant to all x-values (a translation) will affect only the intercept but not the regression coefficient (since it is defined in terms of deviations from the mean, which are unaffected by a translation). So we could *zero-centre* the x-values by subtracting $\overline{x}$, in which case the intercept is equal to $\overline{y}$. We could even subtract $\overline{y}$ from all y-values to achieve a zero intercept, without changing the problem in an essential way.

Furthermore, suppose we replace x_i with $x'_i = x_i/\sigma_{xx}$ and likewise $\overline{x}$ with $\overline{x'} = \overline{x}/\sigma_{xx}$, then we have that $\hat{b} = \frac{1}{n}\sum_{i=1}^{n}(x'_i - \overline{x'})(y_i - \overline{y}) = \sigma_{x'y}$. In other words, if we *normalise* x by dividing all its values by x's variance, we can take the covariance between the normalised feature and the target variable as regression coefficient. In other words, univariate linear regression can be understood as consisting of two steps:

1. normalisation of the feature by dividing its values by the feature's variance;
2. calculating the covariance of the target variable and the normalised feature.

We will see below how these two steps change when dealing with more than one feature.

Another important point to note is that the sum of the residuals of the least-squares solution is zero:

$$\sum_{i=1}^{n}(y_i - (\hat{a} + \hat{b}x_i)) = n(\overline{y} - \hat{a} - \hat{b}\overline{x}) = 0$$

The result follows because $\hat{a} = \overline{y} - \hat{b}\overline{x}$, as derived in Example 7.1. While this property is intuitively appealing, it is worth keeping in mind that it also makes linear regression susceptible to *outliers*: points that are far removed from the regression line, often because of measurement errors.

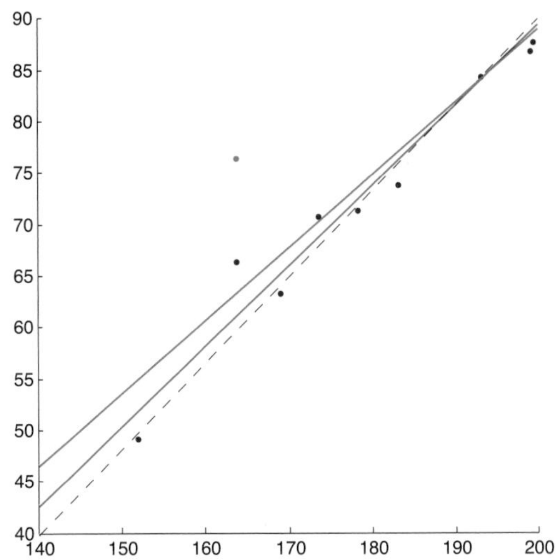

Figure 7.2. The effect of an outlier in univariate regression. One of the blue points got moved up 10 units to the green point, changing the red regression line to the green line.

Example 7.2 (The effect of outliers). Suppose that, as the result of a transcription error, one of the weight values in Figure 7.1 is increased by 10 kg. Figure 7.2 shows that this has a considerable effect on the least-squares regression line.

Despite this sensitivity to outliers, the least-squares method usually works surprisingly well for such a simple method. How can it be justified? One way to look at this is to assume that the true function f is indeed linear, but that the observed y-values are contaminated with random noise. That is, our examples are $(x_i, f(x_i) + \epsilon_i)$ rather than $(x_i, f(x_i))$, and we assume that $f(x) = ax + b$ for some a and b. If we knew a and b we could work out exactly what the residuals are, and if we knew σ^2 we could calculate the probability of observing that set of residuals. Since we don't know a and b we have to estimate them, and the estimate we want is the value of a and b that maximises the probability of the residuals. We will see in Chapter 9 that this so-called ☞*maximum-likelihood estimate* is exactly the least-squares solution.

Variants of the least-squares method exist. Here we discussed *ordinary* least squares, which assumes that only the y-values are contaminated with random noise. *Total* least squares generalises this to the situation that both x- and y-values are noisy, but this does not necessarily have a unique solution.

$\mathbf{X}$ usually denotes an n-by-d data matrix containing n instances in rows described by d features or variables in columns. $\mathbf{X}_{r\cdot}$ denotes the r-th row of $\mathbf{X}$, $\mathbf{X}_{\cdot c}$ denotes the c-th column, and $\mathbf{X}_{rc}$ denotes the entry in the r-th row and c-th column. We also use i and j to range over rows and columns, respectively. The j-th column mean is defined as $\mu_j = \frac{1}{n}\sum_{i=1}^{n}\mathbf{X}_{ij}$; $\boldsymbol{\mu}^{\mathrm{T}}$ is a row vector containing all column means. If $\mathbf{1}$ is an n-vector containing only ones, then $\mathbf{1}\boldsymbol{\mu}^{\mathrm{T}}$ is an n-by-d matrix whose rows are $\boldsymbol{\mu}^{\mathrm{T}}$; hence $\mathbf{X}' = \mathbf{X} - \mathbf{1}\boldsymbol{\mu}^{\mathrm{T}}$ has mean zero in each column and is referred to as the *zero-centred* data matrix.

The *scatter matrix* is the d-by-d matrix $\mathbf{S} = \mathbf{X}'^{\mathrm{T}}\mathbf{X}' = \left(\mathbf{X} - \mathbf{1}\boldsymbol{\mu}^{\mathrm{T}}\right)^{\mathrm{T}}\left(\mathbf{X} - \mathbf{1}\boldsymbol{\mu}^{\mathrm{T}}\right) = \mathbf{X}^{\mathrm{T}}\mathbf{X} - n\mathbf{M}$, where $\mathbf{M} = \boldsymbol{\mu}\boldsymbol{\mu}^{\mathrm{T}}$ is a d-by-d matrix whose entries are products of column means $\mathbf{M}_{jc} = \mu_j\mu_c$. The *covariance matrix* of $\mathbf{X}$ is $\boldsymbol{\Sigma} = \frac{1}{n}\mathbf{S}$ whose entries are the pairwise covariances $\sigma_{jc} = \frac{1}{n}\sum_{i=1}^{n}\left(\mathbf{X}_{ij} - \mu_j\right)\left(\mathbf{X}_{ic} - \mu_c\right) = \frac{1}{n}\left(\sum_{i=1}^{n}\mathbf{X}_{ij}\mathbf{X}_{ic} - \mu_i\mu_c\right)$. Two uncorrelated features have a covariance close to 0; positively correlated features have a positive covariance, indicating a certain tendency to increase or decrease together; a negative covariance indicates that if one feature increases, the other tends to decrease and vice versa. $\sigma_{jj} = \frac{1}{n}\sum_{i=1}^{n}\left(\mathbf{X}_{ij} - \mu_j\right)^2 = \frac{1}{n}\left(\sum_{i=1}^{n}\mathbf{X}_{ij}^2 - \mu_j^2\right)$ is the *variance* of column j, also denoted as σ_j^2. The variance is always positive and indicates the spread of the values of a feature around their mean.

A small example clarifies these definitions:

$$\mathbf{X} = \begin{pmatrix} 5 & 0 \\ 3 & 5 \\ 1 & 7 \end{pmatrix} \quad \mathbf{1}\boldsymbol{\mu}^{\mathrm{T}} = \begin{pmatrix} 3 & 4 \\ 3 & 4 \\ 3 & 4 \end{pmatrix} \quad \mathbf{X}' = \begin{pmatrix} 2 & -4 \\ 0 & 1 \\ -2 & 3 \end{pmatrix} \quad \mathbf{G} = \begin{pmatrix} 25 & 15 & 5 \\ 15 & 34 & 38 \\ 5 & 38 & 50 \end{pmatrix}$$

$$\mathbf{X}^{\mathrm{T}}\mathbf{X} = \begin{pmatrix} 35 & 22 \\ 22 & 74 \end{pmatrix} \quad \mathbf{M} = \begin{pmatrix} 9 & 12 \\ 12 & 16 \end{pmatrix} \quad \mathbf{S} = \begin{pmatrix} 8 & -14 \\ -14 & 26 \end{pmatrix} \quad \boldsymbol{\Sigma} = \begin{pmatrix} 8/3 & -14/3 \\ -14/3 & 26/3 \end{pmatrix}$$

We see that the two features are negatively correlated and that the second feature has the larger variance. Another way to calculate the scatter matrix is as a sum of outer products, one for each data point: $\mathbf{S} = \sum_{i=1}^{n}\left(\mathbf{X}_{i\cdot} - \boldsymbol{\mu}^{\mathrm{T}}\right)^{\mathrm{T}}\left(\mathbf{X}_{i\cdot} - \boldsymbol{\mu}^{\mathrm{T}}\right)$. In our example we have

$$\left(\mathbf{X}_{1\cdot} - \boldsymbol{\mu}^{\mathrm{T}}\right)^{\mathrm{T}}\left(\mathbf{X}_{1\cdot} - \boldsymbol{\mu}^{\mathrm{T}}\right) = \begin{pmatrix} 2 \\ -4 \end{pmatrix}\begin{pmatrix} 2 & -4 \end{pmatrix} = \begin{pmatrix} 4 & -8 \\ -8 & 16 \end{pmatrix}$$

$$\left(\mathbf{X}_{2\cdot} - \boldsymbol{\mu}^{\mathrm{T}}\right)^{\mathrm{T}}\left(\mathbf{X}_{2\cdot} - \boldsymbol{\mu}^{\mathrm{T}}\right) = \begin{pmatrix} 0 \\ 1 \end{pmatrix}\begin{pmatrix} 0 & 1 \end{pmatrix} = \begin{pmatrix} 0 & 0 \\ 0 & 1 \end{pmatrix}$$

$$\left(\mathbf{X}_{3\cdot} - \boldsymbol{\mu}^{\mathrm{T}}\right)^{\mathrm{T}}\left(\mathbf{X}_{3\cdot} - \boldsymbol{\mu}^{\mathrm{T}}\right) = \begin{pmatrix} -2 \\ 3 \end{pmatrix}\begin{pmatrix} -2 & 3 \end{pmatrix} = \begin{pmatrix} 4 & -6 \\ -6 & 9 \end{pmatrix}$$

Background 7.2. Some more matrix notation.

Multivariate linear regression

In order to deal with an arbitrary number of features it will be useful to employ matrix notation (see Background 7.2). We can write univariate linear regression in matrix form as

$$\begin{pmatrix} y_1 \\ \vdots \\ y_n \end{pmatrix} = \begin{pmatrix} 1 \\ \vdots \\ 1 \end{pmatrix} a + \begin{pmatrix} x_1 \\ \vdots \\ x_n \end{pmatrix} b + \begin{pmatrix} \epsilon_1 \\ \vdots \\ \epsilon_n \end{pmatrix}$$

$$\mathbf{y} = \mathbf{a} + \mathbf{X}\mathbf{b} + \epsilon$$

In the second form of this equation, $\mathbf{y}$, $\mathbf{a}$, $\mathbf{X}$ and ϵ are n-vectors, and $\mathbf{b}$ is a scalar. In case of d features, all that changes is that $\mathbf{X}$ becomes an n-by-d matrix, and $\mathbf{b}$ becomes a d-vector of regression coefficients.

We can apply the by now familiar trick of using homogeneous coordinates to simplify these equations as follows:

$$\begin{pmatrix} y_1 \\ \vdots \\ y_n \end{pmatrix} = \begin{pmatrix} 1 & x_1 \\ \vdots & \vdots \\ 1 & x_n \end{pmatrix} \begin{pmatrix} a \\ b \end{pmatrix} + \begin{pmatrix} \epsilon_1 \\ \vdots \\ \epsilon_n \end{pmatrix}$$

$$\mathbf{y} = \mathbf{X}^{\circ}\mathbf{w} + \epsilon$$

with $\mathbf{X}^{\circ}$ an n-by-$(d+1)$ matrix whose first column is all 1s and the remaining columns are the columns of $\mathbf{X}$, and $\mathbf{w}$ has the intercept as its first entry and the regression coefficients as the remaining d entries. For convenience we will often blur the distinction between these two formulations and state the regression equation as $\mathbf{y} = \mathbf{X}\mathbf{w} + \epsilon$ with $\mathbf{X}$ having d columns and $\mathbf{w}$ having d rows – from the context it will be clear whether we are representing the intercept by means of homogeneous coordinates, or have rather zero-centred the target and features to achieve a zero intercept.

In the univariate case we were able to obtain a closed-form solution for $\mathbf{w}$: can we do the same in the multivariate case? First, we are likely to need the covariances between every feature and the target variable. Consider the expression $\mathbf{X}^{\mathrm{T}}\mathbf{y}$, which is an n-vector, the j-th entry of which is the product of the j-th row of $\mathbf{X}^{\mathrm{T}}$ – i.e., the j-th column of $\mathbf{X}$, which is $(x_{1j}, \ldots, x_{nj})$ – with $(y_1, \ldots, y_n)$:

$$(\mathbf{X}^{\mathrm{T}}\mathbf{y})_j = \sum_{i=1}^{n} x_{ij} y_i = \sum_{i=1}^{n} (x_{ij} - \mu_j)(y_i - \overline{y}) + n\mu_j \overline{y} = n(\sigma_{jy} + \mu_j \overline{y})$$

Assuming for the moment that every feature is zero-centred, we have $\mu_j = 0$ and thus $\mathbf{X}^{\mathrm{T}}\mathbf{y}$ is an n-vector holding all the required covariances (times n).

In the univariate case we needed to normalise the features to have unit variance. In the multivariate case we can achieve this by means of a d-by-d scaling matrix: a diagonal matrix with diagonal entries $1/n\sigma_{jj}$. If $\mathbf{S}$ is a diagonal matrix with diagonal entries $n\sigma_{jj}$, we can get the required scaling matrix by simply inverting $\mathbf{S}$. So our first stab at a solution for the *multivariate regression* problem is

$$\hat{\mathbf{w}} = \mathbf{S}^{-1}\mathbf{X}^{\mathrm{T}}\mathbf{y} \tag{7.2}$$

As it turns out, the general case requires a more elaborate matrix instead of $\mathbf{S}$:

$$\hat{\mathbf{w}} = (\mathbf{X}^{\mathrm{T}}\mathbf{X})^{-1}\mathbf{X}^{\mathrm{T}}\mathbf{y} \tag{7.3}$$

Let us try to understand the term $(\mathbf{X}^{\mathrm{T}}\mathbf{X})^{-1}$ a bit better. Assume that the features are uncorrelated (meaning the covariance between every pair of different features is 0) in addition to being zero-centred. In the notation of Background 7.2, the covariance matrix $\mathbf{\Sigma}$ is diagonal with entries σ_{jj}. Since $\mathbf{X}^{\mathrm{T}}\mathbf{X} = n(\mathbf{\Sigma} + \mathbf{M})$, and since the entries of $\mathbf{M}$ are 0 because the columns of $\mathbf{X}$ are zero-centred, this matrix is also diagonal with entries $n\sigma_{jj}$ – in fact, it is the matrix $\mathbf{S}$ referred to above. In other words, assuming zero-centred and uncorrelated features, $(\mathbf{X}^{\mathrm{T}}\mathbf{X})^{-1}$ reduces to our scaling matrix $\mathbf{S}^{-1}$. In the general case we cannot make any assumptions about the features, and $(\mathbf{X}^{\mathrm{T}}\mathbf{X})^{-1}$ *acts as a transformation that decorrelates, centres and normalises the features*.

To make this a bit more concrete, the next example shows how this works out in the bivariate case.

Example 7.3 (Bivariate linear regression in matrix notation). First, we derive the basic expressions.

$$\begin{aligned}
\mathbf{X}^{\mathrm{T}}\mathbf{X} &= \begin{pmatrix} x_{11} & \cdots & x_{n1} \\ x_{12} & \cdots & x_{n2} \end{pmatrix} \begin{pmatrix} x_{11} & x_{12} \\ \vdots & \vdots \\ x_{n1} & x_{n2} \end{pmatrix} = n \begin{pmatrix} \sigma_{11} + \overline{x_1}^2 & \sigma_{12} + \overline{x_1}\,\overline{x_2} \\ \sigma_{12} + \overline{x_1}\,\overline{x_2} & \sigma_{22} + \overline{x_2}^2 \end{pmatrix} \\
(\mathbf{X}^{\mathrm{T}}\mathbf{X})^{-1} &= \frac{1}{nD} \begin{pmatrix} \sigma_{22} + \overline{x_2}^2 & -\sigma_{12} - \overline{x_1}\,\overline{x_2} \\ -\sigma_{12} - \overline{x_1}\,\overline{x_2} & \sigma_{11} + \overline{x_1}^2 \end{pmatrix} \\
D &= (\sigma_{11} + \overline{x_1}^2)(\sigma_{22} + \overline{x_2}^2) - (\sigma_{12} + \overline{x_1}\,\overline{x_2})^2 \\
\mathbf{X}^{\mathrm{T}}\mathbf{y} &= \begin{pmatrix} x_{11} & \cdots & x_{n1} \\ x_{12} & \cdots & x_{n2} \end{pmatrix} \begin{pmatrix} y_1 \\ \vdots \\ y_n \end{pmatrix} = n \begin{pmatrix} \sigma_{1y} + \overline{x_1}\,\overline{y} \\ \sigma_{2y} + \overline{x_2}\,\overline{y} \end{pmatrix}
\end{aligned}$$

We now consider two special cases. The first is that $\mathbf{X}$ is in homogeneous coordinates, i.e., we are really dealing with a univariate problem. In that case we have

$x_{i1} = 1$ for $1 \le i \le n$; $\overline{x_1} = 1$; and $\sigma_{11} = \sigma_{12} = \sigma_{1y} = 0$. We then obtain (we write x instead of x_2, σ_{xx} instead of σ_{22} and σ_{xy} instead of σ_{2y}):

$$
\begin{aligned}
(\mathbf{X}^{\mathrm{T}}\mathbf{X})^{-1} &= \frac{1}{n\sigma_{xx}} \begin{pmatrix} \sigma_{xx} + \overline{x}^2 & -\overline{x} \\ -\overline{x} & 1 \end{pmatrix} \\
\mathbf{X}^{\mathrm{T}}\mathbf{y} &= n \begin{pmatrix} \overline{y} \\ \sigma_{xy} + \overline{x}\,\overline{y} \end{pmatrix} \\
\hat{\mathbf{w}} = (\mathbf{X}^{\mathrm{T}}\mathbf{X})^{-1}\mathbf{X}^{\mathrm{T}}\mathbf{y} &= \frac{1}{\sigma_{xx}} \begin{pmatrix} \sigma_{xx}\overline{y} - \sigma_{xy}\overline{x} \\ \sigma_{xy} \end{pmatrix}
\end{aligned}
$$

This is the same result as obtained in Example 7.1.

The second special case we consider is where we assume x_1, x_2 and y to be zero-centred, which means that the intercept is zero and $\mathbf{w}$ contains the two regression coefficients. In this case we obtain

$$
\begin{aligned}
(\mathbf{X}^{\mathrm{T}}\mathbf{X})^{-1} &= \frac{1}{n(\sigma_{11}\sigma_{22} - \sigma_{12}^2)} \begin{pmatrix} \sigma_{22} & -\sigma_{12} \\ -\sigma_{12} & \sigma_{11} \end{pmatrix} \\
\mathbf{X}^{\mathrm{T}}\mathbf{y} &= n \begin{pmatrix} \sigma_{1y} \\ \sigma_{2y} \end{pmatrix} \\
\hat{\mathbf{w}} = (\mathbf{X}^{\mathrm{T}}\mathbf{X})^{-1}\mathbf{X}^{\mathrm{T}}\mathbf{y} &= \frac{1}{(\sigma_{11}\sigma_{22} - \sigma_{12}^2)} \begin{pmatrix} \sigma_{22}\sigma_{1y} - \sigma_{12}\sigma_{2y} \\ \sigma_{11}\sigma_{2y} - \sigma_{12}\sigma_{1y} \end{pmatrix}
\end{aligned}
$$

The last expression shows, e.g., that the regression coefficient for x_1 may be non-zero even if x_1 doesn't correlate with the target variable ($\sigma_{1y} = 0$), on account of the correlation between x_1 and x_2 ($\sigma_{12} \neq 0$).

Notice that if we do assume $\sigma_{12} = 0$ then the components of $\hat{\mathbf{w}}$ reduce to σ_{jy}/σ_{jj}, which brings us back to Equation 7.2. *Assuming uncorrelated features effectively decomposes a multivariate regression problem into d univariate problems.* We shall see several other examples of decomposing multivariate learning problems into univariate problems in this book – in fact, we have already seen an example in the form of the ☞ *naive Bayes* classifier in Chapter 1. So, you may wonder, why take feature correlation into account at all?

The answer is that ignoring feature correlation can be harmful in certain situations. Consider Figure 7.3: on the left, there is little correlation among the features, and as a result the samples provide a lot of information about the true function. On

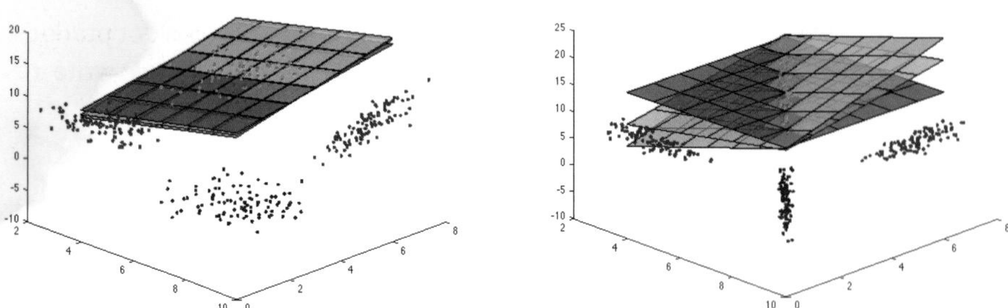

Figure 7.3. (left) Regression functions learned by linear regression. The true function is $y = x_1 + x_2$ (red plane). The red points are noisy samples of this function; the black points show them projected onto the (x_1, x_2)-plane. The green plane indicates the function learned by linear regression; the blue plane is the result of decomposing the problem into two univariate regression problems (blue points). Both are good approximations of the true function. **(right)** The same function, but now x_1 and x_2 are highly (negatively) correlated. The samples now give much less information about the true function: indeed, from the univariate decomposition it appears that the function is constant.

the right, the features are highly negatively correlated in such a way that the sampled values $y = x_1 + x_2 + \epsilon$ appear nearly constant, as any increase in one feature is accompanied by a nearly equal decrease in the other. As a result, decomposing the problem into two univariate regression problems leads to learning a nearly constant function. To be fair, taking the full covariance matrix into account doesn't do so well either in this example. However, although we will not explore the details here, one advantage of the full covariance approach is that it allows us to recognise that we can't place much confidence in our estimates of the regression parameters in this situation. The computational cost of computing the closed-form solution in Equation 7.3 lies in inverting the d-by-d matrix $\mathbf{X}^{\mathrm{T}}\mathbf{X}$, which can be prohibitive in high-dimensional feature spaces.

Regularised regression

We have just seen a situation in which least-squares regression can become *unstable*: i.e., highly dependent on the training data. Instability is a manifestation of a tendency to overfit. *Regularisation* is a general method to avoid such overfitting by applying additional constraints to the weight vector. A common approach is to make sure the weights are, on average, small in magnitude: this is referred to as *shrinkage*. To show how this can be achieved, we first write down the least-squares regression problem as an optimisation problem:

$$\mathbf{w}^* = \operatorname*{arg\,min}_{\mathbf{w}} (\mathbf{y} - \mathbf{X}\mathbf{w})^{\mathrm{T}}(\mathbf{y} - \mathbf{X}\mathbf{w})$$

The right-hand side is just a way to write the sum of squared residuals as a dot product. The regularised version of this optimisation is then as follows:

$$\mathbf{w}^* = \arg\min_{\mathbf{w}} (\mathbf{y}-\mathbf{X}\mathbf{w})^{\mathrm{T}}(\mathbf{y}-\mathbf{X}\mathbf{w}) + \lambda||\mathbf{w}||^2 \tag{7.4}$$

where $||\mathbf{w}||^2 = \sum_i w_i^2$ is the squared norm of the vector $\mathbf{w}$, or, equivalently, the dot product $\mathbf{w}^{\mathrm{T}}\mathbf{w}$; λ is a scalar determining the amount of regularisation. This regularised problem still has a closed-form solution:

$$\hat{\mathbf{w}} = (\mathbf{X}^{\mathrm{T}}\mathbf{X} + \lambda\mathbf{I})^{-1}\mathbf{X}^{\mathrm{T}}\mathbf{y} \tag{7.5}$$

where $\mathbf{I}$ denotes the identity matrix with 1s on the diagonal and 0s everywhere else. Comparing this with Equation 7.3 on p.202 we see that regularisation amounts to adding λ to the diagonal of $\mathbf{X}^{\mathrm{T}}\mathbf{X}$, a well-known trick to improve the numerical stability of matrix inversion. This form of least-squares regression is known as *ridge regression*.

An interesting alternative form of regularised regression is provided by the *lasso*, which stands for 'least absolute shrinkage and selection operator'. It replaces the ridge regularisation term $\sum_i w_i^2$ with the sum of absolute weights $\sum_i |w_i|$. (Using terminology that will be introduced in Definition 8.2 on p.235: lasso uses L_1 regularisation where ridge regression uses the L_2 norm.) The result is that some weights are shrunk, but others are set to 0, and so the lasso regression favours *sparse solutions*. It should be added that lasso regression is quite sensitive to the regularisation parameter λ, which is usually set on hold-out data or in cross-validation. Also, there is no closed-form solution and so some numerical optimisation technique must be applied.

Using least-squares regression for classification

So far we have used the least-squares method to construct function approximators. Interestingly, we can also use linear regression to learn a binary classifier by encoding the two classes as real numbers. For instance, we can label the *Pos* positive examples with $y^{\oplus} = +1$ and the *Neg* negative examples with $y^{\ominus} = -1$. It then follows that $\mathbf{X}^{\mathrm{T}}\mathbf{y} = Pos\,\boldsymbol{\mu}^{\oplus} - Neg\,\boldsymbol{\mu}^{\ominus}$, where $\boldsymbol{\mu}^{\oplus}$ and $\boldsymbol{\mu}^{\ominus}$ are d-vectors containing each feature's mean values for the positive and negative examples, respectively.

Example 7.4 (Univariate least-squares classifier). In the univariate case we have $\sum_i x_i y_i = Pos\,\mu^{\oplus} - Neg\,\mu^{\ominus}$; we also know (see Example 7.3) that $\sum_i x_i y_i = n(\sigma_{xy} + \overline{x}\,\overline{y})$, and so $\sigma_{xy} = pos\,\mu^{\oplus} - neg\,\mu^{\ominus} - \overline{x}\,\overline{y}$. Since $\overline{x} = pos\,\mu^{\oplus} + neg\,\mu^{\ominus}$ and $\overline{y} = pos - neg$, we can rewrite the covariance between x and y as $\sigma_{xy} =$

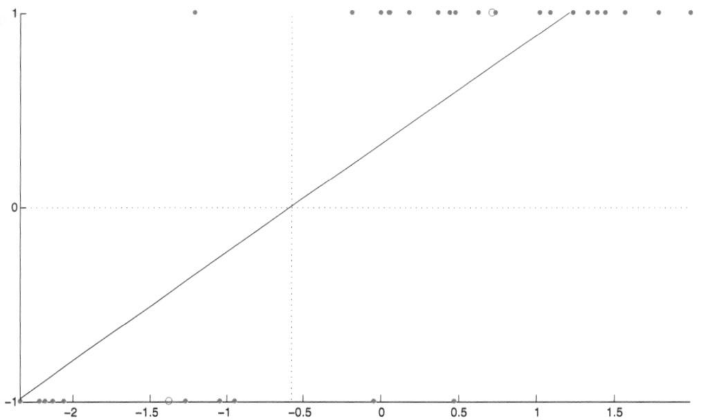

Figure 7.4. Using univariate linear regression to obtain a decision boundary. The 10 negative examples are labelled with $y^{\ominus} = -1$ and the 20 positive examples are labelled $y^{\oplus} = +1$. $\mu^{\ominus}$ and $\mu^{\oplus}$ are indicated by red circles. The blue line is the linear regression line $y = \overline{y} + \hat{b}(x - \overline{x})$, and the crosshair indicates the decision boundary $x_0 = \overline{x} - \overline{y}/\hat{b}$. This results in three examples being misclassified – notice that this is the best that can be achieved with the given data.

$2pos \cdot neg\,(\mu^{\oplus} - \mu^{\ominus})$, and so the slope of the regression line is

$$\hat{b} = 2pos \cdot neg \frac{\mu^{\oplus} - \mu^{\ominus}}{\sigma_{xx}} \tag{7.6}$$

This equation shows that the slope of the regression line increases with the separation between the classes (measured as the distance between the class means in proportion to the feature's variance), but also decreases if the class distribution becomes skewed.

The regression equation $y = \overline{y} + \hat{b}(x - \overline{x})$ can then be used to obtain a decision boundary. We need to determine the point (x_0, y_0) such that y_0 is half-way between $y^{\oplus}$ and $y^{\ominus}$ (i.e., $y_0 = 0$ in our case). We then have

$$x_0 = \overline{x} + \frac{y_0 - \overline{y}}{\hat{b}} = \overline{x} - \frac{pos - neg}{2pos \cdot neg} \frac{\sigma_{xx}}{\mu^{\oplus} - \mu^{\ominus}}$$

That is, if there are equal numbers of positive and negative examples we simply threshold the feature at the feature mean $\overline{x}$; in case of unequal class distribution we shift this threshold to the left or right as appropriate (Figure 7.4).

In the general case, the *least-squares classifier* learns the decision boundary $\mathbf{w} \cdot \mathbf{x} = t$ with

$$\mathbf{w} = (\mathbf{X}^{\mathrm{T}}\mathbf{X})^{-1}(Pos\,\boldsymbol{\mu}^{\oplus} - Neg\,\boldsymbol{\mu}^{\ominus}) \tag{7.7}$$

We would hence assign class $\hat{y} = \text{sign}(\mathbf{w}\cdot\mathbf{x} - t)$ to instance $\mathbf{x}$, where

$$\text{sign}(x) = \begin{cases} +1 & \text{if } x > 0 \\ 0 & \text{if } x = 0 \\ -1 & \text{if } x < 0 \end{cases}$$

Various simplifying assumptions can be made, including zero-centred features, equal-variance features, uncorrelated features and equal class prevalences. In the simplest case, when all these assumptions are made, Equation 7.7 reduces to $\mathbf{w} = c(\boldsymbol{\mu}^{\oplus} - \boldsymbol{\mu}^{\ominus})$ where c is some scalar that can be incorporated in the decision threshold t. We recognise this as the ☞*basic linear classifier* that was introduced in the Prologue. Equation 7.7 thus tells us how to adapt the basic linear classifier, using the least-squares method, in order to take feature correlation and unequal class distributions into account.

In summary, *a general way of constructing a linear classifier with decision boundary* $\mathbf{w}\cdot\mathbf{x} = t$ *is by constructing* $\mathbf{w}$ *as* $\mathbf{M}^{-1}(n^{\oplus}\boldsymbol{\mu}^{\oplus} - n^{\ominus}\boldsymbol{\mu}^{\ominus})$, with different possible choices of $\mathbf{M}$, $n^{\oplus}$ and $n^{\ominus}$. The full covariance approach with $\mathbf{M} = \mathbf{X}^{\mathrm{T}}\mathbf{X}$ has time complexity $O(n^2 d)$ for construction of $\mathbf{M}$ and $O(d^3)$ for inverting it,[1] so this approach becomes unfeasible with large numbers of features.

7.2 The perceptron

Recall from Chapter 1 that labelled data is called ☞*linearly separable* if there exists a linear decision boundary separating the classes. The least-squares classifier may find a perfectly separating decision boundary if one exists, but this is not guaranteed. To see this, suppose that the basic linear classifier achieves perfect separation for a given training set. Now, move all but one of the positive points away from the negative class. The decision boundary will also move away from the negative class, at some point crossing the one positive that remains fixed. By construction, the modified data is still linearly separable, since the original decision boundary separates it; however, the statistics of the modified data are such that the basic linear classifier will misclassify the one positive outlier.

A linear classifier that will achieve perfect separation on linearly separable data is the *perceptron*, originally proposed as a simple neural network. The perceptron iterates over the training set, updating the weight vector every time it encounters an incorrectly classified example. For example, let $\mathbf{x}_i$ be a misclassified positive example, then we have $y_i = +1$ and $\mathbf{w}\cdot\mathbf{x}_i < t$. We therefore want to find $\mathbf{w}'$ such that $\mathbf{w}'\cdot\mathbf{x}_i > \mathbf{w}\cdot\mathbf{x}_i$, which moves the decision boundary towards and hopefully past x_i. This can be achieved by calculating the new weight vector as $\mathbf{w}' = \mathbf{w} + \eta\mathbf{x}_i$, where $0 < \eta \leq 1$ is the *learning rate*. We then have $\mathbf{w}'\cdot\mathbf{x}_i = \mathbf{w}\cdot\mathbf{x}_i + \eta\mathbf{x}_i\cdot\mathbf{x}_i > \mathbf{w}\cdot\mathbf{x}_i$ as required. Similarly, if $\mathbf{x}_j$ is a misclassified

[1] A more sophisticated algorithm can achieve $O(d^{2.8})$, but this is probably the best we can do.

negative example, then we have $y_j = -1$ and $\mathbf{w}\cdot\mathbf{x}_j > t$. In this case we calculate the new weight vector as $\mathbf{w}' = \mathbf{w} - \eta\mathbf{x}_j$, and thus $\mathbf{w}'\cdot\mathbf{x}_j = \mathbf{w}\cdot\mathbf{x}_j - \eta\mathbf{x}_j\cdot\mathbf{x}_j < \mathbf{w}\cdot\mathbf{x}_j$. The two cases can be combined in a single update rule:

$$\mathbf{w}' = \mathbf{w} + \eta y_i \mathbf{x}_i \tag{7.8}$$

The perceptron training algorithm is given in Algorithm 7.1. It iterates through the training examples until all examples are correctly classified. The algorithm can easily be turned into an *online* algorithm that processes a stream of examples, updating the weight vector only if the last received example is misclassified. The perceptron is guaranteed to converge to a solution if the training data is linearly separable, but it won't converge otherwise. Figure 7.5 gives a graphical illustration of the perceptron training algorithm. In this particular example I initialised the weight vector to the basic linear classifier, which means the learning rate does have an effect on how quickly we move away from the initial decision boundary. However, if the weight vector is initialised to the zero vector, it is easy to see that the learning rate is just a constant factor that does not affect convergence. We will set it to 1 in the remainder of this section.

The key point of the perceptron algorithm is that, every time an example $\mathbf{x}_i$ is misclassified, we add $y_i\mathbf{x}_i$ to the weight vector. After training has completed, each example has been misclassified zero or more times – denote this number α_i for example $\mathbf{x}_i$.

Algorithm 7.1: Perceptron(D, η) – train a perceptron for linear classification.

Input : labelled training data D in homogeneous coordinates;
learning rate η.
Output : weight vector $\mathbf{w}$ defining classifier $\hat{y} = \text{sign}(\mathbf{w}\cdot\mathbf{x})$.

$\mathbf{w} \leftarrow \mathbf{0}$; // Other initialisations of the weight vector are possible
converged←false;
while *converged* = false **do**
  converged←true;
  for $i = 1$ to $|D|$ **do**
    if $y_i \mathbf{w}\cdot\mathbf{x}_i \le 0$ // i.e., $\hat{y}_i \neq y_i$
    then
      $\mathbf{w} \leftarrow \mathbf{w} + \eta y_i \mathbf{x}_i$;
      converged←false; // We changed $\mathbf{w}$ so haven't converged yet
    end
  end
end

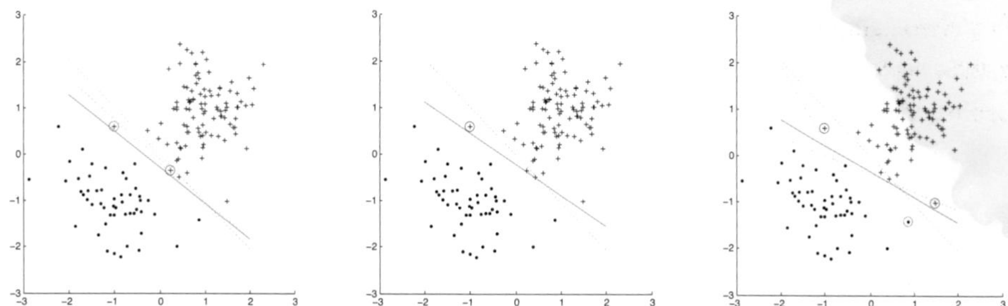

Figure 7.5. (left) A perceptron trained with a small learning rate ($\eta = 0.2$). The circled examples are the ones that trigger the weight update. **(middle)** Increasing the learning rate to $\eta = 0.5$ leads in this case to a rapid convergence. **(right)** Increasing the learning rate further to $\eta = 1$ may lead to too aggressive weight updating, which harms convergence. The starting point in all three cases was the basic linear classifier.

Using this notation the weight vector can be expressed as

$$\mathbf{w} = \sum_{i=1}^{n} \alpha_i y_i \mathbf{x}_i \tag{7.9}$$

In other words, the weight vector is a linear combination of the training instances. The perceptron shares this property with, e.g., the basic linear classifier:

$$\mathbf{w}_{blc} = \boldsymbol{\mu}^{\oplus} - \boldsymbol{\mu}^{\ominus} = \frac{1}{Pos} \sum_{\mathbf{x}^{\oplus} \in Tr^{\oplus}} \mathbf{x}^{\oplus} - \frac{1}{Neg} \sum_{\mathbf{x}^{\ominus} \in Tr^{\ominus}} \mathbf{x}^{\ominus} = \sum_{\mathbf{x}^{\oplus} \in Tr^{\oplus}} \alpha^{\oplus} c(\mathbf{x}^{\oplus}) \mathbf{x}^{\oplus} + \sum_{\mathbf{x}^{\ominus} \in Tr^{\ominus}} \alpha^{\ominus} c(\mathbf{x}^{\ominus}) \mathbf{x}^{\ominus} \tag{7.10}$$

Algorithm 7.2: DualPerceptron(D) – perceptron training in dual form.

Input : labelled training data D in homogeneous coordinates.
Output : coefficients α_i defining weight vector $\mathbf{w} = \sum_{i=1}^{|D|} \alpha_i y_i \mathbf{x}_i$.

```
αᵢ ← 0 for 1 ≤ i ≤ |D|;
converged←false;
while converged = false do
    converged←true;
    for i = 1 to |D| do
        if yᵢ Σ_{j=1}^{|D|} αⱼ yⱼ xᵢ · xⱼ ≤ 0 then
            αᵢ ← αᵢ + 1;
            converged←false;
        end
    end
end
```

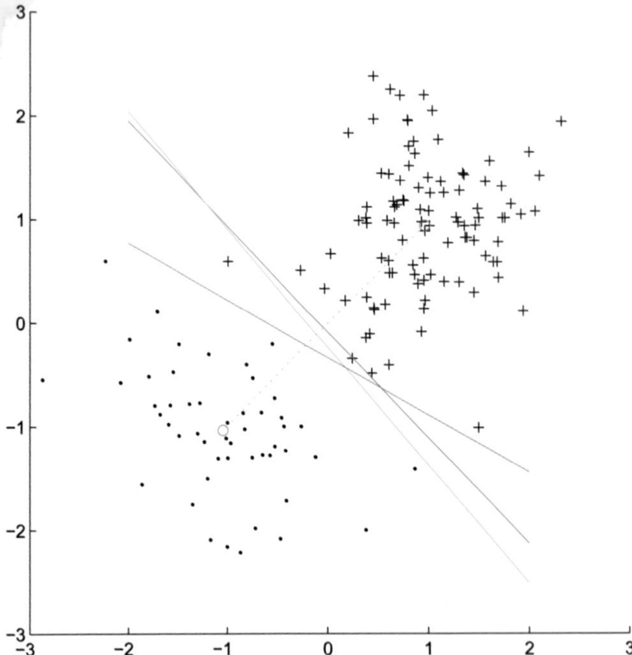

Figure 7.6. Three differently trained linear classifiers on a data set of 100 positives (top-right) and 50 negatives (bottom-left): the basic linear classifier in red, the least-squares classifier in orange and the perceptron in green. Notice that the perceptron perfectly separates the training data, but its heuristic approach may lead to overfitting in certain situations.

where $c(\mathbf{x})$ is the true class of example $\mathbf{x}$ (i.e., +1 or −1), $\alpha^{\oplus} = 1/Pos$ and $\alpha^{\ominus} = 1/Neg$. *In the dual, instance-based view of linear classification we are learning instance weights α_i rather than feature weights w_j.* In this dual perspective, an instance $\mathbf{x}$ is classified as $\hat{y} = \text{sign}\left(\sum_{i=1}^{n} \alpha_i y_i \mathbf{x}_i \cdot \mathbf{x}\right)$. This means that, during training, the only information needed about the training data is all pairwise dot products: the n-by-n matrix $\mathbf{G} = \mathbf{X}\mathbf{X}^{\mathrm{T}}$ containing these dot products is called the *Gram matrix*. Algorithm 7.2 gives the dual form of the perceptron training algorithm. We will encounter this instance-based perspective again when we discuss support vector machines in the next section.

Figure 7.6 demonstrates the difference between the basic linear classifier, the least-squares classifier and the perceptron on some random data. For this particular data set, neither the basic linear classifier nor the least-squares classifier achieves perfect separation, but the perceptron does. One difference with other linear methods is that we cannot derive a closed-form solution for the weight vector learned by the perceptron, so it is a more heuristic approach.

The perceptron can easily be turned into a linear function approximator (Algorithm 7.3). To this end the update rule is changed to $\mathbf{w}' = \mathbf{w} + (y_i - \hat{y}_i)^2 \mathbf{x}_i$, which uses squared residuals. This is unlikely to converge to the exact function, so the algorithm simply runs for a fixed number of training epochs (an epoch is one complete run through the training data). Alternatively, one could run the algorithm until a bound on the sum of squared residuals is reached.

7.3 Support vector machines

Linearly separable data admits infinitely many decision boundaries that separate the classes, but intuitively some of these are better than others. For example, the left and middle decision boundaries in Figure 7.5 seem to be unnecessarily close to some of the positives; while the one on the right leaves a bit more space on either side, it doesn't seem particularly good either. To make this a bit more precise, recall that in Section 2.2 we defined the ☞*margin* of an example assigned by a scoring classifier as $c(x)\hat{s}(x)$, where $c(x)$ is $+1$ for positive examples and -1 for negative examples and $\hat{s}(x)$ is the score of example x. If we take $\hat{s}(\mathbf{x}) = \mathbf{w}\cdot\mathbf{x} - t$, then a true positive $\mathbf{x}_i$ has margin $\mathbf{w}\cdot\mathbf{x}_i - t > 0$ and a true negative $\mathbf{x}_j$ has margin $-(\mathbf{w}\cdot\mathbf{x}_j - t) > 0$. For a given training set and decision boundary, let $m^{\oplus}$ be the smallest margin of any positive, and $m^{\ominus}$ the smallest margin of any negative, then we want the sum of these to be as large as possible. This sum is independent of the decision threshold t, as long as we keep the nearest positives and negatives at the right sides of the decision boundary, and so we re-adjust t such that $m^{\oplus}$ and $m^{\ominus}$ become equal. Figure 7.7 depicts this graphically in a two-dimensional instance space. The training examples nearest to the decision boundary are called *support vectors*: as we shall see, the decision boundary of a support vector machine (SVM) is defined as a linear combination of the support vectors.

The *margin* is thus defined as $m/||\mathbf{w}||$, where m is the distance between the decision boundary and the nearest training instances (at least one of each class) as

---

Algorithm 7.3: PerceptronRegression(D, T) – train a perceptron for regression.

Input : labelled training data D in homogeneous coordinates;
maximum number of training epochs T.

Output : weight vector $\mathbf{w}$ defining function approximator $\hat{y} = \mathbf{w}\cdot\mathbf{x}$.

$\mathbf{w} \leftarrow \mathbf{0}$; $t \leftarrow 0$;
while $t < T$ **do**
  for $i = 1$ to $|D|$ **do**
    $\mathbf{w} \leftarrow \mathbf{w} + (y_i - \hat{y}_i)^2 \mathbf{x}_i$;
  end
  $t \leftarrow t + 1$;
end

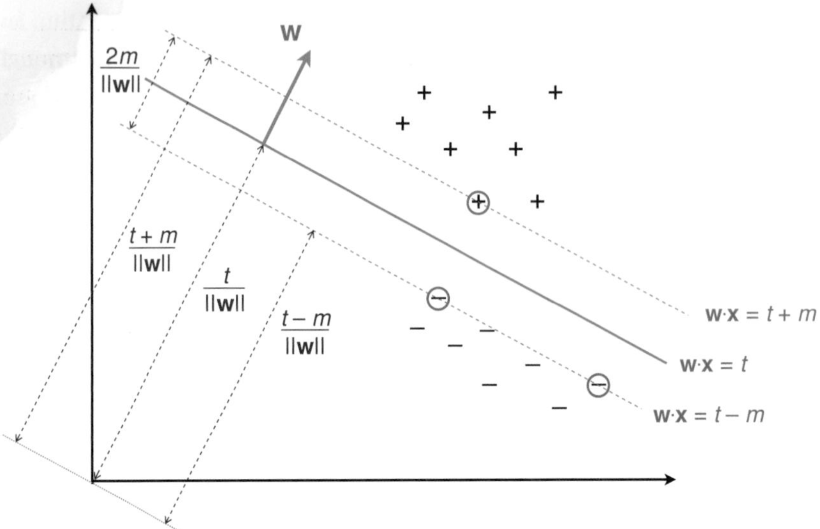

Figure 7.7. The geometry of a support vector classifier. The circled data points are the support vectors, which are the training examples nearest to the decision boundary. The support vector machine finds the decision boundary that maximises the margin $m/||\mathbf{w}||$.

measured along **w**. Since we are free to rescale t, $||\mathbf{w}||$ and m, it is customary to choose $m = 1$. Maximising the margin then corresponds to minimising $||\mathbf{w}||$ or, more conveniently, $\frac{1}{2}||\mathbf{w}||^2$, provided of course that none of the training points fall inside the margin. This leads to a quadratic, constrained optimisation problem:

$$\mathbf{w}^*, t^* = \operatorname*{arg\,min}_{\mathbf{w},t} \frac{1}{2}||\mathbf{w}||^2 \qquad \text{subject to } y_i(\mathbf{w}\cdot\mathbf{x}_i - t) \geq 1, 1 \leq i \leq n$$

We will approach this using the method of Lagrange multipliers (see Background 7.3). Adding the constraints with multipliers α_i for each training example gives the Lagrange function

$$\begin{aligned}
\Lambda(\mathbf{w}, t, \alpha_1, \ldots, \alpha_n) &= \frac{1}{2}||\mathbf{w}||^2 - \sum_{i=1}^{n} \alpha_i (y_i(\mathbf{w}\cdot\mathbf{x}_i - t) - 1) \\
&= \frac{1}{2}||\mathbf{w}||^2 - \sum_{i=1}^{n} \alpha_i y_i (\mathbf{w}\cdot\mathbf{x}_i) + \sum_{i=1}^{n} \alpha_i y_i t + \sum_{i=1}^{n} \alpha_i \\
&= \frac{1}{2}\mathbf{w}\cdot\mathbf{w} - \mathbf{w}\cdot\left(\sum_{i=1}^{n} \alpha_i y_i \mathbf{x}_i\right) + t\left(\sum_{i=1}^{n} \alpha_i y_i\right) + \sum_{i=1}^{n} \alpha_i
\end{aligned}$$

While this looks like a formidable formula, some further analysis will allow us to derive the simpler dual form of the Lagrange function.

By taking the partial derivative of the Lagrange function with respect to t and setting it to 0 we find that for the optimal threshold t we have $\sum_{i=1}^{n} \alpha_i y_i = 0$. Similarly, by

---

Optimisation is a broad term denoting the problem of finding the best item or value among a set of alternatives. We have already seen a very simple, unconstrained form of optimisation in Example 7.1 on p.197, where we found the values of a and b minimising the sum of squared residuals $f(a,b) = \sum_{i=1}^{n}(w_i - (a + bh_i))^2$; this can be denoted as

$$a^*, b^* = \operatorname*{arg\,min}_{a,b} f(a,b)$$

f is called the *objective function*; it can be linear, quadratic (as in this case), or more complex. We found the minimum of f by setting the partial derivatives of f with respect to a and b to 0, and solving for a and b; the vector of these partial derivatives is called the *gradient* and denoted ∇f, so a succinct way of defining the unconstrained optimisation problem is: find a and b such that $\nabla f(a,b) = \mathbf{0}$. In this particular case the objective function is *convex*, which essentially means that there is a unique global minimum. This is, however, not always the case.

A *constrained optimisation* problem is one where the alternatives are subject to constraints, for instance

$$a^*, b^* = \operatorname*{arg\,min}_{a,b} f(a,b) \qquad \text{subject to } g(a,b) = c$$

If the relationship expressed by the constraint is linear, say $a - b = 0$, we can of course eliminate one of the variables and solve the simpler, unconstrained problem. However, this may not be possible if the constraints are non-linear. *Lagrange multipliers* are a powerful way of dealing with the general case. We form the Lagrange function defined by

$$\Lambda(a,b,\lambda) = f(a,b) - \lambda(g(a,b) - c)$$

where λ is the Lagrange multiplier, and solve the unconstrained problem $\nabla\Lambda(a,b,\lambda) = \mathbf{0}$. Since $\nabla_{a,b}\Lambda(a,b,\lambda) = \nabla f(a,b) - \lambda\nabla g(a,b)$ and $\nabla_{\lambda}\Lambda(a,b,\lambda) = g(a,b) - c$, this is a succinct way of requiring (*i*) that the gradients of f and g point in the same direction, and (*ii*) that the constraint is satisfied. We can include multiple equality constraints and also inequality constraints, each with their own Lagrange multiplier.

From the Lagrange function it is possible to derive a *dual* optimisation problem where we find the optimal values of the Lagrange multipliers. In general, the solution to the dual problem is only a lower bound on the solution to the *primal* problem, but under a set of conditions known as the *Karush–Kuhn–Tucker conditions* (*KKT*) the two solutions become equal. The quadratic optimisation problem posed by support vector machines is usually solved in its dual form.

Background 7.3. Basic concepts and terminology in mathematical optimisation.

taking the partial derivative of the Lagrange function with respect to **w** we see that the Lagrange multipliers define the weight vector as a linear combination of the training examples:

$$\frac{\partial}{\partial \mathbf{w}}\Lambda(\mathbf{w},t,\alpha_1,\ldots,\alpha_n) = \frac{\partial}{\partial \mathbf{w}}\frac{1}{2}\mathbf{w}\cdot\mathbf{w} - \frac{\partial}{\partial \mathbf{w}}\mathbf{w}\cdot\left(\sum_{i=1}^{n}\alpha_i y_i \mathbf{x}_i\right) = \mathbf{w} - \sum_{i=1}^{n}\alpha_i y_i \mathbf{x}_i$$

Since this partial derivative is 0 for an optimal weight vector we conclude $\mathbf{w} = \sum_{i=1}^{n}\alpha_i y_i \mathbf{x}_i$ – the same expression as we derived for the perceptron in Equation 7.9 on p.209. For the perceptron, the instance weights α_i are non-negative integers denoting the number of times an example has been misclassified in training. For a support vector machine, the α_i are non-negative reals. What they have in common is that, if $\alpha_i = 0$ for a particular example $\mathbf{x}_i$, that example could be removed from the training set without affecting the learned decision boundary. In the case of support vector machines this means that $\alpha_i > 0$ only for the support vectors: the training examples nearest to the decision boundary.

Now, by plugging the expressions $\sum_{i=1}^{n}\alpha_i y_i = 0$ and $\mathbf{w} = \sum_{i=1}^{n}\alpha_i y_i \mathbf{x}_i$ back into the Lagrangian we are able to eliminate **w** and t, and hence obtain the dual optimisation problem, which is entirely formulated in terms of the Lagrange multipliers:

$$\begin{aligned}\Lambda(\alpha_1,\ldots,\alpha_n) &= -\frac{1}{2}\left(\sum_{i=1}^{n}\alpha_i y_i \mathbf{x}_i\right)\cdot\left(\sum_{i=1}^{n}\alpha_i y_i \mathbf{x}_i\right) + \sum_{i=1}^{n}\alpha_i \\ &= -\frac{1}{2}\sum_{i=1}^{n}\sum_{j=1}^{n}\alpha_i\alpha_j y_i y_j \mathbf{x}_i\cdot\mathbf{x}_j + \sum_{i=1}^{n}\alpha_i\end{aligned}$$

The dual problem is to maximise this function under positivity constraints and one equality constraint:

$$\alpha_1^*,\ldots,\alpha_n^* = \mathop{\arg\max}_{\alpha_1,\ldots,\alpha_n} -\frac{1}{2}\sum_{i=1}^{n}\sum_{j=1}^{n}\alpha_i\alpha_j y_i y_j \mathbf{x}_i\cdot\mathbf{x}_j + \sum_{i=1}^{n}\alpha_i$$

$$\text{subject to } \alpha_i \geq 0, 1 \leq i \leq n \text{ and } \sum_{i=1}^{n}\alpha_i y_i = 0$$

The dual form of the optimisation problem for support vector machines illustrates two important points. First, it shows that searching for the maximum-margin decision boundary is equivalent to searching for the support vectors: they are the training examples with non-zero Lagrange multipliers, and through $\mathbf{w} = \sum_{i=1}^{n}\alpha_i y_i \mathbf{x}_i$ they completely determine the decision boundary. Secondly, it shows that the optimisation problem is entirely defined by pairwise dot products between training instances: the entries of the Gram matrix. As we shall see in Section 7.5, this paves the way for a powerful adaptation of support vector machines that allows them to learn non-linear decision boundaries.

The following example makes these issues a bit more concrete by showing detailed calculations on some toy data.

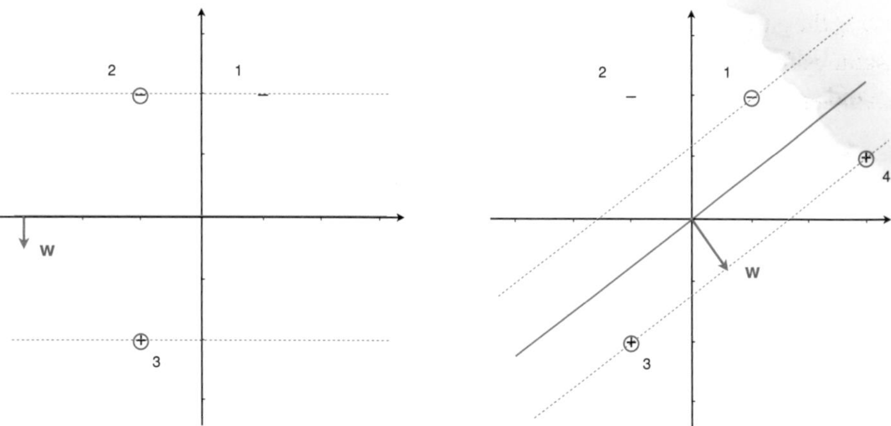

Figure 7.8. **(left)** A maximum-margin classifier built from three examples, with $\mathbf{w} = (0, -1/2)$ and margin 2. The circled examples are the support vectors: they receive non-zero Lagrange multipliers and define the decision boundary. **(right)** By adding a second positive the decision boundary is rotated to $\mathbf{w} = (3/5, -4/5)$ and the margin decreases to 1.

Example 7.5 (Two maximum-margin classifiers and their support vectors). Let the data points and labels be as follows (see Figure 7.8 (left)):

$$\mathbf{X} = \begin{pmatrix} 1 & 2 \\ -1 & 2 \\ -1 & -2 \end{pmatrix} \quad \mathbf{y} = \begin{pmatrix} -1 \\ -1 \\ +1 \end{pmatrix} \quad \mathbf{X}' = \begin{pmatrix} -1 & -2 \\ 1 & -2 \\ -1 & -2 \end{pmatrix}$$

The matrix $\mathbf{X}'$ on the right incorporates the class labels; i.e., the rows are $y_i \mathbf{x}_i$. The Gram matrix is (without and with class labels):

$$\mathbf{X}\mathbf{X}^{\mathrm{T}} = \begin{pmatrix} 5 & 3 & -5 \\ 3 & 5 & -3 \\ -5 & -3 & 5 \end{pmatrix} \quad \mathbf{X}'\mathbf{X}'^{\mathrm{T}} = \begin{pmatrix} 5 & 3 & 5 \\ 3 & 5 & 3 \\ 5 & 3 & 5 \end{pmatrix}$$

The dual optimisation problem is thus

$$\begin{aligned} &\operatorname*{argmax}_{\alpha_1,\alpha_2,\alpha_3} -\frac{1}{2}\big(5\alpha_1^2 + 3\alpha_1\alpha_2 + 5\alpha_1\alpha_3 + 3\alpha_2\alpha_1 + 5\alpha_2^2 + 3\alpha_2\alpha_3 + 5\alpha_3\alpha_1 \\ &\qquad\qquad + 3\alpha_3\alpha_2 + 5\alpha_3^2\big) + \alpha_1 + \alpha_2 + \alpha_3 \\ &= \operatorname*{argmax}_{\alpha_1,\alpha_2,\alpha_3} -\frac{1}{2}\big(5\alpha_1^2 + 6\alpha_1\alpha_2 + 10\alpha_1\alpha_3 + 5\alpha_2^2 + 6\alpha_2\alpha_3 + 5\alpha_3^2\big) + \alpha_1 + \alpha_2 + \alpha_3 \end{aligned}$$

subject to $\alpha_1 \geq 0, \alpha_2 \geq 0, \alpha_3 \geq 0$ and $-\alpha_1 - \alpha_2 + \alpha_3 = 0$. While in practice such problems are solved by dedicated quadratic optimisation solvers, here we will show how to solve this toy problem by hand.

Using the equality constraint we can eliminate one of the variables, say α_3, and simplify the objective function to

$$\begin{aligned}\operatorname*{arg\,max}_{\alpha_1,\alpha_2,\alpha_3} -\frac{1}{2}\left(5\alpha_1^2+6\alpha_1\alpha_2+10\alpha_1(\alpha_1+\alpha_2)+5\alpha_2^2+6\alpha_2(\alpha_1+\alpha_2)+5(\alpha_1+\alpha_2)^2\right)\\ +2\alpha_1+2\alpha_2\end{aligned}$$

$$=\operatorname*{arg\,max}_{\alpha_1,\alpha_2,\alpha_3} -\frac{1}{2}\left(20\alpha_1^2+32\alpha_1\alpha_2+16\alpha_2^2\right)+2\alpha_1+2\alpha_2$$

Setting partial derivatives to 0 we obtain $-20\alpha_1-16\alpha_2+2=0$ and $-16\alpha_1-16\alpha_2+2=0$ (notice that, because the objective function is quadratic, these equations are guaranteed to be linear). We therefore obtain the solution $\alpha_1=0$ and $\alpha_2=\alpha_3=1/8$. We then have $\mathbf{w}=1/8(\mathbf{x}_3-\mathbf{x}_2)=\begin{pmatrix}0\\-1/2\end{pmatrix}$, resulting in a margin of $1/||\mathbf{w}||=2$. Finally, t can be obtained from any support vector, say $\mathbf{x}_2$, since $y_2(\mathbf{w}\cdot\mathbf{x}_2-t)=1$; this gives $-1\cdot(-1-t)=1$, hence $t=0$. The resulting maximum-margin classifier is depicted in Figure 7.8 (left). Notice that the first example $\mathbf{x}_1$ is not a support vector, even though it is on the margin: this is because removing it will not affect the decision boundary.

We now add an additional positive at $(3,1)$. This gives the following data matrices:

$$\mathbf{X}'=\begin{pmatrix}-1 & -2\\ 1 & -2\\ -1 & -2\\ 3 & 1\end{pmatrix}\qquad \mathbf{X}'\mathbf{X}'^{\mathrm{T}}=\begin{pmatrix}5 & 3 & 5 & -5\\ 3 & 5 & 3 & 1\\ 5 & 3 & 5 & -5\\ -5 & 1 & -5 & 10\end{pmatrix}$$

It can be verified by similar calculations to those above that the margin decreases to 1 and the decision boundary rotates to $\mathbf{w}=\begin{pmatrix}3/5\\-4/5\end{pmatrix}$ (Figure 7.8 (right)). The Lagrange multipliers now are $\alpha_1=1/2$, $\alpha_2=0$, $\alpha_3=1/10$ and $\alpha_4=2/5$. Thus, only $\mathbf{x}_3$ is a support vector in both the original and the extended data set.

Soft margin SVM

If the data is not linearly separable, then the constraints $\mathbf{w}\cdot\mathbf{x}_i-t\geq 1$ posed by the examples are not jointly satisfiable. However, there is a very elegant way of adapting the optimisation problem such that it admits a solution even in this case. The idea is to introduce *slack variables* ξ_i, one for each example, which allow some of them to be inside the margin or even at the wrong side of the decision boundary – we will call these *margin errors*. Thus, we change the constraints to $\mathbf{w}\cdot\mathbf{x}_i-t\geq 1-\xi_i$ and add the sum of all slack variables to the objective function to be minimised, resulting in the following *soft margin* optimisation problem:

$$\mathbf{w}^*, t^*, \xi_i^* = \operatorname*{arg\,min}_{\mathbf{w},t,\xi_i} \frac{1}{2}||\mathbf{w}||^2 + C\sum_{i=1}^{n} \xi_i$$

$$\text{subject to } y_i(\mathbf{w}\cdot\mathbf{x}_i - t) \geq 1 - \xi_i \text{ and } \xi_i \geq 0, 1 \leq i \leq n \tag{7.11}$$

C is a user-defined parameter trading off margin maximisation against slack variable minimisation: a high value of C means that margin errors incur a high penalty, while a low value permits more margin errors (possibly including misclassifications) in order to achieve a large margin. If we allow more margin errors we need fewer support vectors, hence C controls to some extent the 'complexity' of the SVM and hence is often referred to as the *complexity parameter*. It can be seen as a form of regularisation similar to that discussed in the context of least-squares regression.

The Lagrange function is then as follows:

$$\begin{aligned}
\Lambda(\mathbf{w}, t, \xi_i, \alpha_i, \beta_i) &= \frac{1}{2}||\mathbf{w}||^2 + C\sum_{i=1}^{n} \xi_i - \sum_{i=1}^{n} \alpha_i(y_i(\mathbf{w}\cdot\mathbf{x}_i - t) - (1-\xi_i)) - \sum_{i=1}^{n} \beta_i\xi_i \\
&= \frac{1}{2}\mathbf{w}\cdot\mathbf{w} - \mathbf{w}\cdot\left(\sum_{i=1}^{n} \alpha_i y_i \mathbf{x}_i\right) + t\left(\sum_{i=1}^{n} \alpha_i y_i\right) + \sum_{i=1}^{n} \alpha_i + \sum_{i=1}^{n} (C - \alpha_i - \beta_i)\xi_i \\
&= \Lambda(\mathbf{w}, t, \alpha_i) + \sum_{i=1}^{n} (C - \alpha_i - \beta_i)\xi_i
\end{aligned}$$

For an optimal solution every partial derivative with respect to ξ_i should be 0, from which it follows that $C - \alpha_i - \beta_i = 0$ for all i, and hence the added term vanishes from the dual problem. Furthermore, since both α_i and β_i are positive, this means that α_i cannot be larger than C, which manifests itself as an additional upper bound on α_i in the dual problem:

$$\alpha_1^*, \ldots, \alpha_n^* = \operatorname*{arg\,max}_{\alpha_1,\ldots,\alpha_n} -\frac{1}{2}\sum_{i=1}^{n}\sum_{j=1}^{n} \alpha_i\alpha_j y_i y_j \mathbf{x}_i \cdot \mathbf{x}_j + \sum_{i=1}^{n} \alpha_i$$

$$\text{subject to } 0 \leq \alpha_i \leq C \text{ and } \sum_{i=1}^{n} \alpha_i y_i = 0 \tag{7.12}$$

This is a remarkable and beautiful result. It follows from the particular way that slack variables were added to the optimisation problem in Equation 7.11. By restricting the slack variables to be positive and adding them to the objective function to be minimised, they function as penalty terms, measuring deviations on the wrong side of the margin only. Furthermore, the fact that the β_i multipliers do not appear in the dual objective follows from the fact that the penalty term in the primal objective is linear in ξ_i. In effect, these slack variables implement what was called *hinge loss* in Figure 2.6 on p.63: a margin $z > 1$ incurs no penalty, and a margin $z = 1 - \xi \leq 1$ incurs a penalty $\xi = 1 - z$.

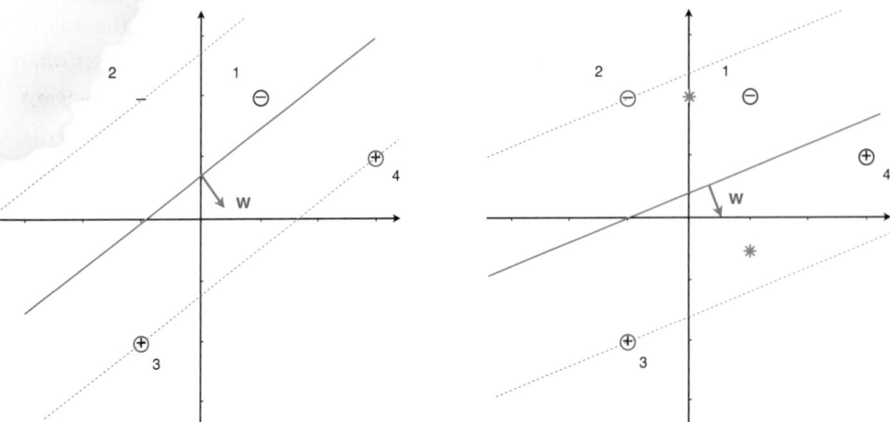

Figure 7.9. (left) The soft margin classifier learned with $C = 5/16$, at which point $\mathbf{x}_2$ is about to become a support vector. **(right)** The soft margin classifier learned with $C = 1/10$: all examples contribute equally to the weight vector. The asterisks denote the class means, and the decision boundary is parallel to the one learned by the basic linear classifier.

What is the significance of the upper bound C on the α_i multipliers? Since $C - \alpha_i - \beta_i = 0$ for all i, $\alpha_i = C$ implies $\beta_i = 0$. The β_i multipliers come from the $\xi_i \geq 0$ constraint, and a multiplier of 0 means that the lower bound is not reached, i.e., $\xi_i > 0$ (analogous to the fact that $\alpha_j = 0$ means that $\mathbf{x}_j$ is not a support vector and hence $\mathbf{w} \cdot \mathbf{x}_j - t > 1$). In other words, a solution to the soft margin optimisation problem in dual form divides the training examples into three cases:

$\alpha_i = 0$	these are outside or on the margin;
$0 < \alpha_i < C$	these are the support vectors on the margin;
$\alpha_i = C$	these are on or inside the margin.

Notice that we still have $\mathbf{w} = \sum_{i=1}^{n} \alpha_i y_i \mathbf{x}_i$, and so both second and third case examples participate in spanning the decision boundary.

Example 7.6 (Soft margins). We continue Example 7.5, where we saw that adding the positive example $\mathbf{x}_4 = (3, 1)$ to the first three examples significantly reduced the margin from 2 to 1. We will now show that soft margin classifiers with larger margins are learned with sufficiently large complexity parameter C.

Recall that the Lagrange multipliers for the classifier in Figure 7.8 (right) are $\alpha_1 = 1/2$, $\alpha_2 = 0$, $\alpha_3 = 1/10$ and $\alpha_4 = 2/5$. So α_1 is the largest multiplier, and as long as $C > \alpha_1 = 1/2$ no margin errors are tolerated. For $C = 1/2$ we have $\alpha_1 = C$, and hence for $C < 1/2$ we have that $\mathbf{x}_1$ becomes a margin error and the optimal classifier is a soft margin classifier. Effectively, with decreasing C the decision boundary and the upper margin move upward, while the lower margin stays the same.

The upper margin reaches $\mathbf{x}_2$ for $C = 5/16$ (Figure 7.9 (left)), at which point we have $\mathbf{w} = \begin{pmatrix} 3/8 \\ -1/2 \end{pmatrix}$, $t = 3/8$ and the margin has increased to 1.6. Furthermore, we have $\xi_1 = 6/8, \alpha_1 = C = 5/16, \alpha_2 = 0, \alpha_3 = 1/16$ and $\alpha_4 = 1/4$.

If we now decrease C further, the decision boundary starts to rotate clockwise, so that $\mathbf{x}_4$ becomes a margin error as well, and only $\mathbf{x}_2$ and $\mathbf{x}_3$ are support vectors. The boundary rotates until $C = 1/10$, at which point we have $\mathbf{w} = \begin{pmatrix} 1/5 \\ -1/2 \end{pmatrix}$, $t = 1/5$ and the margin has increased to 1.86. Furthermore, we have $\xi_1 = 4/10$ and $\xi_4 = 7/10$, and all multipliers have become equal to C (Figure 7.9 (right)).

Finally, when C decreases further the decision boundary stays where it is, but the norm of the weight vector gradually decreases and all points become margin errors.

Example 7.6 illustrates an important point: for low enough C, all examples receive the same multiplier C, and hence we have $\mathbf{w} = C\sum_{i=1}^{n} y_i\mathbf{x}_i = C(Pos \cdot \boldsymbol{\mu}^{\oplus} - Neg \cdot \boldsymbol{\mu}^{\ominus})$, where $\boldsymbol{\mu}^{\oplus}$ and $\boldsymbol{\mu}^{\ominus}$ are the means of the positive and negative examples, respectively. In other words, *a minimal-complexity soft margin classifier summarises the classes by their class means in a way very similar to the basic linear classifier.* For intermediate values of C the decision boundary is spanned by the support vectors and the per-class means of the margin errors.

In summary, support vector machines are linear classifiers that construct the unique decision boundary that maximises the distance to the nearest training examples (the support vectors). The complexity parameter C can be used to adjust the number and severity of allowed margin violations. Training an SVM involves solving a large quadratic optimisation problem and is usually best left to a dedicated numerical solver.

7.4 Obtaining probabilities from linear classifiers

As we have seen, a linear classifier produces scores $\hat{s}(\mathbf{x}_i) = \mathbf{w}\cdot\mathbf{x}_i - t$ that are thresholded at 0 in order to classify examples. Owing to the geometric nature of linear classifiers, such scores can be used to obtain the (signed) distance of $\mathbf{x}_i$ from the decision boundary. To see this, notice that the length of the projection of $\mathbf{x}_i$ onto $\mathbf{w}$ is $||\mathbf{x}_i||\cos\theta$, where

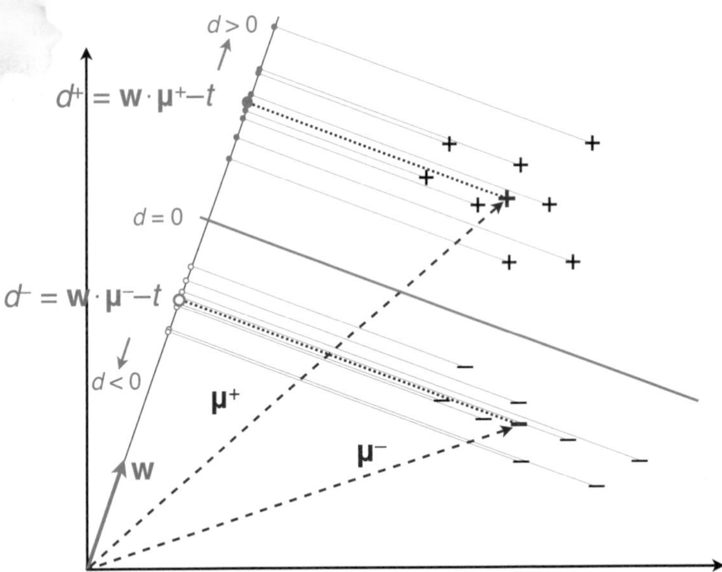

Figure 7.10. We can think of a linear classifier as a projection onto the direction given by **w**, here assumed to be a unit vector. $\mathbf{w}\cdot\mathbf{x}-t$ gives the signed distance from the decision boundary on the projection line. Also indicated are the class means $\boldsymbol{\mu}^{\oplus}$ and $\boldsymbol{\mu}^{\ominus}$, and the corresponding mean distances $d^{\oplus}$ and $d^{\ominus}$.

θ is the angle between $\mathbf{x}_i$ and $\mathbf{w}$. Since $\mathbf{w}\cdot\mathbf{x}_i = ||\mathbf{w}||\,||\mathbf{x}_i||\cos\theta$, we can write this length as $(\mathbf{w}\cdot\mathbf{x}_i)/||\mathbf{w}||$. This gives the following signed distance:

$$d(\mathbf{x}_i) = \frac{\hat{s}(\mathbf{x}_i)}{||\mathbf{w}||} = \frac{\mathbf{w}\cdot\mathbf{x}_i - t}{||\mathbf{w}||} = \mathbf{w}'\cdot\mathbf{x}_i - t'$$

with $\mathbf{w}' = \mathbf{w}/||\mathbf{w}||$ rescaled to unit length and $t' = t/||\mathbf{w}||$ the corresponding rescaled intercept. The sign of this quantity tells us which side of the decision boundary we are on: positive distances for points on the 'positive' side of the decision boundary (the direction in which **w** points) and negative distances on the other side (Figure 7.10).

This geometric interpretation of the scores produced by linear classifiers offers an interesting possibility for turning them into probabilities, a process that was called ☞*calibration* in Section 2.3. Let $\overline{d}^{\oplus}$ denote the mean distance of the positive examples to the decision boundary: i.e., $\overline{d}^{\oplus} = \mathbf{w}\cdot\boldsymbol{\mu}^{\oplus} - t$, where $\boldsymbol{\mu}^{\oplus}$ is the mean of the positive examples and **w** is unit length (although the latter assumption is not strictly necessary, as it will turn out that the weight vector will be rescaled). It would not be unreasonable to expect that the distance of positive examples to the decision boundary is normally distributed around this mean:[2] that is, when plotting a histogram of these distances,

[2]For instance, with sufficiently many examples this could be justified by the *central limit theorem*: the sum of a large number of identically distributed independent random variables is approximately normally distributed.

we would expect the familiar bell curve to appear. Under this assumption, the probability density function of d is $P(d|\oplus) = \frac{1}{\sqrt{2\pi}\sigma}\exp\left(-\frac{(d-\overline{d}^{\oplus})^2}{2\sigma^2}\right)$ (see Background 9.1 on p.267 if you need to remind yourself about the normal distribution). Similarly, the distances of negative examples to the decision boundary can be expected to be normally distributed around $\overline{d}^{\ominus} = \mathbf{w}\cdot\boldsymbol{\mu}^{\ominus} - t$, with $\overline{d}^{\ominus} < 0 < \overline{d}^{\oplus}$. We will assume that both normal distributions have the same variance σ^2.

Suppose we now observe a point $\mathbf{x}$ with distance $d(\mathbf{x})$. We classify this point as positive if $d(\mathbf{x}) > 0$ and as negative if $d(\mathbf{x}) < 0$, but we want to attach a probability $\hat{p}(\mathbf{x}) = P(\oplus|d(\mathbf{x}))$ to these predictions. Using Bayes' rule we obtain

$$P(\oplus|d(\mathbf{x})) = \frac{P(d(\mathbf{x})|\oplus)P(\oplus)}{P(d(\mathbf{x})|\oplus)P(\oplus) + P(d(\mathbf{x})|\ominus)P(\ominus)} = \frac{LR}{LR + 1/clr}$$

where LR is the likelihood ratio obtained from the normal score distributions, and clr is the class ratio. We will assume for simplicity that $clr = 1$ in the derivation below. Furthermore, assume for now that $\sigma^2 = 1$ and $\overline{d}^{\oplus} = -\overline{d}^{\ominus} = 1/2$ (we will relax this in a moment). We then have

$$\begin{aligned} LR = \frac{P(d(\mathbf{x})|\oplus)}{P(d(\mathbf{x})|\ominus)} &= \frac{\exp\left(-(d(\mathbf{x}) - 1/2)^2/2\right)}{\exp\left(-(d(\mathbf{x}) + 1/2)^2/2\right)} \\ &= \exp\left(-(d(\mathbf{x}) - 1/2)^2/2 + (d(\mathbf{x}) + 1/2)^2/2\right) = \exp(d(\mathbf{x})) \end{aligned}$$

and so

$$P(\oplus|d(\mathbf{x})) = \frac{\exp(d(\mathbf{x}))}{\exp(d(\mathbf{x})) + 1} = \frac{\exp(\mathbf{w}\cdot\mathbf{x} - t)}{\exp(\mathbf{w}\cdot\mathbf{x} - t) + 1}$$

So, in order to obtain probability estimates from a linear classifier outputting distance scores d, we convert d into a probability by means of the mapping $d \mapsto \frac{\exp(d)}{\exp(d)+1}$ (or, equivalently, $d \mapsto \frac{1}{1+\exp(-d)}$). This S-shaped or *sigmoid* function is called the *logistic function*; it finds applications in a wide range of areas (Figure 7.11).

Suppose now that $\overline{d}^{\oplus} = -\overline{d}^{\ominus}$ as before, but we do not assume anything about the magnitude of these mean distances or of σ^2. In this case we have

$$\begin{aligned} LR &= \exp\left(\frac{-(d(\mathbf{x}) - \overline{d}^{\oplus})^2 + (d(\mathbf{x}) - \overline{d}^{\ominus})^2}{2\sigma^2}\right) \\ &= \exp\left(\frac{2\overline{d}^{\oplus} d(\mathbf{x}) - \left(\overline{d}^{\oplus}\right)^2 - 2\overline{d}^{\ominus} d(\mathbf{x}) + \left(\overline{d}^{\ominus}\right)^2}{2\sigma^2}\right) = \exp\left(\gamma d(\mathbf{x})\right) \end{aligned}$$

with $a = (\overline{d}^{\oplus} - \overline{d}^{\ominus})/\sigma^2$ a scaling factor that rescales the weight vector so that the mean distances per class are one unit of variance apart. In other words, by taking the scaling factor γ into account, we can drop our assumption that $\mathbf{w}$ is a unit vector.

If we also drop the assumption that $\overline{d}^{\oplus}$ and $\overline{d}^{\ominus}$ are symmetric around the decision

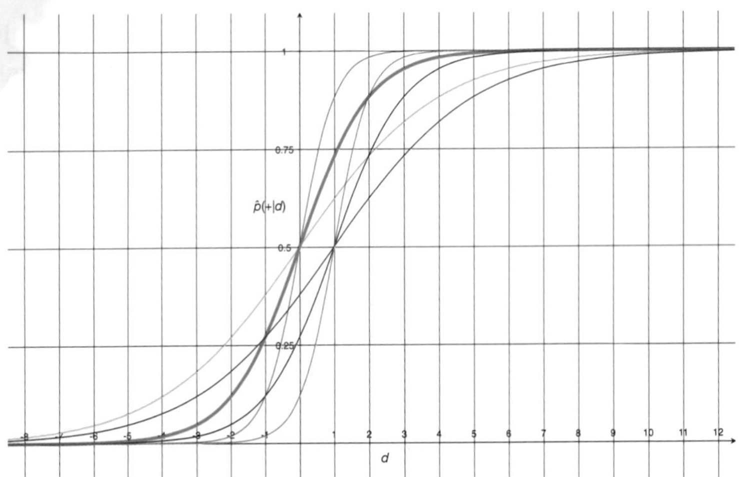

Figure 7.11. The logistic function, a useful function for mapping distances from a linear decision boundary into an estimate of the positive posterior probability. The **fat** red line indicates the standard logistic function $\hat{p}(d) = \frac{1}{1+\exp(-d)}$; this function can be used to obtain probability estimates if the two classes are equally prevalent and the class means are equidistant from the decision boundary and one unit of variance apart. The steeper and flatter red lines show how the function changes if the class means are 2 and 1/2 units of variance apart, respectively. The three blue lines show how these curves change if $d_0 = 1$, which means that the positives are on average further away from the decision boundary.

boundary, then we obtain the most general form

$$LR = \frac{P(d(\mathbf{x})|\oplus)}{P(d(\mathbf{x})|\ominus)} = \exp\left(\gamma(d(\mathbf{x}) - d_0)\right) \tag{7.13}$$

$$\gamma = \frac{\overline{d}^{\oplus} - \overline{d}^{\ominus}}{\sigma^2} = \frac{\mathbf{w}\cdot(\boldsymbol{\mu}^{\oplus} - \boldsymbol{\mu}^{\ominus})}{\sigma^2}, \quad d_0 = \frac{\overline{d}^{\oplus} + \overline{d}^{\ominus}}{2} = \frac{\mathbf{w}\cdot(\boldsymbol{\mu}^{\oplus} + \boldsymbol{\mu}^{\ominus})}{2} - t$$

d_0 has the effect of moving the decision boundary from $\mathbf{w}\cdot\mathbf{x} = t$ to $\mathbf{x} = (\boldsymbol{\mu}^{\oplus} + \boldsymbol{\mu}^{\ominus})/2$, that is, halfway between the two class means. The logistic mapping thus becomes $d \mapsto \frac{1}{1+\exp(-\gamma(d-d_0))}$, and the effect of the two parameters is visualised in Figure 7.11.

Example 7.7 (Logistic calibration of a linear classifier). Logistic calibration has a particularly simple form for the basic linear classifier, which has $\mathbf{w} = \boldsymbol{\mu}^{\oplus} - \boldsymbol{\mu}^{\ominus}$. It follows that

$$\overline{d}^{\oplus} - \overline{d}^{\ominus} = \frac{\mathbf{w}\cdot(\boldsymbol{\mu}^{\oplus} - \boldsymbol{\mu}^{\ominus})}{||\mathbf{w}||} = \frac{||\boldsymbol{\mu}^{\oplus} - \boldsymbol{\mu}^{\ominus}||^2}{||\boldsymbol{\mu}^{\oplus} - \boldsymbol{\mu}^{\ominus}||} = ||\boldsymbol{\mu}^{\oplus} - \boldsymbol{\mu}^{\ominus}||$$

and hence $\gamma = ||\boldsymbol{\mu}^{\oplus} - \boldsymbol{\mu}^{\ominus}||/\sigma^2$. Furthermore, $d_0 = 0$ as $(\boldsymbol{\mu}^{\oplus} + \boldsymbol{\mu}^{\ominus})/2$ is already on the decision boundary. So in this case logistic calibration does not move the

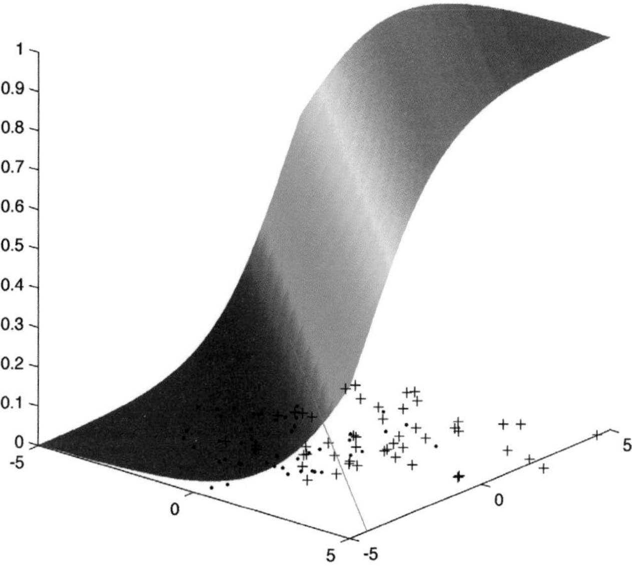

Figure 7.12. The surface shows the sigmoidal probability estimates resulting from logistic calibration of the basic linear classifier on random data satisfying the assumptions of logistic calibration.

decision boundary, and only adjusts the steepness of the sigmoid according to the separation of the classes. Figure 7.12 illustrates this for some data sampled from two normal distributions with the same diagonal covariance matrix.

To summarise: in order to get calibrated probability estimates out of a linear classifier, we first calculate the mean distances $\overline{d}^{\oplus}$ and $\overline{d}^{\ominus}$ and the variance σ^2, and from those the location parameter d_0 and the scaling parameter γ. The likelihood ratio is then $LR = \exp\left(\gamma(d(\mathbf{x}) - d_0)\right) = \exp\left(\gamma(\mathbf{w}\cdot\mathbf{x} - t - d_0)\right)$. Since the logarithm of the likelihood ratio is linear in $\mathbf{x}$, such models are called *log-linear models*. Notice that $\gamma(\mathbf{w}\cdot\mathbf{x} - t - d_0) = \mathbf{w}'\cdot\mathbf{x} - t'$ with $\mathbf{w}' = \gamma\mathbf{w}$ and $t' = \gamma(t + d_0)$. This means that the logistic calibration procedure can change the location of the decision boundary but not its direction. However, there may be an alternative weight vector with a different direction that assigns a higher likelihood to the data. Finding the maximum-likelihood linear classifier using the logistic model is called ☞*logistic regression*, and will be discussed in Section 9.3.

As an alternative to logistic calibration, we can also use the isotonic calibration

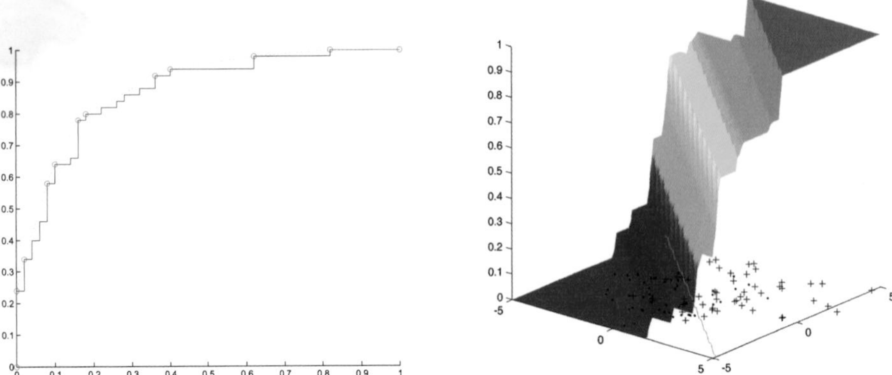

Figure 7.13. **(left)** ROC curve and convex hull of the same model and data as in Figure 7.12. **(right)** The convex hull can be used as a non-parametric calibration method. Each segment of the convex hull corresponds to a plateau of the probability surface.

method discussed in Section 2.3. Figure 7.13 (left) shows the ROC curve of the basic linear classifier on the data in Figure 7.12 as well as its convex hull. We can then construct a piecewise linear calibration function with plateaus corresponding to the convex hull segments, as shown in Figure 7.13 (right). In contrast with the logistic method this calibration method is non-parametric and hence does not make any assumptions about the data. In order to avoid overfitting, non-parametric methods typically need more data than parametric methods. It is interesting to note that no grading takes place on the plateaus, which are rather similar to the segments of a grouping model. In other words, convex hull calibration can potentially produce a hybrid between grouping and grading models.

7.5 Going beyond linearity with kernel methods

In this chapter we have looked at linear methods for classification and regression. Starting with the least-squares method for regression, we have seen how to adapt it to binary classification, resulting in a version of the basic linear classifier that takes feature correlation into account by constructing the matrix $(\mathbf{X}^{\mathrm{T}}\mathbf{X})^{-1}$ and is sensitive to unequal class distributions. We then looked at the heuristic perceptron algorithm for linearly separable data, and the support vector machine which finds the unique decision boundary with maximum margin and which can be adapted to non-separable data. In this section we show that these techniques can be adapted to learn non-linear decision boundaries. The main idea is simple (and was already explored in Example 1.9 on p.43): to transform the data non-linearly to a feature space in which linear classification can be applied.

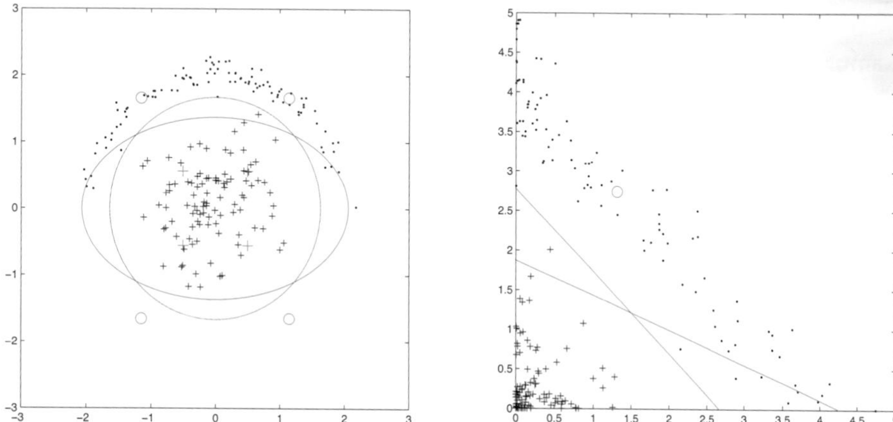

Figure 7.14. (left) Decision boundaries learned by the basic linear classifier and the perceptron using the square of the features. **(right)** Data and decision boundaries in the transformed feature space.

Example 7.8 (Learning a quadratic decision boundary). The data in Figure 7.14 (left) is not linearly separable, but both classes have a clear circular shape. Figure 7.14 (right) shows the same data with the feature values squared. In this transformed feature space the data has become linearly separable, and the perceptron is able to separate the classes. The resulting decision boundary in the original space is a near-circle. Also shown is the decision boundary learned by the basic linear classifier in the quadratic feature space, corresponding to an ellipse in the original space.

In general, mapping points back from the feature space to the instance space is non-trivial. E.g., in this example each class mean in feature space maps back to four points in the original space, owing to the quadratic mapping.

It is customary to call the transformed space the *feature space* and the original space the *input space*. The approach thus appears to be to transform the training data to feature space and learn a model there. In order to classify new data we transform that to feature space as well and apply the model. However, the remarkable thing is that in many cases the feature space does not have to be explicitly constructed, as we can perform all necessary operations in input space.

Take the perceptron algorithm in dual form, for example (Algorithm 7.2 on p.209). The algorithm is a simple counting algorithm – the only operation that is somewhat involved is testing whether example $\mathbf{x}_i$ is correctly classified by evaluating $y_i \sum_{j=1}^{|D|} \alpha_j y_j \mathbf{x}_i \cdot$

$\mathbf{x}_j$. The key component of this calculation is the dot product $\mathbf{x}_i \cdot \mathbf{x}_j$. Assuming bivariate examples $\mathbf{x}_i = (x_i, y_i)$ and $\mathbf{x}_j = (x_j, y_j)$ for notational simplicity, the dot product can be written as $\mathbf{x}_i \cdot \mathbf{x}_j = x_i x_j + y_i y_j$. The corresponding instances in the quadratic feature space are (x_i^2, y_i^2) and (x_j^2, y_j^2), and their dot product is

$$(x_i^2, y_i^2) \cdot (x_j^2, y_j^2) = x_i^2 x_j^2 + y_i^2 y_j^2$$

This is almost equal to

$$(\mathbf{x}_i \cdot \mathbf{x}_j)^2 = (x_i x_j + y_i y_j)^2 = (x_i x_j)^2 + (y_i y_j)^2 + 2 x_i x_j y_i y_j$$

but not quite because of the third term of cross-products. We can capture this term by extending the feature vector with a third feature $\sqrt{2}xy$. This gives the following feature space:

$$\phi(\mathbf{x}_i) = \left(x_i^2, y_i^2, \sqrt{2} x_i y_i\right) \qquad \phi(\mathbf{x}_j) = \left(x_j^2, y_j^2, \sqrt{2} x_j y_j\right)$$
$$\phi(\mathbf{x}_i) \cdot \phi(\mathbf{x}_j) = x_i^2 x_j^2 + y_i^2 y_j^2 + 2 x_i x_j y_i y_j = (\mathbf{x}_i \cdot \mathbf{x}_j)^2$$

We now define $\kappa(\mathbf{x}_i, \mathbf{x}_j) = (\mathbf{x}_i \cdot \mathbf{x}_j)^2$, and replace $\mathbf{x}_i \cdot \mathbf{x}_j$ with $\kappa(\mathbf{x}_i, \mathbf{x}_j)$ in the dual perceptron algorithm to obtain the *kernel perceptron* (Algorithm 7.4), which is able to learn the kind of non-linear decision boundaries illustrated in Example 7.8.

The introduction of kernels opens up a whole range of possibilities. Clearly we can define a polynomial kernel of any degree p as $\kappa(\mathbf{x}_i, \mathbf{x}_j) = (\mathbf{x}_i \cdot \mathbf{x}_j)^p$. This transforms

---

Algorithm 7.4: KernelPerceptron(D, κ) – perceptron training algorithm using a kernel.

Input : labelled training data D in homogeneous coordinates;
kernel function κ.

Output : coefficients α_i defining non-linear decision boundary.

$\alpha_i \leftarrow 0$ for $1 \le i \le |D|$;
converged←false;
while *converged* = false **do**
    converged←true;
    for $i = 1$ to $|D|$ **do**
        if $y_i \sum_{j=1}^{|D|} \alpha_j y_j \kappa(\mathbf{x}_i, \mathbf{x}_j) \le 0$ **then**
            $\alpha_i \leftarrow \alpha_i + 1$;
            converged←false;
        end
    end
end

---

a d-dimensional input space into a high-dimensional feature space, such that each new feature is a product of p terms (possibly repeated). If we include a constant, say $\kappa(\mathbf{x}_i, \mathbf{x}_j) = (\mathbf{x}_i \cdot \mathbf{x}_j + 1)^p$, we would get all lower-order terms as well. So, for example, in a bivariate input space and setting $p = 2$ the resulting feature space is

$$\phi(\mathbf{x}) = \left(x^2, y^2, \sqrt{2}xy, \sqrt{2}x, \sqrt{2}y, 1\right)$$

with linear as well as quadratic features.

But we are not restricted to polynomial kernels. An often-used kernel is the *Gaussian kernel*, defined as

$$\kappa(\mathbf{x}_i, \mathbf{x}_j) = \exp\left(\frac{-||\mathbf{x}_i - \mathbf{x}_j||^2}{2\sigma^2}\right) \tag{7.14}$$

where σ is a parameter known as the *bandwidth*. To understand the Gaussian kernel a bit better, notice that $\kappa(\mathbf{x}, \mathbf{x}) = \phi(\mathbf{x}) \cdot \phi(\mathbf{x}) = ||\phi(\mathbf{x})||^2$ for any kernel obeying a number of standard properties referred to as 'positive semi-definiteness'. In this case we have $\kappa(\mathbf{x}, \mathbf{x}) = 1$, which means that all points $\phi(\mathbf{x})$ lie on a hypersphere around the feature space origin – which is however of infinite dimension, so geometric considerations don't help us much here. It is more helpful to think of a Gaussian kernel as imposing a Gaussian (i.e., multivariate normal, see Background 9.1 on p.267) surface on each support vector in instance space, so that the decision boundary is defined in terms of those Gaussian surfaces.

Kernel methods are best known in combination with support vector machines. Notice that the soft margin optimisation problem (Equation 7.12 on p.217) is defined in terms of dot products between training instances and hence the 'kernel trick' can be applied:

$$\alpha_1^*, \ldots, \alpha_n^* = \underset{\alpha_1, \ldots, \alpha_n}{\arg\max} -\frac{1}{2} \sum_{i=1}^{n} \sum_{j=1}^{n} \alpha_i \alpha_j y_i y_j \kappa(\mathbf{x}_i, \mathbf{x}_j) + \sum_{i=1}^{n} \alpha_i$$

$$\text{subject to } 0 \le \alpha_i \le C \text{ and } \sum_{i=1}^{n} \alpha_i y_i = 0$$

One thing to keep in mind is that the decision boundary learned with a non-linear kernel cannot be represented by a simple weight vector in input space. Thus, in order to classify a new example $\mathbf{x}$ we need to evaluate $y_i \sum_{j=1}^{n} \alpha_j y_j \kappa(\mathbf{x}, \mathbf{x}_j)$ which is an $O(n)$ computation involving all training examples, or at least the ones with non-zero multipliers α_j. This is why support vector machines are a popular choice as a kernel method, since they naturally promote sparsity in the support vectors. Although we have restricted attention to numerical features here, it is worth stressing that kernels can be defined over discrete structures, including trees, graphs, and logical formulae, and thus open the way to extending geometric models to non-numerical data.

7.6 Linear models: Summary and further reading

After considering logical models in the previous three chapters we had a good look at linear models in this chapter. Logical models are inherently non-numerical, and so deal with numerical features by using thresholds to convert them into two or more intervals. Linear models are almost diametrically opposite in that they can deal with numerical features directly but need to pre-process non-numerical features.[3] Geometrically, linear models use lines and planes to build the model, which essentially means that a certain increase or decrease in one of the features has the same effect, regardless of that feature's value or any of the other features. They are simple and robust to variations in the training data, but sometimes suffer from underfitting as a consequence.

- ☞ In Section 7.1 we considered the least-squares method that was originally conceived to solve a regression problem. This classical method, which derives its name from minimising the sum of squared residuals between predicted and actual function values, is described in innumerable introductory mathematics and engineering texts (and was one of the example programs I remember running on my father's Texas Instruments TI-58 programmable calculator). We first had a look at the problem in univariate form, and then derived the general solution as $\hat{\mathbf{w}} = (\mathbf{X}^{\mathrm{T}}\mathbf{X})^{-1}\mathbf{X}^{\mathrm{T}}\mathbf{y}$, where $(\mathbf{X}^{\mathrm{T}}\mathbf{X})^{-1}$ is a transformation that decorrelates, centres and normalises the features. We then discussed regularised versions of linear regression: ridge regression was introduced by Hoerl and Kennard (1970), and the lasso which naturally leads to sparse solutions was introduced by Tibshirani (1996). We saw how the least-squares method could be applied to binary classification by encoding the classes by +1 and −1, leading to the solution $\hat{\mathbf{w}} = (\mathbf{X}^{\mathrm{T}}\mathbf{X})^{-1}(Pos\,\boldsymbol{\mu}^{\oplus} - Neg\,\boldsymbol{\mu}^{\ominus})$. This generalises the basic linear classifier by taking feature correlation and unequal class prevalence into account, but at a considerably increased computational cost (quadratic in the number of instances and cubic in the number of features).

- ☞ Section 7.2 presented another classical linear model, the perceptron. Unlike the least-squares method, which always finds the optimal solution in terms of sum of squared residuals, the perceptron is a heuristic algorithm that depends, for one thing, on the order in which the examples are presented. Invented by Rosenblatt (1958), its convergence for linearly separable data was proved by Novikoff (1962), who gave an upper bound on the number of mistakes made before the perceptron converged. Minsky and Papert (1969) proved further formal properties of the perceptron, but also demonstrated the limitations of a linear classifier. These were overcome with the development, over an extended period of time and with contributions from many people, of the multilayer perceptron and its

[3] Ways to pre-process non-numerical features for use in linear models are discussed in Chapter 10.

back-propagation training algorithm (Rumelhart, Hinton and Williams, 1986). In this section we also learned about the dual, instance-based view of linear classification in which we are learning instance weights rather than feature weights. For the perceptron these weights are the number of times the example has been misclassified during training.

☞ Maximum-margin classification with support vector machines was the topic of Section 7.3. The approach was proposed by Boser, Guyon and Vapnik (1992). Using the dual formulation, the instance weights are non-zero only for the support vectors, which are the training instances on the margin. The soft-margin generalisation is due to Cortes and Vapnik (1995). Margin errors are allowed, but the total margin error is added as a regularisation term to the objective function to be minimised, weighted by the complexity parameter C; all instances inside the margin receive instance weight C. As we have seen, by making C sufficiently small the support vector machine summarises the classes by their unweighted class means and hence is very similar to the basic linear classifier. A general introduction to SVMs is provided by Cristianini and Shawe-Taylor (2000). The sequential minimal optimisation algorithm is an often-used solver which iteratively selects pairs of multipliers to optimise analytically and is due to Platt (1998).

☞ In Section 7.4 we considered two methods to turn linear classifiers into probability estimators by converting the signed distance from the decision boundary into class probabilities. One well-known method is to use the logistic function, either straight out of the box or by fitting location and spread parameters to the data. Although this is often presented as a simple trick, we saw how it can be justified by assuming that the distances per class are normally distributed with the same variance; this latter assumption is needed to make the transformation monotonic. A non-parametric alternative is to use the ROC convex hull to obtain calibrated probability estimates. As was already mentioned in the summary of Chapter 2, the approach has its roots in isotonic regression (Best and Chakravarti, 1990) and was introduced to the machine learning community by Zadrozny and Elkan (2002). Fawcett and Niculescu-Mizil (2007) and Flach and Matsubara (2007) show its equivalence to calibration by means of the ROC convex hull.

☞ Finally, Section 7.5 discussed briefly how to go beyond linearity with kernel methods. The 'kernel trick' can be applied to any learning algorithm that can be entirely described in terms of dot products, which includes most approaches discussed in this chapter. The beauty is that we are implicitly classifying in a high-dimensional feature space, without having to construct the space explicitly. I gave the kernel perceptron as a simple example of a kernelised algorithm; in the next chapter we will see another example. Shawe-Taylor and Cristianini (2004) provide an excellent reference bringing together a wealth of material on the use of kernels in machine learning, and Gärtner (2009) discusses how kernel methods can be applied to structured, non-numerical data.

CHAPTER 8

Distance-based models

MANY FORMS OF LEARNING are based on generalising from training data to unseen data by exploiting the similarities between the two. With grouping models such as decision trees these similarities take the form of an equivalence relation or partition of the instance space: two instances are similar whenever they end up in the same segment of this partition. In this chapter we consider learning methods that utilise more graded forms of similarity. There are many different ways in which similarity can be measured, and in Section 8.1 we take a look at the most important of them. Section 8.2 is devoted to a discussion of two key concepts in distance-based machine learning: neighbours and exemplars. In Section 8.3 we consider what is perhaps the best-known distance-based learning method: the nearest-neighbour classifier. Section 8.4 investigates K-means clustering and close relatives, and Section 8.5 looks at hierarchical clustering by constructing dendrograms. Finally, in Section 8.6 we discuss how several of these methods can be extended using the kind of kernels that we saw in the previous chapter.

8.1 So many roads...

It may seem odd at first that there should be many ways to measure distance. I am not referring to the fact that distance can be measured on different scales (kilometres, miles, nautical miles, and so on), as such changes of scale are simple monotonic trans-

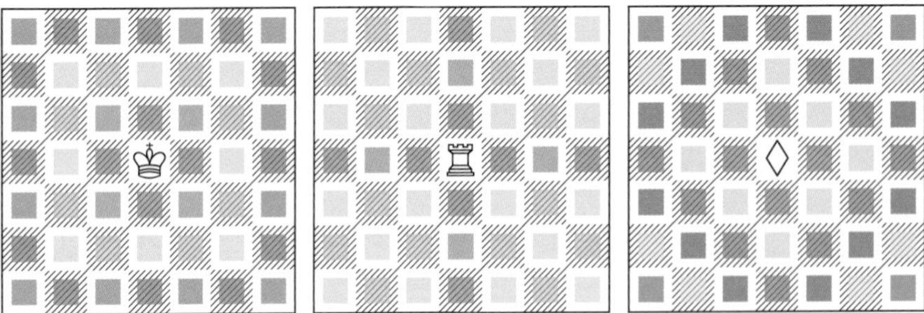

Figure 8.1. **(left)** Distance as experienced by a King on a chessboard: green squares are one move away, orange ones two moves and red ones three moves. The shape formed by equidistant squares from the current position is itself a square. **(middle)** A Rook can travel any number of squares in one move, but only horizontally or vertically. No square is further than two moves away. **(right)** The (fictional) KRook combines the restrictions of King and Rook: it can move only one square at a time, and only horizontally or vertically. Equidistant squares now form a lozenge.

formations and do not fundamentally alter the distance measure. A better intuition is obtained by taking the mode of travel into account. Clearly, when travelling from Bristol to Amsterdam by train you travel a larger distance then when travelling by plane, because planes are less restricted in their paths than trains. We will explore this a bit further by considering the game of chess.

In chess, each piece is governed by a set of rules that restrict its possible moves. These restrictions can be directional: for instance, King and Queen can move horizontally, vertically and diagonally, while a Bishop can only move diagonally, a Rook only horizontally and vertically, and pawns only upwards. King and pawn are further restricted by the fact that they can move only one square at a time, whereas Queen, Rook and Bishop can move any number of squares in a single allowed direction. Finally, a Knight moves according to a very specific pattern (one diagonal step and one horizontal or vertical step in a single move).

Although these pieces move around on the same board, they experience distances in very different ways. For example, the next square down is one move away for King, Queen and Rook; three moves away for a Knight; and unreachable for Bishop or pawn. This is, of course, very similar to our experience in the real world. Trains and cars can only move along tracks or roads, like a Bishop, which leaves remote places unreachable. A mountain range can mean large detours when travelling by car, train or on foot, but is easy to cross when flying. On an underground, two stations a few streets away may be only reachable with several changes of line, not unlike the way a Knight can reach a nearby square only in two or three moves. And on foot we are most flexible but

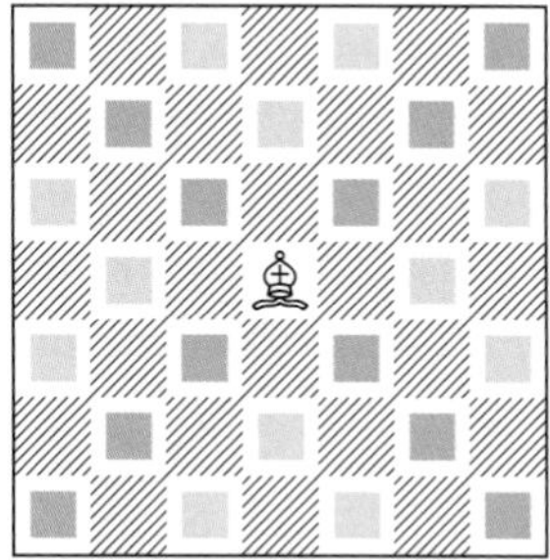
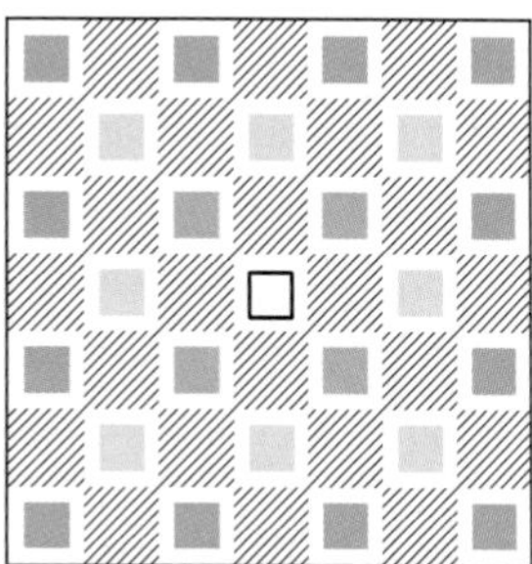

Figure 8.2. (left) The Bishop's world: squares are either one or two moves away, or else unreachable. **(right)** The fictional Bing combines the restrictions of King and Bishop: it can only move one square at a time, and only diagonally. Equidistant squares now form a punctuated square.

also slow, like a King.

Figure 8.1 visualises the distances experienced by King and Rook. Both can reach all parts of the chessboard, but a Rook can travel much faster. In fact, a Rook can reach any square in either one or two moves (assuming no other pieces are in its way). All squares one move away form a cross, and the remaining squares are one additional move away. A King will often have to travel more than two moves to reach a particular square (although there are also squares that the King can reach in one move while a Rook needs two). The squares one move away form a small square shape around the current position; those two moves away form a larger square around the smaller square; and so on. Figure 8.1 (right) shows a piece that doesn't exist in chess, but could. It combines the restrictions of King and Rook, and I therefore call it a KRook. Like a King, it can only move one square at a time; and like a Rook, it can only move horizontally and vertically. For the KRook, equidistant squares form a sort of lozenge around the current position.

Figure 8.2 (left) visualises the Bishop's moves. The Bishop is somewhat similar to the Rook in that some squares (those of the same colour as its current square) are never more than two moves away; however, the remaining squares of the other colour are unreachable. Combining the restrictions of the Bishop (only diagonal moves) with those of the King (one square per move) we obtain another fictional piece, the Bing (Figure 8.2 (right)). We could say that the world of Bishops and Bings is rotated 45 degrees, compared with the world of Rooks and KRooks.

What's the relevance of all this when trying to understand distance-based machine learning, you may ask? Well, the rank (row) and file (column) on a chessboard is not unlike a discrete or categorical feature in machine learning (in fact, since ranks and files are ordered, they are ☞*ordinal features*, as we will further discuss in Chapter 10). We can switch to real-valued features by imagining a 'continuous' chessboard with infinitely many, infinitesimally narrow ranks and files. Squares now become points, and distances are not expressed as the number of squares travelled, but simply as a real number on some scale. If we now look at the shapes obtained by connecting equidistant points, we see that many of these carry over from the discrete to the continuous case. For a King, for example, all points a given fixed distance away still form a square around the current position; and for a KRook they still form a square rotated 45 degrees. As it happens, these are special cases of the following generic concept.

Definition 8.1 (Minkowski distance). *If* $\mathscr{X} = \mathbb{R}^d$, *the* Minkowski distance *of order* $p > 0$ *is defined as*

$$\mathrm{Dis}_p(\mathbf{x},\mathbf{y}) = \left(\sum_{j=1}^{d} |x_j - y_j|^p\right)^{1/p} = ||\mathbf{x}-\mathbf{y}||_p$$

where $||\mathbf{z}||_p = \left(\sum_{j=1}^{d} |z_j|^p\right)^{1/p}$ *is the* p-norm *(sometimes denoted* L_p *norm) of the vector* $\mathbf{z}$. *We will often refer to* Dis_p *simply as the* p*-norm.*

So, the *2-norm* refers to the familiar *Euclidean distance*

$$\mathrm{Dis}_2(\mathbf{x},\mathbf{y}) = \sqrt{\sum_{j=1}^{d} (x_j - y_j)^2} = \sqrt{(\mathbf{x}-\mathbf{y})^{\mathrm{T}}(\mathbf{x}-\mathbf{y})}$$

which measures distance 'as the crow flies'. Two other values of p can be related back to the chess example. The *1-norm* denotes *Manhattan distance*, also called *cityblock distance*:

$$\mathrm{Dis}_1(\mathbf{x},\mathbf{y}) = \sum_{j=1}^{d} |x_j - y_j|$$

This is the distance if we can only travel along coordinate axes: similar to a taxi in Manhattan or other cities whose streets follow a regular grid pattern, but also the distance experienced by our fictional KRook piece. If we now let p grow larger, the distance will be more and more dominated by the largest coordinate-wise distance, from which we can infer that $\mathrm{Dis}_\infty(\mathbf{x},\mathbf{y}) = \max_j |x_j - y_j|$. This is the distance experienced by the King on a chessboard, who can move diagonally as well as horizontally and vertically but only one step at a time; it is also called *Chebyshev distance*. Figure 8.3 (left) visualises equidistant points from the origin using Minkowski distances of various orders. It can be seen that Euclidean distance is the only Minkowski distance that is rotation-invariant – in other words, special significance is given to the directions of the coordinate axes whenever $p \neq 2$. Minkowski distances do not refer to a particular choice of origin and are therefore translation-invariant, but none of them are scaling-invariant.

You will sometimes see references to the *0-norm* (or L_0 norm) which counts the number of non-zero elements in a vector. The corresponding distance then counts the

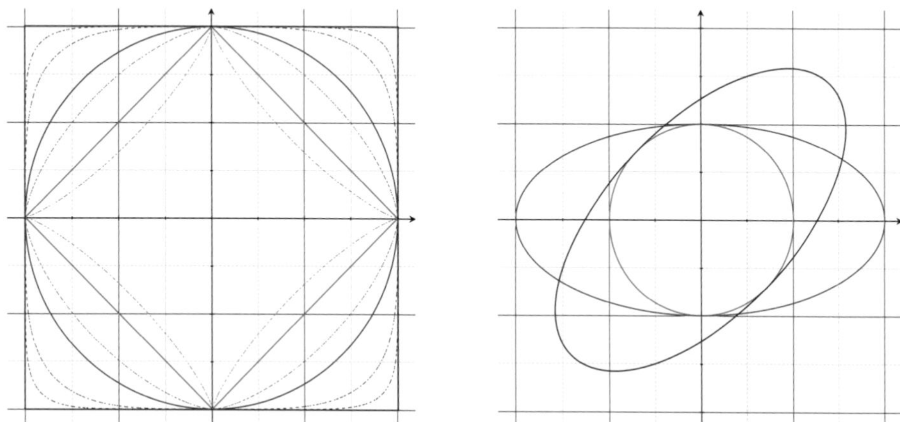

Figure 8.3. **(left)** Lines connecting points at order-p Minkowski distance 1 from the origin for (from inside) $p = 0.8$; $p = 1$ (Manhattan distance, the rotated square in red); $p = 1.5$; $p = 2$ (Euclidean distance, the violet circle); $p = 4$; $p = 8$; and $p = \infty$ (Chebyshev distance, the blue rectangle). Notice that for points on the coordinate axes all distances agree. For the other points, our reach increases with p; however, if we require a rotation-invariant distance metric then Euclidean distance is our only choice. **(right)** The rotated ellipse $\mathbf{x}^{\mathrm{T}}\mathbf{R}^{\mathrm{T}}\mathbf{S}^2\mathbf{R}\mathbf{x} = 1/4$; the axis-parallel ellipse $\mathbf{x}^{\mathrm{T}}\mathbf{S}^2\mathbf{x} = 1/4$; and the circle $\mathbf{x}^{\mathrm{T}}\mathbf{x} = 1/4$ (**R** and **S** as in Example 8.1).

number of positions in which vectors **x** and **y** differ. This is not strictly a Minkowski distance; however, we can define it as

$$\mathrm{Dis}_0(\mathbf{x},\mathbf{y}) = \sum_{j=1}^{d}(x_j - y_j)^0 = \sum_{j=1}^{d} I[x_j = y_j]$$

under the understanding that $x^0 = 0$ for $x = 0$ and 1 otherwise. This is actually the distance experienced by a Rook on the chessboard: if both rank and file are different the square is two moves away, if only one of them is different the square is one move away. If **x** and **y** are binary strings, this is also called the *Hamming distance*. Alternatively, we can see the Hamming distance as the number of bits that need to be flipped to change **x** into **y**; for non-binary strings of unequal length this can be generalised to the notion of *edit distance* or *Levenshtein distance*.

Do all of these mathematical constructs make sense as a notion of distance? In order to answer that question we can draw up a list of properties that a proper distance measure should have, such as non-negativity and symmetry. The generally agreed-upon list defines what is known as a metric.

Definition 8.2 (Distance metric). *Given an instance space* $\mathscr{X}$, *a* distance metric *is a function* $\mathrm{Dis} : \mathscr{X} \times \mathscr{X} \to \mathbb{R}$ *such that for any* $x, y, z \in \mathscr{X}$*:*

1. *distances between a point and itself are zero:* $\mathrm{Dis}(x,x) = 0$;

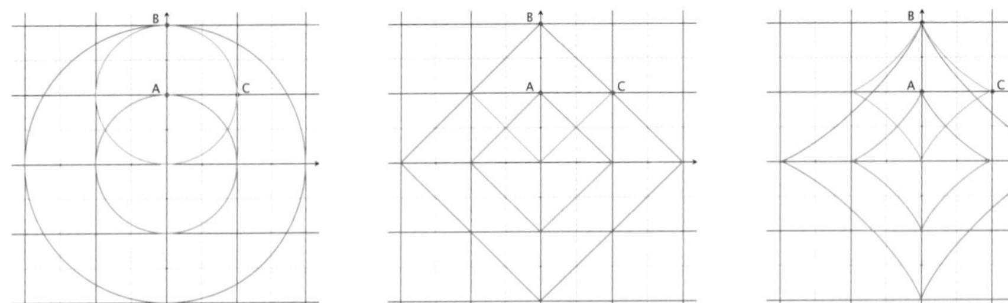

Figure 8.4. (left) The green circle connects points the same Euclidean distance (i.e., Minkowski distance of order $p = 2$) away from the origin as A. The orange circle shows that B and C are equidistant from A. The red circle demonstrates that C is closer to the origin than B, which conforms to the triangle inequality. **(middle)** With Manhattan distance ($p = 1$), B and C are equally close to the origin and also equidistant from A. **(right)** With $p < 1$ (here, $p = 0.8$) C is further away from the origin than B; since both are again equidistant from A, it follows that travelling from the origin to C via A is quicker than going there directly, which violates the triangle inequality.

2. *all other distances are larger than zero: if* $x \neq y$ *then* $\text{Dis}(x, y) > 0$*;*
3. *distances are symmetric:* $\text{Dis}(y, x) = \text{Dis}(x, y)$*;*
4. *detours can not shorten the distance:* $\text{Dis}(x, z) \leq \text{Dis}(x, y) + \text{Dis}(y, z)$.

If the second condition is weakened to a non-strict inequality – i.e., $\text{Dis}(x, y)$ *may be zero even if* $x \neq y$ *– the function* Dis *is called a* pseudo-metric.

The last condition is called the *triangle inequality* (or sub-additivity, as it really concerns the interaction between distance and addition). Figure 8.4 investigates this for Minkowski distances of various orders. The triangle inequality dictates that the distance from the origin to C is no more than the sum of the distances from the origin to A ($\text{Dis}(\text{O}, \text{A})$) and from A to C ($\text{Dis}(\text{A}, \text{C})$). B is at the same distance from A as C, regardless of the distance measure used; so $\text{Dis}(\text{O}, \text{A}) + \text{Dis}(\text{A}, \text{C})$ is equal to the distance from the origin to B. So, if we draw a circle around the origin through B, the triangle inequality dictates that C not be outside that circle. As we see in the left figure for Euclidean distance, B is the only point where the circles around the origin and around A intersect, so everywhere else the triangle inequality is a strict inequality.

The middle figure shows the same situation for Manhattan distance ($p = 1$). Now, B and C are in fact equidistant from the origin, and so travelling via A to C is no longer a detour, but just one of the many shortest routes. However, if we now decrease p further, we see that C ends up outside the red shape, and is thus further away than B when seen from the origin, whereas of course the sum of the distances from the origin to A and from A to C is still equal to the distance from the origin to B. At this point, our intuition breaks down: Minkowski distances with $p < 1$ are simply not very useful as distances since they all violate the triangle inequality.

Sometimes it is useful to use different scales for different coordinates if they are traversed with different speeds. For instance, for people horizontal distances can be traversed more easily than vertical differences, and consequently it is more realistic to use an ellipse rather than a circle to identify points that can be reached in a fixed amount of time, with the major axis of the ellipse indicating directions that can be traversed at larger speed. The ellipse can also be rotated, so that the major axis is not aligned with any of the coordinates: for instance, this could be the direction of a motorway, or the wind direction. Mathematically, while hyper-spheres (circles in $d \geq 2$ dimensions) of radius r can be defined by the equation $\mathbf{x}^{\mathrm{T}}\mathbf{x} = r^2$, hyper-ellipses are defined by $\mathbf{x}^{\mathrm{T}}\mathbf{M}\mathbf{x} = r^2$, where $\mathbf{M}$ is a matrix describing the appropriate rotation and scaling.

Example 8.1 (Elliptical distance). Consider the following matrices

$$\mathbf{R} = \begin{pmatrix} 1/\sqrt{2} & 1/\sqrt{2} \\ -1/\sqrt{2} & 1/\sqrt{2} \end{pmatrix} \quad \mathbf{S} = \begin{pmatrix} 1/2 & 0 \\ 0 & 1 \end{pmatrix} \quad \mathbf{M} = \begin{pmatrix} 5/8 & -3/8 \\ -3/8 & 5/8 \end{pmatrix}$$

The matrix $\mathbf{R}$ describes a clockwise rotation of 45 degrees, and the diagonal matrix $\mathbf{S}$ scales the x-axis by a factor 1/2. The equation

$$(\mathbf{SRx})^{\mathrm{T}}(\mathbf{SRx}) = \mathbf{x}^{\mathrm{T}}\mathbf{R}^{\mathrm{T}}\mathbf{S}^{\mathrm{T}}\mathbf{SRx} = \mathbf{x}^{\mathrm{T}}\mathbf{R}^{\mathrm{T}}\mathbf{S}^2\mathbf{Rx} = \mathbf{x}^{\mathrm{T}}\mathbf{Mx} = 1/4$$

describes a shape which, after clockwise rotation of 45 degrees and scaling of the x-axis by a factor 1/2, is a circle with radius 1/2 – i.e., the 'ascending' ellipse in Figure 8.3 (right). The ellipse equation is $(5/8)x^2 + (5/8)y^2 - (3/4)xy = 1/2$.

Often, the shape of the ellipse is estimated from data as the inverse of the covariance matrix: $\mathbf{M} = \mathbf{\Sigma}^{-1}$. This leads to the definition of the *Mahalanobis distance*

$$\mathrm{Dis}_M(\mathbf{x}, \mathbf{y}|\mathbf{\Sigma}) = \sqrt{(\mathbf{x}-\mathbf{y})^{\mathrm{T}}\mathbf{\Sigma}^{-1}(\mathbf{x}-\mathbf{y})} \tag{8.1}$$

Using the covariance matrix in this way has the effect of decorrelating and normalising the features, as we saw in Section 7.1. Clearly, Euclidean distance is a special case of Mahalanobis distance with the identity matrix $\mathbf{I}$ as covariance matrix: $\mathrm{Dis}_2(\mathbf{x}, \mathbf{y}) = \mathrm{Dis}_M(\mathbf{x}, \mathbf{y}|\mathbf{I})$.

8.2 Neighbours and exemplars

Now that we understand the basics of measuring distance in instance space, we proceed to consider the key ideas underlying distance-based models. The two most important of these are: formulating the model in terms of a number of prototypical instances or *exemplars*, and defining the decision rule in terms of the nearest exemplars or *neighbours*. We can understand these concepts by revisiting our old friend, the basic linear classifier. This classifier uses the two class means $\boldsymbol{\mu}^{\oplus}$ and $\boldsymbol{\mu}^{\ominus}$ as exemplars, as a summary of all we need to know about the training data in order to build the classifier. A fundamental property of the mean of a set of vectors is that it minimises the sum of squared Euclidean distances to those vectors.

Theorem 8.1 (The arithmetic mean minimises squared Euclidean distance). *The arithmetic mean $\boldsymbol{\mu}$ of a set of data points D in a Euclidean space is the unique point that minimises the sum of squared Euclidean distances to those data points.*

Proof. We will show that $\arg\min_{\mathbf{y}} \sum_{\mathbf{x}\in D} ||\mathbf{x}-\mathbf{y}||^2 = \boldsymbol{\mu}$, where $||\cdot||$ denotes the 2-norm. We find this minimum by taking the gradient (the vector of partial derivatives with respect to y_i) of the sum and setting it to the zero vector:

$$\nabla_{\mathbf{y}} \sum_{\mathbf{x}\in D} ||\mathbf{x}-\mathbf{y}||^2 = -2\sum_{\mathbf{x}\in D}(\mathbf{x}-\mathbf{y}) = -2\sum_{\mathbf{x}\in D}\mathbf{x} + 2|D|\mathbf{y} = \mathbf{0}$$

from which we derive $\mathbf{y} = \frac{1}{|D|}\sum_{\mathbf{x}\in D}\mathbf{x} = \boldsymbol{\mu}$. ∎

Notice that minimising the sum of squared Euclidean distances of a given set of points is the same as minimising the *average* squared Euclidean distance. You may wonder what happens if we drop the square here: wouldn't it be more natural to take the point that minimises total Euclidean distance as exemplar? This point is known as the *geometric median*, as for univariate data it corresponds to the median or 'middle value' of a set of numbers. However, for multivariate data there is no closed-form expression for the geometric median, which needs to be calculated by successive approximation. This computational advantage is the main reason why distance-based methods tend to use squared Euclidean distance.

In certain situations it makes sense to restrict an exemplar to be one of the given data points. In that case, we speak of a *medoid*, to distinguish it from a *centroid* which is an exemplar that doesn't have to occur in the data. Finding a medoid requires us to calculate, for each data point, the total distance to all other data points, in order to choose the point that minimises it. Regardless of the distance metric used, this is an $O(n^2)$ operation for n points, so for medoids there is no compuational reason to prefer one distance metric over another. Figure 8.5 shows a set of 10 data points where the different ways of determining exemplars all give different results. In particular, the mean and squared 2-norm medoid can be overly sensitive to outliers.

Once we have determined the exemplars, the basic linear classifier constructs the decision boundary as the perpendicular bisector of the line segment connecting the two exemplars. An alternative, distance-based way to classify instances without direct

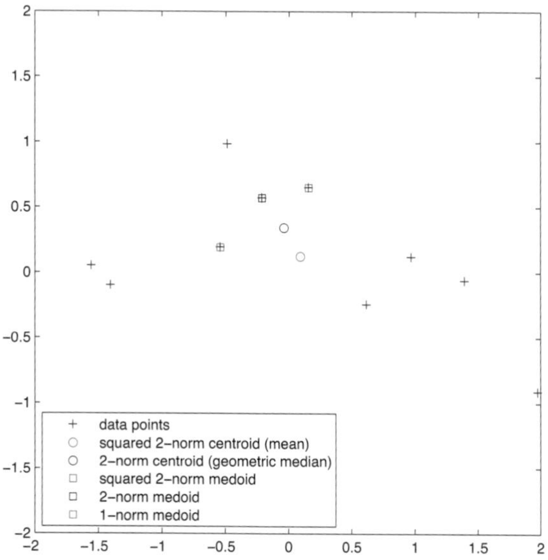

Figure 8.5. A small data set of 10 points, with circles indicating centroids and squares indicating medoids (the latter must be data points), for different distance metrics. Notice how the outlier on the bottom-right 'pulls' the mean away from the geometric median; as a result the corresponding medoid changes as well.

reference to a decision boundary is by the following decision rule: if $\mathbf{x}$ is nearest to $\boldsymbol{\mu}^{\oplus}$ then classify it as positive, otherwise as negative; or equivalently, classify an instance to the class of the *nearest* exemplar. If we use Euclidean distance as our closeness measure, simple geometry tells us we get exactly the same decision boundary (Figure 8.6 (left)).

So *the basic linear classifier can be interpreted from a distance-based perspective as constructing exemplars that minimise squared Euclidean distance within each class, and then applying a nearest-exemplar decision rule.* This change of perspective opens up many new possibilities. For example, we can investigate what the decision boundary looks like if we use Manhattan distance for the decision rule (Figure 8.6 (right)). It turns out that the decision boundary can only run along a number of fixed angles: in two dimensions these are horizontal, vertical and at (plus or minus) 45 degrees. This can be understood as follows. Suppose the two exemplars have different x- and y-coordinates, then they span a rectangle (I'll assume a tall rectangle, as in the figure). Imagine yourself in the centre of that rectangle, then clearly you are at equal distances from both exemplars (in fact, that same point is part of the 2-norm decision boundary). Now, imagine that you move one horizontal step, then you will move closer to one exemplar and away from the other; in order to compensate for that, you will also need to make a vertical step. So, within the rectangle, you maintain equal distance

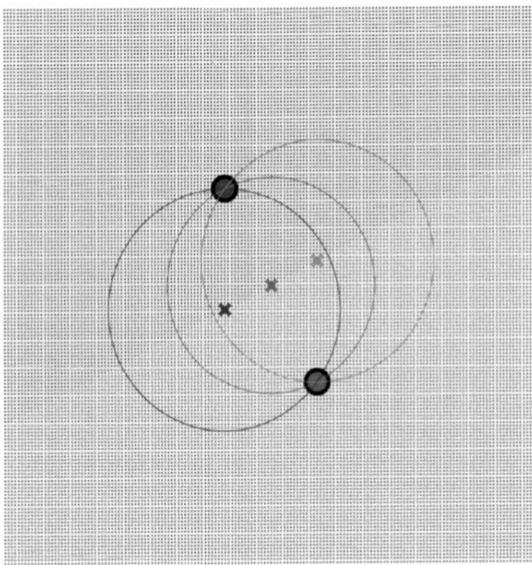

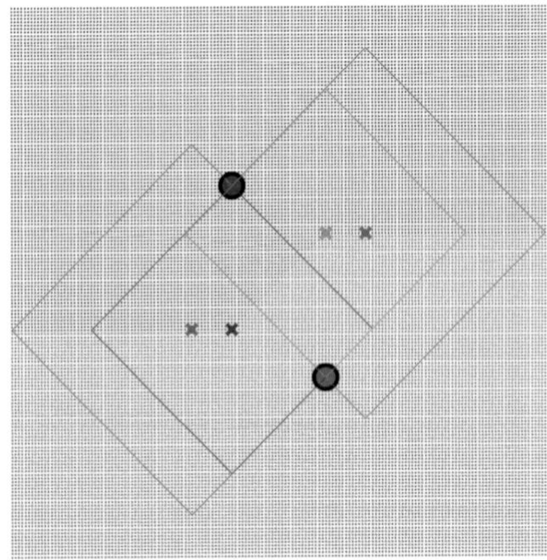

Figure 8.6. (left) For two exemplars the nearest-exemplar decision rule with Euclidean distance results in a linear decision boundary coinciding with the perpendicular bisector of the line connecting the two exemplars. The crosses denote different locations on the decision boundary, and the circles centred at those locations demonstrate that the exemplars are equidistant from each of them. When travelling along the decision boundary from bottom-left to top-right, these circles first shrink then grow again after passing the location halfway between the two exemplars. **(right)** Using Manhattan distance the circles are replaced by diamonds. Travelling from left to right, the diamonds shrink along the left-most horizontal segment of the decision boundary, then stay the same size along the 45-degree segment, and then grow again along the right-most horizontal segment.

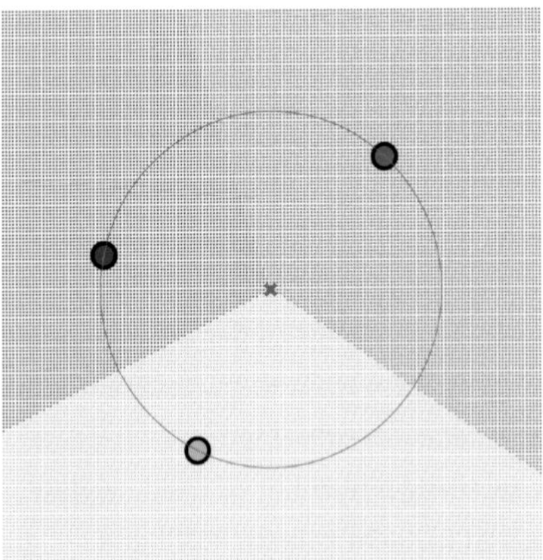

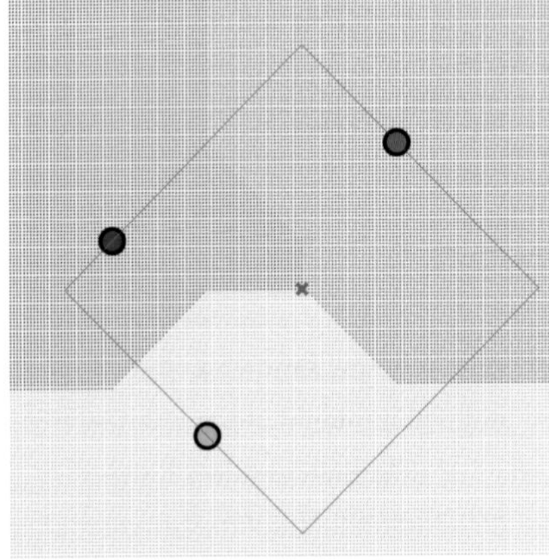

Figure 8.7. (left) Decision regions defined by the 2-norm nearest-exemplar decision rule for three exemplars. **(right)** With Manhattan distance the decision regions become non-convex.

from the exemplars by moving at a 45 degree angle. Once you reach the perimeter of the rectangle you will walk away from both exemplars by making horizontal steps, so from there the decision boundary runs horizontally.

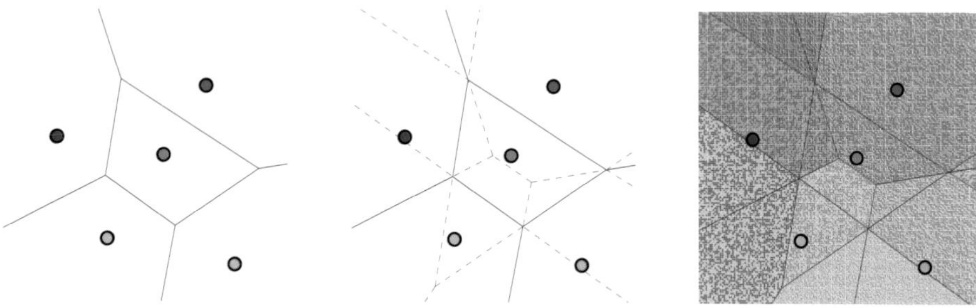

Figure 8.8. **(left)** Voronoi tesselation for five exemplars. **(middle)** Taking the two nearest exemplars into account leads to a further subdivision of each Voronoi cell. **(right)** The shading indicates which exemplars contribute to which cell.

Another useful consequence of switching to the distance-based perspective is that the nearest-exemplar decision rule works equally well for more than two exemplars, which gives us a multi-class version of the basic linear classifier.[1] Figure 8.7 (left) illustrates this for three exemplars. Each decision region is now bounded by two line segments. As you would expect, the 2-norm decision boundaries are more regular than the 1-norm ones: mathematicians say that the 2-norm decision regions are *convex*, which means that linear interpolation between any two points in the region can never go outside it. Clearly, this doesn't hold for 1-norm decision regions (Figure 8.7 (right)).

Increasing the number of exemplars further means that some of the regions become closed convex 'cells' (we are assuming Euclidean distance for the remainder of this section), giving rise to what is known as a *Voronoi tesselation*. Since the number of classes is typically much lower than the number of exemplars, decision rules often take more than one nearest exemplar into account. This increases the number of decision regions further.

Example 8.2 (Two neighbours know more than one). Figure 8.8 (left) gives a Voronoi tesselation for five exemplars. Each line segment is part of the perpendicular bisector of two exemplars. There are $\binom{5}{2} = 10$ pairs of exemplars, but two of these pairs are too far away from each other so we observe only eight line segments in the Voronoi tesselation.

If we now also take the second-nearest exemplars into account, each Voronoi cell is further subdivided: for instance, since the central point has four neighbours, the central cell is divided into four subregions (Figure 8.8 (middle)). You can think of those additional line segments as being part of the Voronoi tessela-

[1] In information retrieval this is often called the *Rocchio classifier*.

tion that results when the central point is removed. The other exemplars have only three immediate neighbours and so their cells are divided into three subregions. We thus obtain 16 '2-nearest exemplar' decision regions, each of which is defined by a different pair of nearest and second-nearest exemplars.

Figure 8.8 (right) shades each of these regions according to the two nearest exemplars spanning it. Notice that we gave each of the two exemplars the same weight, and so there are pairs of adjacent regions (across each of the original Voronoi boundaries) receiving the same shading, resulting in eight different shadings in all. This will be relevant later on, when we discuss the refinement of nearest-neighbour classifiers.

To summarise, the main ingredients of distance-based models are

- distance metrics, which can be Euclidean, Manhattan, Minkowski or Mahalanobis, among many others;
- exemplars: centroids that find a centre of mass according to a chosen distance metric, or medoids that find the most centrally located data point; and
- distance-based decision rules, which take a vote among the k nearest exemplars.

In the next sections these ingredients are combined in various ways to obtain supervised and unsupervised learning algorithms.

8.3 Nearest-neighbour classification

In the previous section we saw how to generalise the basic linear classifier to more than two classes, by learning an exemplar for each class and using the nearest-exemplar decision rule to classify new data. In fact, the most commonly used distance-based classifier is even more straightforward than that: it simply uses each training instance as an exemplar. Consequently, 'training' this classifier requires nothing more than memorising the training data. This extremely simple classifier is known as the *nearest-neighbour classifier*. Its decision regions are made up of the cells of a Voronoi tesselation, with piecewise linear decision boundaries selected from the Voronoi boundaries (since adjacent cells may be labelled with the same class).

What are the properties of the nearest-neighbour classifier? First, notice that, unless the training set contains identical instances from different classes, we will be able to separate the classes perfectly on the training set – not really a surprise, as we memorised all training examples! Furthermore, by choosing the right exemplars we can more or less represent any decision boundary, or at least an arbitrarily close piecewise linear approximation. It follows that the nearest-neighbour classifier has low bias, but also high variance: move any of the exemplars spanning part of the decision boundary, and you will also change the boundary. This suggests a risk of overfitting if the training data is limited, noisy or unrepresentative.

From an algorithmic point of view, training the nearest-neighbour classifier is very fast, taking only $O(n)$ time for storing n exemplars. The downside is that classifying a single instance also takes $O(n)$ time, as the instance will need to be compared with every exemplar to determine which one is the nearest. It is possible to reduce classification time at the expense of increased training time by storing the exemplars in a more elaborate data structure, but this tends not to scale well to large numbers of features.

In fact, high-dimensional instance spaces can be problematic for another reason: the infamous *curse of dimensionality*. High-dimensional spaces tend to be extremely sparse, which means that every point is far away from virtually every other point, and hence pairwise distances tend to be uninformative. However, whether or not you are hit by the curse of dimensionality is not simply a matter of counting the number of features, as there are several reasons why the effective dimensionality of the instance space may be much smaller than the number of features. For example, some of the features may be irrelevant and drown out the relevant features' signal in the distance calculations. In such a case it would be a good idea, before building a distance-based model, to reduce dimensionality by performing ☞*feature selection*, as will be discussed in Chapter 10. Alternatively, the data may live on a *manifold* of lower dimension than the instance space (e.g., the surface of a sphere is a two-dimensional manifold wrapped around a three-dimensional object), which allows other dimensionality-reduction techniques such as ☞*principal component analysis*, which will be explained in the same chapter. In any case, before applying nearest-neighbour classification it is a good idea to plot a histogram of pairwise distances of a sample to see if they are sufficiently varied.

Notice that the nearest-neighbour method can easily be applied to regression problems with a real-valued target variable. In fact, the method is completely oblivious to the type of target variable and can be used to output text documents, images and videos. It is also possible to output the exemplar itself instead of a separate target, in which case we usually speak of *nearest-neighbour retrieval*. Of course we can only output targets (or exemplars) stored in the exemplar database, but if we have a way of aggregating these we can go beyond this restriction by applying the *k-nearest neighbour* method. In its simplest form, the k-nearest neighbour classifier takes a vote between the $k \geq 1$ nearest exemplars of the instance to be classified, and predicts the majority class. We can easily turn this into a probability estimator by returning the normalised class counts as a probability distribution over classes.

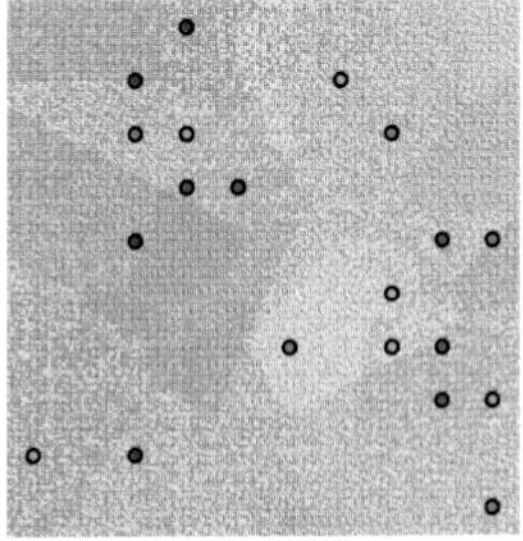
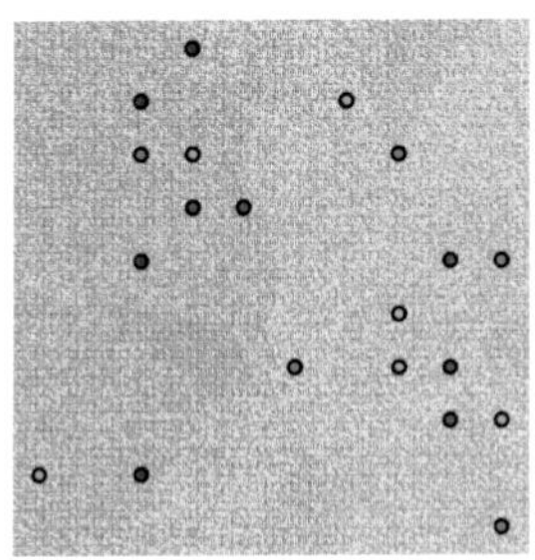
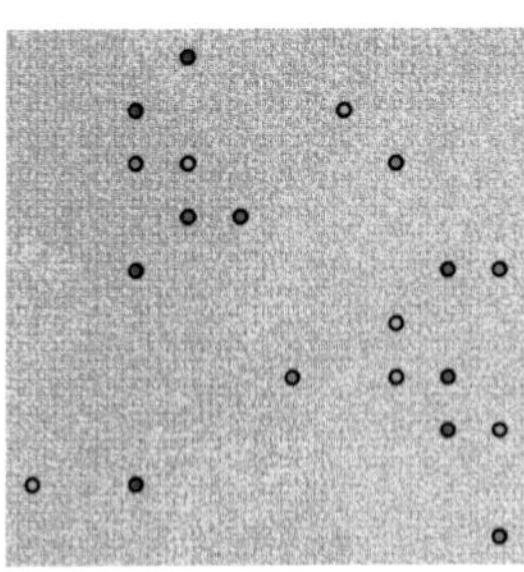

Figure 8.9. (left) Decision regions of a 3-nearest neighbour classifier; the shading represents the predicted probability distribution over the five classes. **(middle)** 5-nearest neighbour. **(right)** 7-nearest neighbour.

Figure 8.9 illustrates this on a small data set of 20 exemplars from five different classes, for $k = 3, 5, 7$. The class distribution is visualised by assigning each test point the class of a uniformly sampled neighbour: so, in a region where two of $k = 3$ neighbours are red and one is orange, the shading is a mix of two-thirds red and one-third orange. While for $k = 3$ the decision regions are still mostly discernible, this is much less so for $k = 5$ and $k = 7$. This may seem at odds with our earlier demonstration of the increase in the number of decision regions with increasing k in Example 8.2. However, this increase is countered by the fact that the probability vectors become more similar to each other. To take an extreme example: if k is equal to the number of exemplars n, every test instance will have the same number of neighbours and will receive the same probability vector which is equal to the prior distribution over the exemplars. If $k = n - 1$ we can reduce one of the class counts by 1, which can be done in c ways: the same number of possibilities as with $k = 1$!

We conclude that the refinement of k-nearest neighbour – the number of different predictions it can make – initially increases with increasing k, then decreases again. Furthermore, we can say that the bias increases and the variance decreases with increasing k. There is no easy recipe to decide what value of k is appropriate for a given data set. However, it is possible to sidestep this question to some extent by applying *distance weighting* to the votes: that is, the closer an exemplar is to the instance to be classified, the more its vote counts. Figure 8.10 demonstrates this, using the reciprocal of the distance to an exemplar as the weight of its vote. This blurs the decision boundaries, as the model now applies a combination of grouping by means of the Voronoi boundaries, and grading by means of distance weighting. Furthermore, since the weights decrease quickly for larger distances, the effect of increasing k is much smaller than with unweighted voting. In fact, with distance weighting we can simply put $k = n$ and still obtain a model that makes different predictions in different parts of the instance space. One could say that distance weighting makes k-nearest neighbour

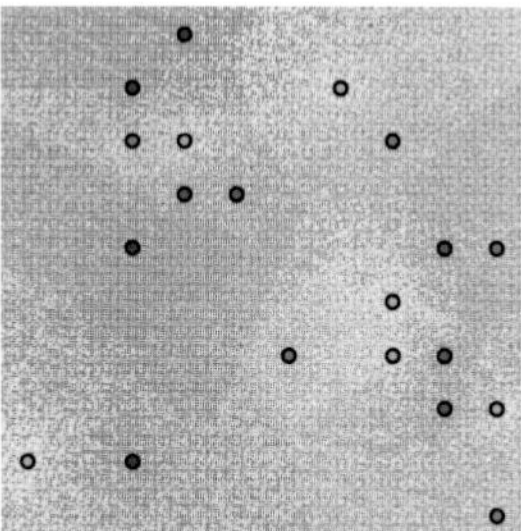
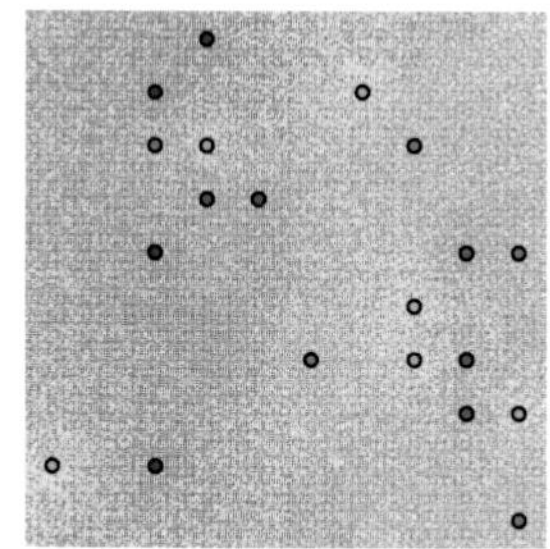
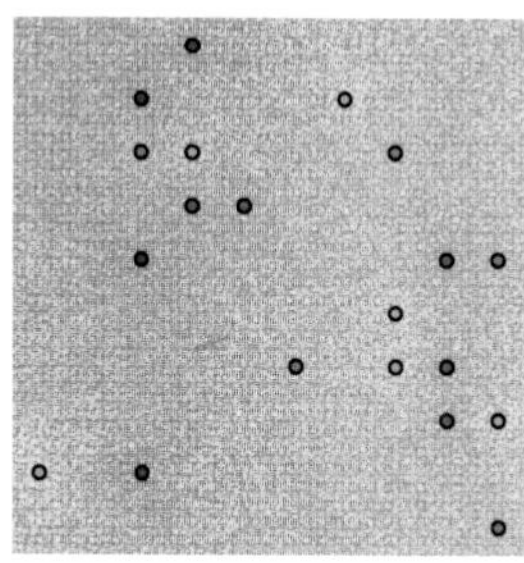

Figure 8.10. **(left)** 3-nearest neighbour with distance weighting on the data from Figure 8.9. **(middle)** 5-nearest neighbour. **(right)** 7-nearest neighbour.

more of a global model, while without it (and for small k) it is more like an aggregation of local models.

If k-nearest neighbour is used for regression problems, the obvious way to aggregate the predictions from the k neighbours is by taking the mean value, which can again be distance-weighted. This would lend the model additional predictive power by predicting values that aren't observed among the stored exemplars. More generally, we can apply k-means to any learning problem where we have an appropriate 'aggregator' for multiple target values.

8.4 Distance-based clustering

In a distance-based context, unsupervised learning is usually taken to refer to clustering, and we will now review a number of distance-based clustering methods. The ones considered in this section are all exemplar-based and hence predictive: they naturally generalise to unseen instances (see Section 3.3 for the distinction between predictive and descriptive clustering). In the next section we consider a clustering method that is not exemplar-based and hence descriptive.

Predictive distance-based clustering methods use the same ingredients as distance-based classifiers: a distance metric, a way to construct exemplars and a distance-based decision rule. In the absence of an explicit target variable, the assumption is that the distance metric indirectly encodes the learning target, so that we aim to find clusters that are *compact* with respect to the distance metric. This requires a notion of cluster compactness that can serve as our optimisation criterion. To that end, we refer back to the scatter matrix introduced in Background 7.2 on p.200.

Definition 8.3 (Scatter). *Given a data matrix* $\mathbf{X}$, *the* scatter matrix *is the matrix*

$$\mathbf{S} = (\mathbf{X} - \mathbf{1}\boldsymbol{\mu})^{\mathrm{T}} (\mathbf{X} - \mathbf{1}\boldsymbol{\mu}) = \sum_{i=1}^{n} (\mathbf{X}_{i\cdot} - \boldsymbol{\mu})^{\mathrm{T}} (\mathbf{X}_{i\cdot} - \boldsymbol{\mu})$$

where $\boldsymbol{\mu}$ is a row vector containing all column means of $\mathbf{X}$. *The* scatter *of* $\mathbf{X}$ *is defined as* $\text{Scat}(\mathbf{X}) = \sum_{i=1}^{n} ||\mathbf{X}_{i\cdot} - \boldsymbol{\mu}||^2$, *which is equal to the trace of the scatter matrix (i.e., the sum of its diagonal elements).*

Imagine now that we partition D into K subsets $D_1 \uplus \ldots \uplus D_K = D$, and let $\boldsymbol{\mu}_j$ denote the mean of D_j. Let $\mathbf{S}$ be the scatter matrix of D, and $\mathbf{S}_j$ be the scatter matrices of D_j. These scatter matrices then have the following relationship:

$$\mathbf{S} = \sum_{j=1}^{K} \mathbf{S}_j + \mathbf{B} \tag{8.2}$$

Here, $\mathbf{B}$ is the scatter matrix that results by replacing each point in D with the corresponding $\boldsymbol{\mu}_j$. Each $\mathbf{S}_j$ is called a *within-cluster scatter matrix* and describes the compactness of the j-th cluster. $\mathbf{B}$ is the *between-cluster scatter matrix* and describes the spread of the cluster centroids. It follows that the traces of these matrices can be decomposed similarly, which gives

$$\text{Scat}(D) = \sum_{j=1}^{K} \text{Scat}(D_j) + \sum_{j=1}^{K} |D_j|\,||\boldsymbol{\mu}_j - \boldsymbol{\mu}||^2 \tag{8.3}$$

What this tells us is that minimising the total scatter over all clusters is equivalent to maximising the (weighted) scatter of the centroids. The *K-means problem* is to find a partition that minimises the total within-cluster scatter.

Example 8.3 (Reducing scatter by partitioning data). Consider the following five points: $(0,3)$, $(3,3)$, $(3,0)$, $(-2,-4)$ and $(-4,-2)$. These points are, conveniently, centred around $(0,0)$. The scatter matrix is

$$\mathbf{S} = \begin{pmatrix} 0 & 3 & 3 & -2 & -4 \\ 3 & 3 & 0 & -4 & -2 \end{pmatrix} \begin{pmatrix} 0 & 3 \\ 3 & 3 \\ 3 & 0 \\ -2 & -4 \\ -4 & -2 \end{pmatrix} = \begin{pmatrix} 38 & 25 \\ 25 & 38 \end{pmatrix}$$

with trace $\text{Scat}(D) = 76$. If we cluster the first two points together in one cluster and the remaining three in another, then we obtain cluster means $\boldsymbol{\mu}_1 = (1.5, 3)$ and $\boldsymbol{\mu}_2 = (-1,-2)$ and within-cluster scatter matrices

$$\mathbf{S}_1 = \begin{pmatrix} 0-1.5 & 3-1.5 \\ 3-3 & 3-3 \end{pmatrix} \begin{pmatrix} 0-1.5 & 3-3 \\ 3-1.5 & 3-3 \end{pmatrix} = \begin{pmatrix} 4.5 & 0 \\ 0 & 0 \end{pmatrix}$$

$$\mathbf{S}_2 = \begin{pmatrix} 3-(-1) & -2-(-1) & -4-(-1) \\ 0-(-2) & -4-(-2) & -2-(-2) \end{pmatrix} \begin{pmatrix} 3-(-1) & 0-(-2) \\ -2-(-1) & -4-(-2) \\ -4-(-1) & -2-(-2) \end{pmatrix} = \begin{pmatrix} 26 & 10 \\ 10 & 8 \end{pmatrix}$$

with traces $\mathrm{Scat}(D_1) = 4.5$ and $\mathrm{Scat}(D_2) = 34$. Two copies of μ_1 and three copies of μ_2 have, by definition, the same centre of gravity as the complete data set: $(0,0)$ in this case. We thus calculate the between-cluster scatter matrix as

$$\mathbf{B} = \begin{pmatrix} 1.5 & 1.5 & -1 & -1 & -1 \\ 3 & 3 & -2 & -2 & -2 \end{pmatrix} \begin{pmatrix} 1.5 & 3 \\ 1.5 & 3 \\ -1 & -2 \\ -1 & -2 \\ -1 & -2 \end{pmatrix} = \begin{pmatrix} 7.5 & 15 \\ 15 & 30 \end{pmatrix}$$

with trace 37.5.

Alternatively, if we treat the first three points as a cluster and put the other two in a second cluster, then we obtain cluster means $\mu_1' = (2,2)$ and $\mu_2' = (-3,-3)$, and within-cluster scatter matrices

$$\mathbf{S}_1' = \begin{pmatrix} 0-2 & 3-2 & 3-2 \\ 3-2 & 3-2 & 0-2 \end{pmatrix} \begin{pmatrix} 0-2 & 3-2 \\ 3-2 & 3-2 \\ 3-2 & 0-2 \end{pmatrix} = \begin{pmatrix} 6 & -3 \\ -3 & 6 \end{pmatrix}$$

$$\mathbf{S}_2' = \begin{pmatrix} -2-(-3) & -4-(-3) \\ -4-(-3) & -2-(-3) \end{pmatrix} \begin{pmatrix} -2-(-3) & -4-(-3) \\ -4-(-3) & -2-(-3) \end{pmatrix} = \begin{pmatrix} 2 & -2 \\ -2 & 2 \end{pmatrix}$$

with traces $\mathrm{Scat}(D_1') = 12$ and $\mathrm{Scat}(D_2') = 4$. The between-cluster scatter matrix is

$$\mathbf{B}' = \begin{pmatrix} 2 & 2 & 2 & -3 & -3 \\ 2 & 2 & 2 & -3 & -3 \end{pmatrix} \begin{pmatrix} 2 & 2 \\ 2 & 2 \\ 2 & 2 \\ -3 & -3 \\ -3 & -3 \end{pmatrix} = \begin{pmatrix} 30 & 30 \\ 30 & 30 \end{pmatrix}$$

with trace 60. Clearly, the second clustering produces tighter clusters whose centroids are further apart.

K-means algorithm

The K-means problem is NP-complete, which means that there is no efficient solution to find the global minimum and we need to resort to a heuristic algorithm. The best-known algorithm is usually also called K-means, although the name 'Lloyd's algorithm' is also used. The outline of the algorithm is given in Algorithm 8.1. The algorithm iterates between partitioning the data using the nearest-centroid decision rule, and

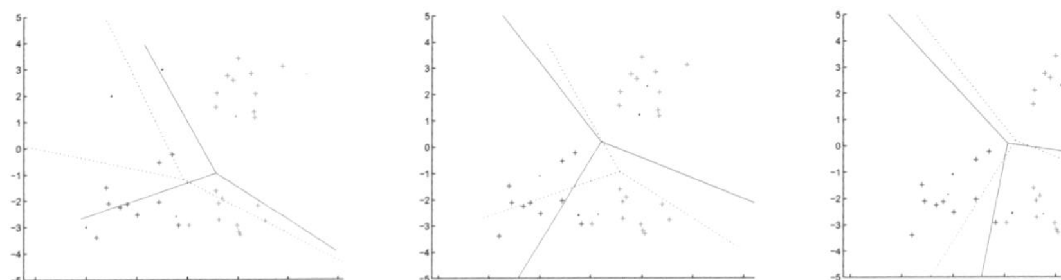

Figure 8.11. **(left)** First iteration of 3-means on Gaussian mixture data. The dotted lines are the Voronoi boundaries resulting from randomly initialised centroids; the violet solid lines are the result of the recalculated means. **(middle)** Second iteration, taking the previous partition as starting point (dotted line). **(right)** Third iteration with stable clustering.

recalculating centroids from a partition. Figure 8.11 demonstrates the algorithm on a small data set with three clusters, and Example 8.4 gives the result on our example data set describing properties of different machine learning methods.

Example 8.4 (Clustering MLM data). Refer back to the MLM data set in Table 1.4 on p.39 (it is also helpful to look at its two-dimensional approximation in Figure 1.7 on p.37). When we run K-means on this data with $K = 3$, we obtain the clusters {Associations, Trees, Rules}, {GMM, naive Bayes}, and a larger cluster with the remaining data points. When we run it with $K = 4$, we get that the large cluster splits into two: {kNN, Linear Classifier, Linear Regression} and

---

Algorithm 8.1: KMeans(D, K) – K-means clustering using Euclidean distance Dis_2.

Input : data $D \subseteq \mathbb{R}^d$; number of clusters $K \in \mathbb{N}$.
Output : K cluster means $\boldsymbol{\mu}_1, \ldots, \boldsymbol{\mu}_K \in \mathbb{R}^d$.

randomly initialise K vectors $\boldsymbol{\mu}_1, \ldots, \boldsymbol{\mu}_K \in \mathbb{R}^d$;
repeat
  assign each $\mathbf{x} \in D$ to $\arg\min_j \text{Dis}_2(\mathbf{x}, \boldsymbol{\mu}_j)$;
  for $j = 1$ to K **do**
    $D_j \leftarrow \{\mathbf{x} \in D | \mathbf{x} \text{ assigned to cluster } j\}$;
    $\boldsymbol{\mu}_j = \frac{1}{|D_j|} \sum_{\mathbf{x} \in D_j} \mathbf{x}$;
  end
until no change in $\boldsymbol{\mu}_1, \ldots, \boldsymbol{\mu}_K$;
return $\boldsymbol{\mu}_1, \ldots, \boldsymbol{\mu}_K$;

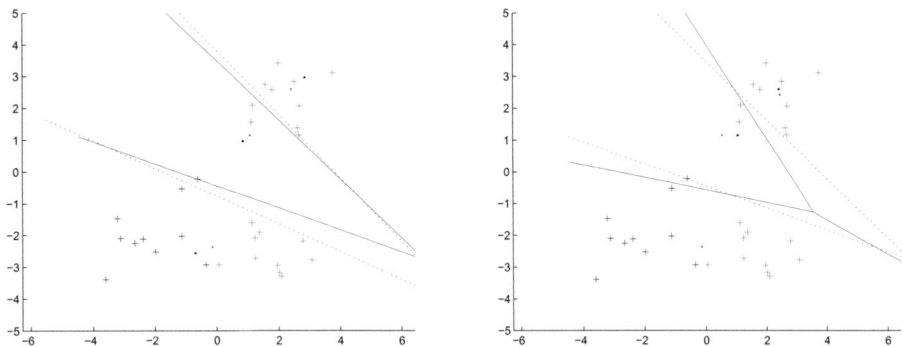

Figure 8.12. **(left)** First iteration of 3-means on the same data as Figure 8.11 with differently initialised centroids. **(right)** 3-means has converged to a sub-optimal clustering.

{Kmeans, Logistic Regression, SVM}; but also that GMM gets reallocated to the latter cluster, and naive Bayes ends up as a singleton.

It can be shown that one iteration of K-means can never increase the within-cluster scatter, from which it follows that the algorithm will reach a *stationary point*: a point where no further improvement is possible. It is worth noting that even the simplest data set will have many stationary points.

Example 8.5 (Stationary points in clustering). Consider the task of dividing the set of numbers $\{8,44,50,58,84\}$ into two clusters. There are four possible partitions that 2-means can find: $\{8\},\{44,50,58,84\}$; $\{8,44\},\{50,58,84\}$; $\{8,44,50\},\{58,84\}$; and $\{8,44,50,58\},\{84\}$. It is easy to verify that each of these establishes a stationary point for 2-means, and hence will be found with a suitable initialisation. Only the first clustering is optimal; i.e., it minimises the total within-cluster scatter.

In general, while K-means converges to a stationary point in finite time, no guarantees can be given about whether the convergence point is in fact the global minimum, or if not, how far we are from it. Figure 8.12 shows how an unfortunate initialisation of the centroids can lead to a sub-optimal solution. In practice it is advisable to run the algorithm a number of times and select the solution with the smallest within-cluster scatter.

Clustering around medoids

It is straightforward to adapt the K-means algorithm to use a different distance metric; note that this will also change the objective function being minimised. Algorithm 8.2 gives the *K-medoids* algorithm, which additionally requires the exemplars to be data points. Notice that calculating the medoid of a cluster requires examining all pairs of points – whereas calculating the mean requires just a single pass through the points – which can be prohibitive for large data sets. Algorithm 8.3 gives an alternative algorithm called *partitioning around medoids* (*PAM*) that tries to improve a clustering locally by swapping medoids with other data points. The quality of a clustering Q is calculated as the total distance over all points to their nearest medoid. Notice that there are $k(n-k)$ pairs of one medoid and one non-medoid, and evaluating Q requires iterating over $n-k$ data points, so the computational cost of one iteration is quadratic in the number of data points. For large data sets one can run PAM on a small sample but evaluate Q on the whole data set, and repeat this a number of times for different samples.

An important limitation of the clustering methods discussed in this section is that they represent clusters only by means of exemplars. This disregards the shape of the clusters, and sometimes leads to counter-intuitive results. The two data sets in Figure 8.13 are identical, except for a rescaling of the y-axis. Nevertheless, K-means finds entirely different clusterings. This is not actually a shortcoming of the K-means algorithm as such, as in Figure 8.13 (right) the two centroids are further away than in the intended solution, and hence this represents a better solution in terms of Equation

---

Algorithm 8.2: KMedoids($D, K,$ Dis) – K-medoids clustering using arbitrary distance metric Dis.

Input : data $D \subseteq \mathscr{X}$; number of clusters $K \in \mathbb{N}$;
distance metric $\text{Dis}: \mathscr{X} \times \mathscr{X} \rightarrow \mathbb{R}$.
Output : K medoids $\boldsymbol{\mu}_1, \ldots, \boldsymbol{\mu}_K \in D$, representing a predictive clustering of $\mathscr{X}$.

randomly pick K data points $\boldsymbol{\mu}_1, \ldots, \boldsymbol{\mu}_K \in D$;
repeat
    assign each $\mathbf{x} \in D$ to $\arg\min_j \text{Dis}(\mathbf{x}, \boldsymbol{\mu}_j)$;
    for $j = 1$ to k **do**
        $D_j \leftarrow \{\mathbf{x} \in D | \mathbf{x} \text{ assigned to cluster } j\}$;
        $\boldsymbol{\mu}_j = \arg\min_{\mathbf{x} \in D_j} \sum_{\mathbf{x}' \in D_j} \text{Dis}(\mathbf{x}, \mathbf{x}')$;
    end
until no change in $\boldsymbol{\mu}_1, \ldots, \boldsymbol{\mu}_K$;
return $\boldsymbol{\mu}_1, \ldots, \boldsymbol{\mu}_K$;

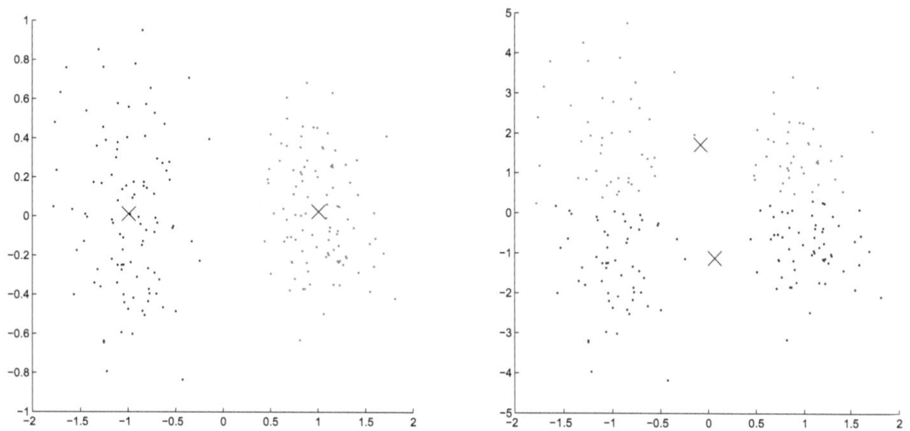

Figure 8.13. **(left)** On this data 2-means detects the right clusters. **(right)** After rescaling the y-axis, this configuration has a higher between-cluster scatter than the intended one.

8.3. The real issue is that in this case we want to estimate the 'shape' of the clusters as well as the cluster centroids, and hence take account of more than just the trace of the scatter matrices. We will discuss this further in the next chapter.

Algorithm 8.3: PAM(D, K, Dis) – Partitioning around medoids clustering using arbitrary distance metric Dis.

Input : data $D \subseteq \mathscr{X}$; number of clusters $K \in \mathbb{N}$;
distance metric $\mathrm{Dis} : \mathscr{X} \times \mathscr{X} \to \mathbb{R}$.

Output : K medoids $\mu_1, \ldots, \mu_K \in D$, representing a predictive clustering of $\mathscr{X}$.

randomly pick K data points $\mu_1, \ldots, \mu_K \in D$;
repeat
  assign each $\mathbf{x} \in D$ to $\arg\min_j \mathrm{Dis}(\mathbf{x}, \mu_j)$;
  for $j = 1$ to k **do**
    $D_j \leftarrow \{\mathbf{x} \in D | \mathbf{x}$ assigned to cluster $j\}$;
  end
  $Q \leftarrow \sum_j \sum_{\mathbf{x} \in D_j} \mathrm{Dis}(\mathbf{x}, \mu_j)$;
  for each medoid $\mathbf{m}$ and each non-medoid $\mathbf{o}$ **do**
    calculate the improvement in Q resulting from swapping $\mathbf{m}$ with $\mathbf{o}$;
  end
  select the pair with maximum improvement and swap;
until no further improvement possible;
return $\mu_1, \ldots, \mu_K$;

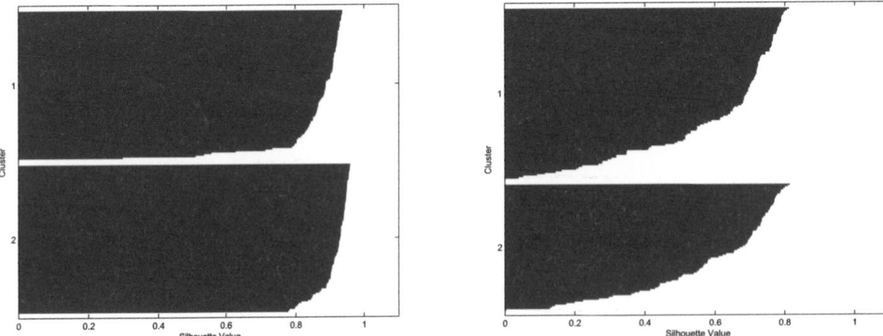

Figure 8.14. (left) Silhouette for the clustering in Figure 8.13 (left), using squared Euclidean distance. Almost all points have a high $s(\mathbf{x})$, which means that they are much closer, on average, to the other members of their cluster than to the members of the neighbouring cluster. **(right)** The silhouette for the clustering in Figure 8.13 (right) is much less convincing.

Silhouettes

How could we detect the poor quality of the clustering in Figure 8.13 (right)? An interesting technique is the use of silhouettes. For any data point $\mathbf{x}_i$, let $d(\mathbf{x}_i, D_j)$ denote the average distance of $\mathbf{x}_i$ to the data points in cluster D_j, and let $j(i)$ denote the index of the cluster that $\mathbf{x}_i$ belongs to. Furthermore, let $a(\mathbf{x}_i) = d(\mathbf{x}_i, D_{j(i)})$ be the average distance of $\mathbf{x}_i$ to the points in its own cluster $D_{j(i)}$, and let $b(\mathbf{x}_i) = \min_{k \neq j(i)} d(\mathbf{x}_i, D_k)$ be the average distance to the points in its neighbouring cluster. We would expect $a(\mathbf{x}_i)$ to be considerably smaller than $b(\mathbf{x}_i)$, but this cannot be guaranteed. So we can take the difference $b(\mathbf{x}_i) - a(\mathbf{x}_i)$ as an indication of how 'well-clustered' $\mathbf{x}_i$ is, and divide this by $b(\mathbf{x}_i)$ to obtain a number less than or equal to 1.

It is, however, conceivable that $a(\mathbf{x}_i) > b(\mathbf{x}_i)$, in which case the difference $b(\mathbf{x}_i) - a(\mathbf{x}_i)$ is negative. This describes the situation that, on average, the members of the neighbouring cluster are closer to $\mathbf{x}_i$ than the members of its own cluster. In order to get a normalised value we divide by $a(\mathbf{x}_i)$ in this case. This leads to the following definition:

$$s(\mathbf{x}_i) = \frac{b(\mathbf{x}_i) - a(\mathbf{x}_i)}{\max(a(\mathbf{x}_i), b(\mathbf{x}_i))} \tag{8.4}$$

A *silhouette* then sorts and plots $s(\mathbf{x})$ for each instance, grouped by cluster. Examples are shown in Figure 8.14 for the two clusterings in Figure 8.13. In this particular case we have used squared Euclidean distance in the construction of the silhouette, but the method can be applied to other distance metrics. We can clearly see that the first clustering is much better than the second. In addition to the graphical representation, we can compute average silhouette values per cluster and over the whole data set.

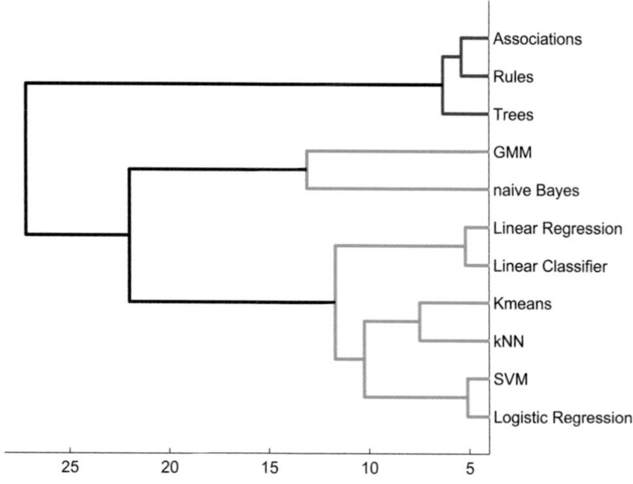

Figure 8.15. A dendrogram (printed left to right to improve readability) constructed by hierarchical clustering from the data in Table 1.4 on p.39.

8.5 Hierarchical clustering

The clustering methods discussed in the previous section use exemplars to represent a predictive clustering: a partition of the entire instance space. In this section we take a look at methods that represent clusters using trees. We previously encountered ☞*clustering trees* in Section 5.3: those trees use features to navigate the instance space, similar to decision trees, and aren't distance-based as such. Here we consider trees called dendrograms, which are purely defined in terms of a distance measure. Because dendrograms use features only indirectly, as the basis on which the distance measure is calculated, they partition the given data rather than the entire instance space, and hence represent a descriptive clustering rather than a predictive one.

Example 8.6 (Hierarchical clustering of MLM data). We continue Example 8.4 on p.248. A hierarchical clustering of the MLM data is given in Figure 8.15. The tree shows that the three logical methods at the top form a strong cluster. If we wanted three clusters, we get the logical cluster, a second small cluster {GMM, naive Bayes}, and the remainder. If we wanted four clusters, we would separate GMM and naive Bayes, as the tree indicates this cluster is the least tight of the three (notice that this is slightly different from the solution found by 4-means). If we wanted five clusters, we would construct {Linear Regression, LinearClassifier} as a separate cluster. This illustrates the key advantage of hierarchical clustering: it doesn't require fixing the number of clusters in advance.

A precise definition of a dendrogram is as follows.

Definition 8.4 (Dendrogram). *Given a data set D, a* dendrogram *is a binary tree with the elements of D at its leaves. An internal node of the tree represents the subset of elements in the leaves of the subtree rooted at that node. The level of a node is the distance between the two clusters represented by the children of the node. Leaves have level 0.*

For this definition to work, we need a way to measure how close two clusters are. You might think that this is straightforward: just calculate the distance between the two cluster means. However, this occasionally leads to problems, as discussed later in this section. Furthermore, taking cluster means as exemplars assumes Euclidean distance, and we may want to use one of the other distance metrics discussed earlier. This has led to the introduction of the so-called linkage function, which is a general way to turn pairwise point distances into pairwise cluster distances.

Definition 8.5 (Linkage function). *A* linkage function $L : 2^{\mathscr{X}} \times 2^{\mathscr{X}} \rightarrow \mathbb{R}$ *calculates the distance between arbitrary subsets of the instance space, given a distance metric* $\mathrm{Dis} : \mathscr{X} \times \mathscr{X} \rightarrow \mathbb{R}$.

The most common linkage functions are as follows:

Single linkage	defines the distance between two clusters as the *smallest* pairwise distance between elements from each cluster.
Complete linkage	defines the distance between two clusters as the *largest* pointwise distance.
Average linkage	defines the cluster distance as the *average* pointwise distance.
Centroid linkage	defines the cluster distance as the point distance between the cluster means.

These linkage functions can be defined mathematically as follows:

$$L_{\text{single}}(A, B) = \min_{x \in A, y \in B} \mathrm{Dis}(x, y)$$

$$L_{\text{complete}}(A, B) = \max_{x \in A, y \in B} \mathrm{Dis}(x, y)$$

$$L_{\text{average}}(A, B) = \frac{\sum_{x \in A, y \in B} \mathrm{Dis}(x, y)}{|A| \cdot |B|}$$

$$L_{\text{centroid}}(A, B) = \mathrm{Dis}\left(\frac{\sum_{x \in A} x}{|A|}, \frac{\sum_{y \in B} y}{|B|}\right)$$

Clearly, all these linkage functions coincide for singleton clusters: $L(\{x\},\{y\}) = \mathrm{Dis}(x, y)$. However, for larger clusters they start to diverge. For example, suppose $\mathrm{Dis}(x, y) < \mathrm{Dis}(x, z)$, then the linkage between $\{x\}$ and $\{y, z\}$ is different in all four cases:

$$
\begin{aligned}
L_{\text{single}}(\{x\},\{y,z\}) &= \mathrm{Dis}(x,y)\\
L_{\text{complete}}(\{x\},\{y,z\}) &= \mathrm{Dis}(x,z)\\
L_{\text{average}}(\{x\},\{y,z\}) &= \big(\mathrm{Dis}(x,y)+\mathrm{Dis}(x,z)\big)/2\\
L_{\text{centroid}}(\{x\},\{y,z\}) &= \mathrm{Dis}(x,(y+z)/2)
\end{aligned}
$$

The general algorithm to build a dendrogram is given in Algorithm 8.4. The tree is built from the data points upwards and is hence a bottom–up or *agglomerative* algorithm. At each iteration the algorithm constructs a new partition of the data by merging the two nearest clusters together. In general, the HAC algorithm gives different results when different linkage functions are used. Single linkage is the easiest case to understand, as it effectively builds a graph by adding increasingly longer links between points, one at a time, such that ultimately there is a path between any pair of points (hence the term 'linkage'). At any point during this process, the connected components are the clusters found at that iteration, and the linkage of the most recently found cluster is the length of the most recently added link. Hierarchical clustering using single linkage can essentially be done by calculating and sorting all pairwise distances between data points, which requires $O(n^2)$ time for n points. The other linkage functions require at least $O(n^2 \log n)$. Notice that the unoptimised algorithm in Algorithm 8.4 has time complexity $O(n^3)$.

Algorithm 8.4: HAC(D, L) – Hierarchical agglomerative clustering.

```
Input  : data D ⊆ 𝒳; linkage function L : 2^𝒳 × 2^𝒳 → ℝ defined in terms of
         distance metric.
Output : a dendrogram representing a descriptive clustering of D.
initialise clusters to singleton data points;
create a leaf at level 0 for every singleton cluster;
repeat
    find the pair of clusters X, Y with lowest linkage l, and merge;
    create a parent of X, Y at level l;
until all data points are in one cluster;
return the constructed binary tree with linkage levels;
```

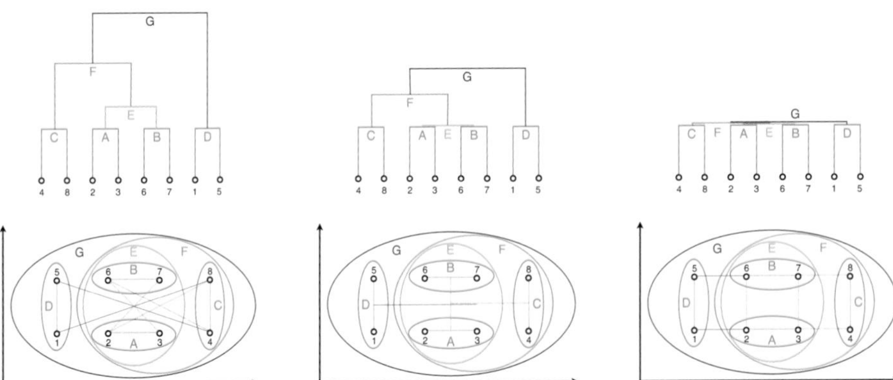

Figure 8.16. **(left)** Complete linkage defines cluster distance as the largest pairwise distance between elements from each cluster, indicated by the coloured lines between data points. The clustering found can be represented as nested partitions (bottom) or a dendrogram (top); the level of a horizontal connection between clusters in the dendrogram corresponds to the length of a linkage line. The example assumes that ties are broken by small irregularities in the grid. **(middle)** Centroid linkage defines the distance between clusters as the distance between their means. Notice that E obtains the same linkage as A and B, and so the latter clusters effectively disappear. **(right)** Single linkage defines the distance between clusters as the smallest pairwise distance. The dendrogram all but collapses, which means that no meaningful clusters are found in the given grid configuration.

Example 8.7 (Linkage matters). We consider a regular grid of 8 points in two rows of four (Figure 8.16). We assume that ties are broken by small irregularities. Each linkage function merges the same clusters in the same order, but the linkages are quite different in each case. Complete linkage gives the impression that D is far removed from the rest, whereas by moving D very slightly to the right it would have been added to E before C. With centroid linkage we see that E has in fact the same linkage as A and B, which means that A and B are not really discernible as separate clusters, even though they are found first. Single linkage seems preferable in this case, as it most clearly demonstrates that there is no meaningful cluster structure in this set of points.

Single and complete linkage both define the distance between clusters in terms of a particular pair of points. Consequently, they cannot take the shape of the cluster into account, which is why average and centroid linkage can offer an advantage. However, centroid linkage can lead to non-intuitive dendrograms, as illustrated in Figure

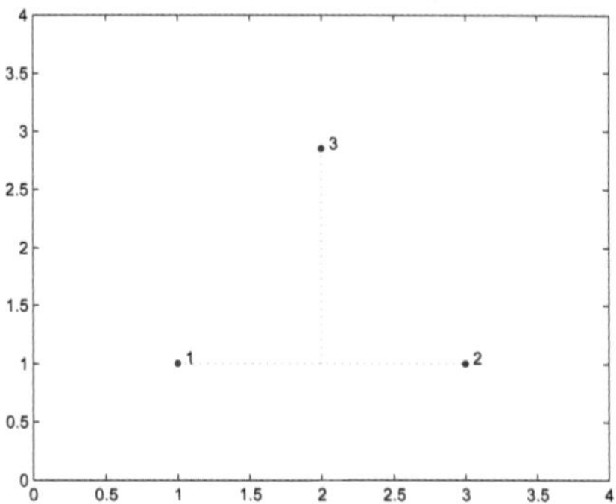

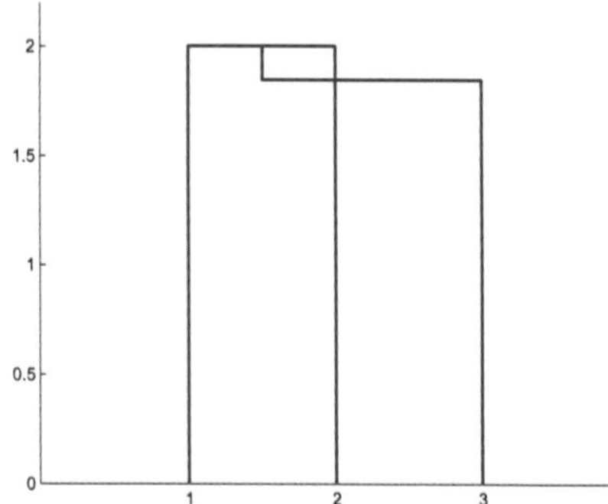

Figure 8.17. (left) Points 1 and 2 are closer to each other than to point 3. However, the distance between point 3 to the centroid of the other two points is less than any of the pairwise distances. **(right)** This results in a decrease in linkage when adding point 3 to cluster $\{1,2\}$, and hence a non-monotonic dendrogram.

8.17. The issue here is that we have $L(\{1\},\{2\}) < L(\{1\},\{3\})$ and $L(\{1\},\{2\}) < L(\{2\},\{3\})$ but $L(\{1\},\{2\}) > L(\{1,2\},\{3\})$. The first two inequalities mean that 1 and 2 are the first to be merged into a cluster; but the second inequality means that the level of cluster $\{1,2,3\}$ in the dendrogram drops below the level of $\{1,2\}$. Centroid linkage violates the requirement of *monotonicity*, which stipulates that $L(A,B) < L(A,C)$ and $L(A,B) < L(B,C)$ implies $L(A,B) < L(A \cup B,C)$ for any clusters A, B and C. The other three linkage functions are monotonic (the example also serves as an illustration why average linkage and centroid linkage are not the same).

Another thing to keep in mind when constructing dendrograms is that the hierarchical clustering method is deterministic and will always construct a clustering. Consider Figure 8.18, which shows a data set of 20 uniformly randomly sampled points. One would be hard-pressed to find any cluster structure in this data; yet a dendrogram constructed with complete linkage and Euclidean distance appears to indicate that there are three or four clearly discernible clusters. But if we look closer, we see that the linkage levels are very close together in the bottom of the tree, and the fact that linkages are higher towards the top comes primarily from the use of complete linkage, which concentrates on maximal pairwise distances. The silhouette in Figure 8.18 (right) confirms that the cluster structure is not very strong. Effectively, we are witnessing here a particular, clustering-related kind of overfitting, already familiar from other tree-based models discussed in Chapter 5. Furthermore, dendrograms – like other tree models – have high variance in that small changes in the data points can lead to large changes in the dendrogram.

In conclusion, hierarchical clustering methods have the distinct advantage that the number of clusters does not need to be fixed in advance. However, this advantage comes at considerable computational cost. Furthermore, we now need to choose not

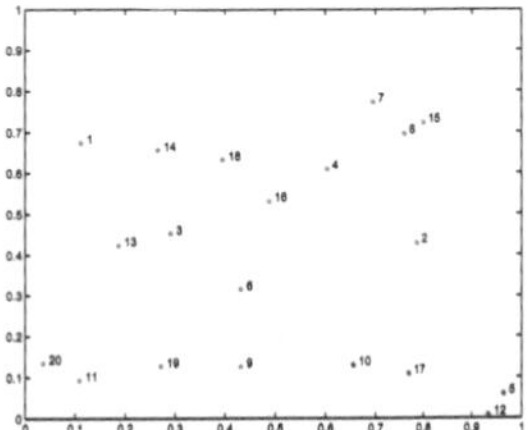
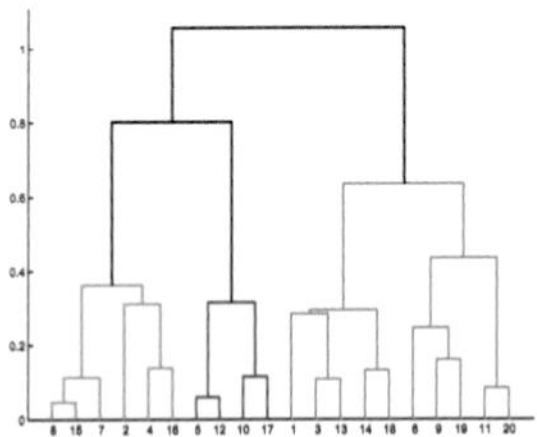
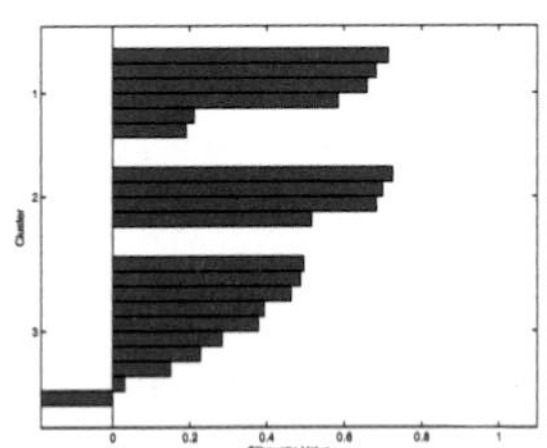

Figure 8.18. **(left)** 20 data points, generated by uniform random sampling. **(middle)** The dendrogram generated from complete linkage. The three clusters suggested by the dendrogram are spurious as they cannot be observed in the data. **(right)** The rapidly decreasing silhouette values in each cluster confirm the absence of a strong cluster structure. Point 18 has a negative silhouette value as it is on average closer to the green points than to the other red points.

just the distance measure used, but also the linkage function.

8.6 From kernels to distances

In Section 7.5 we discussed how kernels can be used to extend the power of linear models considerably. Recall that a kernel is a function $\kappa(\mathbf{x}_i, \mathbf{x}_j) = \phi(\mathbf{x}_i) \cdot \phi(\mathbf{x}_j)$ that calculates a dot product in some feature space, but without constructing the feature vectors $\phi(\mathbf{x})$ explicitly. Any learning method that can be defined purely in terms of dot products of data points is amenable to such 'kernelisation'. Because of the close connection between Euclidean distance and dot products we can apply the same 'kernel trick' to many distance-based learning methods.

The key insight is that Euclidean distance can be rewritten in terms of dot products:

$$\text{Dis}_2(\mathbf{x}, \mathbf{y}) = ||\mathbf{x} - \mathbf{y}||_2 = \sqrt{(\mathbf{x} - \mathbf{y}) \cdot (\mathbf{x} - \mathbf{y})} = \sqrt{\mathbf{x} \cdot \mathbf{x} - 2\mathbf{x} \cdot \mathbf{y} + \mathbf{y} \cdot \mathbf{y}}$$

This formula clearly shows that the distance between $\mathbf{x}$ and $\mathbf{y}$ decreases whenever the dot product $\mathbf{x} \cdot \mathbf{y}$ increases, which suggests that the dot product itself is a kind of similarity measure. However, it is not translation-invariant, because it depends on the location of the origin. The two terms $\mathbf{x} \cdot \mathbf{x}$ and $\mathbf{y} \cdot \mathbf{y}$ have the effect of making the overall expression translation-invariant. Replacing the dot product with a kernel function κ, we can construct the following kernelised distance:

$$\text{Dis}_\kappa(\mathbf{x}, \mathbf{y}) = \sqrt{\kappa(\mathbf{x}, \mathbf{x}) - 2\kappa(\mathbf{x}, \mathbf{y}) + \kappa(\mathbf{y}, \mathbf{y})} \tag{8.5}$$

It turns out that Dis_κ defines a pseudo-metric (see Definition 8.2 on p.235) whenever κ is a positive semi-definite kernel.[2]

[2]It is only a metric if the feature mapping ϕ is injective: suppose not, then some distinct $\mathbf{x}$ and $\mathbf{y}$ are mapped to the same feature vector $\phi(\mathbf{x}) = \phi(\mathbf{y})$, from which we derive $\kappa(\mathbf{x}, \mathbf{x}) - 2\kappa(\mathbf{x}, \mathbf{y}) + \kappa(\mathbf{y}, \mathbf{y}) = \phi(\mathbf{x}) \cdot \phi(\mathbf{x}) - 2\phi(\mathbf{x}) \cdot \phi(\mathbf{y}) + \phi(\mathbf{y}) \cdot \phi(\mathbf{y}) = 0$.

As an illustration, Algorithm 8.5 adapts the ☞*K-means* algorithm (Algorithm 8.1 on p.248) to use a kernelised distance. So, the algorithm clusters according to a non-linear distance in instance space, corresponding to Euclidean distance in an implicit feature space. However, one complication arises, which is that Theorem 8.1 doesn't apply to non-linear distances, and so we cannot construct cluster means in instance space. For this reason Algorithm 8.5 treats the clustering as a partition rather than a set of exemplars. Consequently, assigning each data point $\mathbf{x}$ to its nearest cluster (step 3) is now of quadratic complexity, since for each cluster we need to sum up the distances of all its members to $\mathbf{x}$. In contrast, this step is linear in $|D|$ for the K-means algorithm.

There is an alternative way to turn dot products into distances. Since the dot product can be written as $||\mathbf{x}|| \cdot ||\mathbf{y}|| \cos\theta$, where θ is the angle between the vectors $\mathbf{x}$ and $\mathbf{y}$, we define the *cosine similarity* as

$$\cos\theta = \frac{\mathbf{x}\cdot\mathbf{y}}{||\mathbf{x}||\cdot||\mathbf{y}||} = \frac{\mathbf{x}\cdot\mathbf{y}}{\sqrt{(\mathbf{x}\cdot\mathbf{x})(\mathbf{y}\cdot\mathbf{y})}} \tag{8.6}$$

Cosine similarity differs from Euclidean distance in that it doesn't depend on the length of the vectors $\mathbf{x}$ and $\mathbf{y}$. On the other hand, it is not translation-independent, but assigns special status to the origin: one way to think of it is as a projection onto a unit sphere around the origin, and measuring distance on that sphere. Cosine similarity is usually turned into a distance metric by taking $1-\cos\theta$. Being defined entirely in terms of dot products, it is as easily kernelised as Euclidean distance.

Algorithm 8.5: Kernel-KMeans(D, K) – K-means clustering using kernelised distance $\text{Dis}_{\mathscr{K}}$.

Input : data $D \subseteq \mathscr{X}$; number of clusters $K \in \mathbb{N}$.
Output : K-fold partition $D_1 \uplus \ldots \uplus D_K = D$.

1 randomly initialise K clusters $D_1, \ldots, D_K$;
2 **repeat**
3   assign each $\mathbf{x} \in D$ to $\arg\min_j \frac{1}{|D_j|} \sum_{\mathbf{y}\in D_j} \text{Dis}_{\mathscr{K}}(\mathbf{x}, \mathbf{y})$;
4   **for** $j = 1$ to K **do**
5         $D_j \leftarrow \{\mathbf{x} \in D | \mathbf{x}$ assigned to cluster $j\}$;
6   **end**
7 **until** no change in $D_1, \ldots, D_K$;
8 **return** $D_1, \ldots, D_K$;

8.7 Distance-based models: Summary and further reading

Along with linear models, distance-based models are the second group of models with strong geometric intuitions. The literature on distance-based models is rich and diverse; in this chapter I've concentrated on getting the main intuitions across.

- ☞ In Section 8.1 we reviewed the most commonly used distance metrics: the Minkowski distance or p-norm with special cases Euclidean distance ($p = 2$) and Manhattan distance ($p = 1$); the Hamming distance, which counts the number of bits or literals that are different; and the Mahalanobis distance, which decorrelates and normalises the features (Mahalanobis, 1936). Other distances can be taken into account, as long as they satisfy the requirements of a distance metric listed in Definition 8.2.

- ☞ Section 8.2 investigated the key concepts of neighbours and exemplars. Exemplars are either centroids that find a centre of mass according to a chosen distance metric, or medoids that find the most centrally located data point. The most commonly used centroid is the arithmetic mean, which minimises squared Euclidean distance to all other points. Other definitions of centroids are possible but harder to compute: e.g., the geometric median is the point minimising Euclidean distance, but does not admit a closed-form solution. The complexity of finding a medoid is always quadratic regardless of the distance metric. We then considered nearest-neighbour decision rules, and looked in particular at the difference between 2-norm and 1-norm nearest-exemplar decision boundaries, and how these get refined by switching to a 2-nearest-exemplars decision rule.

- ☞ In Section 8.3 we discussed nearest-neighbour models which simply use the training data as exemplars. This is a very widely used model for classification, the origins of which can be traced back to Fix and Hodges (1951). Despite its simplicity, it can be shown that with sufficient training data the error rate is at most twice the optimal error rate (Cover and Hart, 1967). The 1-nearest neighbour classifier has low bias but high variance; by increasing the number of neighbours over which we aggregate we can reduce the variance but at the same time increase the bias. The nearest-neighbour decision rule can also be applied to real-valued target variables, and more generally to any task where we have an appropriate aggregator for multiple target values.

- ☞ Section 8.4 considered a number of algorithms for distance-based clustering using either arithmetic means or medoids. The K-means algorithm is a simple heuristic approach to solve the K-means problem that was originally proposed in 1957 and is sometimes referred to as Lloyd's algorithm (Lloyd, 1982). It is dependent on the initial configuration and can easily converge to the wrong stationary point. We also looked at the K-medoids and partitioning around medoids algorithms, the latter due to Kaufman and Rousseeuw (1990). These are computationally more expensive due to the use of medoids. Silhouettes (Rousseeuw, 1987) are a useful technique to check whether points are on average closer to the other members of their cluster than they are to the members of the neighbouring cluster. Much more detail about these and other clustering methods is provided by Jain, Murty and Flynn (1999).

☞ Whereas the previous clustering methods all result in a partition of the instance space and are therefore predictive, hierarchical clustering discussed in Section 8.5 applies only to the given data and is hence descriptive. A distinct advantage is that the clustering is constructed in the form of a dendrogram, which means that the number of clusters does not need to be specified in advance and can be chosen by inspecting the dendrogram. However, the method is computationally expensive and infeasible for large data sets. Furthermore, it is not always obvious which of the possible linkage functions to choose.

☞ Finally, in Section 8.6 we briefly considered how distances can be 'kernelised', and we gave one example in the form of kernel K-means. The use of a non-Euclidean distance metric leads to quadratic complexity of recalculating the clusters in each iteration.

CHAPTER 9

Probabilistic models

THE THIRD AND FINAL FAMILY of machine learning models considered in this book are probabilistic models. We have already seen how probabilities can be useful to express a model's expectation about the class of a given instance. For example, a ☞*probability estimation tree* (Section 5.2) attaches a class probability distribution to each leaf of the tree, and each instance that gets filtered down to a particular leaf in a tree model is labelled with that particular class distribution. Similarly, a calibrated linear model translates the distance from the decision boundary into a class probability (Section 7.4). These are examples of what are called *discriminative* probabilistic models. They model the posterior probability distribution $P(Y|X)$, where Y is the target variable and X are the features. That is, given X they return a probability distribution over Y.

The other main class of probabilistic models are called *generative* models. They model the joint distribution $P(Y,X)$ of the target Y and the feature vector X. Once we have access to this joint distribution we can derive any conditional or marginal distribution involving the same variables. In particular, since $P(X) = \sum_y P(Y = y, X)$ it follows that the posterior distribution can be obtained as

$$P(Y|X) = \frac{P(Y,X)}{\sum_y P(Y = y, X)}$$

Alternatively, generative models can be described by the likelihood function $P(X|Y)$, since $P(Y,X) = P(X|Y)P(Y)$ and the target or prior distribution (usually abbreviated to 'prior') can be easily estimated or postulated. Such models are called 'generative' because we can sample from the joint distribution to obtain new data points together with their labels. Alternatively, we can use $P(Y)$ to sample a class and $P(X|Y)$ to sample an instance for that class – this was illustrated for the spam e-mail example on p.29. In contrast, a discriminative model such as a probability estimation tree or a linear classifier models $P(Y|X)$ but not $P(X)$, and hence can be used to label data but not generate it.

Since generative models can do anything that discriminative models do, they may seem preferable. However, they have a number of drawbacks as well. First of all, note that storing the joint distribution requires space exponential in the number of features. This necessitates simplifying assumptions such as independence between features, which may lead to inaccuracies if they are not valid in a particular domain. The most common criticism levied against generative models is that accuracy in modelling $P(X)$ may actually be achieved at the expense of less accurate modelling of $P(Y|X)$. However, the issue is not yet fully understood, and there are certainly situations where knowledge of $P(X)$ provides welcome additional understanding of the domain. For example, we may be less concerned about misclassifying certain instances if they are unlikely according to $P(X)$.

One of the most attractive features of the probabilistic perspective is that it allows us to view learning as a process of reducing uncertainty. For instance, a uniform class prior tells us that, before knowing anything about the instance to be classified, we are maximally uncertain about which class to assign. If the posterior distribution after observing the instance is less uniform, we have reduced our uncertainty in favour of one class or the other. We can repeat this process every time we receive new information, using the posterior obtained in the previous step as the prior for the next step. This process can be applied, in principle, to any unknown quantity that we come across.

Example 9.1 (Spam or not?). Suppose we want to estimate the probability θ that an arbitrary e-mail is spam, so that we can use the appropriate prior distribution. The natural thing to do is to inspect n e-mails, determine the number of spam e-mails d, and set $\hat{\theta} = d/n$; we don't really need any complicated statistics to tell us that. However, while this is the most likely estimate of θ – the maximum a posteriori (MAP) estimate, using the terminology introduced on p.28 – this doesn't mean that other values of θ are completely ruled out. We model this by a probability distribution over θ which is updated each time new information comes in. This is further illustrated in Figure 9.1 for a distribution that is more and more skewed towards spam.

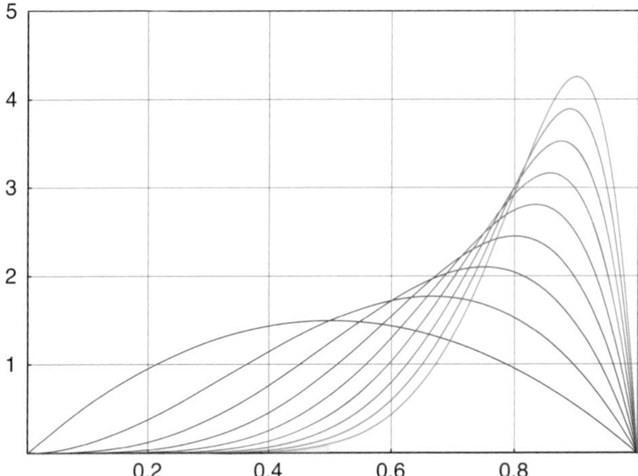

Figure 9.1. Each time we inspect an e-mail, we are reducing our uncertainty regarding the prior spam probability θ. After we inspect two e-mails and observe one spam, the possible θ values are characterised by a symmetric distribution around 1/2. If we inspect a third, fourth, ..., tenth e-mail and each time (except the first one) it is spam, then this distribution narrows and shifts a little bit to the right each time. As you would expect, the distribution for n e-mails reaches its maximum at $\hat{\theta}_{\text{MAP}} = \frac{n-1}{n}$ (e.g., $\hat{\theta}_{\text{MAP}} = 0.8$ for $n = 5$); however, asymmetric distributions like these contain information that cannot be conveyed by single numbers such as the mean or the maximum.

Explicitly modelling the posterior distribution over the parameter θ has a number of advantages that are usually associated with the 'Bayesian' perspective:

☞ We can precisely characterise the uncertainty that remains about our estimate by quantifying the spread of the posterior distribution.

☞ We can obtain a generative model for the parameter by sampling from the posterior distribution, which contains much more information than a summary statistic such as the MAP estimate can convey – so, rather than using a single e-mail with $\theta = \theta_{\text{MAP}}$, our generative model can contain a number of e-mails with θ sampled from the posterior distribution.

☞ We can quantify the probability of statements such as 'e-mails are biased towards ham' (the tiny shaded area in Figure 9.1 demonstrates that after observing one ham and nine spam e-mails this probability is very small, about 0.6%).

☞ We can use one of these distributions to encode our prior beliefs: e.g., if we believe that the proportions of spam and ham are typically 50–50, we can take the distribution for $n = 2$ (the lowest, symmetric one in Figure 9.1) as our prior.[1]

[1]Statisticians call a prior that has the same mathematical form as a posterior distribution a *conjugate*

The key point is that *probabilities do not have to be interpreted as estimates of relative frequencies, but can carry the more general meaning of (possibly subjective) degrees of belief*. Consequently, we can attach a probability distribution to almost anything: not just features and targets, but also model parameters and even models. For instance, in the example just given we were considering the distribution $P(\theta|D)$, where D represents the data (i.e., the classes of the inspected e-mails).

An important concept related to probabilistic models is *Bayes-optimality*. A classifier is Bayes-optimal if it always assigns $\arg\max_y P^*(Y = y|X = x)$ to an instance x, where P^* denotes the true posterior distribution. Even if we almost never know the true distribution in a practical situation, there are several ways in which we can make this concrete. For example, we can perform experiments with artificially generated data for which we have chosen the true distribution ourselves: this allows us to experimentally evaluate how close the performance of a model is to being Bayes-optimal. Alternatively, the derivation of a probabilistic learning method usually makes certain assumptions about the true distribution, which allows us to prove theoretically that the model will be Bayes-optimal provided these assumptions are met. For example, later on in this chapter we will state the conditions under which the basic linear classifier is Bayes-optimal. The property is therefore best understood as a yardstick by which we measure the performance of probabilistic models.

Since many models discussed in previous chapters are able to estimate class probabilities and hence are discriminative probabilistic models, it is worth pointing out that the choice of a single model, often referred to as *model selection*, does not necessarily lead to Bayes-optimality – even if the model chosen is the one that performs best under the true distribution. To illustrate this, let m^* be the best probability estimation tree we have learned from a sufficient amount of data. Using m^* we would predict $\arg\max_y P(Y = y|M = m^*, X = x)$ for an instance x, where M is a random variable ranging over the model class m^* was chosen from. However, these predictions are not necessarily Bayes-optimal since

$$
\begin{aligned}
P(Y|X = x) &= \sum_{m \in M} P(Y, M = m|X = x) && \text{by marginalising over } M \\
&= \sum_{m \in M} P(Y|M = m, X = x)P(M = m|X = x) && \text{by the chain rule} \\
&= \sum_{m \in M} P(Y|M = m, X = x)P(M = m) && \text{by independence of } M \text{ and } X
\end{aligned}
$$

Here, $P(M)$ can be interpreted as a posterior distribution over models after seeing the training data (the MAP model is therefore $m^* = \arg\max_m P(M = m)$). The final

---

prior – in this case we have used the Beta distribution, which is conjugate to the binomial distribution. Conjugate priors not only simplify the mathematics, but also allow more intuitive interpretations: in this case we pretend we have already inspected two e-mails, one of which was spam – a very useful idea that we have in fact already used in the form of the ☞*Laplace correction* in Section 2.3.

expression in the preceding derivation tells us to average the predictions of all models, weighted by their posterior probabilities. Clearly, this distribution is only equal to $P(Y|M = m^*, X = x)$ if $P(M)$ is zero for all models other than m^*, i.e., if we have seen sufficient training data to rule out all but one remaining model. This is obviously unrealistic.[2]

The outline of the chapter is as follows. In Section 9.1 we will see some useful connections between the geometric perspective and the probabilistic viewpoint, which come about when features are normally distributed. This allows us, as already mentioned, to state the conditions under which the basic linear classifier is Bayes-optimal. In Section 9.2 we consider the case of categorical features, leading to the well-known naive Bayes classifier. Section 9.3 revisits the linear classifier from a probabilistic perspective, which results in a new training algorithm explicitly aimed at optimising the posterior probability of the examples. Section 9.4 discusses ways to deal with hidden variables. Finally, in Section 9.5 we briefly look at compression-based learning methods, which can be given a probabilistic interpretation by means of information-theoretic notions.

9.1 The normal distribution and its geometric interpretations

We can draw a connection between probabilistic and geometric models by considering probability distributions defined over Euclidean spaces. The most common such distributions are *normal distributions*, also called *Gaussians*; Background 9.1 recalls the most important facts concerning univariate and multivariate normal distributions. We start by considering the univariate, two-class case. Suppose the values of $x \in \mathbb{R}$ follow a *mixture model*: i.e., each class has its own probability distribution (a *component* of the mixture model). We will assume a Gaussian mixture model, which means that the components of the mixture are both Gaussians. We thus have

$$P(x|\oplus) = \frac{1}{\sqrt{2\pi}\sigma^{\oplus}} \exp\left(-\frac{1}{2}\left[\frac{x-\mu^{\oplus}}{\sigma^{\oplus}}\right]^2\right) \qquad P(x|\ominus) = \frac{1}{\sqrt{2\pi}\sigma^{\ominus}} \exp\left(-\frac{1}{2}\left[\frac{x-\mu^{\ominus}}{\sigma^{\ominus}}\right]^2\right)$$

where $\mu^{\oplus}$ and $\sigma^{\oplus}$ are the mean and standard deviation for the positive class, and $\mu^{\ominus}$ and $\sigma^{\ominus}$ are the mean and standard deviation for the negative class. This gives the following likelihood ratio:

$$\mathrm{LR}(x) = \frac{P(x|\oplus)}{P(x|\ominus)} = \frac{\sigma^{\ominus}}{\sigma^{\oplus}} \exp\left(-\frac{1}{2}\left[\left(\frac{x-\mu^{\oplus}}{\sigma^{\oplus}}\right)^2 - \left(\frac{x-\mu^{\ominus}}{\sigma^{\ominus}}\right)^2\right]\right) \tag{9.1}$$

---

[2] Note that we do not require the two distributions to be equal, but rather that they reach the same maximum for Y. It is not hard to demonstrate that this, too, is not generally the case.

The univariate normal or Gaussian distribution has the following probability density function:

$$P(x|\mu,\sigma) = \frac{1}{\sqrt{2\pi}\sigma}\exp\left(-\frac{(x-\mu)^2}{2\sigma^2}\right) = \frac{1}{E}\exp\left(-\frac{1}{2}\left[\frac{x-\mu}{\sigma}\right]^2\right) = \frac{1}{E}\exp\left(-z^2/2\right), \quad E = \sqrt{2\pi}\sigma$$

The distribution has two parameters: μ, which is the mean or expected value, as well as the median (i.e., the point where the area under the density function is split in half) and the mode (i.e., the point where the density function reaches its maximum); and σ, which is the standard deviation and determines the width of the bell-shaped curve.

$z = (x-\mu)/\sigma$ is the *z-score* associated with x; it measures the number of standard deviations between x and the mean (it has itself mean 0 and standard deviation 1). It follows that $P(x|\mu,\sigma) = \frac{1}{\sigma}P(z|0,1)$, where $P(z|0,1)$ denotes the *standard normal distribution*. In other words, any normal distribution can be obtained from the standard normal distribution by scaling the x-axis with a factor σ, scaling the y-axis with a factor $1/\sigma$ (so the area under the curve remains 1), and translating the origin over μ.

The *multivariate normal distribution* over d-vectors $\mathbf{x} = (x_1,\ldots,x_d)^{\mathrm{T}} \in \mathbb{R}^d$ is

$$P(\mathbf{x}|\boldsymbol{\mu},\boldsymbol{\Sigma}) = \frac{1}{E_d}\exp\left(-\frac{1}{2}(\mathbf{x}-\boldsymbol{\mu})^{\mathrm{T}}\boldsymbol{\Sigma}^{-1}(\mathbf{x}-\boldsymbol{\mu})\right), \quad E_d = (2\pi)^{d/2}\sqrt{|\boldsymbol{\Sigma}|} \tag{9.2}$$

The parameters are the mean vector $\boldsymbol{\mu} = (\mu_1,\ldots,\mu_d)^{\mathrm{T}}$ and the d-by-d covariance matrix $\boldsymbol{\Sigma}$ (see Background 7.2 on p.200). $\boldsymbol{\Sigma}^{-1}$ is the inverse of the covariance matrix, and $|\boldsymbol{\Sigma}|$ is its determinant. The components of $\mathbf{x}$ may be thought of as d features that are possibly correlated.

If $d = 1$, then $\boldsymbol{\Sigma} = \sigma^2 = |\boldsymbol{\Sigma}|$ and $\boldsymbol{\Sigma}^{-1} = 1/\sigma^2$, which gives us the univariate Gaussian as a special case. For $d = 2$ we have $\boldsymbol{\Sigma} = \begin{pmatrix} \sigma_1^2 & \sigma_{12} \\ \sigma_{12} & \sigma_2^2 \end{pmatrix}$, $|\boldsymbol{\Sigma}| = \sigma_1^2\sigma_2^2 - (\sigma_{12})^2$ and $\boldsymbol{\Sigma}^{-1} = \frac{1}{|\boldsymbol{\Sigma}|}\begin{pmatrix} \sigma_2^2 & -\sigma_{12} \\ -\sigma_{12} & \sigma_1^2 \end{pmatrix}$. Using z-scores we derive the following expression for the bivariate normal distribution:

$$P(x_1,x_2|\mu_1,\mu_2,\sigma_1,\sigma_2,\rho) = \frac{1}{E_2}\exp\left(-\frac{1}{2(1-\rho^2)}(z_1^2+z_2^2-2\rho z_1 z_2)\right), \quad E_2 = 2\pi\sigma_1\sigma_2\sqrt{1-\rho^2} \tag{9.3}$$

where $z_i = (x_i-\mu_i)/\sigma_i$ for $i = 1,2$, and $\rho = \sigma_{12}/\sigma_1\sigma_2$ is the *correlation coefficient* between the two features.

The *multivariate standard normal distribution* has $\boldsymbol{\mu} = \mathbf{0}$ (a d-vector with all 0s) and $\boldsymbol{\Sigma} = \mathbf{I}$ (the d-by-d identity matrix), and thus $P(\mathbf{x}|\mathbf{0},\mathbf{I}) = \frac{1}{(2\pi)^{d/2}}\exp\left(-\frac{1}{2}\mathbf{x}\cdot\mathbf{x}\right)$.

Background 9.1. The normal distribution.

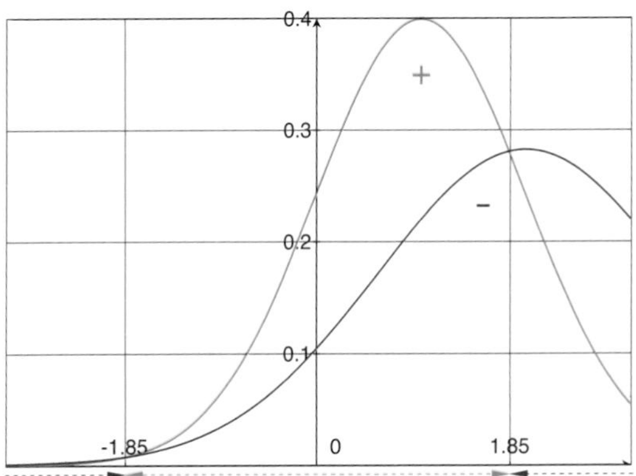

Figure 9.2. If positive examples are drawn from a Gaussian with mean and standard deviation 1 and negatives from a Gaussian with mean and standard deviation 2, then the two distributions cross at $x = \pm 1.85$. This means that the maximum-likelihood region for positives is the closed interval $[-1.85, 1.85]$, and hence the negative region is non-contiguous.

Let's first consider the case that both components have the same standard deviation, i.e., $\sigma^{\oplus} = \sigma^{\ominus} = \sigma$. We can then simplify the exponent in Equation 9.1 as follows:

$$\begin{aligned}
-\frac{1}{2\sigma^2}\left[(x-\mu^{\oplus})^2 - (x-\mu^{\ominus})^2\right] &= -\frac{1}{2\sigma^2}\left[x^2 - 2\mu^{\oplus}x + \mu^{\oplus 2} - (x^2 - 2\mu^{\ominus}x + \mu^{\ominus 2})\right] \\
&= -\frac{1}{2\sigma^2}\left[-2(\mu^{\oplus} - \mu^{\ominus})x + (\mu^{\oplus 2} - \mu^{\ominus 2})\right] \\
&= \frac{\mu^{\oplus} - \mu^{\ominus}}{\sigma^2}\left[x - \frac{\mu^{\oplus} + \mu^{\ominus}}{2}\right]
\end{aligned}$$

The likelihood ratio can thus be written as $\mathrm{LR}(x) = \exp\left(\gamma(x-\mu)\right)$, with two parameters: $\gamma = (\mu^{\oplus} - \mu^{\ominus})/\sigma^2$ is the difference between the means in proportion to the variance, and $\mu = (\mu^{\oplus} + \mu^{\ominus})/2$ is the midpoint between the two class means. It follows that the maximum-likelihood decision threshold (the value of x such that $\mathrm{LR}(x) = 1$) is $x_{\mathrm{ML}} = \mu$.

If $\sigma^{\oplus} \neq \sigma^{\ominus}$, the x^2 terms in Equation 9.1 do not cancel. This results in two decision boundaries and a non-contiguous decision region for one of the classes.

Example 9.2 (Univariate mixture model with unequal variances). Suppose $\mu^{\oplus} = 1$, $\mu^{\ominus} = 2$ and $\sigma^{\ominus} = 2\sigma^{\oplus} = 2$, then $\mathrm{LR}(x) = 2\exp\left(-[(x-1)^2 - (x-2)^2/4]/2\right) = 2\exp\left(3x^2/8\right)$. It follows that the ML decision boundaries are $x = \pm(8/3)\ln 2 = \pm 1.85$. As can be observed in Figure 9.2, these are the points where the two Gaussians cross. In contrast, if $\sigma^{\ominus} = \sigma^{\oplus}$ then we get a single ML decision boundary at $x = 1.5$.

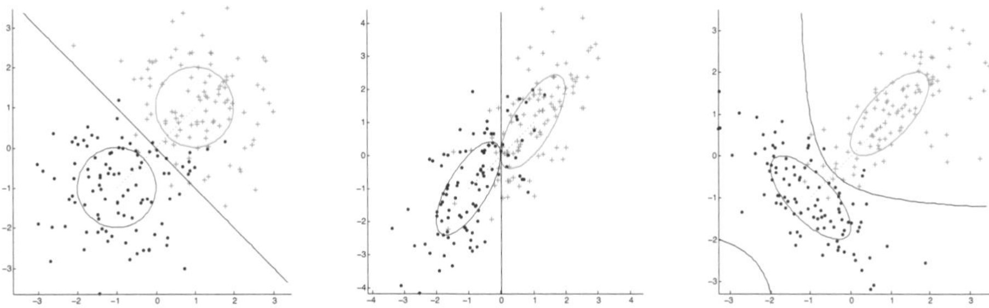

Figure 9.3. (left) If the features are uncorrelated and have the same variance, maximum-likelihood classification leads to the basic linear classifier, whose decision boundary is orthogonal to the line connecting the means. **(middle)** As long as the per-class covariance matrices are identical, the Bayes-optimal decision boundary is linear – if we were to decorrelate the features by rotation and scaling, we would again obtain the basic linear classifier. **(right)** Unequal covariance matrices lead to hyperbolic decision boundaries, which means that one of the decision regions is non-contiguous.

Non-contiguous decision regions can also occur in higher-dimensional spaces. The following example demonstrates this for $m = 2$.

Example 9.3 (Bivariate Gaussian mixture). We use Equation 9.3 on p.267 to obtain explicit expressions for the ML decision boundary in the bivariate case. Throughout the example we assume $\mu_1^{\oplus} = \mu_2^{\oplus} = 1$ and $\mu_1^{\ominus} = \mu_2^{\ominus} = -1$.

(*i*) If all variances are 1 and both correlations are 0, then the ML decision boundary is given by $(x_1-1)^2+(x_2-1)^2-(x_1+1)^2-(x_2+1)^2 = -2x_1-2x_2-2x_1-2x_2 = 0$, i.e., $x_1+x_2 = 0$ (Figure 9.3 (left)).

(*ii*) If $\sigma_1^{\oplus} = \sigma_1^{\ominus} = 1$, $\sigma_2^{\oplus} = \sigma_2^{\ominus} = \sqrt{2}$ and $\rho^{\oplus} = \rho^{\ominus} = \sqrt{2}/2$, then the ML decision boundary is $(x_1-1)^2+(x_2-1)^2/2-\sqrt{2}(x_1-1)(x_2-1)/\sqrt{2}-(x_1+1)^2-(x_2+1)^2/2+\sqrt{2}(x_1+1)(x_2+1)/\sqrt{2} = -2x_1 = 0$ (Figure 9.3 (middle)).

(*iii*) If all variances are 1 and $\rho^{\oplus} = -\rho^{\ominus} = \rho$, then the ML decision boundary is given by $(x_1-1)^2+(x_2-1)^2-2\rho(x_1-1)(x_2-1)-(x_1+1)^2-(x_2+1)^2-2\rho(x_1+1)(x_2+1) = -4x_1-4x_2-4\rho x_1x_2-4\rho = 0$, i.e., $x_1+x_2+\rho x_1x_2+\rho = 0$, which is a hyperbole. Figure 9.3 (right) illustrates this for $\rho = 0.7$. Notice that the bottom left of the instance space is a positive decision region, even though it contains no training examples and it is closer to the negative mean than to the positive mean.

Notice the circles and ellipses in Figure 9.3, which provide a visual summary of the covariance matrix. By projecting the shape for the positive class down to the x-axis we obtain the interval $[\mu_1{}^{\oplus}-\sigma_1{}^{\oplus}, \mu_1{}^{\oplus}+\sigma_1{}^{\oplus}]$ – i.e., one standard deviation around the mean – and similar for the negative class and the y-axis. Three cases can be distinguished: (*i*) both x and y standard deviations are equal and the correlation coefficient is zero, in which case the shape is a circle; (*ii*) the standard deviations are different and the correlation coefficient is zero, which means the shape is an ellipse parallel to the axis with the largest standard deviation; (*iii*) the correlation coefficient is non-zero: the orientation of the ellipse gives the sign of the correlation coefficient, and its width varies with the magnitude of the correlation coefficient.[3] Mathematically, these shapes are defined by setting $f(\mathbf{x})$ in $\frac{1}{E_d}\exp\left(-\frac{1}{2}f(\mathbf{x})\right)$ to 1 and solving for $\mathbf{x}$, in order to capture the points that are one standard deviation away from the mean. For the bivariate case this leads to $(z_1^2+z_2^2-2\rho z_1 z_2) = 1-\rho^2$, which can be translated into an elliptic equation for x_1 and x_2 by expanding the z-scores. Notice that for $\rho = 0$ this is a circle around the origin, and when $\rho \to 1$ this approaches the line $z_2 = z_1$ (we can't put $\rho = 1$ because this leads to a singular covariance matrix).

In the general multivariate case the condition $(\mathbf{x}-\boldsymbol{\mu})^{\mathrm{T}}\boldsymbol{\Sigma}^{-1}(\mathbf{x}-\boldsymbol{\mu}) = 1$ defines a hyper-ellipse, because $\boldsymbol{\Sigma}^{-1}$ satisfies certain properties.[4] For a standard normal distribution, one-standard-deviation contours lie on a hyper-sphere (a circle in d dimensions) defined by $\mathbf{x}\cdot\mathbf{x} = 1$. A very useful geometric intuition is that, just as hyper-spheres can be turned into arbitrary hyper-ellipses by scaling and rotation, any multivariate Gaussian can be obtained from the standard Gaussian by scaling and rotation (to obtain the desired covariance matrix) and translation (to obtain the desired mean). Conversely, we can turn an arbitrary multivariate Gaussian into a standard normal distribution by translation, rotation and scaling, as was already suggested in Background 1.2 on p.24. This results in decorrelated and normalised features.

The general form of the likelihood ratio can be derived from Equation 9.2 on p.267 as

$$\mathrm{LR}(\mathbf{x}) = \sqrt{\frac{|\boldsymbol{\Sigma}^{\ominus}|}{|\boldsymbol{\Sigma}^{\oplus}|}}\exp\left(-\frac{1}{2}\left[(\mathbf{x}-\boldsymbol{\mu}^{\oplus})^{\mathrm{T}}(\boldsymbol{\Sigma}^{\oplus})^{-1}(\mathbf{x}-\boldsymbol{\mu}^{\oplus}) - (\mathbf{x}-\boldsymbol{\mu}^{\ominus})^{\mathrm{T}}(\boldsymbol{\Sigma}^{\ominus})^{-1}(\mathbf{x}-\boldsymbol{\mu}^{\ominus})\right]\right)$$

where $\boldsymbol{\mu}^{\oplus}$ and $\boldsymbol{\mu}^{\ominus}$ are the class means, and $\boldsymbol{\Sigma}^{\oplus}$ and $\boldsymbol{\Sigma}^{\ominus}$ are the covariance matrices for each class. To understand this a bit better, assume that $\boldsymbol{\Sigma}^{\oplus} = \boldsymbol{\Sigma}^{\ominus} = \mathbf{I}$ (i.e., in each class the features are uncorrelated and have unit variance), then we have

$$\begin{aligned}\mathrm{LR}(\mathbf{x}) &= \exp\left(-\frac{1}{2}\left[(\mathbf{x}-\boldsymbol{\mu}^{\oplus})^{\mathrm{T}}(\mathbf{x}-\boldsymbol{\mu}^{\oplus}) - (\mathbf{x}-\boldsymbol{\mu}^{\ominus})^{\mathrm{T}}(\mathbf{x}-\boldsymbol{\mu}^{\ominus})\right]\right)\\ &= \exp\left(-\frac{1}{2}\left[||\mathbf{x}-\boldsymbol{\mu}^{\oplus}||^2 - ||\mathbf{x}-\boldsymbol{\mu}^{\ominus}||^2\right]\right)\end{aligned}$$

---

[3] A common mistake is to think that the angle of rotation of the ellipse depends on the correlation coefficient; in fact, it is solely determined by the relative magnitudes of the marginal standard deviations.

[4] Specifically, $\mathbf{x}^{\mathrm{T}}\mathbf{A}\mathbf{x}$ defines a hyper-ellipse if $\mathbf{A}$ is symmetric and positive definite. Both properties are satisfied if $\mathbf{A}$ is the inverse of a non-singular covariance matrix.

It follows that $\mathrm{LR}(\mathbf{x}) = 1$ for any $\mathbf{x}$ equidistant from $\boldsymbol{\mu}^{\oplus}$ and $\boldsymbol{\mu}^{\ominus}$. But this means that the ML decision boundary is a straight line at equal distances from the class means – in which we recognise our old friend, the basic linear classifier! In other words, *for uncorrelated, unit-variance Gaussian features, the basic linear classifier is Bayes-optimal*. This is a good example of how a probabilistic viewpoint can justify particular models.

More generally, as long as the per-class covariance matrices are equal, the ML decision boundary will be linear, intersecting $\boldsymbol{\mu}^{\oplus} - \boldsymbol{\mu}^{\ominus}$ in the middle, but not at right angles if the features are correlated. This means that the basic linear classifier is only Bayes-optimal in this case if we first decorrelate and normalise the features. With non-equal class covariances the decision boundary will be hyperbolic. So, the three cases in Figure 9.3 generalise to the multivariate case.

We have now seen several examples of how the normal distribution links the probabilistic and geometric viewpoints. The multivariate normal distribution essentially translates distances into probabilities. This becomes obvious when we plug the definition of ☞*Mahalanobis distance* (Equation 8.1 on p.237) into Equation 9.2:

$$P(\mathbf{x}|\boldsymbol{\mu},\boldsymbol{\Sigma}) = \frac{1}{E_d}\exp\left(-\frac{1}{2}\left(\mathrm{Dis}_M(\mathbf{x},\boldsymbol{\mu}|\boldsymbol{\Sigma})\right)^2\right) \tag{9.4}$$

Similarly, the standard normal distribution translates Euclidean distances into probabilities:

$$P(\mathbf{x}|\mathbf{0},\mathbf{I}) = \frac{1}{(2\pi)^{d/2}}\exp\left(-\frac{1}{2}\left(\mathrm{Dis}_2(\mathbf{x},\mathbf{0})\right)^2\right)$$

Conversely, we see that *the negative logarithm of the Gaussian likelihood can be interpreted as a squared distance*:

$$-\ln P(\mathbf{x}|\boldsymbol{\mu},\boldsymbol{\Sigma}) = \ln E_d + \frac{1}{2}\left(\mathrm{Dis}_M(\mathbf{x},\boldsymbol{\mu}|\boldsymbol{\Sigma})\right)^2$$

The intuition is that the logarithm transforms the multiplicative probability scale into an additive scale (which, in the case of Gaussian distributions, corresponds to a squared distance). Since additive scales are often easier to handle, log-likelihoods are a common concept in statistics.

Another example of the link between the geometric and the probabilistic perspective occurs when we consider the question of estimating the parameters of a normal distribution. For example, suppose we want to estimate the mean $\boldsymbol{\mu}$ of a multivariate Gaussian distribution with given covariance matrix $\boldsymbol{\Sigma}$ from a set of data points X. The principle of *maximum-likelihood estimation* states that we should find the value of $\boldsymbol{\mu}$ that maximises the joint likelihood of X. Assuming that the elements of X were independently sampled, the joint likelihood decomposes into a product over the individual data points in X, and the maximum-likelihood estimate can be found as follows:

$$\begin{aligned}
\hat{\mu} &= \arg\max_{\mu} \prod_{\mathbf{x}\in X} P(\mathbf{x}|\mu,\mathbf{\Sigma}) \\
&= \arg\max_{\mu} \prod_{\mathbf{x}\in X} \frac{1}{E_d}\exp\left(-\frac{1}{2}\left(\text{Dis}_M(\mathbf{x},\mu|\mathbf{\Sigma})\right)^2\right) && \text{using Equation 9.4} \\
&= \arg\min_{\mu} \sum_{\mathbf{x}\in X} \left[\ln E_d + \frac{1}{2}\left(\text{Dis}_M(\mathbf{x},\mu|\mathbf{\Sigma})\right)^2\right] && \text{taking negative logarithms} \\
&= \arg\min_{\mu} \sum_{\mathbf{x}\in X} \left(\text{Dis}_M(\mathbf{x},\mu|\mathbf{\Sigma})\right)^2 && \text{dropping constant term and factor}
\end{aligned}$$

We thus find that the maximum-likelihood estimate of the mean of a multivariate distribution is the point that minimises the total squared Mahalanobis distance to all points in X. For the identity covariance matrix $\mathbf{\Sigma} = \mathbf{I}$ we can replace Mahalanobis distance with Euclidean distance, and by Theorem 8.1 the point minimising total squared Euclidean distance to all points in X is the arithmetic mean $\frac{1}{|X|}\sum_{\mathbf{x}\in X}\mathbf{x}$.

As a final example of how geometric and probabilistic views of the same problem can be strongly connected I will now demonstrate how the ☞*least-squares solution to a linear regression problem* (Section 7.1) can be derived as a maximum-likelihood estimate. For ease of notation we will look at the univariate case discussed in Example 7.1. The starting point is the assumption that our training examples (h_i, y_i) are noisy measurements of true function points $(x_i, f(x_i))$: i.e., $y_i = f(x_i) + \epsilon_i$, where the ϵ_i are independently and identically distributed errors. (Notice the slight change of notation as y_i is now no longer the true function value.) We want to derive the maximum-likelihood estimates $\hat{y}_i$ of $f(x_i)$. We can derive this if we assume a particular noise distribution, for example Gaussian with variance σ_2. It then follows that each y_i is normally distributed with mean $a + bx_i$ and variance σ^2, and thus

$$P(y_i|a,b,\sigma^2) = \frac{1}{\sqrt{2\pi\sigma^2}}\exp\left(-\frac{\left(y_i-(a+bx_i)\right)^2}{2\sigma^2}\right)$$

Since the noise terms ϵ_i are independent for different i, so are the y_i and so the joint probability over all i is simply the product of n of these Gaussians:

$$\begin{aligned}
P(y_1,\ldots,y_n|a,b,\sigma^2) &= \prod_{i=1}^{n} \frac{1}{\sqrt{2\pi\sigma^2}}\exp\left(-\frac{\left(y_i-(a+bx_i)\right)^2}{2\sigma^2}\right) \\
&= \left(\frac{1}{\sqrt{2\pi\sigma^2}}\right)^n \exp\left(-\frac{\sum_{i=1}^{n}\left(y_i-(a+bx_i)\right)^2}{2\sigma^2}\right)
\end{aligned}$$

For ease of algebraic manipulation we take the negative natural logarithm:

$$-\ln P(y_1,\ldots,y_n|a,b,\sigma^2) = \frac{n}{2}\ln 2\pi + \frac{n}{2}\ln\sigma^2 + \frac{\sum_{i=1}^{n}\left(y_i-(a+bx_i)\right)^2}{2\sigma^2}$$

Taking the partial derivatives with respect to a, b and σ^2 and setting to zero in order to maximise the negative log likelihood gives the following three equations:

$$\sum_{i=1}^{n} y_i - (a + bx_i) = 0$$

$$\sum_{i=1}^{n} \left(y_i - (a + bx_i)\right) x_i = 0$$

$$\frac{n}{2}\frac{1}{\sigma^2} - \frac{\sum_{i=1}^{n}\left(y_i - (a + bx_i)\right)^2}{2(\sigma^2)^2} = 0$$

The first two equations are essentially the same as derived in Example 7.1 and give us $\hat{a} = \overline{y} - \hat{b}\overline{x}$ and $\hat{b} = \sigma_{xy}/\sigma_{xx}$, respectively. The third equation tells us that the sum of squared residuals is equal to $n\sigma^2$ and gives the maximum-likelihood estimate of the noise variance as $\left(\sum_{i=1}^{n}\left(y_i - (a + bx_i)\right)^2\right)/n$.

It is reassuring that the probabilistic viewpoint allows us to derive (ordinary) east-squares regression from first principles. On the other hand, a full treatment would require noise on the x-values as well (total least squares), but this complicates the mathematics and does not necessarily have a unique solution. This illustrates that *a good probabilistic treatment of a machine learning problem achieves a balance between solid theoretical foundations and the pragmatism required to obtain a workable solution.*

9.2 Probabilistic models for categorical data

To kill time during long drives to some faraway holiday destination, my sisters and I would often play games involving passing cars. For example, we would ask each other to look out for cars that had a particular colour, were from a particular country or had a particular letter on the numberplate. A binary question such as 'is the car blue?' is called a *Bernoulli trial* by statisticians. They are modelled as a binary random variable whose probability of success is fixed over each independent trial. We used a Bernoulli distribution to model the event of an e-mail being ham in Example 9.1. On top of such a random variable, other probability distributions can be built. For example, we may want to guess how many of the next n cars are blue: this is governed by the binomial distribution. Or the task may be to estimate how many cars we need to see until the first Dutch one: this number follows a geometric definition. Background 9.2 will help to refresh your memory regarding the main definitions.

Categorical variables or features (also called discrete or nominal) are ubiquitous in machine learning. Perhaps the most common form of the Bernoulli distribution models whether or not a word occurs in a document. That is, for the i-th word in our vocabulary we have a random variable X_i governed by a Bernoulli distribution. The joint distribution over the *bit vector* $X = (X_1, \ldots, X_k)$ is called a *multivariate Bernoulli distribution*. Variables with more than two outcomes are also common: for example,

---

The *Bernoulli distribution*, named after the Swiss seventeenth century mathematician Jacob Bernoulli, concerns Boolean or binary events with two possible outcomes: success or 1, and failure or 0. A Bernoulli distribution has a single parameter θ which gives the probability of success: hence $P(X=1)=\theta$ and $P(X=0)=1-\theta$. The Bernoulli distribution has expected value $\mathbb{E}[X]=\theta$ and variance $\mathbb{E}\left[(X-\mathbb{E}[X])^2\right]=\theta(1-\theta)$.

The *binomial distribution* arises when counting the number of successes S in n independent Bernoulli trials with the same parameter θ. It is described by

$$P(S=s)=\binom{n}{s}\theta^s(1-\theta)^{n-s} \text{ for } s\in\{0,\ldots,n\}$$

This distribution has expected value $\mathbb{E}[S]=n\theta$ and variance $\mathbb{E}\left[(S-\mathbb{E}[S])^2\right]=n\theta(1-\theta)$.

The *categorical distribution* generalises the Bernoulli distribution to $k\geq 2$ outcomes. The parameter of the distribution is a k-vector $\boldsymbol{\theta}=(\theta_1,\ldots,\theta_k)$ such that $\sum_{i=1}^k\theta_i=1$.

Finally, the *multinomial distribution* tabulates the outcomes of n independent and identically distributed (i.i.d.) categorical trials. That is, $\mathbf{X}=(X_1,\ldots,X_k)$ is a k-vector of integer counts, and

$$P(\mathbf{X}=(x_1,\ldots,x_k))=n!\frac{\theta_1^{x_1}}{x_1!}\cdots\frac{\theta_k^{x_k}}{x_k!}$$

with $\sum_{i=1}^k x_i=n$. Notice that setting $n=1$ gives us an alternative way of stating the categorical distribution as $P(\mathbf{X}=(x_1,\ldots,x_k))=\theta_1^{x_1}\cdots\theta_k^{x_k}$, with exactly one of the x_i equal to 1 and the rest set to 0. Furthermore, setting $k=2$ gives an alternative expression for the Bernoulli distribution as $P(X=x)=\theta^x(1-\theta)^{1-x}$ for $x\in\{0,1\}$. It is also useful to note that if $\mathbf{X}$ follows a multinomial distribution, then each component X_i follows a binomial distribution with parameter θ_i.

We can estimate the parameters of these distributions by counting in a straightforward way. Suppose $a\ b\ a\ c\ c\ b\ a\ a\ b\ c$ is a sequence of words. We might be interested in individual words being a or not, and interpret the data as coming from 10 i.i.d. Bernoulli trials, which would allow us to estimate $\hat{\theta}_a=4/10=0.4$. This same parameter generates a binomial distribution of the number of occurrences of the word a in similar sequences. Alternatively, we can estimate the parameters of the categorical (word occurrences) and multinomial (word counts) distributions as $\hat{\boldsymbol{\theta}}=(0.4,0.3,0.3)$.

It is almost always a good idea to smooth these distributions by including *pseudo-counts*. Imagine our vocabulary includes the word d but we haven't yet observed it, then a maximum-likelihood estimate would set $\hat{\theta}_d=0$. We can smooth this by adding a virtual occurrence of each word to our observations, leading to $\hat{\boldsymbol{\theta}}'=(5/14,4/14,4/14,1/14)$. In the case of a binomial this is the Laplace correction.

Background 9.2. Probability distributions for categorical data.

every word position in an e-mail corresponds to a categorical variable with k outcomes, where k is the size of the vocabulary. The multinomial distribution manifests itself as a *count vector*: a histogram of the number of occurrences of all vocabulary words in a document. This establishes an alternative way of modelling text documents that allows the number of occurrences of a word to influence the classification of a document.

Both these document models are in common use. Despite their differences, they both assume independence between word occurrences, generally referred to as the *naive Bayes assumption*. In the multinomial document model, this follows from the very use of the multinomial distribution, which assumes that words at different word positions are drawn independently from the same categorical distribution. In the multivariate Bernoulli model we assume that the bits in a bit vector are statistically independent, which allows us to compute the joint probability of a particular bit vector $(x_1, \ldots, x_k)$ as the product of the probabilities of each component $P(X_i = x_i)$. In practice, such word independence assumptions are often not true: if we know that an e-mail contains the word 'Viagra', we can be quite sure that it will also contain the word 'pill'. In any case, the experience is that, while the naive Bayes assumption almost certainly leads to poor probability estimates, it often doesn't harm ranking performance. This means that, provided the classification threshold is chosen with some care, we can usually get good classification performance too.

Using a naive Bayes model for classification

Assume that we have chosen one of the possible distributions to model our data X. In a classification context, we furthermore assume that the distribution depends on the class, so that $P(X|Y = \mathsf{spam})$ and $P(X|Y = \mathsf{ham})$ are different distributions. The more different these two distributions are, the more useful the features X are for classification. Thus, for a specific e-mail x we calculate both $P(X = x|Y = \mathsf{spam})$ and $P(X = x|Y = \mathsf{ham})$, and apply one of several possible decision rules:

maximum likelihood (ML) – predict $\arg\max_y P(X = x|Y = y)$;

maximum a posteriori (MAP) – predict $\arg\max_y P(X = x|Y = y)P(Y = y)$;

recalibrated likelihood – predict $\arg\max_y w_y P(X = x|Y = y)$.

The relation between the first two decision rules is that ML classification is equivalent to MAP classification with a uniform class distribution. The third decision rule generalises the first two in that it replaces the class distribution with a set of weights learned from the data: this makes it possible to correct for estimation errors in the likelihoods, as we shall see later.

Example 9.4 (Prediction using a naive Bayes model). Suppose our vocabulary contains three words a, b and c, and we use a multivariate Bernoulli model for our e-mails, with parameters

$$\boldsymbol{\theta}^{\oplus} = (0.5, 0.67, 0.33) \qquad \boldsymbol{\theta}^{\ominus} = (0.67, 0.33, 0.33)$$

This means, for example, that the presence of b is twice as likely in spam (+), compared with ham.

The e-mail to be classified contains words a and b but not c, and hence is described by the bit vector $\mathbf{x} = (1, 1, 0)$. We obtain likelihoods

$$P(\mathbf{x}|\oplus) = 0.5 \cdot 0.67 \cdot (1 - 0.33) = 0.222 \qquad P(\mathbf{x}|\ominus) = 0.67 \cdot 0.33 \cdot (1 - 0.33) = 0.148$$

The ML classification of $\mathbf{x}$ is thus spam. In the case of two classes it is often convenient to work with likelihood ratios and odds. The likelihood ratio can be calculated as $\frac{P(\mathbf{x}|\oplus)}{P(\mathbf{x}|\ominus)} = \frac{0.5}{0.67}\frac{0.67}{0.33}\frac{1-0.33}{1-0.33} = 3/2 > 1$. This means that the MAP classification of $\mathbf{x}$ is also spam if the prior odds are more than $2/3$, but ham if they are less than that. For example, with 33% spam and 67% ham the prior odds are $\frac{P(\oplus)}{P(\ominus)} = \frac{0.33}{0.67} = 1/2$, resulting in a posterior odds of $\frac{P(\oplus|\mathbf{x})}{P(\ominus|\mathbf{x})} = \frac{P(\mathbf{x}|\oplus)}{P(\mathbf{x}|\ominus)}\frac{P(\oplus)}{P(\ominus)} = 3/2 \cdot 1/2 = 3/4 < 1$. In this case the likelihood ratio for $\mathbf{x}$ is not strong enough to push the decision away from the prior.

Alternatively, we can employ a multinomial model. The parameters of a multinomial establish a distribution over the words in the vocabulary, say

$$\boldsymbol{\theta}^{\oplus} = (0.3, 0.5, 0.2) \qquad \boldsymbol{\theta}^{\ominus} = (0.6, 0.2, 0.2)$$

The e-mail to be classified contains three occurrences of word a, one single occurrence of word b and no occurrences of word c, and hence is described by the count vector $\mathbf{x} = (3, 1, 0)$. The total number of vocabulary word occurrences is $n = 4$. We obtain likelihoods

$$P(\mathbf{x}|\oplus) = 4!\frac{0.3^3}{3!}\frac{0.5^1}{1!}\frac{0.2^0}{0!} = 0.054 \qquad P(\mathbf{x}|\ominus) = 4!\frac{0.6^3}{3!}\frac{0.2^1}{1!}\frac{0.2^0}{0!} = 0.1728$$

The likelihood ratio is $\left(\frac{0.3}{0.6}\right)^3\left(\frac{0.5}{0.2}\right)^1\left(\frac{0.2}{0.2}\right)^0 = 5/16$. The ML classification of $\mathbf{x}$ is thus ham, the opposite of the multivariate Bernoulli model. This is mainly because of the three occurrences of word a, which provide strong evidence for ham.

Notice how the likelihood ratio for the multivariate Bernoulli model is a product of factors $\theta_i^{\oplus}/\theta_i^{\ominus}$ if $x_i = 1$ in the bit vector to be classified, and $(1-\theta_i^{\oplus})/(1-\theta_i^{\ominus})$ if $x_i = 0$. For the multinomial model the factors are $\left(\theta_i^{\oplus}/\theta_i^{\ominus}\right)^{x_i}$. One consequence of this is that the multinomial model only takes the presence of words into account, whereas in the multivariate Bernoulli model absent words can make a difference. In the previous example, not containing word b corresponds to a factor of $(1-0.67)/(1-0.33) = 1/2$ in the likelihood ratio. The other main difference between the two models is that multiple occurrences of words are treated like duplicated features in the multinomial model, through the exponential 'weight' x_i. This becomes clearer by taking the logarithm of the likelihood ratio, which is $\sum_i x_i(\ln\theta_i^{\oplus} - \ln\theta_i^{\ominus})$: this expression is linear in $\ln\theta_i^{\oplus}$ and $\ln\theta_i^{\ominus}$ with x_i as weights. Notice that this does not mean that naive Bayes classifiers are linear in the sense discussed in Chapter 7 unless we can demonstrate a linear relationship between $\ln\theta$ and the corresponding feature value. But we can say that naive Bayes models are linear in a particular space (the 'log-odds' space) obtained by applying a well-defined transformation to the features. We will return to this point when we discuss ☞*feature calibration* in Section 10.2.

The fact that the joint likelihood ratio of a naive Bayes model factorises as a product of likelihood ratios of individual words is a direct consequence of the naive Bayes assumption. In other words, the learning task decomposes into univariate tasks, one for each word in the vocabulary. We have encountered such a decomposition before when we discussed ☞*multivariate linear regression* in Section 7.1. There, we saw an example of how ignoring feature correlation could be harmful. Can we come up with similar examples for naive Bayes classifiers? Consider the situation when a particular word occurs twice in the vocabulary. In that case, we have the same factor occurring twice in the product for the likelihood ratio, and are effectively giving the word in question twice the weight of other words. While this is an extreme example, such double-counting does have noticeable effects in practice. I previously gave the example that if a spam e-mail contains the word 'Viagra', it is also expected to contain the word 'pill', so seeing the two words together should not give much more evidence for spam than seeing the first word on its own, and the likelihood ratio for the two words should not be much higher than that of the first word. However, multiplying two likelihood ratios larger than 1 will result in an even larger likelihood ratio. As a result, the probability estimates of a naive Bayes classifier are often pushed too far towards 0 or 1.

This may not seem such a big deal if we are only interested in classification, and not in the probability estimates as such. However, *an often overlooked consequence of having uncalibrated probability estimates such as those produced by naive Bayes is that both the ML and MAP decision rules become inadequate*. Unless we have evidence that the model assumptions are satisfied, the only sensible thing to do in this case is to invoke the *recalibrated likelihood decision rule*, which requires one to learn a weight vector

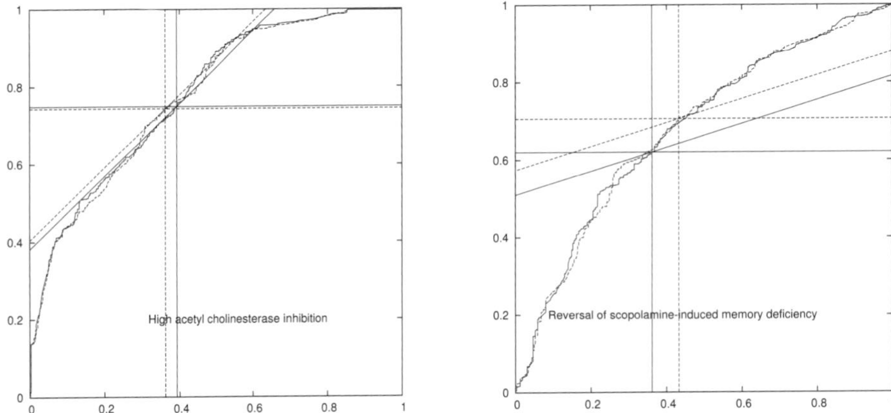

Figure 9.4. (left) ROC curves produced by two naive Bayes classifiers (solid line: a variant of the multivariate Bernoulli model; dashed line: a variant of the multinomial model). Both models have similar ranking performance and yield almost the same – more or less optimal – MAP decision threshold. **(right)** On a different data set from the same domain, the multinomial model's MAP threshold is slightly better, hinting at somewhat better calibrated probability estimates. But since the slope of the accuracy isometrics indicates that there are about four positives for every negative, the optimal decision rule is in fact to always predict positive.

over the classes, in order to correct for the estimation errors in the likelihoods. Specifically, we want to find weights w_i such that predicting $\arg\max_y w_y P(X = x|Y = y)$ results in the smallest possible loss – e.g., the number of misclassified examples – over a test set. For two classes this can be solved by the same procedure we considered for ☞*turning rankers into classifiers* in Section 2.2. To see this, notice that for two classes the recalibrated likelihood decision rule can be rewritten as

☞ predict positive if $w^{\oplus}P(X = x|Y = \oplus) > w^{\ominus}P(X = x|Y = \ominus)$ and negative otherwise; which is equivalent to

☞ predict positive if $P(X = x|Y = \oplus)/P(X = x|Y = \ominus) > w^{\ominus}/w^{\oplus}$ and negative otherwise

This demonstrates that in the two-class case we really have just one degree of freedom, as multiplying the weights by a constant does not affect the decisions. In other words, what we are interested in is finding the best threshold $t = w^{\ominus}/w^{\oplus}$ on the likelihood ratio, which is essentially the same problem as finding the best operating point on an ROC curve. The solution is given by the point on the highest accuracy isometric. Figure 9.4 illustrates this on two real-life data sets: in the left figure we see that the MAP decision threshold is more or less optimal, whereas in the right figure the optimal point is in the top right-hand corner.

For more than two classes, finding a globally optimal weight vector is computationally intractable, which means that we need to resort to a heuristic method. In Section 3.1 such a method was demonstrated for three classes. The idea is to fix the weights one by one, using some ordering of the classes. That is, we use the two-class procedure to optimally separate the i-th class from the previous $i-1$ classes.

Training a naive Bayes model

Training a probabilistic model usually involves estimating the parameters of the distributions used in the model. The parameter of a Bernoulli distribution can be estimated by counting the number of successes d in n trials and setting $\hat{\theta} = d/n$. In other words, we count, for each class, how many e-mails contain the word in question. Such relative frequency estimates are usually smoothed by including *pseudo-counts*, representing the outcome of virtual trials according to some fixed distributions. In the case of a Bernoulli distribution the most common smoothing operation is the Laplace correction, which involves two virtual trials, one of which results in success and the other in failure. Consequently, the relative frequency estimate is changed to $(d+1)/(n+2)$. From a Bayesian perspective this amounts to adopting a uniform prior, representing our initial belief that success and failure are equally likely. If appropriate, we can strengthen the influence of the prior by including a larger number of virtual trials, which means that more data is needed to move the estimate away from the prior. For a categorical distribution smoothing adds one pseudo-count to each of the k categories, leading to the smoothed estimate $(d+1)/(n+k)$. The *m-estimate* generalises this further by making both the total number of pseudo-counts m and the way they are distributed over the categories into parameters. The estimate for the i-th category is defined as $(d+p_i m)/(n+m)$, where p_i is a distribution over the categories (i.e., $\sum_{i=1}^{k} p_i = 1$). Notice that smoothed relative frequency estimates – and hence products of such estimates – can never attain the extreme values $\hat{\theta} = 0$ or $\hat{\theta} = 1$.

Example 9.5 (Training a naive Bayes model). We now show how the parameter vectors in the previous example might have been obtained. Consider the following e-mails consisting of five words a, b, c, d, e:

e_1: $b\ d\ e\ b\ b\ d\ e$	e_5: $a\ b\ a\ b\ a\ b\ a\ e\ d$
e_2: $b\ c\ e\ b\ b\ d\ d\ e\ c\ c$	e_6: $a\ c\ a\ c\ a\ c\ a\ e\ d$
e_3: $a\ d\ a\ d\ e\ a\ e\ e$	e_7: $e\ a\ e\ d\ a\ e\ a$
e_4: $b\ a\ d\ b\ e\ d\ a\ b$	e_8: $d\ e\ d\ e\ d$

We are told that the e-mails on the left are spam and those on the right are ham, and so we use them as a small training set to train our Bayesian classifier. First,

E-mail	#a	#b	#c	Class
e_1	0	3	0	+
e_2	0	3	3	+
e_3	3	0	0	+
e_4	2	3	0	+
e_5	4	3	0	−
e_6	4	0	3	−
e_7	3	0	0	−
e_8	0	0	0	−

E-mail	a?	b?	c?	Class
e_1	0	1	0	+
e_2	0	1	1	+
e_3	1	0	0	+
e_4	1	1	0	+
e_5	1	1	0	−
e_6	1	0	1	−
e_7	1	0	0	−
e_8	0	0	0	−

Table 9.1. **(left)** A small e-mail data set described by count vectors. **(right)** The same data set described by bit vectors.

we decide that d and e are so-called *stop words* that are too common to convey class information. The remaining words, a, b and c, constitute our vocabulary.

For the multinomial model, we represent each e-mail as a count vector, as in Table 9.1 (left). In order to estimate the parameters of the multinomial, we sum up the count vectors for each class, which gives $(5,9,3)$ for spam and $(11,3,3)$ for ham. To smooth these probability estimates we add one pseudo-count for each vocabulary word, which brings the total number of occurrences of vocabulary words to 20 for each class. The estimated parameter vectors are thus $\hat{\boldsymbol{\theta}}^{\oplus} = (6/20, 10/20, 4/20) = (0.3, 0.5, 0.2)$ for spam and $\hat{\boldsymbol{\theta}}^{\ominus} = (12/20, 4/20, 4/20) = (0.6, 0.2, 0.2)$ for ham.

In the multivariate Bernoulli model e-mails are represented by bit vectors, as in Table 9.1 (right). Adding the bit vectors for each class results in $(2,3,1)$ for spam and $(3,1,1)$ for ham. Each count is to be divided by the number of documents in a class, in order to get an estimate of the probability of a document containing a particular vocabulary word. Probability smoothing now means adding two pseudo-documents, one containing each word and one containing none of them. This results in the estimated parameter vectors $\hat{\boldsymbol{\theta}}^{\oplus} = (3/6, 4/6, 2/6) = (0.5, 0.67, 0.33)$ for spam and $\hat{\boldsymbol{\theta}}^{\ominus} = (4/6, 2/6, 2/6) = (0.67, 0.33, 0.33)$ for ham.

Many other variations of the naive Bayes classifier exist. In fact, what is normally understood as 'the' naive Bayes classifier employs neither a multinomial nor a multivariate Bernoulli model, but rather a multivariate categorical model. This means that features are categorical, and the probability of the i-th feature taking on its l-th value for class c examples is given by $\theta_{il}^{(c)}$, under the constraint that $\sum_{l=1}^{k_i} \theta_{il}^{(c)} = 1$, where k_i

is the number of values of the i-th feature. These parameters can be estimated by smoothed relative frequencies in the training set, as in the multivariate Bernoulli case. We again have that the joint probability of the feature vector is the product of the individual feature probabilities, and hence $P(F_i, F_j|C) = P(F_i|C)P(F_j|C)$ for all pairs of features and for all classes.

Notice, by the way, that conditional independence is quite different from unconditional independence: neither implies the other. To see that conditional independence does not imply unconditional independence, imagine two words that are very likely to occur in spam, but they are independent (i.e., the probability of both of them occurring in a spam e-mail is the product of the marginal probabilities). Imagine further that they are very unlikely – but also independent – in ham. Suppose I tell you an unclassified e-mail contains one of the words: you would probably guess that it is a spam e-mail, from which you would further guess that it also contains the other word – demonstrating that the words are not unconditionally independent. To see that unconditional independence does not imply conditional independence, consider two different independent words, and let an e-mail be spam if it contains at least one of the words and ham otherwise, then among spam e-mails the two words are dependent (since if I know that a spam e-mail doesn't contain one of the words, then it must contain the other).

Another extension of the naive Bayes model is required when some of the features are real-valued. One option is to discretise the real-valued features in a pre-processing stage: this will be discussed in Chapter 10. Another option is to assume that the feature values are normally distributed within each class, as discussed in the previous section. In this context it is worth noting that the naive Bayes assumption boils down to assuming a diagonal covariance matrix within each class, so that each feature can be treated independently. A third option that is also used in practice is to model the class-conditional likelihood of each feature by a non-parametric density estimator. These three options are illustrated in Figure 9.5.

In summary, the naive Bayes model is a popular model for dealing with textual, categorical and mixed categorical/real-valued data. Its main shortcoming as a probabilistic model – poorly calibrated probability estimates – are outweighed by generally good ranking performance. Another apparent paradox with naive Bayes is that it isn't particularly Bayesian at all! For one thing, we have seen that the poor probability estimates necessitate the use of reweighted likelihoods, which avoids using Bayes' rule altogether. Secondly, in training a naive Bayes model we use maximum-likelihood parameter estimation, whereas a fully fledged Bayesian approach would not commit to a particular parameter value, but rather employ a full posterior distribution. Personally, I think the essence of naive Bayes is the decomposition of joint likelihoods into marginal likelihoods. This decomposition is evocatively visualised by the Scottish tartan pattern in Figure 1.3 on p.31, which is why I like to call naive Bayes the 'Scottish classifier'.

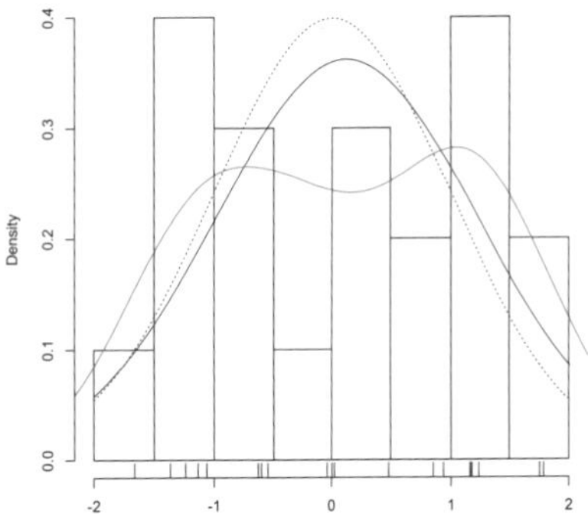

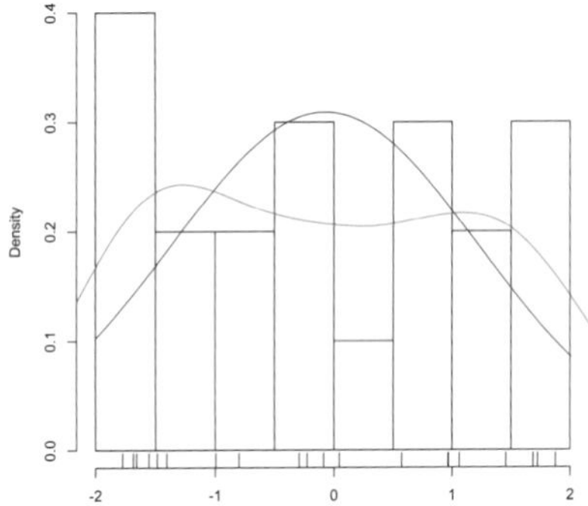

Figure 9.5. **(left)** Examples of three density estimators on 20 points sampled from a normal distribution with zero mean and unit variance (dotted line)). A histogram is a simple non-parametric method which employs a fixed number of equal-width intervals. A kernel density estimator (in red) applies interpolation to obtain a smooth density function. The solid bell curve (in blue) is obtained by estimating the sample mean and variance, assuming the true distribution is normal. **(right)** Here, the 20 points are sampled uniformly from $[-2,2]$, and the non-parametric methods generally do better.

9.3 Discriminative learning by optimising conditional likelihood

In the introduction to this chapter we distinguished between generative and discriminative probabilistic models. Naive Bayes models are generative: after training they can be used to generate data. In this section we look at one of the most commonly used discriminative models: *logistic regression*.[5] The easiest way to understand logistic regression is as a linear classifier whose probability estimates have been logistically calibrated using the method described in Section 7.4, but with one crucial difference: calibration is an integral part of the training algorithm, rather than a post-processing step. While in generative models the decision boundary is a by-product of modelling the distributions of each class, logistic regression models the decision boundary directly. For example, if the classes are overlapping then logistic regression will tend to locate the decision boundary in an area where classes are maximally overlapping, regardless of the 'shapes' of the samples of each class. This results in decision boundaries that are noticeably different from those learned by generative classifiers (Figure 9.6).

Equation 7.13 on p.222 expresses the likelihood ratio as $\exp\big(\gamma(d(\mathbf{x})-d_0)\big)$ with $d(\mathbf{x}) = \mathbf{w}\cdot\mathbf{x}-t$. Since we are learning the parameters all at once in discriminative learning, we can absorb γ and d_0 into $\mathbf{w}$ and t. So the logistic regression model is

[5]Notice that the term 'regression' is a bit of a misnomer here, since, even though a probability estimator approximates an unknown function, the training labels are classes rather than true function values.

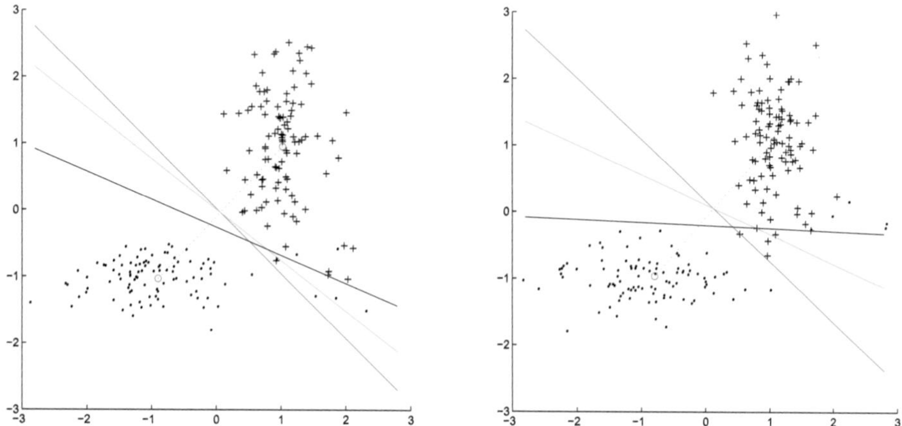

Figure 9.6. (left) On this data set, logistic regression (in blue) outperforms the basic linear classifier (in red) and the least squares classifier (in orange) because the latter two are more sensitive to the shape of the classes, while logistic regression concentrates on where the classes overlap. **(right)** On this slightly different set of points, logistic regression is outperformed by the other two methods because it concentrates too much on tracking the transition from mostly positive to mostly negative.

simply given by

$$\hat{p}(\mathbf{x}) = \frac{\exp(\mathbf{w}\cdot\mathbf{x} - t)}{\exp(\mathbf{w}\cdot\mathbf{x} - t) + 1} = \frac{1}{1 + \exp(-(\mathbf{w}\cdot\mathbf{x} - t))}$$

Assuming the class labels are $y = 1$ for positives and $y = 0$ for negatives, this defines a Bernoulli distribution for each training example:

$$P(y_i|\mathbf{x}_i) = \hat{p}(\mathbf{x}_i)^{y_i}(1 - \hat{p}(\mathbf{x}_i))^{(1-y_i)}$$

It is important to note that the parameters of these Bernoulli distributions are linked through $\mathbf{w}$ and t, and consequently there is one parameter for every feature dimension, rather than for every training instance.

The likelihood function is

$$\mathrm{CL}(\mathbf{w}, t) = \prod_i P(y_i|\mathbf{x}_i) = \prod_i \hat{p}(\mathbf{x}_i)^{y_i}(1 - \hat{p}(\mathbf{x}_i))^{(1-y_i)}$$

This is called *conditional likelihood* to stress that it gives us the *conditional* probability $P(y_i|\mathbf{x}_i)$ rather than $P(\mathbf{x}_i)$ as in a generative model. Notice that our use of the product requires the assumption that the y-values are independent given $\mathbf{x}$; but this is an entirely reasonable assumption and not nearly as strong as the naive Bayes assumption of $\mathbf{x}$ being independent within each class. As usual, the logarithm of the likelihood function is easier to work with:

$$\mathrm{LCL}(\mathbf{w},t) = \sum_i y_i \ln \hat{p}(\mathbf{x}_i) + (1-y_i)\ln(1-\hat{p}(\mathbf{x}_i)) = \sum_{\mathbf{x}^{\oplus}\in Tr^{\oplus}} \ln \hat{p}(\mathbf{x}^{\oplus}) + \sum_{\mathbf{x}^{\ominus}\in Tr^{\ominus}} \ln(1-\hat{p}(\mathbf{x}^{\ominus}))$$

We want to maximise the log-conditional likelihood with respect to these parameters, which means that all partial derivatives must be zero:

$$\nabla_{\mathbf{w}}\mathrm{LCL}(\mathbf{w},t) = \mathbf{0}$$
$$\frac{\partial}{\partial t}\mathrm{LCL}(\mathbf{w},t) = 0$$

Although these equations do not yield an analytic solution, they can be used to obtain further insight into the nature of logistic regression. Concentrating on t, we first need to do some algebraic groundwork.

$$\begin{aligned}
\ln \hat{p}(\mathbf{x}) &= \ln \frac{\exp(\mathbf{w}\cdot\mathbf{x}-t)}{\exp(\mathbf{w}\cdot\mathbf{x}-t)+1} \\
&= \mathbf{w}\cdot\mathbf{x} - t - \ln(\exp(\mathbf{w}\cdot\mathbf{x}-t)+1) \\
\frac{\partial}{\partial t}\ln \hat{p}(\mathbf{x}) &= -1 - \frac{\partial}{\partial t}\ln(\exp(\mathbf{w}\cdot\mathbf{x}-t)+1) \\
&= -1 - \frac{1}{\exp(\mathbf{w}\cdot\mathbf{x}-t)+1}\exp(\mathbf{w}\cdot\mathbf{x}-t)\cdot(-1) \\
&= \hat{p}(\mathbf{x}) - 1
\end{aligned}$$

Similarly for the negatives:

$$\begin{aligned}
\ln(1-\hat{p}(\mathbf{x})) &= \ln \frac{1}{\exp(\mathbf{w}\cdot\mathbf{x}-t)+1} \\
&= -\ln(\exp(\mathbf{w}\cdot\mathbf{x}-t)+1) \\
\frac{\partial}{\partial t}\ln(1-\hat{p}(\mathbf{x})) &= \frac{\partial}{\partial t} - \ln(\exp(\mathbf{w}\cdot\mathbf{x}-t)+1) \\
&= \frac{-1}{\exp(\mathbf{w}\cdot\mathbf{x}-t)+1}\exp(\mathbf{w}\cdot\mathbf{x}-t)\cdot(-1) \\
&= \hat{p}(\mathbf{x})
\end{aligned}$$

It follows that the partial derivative of LCL with respect to t has a simple form:

$$\begin{aligned}
\frac{\partial}{\partial t}\mathrm{LCL}(\mathbf{w},t) &= \sum_{\mathbf{x}^{\oplus}\in Tr^{\oplus}} (\hat{p}(\mathbf{x})-1) + \sum_{\mathbf{x}^{\ominus}\in Tr^{\ominus}} \hat{p}(\mathbf{x}^{\ominus}) \\
&= \sum_{\mathbf{x}_i\in Tr} (\hat{p}(\mathbf{x}_i) - y_i)
\end{aligned}$$

For the optimal solution this partial derivative is zero. What this means is that, on average, the predicted probability should be equal to the proportion of positives *pos*. This is a satisfying result, as it is clearly a desirable global property of a calibrated classifier.

Notice that grouping models such as probability estimating trees have this property by construction, as they set the predicted probability equal to the empirical probability in a segment.

A very similar derivation leads to the partial derivative of the log-conditional likelihood with respect to the j-th weight w_j. The point to note here is that, whereas $\frac{\partial}{\partial t}(\mathbf{w}\cdot\mathbf{x}-t) = -1$, we have $\frac{\partial}{\partial w_j}(\mathbf{w}\cdot\mathbf{x}-t) = \frac{\partial}{\partial w_j}\left(\sum_j w_j x_j - t\right) = x_j$, the instance's j-th feature value. This then leads to

$$\frac{\partial}{\partial w_j}\text{LCL}(\mathbf{w},t) = \sum_{\mathbf{x}_i \in Tr}(y_i - \hat{p}(\mathbf{x}_i))x_{ij} \tag{9.5}$$

Setting this partial derivative to zero expresses another, feature-wise calibration property. For example, if the j-th feature is a sparse Boolean feature that is mostly zero, then this calibration property only involves the instances $\mathbf{x}_i$ for which $x_{ij} = 1$: on average, those instances should have their predicted probability equal the proportion of positives among them.

Example 9.6 (Univariate logistic regression). Consider the data in Figure 9.7 with 20 points in each class. Although both classes were generated from normal distributions, class overlap in this particular sample is less than what could be expected on the basis of the class means. Logistic regression is able to take advantage of this and gives a much steeper sigmoid than the basic linear classifier with logistic calibration (explained in Example 7.7 on p.222), which is entirely formulated in terms of class means and variance. Also shown are the probability estimates obtained from the convex hull of the ROC curve (see Figure 7.13 on p.224); this calibration procedure is non-parametric and hence better able to detect the limited class overlap.

In terms of statistics, logistic regression has better mean squared error (0.040) than the logistically calibrated classifier (0.057). Isotonic calibration leads to the lowest error (0.021), but note that no probability smoothing has been applied to mitigate the risk of overfitting. The sum of predicted probabilities is 18.7 for the logistically calibrated classifier and 20 for the other two – i.e., equal to the number of examples, which is a necessary condition for full calibration. Finally, $\sum_{\mathbf{x}_i \in Tr}(y_i - \hat{p}(\mathbf{x}_i))x_i$ is 2.6 for the logistically calibrated classifier, 4.7 for the ROC-calibrated classifier, and 0 for logistic regression as expected from Equation 9.5.

In order to train a logistic regression model we need to find

$$\mathbf{w}^*, t^* = \underset{\mathbf{w},t}{\arg\max}\,\text{CL}(\mathbf{w},t) = \underset{\mathbf{w},t}{\arg\max}\,\text{LCL}(\mathbf{w},t)$$

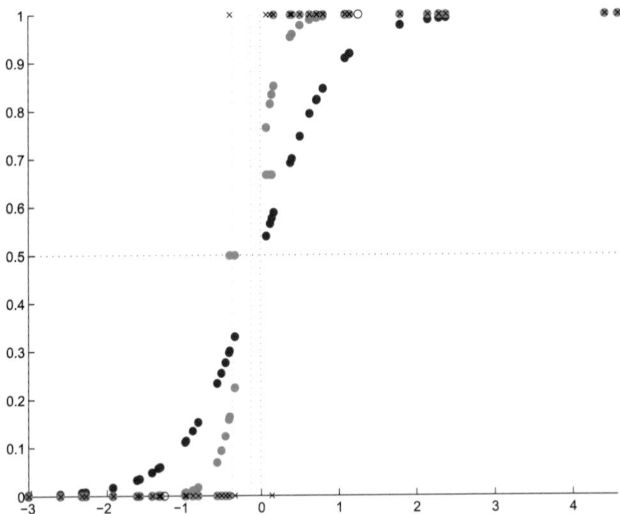

Figure 9.7. Logistic regression (in red) compared with probability estimates obtained by logistic calibration (in blue) and isotonic calibration (in green); the latter two are applied to the basic linear classifier (estimated class means are indicated by circles). The corresponding three decision boundaries are shown as vertical dotted lines.

This can be shown to be a convex optimisation problem, which means that there is only one maximum. A range of optimisation techniques can be applied. One simple approach is inspired by the perceptron algorithm and iterates over examples, using the following update rule:

$$\mathbf{w} = \mathbf{w} + \eta(y_i - \hat{p}_i)\mathbf{x}_i$$

where η is the learning rate. Notice the relationship with the partial derivative in Equation 9.5. Essentially, we are using single examples to approximate the direction of steepest ascent.

9.4 Probabilistic models with hidden variables

Suppose you are dealing with a four-class classification problem with classes A, B, C and D. If you have a sufficiently large and representative training sample of size n, you can use the relative frequencies in the sample $n_A, \ldots, n_D$ to estimate the class prior $\hat{p}_A = n_A/n, \ldots, \hat{p}_D = n_D/n$, as we have done many times before.[6] Conversely, if you know the prior and want to know the most likely class distribution in a random

[6]Of course, if you're not sure whether the sample is large enough it is better to smooth these relative frequency estimates by, e.g., the ☞*Laplace correction* (Section 2.3).

sample of n instances, you would use the prior to calculate expected values $\mathbb{E}[n_A] = p_A \cdot n, \ldots, \mathbb{E}[n_D] = p_D \cdot n$. So, complete knowledge of one allows us to estimate or infer the other. However, sometimes we have a bit of knowledge about both. For example, we may know that $p_A = 1/2$ and that C is twice as likely as B, without knowing the complete prior. And we may know that the sample we saw last week was evenly split between $A \cup B$ and $C \cup D$, and that C and D were equally large, but we can't remember the size of A and B separately. What should we do?

Formalising what we know about the prior, we have $p_A = 1/2$; $p_B = \beta$, as yet unknown; $p_C = 2\beta$, since it is twice p_B; and $p_D = 1/2 - 3\beta$, since the four cases need to add up to 1. Furthermore: $n_A + n_B = a + b = s$, $n_C = c$ and $n_D = d$, with s, c and d known. We want to infer a, b and β: however, it seems we are stuck in a chicken-and-egg problem. If we knew β we would have full knowledge about the prior and we could use that to infer expected values for a and b:

$$\frac{\mathbb{E}[a]}{\mathbb{E}[b]} = \frac{1/2}{\beta} \qquad \mathbb{E}[a] + \mathbb{E}[b] = s$$

from which we could derive

$$\mathbb{E}[a] = \frac{1}{1+2\beta} s \qquad \mathbb{E}[b] = \frac{2\beta}{1+2\beta} s \tag{9.6}$$

So, for example, if $s = 20$ and $\beta = 1/10$, then $\mathbb{E}[a] = 16\frac{2}{3}$ and $\mathbb{E}[b] = 3\frac{1}{3}$.

Conversely, if we knew a and b, then we could estimate β by maximum-likelihood estimation, using a multinomial distribution for a, b, c and d:

$$P(a,b,c,d|\beta) = K(1/2)^a \beta^b (2\beta)^c (1/2 - 3\beta)^d$$
$$\ln P(a,b,c,d|\beta) = \ln K + a\ln(1/2) + b\ln\beta + c\ln(2\beta) + d\ln(1/2 - 3\beta)$$

Here, K is a combinatorial constant that doesn't affect the value of β which maximises the likelihood. Taking the partial derivative with respect to β gives

$$\frac{\partial}{\partial\beta} \ln P(a,b,c,d|\beta) = \frac{b}{\beta} + \frac{2c}{2\beta} - \frac{3d}{1/2 - 3\beta}$$

Setting to 0 and solving for β finally gives

$$\hat{\beta} = \frac{b+c}{6(b+c+d)} \tag{9.7}$$

So, for example, if $b = 5$ and $c = d = 10$, then $\hat{\beta} = 1/10$.

The way out of this chicken-and-egg problem is to iterate the following two steps: (*i*) calculate an expected value of the missing frequencies a and b from an assumed or previously estimated value of the parameter β; and (*ii*) calculate a maximum-likelihood estimate of the parameter β from assumed or expected values of the missing frequencies a and b. These two steps are iterated until a stationary configuration is reached.

So, if we start with $a = 15$, $b = 5$ and $c = d = 10$, then we have just seen that $\hat{\beta} = 1/10$. Plugging this value of β into Equation 9.6 gives us $\mathbb{E}[a] = 16\frac{2}{3}$ and $\mathbb{E}[b] = 3\frac{1}{3}$. Plugging these values back into Equation 9.7 yields $\hat{\beta} = 2/21$, which in turn gives $\mathbb{E}[a] = 16.8$ and $\mathbb{E}[b] = 3.2$, and so on. A stationary configuration with $\beta = 0.0948$, $a = 16.813$ and $b = 3.187$ is reached in fewer than 10 iterations. In this simple case this is a global optimum that is reached regardless of the starting point, essentially because the relationship between b and β is monotonic ($\mathbb{E}[b]$ increases with β according to Equation 9.6 and $\hat{\beta}$ increases with b according to Equation 9.7). However, this is not normally the case: we will return to this point later.

Expectation-Maximisation

The problem that we have just discussed is an example of a problem with missing data, where the full data Y separates into observed variables X and *hidden variables* Z (also called *latent variables*). In the example, the observed variables are c, d and s, and the hidden variables are a and b. We also have model parameter(s) θ, which is β in the example.[7] Denote the estimate of θ in the t-th iteration as θ^t. We have two relevant quantities:

- the expectation $\mathbb{E}\left[Z|X,\theta^t\right]$ of the hidden variables given the observed variables and the current estimate of the parameters (so in Equation 9.6 the expectations of a and b depend on s and β);
- the likelihood $P(Y|\theta)$, which is used to find the maximising value of θ.

In the likelihood function we need values for $Y = X \cup Z$. We obviously use the observed values for X, but we need to use previously calculated expectations for Z. This means that we really want to maximise $P(X \cup \mathbb{E}\left[Z|X,\theta^t\right]|\theta)$, or equivalently, the logarithm of that function. We now make the assumption that the logarithm of the likelihood function is linear in Y: notice that this assumption is valid in the example above. For any linear function f, $f(\mathbb{E}[Z]) = \mathbb{E}\left[f(Z)\right]$ and thus we can bring the expectation outside in our objective function:

$$\ln P(X \cup \mathbb{E}\left[Z|X,\theta^t\right]|\theta) = \mathbb{E}\left[\ln P(X \cup Z|\theta)|X,\theta^t\right] = \mathbb{E}\left[\ln P(Y|\theta)|X,\theta^t\right] \tag{9.8}$$

This last expression is usually denoted as $Q(\theta|\theta^t)$, as it essentially tells us how to calculate the next value of θ from the current one:

$$\theta^{t+1} = \arg\max_{\theta} Q(\theta|\theta^t) = \arg\max_{\theta} \mathbb{E}\left[\ln P(Y|\theta)|X,\theta^t\right] \tag{9.9}$$

[7] Model parameters are also 'hidden' in a sense, but they are different from hidden variables in that you would never expect to observe the value of a parameter (e.g., a class mean), whereas a hidden variable could be observed in principle but happens to be unobserved in the case at hand.

This, then, is the general form of the celebrated *Expectation-Maximisation* (*EM*) algorithm, which is a powerful approach to probabilistic modelling with hidden variables or missing data. Similar to the example above, we iterate over assigning an expected value to the hidden variables given our current estimates of the parameters, and re-estimating the parameters from these updated expectations, until a stationary configuration is reached. We can start the iteration by initialising either the parameters or the hidden variables in some way. The algorithm bears a striking resemblance to the ☞*K-means* algorithm (Algorithm 8.1 on p.248), which also iterates over assigning data points to current cluster means, and re-estimating the cluster means from the new assignments. This resemblance is not accidental, as we shall see in a moment. Like the K-means algorithm, EM can be proved to always converge to a stationary configuration for a wide class of probabilistic models. However, EM can get trapped in a local optimum that is dependent on the initial configuration.

Gaussian mixture models

A common application of Expectation-Maximisation is to estimate the parameters of a *Gaussian mixture model* from data. In such a model the data points are generated by K normal distributions, each with their own mean $\boldsymbol{\mu}_j$ and covariance matrix $\boldsymbol{\Sigma}_j$, and the proportion of points coming from each Gaussian is governed by a prior $\boldsymbol{\tau} = (\tau_1, \ldots, \tau_K)$. If each data point in a sample were labelled with the index of the Gaussian it came from this would be a straightforward classification problem, which could be solved easily by estimating each Gaussian's $\boldsymbol{\mu}_j$ and $\boldsymbol{\Sigma}_j$ separately from the data points belonging to class j. However, we are now considering the much harder predictive clustering problem in which the class labels are hidden and need to be reconstructed from the observed feature values.

A convenient way to model this is to have for each data point $\mathbf{x}_i$ a Boolean vector $\mathbf{z}_i = (z_{i1}, \ldots, z_{iK})$ such that exactly one bit z_{ij} is set to 1 and the rest set to 0, signalling that the i-th data point comes from the j-th Gaussian. Using this notation we can adapt the expression for the ☞*multivariate normal distribution* (Equation 9.2 on p.267) to obtain a general expression for a Gaussian mixture model:

$$P(\mathbf{x}_i, \mathbf{z}_i | \theta) = \sum_{j=1}^{K} z_{ij} \tau_j \frac{1}{(2\pi)^{d/2} \sqrt{|\boldsymbol{\Sigma}_j|}} \exp\left(-\frac{1}{2} (\mathbf{x}_i - \boldsymbol{\mu}_j)^{\mathrm{T}} \boldsymbol{\Sigma}_j^{-1} (\mathbf{x}_i - \boldsymbol{\mu}_j) \right) \tag{9.10}$$

Here, θ collects all the parameters τ, $\boldsymbol{\mu}_1, \ldots, \boldsymbol{\mu}_K$ and $\boldsymbol{\Sigma}_1, \ldots, \boldsymbol{\Sigma}_K$. The interpretation as a generative model is as follows: we first randomly select a Gaussian using the prior $\boldsymbol{\tau}$, and then we invoke the corresponding Gaussian using the indicator variables z_{ij}.

In order to apply Expectation-Maximisation we form the Q function:

$$
\begin{aligned}
Q(\theta|\theta^t) &= \mathbb{E}\left[\ln P(\mathbf{X}\cup\mathbf{Z}|\theta)|\mathbf{X},\theta^t\right]\\
&= \mathbb{E}\left[\ln\prod_{i=1}^{n} P(\mathbf{x}_i\cup\mathbf{z}_i|\theta)\middle|\mathbf{X},\theta^t\right]\\
&= \mathbb{E}\left[\sum_{i=1}^{n}\ln P(\mathbf{x}_i\cup\mathbf{z}_i|\theta)\middle|\mathbf{X},\theta^t\right]\\
&= \mathbb{E}\left[\sum_{i=1}^{n}\ln\sum_{j=1}^{K} z_{ij}\tau_j\frac{1}{(2\pi)^{d/2}\sqrt{|\boldsymbol{\Sigma}_j|}}\exp\left(-\frac{1}{2}(\mathbf{x}_i-\boldsymbol{\mu}_j)^{\mathrm{T}}\boldsymbol{\Sigma}_j^{-1}(\mathbf{x}_i-\boldsymbol{\mu}_j)\right)\middle|\mathbf{X},\theta^t\right]\\
&= \mathbb{E}\left[\sum_{i=1}^{n}\sum_{j=1}^{K} z_{ij}\ln\left(\tau_j\frac{1}{(2\pi)^{d/2}\sqrt{|\boldsymbol{\Sigma}_j|}}\exp\left(-\frac{1}{2}(\mathbf{x}_i-\boldsymbol{\mu}_j)^{\mathrm{T}}\boldsymbol{\Sigma}_j^{-1}(\mathbf{x}_i-\boldsymbol{\mu}_j)\right)\right)\middle|\mathbf{X},\theta^t\right] \qquad (*)\\
&= \mathbb{E}\left[\sum_{i=1}^{n}\sum_{j=1}^{K} z_{ij}\left(\ln\tau_j-\frac{d}{2}\ln(2\pi)-\frac{1}{2}\ln|\boldsymbol{\Sigma}_j|-\frac{1}{2}(\mathbf{x}_i-\boldsymbol{\mu}_j)^{\mathrm{T}}\boldsymbol{\Sigma}_j^{-1}(\mathbf{x}_i-\boldsymbol{\mu}_j)\right)\middle|\mathbf{X},\theta^t\right]\\
&= \sum_{i=1}^{n}\sum_{j=1}^{K}\mathbb{E}\left[z_{ij}\middle|\mathbf{X},\theta^t\right]\left(\ln\tau_j-\frac{d}{2}\ln(2\pi)-\frac{1}{2}\ln|\boldsymbol{\Sigma}_j|-\frac{1}{2}(\mathbf{x}_i-\boldsymbol{\mu}_j)^{\mathrm{T}}\boldsymbol{\Sigma}_j^{-1}(\mathbf{x}_i-\boldsymbol{\mu}_j)\right)
\end{aligned}
\tag{9.11}
$$

The step marked (*) is possible because for a given i only one z_{ij} is switched on, hence we can bring the indicator variables outside the logarithm. The last line shows the Q function in the desired form, involving on the one hand expectations over the hidden variables conditioned on the observable data $\mathbf{X}$ and the previously estimated parameters θ^t, and on the other hand expressions in θ that allow us to find θ^{t+1} by maximisation.

The Expectation step of the EM algorithm is thus the calculation of the expected values of the indicator variables $\mathbb{E}\left[z_{ij}\middle|\mathbf{X},\theta^t\right]$. Notice that expectations of Boolean variables take values on the entire interval $[0,1]$, under the constraint that $\sum_{j=1}^{K} z_{ij} = 1$ for all i. In effect, the hard cluster assignment of K-means is changed into a soft assignment – one of the ways in which Gaussian mixture models generalise K-means. Now, suppose that $K = 2$ and we expect both clusters to be of equal size and with equal covariances. If a given data point $\mathbf{x}_i$ is equidistant from the two cluster means (or rather, our current estimates of these), then clearly $\mathbb{E}\left[z_{i1}|\mathbf{X},\theta^t\right] = \mathbb{E}\left[z_{i2}|\mathbf{X},\theta^t\right] = 1/2$. In the general case these expectations are apportioned proportionally to the probability mass assigned to the point by each Gaussian:

$$
\mathbb{E}\left[z_{ij}\middle|\mathbf{X},\theta^t\right] = \frac{\tau_j^t f(\mathbf{x}_i|\boldsymbol{\mu}_j^t,\boldsymbol{\Sigma}_j^t)}{\sum_{k=1}^{K}\tau_k^t f(\mathbf{x}_i|\boldsymbol{\mu}_k^t,\boldsymbol{\Sigma}_k^t)} \tag{9.12}
$$

where $f(\mathbf{x}|\boldsymbol{\mu},\boldsymbol{\Sigma})$ stands for the multivariate Gaussian density function.

For the Maximisation step we optimise the parameters in Equation 9.11. Notice there is no interaction between the terms containing τ_j and the terms containing the other parameters, and so the prior distribution $\boldsymbol{\tau}$ can be optimised separately:

$$\boldsymbol{\tau}^{t+1} = \underset{\boldsymbol{\tau}}{\arg\max} \sum_{i=1}^{n} \sum_{j=1}^{K} \mathbb{E}\left[z_{ij} \middle| \mathbf{X}, \theta^t \right] \ln \tau_j$$

$$= \underset{\boldsymbol{\tau}}{\arg\max} \sum_{j=1}^{K} E_j \ln \tau_j \qquad \text{under the constraint} \sum_{j=1}^{K} \tau_j = 1$$

where I have written E_j for $\sum_{i=1}^{n} \mathbb{E}\left[z_{ij} \middle| \mathbf{X}, \theta^t \right]$, which is the total (partial) membership of the j-th cluster – notice that $\sum_{j=1}^{K} E_j = n$. For simplicity we assume $K = 2$, so that $\tau_2 = 1 - \tau_1$: then

$$\tau_1^{t+1} = \underset{\tau_1}{\arg\max} E_1 \ln \tau_1 + E_2 \ln(1 - \tau_1)$$

Setting the derivative with respect to τ_1 to zero and solving for τ_1, it can be easily verified that $\tau_1^{t+1} = E_1/(E_1 + E_2) = E_1/n$ and thus $\tau_2^{t+1} = E_2/n$. In the general case of K clusters we have analogously

$$\tau_j^{t+1} = \frac{E_j}{\sum_{k=1}^{K} E_k} = \frac{1}{n} \sum_{i=1}^{n} \mathbb{E}\left[z_{ij} \middle| \mathbf{X}, \theta^t \right] \tag{9.13}$$

The means and covariance matrices can be optimised for each cluster separately:

$$\boldsymbol{\mu}_j^{t+1}, \boldsymbol{\Sigma}_j^{t+1} = \underset{\boldsymbol{\mu}_j, \boldsymbol{\Sigma}_j}{\arg\max} \sum_{i=1}^{n} \mathbb{E}\left[z_{ij} \middle| \mathbf{X}, \theta^t \right] \left(-\frac{1}{2} \ln |\boldsymbol{\Sigma}_j| - \frac{1}{2} (\mathbf{x}_i - \boldsymbol{\mu}_j)^{\mathrm{T}} \boldsymbol{\Sigma}_j^{-1} (\mathbf{x}_i - \boldsymbol{\mu}_j) \right)$$

$$= \underset{\boldsymbol{\mu}_j, \boldsymbol{\Sigma}_j}{\arg\min} \sum_{i=1}^{n} \mathbb{E}\left[z_{ij} \middle| \mathbf{X}, \theta^t \right] \left(\frac{1}{2} \ln |\boldsymbol{\Sigma}_j| + \frac{1}{2} (\mathbf{x}_i - \boldsymbol{\mu}_j)^{\mathrm{T}} \boldsymbol{\Sigma}_j^{-1} (\mathbf{x}_i - \boldsymbol{\mu}_j) \right)$$

Notice that the term between brackets is a squared-distance term with the expectations functioning as instance weights on each instance. This describes a generalised version of the problem of finding the point that ☞*minimises the sum of squared Euclidean distances* to a set of points (Theorem 8.1 on p.238). While that problem is solved by the arithmetic mean, here we simply take the *weighted* average over all the points:

$$\boldsymbol{\mu}_j^{t+1} = \frac{1}{E_j} \sum_{i=1}^{n} \mathbb{E}\left[z_{ij} \middle| \mathbf{X}, \theta^t \right] \mathbf{x}_i = \frac{\sum_{i=1}^{n} \mathbb{E}\left[z_{ij} \middle| \mathbf{X}, \theta^t \right] \mathbf{x}_i}{\sum_{i=1}^{n} \mathbb{E}\left[z_{ij} \middle| \mathbf{X}, \theta^t \right]} \tag{9.14}$$

Similarly, the covariance matrix is computed as a weighted average of covariance matrices obtained from each data point, taking into account the newly estimated mean:

$$\boldsymbol{\Sigma}_j^{t+1} = \frac{1}{E_j} \sum_{i=1}^{n} \mathbb{E}\left[z_{ij} \middle| \mathbf{X}, \theta^t \right] (\mathbf{x}_i - \boldsymbol{\mu}_j^{t+1})(\mathbf{x}_i - \boldsymbol{\mu}_j^{t+1})^{\mathrm{T}}$$

$$= \frac{\sum_{i=1}^{n} \mathbb{E}\left[z_{ij} \middle| \mathbf{X}, \theta^t \right] (\mathbf{x}_i - \boldsymbol{\mu}_j^{t+1})(\mathbf{x}_i - \boldsymbol{\mu}_j^{t+1})^{\mathrm{T}}}{\sum_{i=1}^{n} \mathbb{E}\left[z_{ij} \middle| \mathbf{X}, \theta^t \right]} \tag{9.15}$$

Equations 9.12–9.15, then, constitute the EM solution to learning a Gaussian mixture model from an unlabelled sample. I have presented it here in its most general

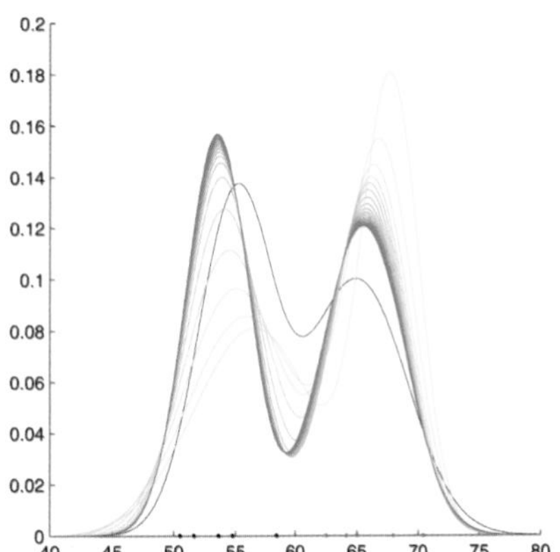

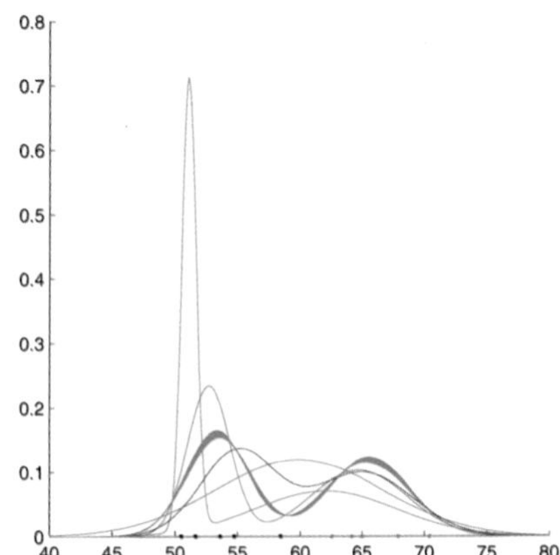

Figure 9.8. (left) The blue line shows the true Gaussian mixture model from which the 10 points on the x-axis were sampled; the colour of the points indicates whether they came from the left or the right Gaussian. The other lines show convergence of Expectation-Maximisation to a stationary configuration from a random initialisation. **(right)** This plot shows four stationary configurations for the same set of points. The EM algorithm was run for 20 iterations; the thickness of one of the lines demonstrates that this configuration takes longer to converge.

form, explicitly modelling unequal cluster sizes and covariance matrices. The latter is important as it allows for clusters of different shapes, unlike the K-means algorithm which assumes that all clusters have the same spherical shape. Consequently, the boundaries between clusters will not be linear, as they are in the clusterings learned by K-means. Figure 9.8 demonstrates the convergence of EM on a simple univariate data set, as well as the existence of multiple stationary configurations.

In conclusion, Expectation-Maximisation is a versatile and powerful method to deal with missing variables in a principled way. As we have seen in detail for the Gaussian mixture model, the main ingredient is an expression for the parametric likelihood function $P(X \cup Z|\theta)$, from which the update equations can be derived by means of the Q function. A word of caution is also in order, since – except in the simplest cases – there will be more than one stationary configuration. Like with K-means, the optimisation should therefore be run multiple times with different starting configurations.

9.5 Compression-based models

We end this chapter with a brief discussion of an approach to machine learning that is both closely related to and quite distinct from the probabilistic approach. Consider the maximum a posteriori decision rule again:

$$y_{\text{MAP}} = \arg\max_{y} P(X = x|Y = y)P(Y = y)$$

Y	$P(\text{Viagra} = 1\|Y)$	$IC(\text{Viagra} = 1\|Y)$	$P(\text{Viagra} = 0\|Y)$	$IC(\text{Viagra} = 0\|Y)$
spam	0.40	**1.32 bits**	0.60	**0.74 bits**
ham	0.12	**3.06 bits**	0.88	**0.18 bits**

Table 9.2. Example marginal likelihoods.

Taking negative logarithms, we can turn this into an equivalent minimisation:

$$y_{\text{MAP}} = \arg\min_{y} -\log P(X = x|Y = y) - \log P(Y = y) \tag{9.16}$$

This follows because for any two probabilities $0 < p < p' < 1$ we have $\infty > -\log p > -\log p' > 0$. If an event has probability p of happening, the negative logarithm of p quantifies the *information content* of the message that the event has indeed happened. This makes intuitive sense, as the less expected an event is, the more information an announcement of the event contains. The unit of information depends on the base of the logarithm: it is customary to take logarithms to the base 2, in which case information is measured in bits. For example, if you toss a fair coin once and tell me it came up heads, this contains $-\log_2 1/2 = 1$ bit of information; if you roll a fair die once and let me know it came up six, the information content of your message is $-\log_2 1/6 = 2.6$ bits. Equation 9.16 tells us that the MAP decision rule chooses the least surprising or the most expected class for an instance x given particular prior distributions and likelihoods. We write $IC(X|Y) = -\log_2 P(X|Y)$ and $IC(Y) = -\log_2 P(Y)$.

Example 9.7 (Information-based classification). Table 9.2 reproduces the left table in Table 1.3 on p.29 together with the relevant information content quantities. If Y is uniformly distributed then $IC(Y = \text{spam}) = 1$ bit and $IC(Y = \text{ham}) = 1$ bit. It follows that

$$\arg\min_{y} \big(IC(\text{Viagra} = 1|Y = y) + IC(Y = y)\big) = \text{spam}$$

$$\arg\min_{y} \big(IC(\text{Viagra} = 0|Y = y) + IC(Y = y)\big) = \text{ham}$$

If ham is four times as likely as spam then $IC(Y = \text{spam}) = 2.32$ bit and $IC(Y = \text{ham}) = 0.32$ bit, and $\arg\min_y \big(IC(\text{Viagra} = 1|Y = y) + IC(Y = y)\big) = \text{ham}$.

Clearly, for a uniform distribution over k outcomes, each outcome has the same information content $-\log_2 1/k = \log_2 k$. For a non-uniform distribution these information contents differ, and hence it makes sense to compute the average information content or *entropy* $\sum_{i=1}^{k} -p_i \log_2 p_i$. We have encountered entropy before as an ☞*impurity measure* in Section 5.1.

So far I have not really told you anything new, other than that there is a one-to-one relationship between probability and information content. What really kicks things off in compression-based learning is a fundamental result from information theory proved by Claude Shannon in 1948. Shannon's result says – loosely speaking – that we cannot transmit information at a rate that surpasses entropy, but we can get arbitrarily close to the optimal rate by designing clever binary codes. Some well-known codes include the Shannon–Fanon code and the Huffman code, which are worth looking up as they employ a simple tree structure to build the code from empirical probabilities. Even more efficient codes, such as arithmetic coding, combine multiple messages into a single code word.

Assuming the availability of a near-optimal code, we can now turn the tables and use information content – or 'description length' as it is more commonly called – as a proxy for probability. One simplified version of the minimum description length (MDL) principle runs as follows.

Definition 9.1 (Minimum description length principle). *Let $L(m)$ denote the length in bits of a description of model m, and let $L(D|m)$ denote the length in bits of a description of data D given model m. According to the minimum description length principle, the preferred model is the one minimising the description length of model and data given model:*

$$m_{\text{MDL}} = \arg\min_{m \in M} (L(m) + L(D|m)) \tag{9.17}$$

In a predictive learning context, 'description of data given model' refers to whatever information we need, in addition to the model and the feature values of the data, to infer the target labels. If the model is 100% accurate no further information is needed, so this term essentially quantifies the extent to which the model is incorrect. For example, in a uniform two-class setting we need one bit for every data point incorrectly classified by the model. The term $L(m)$ quantifies the complexity of the model. For instance, if we are fitting a polynomial to the data we need to encode the degree of the polynomial as well as its roots, up to a certain resolution. MDL learning thus trades off accuracy and complexity of a model: the complexity term serves to avoid overfitting in a similar way to the ☞*regularisation* term in ridge regression in Section 7.1 and the ☞*slack variable* term in soft-margin SVMs in Section 7.3.

What encoding to use in order to determine the model complexity $L(m)$ is often not straightforward and to some extent subjective. This is similar to the Bayesian perspective, where we need to define a prior distribution on models. The MDL viewpoint offers a concrete way of defining model priors by means of codes.

9.6 Probabilistic models: Summary and further reading

In this chapter we covered a range of machine learning models that are all based on the idea that features and target variables can be modelled as random variables, giving the opportunity to explicitly represent and manipulate the level of certainty we have about those variables. Such models are usually predictive in that they result in a conditional distribution $P(Y|X)$ with which Y can be predicted from X. Generative models estimate the joint distribution $P(Y,X)$ – often through the likelihood $P(X|Y)$ and the prior $P(Y)$ – from which the posterior $P(Y|X)$ can be obtained, while conditional models learn the posterior $P(Y|X)$ directly without spending resources on learning $P(X)$. The 'Bayesian' approach to machine learning is characterised by concentrating on the full posterior distribution wherever this is feasible, rather than just deriving a maximising value.

☞ In Section 9.1 we saw that the normal or Gaussian distribution supports many useful geometric intuitions, essentially because the negative logarithm of the Gaussian likelihood can be interpreted as a squared distance. Straight decision boundaries result from having the same per-class covariance matrices, which means that models resulting in such linear boundaries, including linear classifiers, linear regression and K-means clustering, can be interpreted from a probabilistic viewpoint that makes their inherent assumptions explicit. Two examples of this are that the basic linear classifier is Bayes-optimal for uncorrelated, unit-variance Gaussian features; and least-squares regression is optimal for linear functions contaminated by Gaussian noise on the target variable.

☞ Section 9.2 was devoted to different versions of the naive Bayes classifier, which makes the simplifying assumption that features are independent within each class. Lewis (1998) gives an overview and history. This model is widely used in information retrieval and text classification as it is often a good ranker if not a good probability estimator. While the model that is usually understood as naive Bayes treats features as categorical or Bernoulli random variables, variants employing a multinomial model tend to better model the number of occurrences of words in a document (McCallum and Nigam, 1998). Real-valued features can be taken into account by either modelling them as normally distributed within each class, or by non-parametric density estimation – John and Langley (1995) suggest that the latter gives better empirical results. Webb, Boughton and Wang (2005) discuss ways of relaxing the strong independence assumptions made by naive Bayes. Probability smoothing by means of the m-estimate was introduced by Cestnik (1990).

☞ Perhaps paradoxically, I don't think there is anything particularly 'Bayesian' about the naive Bayes classifier. While it is a generative probabilistic model estimating the posterior $P(Y|X)$ through the joint $P(Y,X)$, in practice the posterior is very poorly calibrated owing to the unrealistic independence assumptions. The reason naive Bayes is often successful is because of the quality of $\arg\max_Y P(Y|X)$ rather than the quality of the posterior as such, as analysed by Domingos and Pazzani (1997). Furthermore, even the use of Bayes' rule in determining the maximising Y can be avoided, as it only serves to transform uncalibrated likelihoods into uncalibrated posteriors. So my recommendation is to use naive Bayes likelihoods as scores on an unknown scale whose decision threshold needs to be calibrated by means of ROC analysis, as has been discussed several times before.

☞ In Section 9.3 we looked at the widely used logistic regression model. The basic idea is to combine a linear decision boundary with logistic calibration, but to train this in a discriminative fashion by optimising conditional likelihood. So, rather than modelling the classes as clouds of points and deriving a decision boundary from those clouds, logistic regression concentrates on areas of class overlap. It is an instance of the larger class of generalised linear models (Nelder and Wedderburn, 1972). Jebara (2004) discusses the advantages of discriminative learning in comparison with generative models. Discriminative learning can also be applied to sequential data in the form of conditional random fields (Lafferty *et al.*, 2001)

☞ Section 9.4 presented the Expectation-Maximisation algorithm as a general way of learning models involving unobserved variables. This general form of EM was proposed by Dempster, Laird and Rubin (1977) based on a variety of earlier work. We have seen how it can be applied to Gaussian mixture models to obtain a more general version of K-means predictive clustering, which is also able to estimate cluster shapes and sizes. However, this increases the number of parameters of the model and thus the risk of getting stuck in a non-optimal stationary configuration. (Little and Rubin, 1987) is a standard reference for dealing with missing data.

☞ Finally, in Section 9.5 we briefly discussed some ideas related to learning as compression. The link with probabilistic modelling is that both seek to model and exploit the non-random aspects of the data. In a simplified setting, the minimum description length principle can be derived from Bayes' rule by taking the negative logarithm, and states that models minimising the description length of the model and of the data given the model should be preferred. The first term quantifies the complexity of the model, and the second term quantifies its accuracy (as only the model's errors need to be encoded explicitly). The advantage of the MDL principle is that encoding schemes are often more tangible and easier to define than prior distributions. However, not just any encoding will do: as with their probabilistic counterparts, these schemes need to be justified in the domain being modelled. Pioneering work in this area has been done by Solomonoff (1964*a,b*); Wallace and Boulton (1968); Rissanen (1978), among others. An excellent introduction and overview is provided by Grünwald (2007).

CHAPTER *10*

Features

PREVIOUSLY I REFERRED to features as 'the workhorses of machine learning' – it is therefore high time to consider them in more detail. Features, also called attributes, are defined as mappings $f_i : \mathscr{X} \to \mathscr{F}_i$ from the instance space $\mathscr{X}$ to the feature domain $\mathscr{F}_i$. We can distinguish features by their domain: common feature domains include real and integer numbers, but also discrete sets such as colours, the Booleans, and so on. We can also distinguish features by the range of permissible operations. For example, we can calculate a group of people's average age but not their average blood type, so taking the average value is an operation that is permissible on some features but not on others. We will take a closer look at different kinds of feature in Section 10.1.

Although many data sets come with pre-defined features, they can be manipulated in many ways. For example, we can change the domain of a feature by rescaling or discretisation; we can select the best features from a larger set and only work with the selected ones; or we can combine two or more features into a new feature. In fact, a model itself is a way of constructing a new feature that solves the task at hand. Feature transformations will be investigated in Section 10.2, while feature construction and selection is the topic of Section 10.3

10.1 Kinds of feature

Consider two features, one describing a person's age and the other their house number. Both features map into the integers, but the way we use those features can be quite different. Calculating the average age of a group of people is meaningful, but an average house number is probably not very useful! In other words, what matters is not just the domain of a feature, but also the range of permissible operations. These, in turn, depend on whether the feature values are expressed on a meaningful *scale*. Despite appearances, house numbers are not really integers but *ordinals*: we can use them to determine that number 10's neighbours are number 8 and number 12, but we cannot assume that the distance between 8 and 10 is the same as the distance between 10 and 12. Because of the absence of a linear scale it is not meaningful to add or subtract house numbers, which precludes operations such as averaging.

Calculations on features

Let's take a closer look at the range of possible calculations on features, often referred to as aggregates or statistics. Three main categories are *statistics of central tendency*, *statistics of dispersion* and *shape statistics*. Each of these can be interpreted either as a theoretical property of an unknown population or a concrete property of a given sample – here we will concentrate on sample statistics.

Starting with statistics of central tendency, the most important ones are

☞ the *mean* or average value;

☞ the *median*, which is the middle value if we order the instances from lowest to highest feature value; and

☞ the *mode*, which is the majority value or values.

Of these statistics, the mode is the one we can calculate whatever the domain of the feature: so, for example, we can say that the most frequent blood type in a group of people is O+. In order to calculate the median, we need to have an ordering on the feature values: so we can calculate both the mode and the median house number in a set of addresses.[1] In order to calculate the mean, we need a feature expressed on some scale: most often this will be a linear scale for which we calculate the familiar arithmetic mean, but Background 10.1 discusses means for some other scales. It is often suggested that the median tends to lie between the mode and the mean, but there are plenty of exceptions to this 'rule'. The famous statistician Karl Pearson suggested a

[1]If our sample contains an even number of instances, there are two middle values. If the feature has a scale it is customary to take the mean of those two values as the median; if the feature doesn't have a scale, or if it is important that we select a value actually occurring in the sample, we can either select both as the lower and upper median, or we can make a random choice.

Imagine a swimmer who swims the same distance d on two different days, taking a seconds one day and b seconds the next. On average, it took her therefore $c = (a+b)/2$ seconds, with an average speed of $d/c = 2d/(a+b)$. Notice how this average speed is *not* calculated as the normal or *arithmetic mean* of the speeds, which would yield $(d/a + d/b)/2$: to calculate average speed over a fixed distance we use a different mean called the *harmonic mean*. Given two numbers x and y (in our swimming example these are the speeds on either day, d/a and d/b), the harmonic mean h is defined as

$$h(x, y) = \frac{2}{1/x + 1/y} = \frac{2xy}{x+y}$$

Since $1/h(x, y) = (1/x + 1/y)/2$, we observe that calculating the harmonic mean on a scale with unit u corresponds to calculating the arithmetic mean on the *reciprocal scale* with unit $1/u$. In the example, speed with fixed distance is expressed on a scale reciprocal to the time scale, and since we use the arithmetic mean to average time, we use the harmonic mean to average speed. (If we average speed over a fixed *time* interval this is expressed on the same scale as distance and thus we would use the arithmetic mean.)

A good example of where the harmonic mean is used in machine learning arises when we average precision and recall of a classifier. Remember that precision is the proportion of positive predictions that is correct ($prec = TP/(TP + FP)$), and recall is the proportion of positives that is correctly predicted ($rec = TP/(TP + FN)$). Suppose we first calculate the number of mistakes averaged over the classes: this is the arithmetic mean $Fm = (FP + FN)/2$. We can then derive

$$\frac{TP}{TP + Fm} = \frac{TP}{TP + (FP + FN)/2} = \frac{2TP}{(TP + FP) + (TP + FN)} = \frac{2}{1/prec + 1/rec}$$

We recognise the last term as the harmonic mean of precision and recall. Since the enumerator of both precision and recall is fixed, taking the arithmetic mean of the denominators corresponds to taking the harmonic mean of the ratios. In information retrieval this harmonic mean of precision and recall is very often used and called the *F-measure*.

Yet other means exist for other scales. In music, going from one note to a note one octave higher corresponds to doubling the frequency. So frequencies f and $4f$ are two octaves apart, and it makes sense to take the octave in between with frequency $2f$ as their mean. This is achieved by the *geometric mean*, which is defined as $g(x, y) = \sqrt{xy}$. Since $\log\sqrt{xy} = (\log xy)/2 = (\log x + \log y)/2$ it follows that the geometric mean corresponds to the arithmetic mean on a logarithmic scale. All these means have in common that the mean of two values is an intermediate value, and that they can easily be extended to more than two values.

Background 10.1. On scales and means.

more specific rule of thumb (with therefore even more exceptions): the median tends to fall one-third of the way from mean to mode.

The second kind of calculation on features are statistics of dispersion or 'spread'. Two well-known statistics of dispersion are the *variance* or average squared deviation from the (arithmetic) mean, and its square root, the *standard deviation*. Variance and standard deviation essentially measure the same thing, but the latter has the advantage that it is expressed on the same scale as the feature itself. For example, the variance of the body weight in kilograms of a group of people is measured in kg^2 (kilograms-squared), whereas the standard deviation is measured in kilograms. The absolute difference between the mean and the median is never larger than the standard deviation – this is a consequence of *Chebyshev's inequality*, which states that at most $1/k^2$ of the values are more than k standard deviations away from the mean.

A simpler dispersion statistic is the difference between maximum and minimum value, which is called the *range*. A natural statistic of central tendency to be used with the range is the *midrange point*, which is the mean of the two extreme values. These definitions assume a linear scale but can be adapted to other scales using suitable transformations. For example, for a feature expressed on a logarithmic scale, such as frequency, we would take the ratio of the highest and lowest frequency as the range, and the harmonic mean of these two extremes as the midrange point.

Other statistics of dispersion include *percentiles*. The p-th percentile is the value such that p per cent of the instances fall below it. If we have 100 instances, the 80th percentile is the value of the 81st instance in a list of increasing values.[2] If p is a multiple of 25 the percentiles are also called *quartiles*, and if it is a multiple of 10 the percentiles are also called *deciles*. Note that the 50th percentile, the 5th decile and the second quartile are all the same as the median. Percentiles, deciles and quartiles are special cases of *quantiles*. Once we have quantiles we can measure dispersion as the distance between different quantiles. For instance, the *interquartile range* is the difference between the third and first quartile (i.e., the 75th and 25th percentile).

Example 10.1 (Percentile plot). Suppose you are learning a model over an instance space of countries, and one of the features you are considering is the gross domestic product (GDP) per capita. Figure 10.1 shows a so-called *percentile plot* of this feature. In order to obtain the p-th percentile, you intersect the line $y = p$ with the dotted curve and read off the corresponding percentile on the x-axis. Indicated in the figure are the 25th, 50th and 75th percentile. Also indicated is the

[2] Similar to the median there are issues with non-integer ranks, and they can be dealt with in different ways; however, significant differences do not arise unless the sample size is very small.

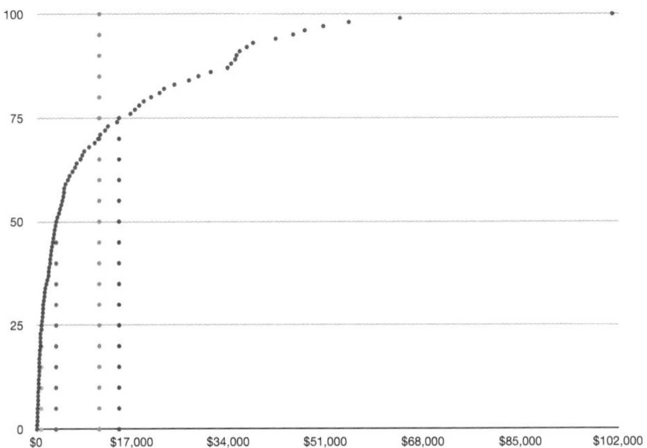

Figure 10.1. Percentile plot of GDP per capita for 231 countries (data obtained from www.wolframalpha.com by means of the query 'GDP per capita').The vertical dotted lines indicate, from left to right: the first quartile ($900); the median ($3600); the mean ($11 284); andthe third quartile ($14 750). The interquartile range is $13 850, while the standard deviation is $16 189.

mean (which has to be calculated from the raw data). As you can see, the mean is considerably higher than the median; this is mainly because of a few countries with very high GDP per capita. In other words, the mean is more sensitive to *outliers* than the median, which is why the median is often preferred to the mean for skewed distributions like this one.

You might think that the way I drew the percentile plot is the wrong way around: surely it would make more sense to have p on the x-axis and the percentiles on the y-axis? One advantage of drawing the plot this way is that, by interpreting the y-axis as probabilities, the plot can be read as a *cumulative probability distribution*: a plot of $P(X \leq x)$ against x for a random variable X. For example, the plot shows that $P(X \leq \mu)$ is approximately 0.70, where $\mu = \$11284$ is the mean GDP per capita. In other words, if you choose a random country the probability that its GDP per capita is less than the average is about 0.70.

Since GDP per capita is a real-valued feature, it doesn't necessarily make sense to talk about its mode, since if you measure the feature precisely enough every country will have a different value. We can get around this by means of a *histogram*, which counts the number of feature values in a particular interval or bin.

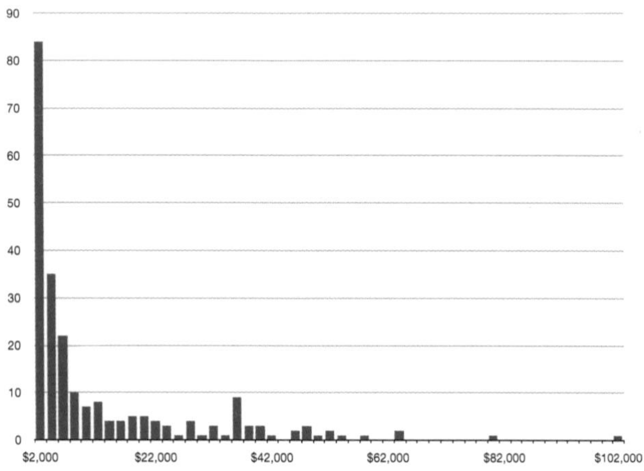

Figure 10.2. Histogram of the data from Figure 10.1, with bins of $2000 wide.

Example 10.2 (Histogram). A histogram of the data from Example 10.1 is shown in Figure 10.2. The left-most bin is the mode, with well over a third of the countries having a GDP per capita of not more than $2000. This demonstrates that the distribution is extremely *right-skewed* (i.e., has a long right tail), resulting in a mean that is considerably higher than the median.

The skew and 'peakedness' of a distribution can be measured by shape statistics such as skewness and kurtosis. The main idea is to calculate the third and fourth *central moment* of the sample. In general, the k-th central moment of a sample $\{x_i, \ldots, x_n\}$ is defined as $m_k = \frac{1}{n}\sum_{i=1}^{n}(x_i - \mu)^k$, where μ is the sample mean. Clearly, the first central moment is the average deviation from the mean – this is always zero, as the positive and negative deviations cancel each other out – and the second central moment is the average squared deviation from the mean, otherwise known as the variance. The third central moment m_3 can again be positive or negative. *Skewness* is then defined as m_3/σ^3, where σ is the sample's standard deviation. A positive value of skewness means that the distribution is right-skewed, which means that the right tail is longer than the left tail. Negative skewness indicates the opposite, left-skewed case. *Kurtosis* is defined as m_4/σ^4. As it can be shown that a normal distribution has kurtosis 3, people often use *excess kurtosis* $m_4/\sigma^4 - 3$ as the statistic of interest. Briefly, positive excess kurtosis means that the distribution is more sharply peaked than the normal distribution.

Kind	*Order*	*Scale*	*Tendency*	*Dispersion*	*Shape*
Categorical	×	×	mode	n/a	n/a
Ordinal	√	×	median	quantiles	n/a
Quantitative	√	√	mean	range, interquartile range, variance, standard deviation	skewness, kurtosis

Table 10.1. Kinds of feature, their properties and allowable statistics. Each kind inherits the statistics from the kinds above it in the table. For instance, the mode is a statistic of central tendency that can be computed for any kind of feature.

Example 10.3 (Skewness and kurtosis). In the GDP per capita example we can calculate skewness as 2.12 and excess kurtosis as 2.53. This confirms that the distribution is heavily right-skewed, and also more sharply peaked than the normal distribution.

Categorical, ordinal and quantitative features

Given these various statistics we can distinguish three main kinds of feature: those with a meaningful numerical scale, those without a scale but with an ordering, and those without either. We will call features of the first type *quantitative*; they most often involve a mapping into the reals (another term in common use is 'continuous'). Even if a feature maps into a subset of the reals, such as age expressed in years, the various statistics such as mean or standard deviation still require the full scale of the reals.

Features with an ordering but without scale are called *ordinal features*. The domain of an ordinal feature is some totally ordered set, such as the set of characters or strings. Even if the domain of a feature is the set of integers, denoting the feature as ordinal means that we have to dispense with the scale, as we did with house numbers. Another common example are features that express a rank order: first, second, third, and so on. Ordinal features allow the mode and median as central tendency statistics, and quantiles as dispersion statistics.

Features without ordering or scale are called *categorical features* (or sometimes 'nominal' features). They do not allow any statistical summary except the mode. One subspecies of the categorical features is the *Boolean feature*, which maps into the truth values true and false. The situation is summarised in Table 10.1.

Models treat these different kinds of feature in distinct ways. First, consider tree models such as decision trees. A split on a categorical feature will have as many children as there are feature values. Ordinal and quantitative features, on the other hand, give rise to a binary split, by selecting a value v_0 such that all instances with a feature value less than or equal to v_0 go to one child, and the remaining instances to the other child. It follows that tree models are insensitive to the scale of quantitative features. For example, whether a temperature feature is measured on the Celsius scale or on the Fahrenheit scale will not affect the learned tree. Neither will switching from a linear scale to a logarithmic scale have any effect: the split threshold will simply be $\log v_0$ instead of v_0. In general, tree models are insensitive to *monotonic* transformations on the scale of a feature, which are those transformations that do not affect the relative order of the feature values. In effect, *tree models ignore the scale of quantitative features, treating them as ordinal*. The same holds for rule models.

Now let's consider the naive Bayes classifier. We have seen that this model works by estimating a likelihood function $P(X|Y)$ for each feature X given the class Y. For categorical and ordinal features with k values this involves estimating $P(X = v_1|Y), \ldots, P(X = v_k|Y)$. In effect, ordinal features are treated as categorical ones, ignoring the order. Quantitative features cannot be handled at all, unless they are discretised into a finite number of bins and thus converted to categoricals. Alternatively, we could assume a parametric form for $P(X|Y)$, for instance a normal distribution. We will return to this later in this chapter when we discuss feature calibration.

While naive Bayes only really handles categorical features, many geometric models go in the other direction: they can only handle quantitative features. Linear models are a case in point: the very notion of linearity assumes a Euclidean instance space in which features act as Cartesian coordinates, and thus need to be quantitative. Distance-based models such as k-nearest neighbour and K-means require quantitative features if their distance metric is Euclidean distance, but we can adapt the distance metric to incorporate categorical features by setting the distance to 0 for equal values and 1 for unequal values (the ☞*Hamming distance* as defined in Section 8.1). In a similar vein, for ordinal features we can count the number of values between two feature values (if we encode the ordinal feature by means of integers, this would simply be their difference). This means that distance-based methods can accommodate all feature types by using an appropriate distance metric. Similar techniques can be used to extend support vector machines and other kernel-based methods to categorical and ordinal features.

Structured features

It is usually tacitly assumed that an instance is a vector of feature values. In other words, the instance space is a Cartesian product of d feature domains: $\mathscr{X} = \mathscr{F}_1 \times \ldots \times \mathscr{F}_d$. This means that there is no other information available about an instance apart from the information conveyed by its feature values. Identifying an instance with its vector of feature values is what computer scientists call an *abstraction*, which is the result of filtering out unnecessary information. Representing an e-mail as a vector of word frequencies is an example of an abstraction.

However, sometimes it is necessary to avoid such abstractions, and to keep more information about an instance than can be captured by a finite vector of feature values. For example, we could represent an e-mail as a long string; or as a sequence of words and punctuation marks; or as a tree that captures the HTML mark-up; and so on. Features that operate on such structured instance spaces are called *structured features*.

Example 10.4 (Structured features). Suppose an e-mail is represented as a sequence of words. This allows us to define, apart from the usual word frequency features, a host of other features, including:

- whether the phrase 'machine learning' – or any other set of consecutive words – occurs in the e-mail;
- whether the e-mail contains at least eight consecutive words in a language other than English;
- whether the e-mail is palindromic, as in 'Degas, are we not drawn onward, we freer few, drawn onward to new eras aged?'

Furthermore, we could go beyond properties of single e-mails and express relations such as whether one e-mail is quoted in another e-mail, or whether two e-mails have one or more passages in common.

Structured features are not unlike *queries* in a database query language such as SQL or a declarative programming language such as Prolog. In fact, we have already seen examples of structured features in Section 6.4 when we looked at learning Prolog clauses such as the following:

```
fish(X):-bodyPart(X,Y).
fish(X):-bodyPart(X,pairOf(Z)).
```

The first clause has a single structured feature in the body which tests for the existence of some unspecified body part, while the second clause has another structured feature testing for the existence of a pair of unspecified body parts. The defining characteristic of structured features is that they involve *local variables* that refer to objects other than the instance itself. In a logical language such as Prolog it is natural to interpret local variables as existentially quantified, as we just did. However, it is equally possible to use other forms of *aggregation* over local variables: e.g., we can count the number of body parts (or pairs of body parts) an instance has.

↓ to, from →	*Quantitative*	*Ordinal*	*Categorical*	*Boolean*
Quantitative	**normalisation**	**calibration**	**calibration**	**calibration**
Ordinal	**discretisation**	**ordering**	**ordering**	**ordering**
Categorical	**discretisation**	**unordering**	**grouping**	
Boolean	**thresholding**	**thresholding**	**binarisation**	

Table 10.2. An overview of possible feature transformations. **Normalisation and calibration** adapt the scale of quantitative features, or add a scale to features that don't have one. **Ordering** adds or adapts the order of feature values without reference to a scale. The other operations abstract away from unnecessary detail, either in a deductive way (**unordering**, **binarisation**) or by introducing new information (**thresholding**, **discretisation**).

Structured features can be constructed either prior to learning a model, or simultaneously with it. The first scenario is often called *propositionalisation* because the features can be seen as a translation from first-order logic to propositional logic without local variables. The main challenge with propositionalisation approaches is how to deal with combinatorial explosion of the number of potential features. Notice that features can be logically related: e.g., the second clause above covers a subset of the instances covered by the first one. It is possible to exploit this if structured feature construction is integrated with model building, as in inductive logic programming.

10.2 Feature transformations

Feature transformations aim at improving the utility of a feature by removing, changing or adding information. We could order feature types by the amount of detail they convey: quantitative features are more detailed than ordinal ones, followed by categorical features, and finally Boolean features. The best-known feature transformations are those that turn a feature of one type into another of the next type down this list. But there are also transformations that change the scale of quantitative features, or add a scale (or order) to ordinal, categorical and Boolean features. Table 10.2 introduces the terminology we will be using.

The simplest feature transformations are entirely deductive, in the sense that they achieve a well-defined result that doesn't require making any choices. *Binarisation* transforms a categorical feature into a set of Boolean features, one for each value of the categorical feature. This loses information since the values of a single categorical feature are mutually exclusive, but is sometimes needed if a model cannot handle more than two feature values. *Unordering* trivially turns an ordinal feature into a categorical one by discarding the ordering of the feature values. This is often required since most learning models cannot handle ordinal features directly. An interesting alternative that

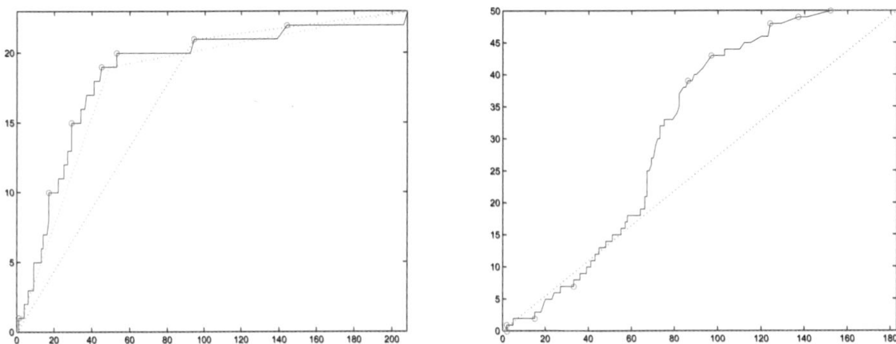

Figure 10.3. (left) Coverage curve obtained by ranking countries on decreasing GDP per capita, using 23 Euro countries as the positive class. The orange split sets the threshold equal to the mean, selecting 19 Euro countries and 49 non-Euro countries. The green split sets the threshold equal to the median, selecting 21 Euro countries and 94 non-Euro countries. The red points are on the convex hull of the coverage curve and indicate potentially optimal splits when the class label is taken into account. **(right)** Coverage curve of the same feature, using 50 countries in the Americas as the positive class. The red splits indicate potentially optimal thresholds with relatively many positives above the threshold, while the green splits indicate potentially optimal thresholds with relatively many positives below the threshold.

we will explore below is to add a scale to the feature by means of calibration.

In the remainder of this section we consider feature transformations that add information, the most important of which are discretisation and calibration.

Thresholding and discretisation

Thresholding transforms a quantitative or an ordinal feature into a Boolean feature by finding a feature value to split on. I briefly alluded to this in Chapter 5 as a way to split on quantitative features in decision trees. Concretely, let $f : \mathscr{X} \to \mathbb{R}$ be a quantitative feature and let $t \in \mathbb{R}$ be a threshold, then $f_t : \mathscr{X} \to \{\text{true}, \text{false}\}$ is a Boolean feature defined by $f_t(x) = \text{true}$ if $f(x) \geq t$ and $f_t(x) = \text{false}$ if $f(x) < t$. We can choose such thresholds in an unsupervised or a supervised way.

Example 10.5 (Unsupervised and supervised thresholding). Consider the GDP per capita feature plotted in Figure 10.1 again. Without knowing how this feature is to be used in a model, the most sensible thresholds are the statistics of central tendency such as the mean and the median. This is referred to as *unsupervised thresholding*.

In a *supervised* learning setting we can do more. For example, suppose we want to use the GDP per capita as a feature in a decision tree to predict whether a country is one of the 23 countries that use the Euro as their official currency (or as one of their currencies). Using the feature as a ranker, we can construct a coverage curve (Figure 10.3 (left)). We see that for this feature the mean is not the most obvious threshold, as it splits right in the middle of a run of negatives. A better split is obtained at the start of that run of negatives, or at the end of the following run of positives, indicated by the red points at either end of the mean split. More generally, any point on the convex hull of the coverage curve represents a candidate threshold; which one to choose is informed by whether we put more value on picking out positives or negatives. As it happens in this example, the median threshold is on the convex hull, but this cannot be guaranteed in general as, by definition, unsupervised thresholding methods select the threshold independently from the target.

Figure 10.3 (right) shows the same feature with a different target: whether a country is in the Americas. We see that part of the curve is below the ascending diagonal, indicating that, in comparison with the whole data set, the initial segment of the ranking contains a smaller proportion of American countries. This means that potentially useful thresholds can also be found on the *lower convex hull*.

In summary, unsupervised thresholding typically involves calculating some statistic over the data, whereas supervised thresholding requires sorting the data on the feature value and traversing down this ordering to optimise a particular objective function such as information gain. Non-optimal split points could be filtered out by means of constructing the upper and lower convex hull, but in practice this is unlikely to be more efficient computationally than a straightforward sweep over the sorted instances.

If we generalise thresholding to multiple thresholds we arrive at one of the most commonly used non-deductive feature transformations. *Discretisation* transforms a quantitative feature into an ordinal feature. Each ordinal value is referred to as a *bin* and corresponds to an interval of the original quantitative feature. Again, we can distinguish between supervised and unsupervised approaches. *Unsupervised discretisation* methods typically require one to decide the number of bins beforehand. A simple method that often works reasonably well is to choose the bins so that each bin has approximately the same number of instances: this is referred to as *equal-frequency discretisation*. If we choose two bins then this method coincides with thresholding on the median. More generally, the bin boundaries are quantiles: for instance, with 10 bins the bin boundaries of equal-width discretisation are deciles. Another unsupervised discretisation method is *equal-width discretisation*, which chooses the bin boundaries so that each interval has the same width. The interval width can be established by dividing the feature range by the number of bins if the feature has upper and lower limits; alternatively, we can take the bin boundaries at an integer number of standard deviations above and below the mean. An interesting alternative is to treat feature discretisation as a univariate clustering problem. For example, in order to generate K bins we can uniformly sample K initial bin centres and run K-means until convergence. We can alternatively use any of the other clustering methods discussed in Chapter 8: K-medoids, partitioning around medoids and hierarchical agglomerative clustering.

Switching now to *supervised discretisation* methods, we can distinguish between *top–down* or *divisive* discretisation methods on the one hand, and *bottom–up* or *agglomerative* discretisation methods on the other. Divisive methods work by progressively splitting bins, whereas agglomerative methods proceed by initially assigning each instance to its own bin and successively merging bins. In either case an important role is played by the *stopping criterion*, which decides whether a further split or merge is worthwhile. We give an example of each strategy. A natural generalisation of thresholding leads to a top–down *recursive partitioning* algorithm (Algorithm 10.1). This discretisation algorithm finds the best threshold according to some scoring function Q, and proceeds to recursively split the left and right bins. One scoring function that is often used is information gain.

Example 10.6 (Recursive partitioning using information gain). Consider the following feature values, which are ordered on increasing value for convenience.

Instance	*Value*	*Class*
e_1	−5.0	⊖
e_2	−3.1	⊕
e_3	−2.7	⊖
e_4	0.0	⊖
e_5	7.0	⊖
e_6	7.1	⊕
e_7	8.5	⊕
e_8	9.0	⊖
e_9	9.0	⊕
e_{10}	13.7	⊖
e_{11}	15.1	⊖
e_{12}	20.1	⊖

This feature gives rise to the following ranking: ⊖⊕⊖⊖⊖⊕⊕[⊖⊕]⊖⊖⊖, where the square brackets indicate a tie between instances e_8 and e_9. The corresponding

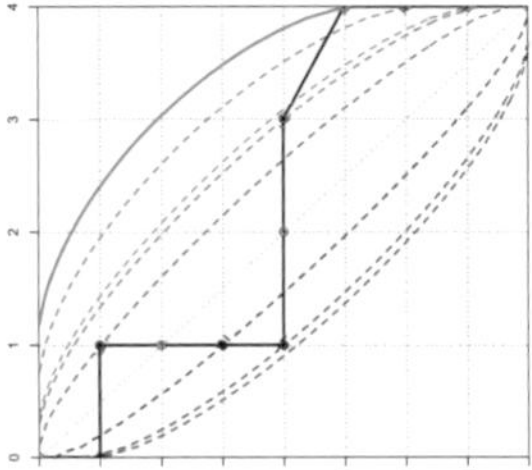
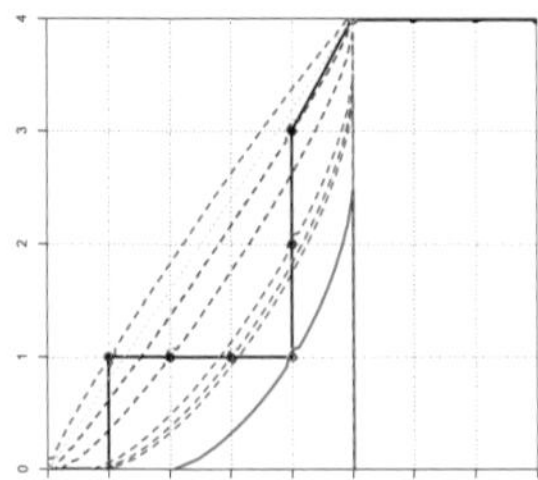
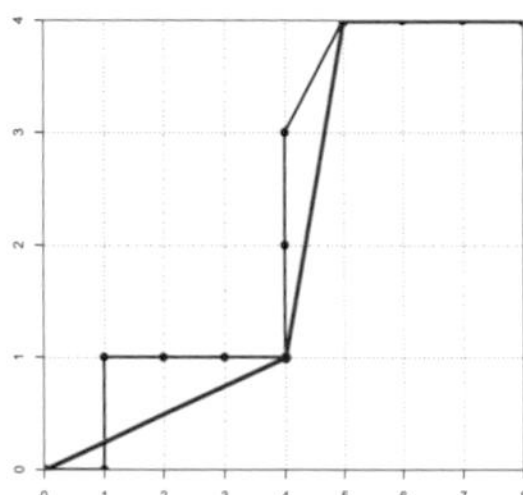

Figure 10.4. **(left)** A coverage curve visualising the ranking of four positive and eight negative examples by a feature to be discretised. The curved lines are information gain isometrics through possible split points; the solid isometric indicates the best split [4+,5−][0+,3−] according to information gain. **(middle)** Recursive partitioning proceeds to split the segment [4+,5−] into [1+,4−][3+,1−]. **(right)** If we stop here, the blue curve visualises the discretised (but still ordinal) feature.

coverage curve is depicted in Figure 10.4. Tracing information gain isometrics through each possible split, we see that the best split is ⊖⊕⊖⊖⊖⊕⊕[⊖⊕]||⊖⊖⊖. Repeating the process once more gives the discretisation ⊖⊕⊖⊖⊖|⊕⊕[⊖⊕]||⊖⊖⊖.

Clearly, we can stop the recursive partitioning algorithm when the empirical probabilities are the same across the ranking; this has pure bins and bins with a constant feature value as special cases. With this stopping criterion, the algorithm will successfully identify all straight line segments in the ranking. In fact, it is not hard to see that this holds true even if we change the scoring function – the split points may be found in a different order, but the end result will be the same. In practice more aggressive stopping criteria are used, which does mean that the end result depends on the

---

Algorithm 10.1: RecPart(S, f, Q) – supervised discretisation by means of recursive partitioning.

Input : set of labelled instances S ranked on feature values $f(x)$; scoring function Q.

Output : sequence of thresholds $t_1, \dots, t_{k-1}$.

if stopping criterion applies **then return** $\varnothing$;

Split S into S_l and S_r using threshold t that optimises Q ;

T_l = RecPart(S_l, f, Q);

T_r = RecPart(S_r, f, Q);

return $T_l \cup \{t\} \cup T_r$;

Algorithm 10.2: AggloMerge(S, f, Q) – supervised discretisation by means of agglomerative merging.

Input : set of labelled instances S ranked on feature values $f(x)$; scoring function Q.
Output : sequence of thresholds.

```
initialise bins to data points with the same scores;
merge consecutive pure bins ;                          // optional optimisation
repeat
    evaluate Q on consecutive bin pairs;
    merge the pairs with best Q (unless they invoke the stopping criterion);
until no further merges are possible;
return thresholds between bins;
```

scoring function. For example, in Figure 10.4 we see that the split ⊖|[⊕⊖]⊕⊕⊖⊖⊖⊕⊕ has the second-highest information gain but ends up not being chosen at all, while with a different scoring function it might have been chosen in the first round. One of the most popular stopping criteria applies a minimum description length argument to decide whether a given bin should be split further.

It should be noted that the data set in Example 10.6 is probably so small that the stopping criterion will kick in straight away and recursive partitioning will be unable to go beyond a single bin. More generally, this kind of discretisation tends to be fairly conservative. For example, on the Euro data in Figure 10.3 (left) recursive partitioning produces two bins, selecting 20 Euro countries and 53 non-Euro countries (the red point in between the mean and median splits). On the American countries data in Figure 10.3 (right) we again obtain two bins, corresponding to the third red point from the right.

An algorithm for bottom–up *agglomerative merging* is given in Algorithm 10.2. Again the algorithm can take various choices for the scoring function and the stopping criterion: a popular choice is to use the χ^2 *statistic* for both.

Example 10.7 (Agglomerative merging using χ^2). We continue Example 10.6. Algorithm 10.2 initialises the bins to ⊖|⊕|⊖⊖⊖|⊕⊕|[⊖⊕]|⊖⊖⊖. We illustrate the calculation of the χ^2 statistic for the last two bins. We construct the following contingency table:

	Left bin	*Right bin*	
⊕	**1**	0	1
⊖	1	**3**	4
	2	3	5

At the basis of the χ^2 statistic lies a comparison of these observed frequencies with expected frequencies obtained from the row and column marginals. For example, the marginals say that the top row contains 20% of the total mass and the left column 40%; so if rows and columns were statistically independent we would expect 8% of the mass – or 0.4 of the five instances – in the top-left cell. Following a clockwise direction, the expected frequencies for the other cells are 0.6, 2.4 and 1.6. If the observed frequencies are close to the expected ones, this suggests that these two bins are candidates for merging since the split appears to have no bearing on the class distribution.

The χ^2 statistic sums the squared differences between the observed and expected frequencies, each term normalised by the expected frequency:

$$\chi^2 = \frac{(1-0.4)^2}{0.4} + \frac{(0-0.6)^2}{0.6} + \frac{(3-2.4)^2}{2.4} + \frac{(1-1.6)^2}{1.6} = 1.88$$

Going left-to-right through the other pairs of consecutive bins, the χ^2 values are 2, 4, 5 and 1.33 (there's an easy way to calculate the χ^2 value for two pure bins, which I'll leave you to discover). This tells us that the fourth and fifth bin are first to be merged, leading to ⊖|⊕|⊖⊖⊖|⊕⊕[⊖⊕]||⊖⊖⊖. We then recompute the χ^2 values (in fact, only those involving the newly merged bin need to be re-computed), yielding 2, 4, 3.94 and 3.94. We now merge the first two bins, giving the partition ⊖⊕|⊖⊖⊖|⊕⊕[⊖⊕]||⊖⊖⊖. This changes the first χ^2 value to 1.88, so we again merge the first two bins, arriving at ⊖⊕⊖⊖⊖|⊕⊕[⊖⊕]||⊖⊖⊖ (the same three bins as in Example 10.6).

In agglomerative discretisation the stopping criterion usually takes the form of a simple threshold on the scoring function. In the case of the χ^2 statistic, the threshold can be derived from the p-value associated with the χ^2 distribution, which is the probability of observing a χ^2 value above the threshold if the two variables are actually independent. For two classes (i.e., one degree of freedom) and a p-value of 0.10 the χ^2 threshold is 2.71, which in our example means that we stop at the above three bins. For a lower p-value of 0.05 the χ^2 threshold is 3.84, which means that we eventually merge all the bins.

Notice that both top–down and bottom–up supervised discretisation bear some resemblance to algorithms we have seen previously: recursive partitioning shares the divide-and-conquer nature of the ☞*decision tree* training algorithm (Algorithm 5.1 on p.132), and agglomerative discretisation by merging consecutive bins is related to ☞*hierarchical agglomerative clustering* (Algorithm 8.4 on p.255). It is also worth mentioning that, although our examples were predominantly drawn from binary classification, most methods can handle more than two classes without complication.

Normalisation and calibration

Thresholding and discretisation are feature transformations that remove the scale of a quantitative feature. We now turn our attention to adapting the scale of a quantitative feature, or adding a scale to an ordinal or categorical feature. If this is done in an unsupervised fashion it is usually called normalisation, whereas calibration refers to supervised approaches taking in the (usually binary) class labels. *Feature normalisation* is often required to neutralise the effect of different quantitative features being measured on different scales. If the features are approximately normally distributed, we can convert them into ☞*z-scores* (Background 9.1 on p.267) by centring on the mean and dividing by the standard deviation. In certain cases it is mathematically more convenient to divide by the variance instead, as we have seen in Section 7.1. If we don't want to assume normality we can centre on the median and divide by the interquartile range.

Sometimes feature normalisation is understood in the stricter sense of expressing the feature on a $[0,1]$ scale. This can be achieved in various ways. If we know the feature's highest and lowest values h and l, then we can simply apply the linear scaling $f \mapsto (f-l)/(h-l)$. We sometimes have to guess the value of h or l, and truncate any value outside $[l,h]$. For example, if the feature measures age in years, we may take $l = 0$ and $h = 100$, and truncate any $f > h$ to 1. If we can assume a particular distribution for the feature, then we can work out a transformation such that almost all feature values fall in a certain range. For instance, we know that more than 99% of the probability mass of a normal distribution falls within $\pm 3\sigma$ of the mean, where σ is the standard deviation, so the linear scaling $f \mapsto (f-\mu)/6\sigma + 1/2$ virtually removes the need for truncation.

Feature calibration is understood as a supervised feature transformation adding a meaningful scale carrying class information to arbitrary features. This has a number of important advantages. For instance, it allows models that require scale, such as linear classifiers, to handle categorical and ordinal features. It also allows the learning algorithm to choose whether to treat a feature as categorical, ordinal or quantitative. We will assume a binary classification context, and so a natural choice for the calibrated feature's scale is the posterior probability of the positive class, conditioned on the feature's value. This has the additional advantage that models that are based on such probabilities, such as naive Bayes, do not require any additional training once the features are calibrated, as we shall see. The problem of feature calibration can thus be stated as follows: given a feature $F : \mathscr{X} \to \mathscr{F}$, construct a calibrated feature $F^c : \mathscr{X} \to [0,1]$ such that $F^c(x)$ estimates the probability $F^c(x) = P(\oplus|v)$, where $v = F(x)$ is the value of the original feature for x.

For categorical features this is as straightforward as collecting relative frequencies from a training set.

Example 10.8 (Calibration of categorical features). Suppose we want to predict whether or not someone has diabetes from categorical features including whether the person is obese or not, whether he or she smokes, and so on. We collect some statistics which tell us that 1 in every 18 obese persons has diabetes while among non-obese people this is 1 in 55 (data obtained from `www.wolframalpha.com` with the query 'diabetes'). If $F(x) = 1$ for person x who is obese and $F(y) = 0$ for person y who isn't, then the calibrated feature values are $F^c(x) = 1/18 = 0.055$ and $F^c(y) = 1/55 = 0.018$.

In fact, it would be better to compensate for the non-uniform class distribution, in order to avoid over-emphasising the class prior, which is better taken into account in the decision rule. This can be achieved as follows. If m of n obese people have diabetes, then this corresponds to a posterior odds of $m/(n-m)$ or a likelihood ratio of $m/c(n-m)$, where c is the prior odds of having diabetes (since posterior odds is likelihood ratio times prior odds). Working with the likelihood ratio is equivalent to assuming a uniform class distribution. Converting the likelihood ratio into a probability gives

$$F^c(x) = \frac{\frac{m}{c(n-m)}}{\frac{m}{c(n-m)} + 1} = \frac{m}{m + c(n-m)}$$

In our example, if the prior odds of having diabetes is $c = 1/48$, then $F^c(x) = 1/(1 + 17/48) = 48/(48+17) = 0.74$. The extent to which this probability is more than 1/2 quantifies the extent to which obese people are more likely than average to have diabetes. For non-obese people the probability is $1/(1+54/48) = 48/(48+54) = 0.47$, so they are slightly less likely than average to have diabetes. Keep in mind also that it is usually a good idea to smooth these probability estimates by means of the Laplace correction, which adds 1 to m and 2 to n. This leads to the final expression for calibrating a categorical feature:

$$F^c(x) = \frac{m+1}{m+1+c(n-m+1)}$$

Ordinal and quantitative features can be discretised and then calibrated as categorical features. In the remainder of this section we look at calibration methods that maintain the ordering of the feature. For example, suppose we want to use body weight as an indicator for diabetes. A calibrated weight feature attaches a probability to every weight, such that these probabilities are non-decreasing with weight. This is related to our discussion of ☞*calibrating classifier scores* in Section 7.4, as those calibrated probabilities should likewise takes the ranking of the classifier's predictions into account. In fact, the two approaches to classifier calibration – by employing the logistic function and by constructing the ROC convex hull – are directly applicable to feature calibration, since a quantitative feature can simply be treated as a univariate scoring classifier.

We briefly reiterate the main points of *logistic calibration*, but with a slight change in notation. Let $F : \mathscr{X} \to \mathbb{R}$ be a quantitative feature with class means $\mu^{\oplus}$ and $\mu^{\ominus}$ and variance σ^2. Assuming the feature is normally distributed within each class with the same variance, we can express the likelihood ratio of a feature value v as

$$LR(v) = \frac{P(v|\oplus)}{P(v|\ominus)} = \exp\left(\frac{-(v-\mu^{\oplus})^2 + (v-\mu^{\ominus})^2}{2\sigma^2}\right)$$

$$= \exp\left(\frac{\mu^{\oplus}-\mu^{\ominus}}{\sigma}\frac{v-(\mu^{\oplus}+\mu^{\ominus})/2}{\sigma}\right) = \exp\left(d'z\right)$$

where $d' = (\mu^{\oplus} - \mu^{\ominus})/\sigma$ is the difference between the means in proportion to the standard deviation, which is known as *d-prime* in signal detection theory; and $z = (v-\mu)/\sigma$ is the z-score associated with v (notice we take the mean as $\mu = (\mu^{\oplus} + \mu^{\ominus})/2$ to simulate an equal class distribution). Again we work directly with the likelihood ratio to neutralise the effect of a non-uniform class distribution, and we obtain the calibrated feature value as

$$F^{c}(x) = \frac{LR(F(x))}{1 + LR(F(x))} = \frac{\exp\left(d'z(x)\right)}{1 + \exp\left(d'z(x)\right)}$$

You may recognise the logistic function we discussed in Chapter 7 (see Figure 7.11 on p.222).

In essence, logistic feature calibration performs the following steps.

1. Estimate the class means $\mu^{\oplus}$ and $\mu^{\ominus}$ and the standard deviation σ.

2. Transform $F(x)$ into z-scores $z(x)$, making sure to use $\mu = (\mu^{\oplus} + \mu^{\ominus}))/2$ as the feature mean.

3. Rescale the z-scores to $F^{d}(x) = d'z(x)$ with $d' = (\mu^{\oplus} - \mu^{\ominus})/\sigma$.

4. Apply a sigmoidal transformation to $F^{d}(x)$ to give calibrated probabilities $F^{c}(x) = \frac{\exp(F^{d}(x))}{1+\exp(F^{d}(x))}$.

Sometimes it is preferred to work directly with $F^{d}(x)$, as it is expressed on a scale linearly related to the original feature's scale, and the Gaussian assumption implies that

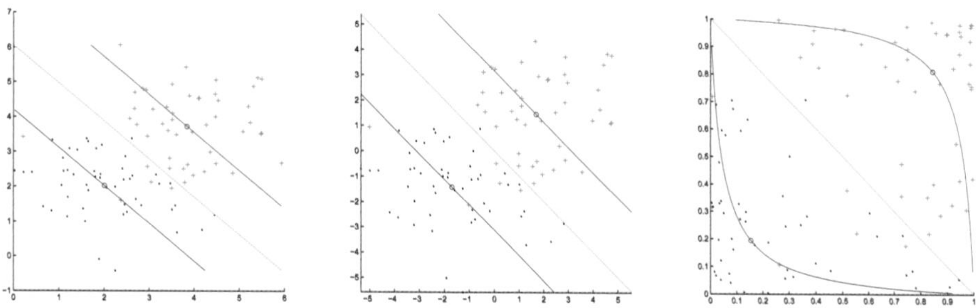

Figure 10.5. (left) Two-class Gaussian data. The middle line is the decision boundary learned by the basic linear classifier; the other two are parallel lines through the class means. **(middle)** Logistic calibration to log-odds space is a linear transformation; assuming unit standard deviations, the basic linear classifier is now the fixed line $F_1^{\mathrm{d}}(x) + F_2^{\mathrm{d}}(x) = 0$. **(right)** Logistic calibration to probability space is a non-linear transformation that pushes data away from the decision boundary.

we expect that scale to be additive. For example, distance-based models expect additive features in order to calculate Euclidean distance. In contrast, the scale of F^{c} is multiplicative. Notice that the two are interdefinable as $F^{\mathrm{d}}(x) = \ln \frac{F^{\mathrm{c}}(x)}{1-F^{\mathrm{c}}(x)} = \ln F^{\mathrm{c}}(x) - \ln(1 - F^{\mathrm{c}}(x))$. I will call the feature space spanned by F^{d} *log-odds space*, since $\exp\left(F^{\mathrm{d}}(x)\right) = LR(x)$ and the likelihood ratio is equal to the odds if we're assuming a uniform class prior. Calibrated features F^{c} live in *probability space*.

Example 10.9 (Logistic calibration of two features). Logistic feature calibration is illustrated in Figure 10.5. I generated two sets of 50 points by sampling bivariate Gaussians with identity covariance matrix, centred at (2,2) and (4,4). I then constructed the basic linear classifier as well as two parallel decision boundaries through the class means. Tracing these three lines in calibrated space will help us understand feature calibration.

In the middle figure we see the transformed data in log-odds space, which is clearly a linear rescaling of the axes. The basic linear classifier is now the line $F_1^{\mathrm{d}}(x) + F_2^{\mathrm{d}}(x) = 0$ through the origin. In other words, for this simple classifier feature calibration has removed the need for further training: instead of fitting a decision boundary to the data, we have fitted the data to a fixed decision boundary! (I should add that I cheated very slightly here, as I fixed $\sigma = 1$ in the calibration process – had I estimated each feature's standard deviation from the data, the decision boundary would most likely have had a slightly different slope.)

On the right we see the transformed data in probability space, which clearly has a non-linear relationship with the other two feature spaces. The basic linear classifier is still linear in this space, but actually this is no longer true for more than two features. To see this, note that $F_1^c(x) + F_2^c(x) = 1$ can be rewritten as

$$\frac{\exp\left(F_1^d(x)\right)}{1+\exp\left(F_1^d(x)\right)} + \frac{\exp\left(F_2^d(x)\right)}{1+\exp\left(F_2^d(x)\right)} = 1$$

which can be simplified to $\exp\left(F_1^d(x)\right)\exp\left(F_2^d(x)\right) = 1$ and hence to $F_1^d(x) + F_2^d(x) = 0$. However, if we add a third feature not all cross-terms cancel and we obtain a non-linear boundary .

The log-odds representation does hold an interest in another respect. An arbitrary linear decision boundary in log-odds space is represented by $\sum_i w_i F_i^d(x) = t$. Taking natural logarithms this can be rewritten as

$$\exp\left(\sum_i w_i F_i^d(x)\right) = \prod_i \exp\left(w_i F_i^d(x)\right) = \prod_i \left(\exp\left(F_i^d(x)\right)\right)^{w_i} = \prod_i LR_i(x)^{w_i} = \exp(t) = t'$$

This exposes a connection with the naive Bayes models discussed in Section 9.2, whose decision boundaries are also defined as products of likelihood ratios for individual features. The basic naive Bayes model has $w_i = 1$ for all i and $t' = 1$, which means that *fitting data to a fixed linear decision boundary in log-odds space by means of feature calibration can be understood as training a naive Bayes model.* Changing the slope of the decision boundary corresponds to introducing non-unit feature weights, which is similar to the way feature weights arose in the multinomial naive Bayes model.

It is instructive to investigate the distribution of the calibrated feature a bit more (I will omit the technical details). Assuming the uncalibrated distributions were two Gaussian bumps, what do the calibrated distributions look like? We have already seen that calibrated data points are pulled away from the decision boundary, so we would expect the peaks of the calibrated distributions to be closer to their extreme values. How much closer depends solely on d'; Figure 10.6 depicts the calibrated distributions for various values of d'.

We move on to *isotonic calibration*, a method that requires order but ignores scale and can be applied to both ordinal and quantitative features. We essentially use the feature as a univariate ranker, and construct its ROC curve and convex hull to obtain a piecewise-constant calibration map. Suppose we have an ROC curve, and suppose the i-th segment of the curve involves n_i training examples, out of which m_i are positives. The corresponding ROC segment has slope $l_i = m_i/(c(n_i - m_i))$, where c is the prior odds. Suppose first the ROC curve is convex: i.e., $i < j$ implies $l_i \geq l_j$. In that case, we can use the same formula as for categorical features to obtain a calibrated feature

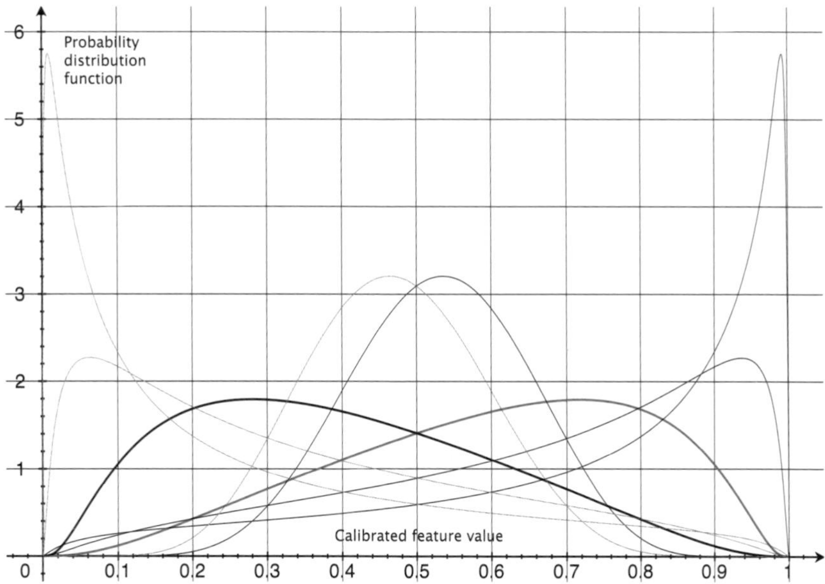

Figure 10.6. Per-class distributions of a logistically calibrated feature for different values of d', the distance between the uncalibrated class means in proportion to the feature's standard deviation. The red and blue curves depict the distributions for the positive and negative class for a feature whose means are one standard deviation apart ($d' = 1$). The other curves are for $d' \in \{0.5, 1.4, 1.8\}$.

value:

$$v_i^{\mathrm{c}} = \frac{m_i + 1}{m_i + 1 + c(n_i - m_i + 1)} \tag{10.1}$$

As before, this achieves both probability smoothing through Laplace correction and compensation for non-uniform class distributions. If the ROC curve is not convex, there exist $i < j$ such that $l_i < l_j$. Assuming we want to maintain the original feature ordering, we first construct the convex hull of the ROC curve. The effect of this is that we join adjacent segments in the ROC curve that are part of a concavity, until no concavities remain. We recalculate the segments and assign calibrated feature values as in Equation 10.1.

Example 10.10 (Isotonic feature calibration). The following table gives sample values of a weight feature in relation to a diabetes classification problem. Figure 10.7 shows the ROC curve and convex hull of the feature and the calibration map obtained by isotonic calibration.

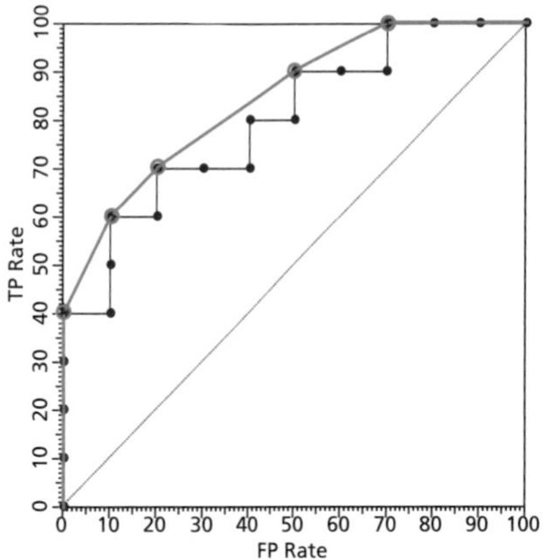

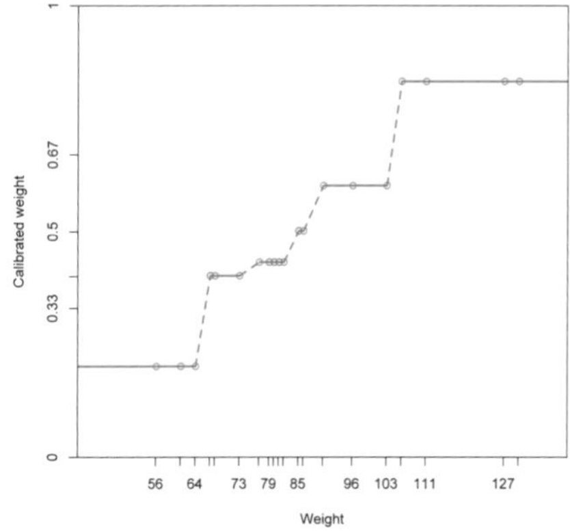

Figure 10.7. **(left)** ROC curve and convex hull of an uncalibrated feature. Calibrated feature values are obtained from the proportion of positives in each segment of the ROC convex hull. **(right)** The corresponding piecewise-constant calibration map, which maps the uncalibrated feature values on the x-axis to the calibrated feature values on the y-axis.

Weight	*Diabetes?*	*Calibrated weight*	*Weight*	*Diabetes?*	*Calibrated weight*
130	⊕	0.83	81	⊖	0.43
127	⊕	0.83	80	⊕	0.43
111	⊕	0.83	79	⊖	0.43
106	⊕	0.83	77	⊕	0.43
103	⊖	0.60	73	⊖	0.40
96	⊕	0.60	68	⊖	0.40
90	⊕	0.60	67	⊕	0.40
86	⊖	0.50	64	⊖	0.20
85	⊕	0.50	61	⊖	0.20
82	⊖	0.43	56	⊖	0.20

For example, a weight of 80 kilograms is calibrated to 0.43, meaning that three out of seven people in that weight interval have diabetes (after Laplace correction).

Example 10.11 gives a bivariate illustration. As is clearly visible, for quantitative features the process amounts to supervised discretisation of the feature values, which means that many points are mapped to the same point in calibrated space. This is different from logistic calibration, which is invertible.

Example 10.11 (Isotonic calibration of two features). Figure 10.8 shows the result of isotonic calibration on the same data as in Example 10.9, both in log-odds

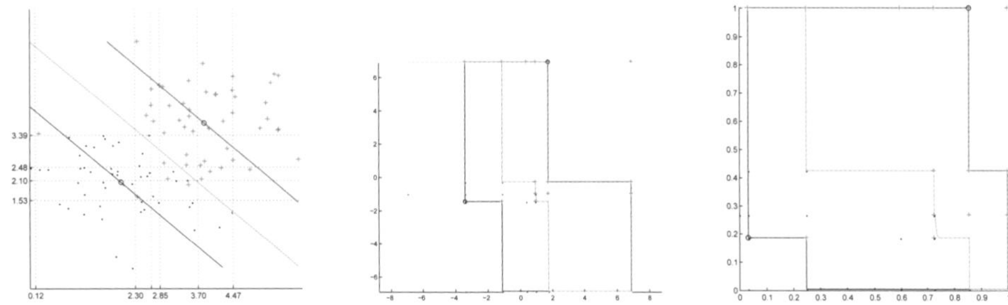

Figure 10.8. (left) The data from Figure 10.5, with grid lines indicating the discretisation obtained by isotonic feature calibration. **(middle)** Isotonically calibrated data in log-odds space. **(right)** Isotonically calibrated data in probability space.

space and in probability space. Because of the discrete nature of isotonic calibration, even the transformation to log-odds space is no longer linear: the basic linear classifier becomes a series of axis-parallel line segments. This is also true in the opposite direction: if we imagine a linear decision boundary in log-odds space or in probability space, this maps to a decision boundary following the dotted lines in the original feature space. Effectively, isotonic feature calibration has changed the linear grading model into a grouping model.

In summary, isotonic feature calibration performs the following steps.

1. Sort the training instances on feature value and construct the ROC curve. The sort order is chosen such that the ROC curve has AUC $\geq 1/2$.
2. Construct the convex hull of this curve, and count the number of positives m_i and the total number of instances n_i in each segment of the convex hull.
3. Discretise the feature according to the convex hull segments, and associate a calibrated feature value $v_i^{\mathrm{c}} = \frac{m_i+1}{m_i+1+c(n_i-m_i+1)}$ with each segment.
4. If an additive scale is required, use $v_i^{\mathrm{d}} = \ln \frac{v_i^{\mathrm{c}}}{1-v_i^{\mathrm{c}}} = \ln v_i^{\mathrm{c}} - \ln(1-v_i^{\mathrm{c}})$.

Incomplete features

At the end of this section on feature transformations we briefly consider what to do if we don't know a feature's value for some of the instances. We encountered this situation in Example 1.2 on p.26, where we discussed how to classify an e-mail if we didn't know whether it contained one of the vocabulary words or not. Probabilistic models handle this rather gracefully by taking a weighted average over all possible values of the feature:

$$P(Y|X) = \sum_z P(Y, Z = z|X) = \sum_z P(Y|X, Z = z)P(Z = z)$$

Here, Y is the target variable as usual, X stands for the features that are observed for the instance to be classified, while Z are the features that are unobserved at classification time. The distribution $P(Z)$ can be obtained from the trained model, at least for a generative model – if our model is discriminative we need to estimate $P(Z)$ separately.

Missing feature values at training time are trickier to handle. First of all, the very fact that a feature value is missing may be correlated with the target variable. For example, the range of medical tests carried out on a patient is likely to depend on their medical history. For such features it may be best to have a designated 'missing' value so that, for instance, a tree model can split on it. However, this would not work for, say, a linear model. In such cases we can complete the feature by 'filling in' the missing values, a process known as *imputation*. For instance, in a classification problem we can calculate the per-class means, medians or modes over the observed values of the feature and use this to impute the missing values. A somewhat more sophisticated method takes feature correlation into account by building a predictive model for each incomplete feature and uses that model to 'predict' the missing value. It is also possible to invoke the ☞*Expectation-Maximisation* algorithm (Section 9.4), which goes roughly as follows: assuming a multivariate model over all features, use the observed values for maximum-likelihood estimation of the model parameters, then derive expectations for the unobserved feature values and iterate.

10.3 Feature construction and selection

The previous section on feature transformation makes it clear that there is a lot of scope in machine learning to play around with the original features given in the data. We can take this one step further by constructing new features from several original features. A simple example of this can be used to improve the ☞*naive Bayes* classifier discussed in Section 9.2. Remember that in text classification applications we have a feature for every word in the vocabulary, which disregards not only the order of words but also their adjacency. This means that sentences such as 'they write about machine learning' and 'they are learning to write about a machine' will be virtually indistinguishable, even though the former is about machine learning and the latter is not. It may therefore sometimes be necessary to include phrases consisting of multiple words in the dictionary and treat them as single features. In the information retrieval literature, a multi-word phrase is referred to as an *n-gram* (unigram, bigram, trigram and so on).

Taking this idea one step further, we can construct a new feature from two Boolean or categorical features by forming their Cartesian product. For example, if we have one feature Shape with values Circle, Triangle and Square, and another feature Colour with values Red, Green and Blue, then their Cartesian product would be the feature (Shape, Colour) with values (Circle, Red), (Circle, Green), (Circle, Blue), (Triangle, Red), and so on. The effect that this would have depends on the model being trained. Constructing Cartesian product features for a naive Bayes classifier means that the two original features are no longer treated as independent, and so this reduces the strong bias that naive Bayes models have. This is not the case for tree models, which can already distinguish between all possible pairs of feature values. On the other hand, a newly introduced Cartesian product feature may incur a high information gain, so it can possibly affect the model learned.

There are many other ways of combining features. For instance, we can take arithmetic or polynomial combinations of quantitative features (we saw examples of this in the use of a ☞*kernel* in Example 1.9 on p.43 and Section 7.5). One attractive possibility is to first apply concept learning or subgroup discovery, and then use these concepts or subgroups as new Boolean features. For instance, in the dolphin domain we could first learn subgroups such as Length = [3, 5] ∧ Gills = no and use these as Boolean features in a subsequent tree model. Notice that this expands the expressive power of tree models through the use of negation: e.g., (Length = [3, 5] ∧ Gills = no) = false is equivalent to the disjunction Length ≠ [3, 5] ∨ Gills = yes, which is not directly expressible by a feature tree.

Once we have constructed new features it is often a good idea to select a suitable subset of them prior to learning. Not only will this speed up learning as fewer candidate features need to be considered, it also helps to guard against overfitting. There are two main approaches to feature selection. The *filter* approach scores features on a particular metric and the top-scoring features are selected. Many of the metrics we have seen so far can be used for feature scoring, including information gain, the χ^2 statistic, the correlation coefficient, to name just a few. An interesting variation is provided by the *Relief* feature selection method, which repeatedly samples a random instance x and finds its nearest hit h (instance of the same class) as well as its nearest miss m (instance of opposite class). The i-th feature's score is then decreased by $\mathrm{Dis}(x_i, h_i)^2$ and increased by $\mathrm{Dis}(x_i, m_i)^2$, where Dis is some distance measure (e.g., Euclidean distance for quantitative features, Hamming distance for categorical features). The intuition is that we want to move closer to the nearest hit while differentiating from the nearest miss.

One drawback of a simple filter approach is that no account is taken of redundancy between features. Imagine, for the sake of the argument, duplicating a promising feature in the data set: both copies score equally high and will be selected, whereas the second one provides no added value in the context of the first one. Secondly, feature filters do not detect dependencies between features as they are solely based on marginal distributions. For example, consider two Boolean features such that half the positives have the value true for both features and the other half have the value false for both, whereas all negatives have opposite values (again distributed half-half over the two possibilities). It follows that each feature in isolation has zero information gain and hence is unlikely to be selected by a feature filter, despite their combination being a perfect classifier. One could say that feature filters are good at picking out possible root features for a decision tree, but not necessarily good at selecting features that are useful further down the tree.

To detect features that are useful in the context of other features we need to evaluate sets of features; this usually goes under the name of *wrapper* approaches. The idea is that feature selection is 'wrapped' in a search procedure that usually involves training and evaluating a model with a candidate set of features. *Forward selection* methods start with an empty set of features and add features to the set one at a time, as long as they improve the performance of the model. *Backward elimination* starts with the full set of features and aims at improving performance by removing features one at a time. Since there are an exponential number of subsets of features it is usually not feasible to search all possible subsets, and most approaches apply a 'greedy' search algorithm that never reconsiders the choices it makes.

Matrix transformations and decompositions

We can also view feature construction and selection from a geometric perspective, assuming quantitative features. To this end we represent our data set as a matrix $\mathbf{X}$ with n data points in rows and d features in columns, which we want to transform into a new matrix $\mathbf{W}$ with n rows and r columns by means of matrix operations. To simplify matters a bit, we assume that $\mathbf{X}$ is zero-centred and that $\mathbf{W} = \mathbf{XT}$ for some d-by-r transformation matrix $\mathbf{T}$. For example, feature scaling corresponds to $\mathbf{T}$ being a d-by-d diagonal matrix; this can be combined with feature selection by removing some of $\mathbf{T}$'s columns. A rotation is achieved by $\mathbf{T}$ being orthogonal, i.e., $\mathbf{TT}^{\mathrm{T}} = \mathbf{I}$. Clearly, several such transformations can be combined (see also Background 1.2 on p.24).

One of the best-known algebraic feature construction methods is *principal component analysis* (*PCA*). Principal components are new features constructed as linear combinations of the given features. The first principal component is given by the direction of maximum variance in the data; the second principal component is the direction of maximum variance orthogonal to the first component, and so on. PCA can be explained in a number of different ways: here, we will derive it by means of the *singular value decomposition* (*SVD*). Any n-by-d matrix can be uniquely written as a product of three matrices with special properties:

$$\mathbf{X} = \mathbf{U\Sigma V}^{\mathrm{T}} \tag{10.2}$$

Here, $\mathbf{U}$ is an n-by-r matrix, $\mathbf{\Sigma}$ is an r-by-r matrix and $\mathbf{V}$ is an d-by-r matrix (for the moment we will assume $r = d < n$). Furthermore, $\mathbf{U}$ and $\mathbf{V}$ are orthogonal (hence rotations) and $\mathbf{\Sigma}$ is diagonal (hence a scaling). The columns of $\mathbf{U}$ and $\mathbf{V}$ are known as the left and right singular vectors, respectively; and the values on the diagonal of $\mathbf{\Sigma}$ are the corresponding singular values. It is customary to order the columns of $\mathbf{V}$ and $\mathbf{U}$ so that the singular values are decreasing from top-left to bottom-right.

Now, consider the n-by-r matrix $\mathbf{W} = \mathbf{U\Sigma}$, and notice that $\mathbf{XV} = \mathbf{U\Sigma V}^{\mathrm{T}}\mathbf{V} = \mathbf{U\Sigma} = \mathbf{W}$ by the orthogonality of $\mathbf{V}$. In other words, we can construct $\mathbf{W}$ from $\mathbf{X}$ by means of the transformation $\mathbf{V}$: this is the reformulation of $\mathbf{X}$ in terms of its principal components. The newly constructed features are found in $\mathbf{U\Sigma}$: the first row is the first principal component, the second row is the second principal component, and so on. These principal components have a geometric interpretation as the directions in which $\mathbf{X}$ has largest, second-largest, ... variance. Assuming the data is zero-centred, these directions can be brought out by a combination of rotation and scaling, which is exactly what PCA does.

We can also use SVD to rewrite the scatter matrix in a standard form:

$$\mathbf{S} = \mathbf{X}^{\mathrm{T}}\mathbf{X} = \left(\mathbf{U\Sigma V}^{\mathrm{T}}\right)^{\mathrm{T}}\left(\mathbf{U\Sigma V}^{\mathrm{T}}\right) = \left(\mathbf{V\Sigma U}^{\mathrm{T}}\right)\left(\mathbf{U\Sigma V}^{\mathrm{T}}\right) = \mathbf{V\Sigma}^2\mathbf{V}^{\mathrm{T}}$$

This is known as the *eigendecomposition* of the matrix $\mathbf{S}$: the columns of $\mathbf{V}$ are the eigenvectors of $\mathbf{S}$, and the elements on the diagonal of $\mathbf{\Sigma}^2$ – which is itself a diagonal matrix – are the eigenvalues. The right singular vectors of the data matrix $\mathbf{X}$ are the eigenvectors of the scatter matrix $\mathbf{S} = \mathbf{X}^{\mathrm{T}}\mathbf{X}$, and the singular values of $\mathbf{X}$ are the square root of the eigenvalues of $\mathbf{S}$. We can derive a similar expression for the Gram matrix $\mathbf{G} = \mathbf{XX}^{\mathrm{T}} = \mathbf{U\Sigma}^2\mathbf{U}^{\mathrm{T}}$, from which we see that the eigenvectors of the Gram matrix are the left singular vectors of $\mathbf{X}$. This demonstrates that in order to perform principal components analysis it is sufficient to perform an eigendecomposition of the scatter or Gram matrices, rather than a full singular value decomposition.

We have seen something resembling SVD in Section 1.1, where we considered the following matrix product:

$$\begin{pmatrix} 1 & 0 & 1 & 0 \\ 0 & 2 & 2 & 2 \\ 0 & 0 & 0 & 1 \\ 1 & 2 & 3 & 2 \\ 1 & 0 & 1 & 1 \\ 0 & 2 & 2 & 3 \end{pmatrix} = \begin{pmatrix} 1 & 0 & 0 \\ 0 & 1 & 0 \\ 0 & 0 & 1 \\ 1 & 1 & 0 \\ 1 & 0 & 1 \\ 0 & 1 & 1 \end{pmatrix} \times \begin{pmatrix} 1 & 0 & 0 \\ 0 & 2 & 0 \\ 0 & 0 & 1 \end{pmatrix} \times \begin{pmatrix} 1 & 0 & 1 & 0 \\ 0 & 1 & 1 & 1 \\ 0 & 0 & 0 & 1 \end{pmatrix}$$

The matrix on the left expresses people's preferences for films (in columns). The right-hand side decomposes or factorises this into film genres: the first matrix quantifies people's appreciation of genres; the last matrix associates films with genres; and the middle matrix tells us the weight of each genre in determining preferences. This is not actually the decomposition computed by SVD, because the left and right matrices in the product are not orthogonal. However, one could argue that this factorisation better captures the data, because the person-by-genre and the film-by-genre matrices are Boolean and sparse, which they won't be in the SVD. The downside is that adding integer or Boolean constraints makes the decomposition problem non-convex (there are local optima) and computationally harder. Matrix decomposition with additional constraints is a very active research area.

These matrix decomposition techniques are often used for dimensionality reduction. The *rank* of an n-by-d matrix is d (assuming $d < n$ and no columns are linear combinations of other columns). The above decompositions are full-rank because $r = d$, and hence the data matrix is reconstructed exactly. A low-rank approximation of a matrix is a factorisation where r is chosen as small as possible while still sufficiently approximating the original matrix. The reconstruction error is usually measured as the sum of the squared differences of the entries in $\mathbf{X}$ and the corresponding entries in $\mathbf{U\Sigma V}^{\mathrm{T}}$. It can be shown that a truncated singular value decomposition with $r < d$ results in the lowest reconstruction error in this sense among all decompositions of rank up to r. Truncated SVD and PCA are popular ways to combine feature construction and feature selection for quantitative features.

One interesting aspect of matrix decompositions such as SVD is that they expose a previously hidden variable in the data. This can be seen as follows. Consider a decomposition or approximation $\mathbf{U\Sigma V}^{\mathrm{T}}$ with diagonal $\mathbf{\Sigma}$ but not necessarily orthogonal $\mathbf{U}$ and $\mathbf{V}$, and denote the i-the column of $\mathbf{U}$ and $\mathbf{V}$ as $\mathbf{U}_{\cdot i}$ (an n-vector) and $\mathbf{V}_{\cdot i}$ (a d-vector). Then $\mathbf{U}_{\cdot i}\sigma_i(\mathbf{V}_{\cdot i})^{\mathrm{T}}$ is an outer product that produces an n-by-d matrix with rank 1 (σ_i denotes the i-th diagonal value of $\mathbf{\Sigma}$). A rank-1 matrix is such that every column is obtained from a single basis vector multiplied by a scalar (and the same for rows). Assuming $\mathbf{U}$ and $\mathbf{V}$ have rank r these basis vectors are independent and so summing up these rank-1 matrices for all i produces the original matrix:

$$\mathbf{U\Sigma V}^{\mathrm{T}} = \sum_{i=1}^{r} \mathbf{U}_{\cdot i}\sigma_i(\mathbf{V}_{\cdot i})^{\mathrm{T}}$$

For example, the film rating matrix can be written as follows:

$$\begin{pmatrix} 1 & 0 & 1 & 0 \\ 0 & 2 & 2 & 2 \\ 0 & 0 & 0 & 1 \\ 1 & 2 & 3 & 2 \\ 1 & 0 & 1 & 1 \\ 0 & 2 & 2 & 3 \end{pmatrix} = \begin{pmatrix} 1 & 0 & 1 & 0 \\ 0 & 0 & 0 & 0 \\ 0 & 0 & 0 & 0 \\ 1 & 0 & 1 & 0 \\ 1 & 0 & 1 & 0 \\ 0 & 0 & 0 & 0 \end{pmatrix} + \begin{pmatrix} 0 & 0 & 0 & 0 \\ 0 & 2 & 2 & 2 \\ 0 & 0 & 0 & 0 \\ 0 & 2 & 2 & 2 \\ 0 & 0 & 0 & 0 \\ 0 & 2 & 2 & 2 \end{pmatrix} + \begin{pmatrix} 0 & 0 & 0 & 0 \\ 0 & 0 & 0 & 0 \\ 0 & 0 & 0 & 1 \\ 0 & 0 & 0 & 0 \\ 0 & 0 & 0 & 1 \\ 0 & 0 & 0 & 1 \end{pmatrix}$$

The matrices on the right can be interpreted as rating models conditioned on genre.

Exposing hidden variables in the data is one of the main applications of matrix decomposition methods. For example, in information retrieval PCA is known under the name *latent semantic indexing* (*LSA*) ('latent' is synonymous with 'hidden'). Instead of film genres, LSA uncovers document topics by decomposing matrices containing word counts per document, under the assumption that the word counts per topic are independent and can thus simply be added up.[3] The other main application of matrix factorisation is *completion* of missing entries in a matrix, the idea being that if we approximate the observed entries in the matrix as closely as possible using a low-rank decomposition, this allows us to infer the missing entries.

10.4 Features: Summary and further reading

In this chapter we have given features some long-overdue attention. Features are the telescopes through which we observe the data universe and therefore an important unifying force in machine learning. Features are related to measurements in science, but there is no widespread consensus on how to formalise and categorise different measurements – I have taken inspiration from Stevens' scales of measurements (Stevens, 1946), but otherwise aimed to stay close to current practice in machine learning.

☞ The main kinds of feature distinguished in Section 10.1 are categorical, ordinal and quantitative features. The latter are expressed on a quantitative scale and admit the calculation of the widest range of statistics of tendency (mean, median, mode; see (von Hippel, 2005) for a discussion of rules of thumb regarding these), dispersion (variance and standard deviation, range, interquartile range) and shape (skewness and kurtosis). In machine learning quantitative features are often referred to as continuous features, but I think this term is inappropriate as it wrongly suggests that their defining feature is somehow an unlimited precision. It is important to realise that quantitative features do not necessarily have an additive scale: e.g., quantitative features expressing a probability are expressed on a multiplicative scale, and the use of Euclidean distance, say, would be inappropriate for non-additive features. Ordinal features have order but not scale; and categorical features (also called nominal or discrete) have neither order nor scale.

☞ Structured features are first-order logical statements that refer to parts of objects by means of local variables and use some kind of aggregation, such as existential quantification or counting, to extract a property of the main object. Constructing first-order features prior to learning is often referred to as propositionalisation;

[3]Other models are possible: e.g., in Boolean matrix decomposition the matrix product is changed to a Boolean product in which integer addition is replaced by Boolean disjunction (so that $1+1=1$), with the effect that additional topics do not provide additional explanatory power for the occurrence of a word in a document.

Kramer *et al.* (2000) and Lachiche (2010) give surveys, and an experimental comparison of different approaches is carried out by Krogel *et al.* (2003).

☞ In Section 10.2 we looked at a number of feature transformations. Discretisation and thresholding are the best-known of these, turning a quantitative feature into a categorical or a Boolean one. One of the most effective discretisation methods is the recursive partitioning algorithm using information gain to find the thresholds and a stopping criterion derived from the minimum description length principle proposed by Fayyad and Irani (1993). Other overviews and proposals are given by Boullé (2004, 2006). The agglomerative merging approach using χ^2 was proposed by Kerber (1992).

☞ We have seen that in a two-class setting, supervised discretisation can be visualised by means of coverage curves. This then naturally leads to the idea of using these coverage curves and their convex hull to calibrate rather than just discretise the features. After all, ordinal and quantitative features are univariate rankers and scoring classifiers and thus the same classifier calibration methods can be applied, in particular logistic and isotonic calibration as discussed in Section 7.4. The calibrated features live in probability space, but we might prefer to work with log-odds space instead as this is additive rather than multiplicative. Fitting data to a fixed linear decision boundary in calibrated log-odds space is closely related to training a naive Bayes model. Isotonic calibration leads to piecewise axis-parallel decision boundaries; owing to the discretising nature of isotonic calibration this can be understood as the constructing of a grouping model, even if the original model in the uncalibrated space was a grading model.

☞ Section 10.3 was devoted to feature construction and selection. Early approaches to feature construction and constructive induction were proposed by Ragavan and Rendell (1993); Donoho and Rendell (1995). The instance-based Relief feature selection method is due to Kira and Rendell (1992) and extended by Robnik-Sikonja and Kononenko (2003). The distinction between filter approaches to feature selection – which evaluate features on their individual merits – and wrapper approaches, which evaluate sets of features, is originally due to Kohavi and John (1997). Hall (1999) proposes a filter approach called correlation-based feature selection that aims at combining the best of both worlds. Guyon and Elisseeff (2003) give an excellent introduction to feature selection.

☞ Finally, we looked at feature construction and selection from a linear algebra perspective. Matrix decomposition and factorisation is an actively researched technique that was instrumental in winning a recent film recommendation challenge worth $1 million (Koren *et al.*, 2009). Decomposition techniques employing additional constraints include non-negative matrix decomposition (Lee *et al.*, 1999).

Boolean matrix decomposition is studied by Miettinen (2009). Mahoney and Drineas (2009) describe a matrix decomposition technique that uses actual columns and rows of the data matrix to preserve sparsity (unlike SVD which produces dense matrices even if the original matrix is sparse). Latent semantic indexing and a probabilistic extension is described by Hofmann (1999). Ding and He (2004) discuss the relationship between K-means clustering and principal component analysis.

❦

CHAPTER *11*

Model ensembles

TWO HEADS ARE BETTER THAN ONE – a well-known proverb suggesting that two minds working together can often achieve better results. If we read 'features' for 'heads' then this is certainly true in machine learning, as we have seen in the preceding chapters. But we can often further improve things by combining not just features but whole models, as will be demonstrated in this chapter. Combinations of models are generally known as *model ensembles*. They are among the most powerful techniques in machine learning, often outperforming other methods. This comes at the cost of increased algorithmic and model complexity.

The topic of model combination has a rich and diverse history, to which we can only partly do justice in this short chapter. The main motivations came from computational learning theory on the one hand, and statistics on the other. It is a well-known statistical intuition that averaging measurements can lead to a more stable and reliable estimate because we reduce the influence of random fluctuations in single measurements. So if we were to build an ensemble of slightly different models from the same training data, we might be able to similarly reduce the influence of random fluctuations in single models. The key question here is how to achieve diversity between these different models. As we shall see, this can often be achieved by training models on random subsets of the data, and even by constructing them from random subsets of the available features.

The motivation from computational learning theory went along the following lines. As we have seen in Section 4.4, learnability of hypothesis languages is studied in the context of a learning model, which determines what we mean by learnability. PAC-learnability requires that a hypothesis be approximately correct most of the time. An alternative learning model called *weak learnability* requires only that a hypothesis is learned that is slightly better than chance. While it appears obvious that PAC-learnability is stricter than weak learnability, it turns out that the two learning models are in fact equivalent: a hypothesis language is PAC-learnable if and only if it is weakly learnable. This was proved constructively by means of an iterative algorithm that repeatedly constructs a hypothesis aimed at correcting the mistakes of the previous hypothesis, thus 'boosting' it. The final model combined the hypotheses learned in each iteration, and therefore establishes an ensemble.

In essence, ensemble methods in machine learning have the following two things in common:

- ☞ they construct multiple, diverse predictive models from adapted versions of the training data (most often reweighted or resampled);
- ☞ they combine the predictions of these models in some way, often by simple averaging or voting (possibly weighted).

It should, however, also be stressed that these commonalities span a very large and diverse space, and that we should correspondingly expect some methods to be practically very different even though superficially similar. For example, it makes a big difference whether the way in which training data is adapted for the next iteration takes the predictions of the previous models into account or not. We will explore this space by means of the two best-known ensemble methods: bagging in Section 11.1 and boosting in Section 11.2. A short discussion of these and related ensemble methods then follows in Section 11.3, before we conclude the chapter in the usual way with a summary and pointers for further reading.

11.1 Bagging and random forests

Bagging, short for 'bootstrap aggregating', is a simple but highly effective ensemble method that creates diverse models on different random samples of the original data set. These samples are taken uniformly with replacement and are known as *bootstrap samples*. Because samples are taken with replacement the bootstrap sample will in general contain duplicates, and hence some of the original data points will be missing even if the bootstrap sample is of the same size as the original data set. This is exactly what we want, as differences between the bootstrap samples will create diversity among the models in the ensemble. To get an idea of how different bootstrap samples

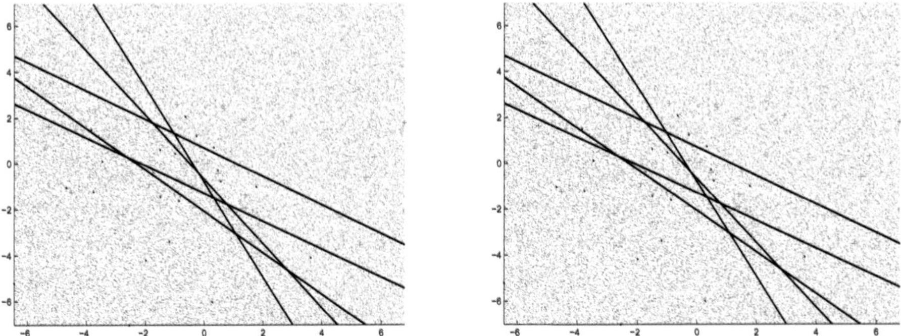

Figure 11.1. (left) An ensemble of five basic linear classifiers built from bootstrap samples with bagging. The decision rule is majority vote, leading to a piecewise linear decision boundary. **(right)** If we turn the votes into probabilities, we see the ensemble is effectively a grouping model: each instance space segment obtains a slightly different probability.

might be, we can calculate the probability that a particular data point is not selected for a bootstrap sample of size n as $(1-1/n)^n$, which for $n = 5$ is about one-third and has limit $1/e = 0.368$ for $n \to \infty$. This means that each bootstrap sample is likely to leave out about a third of the data points.

Algorithm 11.1 gives the basic bagging algorithm, which returns the ensemble as a set of models. We can choose to combine the predictions from the different models by voting – the class predicted by the majority of models wins – or by averaging, which is more appropriate if the base classifiers output scores or probabilities. An illustration is given in Figure 11.1. I trained five basic linear classifiers on bootstrap samples from 20 positive and 20 negative examples. We can clearly see the diversity of the five linear classifiers, which is helped by the fact that the data set is quite small. The

---

Algorithm 11.1: Bagging$(D, T, \mathscr{A})$ – train an ensemble of models from bootstrap samples.

Input : data set D; ensemble size T; learning algorithm $\mathscr{A}$.
Output : ensemble of models whose predictions are to be combined by voting or averaging.

for $t = 1$ to T **do**
  build a bootstrap sample D_t from D by sampling $|D|$ data points with replacement;
  run $\mathscr{A}$ on D_t to produce a model M_t;
end
return $\{M_t | 1 \le t \le T\}$

---

figure demonstrates the difference between combining predictions through voting (Figure 11.1 (left)) and creating a probabilistic classifier by averaging (Figure 11.1 (right)). With voting we see that bagging creates a piecewise linear decision boundary, something that is impossible with a single linear classifier. If we transform the votes from each model into probability estimates, we see that the different decision boundaries partition the instance space into segments that can potentially each receive a different score.

Bagging is particularly useful in combination with tree models, which are quite sensitive to variations in the training data. When applied to tree models, bagging is often combined with another idea: to build each tree from a different random subset of the features, a process also referred to as *subspace sampling*. This encourages the diversity in the ensemble even more, and has the additional advantage that the training time of each tree is reduced. The resulting ensemble method is called *random forests*, and the algorithm is given in Algorithm 11.2.

Since a decision tree is a grouping model whose leaves partition the instance space, so is a random forest: its corresponding instance space partition is essentially the intersection of the partitions of the individual trees in the ensemble. While the random forest partition is therefore finer than most tree partitions, it can in principle be mapped back to a single tree model (because intersection corresponds to combining the branches of two different trees). This is different from bagging linear classifiers, where the ensemble has a decision boundary that can't be learned by a single base classifier. One could say, therefore, that the random forest algorithm implements an alternative training algorithm for tree models.

Algorithm 11.2: RandomForest(D, T, d) – train an ensemble of tree models from bootstrap samples and random subspaces.

Input : data set D; ensemble size T; subspace dimension d.
Output : ensemble of tree models whose predictions are to be combined by voting or averaging.

for $t = 1$ to T **do**
    build a bootstrap sample D_t from D by sampling $|D|$ data points with replacement;
    select d features at random and reduce dimensionality of D_t accordingly;
    train a tree model M_t on D_t without pruning;
end
return $\{M_t | 1 \le t \le T\}$

11.2 Boosting

Boosting is an ensemble technique that is superficially similar to bagging, but uses a more sophisticated technique than bootstrap sampling to create diverse training sets. The basic idea is simple and appealing. Suppose we train a linear classifier on a data set and find that its training error rate is ϵ. We want to add another classifier to the ensemble that does better on the misclassifications of the first classifier. One way to do that is to duplicate the misclassified instances: if our base model is the basic linear classifier, this will shift the class means towards the duplicated instances. A better way to achieve the same thing is to give the misclassified instances a higher weight, and to modify the classifier to take these weights into account (e.g., the basic linear classifier can calculate the class means as a weighted average).

But how much should the weights change? The idea is that half of the total weight is assigned to the misclassified examples, and the other half to the rest. Since we started with uniform weights that sum to 1, the current weight assigned to the misclassified examples is exactly the error rate ϵ, so we multiply their weights by $1/2\epsilon$. Assuming $\epsilon < 0.5$ this is an increase in weight as desired. The weights of the correctly classified examples get multiplied by $1/2(1-\epsilon)$, so the adjusted weights again sum to 1. In the next round we do exactly the same, except we take the non-uniform weights into account when evaluating the error rate.

Example 11.1 (Weight updates in boosting). Suppose a linear classifier achieves performance as in the contingency table on the left. The error rate is $\epsilon = (9+16)/100 = 0.25$. The weight update for the misclassified examples is a factor $1/2\epsilon = 2$ and for the correctly classified examples $1/2(1-\epsilon) = 2/3$.

	Predicted ⊕	*Predicted* ⊖	
Actual ⊕	**24**	**16**	40
Actual ⊖	**9**	**51**	60
	33	67	100

	⊕	⊖	
⊕	**16**	**32**	48
⊖	**18**	**34**	52
	34	66	100

Taking these updated weights into account leads to the contingency table on the right, which has a (weighted) error rate of 0.5.

We need one more ingredient in our boosting algorithm and that is a confidence factor α for each model in the ensemble, which we will use to form an ensemble prediction that is a weighted average of each individual model. Clearly we want α to increase with decreasing ϵ: a common choice is

$$\alpha_t = \frac{1}{2}\ln\frac{1-\epsilon_t}{\epsilon_t} = \ln\sqrt{\frac{1-\epsilon_t}{\epsilon_t}} \tag{11.1}$$

which we will justify in a moment. The basic boosting algorithm is given in Algorithm 11.3. Figure 11.2 (left) illustrates how a boosted ensemble of five basic linear classifiers can achieve zero training error. It is clear that the resulting decision boundary is much more complex than could be achieved by a single basic linear classifier. In contrast, a bagged ensemble of basic linear classifiers has learned five very similar decision boundaries, the reason being that on this data set the bootstrap samples are all very similar.

I will now justify the particular choice for α_t in Equation 11.1. First, I will show that the two weight updates for the misclassified instances and the correctly classified instances can be written as reciprocal terms δ_t and $1/\delta_t$ normalised by some term Z_t:

$$\frac{1}{2\epsilon_t} = \frac{\delta_t}{Z_t} \qquad\qquad \frac{1}{2(1-\epsilon_t)} = \frac{1/\delta_t}{Z_t}$$

The second expression gives $\delta_t = 2(1-\epsilon_t)/Z_t$; substituting this back into the first expression yields

$$Z_t = 2\sqrt{\epsilon_t(1-\epsilon_t)} \qquad\qquad \delta_t = \sqrt{\frac{1-\epsilon_t}{\epsilon_t}} = \exp(\alpha_t) \tag{11.2}$$

Algorithm 11.3: Boosting($D, T, \mathscr{A}$) – train an ensemble of binary classifiers from reweighted training sets.

Input : data set D; ensemble size T; learning algorithm $\mathscr{A}$.
Output : weighted ensemble of models.

$w_{1i} \leftarrow 1/|D|$ for all $x_i \in D$; // start with uniform weights
for $t = 1$ to T **do**
  run $\mathscr{A}$ on D with weights w_{ti} to produce a model M_t;
  calculate weighted error ϵ_t;
  if $\epsilon_t \geq 1/2$ **then**
    set $T \leftarrow t-1$ and break
  end
  $\alpha_t \leftarrow \frac{1}{2}\ln\frac{1-\epsilon_t}{\epsilon_t}$; // confidence for this model
  $w_{(t+1)i} \leftarrow \frac{w_{ti}}{2\epsilon_t}$ for misclassified instances $x_i \in D$; // increase weight
  $w_{(t+1)j} \leftarrow \frac{w_{tj}}{2(1-\epsilon_t)}$ for correctly classified instances $x_j \in D$; // decrease weight
end
return $M(x) = \sum_{t=1}^{T} \alpha_t M_t(x)$

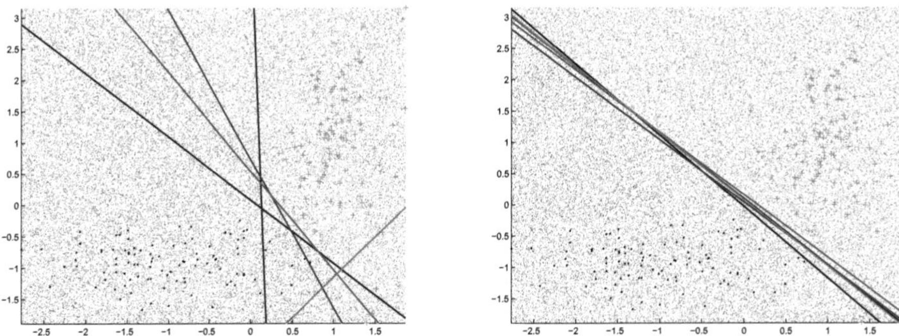

Figure 11.2. (left) An ensemble of five boosted basic linear classifiers with majority vote. The linear classifiers were learned from blue to red; none of them achieves zero training error, but the ensemble does. **(right)** Applying bagging results in a much more homogeneous ensemble, indicating that there is little diversity in the bootstrap samples.

So the weight update for misclassified instances is $\exp(\alpha_t)/Z_t$ and for correctly classified instances $\exp(-\alpha_t)/Z_t$. Using the fact that $y_i M_t(x_i) = +1$ for instances correctly classified by model M_t and -1 otherwise, we can write the weight update as

$$w_{(t+1)i} = w_{ti}\frac{\exp\left(-\alpha_t y_i M_t(x_i)\right)}{Z_t}$$

which is the expression commonly found in the literature.

Let us now step back and pretend that we haven't yet decided what α_t should be in each round. Since the weight updates are multiplicative, we have

$$w_{(T+1)i} = w_{1i}\prod_{t=1}^{T}\frac{\exp\left(-\alpha_t y_i M_t(x_i)\right)}{Z_t} = \frac{1}{|D|}\frac{\exp\left(-y_i M(x_i)\right)}{\prod_{t=1}^{T} Z_t}$$

where $M(x_i) = \sum_{t=1}^{T}\alpha_t M_t(x_i)$ is the model represented by the boosted ensemble. The weights always add up to 1 over the instance space, and so

$$\prod_{t=1}^{T} Z_t = \frac{1}{|D|}\sum_{i=1}^{|D|}\exp\left(-y_i M(x_i)\right)$$

Notice that $\exp\left(-y_i M(x_i)\right)$ is always positive and at least 1 if $-y_i M(x_i)$ is positive, which happens if x_i is misclassified by the ensemble (i.e., $\text{sign}(M(x_i) \neq y_i)$. So the right-hand side of this expression is at least equal to the training error of the boosted ensemble, and $\prod_{t=1}^{T} Z_t$ is an upper bound on that training error. A simple heuristic would therefore be to greedily minimise

$$Z_t = \sum_{i=1}^{|D|} w_{ti}\exp\left(-\alpha_t y_i M_t(x_i)\right) \tag{11.3}$$

in each boosting round. Now, the sum of the weights of instances incorrectly classified by M_t is ϵ_t, and so

$$Z_t = \epsilon_t \exp(\alpha_t) + (1 - \epsilon_t)\exp(-\alpha_t)$$

Taking the derivative with respect to α_t, setting it to zero and solving for α_t yields α_t as given in Equation 11.1 and Z_t as given in Equation 11.2.

Notice that Equation 11.3 demonstrates that the loss function minimised by boosting is ☞*exponential loss* $\exp(-y\hat{s}(x))$ which we already encountered in Figure 2.6 on p.63. Notice, furthermore, that minimising Z_t means minimising $2\sqrt{\epsilon_t(1-\epsilon_t)}$ according to Equation 11.2. You may recognise this as the ☞$\sqrt{\text{Gini}}$ *impurity measure* we investigated in Chapter 5. There, we saw that this splitting criterion is insensitive to changes in the class distribution (see Figure 5.7 on p.146). Here, it arises essentially because of the way weight updates are implemented in the boosting algorithm.

Boosted rule learning

An interesting variant of boosting arises when our base models are partial classifiers that sometimes abstain from making a prediction. For example, suppose that our base classifiers are conjunctive rules whose head is fixed to predicting the positive class. An individual rule therefore either predicts the positive class for those instances it covers, or otherwise abstains from making a prediction. We can use boosting to learn an ensemble of such rules that takes a weighted vote among its members.

We need to make some small adjustments to the boosting equations, as follows. Notice that ϵ_t is the weighted error of the t-th base classifier. Since our rules always predict positive for covered instances, these errors only concern covered negatives, which we will indicate by $\epsilon_t^{\ominus}$. Similarly, we indicate the weighted sum of covered positives as $\epsilon_t^{\oplus}$, which will play the role of $1-\epsilon_t$. However, with abstaining rules there is a third component, indicated as ϵ_t^0, which is the weighted sum of instances which the rule doesn't cover ($\epsilon_t^0 + \epsilon_t^{\oplus} + \epsilon_t^{\ominus} = 1$). We then have

$$Z_t = \epsilon_t^0 + \epsilon_t^{\ominus}\exp(\alpha_t) + \epsilon_t^{\oplus}\exp(-\alpha_t)$$

The value of α_t which maximises this is

$$\alpha_t = \frac{1}{2}\ln\frac{\epsilon_t^{\oplus}}{\epsilon_t^{\ominus}} = \ln\sqrt{\frac{\epsilon_t^{\oplus}}{\epsilon_t^{\ominus}}} \tag{11.4}$$

which gives

$$Z_t = \epsilon_t^0 + 2\sqrt{\epsilon_t^{\oplus}\epsilon_t^{\ominus}} = 1 - \epsilon_t^{\oplus} - \epsilon_t^{\ominus} + 2\sqrt{\epsilon_t^{\oplus}\epsilon_t^{\ominus}} = 1 - \left(\sqrt{\epsilon_t^{\oplus}} - \sqrt{\epsilon_t^{\ominus}}\right)^2$$

This means that in each boosting round we construct a rule that maximises $\left|\sqrt{\epsilon_t^{\oplus}} - \sqrt{\epsilon_t^{\ominus}}\right|$, and set its confidence factor to α_t as in Equation 11.4. In order to obtain a prediction from the ensemble, we add up the confidence factors of all rules covering it. Note that these confidence factors are negative if $\epsilon_t^{\oplus} < \epsilon_t^{\ominus}$, which indicates that the rule correlates with the negative class; this is not a problem as such, but can be avoided by changing the objective function for individual rules to $\sqrt{\epsilon_t^{\oplus}} - \sqrt{\epsilon_t^{\ominus}}$.

The weight updates after each iteration of boosting are the same as previously, except that the weights of examples not covered by the rule do not change. Boosted rule learning is therefore similar to the ☞*weighted covering* (Algorithm 6.5 on p.182) algorithm for subgroup discovery. The difference is that there we wanted to promote rule overlap without reference to the class and hence decrease the weight of all covered examples, whereas here we decrease the weight of covered positives and increase the weight of covered negatives.

11.3 Mapping the ensemble landscape

Now that we have looked at two often-used ensemble methods in somewhat more detail, we consider how their differences in performance might be explained, before turning attention to some of the many other ensemble methods in the literature.

Bias, variance and margins

Ensemble methods are a good vehicle to further understand the ☞*bias–variance dilemma* we discussed in the context of regression in Section 3.2. Broadly speaking, there are three reasons why a model may misclassify a test instance. First, it may simply be unavoidable in the given feature space if instances from different classes are described by the same feature vectors. In a probabilistic context this happens when the per-class distributions $P(X|Y)$ overlap, so that the same instance has non-zero likelihoods for several classes. In such a situation, the best we can hope to do is to approximate the target concept.

The second reason for classification errors is that the model lacks expressivity to exactly represent the target concept. For example, if the data is not linearly separable then even the best linear classifier will make mistakes. This is the bias of a classifier, and it is inversely related to its expressivity. Although there is no generally agreed way to measure expressivity or bias of a classifier[1] it is intuitively clear that, say, a hyperbolic decision boundary has lower bias than a linear one. It is also clear that tree models have the lowest possible bias, as their leaves can be made arbitrarily small to cover singleton instances.

It may seem that low-bias models are generally preferable. However, a practical rule of thumb in machine learning is that *low-bias models tend to have high variance, and*

[1] While squared loss nicely decomposes into squared bias and variance as shown in Equation 3.2 on p.93, loss functions used in classification such as 0–1 loss can be decomposed in several ways.

vice versa. Variance is the third source of classification errors. A model has high variance if its decision boundary is highly dependent on the training data. For example, the nearest-neighbour classifier's instance space segments are determined by a single training point, so if I move a training point in a segment bordering on the decision boundary, that boundary will change. Tree models have high variance for a different reason: if I change the training data sufficiently for another feature to be selected at the root of the tree, then the rest of the tree is likely to be different as well. An example of a low-variance model is the basic linear classifier, because it averages over all the points in a class.

Now look back at Figure 11.1 on p.332. The bagged ensemble of basic linear classifiers has learned a piecewise linear decision boundary that exceeds the expressivity of a single linear classifier. This illustrates that bagging, like any ensemble method, is capable of reducing the bias of a high-bias base model such as a linear classifier. However, if we compare this with boosting in Figure 11.2 on p.336, we see that the reduction in bias resulting from bagging is much smaller than that of boosting. In fact, *bagging is predominantly a variance-reduction technique, while boosting is primarily a bias-reduction technique*. This explains why bagging is often used in combination with high-variance models such as tree models (☞*random forests* in Algorithm 11.2), whereas boosting is typically used with high-bias models such as linear classifiers or univariate decision trees (also called *decision stumps*).

Another way to understand boosting is in terms of margins. Intuitively, the margin is the signed distance from the decision boundary, with the sign indicating whether we are on the correct or the wrong side. It has been observed in experiments that boosting is effective in increasing the margins of examples, even if they are already on the correct side of the decision boundary. The effect is that boosting may continue to improve performance on the test set even after the training error has been reduced to zero. Given that boosting was originally conceived in a PAC-learning framework, which is not specifically aimed at increasing margins, this was a surprising result.

Other ensemble methods

There are many other ensemble methods beyond bagging and boosting. The main variation lies in the way predictions of the base models are combined. Notice that this could itself be defined as a learning problem: given the predictions of some base classifiers as features, learn a *meta-model* that best combines their predictions. For example, in boosting we could learn the weights α_t rather than deriving them from each base model's error rate. Learning a linear meta-model is known as *stacking*. Several variations on this theme exist: e.g., decision trees have been used as the meta-model.

It is also possible to combine different base models into a heterogeneous ensemble: in this way the base model diversity derives from the fact that base models are trained by different learning algorithms, and so they can all use the same training set. Some of these base models might employ different settings of a parameter: for example, the ensemble might include several support vector machines with different values of the complexity parameter which regulates the extent to which margin errors are tolerated.

Generally speaking, then, model ensembles consist of a set of base models and a meta-model that is trained to decide how base model predictions should be combined. Implicitly, training a meta-model involves an assessment of the quality of each base model: for instanceif the meta-model is linear as in stacking, a weight close to zero means that the corresponding base classifier does not contribute much to the ensemble. It is even conceivable that a base classifier obtains a negative weight, meaning that in the context of the other base models its predictions are best inverted. We could go one step further and try to *predict* how well a base model is expected to perform, even before we train it! By formulating this as a learning problem at the meta-level, we arrive at the field of meta-learning.

Meta-learning

Meta-learning first involves training a variety of models on a large collection of data sets. The aim is then to construct a model that can help us answer questions such as the following:

- ☞ In which situations is a decision tree likely to outperform a support vector machine?
- ☞ When can a linear classifier be expected to perform poorly?
- ☞ Can the data be used to give suggestions for setting particular parameters?

The key question in meta-learning is how to design the features on which the meta-model is built. These features should combine data set characteristics and relevant aspects of the trained model. Data set characteristics should go much further than simply listing the number and kind of features and the number of instances, as it is unlikely that anything can be predicted about a model's performance from just that information. For example, we can try to assess the noise level of a data set by measuring the size of a trained decision tree before and after pruning. Training simple models such as decision stumps on a data set and measuring their performance also gives useful information.

In Background 1.1 on p.20 we referred to the no free lunch theorem, which states that no learning algorithm can outperform any other learning algorithm over the set of all possible learning problems. As a corollary, we have that meta-learning over all possible learning problems is futile: if it wasn't, we could build a single hybrid model that uses a meta-model to tell us which base model would achieve better than random performance on a particular data set. It follows that we can only hope to achieve useful meta-learning over non-uniform distributions of learning problems.

11.4 Model ensembles: Summary and further reading

In this short chapter we have discussed some of the fundamental ideas underlying ensemble methods. What all ensemble methods have in common is that they construct several base models from adapted versions of the training data, on top of which some technique is employed to combine the predictions or scores from the base models into a single prediction of the ensemble. We focused on bagging and boosting as two of the most commonly used ensemble methods. A good introduction to model ensembles is given by Brown (2010). The standard reference on classifier combination is Kuncheva (2004) and a more recent overview is given by Zhou (2012).

☞ In Section 11.1 we discussed bagging and random forests. Bagging trains diverse models from samples of the training data, and was introduced by Breiman (1996*a*). Random forests, usually attributed to Breiman (2001), combine bagged decision trees with random subspaces; similar ideas were developed by Ho (1995) and Amit and Geman (1997). These techniques are particularly useful to reduce the variance of low-bias models such as tree models.

☞ Boosting was discussed in Section 11.2. The key idea is to train diverse models by increasing the weight of previously misclassified examples. This helps to reduce the bias of otherwise stable learners such as linear classifiers or decision stumps. An accessible overview is given by Schapire (2003). Kearns and Valiant (1989, 1994) posed the question whether a weak learning algorithm that performs just slightly better than random guessing can be boosted into an arbitrarily accurate strong learning algorithm. Schapire (1990) introduced a theoretical form of boosting to show the equivalence of weak and strong learnability. The AdaBoost algorithm on which Algorithm 11.3 is based was introduced by Freund and Schapire (1997). Schapire and Singer (1999) give multi-class and multi-label extensions of AdaBoost. A ranking version of AdaBoost was proposed by Freund *et al.* (2003). The boosted rule learning approach that can handle classifiers that may abstain was inspired by Slipper (Cohen and Singer, 1999), a boosted version of Ripper (Cohen, 1995).

☞ In Section 11.3 we discussed bagging and boosting in terms of bias and variance. Schapire, Freund, Bartlett and Lee (1998) provide a detailed theoretical and experimental analysis of boosting in terms of improving the margin distribution. I also mentioned some other ensemble methods that train a meta-model for combining the base models. Stacking employs a linear meta-model and was introduced by Wolpert (1992) for classification and extended by Breiman (1996*b*) for regression. Meta-decision trees were introduced by Todorovski and Dzeroski (2003).

☞ We also briefly discussed meta-learning as a technique for learning about the performance of learning algorithms. The field originated from an early empirical study documented by Michie *et al.* (1994). Recent references are Brazdil *et al.* (2009, 2010). Unpruned and unpruned decision trees were used to obtain data set characteristics by Peng *et al.* (2002). The idea of training simple models to obtain further data characteristics is known as landmarking (Pfahringer *et al.*, 2000).

CHAPTER *12*

Machine learning experiments

MACHING LEARNING IS a practical subject as much as a computational one. While we may be able to prove that a particular learning algorithm converges to the theoretically optimal model under certain assumptions, we need actual data to investigate, e.g., the extent to which those assumptions are actually satisfied in the domain under consideration, or whether convergence happens quickly enough to be of practical use. We thus evaluate or run particular models or learning algorithms on one or more data sets, obtain a number of measurements and use these to answer particular questions we might be interested in. This broadly characterises what is known as machine learning *experiments.*

In the natural sciences, an experiment can be seen as a question to nature about a scientific theory. For example, Arthur Eddington's famous 1919 experiment to verify Einstein's theory of general relativity asked the question: Are rays of light bent by gravitational fields produced by large celestial objects such as the Sun? To answer this question, the perceived position of stars was recorded under several conditions including a total solar eclipse. Eddington was able to show that these measurements indeed differed to an extent unexplained by Newtonian physics but consistent with general relativity.

While you don't have to travel to the island of Príncipe to perform machine learning experiments, they bear some similarity to experiments in physics in that *machine learning experiments pose questions about models that we try to answer by means of measurements on data.* The following are common examples of the types of question we are interested in:

☞ How does model m perform on data from domain $\mathscr{D}$?

☞ Which of these models has the best performance on data from domain $\mathscr{D}$?

☞ How do models produced by learning algorithm $\mathscr{A}$ perform on data from domain $\mathscr{D}$?

☞ Which of these learning algorithms gives the best model on data from domain $\mathscr{D}$?

Assuming we have access to data from domain $\mathscr{D}$, we perform measurements on our models using this data in order to answer these questions.[1] There is a large statistical literature about the technicalities of data experiments, and it is all too easy to mistake the forest for the trees. What I mean is that there is a certain tendency in the machine learning literature to approach experimentation in a formulaic manner, recording a fixed set of measurements and significance tests (the trees) with scant consideration for the question we are aiming to answer (the forest). My aim in this short chapter is not to get buried in technicalities, but rather to give you some appreciation of the importance of choosing measurements that are appropriate for your particular experimental objective (Section 12.1). In Sections 12.2 and 12.3 we take a closer look at how to measure and interpret them.

12.1 What to measure

A good starting point for our measurements are the ☞*evaluation measures* in Table 2.3 on p.57. However, measurements don't have to be scalars: a ROC or coverage curve also counts as a measurement in this context. The appropriateness of any of these for our purposes depends on how we define performance in relation to the question the experiment is designed to answer: let's call it our *experimental objective*. It is important not to confuse performance measures and experimental objectives: the former is something we can measure, while the latter is what we are really interested in. There is often a discrepancy between the two. For example, in psychology our experimental objective may be to quantify a person's intelligence level, and our chosen measurement may be the IQ score achieved on a standardised test – while the IQ score may correlate with intelligence level, it is clear they are not the same thing.

[1] It is much harder to answer questions about a new domain given measurements on different domains, although that is what we are ultimately interested in.

In machine learning the situation is usually more concrete, and our experimental objective – accuracy, say – is something we can measure in principle, or at least estimate (since we're generally interested in accuracy on unseen data). However, there may be unknown factors we have to account for. For example, the model may need to operate in different *operating contexts* with different class distributions. In such a case we can treat accuracy on future data as a random variable and take its expectation, assuming some probability distribution over the proportion of positives *pos*. Since $acc = pos \cdot tpr + (1 - pos) \cdot tnr$, and assuming we can measure true positive and negative rates independently of the class distribution, we have (assuming a uniform distribution over *pos*)

$$\begin{aligned}\mathbb{E}[acc] &= \mathbb{E}\left[pos \cdot tpr + (1-pos) \cdot tnr\right] = \mathbb{E}\left[pos\right] tpr + \mathbb{E}\left[1-pos\right] tnr \\ &= tpr/2 + tnr/2 = avg\text{-}rec\end{aligned}$$

In other words, even though estimating accuracy in future contexts is our experimental objective, the fact that we are anticipating the widest possible range of class distributions suggests that the evaluation measure we should use on our test data is not accuracy, but average recall.

Example 12.1 (Expected accuracy for unknown class distributions). Imagine your classifier achieves the following result on a test data set:

	Predicted ⊕	*Predicted* ⊖	
Actual ⊕	**60**	20	80
Actual ⊖	0	**20**	20
	60	40	100

This gives $tpr = 0.75$, $tnr = 1.00$ and $acc = 0.80$. However, this is conditioned on having four times as many positives as negatives. If we take the expectation over *pos* uniformly sampled from the unit interval, expected accuracy increases to $(tpr + tnr)/2 = 0.88 = avg\text{-}rec$. This is higher because the test data underemphasises the classifier's good performance on the negatives.

Suppose you have a second classifier achieving the following result on the test set:

	Predicted ⊕	*Predicted* ⊖	
Actual ⊕	**75**	5	80
Actual ⊖	**10**	**10**	20
	85	15	100

This gives $tpr = 0.94$, $tnr = 0.50$, $acc = 0.85$ and $avg\text{-}rec = 0.72$. These experimental results tell you that the second model is better if the class distribution in the test set is representative, but the first model should be chosen if we have no prior information about the class distribution in the operating context.

As the example demonstrates, if you choose accuracy as your evaluation measure, you are making an implicit assumption that the class distribution in the test set is representative for the operating context in which the model is going to be deployed. Furthermore, if all you recorded in your experiments is accuracy, you will not be able to switch to average recall later if you realise that you need to incorporate varying class distributions. It is therefore good practice to record sufficient information to be able to reproduce the contingency table if needed. A sufficient set of measurements would be true positive rate, true negative rate (or false positive rate), the class distribution and the size of the test set.

As a second example of how your choice of evaluation measures can carry implicit assumptions we consider the case of precision and recall as often reported in the information retrieval literature.

Example 12.2 (Precision and recall as evaluation measures). In the second contingency table in Example 12.1 we have precision $prec = 75/85 = 0.88$ and recall $rec = 75/80 = 0.94$ (remember that recall and true positive rate are different names for the same measure). The F-measure is the harmonic mean of precision and recall (see Background 10.1), which is 0.91.

Now consider the following contingency table:

	Predicted ⊕	*Predicted* ⊖	
Actual ⊕	**75**	5	80
Actual ⊖	10	**910**	920
	85	915	1000

We have a much higher number of true negatives and therefore a much higher true negative rate and accuracy (both rounded to 0.99). On the other hand, true positive rate/recall, precision and F-measure stay exactly the same.

This example demonstrates that *the combination of precision and recall, and therefore the F-measure, is insensitive to the number of true negatives*. This is not a deficiency of the F-measure: quite the contrary, it is very useful in domains where negatives abound, and it would therefore be very easy to achieve high accuracy by always predicting negative. Examples of such domains include search and query engines (most search items are not answers to most queries) and link prediction in networks (most pairs of nodes are not linked). The point is rather to emphasise that if you choose F-measure as your evaluation measure, you are making an implicit assertion that true negatives are not relevant for your operating context.

Finally, I would like to draw attention to a much-neglected evaluation measure that has, nevertheless, practical significance. This is the *predicted positive rate* which is the number of positive predictions (the sum of the left column in the contingency table) in proportion to the number of instances:

$$ppr = \frac{TP + FP}{Pos + Neg} = pos \cdot tpr + (1 - pos) \cdot fpr$$

While the predicted positive rate doesn't tell us much about the classification performance of the classifier, it does tell us what the classifier estimates the class distribution to be. It is also something that is normally under control of a ranker or scoring classifier if the entire test set is given: e.g., a predicted positive rate of 1/2 is simply achieved by setting the threshold such that the ranking splits into equal parts. This suggests a connection between classification accuracy and ranking accuracy: for example, it can be shown that if we split a ranking of n instances at one of the $n+1$ possible split points chosen uniformly at random, the expected accuracy is equal to

$$\mathbb{E}[acc] = \frac{n}{n+1}\frac{2\text{AUC}-1}{4} + 1/2$$

Example 12.3 (Expected accuracy and AUC**).** Suppose a ranker obtains the following ranking on a small test set: ⊕⊕⊖⊖⊕⊖. This corresponds to two ranking errors out of a possible nine, so has AUC = 7/9. There are seven potential split points, corresponding to predicted positive rates of (from left to right) $0, 1/6, \ldots, 5/6, 1$ and corresponding accuracies $3/6, 4/6, 5/6, 4/6, 3/6, 4/6, 3/6$. The expected accuracy over all possible split points is $(3+4+5+4+3+4+3)/(6\cdot 7) = 26/42$. On the other hand, $(2\text{AUC}-1)/4 = 5/36$ and so $\frac{n}{n+1}(2\text{AUC}-1)/4 + 1/2 = 5/42 + 1/2 = 26/42$.

This discussion is intended to highlight two things. First, if a model is a good ranker but its probability estimates are not well-calibrated, it might be a good idea to set the decision threshold such that it achieves a particular predicted positive rate (e.g., $ppr = pos$) rather than invoking the MAP decision rule. Secondly, in such situations AUC is a good evaluation measure because it is linearly related to expected accuracy in that scenario.

In summary, your choice of evaluation measures should reflect the assumptions you are making about your experimental objective as well as possible contexts in which your models operate. We have looked at the following cases:

☞ Accuracy is a good evaluation measure if the class distribution in your test set is representative for the operating context.

☞ Average recall is the evaluation measure of choice if all class distributions are equally likely.

☞ Precision and recall shift the focus from classification accuracy to a performance analysis ignoring the true negatives.

☞ Predicted positive rate and AUC are relevant measures in a ranking context.

In the next section we consider how to estimate these evaluation measures from data.

12.2 How to measure it

The evaluation measures we discussed in the previous section are all calculated from a contingency table. The question of 'how to measure it' thus seems to have a very straightforward answer: construct the contingency table from a test set and perform the relevant calculations. However, two issues demand our attention: (*i*) which data to base our measurements on, and (*ii*) how to assess the inevitable uncertainty associated with every measurement. In this section we are concerned with the first issue; the second issue will be discussed in the next section.

When we measure something – say, a person's height – several times, we expect some variation to occur from one measurement to the next. This is inherent to the measurement process: e.g., you may be stretching the tape measure a bit less for the second measurement, or you may be reading it from a slightly different angle.[2] This variation can be modelled by treating our measurement as a random variable characterised by its mean – the value we are trying to measure – and variance σ^2, both of which are unknown but can be estimated. It follows from this model that if you measure a person's height many times, the sample variance in the measured values converges to σ^2. A standard trick is to average k measurements, as this gets the variance in your estimate down to σ^2/k. What this means is that, if you repeated this averaging for many sets of k measurements, the averages have a sample variance σ^2/k. Crucially,

[2] Some variation is also due to the fact that somebody tends to be taller fresh out of bed in the morning than at the end of a day of sitting and standing up, but I ignore that here and assume an unambiguous true value that we are trying to measure.

this assumes that your measurements are independent: if you are introducing a systematic error by using a faulty tape measure, averaging won't help!

Now suppose you are measuring a classifier's accuracy (or its true positive rate, or the predicted positive rate, or any other evaluation measure discussed earlier), rather than a person's height. The natural model here is that each test instance represents a Bernoulli trial with success probability a, the true but unknown accuracy of the classifier. We estimate a by counting the number of correctly classified test instances A and setting $\hat{a} = A/n$; notice that A has a binomial distribution. The variance of a single Bernoulli trial is $a(1-a)$; averaged over n test instances it is $a(1-a)/n$, assuming the test instances are chosen independently. We can estimate the variance by plugging in our estimate for a: this will help us to assess the uncertainty in $\hat{a}$, as we shall see in the next section. Under certain conditions we can improve our estimate by averaging k independent estimates $\hat{a}_i$ and take their sample variance $\frac{1}{k-1}\sum_{i=1}^{k}(\hat{a}_i - \overline{a})^2$ instead, with $\overline{a} = \frac{1}{k}\sum_{i=1}^{k}\hat{a}_i$ the sample mean.[3]

How do we obtain k independent estimates of a? If we have plenty of data, we can sample k independent test sets of size n and estimate a on each of them. Notice that if we are evaluating a learning algorithm rather than a given model we need to set aside training data which needs to be separate from the test data. If we don't have a lot of data, the following *cross-validation* procedure is often applied: randomly partition the data in k parts or 'folds', set one fold aside for testing, train a model on the remaining $k-1$ folds and evaluate it on the test fold. This process is repeated k times until each fold has been used for testing once. This may seem curious at first since we are evaluating k models rather than a single one, but this makes sense if we are evaluating a learning algorithm (whose output is a model, so we want to average over models) rather than a single model (whose outputs are instance labels, so we want to average over those). By averaging over training sets we get a sense of the variance of the learning algorithm (i.e., its dependence on variations in the training data), although it should be noted that the training sets in cross-validation have considerable overlap and are clearly not independent. Once we are satisfied with the performance of our learning algorithm, we can run it over the entire data set to obtain a single model.

Cross-validation is conventionally applied with $k = 10$, although this is somewhat arbitrary. A rule of thumb is that individual folds should contain at least 30 instances, as this allows us to approximate the binomial distribution of the number of correctly classified instances in a fold by a normal distribution. So if we have fewer than 300 instances we need to adjust k accordingly. Alternatively, we can set $k = n$ and train on all but one test instance, repeated n times: this is known as *leave-one-out* cross-validation (or the jackknife in statistics). This means that in each single-instance 'fold'

[3]Notice that we divide by $k-1$ rather than k in the expression for the sample variance, to account for the uncertainty in our estimate of the sample mean.

our accuracy estimate is 0 or 1, but by averaging n of those we get an approximately normal distribution by the central limit theorem. If we expect the learning algorithm to be sensitive to the class distribution we should apply *stratified cross-validation*: this aims at achieving roughly the same class distribution in each fold. Cross-validation runs can be repeated for different random partitions into folds and the results averaged again to further reduce variance in our estimates: this is referred to as, e.g., 10 times 10-fold cross-validation. It should be kept in mind that this leads increasingly to independence assumptions being violated – if we take this too far our accuracy estimate will overfit the given data and not be representative for new data.

Example 12.4 (Cross-validation). The following table gives a possible result of evaluating three learning algorithms on a data set with 10-fold cross-validation:

Fold	*Naive Bayes*	*Decision tree*	*Nearest neighbour*
1	0.6809	0.7524	0.7164
2	0.7017	0.8964	0.8883
3	0.7012	0.6803	0.8410
4	0.6913	0.9102	0.6825
5	0.6333	0.7758	0.7599
6	0.6415	0.8154	0.8479
7	0.7216	0.6224	0.7012
8	0.7214	0.7585	0.4959
9	0.6578	0.9380	0.9279
10	0.7865	0.7524	0.7455
avg	0.6937	0.7902	0.7606
stdev	0.0448	0.1014	0.1248

The last two lines give the average and standard deviation over all ten folds. We can see that nearest neighbour has the highest standard deviation. Clearly the decision tree achieves the best result, but should we completely discard nearest neighbour?

Cross-validation can also be applied to ROC curves obtained from a scoring classifier. This is because every instance participates in exactly one test fold and receives a score from the corresponding model. We can therefore simply merge all test folds which produces a single ranking.

12.3 How to interpret it

Once we have estimates of a relevant evaluation measure for our models or learning algorithms we can use them to select the best one. The fundamental issue here is how to deal with the inherent uncertainty in these estimates. We will discuss two key concepts: confidence intervals and significance tests. An understanding of these concepts is necessary if you want to appreciate current practice in interpreting results from machine learning experiments – however, it is good to realise that current practice is coming under increasing scrutiny. It should also be noted that the methods described here represent only a tiny fraction of the vast spectrum of possibilities.

Suppose our estimate $\hat{a}$ follows a normal distribution around the true mean a with standard deviation σ. Assuming for the moment that we know these parameters, we can calculate for any interval the likelihood of the estimate falling in the interval, by calculating the area under the normal density function in that interval. For example, the likelihood of obtaining an estimate within ± 1 standard deviation around the mean is 68%. Thus, if we take 100 estimates from independent test sets, we expect 68 of them to be within one standard deviation on either side of the mean – or equivalently, we expect the true mean to fall within one standard deviation on either side of the estimate in 68 cases. This is called the 68% *confidence interval* of the estimate. For two standard deviations the confidence level is 95% – these values can be looked up in probability tables or calculated using statistical packages such as Matlab or R. Notice that confidence intervals for normally distributed estimates are symmetric because the normal distribution is symmetric, but this is not generally the case: e.g., the binomial distribution is asymmetric (except for $p = 1/2$). Notice also that, in case of symmetry, we can easily change the interval into a one-sided interval: for example, we expect the mean to be more than one standard deviation *above* the estimate in 16 cases out of 100, which gives a one-sided 84% confidence interval from minus infinity to the mean plus one standard deviation.

More generally, in order to construct confidence intervals we need to know (*i*) the sampling distribution of the estimates, and (*ii*) the parameters of that distribution. We saw previously that accuracy estimated from a single test set with n instances follows a scaled binomial distribution with variance $\hat{a}(1-\hat{a})/n$. This would lead to asymmetric confidence intervals, but the skew in the binomial distribution is only really noticeable if $na(1-a) < 5$: if that is not the case the normal distribution is a good approximation for the binomial one. So we use the binomial expression for the variance and use the normal distribution to construct the confidence intervals.

Example 12.5 (Confidence interval). Suppose 80 out of 100 test instances are correctly classified. We have $\hat{a} = 0.80$ with an estimated variance of $\hat{a}(1-\hat{a})/n = 0.0016$ or a standard deviation of $\sqrt{\hat{a}(1-\hat{a})/n} = 0.04$. Notice $n\hat{a}(1-\hat{a}) = 16 \geq 5$ so the 68% confidence interval is estimated as $[0.76, 0.84]$ in accordance with the normal distribution, and the 95% interval is $[0.72, 0.88]$.

If we reduce the size of our test sample to 50 and find that 40 test instances are correctly classified, then the standard deviation increases to 0.06 and the 95% confidence interval widens to $[0.68, 0.92]$. If the test sample drops to less than 30 instances we would need to construct an asymmetric confidence interval using tables for the binomial distribution.

Notice that *confidence intervals are statements about estimates rather than statements about the true value of the evaluation measure*. The statement 'assuming the true accuracy a is 0.80, the probability that a measurement m falls in the interval $[0.72, 0.88]$ is 0.95' is correct, but we cannot reverse this to say 'assuming a measurement $m = 0.80$, the probability that the true accuracy falls in the interval $[0.72, 0.88]$ is 0.95'. To infer $P(a \in [0.72, 0.88] | m = 0.80)$ from $P(m \in [0.72, 0.88] | a = 0.80)$ we must somehow invoke Bayes' rule, but this requires meaningful prior distributions over both true accuracies and measurements, which we don't generally have.

We can, however, use similar reasoning to test a particular *null hypothesis* we have about a. For example, suppose our null hypothesis is that the true accuracy is 0.5 and that the standard deviation derived from the binomial distribution is therefore $\sqrt{0.5(1-0.5)/100} = 0.05$. Given our estimate of 0.80, we then calculate the *p-value*, which is the probability of obtaining a measurement of 0.80 or higher given the null hypothesis. The p-value is then compared with a pre-defined significance level, say $\alpha = 0.05$: this corresponds to a confidence of 95%. The null hypothesis is rejected if the p-value is smaller than α; in our case this applies since $p = 1.9732 \cdot 10^{-9}$.

This idea of *significance testing* can be extended to learning algorithms evaluated in cross-validation. For a pair of algorithms we calculate the difference in accuracy on each fold. The difference between two normally distributed variables is also normally distributed. Our null hypothesis is that the true difference is 0, so that any differences in performance are attributed to chance. We calculate a p-value using the normal distribution, and reject the null hypothesis if the p-value is below our significance level α. The one complication is that we don't have access to the true standard deviation in the differences, which therefore needs to be estimated. This introduces additional uncertainty into the process, which means that the sampling distribution is bell-shaped like the normal distribution but slightly more heavy-tailed. This distribution is referred to as Student's t-distribution or simply the *t-distribution*.[4] The extent to which the t-distribution is more heavy-tailed than the normal distribution is regulated by the number of *degrees of freedom*: in our case this is equal to 1 less than the number of folds (since the final fold is completely determined by the other ones). The whole procedure is known as the *paired t-test*.

Example 12.6 (Paired t-test). The following table demonstrates the calculation of a paired t-test on the results in Example 12.4. The numbers show pairwise differences in each fold. The null hypothesis in each case is that the differences come from a normal distribution with mean 0 and unknown standard deviation.

Fold	*NB–DT*	*NB–NN*	*DT–NN*
1	-0.0715	-0.0355	0.0361
2	-0.1947	-0.1866	0.0081
3	0.0209	-0.1398	-0.1607
4	-0.2189	0.0088	0.2277
5	-0.1424	-0.1265	0.0159
6	-0.1739	-0.2065	-0.0325
7	0.0992	0.0204	-0.0788
8	-0.0371	0.2255	0.2626
9	-0.2802	-0.2700	0.0102
10	0.0341	0.0410	0.0069
avg	-0.0965	-0.0669	0.0295
stdev	0.1246	0.1473	0.1278
p-value	**0.0369**	**0.1848**	**0.4833**

The p-value in the last line of the table is calculated by means of the t-distribution with $k-1=9$ degrees of freedom, and only the difference between the naive Bayes and decision tree algorithms is found significant at the $\alpha = 0.05$ level.

---

[4] It was published by William Sealy Gosset in 1908 under the pseudonym 'Student' because his employer, the Guinness brewery in Dublin, did not want the competition to know that they were using statistics.

Interpretation of results over multiple data sets

The t-test can be applied for comparing two learning algorithms over a single data set, typically using results obtained in cross-validation. It is not appropriate for multiple data sets because performance measures cannot be compared across data sets (they are not 'commensurate'). In order to compare two learning algorithms over multiple data sets we need to use a test specifically designed for that purpose such as *Wilcoxon's signed-rank test*. The idea is to rank the performance differences in absolute value, from smallest (rank 1) to largest (rank n). We then calculate the sum of ranks for positive and negative differences separately, and take the smaller of these sums as our test statistic. For a large number of data sets (at least 25) this statistic can be converted to one which is approximately normally distributed, but for smaller numbers the *critical value* (the value of the statistic at which the p-value equals α) can be found in a statistical table.

Example 12.7 (Wilcoxon's signed-rank test). We use the performance differences between naive Bayes and decision tree as in the previous example, but now assume for the sake of argument that they come from 10 different data sets.

Data set	*NB–DT*	*Rank*
1	-0.0715	**4**
2	-0.1947	**8**
3	0.0209	1
4	-0.2189	**9**
5	-0.1424	**6**
6	-0.1739	**7**
7	0.0992	5
8	-0.0371	**3**
9	-0.2802	**10**
10	0.0341	2

The sum of ranks for positive differences is $1+5+2=8$ and for negative differences $4+8+9+6+7+3+10=47$. The critical value for 10 data sets at the $\alpha = 0.05$ level is 8, which means that if the smallest of the two sums of ranks is less than or equal to 8 the null hypothesis that the ranks are distributed the same for positive and negative differences can be rejected. This applies in this case, so we conclude that the performance difference between naive Bayes and decision trees is significant according to Wilcoxon's signed-rank test (as it was for the paired t-test in Example 12.6).

The Wilcoxon signed-rank test assumes that larger performance differences are better than smaller ones, but otherwise makes no assumption about their commensurability – in other words, performance differences are treated as ordinals rather than real-valued. Furthermore, there is no normality assumption regarding the distribution of these differences[5] which means, among other things, that the test is less sensitive to outliers.

If we want to compare k algorithms over n data sets we need to use specialised significance tests to avoid that our confidence level drops with each additional pairwise comparison between algorithms. The *Friedman test* is designed for exactly this situation. Like the Wilcoxon signed-rank test it is based on ranked rather than absolute performance, and hence makes no assumption regarding the distribution of the performance measurements.[6] The idea is to rank the performance of all k algorithms per data set, from best performance (rank 1) to worst performance (rank k). Let R_{ij} denote the rank of the j-th algorithm on the i-th data set, and let $R_j = \left(\sum_i R_{ij}\right)/n$ be the average rank of the j-th algorithm. Under the null hypothesis that all algorithms perform equally these average ranks R_j should be the same. In order to test this we calculate the following quantities:

1. the average rank $\overline{R} = \frac{1}{nk}\sum_{ij} R_{ij} = \frac{k+1}{2}$;
2. the sum of squared differences $n\sum_j (R_j - \overline{R})^2$; and
3. the sum of squared differences $\frac{1}{n(k-1)}\sum_{ij}(R_{ij} - \overline{R})^2$.

There is an analogy with clustering here, in that the second quantity measures the spread between the rank 'centroids' – which we want to be large – and the third quantity measures the spread over all ranks. The Friedman statistic is the ratio of the former and latter quantities.

---

[5] In statistical terminology the test is 'non-parametric' as opposed to a parametric test such as the t-test which assumes a particular distribution. Parametric tests are generally more powerful when that assumed distribution is appropriate but can be misleading when it is not.

[6] A well-known parametric alternative to the Friedman test is *analysis of variance* (ANOVA).

Example 12.8 (Friedman test). We use the data from Example 12.4, assuming it comes from different data sets rather than cross-validation folds. The following table shows the ranks in brackets:

Data set	*Naive Bayes*	*Decision tree*	*Nearest neighbour*
1	0.6809 (3)	0.7524 (1)	0.7164 (2)
2	0.7017 (3)	0.8964 (1)	0.8883 (2)
3	0.7012 (2)	0.6803 (3)	0.8410 (1)
4	0.6913 (2)	0.9102 (1)	0.6825 (3)
5	0.6333 (3)	0.7758 (1)	0.7599 (2)
6	0.6415 (3)	0.8154 (2)	0.8479 (1)
7	0.7216 (1)	0.6224 (3)	0.7012 (2)
8	0.7214 (2)	0.7585 (1)	0.4959 (3)
9	0.6578 (3)	0.9380 (1)	0.9279 (2)
10	0.7865 (1)	0.7524 (2)	0.7455 (3)
avg rank	2.3	1.6	2.1

We have $\overline{R} = 2$, $n\sum_j (R_j - \overline{R})^2 = 2.6$ and $\frac{1}{n(k-1)} \sum_{ij} (R_{ij} - \overline{R})^2 = 1$, so the Friedman statistic is 2.6. The critical value for $k = 3$ and $n = 10$ at the $\alpha = 0.05$ level is 7.8, so we cannot reject the null hypothesis that all algorithms perform equally. In comparison, if the average ranks were 2.7, 1.3 and 2.0, then the null hypothesis would be rejected at that significance level.

The Friedman test tells us whether the average ranks as a whole display significant differences, but further analysis is needed on a pairwise level. This is achieved by applying a *post-hoc test* once the Friedman test gives significance. The idea is to calculate the *critical difference* (*CD*) against which the difference in average rank between two algorithms is compared. The *Nemenyi test* calculates the critical difference as follows:

$$\mathrm{CD} = q_\alpha \sqrt{\frac{k(k+1)}{6n}} \tag{12.1}$$

where q_α depends on the significance level α as well as k: for $\alpha = 0.05$ and $k = 3$ it is 2.343, leading to a critical difference of 1.047 in our example. If the average ranks are 2.7, 1.3 and 2.0, then only the difference between the first and second algorithm exceeds the critical difference. Figure 12.1 (top) demonstrates a useful visual representation of the results of the Nemenyi post-hoc test.

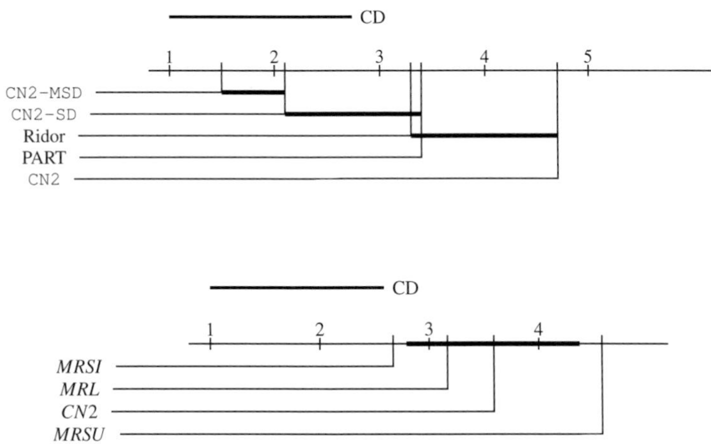

Figure 12.1. **(top)** Critical difference diagram for the pairwise Nemenyi test. Average ranks for each algorithm are plotted on the real axis. The critical difference is shown as a bar above the figure, and any group of consecutively ranked algorithms such that the outermost ones are less than the critical difference apart are connected by a horizontal thick line. The diagram shows, e.g., that the performance of the top ranked algorithm is significantly better than the bottom three. **(bottom)** Critical difference diagram for the Bonferroni–Dunn test with CN2 as control. The critical differences are now drawn symmetrically around the average rank of the control. The top ranked algorithm is significantly better than the control, and the bottom ranked one is significantly worse. (Figures courtesy of Tarek Abudawood (2011)).

A variant of the Nemenyi test called the *Bonferroni–Dunn test* can be applied when we perform pairwise tests only against a control algorithm. The calculation of the critical difference is the same, except q_α is adjusted to reflect the fact that we make $k-1$ pairwise comparisons rather than $k(k-1)/2$. For example, for $\alpha = 0.05$ and $k = 3$ we have $q_\alpha = 2.241$, which is slightly lower than the value used for the Nemenyi test, leading to a tighter critical difference. Figure 12.1 (bottom) shows a graphical representation of the Bonferroni–Dunn post-hoc test.

12.4 Machine learning experiments: Summary and further reading

In this chapter we have taken a look at how we can use data to answer questions about the performance of models and learning algorithms. A 'machine learning experimenter' needs to address three questions: (*i*) what to measure, (*ii*) how to measure it, and (*iii*) how to interpret it. An excellent source – particularly for the last two questions – is Japkowicz and Shah (2011).

☞ In order to decide what to measure, we first need to explicate our experimental objective. We also need to consider the operating context: performance aspects that might change when using the model. For example, the operating context might be given by the class distribution, but we may have no prior knowledge telling us that certain distributions are more likely than others. Example 12.1 on p.345 demonstrated that in such a case average recall would be more appropriate as a performance measure, even if the experimental objective is accuracy. We also looked at the difference between a precision–recall analysis which ignores the true negatives, and a true/false positive rate analysis which takes them into account; a fuller analysis is provided by Davis and Goadrich (2006). The relation between accuracy as experimental objective and AUC as performance measure is studied by Hernández-Orallo *et al.* (2011).

☞ Once we decided what to measure, we need to establish a measuring protocol. The most common approach is k-fold cross-validation, which divides the data into k folds, repeatedly trains on $k-1$ of those and tests on the remaining one. It is of paramount importance that there be no information leak between the training data used to learn the model and the test data used to evaluate it. A common mistake is to use cross-validation to find the best setting of one or more parameters of a learning algorithm, say the complexity parameter of a support vector machine. This is methodologically wrong as parameter tuning should be carried out as part of the training process, without any access to the test data. A methodologically sound option is to use *internal cross-validation* by setting aside a validation fold in each cross-validation run for parameter tuning. Experimental studies regarding cross-validation are carried out by Dietterich (1998) and Bouckaert and Frank (2004): the former recommends five times two-fold cross-validation and the latter ten times ten-fold. ROC curves can be drawn in cross-validation as each instance appears in a test fold exactly once, and so we can collect the scores on all test folds. Fawcett (2006) considers alternatives including horizontal and vertical averaging.

☞ In the context of interpreting experimental results we looked at confidence intervals and significance tests. Confidence intervals have a clear statistical interpretation: they quantify the likelihood of a measurement falling in a particular interval, assuming a particular true value. Significance tests extend this to reasoning about a particular null hypothesis, such as 'these learning algorithms do not perform differently on these data sets'. Significance tests are designed for particular protocols: the t-test can be used for evaluating two learning algorithms on two data sets, Wilcoxon's signed-rank test is applicable for comparing two algorithms over multiple data sets, and Friedman's test (or analysis of variance) compares multiple algorithms over multiple data sets. An excellent discussion of these and related tests is provided by Demšar (2006).

☞ It should be mentioned that there is much discussion on the use of significance tests in machine learning, and on the wider issue regarding machine learning as an experimental science. The importance of experiments in machine learning was stressed early on by Pat Langley in two influential papers (Langley, 1988; Kibler and Langley, 1988); however, more recently he expressed criticism at the way experimental methodology in machine learning has become rather inflexible (Langley, 2011). Other authors critical of current practice include Drummond (2006) and Demšar (2008).

Epilogue: Where to go from here

AND SO WE HAVE come to the end of our journey through the 'making sense of data' landscape. We have seen how machine learning can build models from features for solving tasks involving data. We have seen how models can be predictive or descriptive; learning can be supervised or unsupervised; and models can be logical, geometric, probabilistic or ensembles of such models. Now that I have equipped you with the basic concepts to understand the literature, there is a whole world out there for you to explore. So it is only natural for me to leave you with a few pointers to areas you may want to learn about next.

One thing that we have often assumed in the book is that the data comes in a form suitable for the task at hand. For example, if the task is to label e-mails we conveniently learn a classifier from data in the form of labelled e-mails. For tasks such as class probability estimation I introduced the output space (for the model) as separate from the label space (for the data) because the model outputs (class probability estimates) are not directly observable in the data and have to be reconstructed. An area where the distinction between data and model output is much more pronounced is *reinforcement learning*. Imagine you want to learn how to be a good chess player. This could be viewed as a classification task, but then you require a teacher to score every move. What happens in practical situations is that every now and then you receive a reward or a punishment – e.g., winning the game, or losing one of your pieces. The challenge is then to assign credit or blame to individual moves that led to such rewards or punishments being incurred. Reinforcement learning is a principled way to learn policies for deciding which action to take in which situation or state. This is currently one of the most active subfields of machine learning. The standard reference is Sutton and Barto (1998), and you should have no trouble finding more recent workshop proceedings or journal special issues.

There are many other tasks that require us to relax some of our assumptions. For example, in multi-class classification we assume that classes are mutually exclusive. In *multi-label classification* we drop that assumption, so that an instance can be labelled with an arbitrary subset of labels. This is natural, e.g., when tagging online material such as blog posts. The dependence between labels is an additional source of information: for example, knowing that the tag 'machine learning' applies makes the tag 'reinforcement learning' more likely. Multi-label learning aims to exploit this information by learning the dependence between the labels as well as the mapping between the features and each individual label. For relevant work in the area see, e.g., Tsoumakas *et al.* (2012). A related area is *preference learning*, where the goal is to learn instance-dependent preferences between class labels (Fürnkranz and Hüllermeier, 2010). Increasing the complexity of the model outputs even further, we arrive at the general area of *structured output prediction* (Bakir *et al.*, 2007).

Going back to multi-label learning, although each label establishes a separate binary classification task, the goal is to avoid learning completely separate models for each task. This is, in fact, a special case of what is called *multi-task learning*. For example, each task could be to predict a separate real-valued target variable on the same instance space, and the learner is aiming to exploit, say, correlations between the target variables. Closely related to this is the area of *transfer learning*, which studies the transfer of models between tasks. A relevant reference for both areas is Silver and Bennett (2008).

Another assumption that deserves closer scrutiny is the availability of data in a single batch. In *online learning*, also called incremental learning, the model needs to be updated each time a new data point arrives. One application of this is in the area of *sequence prediction* (Cesa-Bianchi and Lugosi, 2006). With the increase in sensor data this setting is rapidly gaining importance, as can be witnessed from the growing area of *learning from data streams* (Gama and Gaber, 2007). Sometimes it is convenient to give the learner a more active role in data acquisition, for example by issuing queries for examples to be labelled by the teacher. *Active learning* studies exactly this setting (Settles, 2011).

Ultimately, machine learning is – and, in all likelihood, will remain – a research area at the nexus of two distinct developments. On the one hand, it is widely recognised that the ability for learning and self-training is necessary for achieving machine intelligence in any form. An area in machine learning that has this quest at heart is *deep learning*, which aims at employing hierarchies of autonomously constructed features (Bengio, 2009). On the other hand, machine learning is an indispensable tool for dealing with the data deluge. Building machine learning models is an essential step in the *data mining* process, which poses specific challenges such as being able to deal with 'big data' and cloud computing platforms. I hope that this book has kindled your interest in one of these exciting developments.

Important points to remember

References

Abudawood, T. (2011). Multi-class subgroup discovery: Heuristics, algorithms and predictiveness. Ph.D. thesis, University of Bristol, Department of Computer Science, Faculty of Engineering. 357

Abudawood, T. and Flach, P.A. (2009). Evaluation measures for multi-class subgroup discovery. In W.L. Buntine, M. Grobelnik, D. Mladenić and J. Shawe-Taylor (eds.), *Proceedings of the European Conference on Machine Learning and Knowledge Discovery in Databases (ECML-PKDD 2009), Part I, LNCS*, volume 5781, pp. 35–50. Springer. 193

Agrawal, R., Imielinski, T. and Swami, A.N. (1993). Mining association rules between sets of items in large databases. In P. Buneman and S. Jajodia (eds.), *Proceedings of the ACM International Conference on Management of Data (SIGMOD 1993)*, pp. 207–216. ACM Press. 103

Agrawal, R., Mannila, H., Srikant, R., Toivonen, H. and Verkamo, A.I. (1996). Fast discovery of association rules. In *Advances in Knowledge Discovery and Data Mining*, pp. 307–328. AAAI/MIT Press. 193

Allwein, E.L., Schapire, R.E. and Singer, Y. (2000). Reducing multiclass to binary: A unifying approach for margin classifiers. In P. Langley (ed.), *Proceedings of the Seventeenth International Conference on Machine Learning (ICML 2000)*, pp. 9–16. Morgan Kaufmann. 102

Amit, Y. and Geman, D. (**1997**). Shape quantization and recognition with randomized trees. *Neural Computation* 9(7):1545–1588. 341

Angluin, D., Frazier, M. and Pitt, L. (**1992**). Learning conjunctions of Horn clauses. *Machine Learning* 9:147–164. 128

Bakir, G., Hofmann, T., Schölkopf, B., Smola, A.J., Taskar, B. and Vishwanathan, S.V.N. (**2007**). *Predicting Structured Data.* MIT Press. 361

Banerji, R.B. (**1980**). *Artificial Intelligence: A Theoretical Approach.* Elsevier Science. 127

Bengio, Y. (**2009**). Learning deep architectures for AI. *Foundations and Trends in Machine Learning* 2(1):1–127. 361

Best, M.J. and Chakravarti, N. (**1990**). Active set algorithms for isotonic regression; a unifying framework. *Mathematical Programming* 47(1):425–439. 80, 229

Blockeel, H. (**2010***a*). Hypothesis language. In C. Sammut and G.I. Webb (eds.), *Encyclopedia of Machine Learning*, pp. 507–511. Springer. 127

Blockeel, H. (**2010***b*). Hypothesis space. In C. Sammut and G.I. Webb (eds.), *Encyclopedia of Machine Learning*, pp. 511–513. Springer. 127

Blockeel, H., De Raedt, L. and Ramon, J. (**1998**). Top-down induction of clustering trees. In J.W. Shavlik (ed.), *Proceedings of the Fifteenth International Conference on Machine Learning (ICML 1998)*, pp. 55–63. Morgan Kaufmann. 103, 156

Blumer, A., Ehrenfeucht, A., Haussler, D. and Warmuth, M.K. (**1989**). Learnability and the Vapnik-Chervonenkis dimension. *Journal of the ACM* 36(4):929–965. 128

Boser, B.E., Guyon, I. and Vapnik, V. (**1992**). A training algorithm for optimal margin classifiers. In *Proceedings of the International Conference on Computational Learning Theory (COLT 1992)*, pp. 144–152. 229

Bouckaert, R. and Frank, E. (**2004**). Evaluating the replicability of significance tests for comparing learning algorithms. In H. Dai, R. Srikant and C. Zhang (eds.), *Advances in Knowledge Discovery and Data Mining, LNCS*, volume 3056, pp. 3–12. Springer. 358

Boullé, M. (**2004**). Khiops: A statistical discretization method of continuous attributes. *Machine Learning* 55(1):53–69. 328

Boullé, M. (**2006**). MODL: A Bayes optimal discretization method for continuous attributes. *Machine Learning* 65(1):131–165. 328

Bourke, C., Deng, K., Scott, S.D., Schapire, R.E. and Vinodchandran, N.V. (2008). On reoptimizing multi-class classifiers. *Machine Learning* 71(2-3):219–242. 102

Brazdil, P., Giraud-Carrier, C.G., Soares, C. and Vilalta, R. (2009). *Metalearning – Applications to Data Mining.* Springer. 342

Brazdil, P., Vilalta, R., Giraud-Carrier, C.G. and Soares, C. (2010). Metalearning. In C. Sammut and G.I. Webb (eds.), *Encyclopedia of Machine Learning,* pp. 662–666. Springer. 342

Breiman, L. (1996*a*). Bagging predictors. *Machine Learning* 24(2):123–140. 341

Breiman, L. (1996*b*). Stacked regressions. *Machine Learning* 24(1):49–64. 342

Breiman, L. (2001). Random forests. *Machine Learning* 45(1):5–32. 341

Breiman, L., Friedman, J.H., Olshen, R.A. and Stone, C.J. (1984). *Classification and Regression Trees.* Wadsworth. 156

Brier, G.W. (1950). Verification of forecasts expressed in terms of probability. *Monthly Weather Review* 78(1):1–3. 80

Brown, G. (2010). Ensemble learning. In C. Sammut and G.I. Webb (eds.), *Encyclopedia of Machine Learning,* pp. 312–320. Springer. 341

Bruner, J.S., Goodnow, J.J. and Austin, G.A. (1956). *A Study of Thinking.* Science Editions. 2nd edn 1986. 127

Cesa-Bianchi, N. and Lugosi, G. (2006). *Prediction, Learning, and Games.* Cambridge University Press. 361

Cestnik, B. (1990). Estimating probabilities: A crucial task in machine learning. In *Proceedings of the European Conference on Artificial Intelligence (ECAI 1990),* pp. 147–149. 296

Clark, P. and Boswell, R. (1991). Rule induction with CN2: Some recent improvements. In Y. Kodratoff (ed.), *Proceedings of the European Working Session on Learning (EWSL 1991), LNCS,* volume 482, pp. 151–163. Springer. 192

Clark, P. and Niblett, T. (1989). The CN2 induction algorithm. *Machine Learning* 3:261–283. 192

Cohen, W.W. (1995). Fast effective rule induction. In A. Prieditis and S.J. Russell (eds.), *Proceedings of the Twelfth International Conference on Machine Learning (ICML 1995),* pp. 115–123. Morgan Kaufmann. 192, 341

Cohen, W.W. and Singer, Y. (1999). A simple, fast, and effictive rule learner. In J. Hendler and D. Subramanian (eds.), *Proceedings of the Sixteenth National Conference on Artificial Intelligence (AAAI 1999)*, pp. 335–342. AAAI Press / MIT Press. 341

Cohn, D. (2010). Active learning. In C. Sammut and G.I. Webb (eds.), *Encyclopedia of Machine Learning*, pp. 10–14. Springer. 128

Cortes, C. and Vapnik, V. (1995). Support-vector networks. *Machine Learning* 20(3):273–297. 229

Cover, T. and Hart, P. (1967). Nearest neighbor pattern classification. *IEEE Transactions on Information Theory* 13(1):21–27. 260

Cristianini, N. and Shawe-Taylor, J. (2000). *An Introduction to Support Vector Machines*. Cambridge University Press. 229

Dasgupta, S. (2010). Active learning theory. In C. Sammut and G.I. Webb (eds.), *Encyclopedia of Machine Learning*, pp. 14–19. Springer. 128

Davis, J. and Goadrich, M. (2006). The relationship between precision-recall and ROC curves. In W.W. Cohen and A. Moore (eds.), *Proceedings of the Twenty-Third International Conference on Machine Learning (ICML 2006)*, pp. 233–240. ACM Press. 358

De Raedt, L. (1997). Logical settings for concept-learning. *Artificial Intelligence* 95(1):187–201. 128

De Raedt, L. (2008). *Logical and Relational Learning*. Springer. 193

De Raedt, L. (2010). Logic of generality. In C. Sammut and G.I. Webb (eds.), *Encyclopedia of Machine Learning*, pp. 624–631. Springer. 128

De Raedt, L. and Kersting, K. (2010). Statistical relational learning. In C. Sammut and G.I. Webb (eds.), *Encyclopedia of Machine Learning*, pp. 916–924. Springer. 193

Dempster, A.P., Laird, N.M. and Rubin, D.B. (1977). Maximum likelihood from incomplete data via the EM algorithm. *Journal of the Royal Statistical Society, Series B (Methodological)* pp. 1–38. 296

Demšar, J. (2008). On the appropriateness of statistical tests in machine learning. In *Proceedings of the ICML'08 Workshop on Evaluation Methods for Machine Learning*. 359

Demšar, J. (2006). Statistical comparisons of classifiers over multiple data sets. *Journal of Machine Learning Research* 7:1–30. 359

Dietterich, T.G. (1998). Approximate statistical tests for comparing supervised classification learning algorithms. *Neural Computation* 10(7):1895–1923. 358

Dietterich, T.G. and Bakiri, G. (1995). Solving multiclass learning problems via error-correcting output codes. *Journal of Artificial Intelligence Research* 2:263–286. 102

Dietterich, T.G., Kearns, M.J. and Mansour, Y. (1996). Applying the weak learning framework to understand and improve c4.5. In *Proceedings of the Thirteenth International Conference on Machine Learning*, pp. 96–104. 156

Ding, C.H.Q. and He, X. (2004). *K*-means clustering via principal component analysis. In C.E. Brodley (ed.), *Proceedings of the Twenty-First International Conference on Machine Learning (ICML 2004)*. ACM Press. 329

Domingos, P. and Pazzani, M. (1997). On the optimality of the simple Bayesian classifier under zero-one loss. *Machine Learning* 29(2):103–130. 296

Donoho, S.K. and Rendell, L.A. (1995). Rerepresenting and restructuring domain theories: A constructive induction approach. *Journal of Artificial Intelligence Research* 2:411–446. 328

Drummond, C. (2006). Machine learning as an experimental science (revisited). In *Proceedings of the AAAI'06 Workshop on Evaluation Methods for Machine Learning*. 359

Drummond, C. and Holte, R.C. (2000). Exploiting the cost (in)sensitivity of decision tree splitting criteria. In P. Langley (ed.), *Proceedings of the Seventeenth International Conference on Machine Learning (ICML 2000)*, pp. 239–246. Morgan Kaufmann. 156

Egan, J.P. (1975). *Signal Detection Theory and ROC Analysis*. Academic Press. 80

Fawcett, T. (2006). An introduction to ROC analysis. *Pattern Recognition Letters* 27(8):861–874. 80, 358

Fawcett, T. and Niculescu-Mizil, A. (2007). PAV and the ROC convex hull. *Machine Learning* 68(1):97–106. 80, 229

Fayyad, U.M. and Irani, K.B. (1993). Multi-interval discretization of continuous-valued attributes for classification learning. In *Proceedings of the International Joint Conference on Artificial Intelligence (IJCAI 1993)*, pp. 1022–1029. 328

Ferri, C., Flach, P.A. and Hernández-Orallo, J. (2002). Learning decision trees using the area under the ROC curve. In C. Sammut and A.G. Hoffmann (eds.), *Proceedings of the Nineteenth International Conference on Machine Learning (ICML 2002)*, pp. 139–146. Morgan Kaufmann. 156

Ferri, C., Flach, P.A. and Hernández-Orallo, J. (**2003**). Improving the AUC of probabilistic estimation trees. In N. Lavrač, D. Gamberger, L. Todorovski and H. Blockeel (eds.), *Proceedings of the European Conference on Machine Learning (ECML 2003), LNCS*, volume 2837, pp. 121–132. Springer. 156

Fix, E. and Hodges, J.L. (**1951**). Discriminatory analysis. Nonparametric discrimination: Consistency properties. Technical report, USAF School of Aviation Medicine, Texas: Randolph Field. Report Number 4, Project Number 21-49-004. 260

Flach, P.A. (**1994**). *Simply Logical – Intelligent Reasoning by Example.* Wiley. 193

Flach, P.A. (**2003**). The geometry of ROC space: Understanding machine learning metrics through ROC isometrics. In T. Fawcett and N. Mishra (eds.), *Proceedings of the Twentieth International Conference on Machine Learning (ICML 2003)*, pp. 194–201. AAAI Press. 156

Flach, P.A. (**2010***a*). First-order logic. In C. Sammut and G.I. Webb (eds.), *Encyclopedia of Machine Learning*, pp. 410–415. Springer. 128

Flach, P.A. (**2010***b*). ROC analysis. In C. Sammut and G.I. Webb (eds.), *Encyclopedia of Machine Learning*, pp. 869–875. Springer. 80

Flach, P.A. and Lachiche, N. (**2001**). Confirmation-guided discovery of first-order rules with Tertius. *Machine Learning* 42(1/2):61–95. 193

Flach, P.A. and Matsubara, E.T. (**2007**). A simple lexicographic ranker and probability estimator. In J.N. Kok, J. Koronacki, R.L. de Mántaras, S. Matwin, D. Mladenic and A. Skowron (eds.), *Proceedings of the Eighteenth European Conference on Machine Learning (ECML 2007), LNCS*, volume 4701, pp. 575–582. Springer. 80, 229

Freund, Y., Iyer, R.D., Schapire, R.E. and Singer, Y. (**2003**). An efficient boosting algorithm for combining preferences. *Journal of Machine Learning Research* 4:933–969. 341

Freund, Y. and Schapire, R.E. (**1997**). A decision-theoretic generalization of on-line learning and an application to boosting. *J. Comput. Syst. Sci.* 55(1):119–139. 341

Fürnkranz, J. (**1999**). Separate-and-conquer rule learning. *Artificial Intelligence Review* 13(1):3–54. 192

Fürnkranz, J. (**2010**). Rule learning. In C. Sammut and G.I. Webb (eds.), *Encyclopedia of Machine Learning*, pp. 875–879. Springer. 192

Fürnkranz, J. and Flach, P.A. (**2003**). An analysis of rule evaluation metrics. In T. Fawcett and N. Mishra (eds.), *Proceedings of the Twentieth International Conference on Machine Learning (ICML 2003)*, pp. 202–209. AAAI Press. 79

Fürnkranz, J. and Flach, P.A. (**2005**). ROC 'n' Rule learning – towards a better understanding of covering algorithms. *Machine Learning* 58(1):39–77. 192

Fürnkranz, J., Gamberger, D. and Lavrač, N. (**2012**). *Foundations of Rule Learning.* Springer. 192

Fürnkranz, J. and Hüllermeier, E. (eds.) (**2010**). *Preference Learning.* Springer. 361

Fürnkranz, J. and Widmer, G. (**1994**). Incremental reduced error pruning. In *Proceedings of the Eleventh International Conference on Machine Learning (ICML 1994)*, pp. 70–77. 192

Gama, J. and Gaber, M.M. (eds.) (**2007**). *Learning from Data Streams: Processing Techniques in Sensor Networks.* Springer. 361

Ganter, B. and Wille, R. (**1999**). *Formal Concept Analysis: Mathematical Foundations.* Springer. 127

Garriga, G.C., Kralj, P. and Lavrač, N. (**2008**). Closed sets for labeled data. *Journal of Machine Learning Research* 9:559–580. 127

Gärtner, T. (**2009**). *Kernels for Structured Data.* World Scientific. 230

Grünwald, P.D. (**2007**). *The Minimum Description Length Principle.* MIT Press. 297

Guyon, I. and Elisseeff, A. (**2003**). An introduction to variable and feature selection. *Journal of Machine Learning Research* 3:1157–1182. 328

Hall, M.A. (**1999**). Correlation-based feature selection for machine learning. Ph.D. thesis, University of Waikato. 328

Han, J., Cheng, H., Xin, D. and Yan, X. (**2007**). Frequent pattern mining: Current status and future directions. *Data Mining and Knowledge Discovery* 15(1):55–86. 193

Hand, D.J. and Till, R.J. (**2001**). A simple generalisation of the area under the ROC curve for multiple class classification problems. *Machine Learning* 45(2):171–186. 102

Haussler, D. (**1988**). Quantifying inductive bias: AI learning algorithms and Valiant's learning framework. *Artificial Intelligence* 36(2):177–221. 128

Hernández-Orallo, J., Flach, P.A. and Ferri, C. (**2011**). Threshold choice methods: The missing link. Available online at `http://arxiv.org/abs/1112.2640`. 358

Ho, T.K. (**1995**). Random decision forests. In *Proceedings of the International Conference on Document Analysis and Recognition*, p. 278. IEEE Computer Society, Los Alamitos, CA, USA. 341

Hoerl, A.E. and Kennard, R.W. (1970). Ridge regression: Biased estimation for nonorthogonal problems. *Technometrics* pp. 55–67. 228

Hofmann, T. (1999). Probabilistic latent semantic indexing. In *Proceedings of the Twenty-Second Annual International ACM Conference on Research and Development in Information Retrieval (SIGIR 1999)*, pp. 50–57. ACM Press. 329

Hunt, E.B., Marin, J. and Stone, P.J. (1966). *Experiments in Induction.* Academic Press. 127, 156

Jain, A.K., Murty, M.N. and Flynn, P.J. (1999). Data clustering: A review. *ACM Computing Surveys* 31(3):264–323. 261

Japkowicz, N. and Shah, M. (2011). *Evaluating Learning Algorithms: A Classification Perspective.* Cambridge University Press. 357

Jebara, T. (2004). *Machine Learning: Discriminative and Generative.* Springer. 296

John, G.H. and Langley, P. (1995). Estimating continuous distributions in Bayesian classifiers. In *Proceedings of the Eleventh Conference on Uncertainty in Artificial Intelligence (UAI 1995)*, pp. 338–345. Morgan Kaufmann. 295

Kaufman, L. and Rousseeuw, P.J. (1990). *Finding Groups in Data: An Introduction to Cluster Analysis.* John Wiley. 261

Kearns, M.J. and Valiant, L.G. (1989). Cryptographic limitations on learning Boolean formulae and finite automata. In D.S. Johnson (ed.), *Proceedings of the Twenty-First Annual ACM Symposium on Theory of Computing (STOC 1989)*, pp. 433–444. ACM Press. 341

Kearns, M.J. and Valiant, L.G. (1994). Cryptographic limitations on learning Boolean formulae and finite automata. *Journal of the ACM* 41(1):67–95. 341

Kerber, R. (1992). Chimerge: Discretization of numeric attributes. In *Proceedings of the Tenth National Conference on Artificial Intelligence (AAAI 1992)*, pp. 123–128. AAAI Press. 328

Kibler, D.F. and Langley, P. (1988). Machine learning as an experimental science. In *Proceedings of the European Working Session on Learning (EWSL 1988)*, pp. 81–92. 359

King, R.D., Srinivasan, A. and Dehaspe, L. (2001). Warmr: A data mining tool for chemical data. *Journal of Computer-Aided Molecular Design* 15(2):173–181. 193

Kira, K. and Rendell, L.A. (1992). The feature selection problem: Traditional methods and a new algorithm. In W.R. Swartout (ed.), *Proceedings of the Tenth National Conference on Artificial Intelligence (AAAI 1992)*, pp. 129–134. AAAI Press / MIT Press. 328

Klösgen, W. (1996). Explora: A multipattern and multistrategy discovery assistant. In *Advances in Knowledge Discovery and Data Mining*, pp. 249–271. MIT Press. 103

Kohavi, R. and John, G.H. (1997). Wrappers for feature subset selection. *Artificial Intelligence* 97(1-2):273–324. 328

Koren, Y., Bell, R. and Volinsky, C. (2009). Matrix factorization techniques for recommender systems. *IEEE Computer* 42(8):30–37. 328

Kramer, S. (1996). Structural regression trees. In *Proceedings of the National Conference on Artificial Intelligence (AAAI 1996)*, pp. 812–819. 156

Kramer, S., Lavrač, N. and Flach, P.A. (2000). Propositionalization approaches to relational data mining. In S. Džeroski and N. Lavrač (eds.), *Relational Data Mining*, pp. 262–286. Springer. 328

Krogel, M.A., Rawles, S., Zelezný, F., Flach, P.A., Lavrač, N. and Wrobel, S. (2003). Comparative evaluation of approaches to propositionalization. In T. Horváth (ed.), *Proceedings of the Thirteenth International Conference on Inductive Logic Programming (ILP 2003), LNCS*, volume 2835, pp. 197–214. Springer. 328

Kuncheva, L.I. (2004). *Combining Pattern Classifiers: Methods and Algorithms*. John Wiley and Sons. 341

Lachiche, N. (2010). Propositionalization. In C. Sammut and G.I. Webb (eds.), *Encyclopedia of Machine Learning*, pp. 812–817. Springer. 328

Lachiche, N. and Flach, P.A. (2003). Improving accuracy and cost of two-class and multi-class probabilistic classifiers using ROC curves. In T. Fawcett and N. Mishra (eds.), *Proceedings of the Twentieth International Conference on Machine Learning (ICML 2003)*, pp. 416–423. AAAI Press. 102

Lafferty, J.D., McCallum, A. and Pereira, F.C.N. (2001). Conditional random fields: Probabilistic models for segmenting and labeling sequence data. In C.E. Brodley and A.P. Danyluk (eds.), *Proceedings of the Eighteenth International Conference on Machine Learning (ICML 2001)*, pp. 282–289. Morgan Kaufmann. 296

Langley, P. (1988). Machine learning as an experimental science. *Machine Learning* 3:5–8. 359

Langley, P. (1994). *Elements of Machine Learning.* Morgan Kaufmann. 156

Langley, P. (2011). The changing science of machine learning. *Machine Learning* 82(3):275–279. 359

Lavrač, N., Kavšek, B., Flach, P.A. and Todorovski, L. (2004). Subgroup discovery with CN2-SD. *Journal of Machine Learning Research* 5:153–188. 193

Lee, D.D., Seung, H.S. *et al.* **(1999)**. Learning the parts of objects by non-negative matrix factorization. *Nature* 401(6755):788–791. 328

Leman, D., Feelders, A. and Knobbe, A.J. (2008). Exceptional model mining. In W. Daelemans, B. Goethals and K. Morik (eds.), *Proceedings of the European Conference on Machine Learning and Knowledge Discovery in Databases (ECML-PKDD 2008), Part II, LNCS,* volume 5212, pp. 1–16. Springer. 103

Lewis, D. (1998). Naive Bayes at forty: The independence assumption in information retrieval. In *Proceedings of the Tenth European Conference on Machine Learning (ECML 1998),* pp. 4–15. Springer. 295

Li, W., Han, J. and Pei, J. (2001). CMAR: Accurate and efficient classification based on multiple class-association rules. In N. Cercone, T.Y. Lin and X. Wu (eds.), *Proceedings of the IEEE International Conference on Data Mining (ICDM 2001),* pp. 369–376. IEEE Computer Society. 193

Little, R.J.A. and Rubin, D.B. (1987). *Statistical Analysis with Missing Data.* Wiley. 296

Liu, B., Hsu, W. and Ma, Y. (1998). Integrating classification and association rule mining. In *Proceedings of the Fourth International Conference on Knowledge Discovery and Data Mining (KDD 1998),* pp. 80–86. AAAI Press. 193

Lloyd, J.W. (2003). *Logic for Learning – Learning Comprehensible Theories from Structured Data.* Springer. 193

Lloyd, S. (1982). Least squares quantization in PCM. *IEEE Transactions on Information Theory* 28(2):129–137. 261

Mahalanobis, P.C. (1936). On the generalised distance in statistics. *Proceedings of the National Institute of Science, India* 2(1):49–55. 260

Mahoney, M.W. and Drineas, P. (2009). CUR matrix decompositions for improved data analysis. *Proceedings of the National Academy of Sciences* 106(3):697. 329

McCallum, A. and Nigam, K. (1998). A comparison of event models for naive Bayes text classification. In *Proceedings of the AAAI-98 Workshop on Learning for Text Categorization,* pp. 41–48. 295

Michalski, R.S. (**1973**). Discovering classification rules using variable-valued logic system VL_1. In *Proceedings of the Third International Joint Conference on Artificial Intelligence*, pp. 162–172. Morgan Kaufmann Publishers. 127

Michalski, R.S. (**1975**). Synthesis of optimal and quasi-optimal variable-valued logic formulas. In *Proceedings of the 1975 International Symposium on Multiple-Valued Logic*, pp. 76–87. 192

Michie, D., Spiegelhalter, D.J. and Taylor, C.C. (**1994**). *Machine Learning, Neural and Statistical Classification.* Ellis Horwood. 342

Miettinen, P. (**2009**). Matrix decomposition methods for data mining: Computational complexity and algorithms. Ph.D. thesis, University of Helsinki. 329

Minsky, M. and Papert, S. (**1969**). *Perceptrons: An Introduction to Computational Geometry.* MIT Press. 228

Mitchell, T.M. (**1977**). Version spaces: A candidate elimination approach to rule learning. In *Proceedings of the Fifth International Joint Conference on Artificial Intelligence*, pp. 305–310. Morgan Kaufmann Publishers. 127

Mitchell, T.M. (**1997**). *Machine Learning.* McGraw-Hill. 128

Muggleton, S. (**1995**). Inverse entailment and Progol. *New Generation Computing* 13(3&4):245–286. 193

Muggleton, S., De Raedt, L., Poole, D., Bratko, I., Flach, P.A., Inoue, K. and Srinivasan, A. (**2012**). ILP turns 20 – biography and future challenges. *Machine Learning* 86(1):3–23. 193

Muggleton, S. and Feng, C. (**1990**). Efficient induction of logic programs. In *Proceedings of the International Conference on Algorithmic Learning Theory (ALT 1990)*, pp. 368–381. 193

Murphy, A.H. and Winkler, R.L. (**1984**). Probability forecasting in meteorology. *Journal of the American Statistical Association* pp. 489–500. 80

Nelder, J.A. and Wedderburn, R.W.M. (**1972**). Generalized linear models. *Journal of the Royal Statistical Society, Series A (General)* pp. 370–384. 296

Novikoff, A.B. (**1962**). On convergence proofs on perceptrons. In *Proceedings of the Symposium on the Mathematical Theory of Automata*, volume 12, pp. 615–622. Polytechnic Institute of Brooklyn, New York. 228

Pasquier, N., Bastide, Y., Taouil, R. and Lakhal, L. (1999). Discovering frequent closed itemsets for association rules. In *Proceedings of the International Conference on Database Theory (ICDT 1999)*, pp. 398–416. Springer. 127

Peng, Y., Flach, P.A., Soares, C. and Brazdil, P. (2002). Improved dataset characterisation for meta-learning. In S. Lange, K. Satoh and C.H. Smith (eds.), *Proceedings of the Fifth International Conference on Discovery Science (DS 2002), LNCS*, volume 2534, pp. 141–152. Springer. 342

Pfahringer, B., Bensusan, H. and Giraud-Carrier, C.G. (2000). Meta-learning by landmarking various learning algorithms. In P. Langley (ed.), *Proceedings of the Seventeenth International Conference on Machine Learning (ICML 2000)*, pp. 743–750. Morgan Kaufmann. 342

Platt, J.C. (1998). Using analytic QP and sparseness to speed training of support vector machines. In M.J. Kearns, S.A. Solla and D.A. Cohn (eds.), *Advances in Neural Information Processing Systems 11 (NIPS 1998)*, pp. 557–563. MIT Press. 229

Plotkin, G.D. (1971). Automatic methods of inductive inference. Ph.D. thesis, University of Edinburgh. 127

Provost, F.J. and Domingos, P. (2003). Tree induction for probability-based ranking. *Machine Learning* 52(3):199–215. 156

Provost, F.J. and Fawcett, T. (2001). Robust classification for imprecise environments. *Machine Learning* 42(3):203–231. 79

Quinlan, J.R. (1986). Induction of decision trees. *Machine Learning* 1(1):81–106. 155

Quinlan, J.R. (1990). Learning logical definitions from relations. *Machine Learning* 5:239–266. 193

Quinlan, J.R. (1993). *C4.5: Programs for Machine Learning.* Morgan Kaufmann. 156

Ragavan, H. and Rendell, L.A. (1993). Lookahead feature construction for learning hard concepts. In *Proceedings of the Tenth International Conference on Machine Learning (ICML 1993)*, pp. 252–259. Morgan Kaufmann. 328

Rajnarayan, D.G. and Wolpert, D. (2010). Bias-variance trade-offs: Novel applications. In C. Sammut and G.I. Webb (eds.), *Encyclopedia of Machine Learning*, pp. 101–110. Springer. 103

Rissanen, J. (1978). Modeling by shortest data description. *Automatica* 14(5):465–471. 297

Rivest, R.L. (1987). Learning decision lists. *Machine Learning* 2(3):229–246. 192

Robnik-Sikonja, M. and Kononenko, I. (2003). Theoretical and empirical analysis of ReliefF and RReliefF. *Machine Learning* 53(1-2):23–69. 328

Rosenblatt, F. (1958). The perceptron: A probabilistic model for information storage and organization in the brain. *Psychological Review* 65(6):386. 228

Rousseeuw, P.J. (1987). Silhouettes: A graphical aid to the interpretation and validation of cluster analysis. *Journal of Computational and Applied Mathematics* 20(0):53–65. 261

Rumelhart, D.E., Hinton, G.E. and Williams, R.J. (1986). Learning representations by back-propagating errors. *Nature* 323(6088):533–536. 229

Schapire, R.E. (1990). The strength of weak learnability. *Machine Learning* 5:197–227. 341

Schapire, R.E. (2003). The boosting approach to machine learning: An overview. In *Nonlinear Estimation and Classification*, pp. 149–172. Springer. 341

Schapire, R.E., Freund, Y., Bartlett, P. and Lee, W.S. (1998). Boosting the margin: A new explanation for the effectiveness of voting methods. *Annals of Statistics* 26(5):1651–1686. 341

Schapire, R.E. and Singer, Y. (1999). Improved boosting algorithms using confidence-rated predictions. *Machine Learning* 37(3):297–336. 341

Settles, B. (2011). *Active Learning.* Morgan & Claypool. 361

Shawe-Taylor, J. and Cristianini, N. (2004). *Kernel Methods for Pattern Analysis.* Cambridge University Press. 230

Shotton, J., Fitzgibbon, A.W., Cook, M., Sharp, T., Finocchio, M., Moore, R., Kipman, A. and Blake, A. (2011). Real-time human pose recognition in parts from single depth images. In *Proceedings of the Twenty-Fourth IEEE Conference on Computer Vision and Pattern Recognition (CVPR 2011)*, pp. 1297–1304. 155

Silver, D. and Bennett, K. (2008). Guest editor's introduction: special issue on inductive transfer learning. *Machine Learning* 73(3):215–220. 361

Solomonoff, R.J. (1964*a*). A formal theory of inductive inference: Part I. *Information and Control* 7(1):1–22. 297

Solomonoff, R.J. (1964*b*). A formal theory of inductive inference: Part II. *Information and Control* 7(2):224–254. 297

Srinivasan, A. (2007). The Aleph manual, version 4 and above. Available online at `www.cs.ox.ac.uk/activities/machlearn/Aleph/`. 193

Stevens, S.S. (**1946**). On the theory of scales of measurement. *Science* 103(2684):677–680. 327

Sutton, R.S. and Barto, A.G. (**1998**). *Reinforcement Learning: An Introduction.* MIT Press. 361

Tibshirani, R. (**1996**). Regression shrinkage and selection via the lasso. *Journal of the Royal Statistical Society, Series B (Methodological)* pp. 267–288. 228

Todorovski, L. and Dzeroski, S. (**2003**). Combining classifiers with meta decision trees. *Machine Learning* 50(3):223–249. 342

Tsoumakas, G., Zhang, M.L. and Zhou, Z.H. (**2012**). Introduction to the special issue on learning from multi-label data. *Machine Learning* 88(1-2):1–4. 361

Tukey, J.W. (**1977**). *Exploratory Data Analysis.* Addison-Wesley. 103

Valiant, L.G. (**1984**). A theory of the learnable. *Communications of the ACM* 27(11):1134–1142. 128

Vapnik, V.N. and Chervonenkis, A.Y. (**1971**). On uniform convergence of the frequencies of events to their probabilities. *Teoriya Veroyatnostei I Ee Primeneniya* 16(2):264–279. 128

Vere, S.A. (**1975**). Induction of concepts in the predicate calculus. In *Proceedings of the Fourth International Joint Conference on Artificial Intelligence*, pp. 281–287. 127

von Hippel, P.T. (**2005**). Mean, median, and skew: Correcting a textbook rule. *Journal of Statistics Education* 13(2). 327

Wallace, C.S. and Boulton, D.M. (**1968**). An information measure for classification. *Computer Journal* 11(2):185–194. 297

Webb, G.I. (**1995**). Opus: An efficient admissible algorithm for unordered search. *Journal of Artificial Intelligence Research* 3:431–465. 192

Webb, G.I., Boughton, J.R. and Wang, Z. (**2005**). Not so naive Bayes: Aggregating one-dependence estimators. *Machine Learning* 58(1):5–24. 295

Winston, P.H. (**1970**). Learning structural descriptions from examples. Technical report, MIT Artificial Intelligence Lab. AITR-231. 127

Wojtusiak, J., Michalski, R.S., Kaufman, K.A. and Pietrzykowski, J. (**2006**). The AQ21 natural induction program for pattern discovery: Initial version and its novel features. In *Proceedings of the Eighteenth IEEE International Conference on Tools with Artificial Intelligence (ICTAI 2006)*, pp. 523–526. 192

Wolpert, D.H. (1992). Stacked generalization. *Neural Networks* 5(2):241–259. 342

Zadrozny, B. and Elkan, C. (2002). Transforming classifier scores into accurate multiclass probability estimates. In *Proceedings of the Eighth ACM International Conference on Knowledge Discovery and Data Mining (SIGKDD 2002)*, pp. 694–699. ACM Press. 80, 229

Zeugmann, T. (2010). PAC learning. In C. Sammut and G.I. Webb (eds.), *Encyclopedia of Machine Learning*, pp. 745–753. Springer. 128

Zhou, Z.H. (2012). *Ensemble Methods: Foundations and Algorithms.* Taylor & Francis. 341

Index